BASIC MARKETING RESEARCH

Applications to Contemporary Issues

NARESH K. MALHOTRA
Georgia Institute of Technology

Prentice Hall
Upper Saddle River, NJ 07458

The assistance of Tyra Mitchell with the section "Marketing Research and TQM" is gratefully acknowledged.

Acquisitions Editor: Wendy Craven
VP/Editor-in-Chief: Jeff Shelstad
Assistant Editor: Melissa Pellerano
Media Project Manager: Anthony Palmiotto
Marketing Manager: Michelle O'Brien
Marketing Assistant: Christine Genneken
Managing Editor (Production): Judy Leale
Production Editor: Theresa Festa
Permissions Coordinator: Suzanne Grappi
Associate Director, Manufacturing: Vincent Scelta
Production Manager: Arnold Vila
Design Manager: Patricia Smythe
Designer: Michael J. Fruhbeis
Cover Design: Michael J. Fruhbeis
Interior Designer: Donna Wickes
Associate Director, Multimedia Production: Karen Goldsmith
Manager, Print Production: Christy Mahon
Full-Service Project Management: Rainbow Graphics
Printer/Binder: Courier/Westford

10 9 8 7 6 5 4 3 2 1
ISBN 0-13-376856-2

To my wife and best friend, Veena,
with love

"A prudent wife is from the LORD."

PROVERBS 19:14

"Husbands, love your wives, even as Christ also loved the church, and gave Himself for it."

EPHESIANS 5:35

BRIEF CONTENTS

CONTENTS

FOREWORD

Basic Marketing Research: Applications to Contemporary Issues is yet another outstanding textbook from a very well-known and highly successful author, Dr. Naresh K. Malhotra. Dr. Malhotra's *Marketing Research: An Applied Orientation* has been translated into Spanish, Portuguese, Hungarian, and published in several English editions including North American, International, European, and Australian editions.

Basic Marketing Research: Applications to Contemporary Issues carries Dr. Malhotra's pedagogical skills and expertise in marketing research even further. With its focus on contemporary issues like international marketing research, technology, and ethics, the book effectively captures the current environment. The application of Web-based marketing research is integrated in a pervasive way throughout the book, which reflects the state-of-the-art orientation of the material presented in this text.

This book is rich in tangible examples that bring the student closer to the business world and every day realities of the marketplace. The opening vignettes, interwoven throughout the respective chapters, further illustrate the marketing research concepts in real-life settings. The case studies and video case studies are a great learning tool and further reinforce the highly applied and managerial orientation of the text. There are several diagrams and figures in each chapter that truly enhance learning. The lessons are conceptually sound, technically accurate, and communicate the basic research concepts with simplicity and clarity. The book is strong in qualitative concepts and imparts the necessary quantitative knowledge and skills, with the use of SPSS and other statistical software.

We at Elrick & Lavidge are pleased to contribute to this book. We have shared our philosophies, technical skills, and experiences. *Basic Marketing Research: Applications to Contemporary Issues* provides a strong foundation that we believe every student should have. This book is unsurpassed as a basis for students to become researchers and intelligent users of marketing research.

HERMAN M. SCHWARZ
President, Elrick & Lavidge

PREFACE

The response to my graduate text, *Marketing Research: An Applied Orientation,* has been truly gratifying, with more than 144 universities adopting the book in the United States. The book has been translated into Spanish, Portuguese, and Hungarian, and an International Edition, a European Edition, and an Australian and New Zealand Edition have also been published. *Basic Marketing Research: Applications to Contemporary Issues* builds on this success and carries it to the undergraduate level.

Audience

The book is suitable for use in a basic marketing research course at the undergraduate level. Basic marketing research concepts and principles are presented so that they are easy to read and understand. An abundance of diagrams, tables, pictures, illustrations, and examples help to explain the concepts. Other features designed for undergraduate students include an opening vignette that is referred to throughout the chapter, acronyms at the end of each chapter summarizing the key concepts, extensive assignment material (questions, problems, and Internet and computer exercises), and activities (role playing, field work, and group discussion).

Organization

The book has four parts, based on a six-step framework for conducting marketing research. Part One provides an introduction to marketing research and discusses problem definition, the first and most important step. It also describes the nature and scope of research undertaken to develop an approach to the problem, the second step in the marketing research process.

Part Two covers research design, the third step, and describes in detail exploratory, descriptive, and causal research designs. The types of information commonly obtained in marketing research are described, as well as the appropriate scales for obtaining such information. Guidelines for designing questionnaires are presented, and the procedures, techniques, and statistical considerations involved in sampling are explained.

Part Three presents a practical and managerially oriented discussion of field work, the fourth step in the marketing research process. It also covers data preparation and analysis, the fifth step. Basic statistical techniques are discussed in detail, with emphasis on procedures, results, and managerial implications. Four statistical packages—SPSS, SAS, MINITAB, and EXCEL—are featured. While four statistical packages are featured, SPSS gets special emphasis. A student version of SPSS is enclosed along with SPSS files for all the data sets used in this book. Communicating the research by preparing and presenting a formal report constitutes the sixth step in the marketing research process, which is also discussed in Part Three. Finally, Part Four contains comprehensive cases and video cases.

Key Features of the Text

The book has several important or unique features in terms of its content and its pedagogy.

CONTENT FEATURES

1. A chapter is devoted to problem definition and developing an approach. These important steps in the marketing research process are discussed thoroughly and extensively (Chapter 2).

2. A chapter covers secondary data analysis. In addition to the traditional sources, computerized databases are also covered extensively. Use of the Internet for secondary data analysis is discussed in detail (Chapter 4).

3. A chapter is devoted to syndicate services. The types of data available from syndicate firms and the applications of such data are described in detail (Chapter 5).

4. A whole chapter is dedicated to qualitative research. Focus groups, depth interviews, and projective techniques are discussed in detail with emphasis on the applications of these procedures. Use of the Internet for qualitative research is discussed in detail (Chapter 6).

5. One chapter presents survey and observation methods (Chapter 7), while another discusses experimentation (Chapter 8). Thus, descriptive and causal designs are covered in detail with due emphasis on the Internet.

6. Two chapters are devoted to scaling techniques. One chapter is devoted to the fundamentals and comparative scaling techniques (Chapter 9). The other chapter covers noncomparative techniques and the basic procedures for assessing their reliability and validity (Chapter 10).

7. A chapter discusses questionnaire design. A step-by-step procedure and several guidelines are provided for constructing questionnaires (Chapter 11).

8. Two chapters cover sampling techniques. One chapter discusses the qualitative issues involved in sampling and the various nonprobability and probability sampling techniques (Chapter 12). The other chapter explains statistical issues, as well as final and initial sample size determination (Chapter 13).

9. A chapter presents field work. We give several guidelines on interviewer training, interviewing, and supervision of field workers (Chapter 14).

10. Four chapters have been devoted to the analysis of marketing research data covering all the basic techniques. Chapters are devoted to:

    a. Data preparation (Chapter 15)

    b. Frequency distribution, cross-tabulation, and hypothesis testing (Chapter 16)

    c. Testing hypotheses related to differences, including the various t-tests and analysis of variance (Chapter 17)

    d. Correlation and regression analysis (Chapter 18)

    The data set used to explain each technique is provided in the beginning of the chapter. Data analysis is illustrated for four statistical packages: SPSS, SAS, MINITAB, and EXCEL. A student version of SPSS and SPSS files for all the datasets we have used are included with the book. A separate section on SPSS appears in the relevant chapters.

11. A chapter covers report preparation and presentation (Chapter 19).

PEDAGOGICAL FEATURES

1. The book has a highly applied and managerial orientation. We illustrate in a pervasive manner how marketing researchers apply the various concepts

and techniques and how managers implement the findings in order to improve marketing practice. The emphasis on applied marketing research is reinforced by featuring Elrick & Lavidge (E&L) in a significant way in each chapter. (The focus on E&L should not be interpreted as an endorsement for E&L over other marketing research firms—I have no business relationship with E&L and have not provided them with any consulting services. The primary intent is to show how a well-established marketing research firm practices the concepts discussed in each chapter.)

2. Several real-life examples are presented in each chapter. These examples describe in some detail how marketing research addresses specific managerial problems and the decisions that were based on these efforts. Often, information available from published sources has been supplemented to make these examples more illustrative.

3. Each part of the book contains short cases. The conciseness of the cases allows you to use them in examinations. Some long cases are also provided, including some cases with statistical data. These cases are current to sustain student interest.

4. Each part of the book contains video cases drawn from the Prentice Hall video library. These video cases have been rewritten from the marketing research perspective. The accompanying questions are all marketing research questions. The videotapes are available to instructors who adopt the book.

5. A contemporary focus has been achieved by integrating the coverage of total quality management, international marketing research, technology, and ethics in marketing research throughout the text.

6. Each chapter also contains a section entitled "Internet Applications." The text discusses how the Internet connects to each step of the marketing research process. Each chapter also contains "Internet and Computer Exercises," which present opportunities to apply these concepts in real-life settings.

7. Each chapter opens with a set of questions to arouse student curiosity and to give the student a sense of the chapter's structure. Each chapter also contains an opening vignette, used as a running example throughout the chapter.

8. Each chapter but the first opens with a diagram that gives the focus of that chapter, its relationship to the previous chapter(s), and its relationship to the marketing research process. Also included is a diagram that provides an overview of the chapter, showing the major topics and linking them to figures and tables.

9. Data analysis procedures are illustrated with respect to SPSS, SAS, MINITAB, and EXCEL, along with other popular computer programs. This book serves well as a text for whatever statistical package the instructor is using. However, special emphasis is given to SPSS and SPSS files are provided for all the datasets used in the book and the statistical outputs in the chapters.

10. Each chapter contains one or more helpful acronyms that summarize the important concepts. Acronyms are the most popular mnemonic technique college students use. Theoretical and empirical evidence supporting the effectiveness of mnemonic techniques and their usefulness as pedagogical tools is discussed in my paper in the *Journal of the Academy of Marketing Science* (Spring 1991): 141–150.

11. Extensive "Exercises" and "Activities," which include Questions, Problems, Internet and Computer Exercises, Role Playing, Field Work, and Group Discussion, appear at the conclusion of each chapter. This section provides ample opportunities for testing the concepts covered in the chapter.

Instructional Support

The book is supported by a rich set of supplements, detailed below.

1. The Web site can be accessed at www.prenhall.com/malhotra. This site contains the following:
   - The entire Instructors' Manual (password-protected)
   - Test Item File (password-protected)
   - Power Point Slides containing a chapter outline and all the figures and tables (password-protected)
   - Data for Cases 3.1 (Ford Taurus), 3.2 (Marriott), 3.3 (Microsoft), 4.1 (DuPont), and 4.2 (Gucci). These data can be downloaded with ease as either text files or SPSS files. SPSS data files are also provided for the data used to illustrate the statistical concepts in Chapters 16, 17, and 18, as well as for the relevant Internet and Computer Exercises in these chapters.
   - Links to other useful Web sites.

   To obtain the user id and password to the Web site, please contact your local Prentice Hall representative or contact me (e-mail: naresh.malhotra@mgt.gatech.edu, tel: 404-894-4358, fax: 404-894-6030).

   The Web site is being enhanced continually.

2. Instructor's Manual. Written by the author, the entire Instructor's Manual is very closely tied to the text. Each chapter contains transparency masters, chapter objectives, author's notes, chapter outlines, teaching suggestions, and answers to all end-of-chapter exercises and activities (questions, problems, Internet and computer exercises, role playing, field work, and group discussion). In addition, solutions are provided to all the cases, including those that involve data analysis. Solutions are also provided to all the video cases. The disk enclosed with the Instuctor's Manual contains the following:
   - SPSS and text files containing data for Cases 3.1 (Ford Taurus), 3.2 (Marriott), 3.3 (Microsoft), 4.1 (DuPont), and 4.2 (Gucci).
   - SPSS data files for Tables 16.1, 17.1, 17.6, and 18.1.
   - SPSS data files for Internet and Computer Exercises in Chapters 16, 17, and 18.
   - SPSS output files for all the analyses presented in Chapters 16, 17, and 18.

3. Test Item File. Written by Andrew Yap, this valuable test item file contains a wide variety of tests for each chapter, which allows you to create your own exams.

4. Video Cases. A set of videotapes containing these cases is available to adopters. The solutions to these cases are provided in the Instructor's Manual and are also available on the Web site. Professor Martha McEnally

(UNC-Greensboro) originally wrote these video cases, which I have rewritten from a marketing research perspective.

5. PowerPoint slides. These slides contain all the figures and all the tables for each chapter of the book.

6. A student version of SPSS and SPSS files for all the datasets used in the book.

ACKNOWLEDGMENTS

Several people have been extremely helpful in writing this textbook. I would like to acknowledge Professor Arun K. Jain (State University of New York at Buffalo), who taught me Marketing Research in a way I will never forget. My students, especially former doctoral students, particularly Ashutosh Dixit, Charla Mathwick, Rick McFarland, and Cassandra Wells, as well as research assistants, Melanie Carter, Dan Nirenberg, and Edward Lindahl have been very helpful in many ways. Tyra Mitchell provided research assistance for the sections on "Marketing Research and TQM." The students in my Marketing Research courses have provided useful feedback, as the material was class tested for several years. My colleagues at Georgia Tech, especially Dean Terry Blum and Professor Fred Allvine, have been very supportive. I also want to thank Roger L. Bacik (Executive Vice President, Elrick & Lavidge, Inc.) for his encouragement, support, and the many contributions from Elrick & Lavidge that appear throughout the book. William D. Neal (founder and senior executive officer of SDR, Inc.) has been very helpful and supportive over the years.

The reviewers have provided many constructive and valuable suggestions. Among others, the help of the following reviewers is gratefully acknowledged.

DENNIS B. ARNETT
University of Texas at San Antonio

ALAN G. SAWYER
University of Florida

PAUL L. SAUER
Canisius College

JERRY KATRICHIS
University of Hartford

The team at Prentice Hall provided outstanding support. Special thanks are due to Judy Leale, Managing Editor; Whitney Blake, Executive Editor; Wendy Craven, Senior Editor; Anthony Palmiotto, Media Project Manager; Melissa Pellerano, Assistant Editor; Theresa Festa, Production Editor; Pam Sourelis, Developmental Editor; and Melinda Alexander, Photo Editor. Special recognition is due to the several field representatives and salespeople who do an outstanding job.

I want to acknowledge with great respect my parents, Mr. and Mrs. H. N. Malhotra. Their love, encouragement, support, and the sacrificial giving of themselves have been exemplary. My heartfelt love and gratitude go to my wife Veena and my children Ruth and Paul, for their constant encouragement and joyful endurance in the arduous process of writing this book and for their countless expressions of faith, hope, and love (1 Corinthians 13:13).

Most of all, I want to acknowledge and thank my Savior and Lord, Jesus Christ, for the abundant grace and favor He has bestowed upon me. This book is, truly, the result of His favor—"For thou, LORD, wilt bless the righteous; with favor wilt thou compass him as with a shield" (Psalms 5:12).

NARESH K. MALHOTRA

ABOUT THE AUTHOR

Dr. Naresh K. Malhotra is Regents Professor (Highest Academic Rank in the University System of Georgia), DuPree College of Management, Georgia Institute of Technology. He has been listed continuously in Marquis *Who's Who in America* since its fifty-first edition in 1997, and in *Who's Who in the World* since 2000.

In an article by Wheatley and Wilson (1987 AMA Educators Proceedings), Professor Malhotra was ranked the number one researcher in the country, based on articles published in the *Journal of Marketing Research* from 1980 through 1985. He also holds the all-time record for the maximum number of publications in the *Journal of Health Care Marketing*. He is ranked number one based on publications in the *Journal of the Academy of Marketing Science* (JAMS) since its inception through Volume 23, 1995. He is also number one, based on publications in JAMS, during the ten-year period from 1986 through 1995.

He has published more than 85 papers in major refereed journals, including the *Journal of Marketing Research, Journal of Consumer Research, Marketing Science, Journal of Marketing, Journal of Academy of Marketing Science, Journal of Retailing, Journal of Health Care Marketing,* and leading journals in statistics, management science, and psychology. In addition, he has also published numerous refereed articles in the proceedings of major national and international conferences. Several articles have received best paper research awards.

He was chairman, Academy of Marketing Science Foundation, 1996–1998, and was president, Academy of Marketing Science, 1994–1996, and chairman, board of governors, 1990–1992. He is a Distinguished Fellow of the Academy, and Fellow, Decision Sciences Institute. He served as an associate editor of *Decision Sciences* for 18 years and has served as section editor, *Health Care Marketing Abstracts, Journal of Health Care Marketing.* Also, he serves on the editorial board of 8 journals.

His book *Marketing Research: An Applied Orientation, Third Edition,* was published by Prentice Hall, Inc. An international edition, European edition, and an Australian edition of his book have also been published, and the book has been translated into Spanish, Portuguese, and Hungarian. The book has received widespread adoption at both the graduate and undergraduate levels, with more than 144 schools using it in the United States.

Dr. Malhotra has consulted for business, non-profit, and government organizations in the United States and abroad, and has served as an expert witness in legal and regulatory proceedings. He is the winner of numerous awards and honors for research, teaching, and service to the profession.

Dr. Malhotra is a member and deacon, First Baptist Church, Atlanta. He lives in the Atlanta area with his wife Veena, and children Ruth and Paul.

Introduction and Early Phases of Marketing Research

I

1

INTRODUCTION TO MARKETING RESEARCH

THE ROLE OF MARKETING RESEARCH IN HELPING MARKETING MANAGERS MAKE SOUND DECISIONS WILL BECOME EVEN MORE CRUCIAL IN THE TWENTY-FIRST CENTURY. TO BE A GOOD MARKETING RESEARCHER YOU HAVE TO BE A GOOD MARKETING MANAGER, AND VICE-VERSA.

Herman M. Schwarz, President, Elrick & Lavidge. Herman Schwarz is responsible for the overall operations and management of the company. He has been with E&L, a division of Ageis Communications Group, since late 2000.

OPENING QUESTIONS

1. How do you define marketing research?
2. What are the major classifications of marketing research, and what is the relationship between problem-identification research and problem-solving research?
3. What are the six steps in the marketing research process?
4. What role does marketing research play in designing and implementing successful marketing programs?
5. What is the marketing research industry, and what roles do internal and external suppliers play?
6. How should a firm select a marketing research supplier?
7. What careers are available in marketing research, and what skills do you need to succeed in them?
8. How is marketing research relevant to decision support systems?
9. Does marketing research play a role in total quality management?
10. Why is international marketing research more complex than domestic marketing research?
11. How can technology improve marketing research?
12. What are the ethical aspects of marketing research? What responsibilities do each of the marketing research stakeholders have to themselves, each other, and the research project?
13. How can you use the Internet to conduct marketing research?

HOW REEBOK FITS SHOES

Reebok International designs, markets, and distributes sportswear, footwear, and sports equipment. For the summer Olympic Games of 2000 in Sydney, Australia, Reebok outfitted 2,500 athletes and coaches with their new line of apparel and footwear. The product manager for the Olympic apparel said, "The Olympic Games present a great honor and challenge for both the athletes and those of us who are responsible for ensuring their complete comfort during training and competition."

In order to provide "complete comfort" for athletes and consumers, Reebok invested much of its efforts into marketing research. Although the slogan belongs to Nike, when it comes to marketing research, Reebok just does it!

Reebok uses "time use" research to determine how consumers spend their spare time. This type of information enables Reebok to identify opportunities for new products and markets and then design its marketing program to take advantage of them, as illustrated by the recently introduced line of footwear, Reebok Classic. The company researches time-use trends using a variety of methods, including analysis of secondary data (data collected for other purposes, for example, data available from publications, the Internet, and commercial sources). It also uses qualitative research such as focus groups (interviews with 8 to 12 people as a group), and survey research by telephone, in the malls, and interviews at consumer homes.

For example, time-use research helped shape the development of recent aerobic athletic products, including shoes, videotapes, and home step products. Analysis of secondary data showed that health club memberships had grown 9 percent in the 1990s. Focus groups indicated that the new popular venue in fitness was step aerobics (standard aerobics courses made more intense by the addition of a three- to seven-inch platform: a step). Reebok then conducted a survey to determine the market potential of step aerobics and found that members of health clubs were spending less time in the clubs by an average of 12 percent.

This research further showed that the percentage of adults who exercised in their homes had grown from 20 percent in 1990 to 30 percent in 2000. Based on these findings, Reebok designed a home step-aerobics line, including home steps, videotapes, aerobic shoes, and body weights. Product research indicated a strong consumer preference for the home step-aerobics line and, therefore, it was launched nationally. This line has been very successful, and the popularity of these products has resulted in a Reebok step workout program on ESPN.

In this project, Reebok's in-house marketing research specialists were actively involved in defining and designing the research. However, Reebok contracted field work or data collection and data analysis to external suppliers. External suppliers may also be used in writing the report, but presentation of the results to the management and assistance in implementation is the primary responsibility of the in-house marketing research department. Reebok makes use of full-service suppliers who provide assistance in all the steps of the marketing research process as well as limited-service suppliers who may handle only one or a few steps of the process. The data and the findings generated by this ongoing research became a part of Reebok's decision support system.[1]

OVERVIEW

Marketing research is one of the most important and fascinating aspects of marketing. As the opening vignette illustrates, marketing research provides a company with valuable information, which guides all of the marketing activities. In this chapter, we define and describe the two broad forms of marketing research: (1) research designed to identify problems and (2) research designed to solve problems. We explain the six steps of the marketing research process and take a look at how marketing research fits into the entire marketing decision process. The marketing research industry consists of a variety of firms, which we describe. And the field offers exciting career opportunities, which we explain. We conclude by describing the contribution of marketing research to marketing information systems (MISs) and decision support systems (DSSs).

Throughout this book, we discuss applications to five contemporary issues that are important in the current marketing and marketing research environment: total quality management (TQM), international marketing research, technology, ethics, and the Internet. This first chapter provides an introduction to these important application areas; an overview is presented in Figure 1.1. It can be seen in Figure 1.1 that the Opening Vignette, the Focus on Elrick & Lavidge, the Application to Contemporary Issues, and the Internet encompass all of the topics discussed in the chapter. This orientation provides a better overall understanding of the key concepts and illustrates how applications can be made in important areas that are discussed throughout the book.

DEFINITION OF MARKETING RESEARCH

marketing research
The systematic and objective identification, collection, analysis, and dissemination of information that is undertaken to improve decision making related to identifying and solving problems (also known as opportunities) in marketing.

In this book, we emphasize the importance of research in marketing decision making. **Marketing research** is the systematic and objective identification, collection, analysis, and dissemination of information, undertaken to improve decision making related to identifying and solving problems (also known as opportunities) in marketing.

This definition gives marketing research a broad scope that opens up a world of opportunities. Several aspects of this definition are noteworthy. Marketing research involves the identification, collection, analysis, and dissemination of information (see Figure 1.2).

EXAMPLE

MARKETING RESEARCH: A WORLD OF OPPORTUNITIES

Diane Bowers, President, Council for Marketing and Opinion Research (CMOR) and Executive Director, Council of American Survey Research Organizations (CASRO), expressed the following viewpoint:

"I think we're on the threshold of opportunity. We should be taking a major leadership position in how information is accessed, how it's disseminated, how it's used, and how it balances those very critical issues of information gathering and individual privacy. So we could be right on the threshold of being considered in the forefront of leadership."[2]

Each phase of this process is important. Marketing research begins with the identification or definition of the research problem or opportunity. *Problems* often lead to *opportunities* in business, so from a research perspective, the two words are used inter-

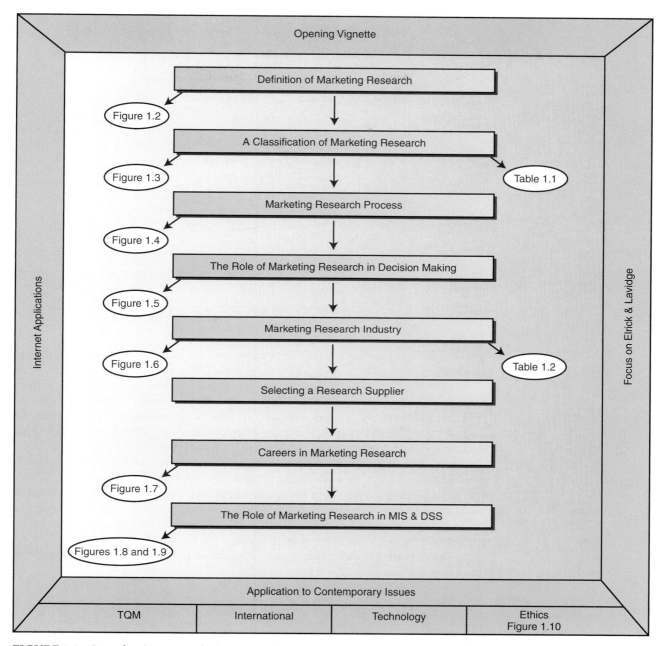

FIGURE 1.1 Introduction to Marketing Research: An Overview

changeably. For example, the discovery that adults were spending less time in health clubs and more time exercising at home represented a problem as well as an opportunity for Reebok. The problem was that when people were spending less time in health clubs, they were also using athletic shoes and equipment to a lesser extent, which resulted in decreased demand. The opportunity was more time spent exercising at home, which represented greater potential for shoes and home exercise equipment. The range of data collection methods and the sources to collect the data vary in sophistication and complexity. The methods used depend on the specific requirements of the project, including budget

FIGURE 1.2   Defining Marketing Research

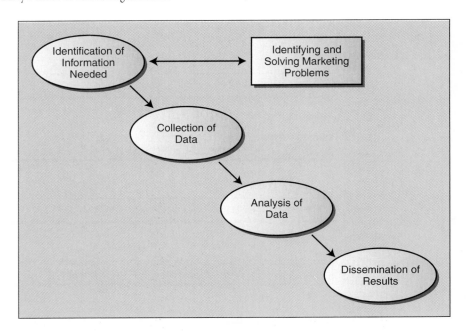

and time constraints. The data are then analyzed and the results are formally presented to the client.

Marketing research is systematic, which means it follows a predictable path. A marketing research project is planned and documented. It has a scientific basis in that data are collected and analyzed to draw conclusions. The time-use research reported in the Reebok vignette is an example. Marketing research obtains its value from its objectivity. While it should be conducted impartially, free from the influence of personal or political biases, this is easier said than done because companies sponsoring the research sometimes pressure the researcher or research firm to generate "support" for a certain desired outcome. But bending to this sort of pressure is a breach of the ethical codes of conduct that guide the profession. The notion of providing an unbiased "outside opinion," or objective opinion, gives marketing research its value. Without that objectivity, results cannot be trusted, and the entire discipline is undermined.

The next section elaborates on this definition of marketing research by classifying different types of marketing research.

A CLASSIFICATION OF MARKETING RESEARCH

Our definition states that organizations engage in marketing research for two reasons: to identify and to solve marketing problems. This distinction serves as a basis for classifying marketing research into problem-identification research and problem-solving research, as shown in Figure 1.3.

problem-identification research
Research undertaken to help identify problems that are not necessarily apparent on the surface and yet exist or are likely to arise in the future.

Problem-identification research involves going below the surface to identify the true underlying problem that the marketing manager is facing. Problem-identification research may be designed to estimate market potential, market share, brand or company image, market characteristics, sales analysis, short-range forecasting, long-range forecasting, or to uncover business trends. Polo may undertake research to determine the size of the market for men's shirts, the projected growth rate, and the market share of major brands. This research may reveal a problem. Say that while Polo's sales of men's shirts have

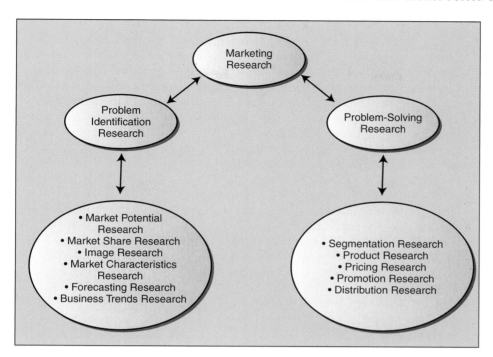

FIGURE 1.3 A Classification of Marketing Research

been increasing, they have not been keeping pace with the growth of the industry. Moreover, Polo has been gradually losing market share to competitors such as Tommy Hilfiger.

Problem identification is the more common of the two forms of research and is undertaken by virtually all marketing firms. This type of research is used to assess the environment and diagnose problems. Information regarding changes in the market provides an initial alert to potential opportunities or problems. A firm that is operating in a growing market but suffering from a declining market share may be dealing with company-specific problems, such as ineffective advertising or high turnover in its sales force. In other instances, problems such as declining demand may be common to all the firms in the industry. Considering economic, social, cultural, or consumer behavior trends may help identify such problems or opportunities.

Once a problem or opportunity has been identified, a firm undertakes **problem-solving research** to address the problem. Most marketing firms conduct problem-solving research as well. Problem-solving research addresses many topics, including segmentation, product, pricing, promotion, and distribution, as shown in Table 1.1. Problem-identification research and problem-solving research go hand in hand, and a given marketing research project may combine both types.

problem-solving research
Research undertaken to help solve specific marketing problems.

EXAMPLE

THE ARCH OF MARKETING RESEARCH AT THE GOLDEN ARCHES

In the decade of the 1960s, McDonald's earned about $170 million domestically; today, the company earns more than that in two days. This growth can be attributed in no small part to marketing research. In 1968, McDonald's formed its marketing research department, which has grown dramatically since its creation. The most prominent aspect of this operation is that 85 percent of all McDonald's are franchises. McDonald's research actively supports these restaurants, providing the franchises with such ideas as breakfast meals and Extra Value Meals.

In the late 1970s, problem-identification research related to market characteristics revealed that more and more people were eating breakfast away from home. To capitalize on this opportunity, McDonald's began serving breakfast in 1979 with the introduction of the Egg McMuffin. The Egg McMuffin—indeed, the entire breakfast concept—was developed based on consumer preferences and feedback obtained via problem-solving research. New product research revealed strong consumer preference for the familiar qualities of McDonald's lunchtime menu, namely, value and convenience, embodied in the Egg McMuffin for breakfast. Today, McDonald's holds 30 percent of the market share for fast-food restaurant breakfast.

In the 1980s, problem-identification research involving focus groups and surveys revealed that customers were clamoring for value. Based on subsequent problem-solving research on product and pricing, McDonald's developed Extra Value Meals to provide convenience and value. Extra Value Meals, which are ordered by number, constitute 50 percent of all transactions in the United States, 90 percent in Mexico, and 60 percent in Japan. According to McDonald's, "It has verified the concept of value beyond price; price brings them in, but value brings them back." This all equates to "the McDonald's experience."

Most fast-food restaurants have a ratio of outlets to business of about one. This means that a fast-food restaurant's percent of market presence (outlets) is directly related to the percent of business the restaurant gains from the market. However, McDonald's has a ratio of almost 1.7. This means that for every percent that McDonald's holds in actual market presence, they gain 1.7 percent of actual fast-food business. It's the feelings the arches evoke. It's the result of problem-identification and problem-solving research that McDonald's undertakes on an ongoing basis.[3]

Classifying marketing research into two main types is useful from a conceptual as well as a practical viewpoint. The McDonald's example illustrates that these two types of research often go hand in hand. Marketing research discovered the consumer's desire for value (problem identification), and the solution was the introduction of value meals designed to meet this need (problem solving). The Reebok International vignette also illustrates this point. Problem identification involving analysis of secondary data, focus groups, and a market potential survey revealed that adults were spending less time in health clubs and more time exercising at home. Problem-solving research in the form of product research led to the development and introduction of the successful home step aerobics line.

TABLE 1.1 **Problem-Solving Research**

SEGMENTATION RESEARCH

Determine basis of segmentation
Establish market potential and responsiveness for various segments
Select target markets and create demographic and lifestyle profiles, media, and product image
    characteristics

PRODUCT RESEARCH

Test concept
Determine optimal product design
Package tests
Product modification
Brand positioning and repositioning
Test marketing
Control store tests

PRICING RESEARCH

Importance of price in brand selection
Pricing policies
Product line pricing
Price elasticity of demand
Initiating and responding to price changes

PROMOTIONAL RESEARCH

Optimal promotional budget
Sales promotion relationship
Optimal promotional mix
Copy decisions
Media decisions
Creative advertising testing
Claim substantiation
Evaluation of advertising effectiveness

DISTRIBUTION RESEARCH

Determine type of distribution
Attitudes of channel members
Intensity of wholesale and retail coverage
Channel margins
Location of retail and wholesale outlets

MARKETING RESEARCH PROCESS

The **marketing research process** consists of six steps (Figure 1.4). Each of these steps is discussed in great detail in subsequent chapters. We will provide only a brief overview here.

Step 1: Defining the Problem

The first step in any marketing research project is to define the problem. This includes not only understanding the purpose of the study but understanding the background issues that go along with it as well. These background issues include answers to such questions

marketing research process
A set of six steps that defines the tasks to be accomplished in conducting a marketing research study: problem definition, developing an approach to the problem, research design formulation, field work, data preparation and analysis, and report generation and presentation.

FIGURE 1.4   The Marketing Research Process

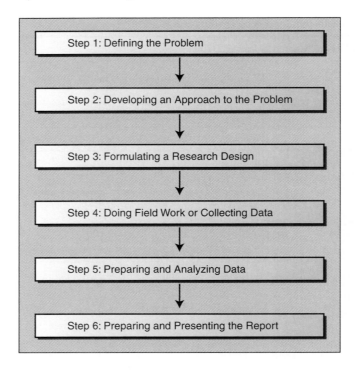

as "What prompted the research?" and "What kind of decisions will be made from it?" Researchers accomplish problem definition through discussions with the decision makers, interviews with industry experts, analysis of secondary data, and perhaps, some qualitative research, such as focus groups. The opening vignette illustrated the use of secondary data and focus groups in defining the marketing research problem. The problem for Reebok was assessing the market potential for home step aerobic products. Once the problem has been precisely defined, the research can be designed and conducted properly. (See Chapter 2.)

Step 2: Developing an Approach to the Problem

Developing an approach to the problem includes formulating an analytical framework and models, research questions, and hypotheses (unproven statements or propositions about a factor or phenomenon that is of interest to the researcher). This process is guided by the same tasks performed to define the problem. (See Chapter 2.)

Step 3: Formulating a Research Design

A research design is a framework or blueprint for conducting the marketing research project. It details the procedures needed to obtain the required information. A study may be designed to test hypotheses of interest or determine possible answers to the research questions, both of which contribute to decision making. Conducting exploratory research, precisely defining the variables, and designing appropriate scales to measure them are also part of the research design. The issue of how the data should be obtained from the respondents (for example, by conducting a survey or an experiment) must be addressed. In the opening vignette, a survey was conducted to assess the market potential for home step-aerobic equipment. It is also necessary to design a questionnaire and a sampling plan to select respondents for the study. These steps are discussed in detail in Chapters 3 through 13.

Step 4: Doing Field Work or Collecting Data

Data collection is accomplished using a staff that operates in the field. Field work involves personal, telephone, mail, or electronic interviewing. Proper selection, training, supervision, and evaluation of the field force are essential to ensure high-quality data collection (see Chapter 14).

Step 5: Preparing and Analyzing Data

Data preparation involves data-processing steps leading up to analysis. This includes the editing, coding, and transcribing of collected data. This entire process must then be verified for accuracy. The editing process involves an initial inspection of questionnaires or observation forms for completeness and reasonableness of responses. After this initial inspection, the response to each question is coded to ensure standardized entry into the computer. The data from the questionnaires are transferred onto storage media and then analyzed using different statistical techniques. These results are then interpreted in order to find conclusions related to the marketing research problem. (See Chapters 15 through 18.)

Step 6: Preparing and Presenting the Report

The entire project should be documented in a written report that addresses the specific research questions; describes the approach, the research design, data collection, and data analysis procedures; and presents the results and the major findings. The written report is supplemented by tables, figures, and graphs to enhance clarity and impact, and is usually accompanied by a formal presentation. (See Chapter 19.)

As can be seen in the following, the marketing research process (Figure 1.4) is very consistent with the definition of marketing research presented earlier (Figure 1.2).

DEFINITION OF MARKETING RESEARCH (FIGURE 1.2)	MARKETING RESEARCH PROCESS (FIGURE 1.4)
Identification of information needed	Step 1: Defining the problem
Collection of data	Step 2: Developing an approach to the problem
	Step 3: Formulating a research design
	Step 4: Doing field work or collecting data
Analysis of data	Step 5: Preparing and analyzing data
Dissemination of results	Step 6: Preparing and presenting the report

EXAMPLE

MARKETING RESEARCH AT MARRIOTT CORPORATION

Marriott functions in three main areas: lodging (Marriott Hotels and Resorts, Renaissance Hotels and Resorts, Marriott Suites, Residence Inns, Courtyards and Fairfield Inns), contract services (Marriott Business Food and Services, Education, Health Care and In-Flight Services, and Host International), and restaurants (family restaurants, Travel Plazas and Hot Shoppes). However, it is probably best known for its lodging operations.

Marketing research at Marriott is done at the corporate level through the Corporate Marketing Services (CMS). The process of research at Marriott is a simple stepwise progression. The first steps are to better define the problem to be addressed and the objectives of the client unit, and to develop an approach to the problem. The next steps are to develop an approach and to formulate a research design. CMS must decide whether to do its own research or to buy it from an outside organization. If it decides to buy from an outside organization, it must decide whether or not to use multiple firms. Once they've made a decision, the research is carried out by collecting and analyzing the data. Then CMS presents the study findings in a detailed report. Part of the final step in the research process is to keep a constant dialogue between the client unit and CMS. During this stage, CMS may help explain the implications of the research findings or make suggestions for future actions.[4]

As the Marriott example indicates, our description of the marketing research process is fairly typical of the research that major companies are undertaking. Reebok International, as discussed in the opening vignette, follows a research process that incorporates all six of these steps.

THE ROLE OF MARKETING RESEARCH IN MARKETING DECISION MAKING

The Reebok vignette illustrates only a few applications of marketing research and its role in the marketing decision-making process. Marketing research, indeed, has a broad range of applications and plays a crucial role in the marketing decision-making process. One way to describe the role of marketing research is in light of the basic marketing paradigm given in Figure 1.5.

A major goal of marketing is to identify and then satisfy customer needs. To do this, marketing managers need information about customers, competitors, and other forces such as environmental trends in the marketplace. In recent years, timely market information has become even more valuable. For example, the speed of new products entering the marketplace, domestic and international competition, and the increase in demanding and well-informed consumers all contribute to the importance of this type of market data.

The task of marketing research is to assess the information needs and provide management with relevant, accurate, reliable, valid, and current information to aid marketing decision making (Figure 1.5). Companies use marketing research to stay competitive and to avoid high costs associated with making poor decisions based on unsound information. Sound decisions are not based on gut feeling, intuition, or even pure judgment; they're based on sound information. Without sound information, management cannot make sound decisions.

The following example illustrates how GM's car design process was improved through the use of marketing research. Due to the new car design process, GM has pleased customers who were initially dissatisfied with certain features of its vehicles. GM reinforces the fact that management cannot make sound decisions without sound information provided by marketing research.

MARKETING RESEARCH MAKES
THE CUSTOMER GM'S DESIGN CHIEF

General Motors (GM) historically had little or no regard for marketing research. The company had the attitude that its size and resource base provided it with a technological edge that was sufficient for continued success. Certainly, the company did not need any input from the customer. Indeed, GM did not form a marketing research division until 1985.

As an example of their "know-all" attitude, GM executives were positive that the popular Camaro and Firebird lines sold because of their exterior design. However, in one of the company's first marketing research projects, consumers indicated that while looks were important, performance and quality rated very high in selecting a car. The consumers went on to say that they were very satisfied with the exterior design, but that they were not as satisfied with the performance and quality. The obvious shortcomings of executive assumptions regarding customer values spawned the birth of "needs-based" market research.

General Motors began compiling information from existing and potential customers in 1986. Since then, GM has conducted interviews with millions of consumers and has amassed a vast portfolio of information on consumer needs in all product segments. Once the information has been gathered, the marketing research team can build a model of the entry-level segment showing the market volume and the number of buyers in the various needs categories, then introduce the factors of incomes and demographics.

Immediate implications of the new research were the planned discontinuance of the Oldsmobile Ninety-Eight model and the realignment of the Oldsmobile Eighty-Eight model. The research revealed that General Motors was not fully using its brand equity and that its models were competing with each other. The Oldsmobile Eighty-Eight and the Buick LeSabre were competing in the same consumer segment, as were the Oldsmobile Ninety-Eight and the Buick Park Avenue. GM decided that the Buick LeSabre would continue in its targeted segment, while the Oldsmobile Eighty-Eight would be reconfigured into a sportier model to target a younger, more demanding consumer. The Buick Park Avenue would remain in its segment as well, while the Oldsmobile Ninety-Eight was phased out. However, the problem remained and on December 12, 2000 GM announced that the entire Oldsmobile line will be phased out.

The real value of this research was improvement of GM's car design process. This research shifted the company's focus from the products of its competitors to the needs of the consumer. Says Chris Cedergren, senior vice president of AutoPacific Group, an automotive marketing and product consultant, "With what GM is doing, it can assess what the needs and desires are 5 to 10 years from now." GM now focuses more on what the consumers say and less on the gut feelings of its executives. All a result of marketing research.[5]

FIGURE 1.5 The Role of Marketing Research in Marketing Decision Making

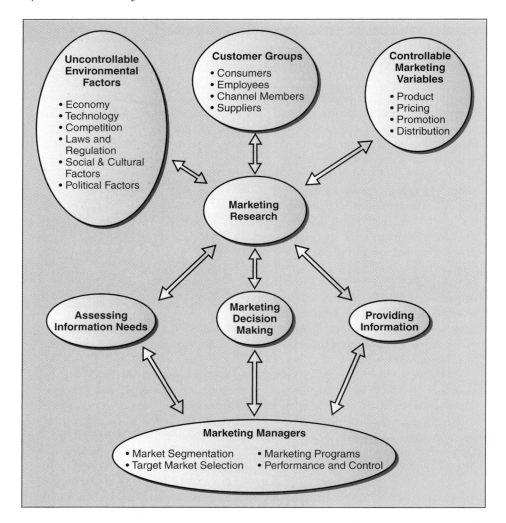

This example from General Motors illustrates the numerous strategic and tactical decisions marketing managers face and how marketing research can be helpful in improving the decision-making process. Identifying and finding solutions to customer needs (a primary goal of marketing) requires the integration of a wide range of factors, not just intuition. Figure 1.5 illustrates this range, which includes decisions about potential opportunities, target market selection, market segmentation, planning and implementing marketing programs, marketing performance, and control. These decisions often result in actions related to product, pricing, promotion, and distribution.

To make the decision process even more complicated, a manager must also consider uncontrollable external factors that influence the marketing process. These include general economic conditions (an economic slow-down or recession), technology (the impact of new technology such as the Internet), public policies and laws (those related to environmental pollution affect automobile companies), political environment (the Republicans are considered pro business), competition (many dot-coms have not been able to survive because of competition), and social and cultural changes (the reversal of traditional marital roles). Another factor in this mix is the complexity of the various customer groups: consumers, employees, shareholders, and suppliers. The marketing manager must attempt to monitor and incorporate all these considerations. Marketing research removes some of the uncertainty and improves the quality of decision making in this highly complex environment.

Traditionally, a clear distinction existed between the responsibilities of marketing researchers and marketing managers. However, these roles are beginning to merge as marketing researchers become more involved in decision making and marketing managers are becoming more involved with research. This trend can be attributed to better training of marketing managers, advances in technology, and use of research as an on-going aspect of the marketing function.[6]

AN OVERVIEW OF THE MARKETING RESEARCH INDUSTRY

The marketing research industry consists of suppliers who provide marketing research services. Figure 1.6 broadly categorizes research suppliers as either internal or external. An **internal supplier** is a marketing research department within the firm. Internal research departments can be found in large organizations across a wide range of industries, including automobile companies (GM, Ford), consumer products firms (Procter & Gamble, Colgate Palmolive, Coca-Cola, Reebok) and banks (Citigroup, JP Morgan Chase). For these larger companies, the research function is often centrally located at the corporate headquarters. For smaller or decentralized firms that operate independent divisions, the market research function is distributed among these separate divisions. In decentralized organizations, divisions may be structured around products, customers, or geographical regions, with marketing research personnel assigned across the country. While companies can be found operating under a number of organizational structures, the recent trend has been toward centralization and a trimming of internal marketing research staff, as illustrated by Hewlett-Packard.

internal suppliers
Marketing research departments located within a firm.

EXAMPLE

CENTRALIZED RESEARCH ENABLES HP TO RESPOND TO THE CENTRAL TRENDS OF A DYNAMIC MARKET PLACE

Hewlett-Packard (HP) operates in a volatile, high-tech market. It makes products such as printers, computers, scanners, workstations, and servers, and provides e-services. Due to the volatility of the market, the decision environment at HP is characterized by rapid change. The rapid evolution in technology demands emphasis on new product development. It is in this environment that marketing research operates.

Marketing Research at HP is a centralized function and operates as a shared resource for the worldwide divisions of the company. This is because not every division has the resources to support a full-time marketing research staff. HP also feels that the centralized approach allows it to bring a clear and fresh perspective to problems within a division. The Marketing Research & Information Center consists of 30 people and three distinct groupings: the Market Information Center (MIC), decision support teams, and regional satellites.

The MIC provides background information on markets, competitors, and the industry in general. It keeps track of all information relevant to the firm that is available from secondary sources such as trade publications, the Internet, and commercial marketing research firms. The decision support teams help integrate HP businesses worldwide. They provide research support and consulting services to the divisions. The regional satellites perform a networking function for HP. This allows different divisions to share information on business problems and solutions, facilitating quick resolutions to problems and reducing the amount of repetitive research.

This centralized and lean structure has made marketing research effective and efficient, allowing HP to identify and respond to the dynamic changes taking place in the industry.[7]

external suppliers
Outside marketing research companies hired to supply marketing research data.

full-service suppliers
Companies that offer the full range of marketing research activities.

syndicated services
Companies that collect and sell common pools of data designed to serve information needs that a number of clients share.

External suppliers are outside firms hired to supply marketing research data. Even firms such as HP and Reebok (see opening vignette) with in-house marketing research departments make at least some use of external suppliers. External suppliers range in size from one- or two-person shops to multinational corporations. Most of the research suppliers are small operations.[8] Table 1.2 lists the top 25 global marketing research suppliers.[9]

External suppliers can provide either full service or limited service. **Full-service suppliers** offer the entire range of marketing research services, from problem definition, developing an approach, questionnaire design, sampling, data collection, data analysis, and interpretation, to report preparation and presentation. The services of these suppliers can be further broken down into syndicated services, customized services, and Internet services (Figure 1.6).

Syndicated services are companies that collect and sell common pools of data designed to serve information needs that a number of clients share. Surveys, diary panels, scanners, and audits are the main means by which these data are collected. For example, the Nielsen Television Index provides information on audience size and demographic characteristics of households watching specific television programs. The Nielsen Company also provides scanner volume tracking data, such as those generated by electronic scanning at checkout counters in supermarkets. The Stanford Research Institute, on the other hand, conducts an annual survey of values and lifestyles that is used to classify people into homogeneous groups for the purpose of market segmentation.

FIGURE 1.6 Marketing Research Industry: Supplier and Services

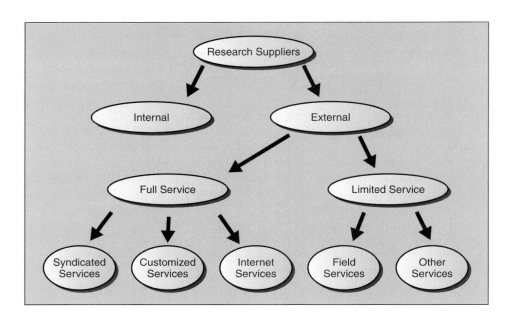

T A B L E   1 . 2   Top 25 Global Research Organizations

2000	1999	Organization	Headquarters	Parent Company	Global Research Revenues[1] (US$ millions)	Percent of Global Revenues from Outside Home Country
1	1	AC Nielsen Corp.	Stamford, Conn.	U.S.	$1,577.0	67.0
2	2	IMS Health Inc.	Westport, Conn.	U.S.	1,131.2	62.5
3	3	The Kantar Group	Fairfield, Conn.	U.K.	928.5	71.4
4	4	Taylor Nelson Sofres plc	London	U.K.	709.6	75.2
5	5	Information Resources Inc.	Chicago	U.S.	531.9	25.0
6	—	VNU Inc.	New York	U.S.	526.9	2.6
7	6	NFO WorldGroup Inc.	Greenwich, Conn.	U.S.	470.5	62.4
8	8	GfK Group	Nuremberg	Germany	444.0	62.4
9	10	Ipsos Group SA	Paris	France	304.2	78.3
10	11	Westat Inc.	Rockville, Md.	U.S.	264.4	0.0
11	9	NOP World	London	U.K.	246.1	60.0
12	14	Aegis Research	London	U.K.	232.2	32.2
13	12	Arbitron Inc.	New York	U.S.	206.8	3.4
14	15	Video Research Ltd.	Tokyo	Japan	174.3*	0.0
15	13	Maritz Research	St. Louis	U.S.	172.0	31.5
16	16	The NPD Group Inc.	Port Washington, N.Y.	U.S.	164.3	17.0
17	18	Opinion Research Corp.	Princeton, N.J.	U.S.	123.9	28.9
18	17	INTAGE Inc.	Tokyo	Japan	119.3*	1.8*
19	19	J.D. Power and Associates	Agoura Hills, Calif.	U.S.	104.0	15.4
20	20	Roper Starch Worldwide Inc.	Harrison, N.Y.	U.S.	73.9	14.3
21	—	Jupiter Media Metrix Inc.	New York	U.S.	69.1	15.0
22	21	Dentsu Research Inc.	Tokyo	Japan	67.6	0.3
23	25	IBOPE Group	Rio de Janeiro	Brazil	60.7	31.8
24	—	Harris Interactive Inc.	Rochester, N.Y.	U.S.	56.0	5.4
25	—	MORPACE International Inc.	Farmington HIlls, Mich.	U.S.	54.3	26.1
		Total			$8,812.7	49.3%

[1]Total revenues that include nonresearch activities for some companies are significantly higher.
*For fiscal year ending March 31, 2001.

Customized services offer a wide variety of marketing research services customized to suit a client's specific needs. Each marketing research project is designed to meet the unique needs of the client. Some of the marketing research firms that offer these services are Burke, Market Facts, and Elrick & Lavidge (featured extensively in this book).

Internet services are offered by several marketing research firms including some who have specialized in conducting marketing research on the Internet, for example, Greenfield Online (www.greenfield.com).

Limited-service suppliers specialize in one or a few steps of the marketing research process. Limited-service suppliers can be found specializing in field services and other services such as coding and data entry and data analysis. **Field services** collect data. They may use the full range of data collection methods (mail, personal, telephone, or electronic interviewing), or they may specialize in only one method. Some field service organizations maintain extensive interviewing facilities across the country for interviewing shoppers in malls. Many offer qualitative data collection services such as focus group interviewing (discussed in Chapter 6). Some firms that offer field services are Field Facts, Field Work Chicago, Quality Controlled Services, and Survey America.

customized services
Companies that tailor the research procedures to best meet the needs of each client.

internet services
Companies that have specialized in conducting marketing research on the Internet.

limited-service suppliers
Companies that specialize in one or a few phases of the marketing research process.

field services
Companies whose primary service offering is their expertise in collecting data for research projects.

coding and data entry services
Companies whose primary service offering is their expertise in converting completed surveys or interviews into a usable database for conducting statistical analysis.

data analysis services
Firms whose primary service is to conduct statistical analysis of quantitative data.

Coding and data entry services provide support services after the data have been collected. The services they perform include editing completed questionnaires, developing a coding scheme, and transcribing the data onto diskettes or magnetic tapes for input into the computer. NRC Data Systems provides such services. **Data analysis services** are offered by firms, also known as tab houses, which specialize in computer analysis of quantitative data such as those obtained in large surveys. Firms such as SDR of Atlanta offer sophisticated data analysis using advanced statistical techniques. Microcomputers and statistical software packages enable firms to perform data analysis in-house. However, the specialized data analysis expertise of outside suppliers is still in demand.

A firm without an internal marketing research department or specialists will be forced to rely on external, generally full-service suppliers. A firm with an internal marketing research staff will make use of both full-service and limited-service suppliers. The need for external suppliers may arise because the firm may not have the resources or the technical expertise to undertake certain phases of a project. Also, political conflict-of-interest issues may determine that a project be conducted by an outside supplier, as in the case of Reebok in the opening vignette. Data collection in almost every case and data analysis in most instances are contracted to external suppliers. Sometimes Reebok also retains full-service suppliers to conduct the entire marketing research project.

SELECTING A RESEARCH SUPPLIER

When initiating a marketing research study, a firm will often need to hire external suppliers for all or part of the project. The process of selecting an outside supplier can be informal, relying primarily on word-of-mouth endorsements, or it may be very formal, involving a "request for proposal." In the latter case, research suppliers are requested to submit formal proposals for evaluation by the hiring firm. The first step involves compiling a list of prospective suppliers from trade publications, professional directories, and personal contacts.

Regardless of the formality of the process, the hiring firm must develop a checklist detailing its criteria governing the selection of outside suppliers. That checklist should go beyond technical requirements, covering the following areas:

- What is the supplier's reputation?
- Does the firm complete projects on schedule? Is it flexible?
- Is it known for maintaining ethical standards?
- Are its research projects of high quality?
- What kind and how much experience does the supplier have?
- Has the firm had experience with projects similar to this one?
- Do the supplier's personnel have both technical and nontechnical expertise?

Reebok International, which subcontracts a great deal of its research to external suppliers, uses a similar checklist. A checklist helps managers examine the working relationships as well as the project requirements. Because of the importance of most research efforts, compatible working relationships and good communication skills can become primary considerations when hiring.

A competitive bidding process often is used in selecting external suppliers, particularly for large jobs. However, awarding projects based on lowest price is not a good rule of thumb. The completeness of the research proposal and the criteria discussed above must all be factored into the hiring decision. Moreover, long-term contracts with research suppliers are preferable to selection on a project-by-project basis.

CAREERS IN MARKETING RESEARCH

Promising career opportunities are available with marketing research firms (e.g., AC Nielsen, Elrick & Lavidge, Burke, M/A/R/C). Equally appealing are careers in business and nonbusiness firms and agencies with in-house marketing research departments (e.g., Procter & Gamble, Coca-Cola, Reebok, the Federal Trade Commission, United States Census Bureau). Advertising agencies (e.g., BBDO International, Ogilvy & Mather, J. Walter Thompson, Young & Rubicam) also conduct substantial marketing research and employ professionals in this field.

A career in research often begins with a supervisory position in field work or data analysis. With experience, the researcher moves up to project management positions, resulting in director and eventually in a vice president–level position. Figure 1.7 gives a sample of marketing research jobs.

The most common entry-level position in the marketing research industry for people with bachelor's degrees (for example, BBA) is operational supervisor. An operational supervisor is responsible for supervising the day-to-day operations of specific aspects of the marketing research process. These may range from field work to data editing to coding for programming and data analysis. Rather than enter the discipline from the operations side, BBAs with strong organizational skills may start as assistant project manager. An assistant project manager will learn and assist in questionnaire design, review field instructions, and monitor timing and costs of studies. As research techniques become more sophisticated, there is a growing preference for people with master's degrees. Those with MBA or equivalent degrees are likely to be employed as project managers. In marketing research firms such as Elrick & Lavidge, the project manager works with the account director in managing the day-to-day operations of a marketing research project.

A researcher entering the profession on the client side would typically begin as a junior research analyst (for BBAs) or research analyst (for MBAs). The junior analyst and the research analyst learn about the particular industry and receive training from a senior staff member, usually the marketing research manager. The junior analyst position includes a training program to prepare individuals for the responsibilities of a research analyst, including coordinating with the marketing department and sales force to develop goals for product exposure. The research analyst's responsibilities include checking all data for accuracy, comparing and contrasting new research with established norms, and analyzing data for the purpose of market forecasting.

As these job titles indicate, careers in marketing research can be either highly technical, specializing in the design and the statistical side of the industry, or they can be of a general management nature, with emphasis on client relationships. To prepare for a career in marketing research, you should:

- Take all the marketing courses you can.
- Take courses in statistics and quantitative methods.
- Acquire computer and Internet skills.
- Take courses in psychology and consumer behavior.
- Acquire effective written and verbal communication skills.
- Think creatively. Creativity and common sense command a premium in marketing research.

It is important for marketing researchers to be liberally educated in order to better understand the problems managers face and then be able to address them from a broad perspective.[10] A career in marketing research will involve working with other bright, en-

A Sample of Marketing Research Jobs

Marketing

Apple Computer has created an environment as progressive and break-through as the products we bring to market. Here, your ideas are heard. And your ability to shape the industry is as un-limited as your ambition. Join us, and we'll give you the freedom to inspire the kind of change that can impact our future . . . and yours.

Senior Customer Research Analyst

Using custom market research, you'll be responsible for answering a wide range of complex marketing and strategic questions, and for advocating the customer's perspective in key Apple decisions. Working with product marketing and corporate decision-makers, you'll assist in setting priorities, and in defining/refining corporate objectives. You'll also design and manage research projects, including studies of positioning, new product benefits, concept testing, etc. Then, you'll present results and make recommendations.

The ideal candidate will have a relevant advanced degree and 5+ years' experience, a BA and 8 years' experience, or an equivalent combination of training and experience, including the management of projects using the full range of research methodology. Superior verbal and written communication skills, and the ability to synthesize research results into persuasive recommendations, are absolutely essential. Fluency in a foreign language and direct experience with PC customers in a non-research capacity are also desirable assets.

Apple Computer has a corporate commitment to the principle of diversity. In that spirit, we welcome applications from all individuals.

 Apple©

©1995 Apple Computer, Inc. All rights reserved. Apple and the Apple logo are registered trademarks of Apple Computer, Inc.

Market Research Manager

Hilti, a worldwide leader in the manufacturing and marketing of construction tools and fasteners for nearly half a century, is presently seeking a Marketing Research Manager for our Tulsa, Oklahoma corporate facility.

Responsible for all primary and secondary Market Research functions, the candidate for this position must be able to perform all functions; surveys, focus groups, analysis, database management and presentation of results. In addition, the incumbent must be able to work with outside suppliers of services.

Qualified candidates must possess:
- Bachelor's degree plus five years of industrial market research
- Specific experience writing and conducting both phone and written surveys including analysis and presentation of the results.
- Complete competency conducting focus groups with customers with responsibility for the entire process.
- Experience utilizing secondary sources such as supplier databases (i.e., Dodge and D&B).
- Absolute wizardry with database programs such as D-base and Access.
- Experience gathering intelligence on competitors from traditional and non-traditional sources.
- Highly developed business writing and presentation skills.

Individuals meeting our requirements and seeking a career will an industry leader offering a competitive salary and excellent benefits should send a resume complete with salary history to:

HILTI INC.
Attn: Personnel Manager, Corporate Division
P.O. Box 21148, Tulsa, OK 74121
Or fax your resume to (918) 250-8089.
Our job line number is (918) 252-6001.

No phone calls or agencies please! Hilti is proud to be an Equal Opportunity Employer MFN.

MARKET RESEARCH

Smith Hanley Associates is the premier resource for the market research professional nationwide. Below is a sample of current openings:
- **Consumer Research**—Financial services, publishing and packaged goods companies seek Master's/MBA with 3–8 yrs. quantitative research experience. Multivariate statistics & project management skills desired. Many locations: NY, CA, D.C., MA, IL, MI, TX, NE, KS, UT, KY, IN, NC. Salary $45–75K.
- **Directors, Market Analysis**—Interactive media, entertainment software or telecommunication ind. exp. desired for high profile opportunities. Stellar MBA w/3–4 yrs. exp. in bus. modeling & sales forecasting. E. Coast Salary $60–80K + Bonus.
- **Management Consulting**—Top tier consulting firm seek PhD/Master's in quantitative discipline for strategic mkt research groups. Survey research and statistical modeling exp. required. Projects include product positioning, market entry, sales force strategy. Boston and New York Salary $50–100K.
- **Direct Marketing**—Red hot field for researchers with a strong technical beat. Positions in publishing, catalogues, and agencies, financial services, and consulting firms. Segmentation modeling and experience with neural nets desired. Dozens of positions worldwide! Salary $40–90K + Bonus.

SMITH HANLEY
Associates, Inc.

Please call or write:
Linda Burtch
312-629-2400
200 W. Madison, Chicago, IL 60606

Sandra Rupp
212-687-9696
99 Park Ave., New York, NY 10016

EXECUTIVE RECRUITERS

FIGURE 1.7 A Sample of Marketing Research Jobs

ergetic people in a fast-paced, dynamic environment. You will get to work on diverse qualitative and quantitative projects with clients in a variety of industries, including e-commerce, travel, telecommunications, pharmaceuticals, government, and nonprofit. The benefits include ongoing training and career development, a competitive salary, comprehensive health and dental plans, a 401k plan, the option to wear business casual attire, and excellent advancement opportunities.

Marketing research is a multibillion-dollar-a-year industry dedicated to providing valuable information to manufacturers and service providers. These companies use the information to develop marketable products and services, and to build and maintain a competitive edge. Marketing researchers help determine answers for such questions as:

- What is the best way to segment the market?
- When should products enter or leave the marketplace?
- How do you predict the results of election polls?
- When is it time to change an advertising campaign?
- How does a company determine customer satisfaction?

College graduates' lack of awareness of marketing research as a career and a growing demand for marketing researchers in the fields of information technology, pharmaceuticals, financial services, and other booming industries has created a shortage of professionals in the field. Marketing research organizations would like to have more incoming talent in order to have a greater presence in senior management in the future. The need for marketing researchers could not be greater. This makes a career worth pursuing for both the short and the long term. For more information on jobs in marketing research, check out the American Marketing Association's career center at *www.ama.org* or *www.marketingpower.com*. The attractive career path marketing research offers is also evident from the comments of Mr. Michael Naples.

EXAMPLE

MARKETING RESEARCH: "A BETTER CAREER PATH"

Michael Naples, President, Advertising Research Foundation (ARF), highly recommends careers in marketing research. In his words:

"It's an information business and information is the revolution we're in, so why wouldn't [marketing] research be a good career path? I think it can only grow in stature as time goes by. I think the fact that the research companies are coming on strong now means they will value their product more and more as they gain strength. They'll invest in their product so it'll be a better career path."[11]

THE ROLE OF MARKETING RESEARCH IN MIS AND DSS

Earlier, we defined marketing research as the systematic and objective identification, collection, analysis, and dissemination of information for use in marketing decision making. Combining external market information with internal billing, production, and other records results in a powerful marketing information system (MIS) (Figure 1.8).

A **marketing information system (MIS)** is a formalized set of procedures for generating, analyzing, storing, and distributing information to marketing decision makers on

marketing information system (MIS)
A formalized set of procedures for generating, analyzing, storing, and distributing pertinent information to marketing decision makers on an ongoing basis.

FIGURE 1.8 The Development of MIS and DSS

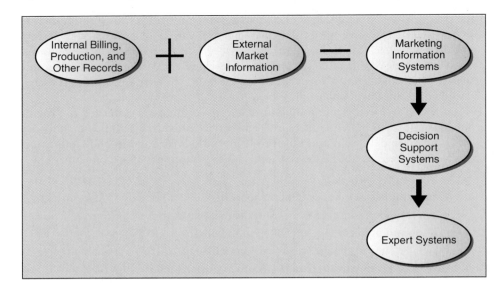

an ongoing basis. MIS is differentiated from marketing research in that it is continuously available. MIS is designed to complement the decision maker's responsibilities, style, and information needs. The power of MIS is in the access it gives managers to vast amounts of information, combining production, invoice, and billing information with marketing intelligence, including marketing research. MIS offers the potential of much more information than can be obtained from ad hoc marketing research projects. However, that potential is often not achieved when the information is structured so rigidly that it cannot be easily manipulated.

Developed to overcome the limitations of MIS, decision support systems (DSSs) have built-in flexibility that allows decision makers to interact directly with databases and analysis models. A **decision support system (DSS)** is an integrated system including hardware, a communications network, database, model base, software base, and the DSS user (decision maker) who collects and interprets information for decision making. Information collected by marketing research becomes a part of the DSS, as in the case of Reebok in the opening vignette. Specifically, marketing research contributes research data to the database, marketing models and analytical techniques to the model base, and specialized programs for analyzing marketing data to the software base. Many firms are building huge internal databases as part of the DSS (see database marketing in Chapter 4). The analytical techniques and the software to analyze these data are also discussed later (Chapters 15 through 18). DSSs differ from MISs in that they combine the models

decision support system (DSS)
An information system that enables decision makers to interact directly with both databases and analysis models. The important components of a DSS include hardware and a communication network, database, model base, software base, and the DSS user (decision maker).

FIGURE 1.9 Marketing Information Systems (MIS) vs. Decision Support Systems (DSS)

MIS	DSS
• Structured problems	• Unstructured problems
• Use of reports	• Use of models
• Information displaying restricted	• Adaptability
• Can improve decision making by clarifying new data	• Can improve decision making by using "what if" analysis

and analytic techniques of traditional marketing research with easy access and retrieval of MISs (see Figure 1.9).

Well-designed DSSs adapt to the decision-making needs of the user with easy interactive processes. In addition to providing easy access to data, DSSs can also enhance decision-making effectiveness by using "what-if" analysis. Reebok International makes use of a sophisticated DSS that enables it to assess the impact of introducing new footwear, making a promotional offer, or opening a new facility at a specific location, when these projects are still in the planning stage.

MISs and DSSs can greatly improve decision making by giving management access to a wide range of information. An advanced form of DSS, called *expert systems,* uses artificial intelligence procedures to incorporate expert judgment. Thus, the expert systems can actually lead to decisions recommending certain courses of action to the management. All these systems can greatly enhance the effectiveness of marketing, as illustrated by Oscar Mayer.

EXAMPLE

MIS AND DSS: THE MAYOR OF OSCAR MAYER

Marketing research activities at Oscar Mayer are broken into two distinct divisions: Brand Research and Marketing Systems and Analytics (MSA). Brand Research is responsible for primary and secondary consumer research, consulting, and reporting trends. MSA is responsible for maintaining the MIS and DSS systems and collects and manipulates internally generated data such as sales.

The MSA databases offer users: (1) formal sales analyses, forecasts, and trends; (2) answers to ad hoc questions not explained by the more formal analysis; and (3) analysis of scanner-based data.

The marketing and sales departments access this information via computers linked to the Oscar Mayer Marketing Information Center. The MIS and DSS have enabled the marketing department to introduce several successful products over the years. For instance, one of the trends revealed by the company's MIS was the people's desire to consume foods that were low fat but rich in taste and flavor. This led to the development of Oscar Mayer Free Hot Dogs, a fat-free frank that still offers the expected taste and texture. This product has been a great success because it met a need in the marketplace.[12]

SUMMARY ILLUSTRATION USING THE OPENING VIGNETTE

To summarize and illustrate the concepts in this chapter, let's return to the opening vignette. Marketing research involves the identification, collection, analysis, and dissemination of information about consumers, channel members, competitors, changes and trends in the marketplace, and other aspects of the firm's environment. In the opening vignette, Reebok used "time use" research in an attempt to discover what consumers do with their spare time. Marketing research may be classified as problem-identification research or problem-solving research. Reebok used problem-identification research involving secondary data analysis, focus groups, and a market potential survey to discover that adults were spending less time in health clubs and more time exercising at home.

Problem-solving research, in the form of product research, then led to the development of the successful home step-aerobics line.

The marketing research process consists of six steps, which must be followed systematically. Reebok follows a very similar marketing research process, and some of these steps were illustrated in the opening vignette. Marketing research may be conducted internally and/or may be purchased from external suppliers. In the case of Reebok, in-house marketing research specialists are actively involved in defining and designing the marketing research project and also have the primary responsibility for presentation of the results to the management and providing assistance in implementation. Reebok also makes use of full-service suppliers who provide assistance in all the steps of the marketing research process as well as limited-service suppliers who may handle only data collection and analysis and assist in report writing.

The marketing research industry offers a wide range of careers in both corporate (e.g., Reebok) and independent service organizations. Information obtained using marketing research can stand alone or is integrated into an MIS and DSS, as in the case of Reebok.

APPLICATION TO CONTEMPORARY ISSUES

While we address several contemporary issues throughout the text, we focus special attention on five major issues: total quality management (TQM), international marketing research, technology and marketing research, ethics in marketing research, and Internet applications. Each of these issues receives a separate section in each chapter of the text (except the data analysis chapters 16 through 18). We show how marketing research principles can be applied to practice TQM and when conducting research in an international setting. Because we live in a technological age, the technological developments that affect marketing research are also discussed. Ethical issues in marketing research are described and the Internet applications identified.

MARKETING RESEARCH AND TQM

Total Quality Management (TQM) has gained increased acceptance as a management practice that helps firms survive and grow in the marketplace. TQM is defined as a company-wide effort that involves all the employees and applies quality to internal and external processes, operations, and results.

The U.S. Department of Commerce established the Malcolm Baldrige Award in 1987 to enhance U.S. competitiveness through quality. The award encourages companies to know who their customers are and how they define quality related to specific products and firms. Marketing research can focus on gathering information that will facilitate the implementation of quality processes in a company. An examination of the marketing research practices of the companies that have won the Malcolm Baldrige National Quality Award indicates a common theme. In all of these firms, there was an emphasis on obtaining information from the ultimate consumers as well as other external and internal customer groups (shareholders, employees, etc.). For example, Federal Express Corporation has extensive data on package delivery reliability, shipments, customer requirements, customer satisfaction, and climate on all customers and in all work groups across the company. The Baldrige Award heavily reflects the importance of collecting and analyzing data to support TQM. In the 2000 examination criteria, about 60 percent of the factors are significantly influenced by the firm's ability to collect, analyze, and act on information about customers, employees, or processes.

FOCUS ON ELRICK & LAVIDGE

■ COMPANY PROFILE

Elrick & Lavidge (E&L), a leading provider of marketing research services, was founded in 1951 by two well-known marketing researchers, Robert F. Elrick and Robert J. Lavidge. E&L, with headquarters in Atlanta, has many branches, including full-service branches in Dallas; San Francisco; Chicago; Paramus, New Jersey; and Kansas City (www.elavidge.com).

■ CAREERS AT E&L

Many professional careers can be found at E&L, but they are essentially divided into two large groupings. The first group has an operational orientation and consists mainly of the people who actually implement the studies, including programmers; computer operators; field workers; telephone operators; and mail, data entry, and coding clerks.

The second group, called Research Services, can be considered the "analysis" side of the company. These people work with clients to design the studies, oversee the implementation of each study, perform much of the analysis on the results of the studies, and present the results to the clients. These people are the traditional marketing researchers, with backgrounds in management, marketing and sales, statistics, and, of course, marketing research.

■ THE MARKETING RESEARCH PROCESS AT E&L

The marketing research process at E&L generally follows the six-step framework of this text.

Step 1: Problem Definition.
It is the research director's job to work with the client to develop an understanding of the nature of the problem.

Step 2: Developing an Approach to the Problem.
This step is done more rigorously in some projects than others. For new projects that are not similar to others that have been done in the past, the research director will use on-staff experts and outside research to develop a suitable approach.

Step 3: Research Design Formulation.
This step is typically done in two phases. The product of the first phase is a high-level design that defines the information needed and addresses the method of data collection (survey, focus group, etc.), the sampling process, and the sample. The purpose of this first phase is to develop a cost and time estimate for the client without expending too much effort on the project before the client has agreed to pay for it. Once the client agrees to the estimate, the next phase begins. The second phase includes the detailed design formulation tasks of any required qualitative research, questionnaire design (including measurement and scaling procedures), and development of the plan of data analysis.

Step 4: Field Work or Data Collection.
This step is done either by E&L staff or by subcontractors who work in particular cities. The field workers collect the data from the appropriate sample of respondents and deliver the information back to E&L for analysis.

Step 5: Data Preparation and Analysis.
Data preparation and analysis differs by client. Some clients perform data preparation and analysis in-house, asking that E&L merely deliver the raw data to them with minimal verification. Other clients ask E&L to perform all of the editing, coding, transcription, and verification of data, and then to analyze the data. These clients also want E&L to present results and conclusions at the end of the project.

Step 6: Report Preparation and Presentation.
Every project involves a report that documents the entire process and includes the work produced from each of the previous steps. In addition, it presents the results of the study and identifies major findings for use in the client's decision making. This report is sent to the client in either paper or electronic form and is often presented orally as well.

Marketing research helps TQM companies determine what their customers value and what aspects of their marketing efforts contribute to quality. This information drives the quality improvement within the company. Thus, marketing research is an integral part of TQM and plays a critical role, as in the life insurance industry.

EXAMPLE

QUALITY AS INSURANCE FOR THE LIFE INSURANCE INDUSTRY

In the late 1990s, the life insurance industry was facing weak sales and an apparent lack of consumer interest toward its products. Marketing research identified the major problem as lack of quality marketing efforts directed to the consumers.

Guided by marketing research, the president and CEO of LIMRA (Life Insurance Market Research Association) International identified the following quality initiatives intended to focus on the consumer.

- **Improve Personnel.** Provide more training, product knowledge, and support to better serve the consumers.
- **Increase Customer Focus.** Understand the consumer's perception of quality through increased marketing research.
- **Growth Through Mergers and Acquisitions.** Improve quality by offering additional products and services unavailable through smaller firms.
- **Add Distribution Channels.** Make life insurance available to consumers through alternative means in order to provide quicker and cheaper service to customers.

The emphasis on building quality in marketing resulted in a turnaround for the life insurance industry.[13]

INTERNATIONAL MARKETING RESEARCH

The United States accounts for only 39 percent of the marketing research expenditures worldwide. About 40 percent of all marketing research is conducted in Western Europe and 9 percent in Japan. Most of the research in Europe is done in Germany, the United Kingdom, France, Italy, and Spain.[14] With the globalization of markets, marketing research has assumed a truly international character, a trend that is likely to continue. Several U.S.-based market research firms are equipped to conduct international marketing research. They include AC Nielsen, IMS Health, Information Resources, and NFO WorldGroup (see Table 1.2). Foreign-based firms include the Kantar Group and Taylor Nelson Sofres (United Kingdom) and the GfK Group (Germany).

International marketing research is much more complex than domestic marketing research. Research of this type should be sensitive to differences in customs, communication, and culture. The environment in the countries or international markets that are being researched influences the way the six steps of the marketing research process should be performed. These factors include marketing, government, and the legal, economic, structural, informational and technological, and sociocultural environment. Properly conducted international marketing research can yield high dividends, as demonstrated by the success of Procter & Gamble in China.

HEAD & SHOULDERS STANDS HEAD AND SHOULDERS ABOVE COMPETITION IN CHINA

P&G products are the largest daily-use consumer products in China. The company has achieved this status by ignoring popular maxims, instead relying on marketing research. The success of P&G comes because it ignored the standard practices used in marketing to a Chinese audience. It did not cater to a wealthy audience, although it was told that none could afford its expensive products. By relying on marketing research, such popular maxims were seen for what they were—misunderstandings. Additionally, by conducting proper cross-cultural research, P&G was able to overcome any Western bias based on erroneous beliefs about China, such as middle-class Chinese could not afford expensive Western products.

Marketing research revealed that dandruff was a major concern as the Chinese have dark hair, where dandruff readily stands out. Furthermore, Chinese shampoos were ineffective in fighting this malady. Research also revealed that most Chinese were willing to pay a premium for a shampoo that addressed this problem.

So in the early 1990s P&G decided to establish its foothold in China by fighting dandruff. P&G targeted a broad segment, rather than just the wealthy. P&G introduced Head & Shoulders as a premium brand, and within three years it was China's leading shampoo. P&G then introduced antidandruff versions of Pert and Pantene. Using careful targeting, both brands performed extremely well. Overall, P&G commands 57 percent of the shampoo market in China, even though its products are priced over 300 percent higher than local brands. These figures show that those who overcome their biases and conduct proper research can stand head and shoulders above the competition.[15]

TECHNOLOGY AND MARKETING RESEARCH

The term *Third Wave,* coined from Alvin Toffler's book of the same name, has come to symbolize the contemporary transition from current ways of viewing and doing things to a new age. The third wave of marketing research will shape not only the way information is used but also our fundamental conception of the role of marketing research in assisting management decisions.

In the First Wave, we progressed from seat-of-the-pants decision making to data-based decisions. The emphasis was on supporting marketing decisions with data. As more data became available, a large problem arose. Marketers were soon floating in a sea of individual facts about their products and markets with very little way of assimilating the data.

In the Second Wave, the progression was from data-based decisions to information-based decision making. Rather than review a multitude of individual facts, the role of marketing research became analyzing data to summarize the underlying patterns. If we could understand the relationships and patterns in the data, so the logic went, this would lead to the insights necessary to make sound marketing decisions.

Now with the Third Wave, we're moving from information-based decision making to system-based decisions. Computer technology, a major driving force behind the Third Wave, allows for a better fit of marketing information to the needs of the market planning process. We can create a better interface and information exchange between marketing researchers and marketing managers resulting in a unique knowledge base that captures the expertise of each group. The Third Wave involves a number of developments centered on decision support systems and expert systems that put the power of marketing information directly into the hands of nontechnical decision makers.

A major goal of this new improved technology is to link the customer to the information superhighway through the Internet, interactive telephone, interactive TV, home shopping channels, and integrated call centers. Such a system knows who is calling based on the customer's phone number and can identify information the customer will likely need. This allows researchers to know in real time what is happening in the marketplace. Cyberspace as a data-collection alternative will rival the telephone in the new century. Researchers will be doing research in an interactive environment. As the leading edge of the Third Wave begins to emerge, one can imagine many intriguing ways that marketing research will be used in the future.[16]

ETHICS IN MARKETING RESEARCH

Business activities are often discussed from the perspective of different stakeholders, those individuals or groups who have an interest in or are directly involved in activities related to business. Marketing research activities affect four stakeholders: (1) the marketing researcher, (2) the client, (3) the respondent, and (4) the public. Ethical questions arise when conflict occurs between these stakeholders (Figure 1.10).

In the face of conflict, the behavior of the stakeholders should be guided by codes of conduct. Several organizations, such as the Marketing Research Association and the American Marketing Association, provide codes in the area of ethical research behavior. Each stakeholder has responsibilities. Neglect of these responsibilities may result in hurting another stakeholder or the research project. It will always damage the research process and the integrity of the profession.[17] These issues are discussed in more detail in subsequent chapters.

FIGURE 1.10
Stakeholders in Marketing Research: An Ethical Perspective

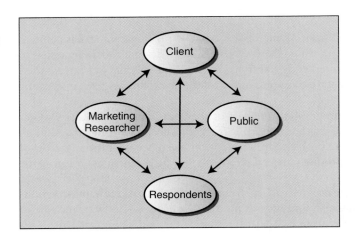

INTERNET APPLICATIONS

The Internet can be useful to marketing researchers in many ways. It can be used as a source of marketing research providers (e.g., *www.greenbook.org*) or secondary data, and for collecting primary data via surveys and other methods. One of the great advantages of doing surveys on the Internet is that the data can be processed as fast as they come in because the data are electronically obtained from the respondents. The Internet is also very useful for project management. Internet e-mail combined with software such as Lotus Notes is being used for communication by researchers and clients, and for coordinating and managing the six steps of the marketing research process. The Internet is also being used to disseminate marketing research results and reports, which can be posted on the Web and made available to managers on a worldwide basis.

The Internet is fast becoming a useful tool in the identification, collection, analysis, and dissemination of information related to marketing research. Throughout this book, we show how the Internet is used in the six steps of the marketing research process.

EXAMPLE

THE WORLD OF MARKETING RESEARCH ON THE INTERNET

The WorldOpinion Web site *(www.worldopinion.com)* is designed to bring you up-to-date news and comprehensive information on the market research industry. Here's how to find what you're looking for and get the most out of your visit.

If you're job hunting or hiring, the classifieds section lists jobs in research, marketing, advertising, public relations, and allied professions. There are literally thousands of current job openings. You're welcome to submit your résumé, or job listing, at no charge.

Looking for the right research company for your project? The directory of researchers lists over 8,500 research locations in 99 countries. Search by company name or search by company type and/or geography.

The news section, updated daily, brings you company, conference, and product news from the world of marketing research.

If you're thinking of attending a marketing or research event or need more information on research education opportunities, check out the WorldOpinion calendar. Hundreds of events and research courses from throughout the world are listed.

There are many other ways the WorldOpinion Web site brings the world of marketing research to you. Explore it!

SPSS

In this book we feature SPSS programs, not merely as a statistical package, but as an integrative package that can be used in the various stages of the marketing research process. We illustrate the use of SPSS for defining the problem, developing an approach, formulating the research design, data collection, data preparation and analysis, and report preparation and presentation. In addition to the BASE module, we also feature other SPSS programs such as Decision Time, What If?, Maps, Data Entry, SamplePower, Missing Values, TextSmart, and SmartViewer.

The data analysis is also illustrated with three other software packages: SAS, MINITAB, and EXCEL.

SUMMARY

Marketing research provides information about consumers, channel members, competitors, changes and trends in the marketplace, and other aspects of the firm's environment. It assesses information needs and provides relevant information in order to improve the marketing decision-making process. Marketing research is a systematic and objective process designed to identify and solve marketing problems. Thus, marketing research can be classified as problem-identification research and problem-solving research. The marketing research process consists of six steps that must be followed systematically.

A firm may conduct its own marketing research or may purchase it from external suppliers. External suppliers can provide full service or they may specialize in one or more aspects of the process. Full-service suppliers provide the entire range of marketing research services, from problem definition to report preparation and presentation. The services provided by these suppliers can be classified as syndicated services, customized services, or Internet services. Limited-service suppliers specialize in one or a few phases of the marketing research project. Services offered by these suppliers can be classified as field services or other services such as coding and data entry and data analysis.

The marketing research industry offers a wide range of careers in both corporate and independent service organizations. Marketing research firms, business and nonbusiness firms, and advertising agencies all employ research professionals. Information obtained using marketing research can stand alone or be integrated into an MIS or a DSS. Marketing research contributes to the DSS by providing research data to the database, marketing models and analytical techniques to the model base, and specialized marketing research programs to the software base.

Marketing research helps to identify, define, and measure how customers define quality, which makes it an integral part of total quality management (TQM). International marketing research is much more complex than domestic research because researchers must consider the environment in the international markets they are researching.

Technological developments are reshaping the role of marketing research as well as the way in which it is conducted. The ethical issues in marketing research involve four stakeholders: (1) the marketing researcher, (2) the client, (3) the respondent, and (4) the public. The Internet can be used at every step of the marketing research process.

KEY TERMS AND CONCEPTS

Marketing research, 4
Problem-identification
   research, 6
Problem-solving
   research, 7
Marketing research
   process, 9
Internal supplier, 15

External suppliers, 16
Full-service suppliers, 16
Syndicated services, 16
Customized services, 17
Internet services, 17
Limited-service
   suppliers, 17
Field services, 17

Coding and data entry
   services, 18
Data analysis services, 18
Marketing information
   system (MIS), 21
Decision support system
   (DSS), 22

ACRONYMS

The role and salient characteristics of marketing research may be described by the acronym RESEARCH:

R ecognition of information needs
E ffective decision making
S ystematic and objective
E xude/disseminate information
A nalysis of information
R ecommendations for action
C ollection of information
H elpful to managers

EXERCISES

1. Define *marketing research.* What are some of the noteworthy aspects of this definition?
2. Describe one classification of marketing research and give examples.
3. Describe the steps in the marketing research process.
4. Describe the task of marketing research and illustrate with an example.
5. What decisions do marketing managers make? How does marketing research help them to make these decisions?
6. Explain one way to classify marketing research suppliers.
7. What are syndicated services and how do they help a firm undertake marketing research?
8. What is the main difference between a full-service and a limited-service supplier?
9. List five guidelines for selecting an external marketing research supplier.
10. What career opportunities are available in marketing research? Are you interested in pursuing such a career? Why or why not?
11. What is a marketing information system?
12. How is DSS different from MIS?
13. Who are the stakeholders in marketing research?

PROBLEMS

1. Look through recent issues of newspapers and magazines to identify five examples of problem-identification research and five examples of problem-solving research.
2. Describe one marketing research project that would be useful to each of the following organizations:
   a. Your campus bookstore.
   b. The public transportation authority in your city.
   c. A major department store in your area.
   d. A restaurant located near your campus.
   e. A zoo in a major city.

INTERNET AND COMPUTER EXERCISES

1. Visit the Web sites of three of the marketing research firms in Table 1.2. Write a report on the services offered by these firms. Use the Framework of Figure 1.6. What statements can you make about the structure of the marketing research industry?

2. Visit Sears's Web site *(www.sears.com)* and write a report discussing the retailing and marketing activities of Sears.
3. Visit the Web sites of MRA *(www.mra-net.org)*, ESOMAR *(www.esomar.nl)*, and MRSA *(www.mrsa.com.au)*, and compare and contrast the information available at these sites. Of the three marketing research associations, which has the most useful Web site, and why?
4. Visit *www.bls.gov*. What is the employment potential for marketing researchers?
5. Examine recent issues of magazines such as *Marketing News, Advertising Age, Quirk's Marketing Research Review,* and *Marketing Research: A Magazine of Management and Applications* to identify one Internet application in each of the following areas:
   a. Identification of information needs
   b. Collection of information
   c. Analysis of information
   d. Provision of information (report preparation)

ACTIVITIES

ROLE PLAYING

1. You are the research director for a major bank. You are to recruit a junior analyst who would be responsible for collecting and analyzing secondary data (data already collected by other agencies that are relevant to your operations). With a fellow student playing the role of an applicant for this position, conduct the interview. Does this applicant have the necessary background and skills? Reverse the roles and repeat the exercise.
2. You are a project director working for a major research supplier. You have just received a telephone call from an irate respondent who believes that an interviewer has violated her privacy by calling at an inconvenient time. The respondent expresses several ethical concerns. Ask a fellow student to play the role of this respondent. Address the respondent's concerns and pacify her.

FIELD WORK

1. Using your local newspaper and national newspapers such as *USA Today,* the *Wall Street Journal,* or the *New York Times,* compile a list of career opportunities in marketing research by looking at the job postings in the classified section.
2. Interview someone who works for a marketing research supplier. What is this person's opinion about career opportunities in marketing research? Write a report of your interview, giving a summary of what was said.
3. Interview someone who works in the marketing research department of a major corporation. What is this person's opinion about career opportunities available in marketing research? Write a report of your interview, giving a summary of what was said.

GROUP DISCUSSION

As a small group of four or five, discuss the following issues:
1. What type of institutional structure is best for a marketing research department in a large business firm?
2. What is the ideal educational background for someone seeking a career in marketing research?
3. Can ethical standards be enforced in marketing research? If so, how?

NOTES

1. Louise Lee, "Burning Rubber at Reebok," *Business Week* (May 15, 2000): 54; Terry Lefton, "Bok in the Saddle Again," *Brandweek* (February 8, 1999): 26–31; Anabelle Perez, "Reebok & DP Rev Up for Home," *Sporting Goods Business*, 30(6) (April 14, 1997): 24; and Joe Schwartz, "How Reebok Fits Shoes," *American Demographics*, 15(3) (March 1993): 54.

2. Doss Struse, "Marketing Research's Top 25 Influences," *Marketing Research*, 11(4) (Winter 1999/Spring 2000: 4–9; and "Marketing Research: On the Threshold of Opportunity? A Roundtable Discussion on the Past, Present and Future of Research," *Quirk's Marketing Research* (March 1996): 34–35, 56–59.

3. Kate MacArthur, "MCD's Serves Up $500 Mil Smile with New Logo," *Advertising Age*, 71(27) (June 26, 2000): 3; Louise Kramer, "More Nimble McDonald's Is Getting Back on Track," *Advertising Age*, 70(3) (January 18, 1999): 6; and "McDonald's Execs Outline Research Philosophy," *Marketing News*, 29(22) (October 23, 1995): 37.

4. Kate Brennan, "Marriott Explores Moderate-Tier Market," *Lodging Hospitality*, 56(6) (May 1, 2000): 18; "Marriott Launches Brand to Capture Moderate Tier," *Hotel & Motel Management*, 214(12) (July 5, 1999): 16; and "Listening to Customers: The Market Research Function at Marriott Corporation," *Marketing Research: A Magazine of Management and Applications* (March 1989).

5. Joe Miller, "GM: New Products at Record Pace," *Automotive News*, 74(5888) (August 14, 2000): 28; Bob Wallace, "Data Warehouse to Drive Online Marketing at GM," *ComputerWorld*, 33(27) (July 5, 1999): 6; Jean Halliday, "Making Ad Research Work for GM," *Advertising Age*, 68(5) (February 3, 1997): S14; and Phil Frame, "GM's Design Chief: The Customer," *Automotive News*, 67(5528) (November 29, 1993): 3.

6. Thomas Leigh, "Research Roundtable," *Marketing Research: A Magazine of Management and Applications*, 11(1) (Spring 1999): 4–19; Naresh K. Malhotra, "Shifting Perspective on the Shifting Paradigm in Marketing Research," *Journal of the Academy of Marketing Science*, 20 (Fall 1992): 379–387; and William Perreault, "The Shifting Paradigm in Marketing Research," *Journal of the Academy of Marketing Science*, 20 (Fall 1992): 367–375.

7. Sami Lais, "Users Focus on Current Products as HP Looks Ahead," *ComputerWorld*, 34(27) (July 3, 2000): 50; Susan Kuchinskas, "Hewlett-Packard: Best Online Campaign," *Brandweek*, 40(26) (June 28, 1999): IQ44; and William R. BonDurant, "Research the HP Way," *Marketing Research: A Magazine of Management and Applications*, 4(2) (June 1992): 28–33.

8. A complete listing and description of the individual firms in the marketing research industry is provided in Ryan P. Green, *International Directory of Marketing Research Houses and Services* (New York Chapter, American Marketing Association, annually).

9. Jack Honomichl, "Top 25 Global Research Organizations," *Marketing News* (August 13, 2001): Special Pullout Section.

10. James Heckman, "Program Introduces Market Research as a Career," *Marketing News*, 33(14) (July 5, 1999): 4; Ralph W. Giacobbe and Madhav N. Segal, "Rethinking Marketing Research Education: A Conceptual, Analytical, and Empirical Investigation," *Journal of Marketing Education*, 16 (Spring 1994): 43–58.

11. Michelle Wirth Fellman, "An Aging Profession," *Marketing Research*, 12(1) (Spring 2000): 33–35; and "Marketing Research: On the Threshold of Opportunity? A Roundtable Discussion on the Past, Present and Future of Research," *Quirk's Marketing Research* (March 1996): 34–35, 56–59.

12. Stephanie Thompson, "Oscar Mayer Hamming It Up for Relaunched Lunch Meats," *Crain's Chicago Business*, 23(33) (August 7, 2000): 53; Judann Pollack, "Ball Park, Oscar Mayer Brands Ready New Tactic," *Advertising Age*, 69(31) (August 3, 1998): 8; and Charlie Etmekjian and John Grede, "Marketing Research Is a Team-Oriented Business: The Oscar Mayer Approach," *Marketing Research: A Magazine of Management and Applications*, 2(4) (December 1990): 6–12.

13. "LIMRA: Pension Sales Saw Double-Digit Gains in 1999," *Best's Review*, 101(3) (July 2000): 118; "A Quest for Education," *LIMRA's MarketFacts*, 18(2) (March/April 1999): 9–11; Stephen Piontek, "Wecker Calls for Commitment to Selling Life Insurance," *National Underwriter* (November 1998): 3, 45; and *www.limra.com*.

14. Jack Honomichl, "Top 25 Global Research Organizations," *Marketing News*, (August 13, 2001): Special Pullout Section.

15. "Getting P&G Righted Again," *Advertising Age*, 71(26) (June 19, 2000): 54; Harriot L. Fox, "Brand Attack on China," *Marketing* (July 2, 1998): 24–25; and "P&G Viewed China As a National Market and Is Conquering It," *Wall Street Journal* (September 12, 1995).

16. Marydee Ojala, "Information Role Models in Market Research," *Online*, 24(2) (March/April 2000): 69–71; Matthew W. Green, Jr., and John A. Fugel, "Third Wave Has Ups and Downs," *Rural Telecommunications*, 15(1): (January/February 1996): 10; and Donald E. Schmidt, "Third Wave of Marketing Research on the Horizon," *Marketing News*, 27(5) (March 1, 1993): 6.

17. Diane K. Bowers, "The Strategic Role of the Telemarketing Sales Rule in the Research Industry," *Marketing Research: A Magazine of Management and Applications*, 11(1) (Spring 1999): 34–35.

2

DEFINING THE MARKETING RESEARCH PROBLEM AND DEVELOPING AN APPROACH

DEFINING THE MARKETING RESEARCH PROBLEM IS ONE OF THE MOST IMPORTANT TASKS IN A MARKETING RESEARCH PROJECT. IT IS ALSO ONE OF THE MOST DIFFICULT.

Opening Questions

1. What is a marketing research problem, and why is it important to define it correctly?

2. What tasks are involved in problem definition?

3. How do environmental factors affect the definition of the research problem, and what are these factors?

4. What is the distinction between the management decision problem and the marketing research problem?

5. How should the marketing research problem be defined?

6. What are the various components of the approach to the problem?

7. How can the problem definition process assist in total quality management?

8. Why are defining the problem and developing an approach more complex processes in international marketing research?

9. How can technology help define the problem and develop an approach?

10. What ethical issues and conflicts arise in defining the problem and developing the approach?

11. How can the Internet aid the researcher in defining the problem and developing an approach?

Roger Bacik, Executive Vice President, Elrick & Lavidge.
Roger L. Bacik has been with the firm since 1965. In his present position, Roger oversees the Sales and Custom Relationship Management Program for the company's custom and syndicated research business. He has several years' experience in a variety of research programs, including customer satisfaction and customer value analysis.

"THE WORLD'S FIRST SPORTS UTILITY WAGON"

The Subaru Outback's unique features and overall driving performance continue to be popular among consumers today. In April 2000, Subaru debuted the new 2001 model Outback wagon at the New York auto show. This luxurious new automobile includes a 3.0-liter six-cylinder boxer engine in which the cylinder heads are at a 180-degree angle to each other. Combined with 212 horsepower, this type of engine provides easy handling and low vibration for a very smooth ride. With this new Outback model, Subaru says, "Now you can conquer the road in style." Due to Subaru's popular vehicles, revenues have nearly tripled and sales have increased by almost 100 percent. *Financial Times Automotive World* magazine named Subaru the "Most Improved Car Company in the World." How was the Outback born?

Subaru of America was trying to identify new opportunities for penetrating the automobile market in the early 1990s. The marketing research firm they hired undertook a comprehensive examination of this marketing situation (a problem audit). The audit enabled the research firm to identify the real problem confronting management (the management decision problem) as "What can Subaru do to expand its share of the automobile market?" The marketing research problem was defined broadly as determining the various needs of automobile users and the extent to which current product offerings were satisfying those needs. However, for marketing research to be conducted effectively and efficiently, the problem had to be defined more precisely. The management and the researcher agreed on the following specific components:

1. What needs do buyers of passenger cars, station wagons, and SUVs seek to satisfy?
2. How well do existing automobile product offerings meet these needs?
3. Is there a segment of the automobile market whose needs are not being adequately met?
4. What automobile features does the segment identified in question 3 desire?
5. What is the demographic and psychographic profile of the identified segment?

The approach to the marketing research problem was developed based on the postulate or framework that buyers first decide on the type of car (station wagon, SUV, passenger car) they want, and then they decide on a particular brand. The researcher also formulated specific research questions and possible answers (hypotheses) to be tested by collecting survey data.

The research indicated a strong market potential for a vehicle that combined the features of a station wagon and a compact SUV. The needs of a sizable male-dominated segment were not being met by either the station wagon or the SUV, and they wanted a hybrid product.

Based on these findings, Subaru of America introduced the 1996 Outback as "the world's first sports utility wagon." Subaru said in a press release that the Outback fills the niche between the SUV and the passenger car. The Outback has several important features that are missing from most SUVs, including an all-wheel-drive system that operates under all road conditions and vehicle speeds, four-wheel independent suspension, antilock brakes, dual air bags, and a side intrusion protection system. It also has a low door threshold for easy passenger entry and exit, and a lower center of gravity for road handling and ride comfort. Inside amenities were also upgraded, and several other features were added.

Cars are subject to regulations in terms of emissions control and Corporate Average Fuel Economy (CAFE). Because Subaru makes primarily high-mileage economy cars, the Outback did not negatively influence its CAFE ratings. But the big automakers could not respond to the Outback because such an introduction would have negatively affected their CAFE ratings.

A TV campaign for Outback featured *Crocodile Dundee*'s Paul Hogan. Viewers liked the ads and, of course, the product. Those taking a test drive were very impressed with the capabilities of the vehicle. The result? Sales were triple what Subaru originally expected.[1]

OVERVIEW

This chapter covers the first two of the six steps of the marketing research process described in Chapter 1: defining the marketing research problem and developing an approach to the problem. Figure 2.1 briefly explains the focus of the chapter, the relationship of this chapter to the previous one, and what steps of the marketing research process this chapter concentrates on.

In the opening vignette, Subaru's introduction of the Outback to exploit a new market segment demonstrates the crucial importance of correctly defining the marketing research problem. Subaru correctly defined the marketing research problem as determining the various needs of automobile users and the extent to which current product offerings were satisfying those needs. Defining the research problem is the most important aspect of the research process. Only when a problem has been clearly and accurately identified can a research project be conducted properly. This is because problem definition sets the course for the entire project. In this chapter we will identify the tasks involved and the factors to be considered at this stage, and will provide guidelines to help the researcher avoid common errors.

The chapter also discusses how to develop an approach to the research problem once it has been identified. The approach lays the foundation for how to conduct the research by specifying the relevant theory and models. It further refines the specific components of the problem by asking more specific questions and formulating the hypotheses that will be tested. The approach also specifies all the information that would need to be collected in the marketing research project. Application to total quality management (TQM) and the special considerations involved in defining the problem and developing

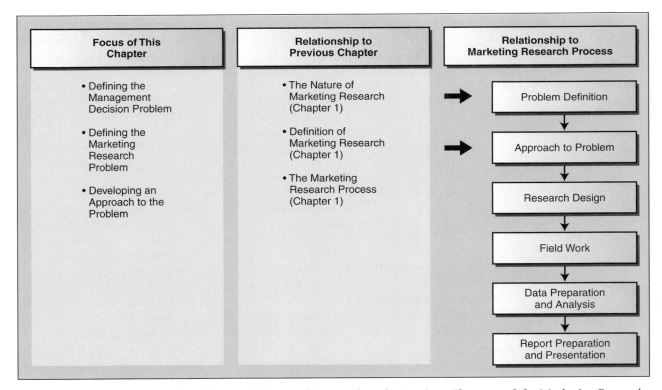

FIGURE 2.1   Relationship of Problem Definition and Approach to the Previous Chapter and the Marketing Research Process

an approach in international marketing research are also discussed. The impact of technology and several ethical issues that arise at this stage of the marketing research process are considered, and Internet applications are discussed. Figure 2.2 gives an overview of the topics discussed in this chapter and how they flow from one to the next.

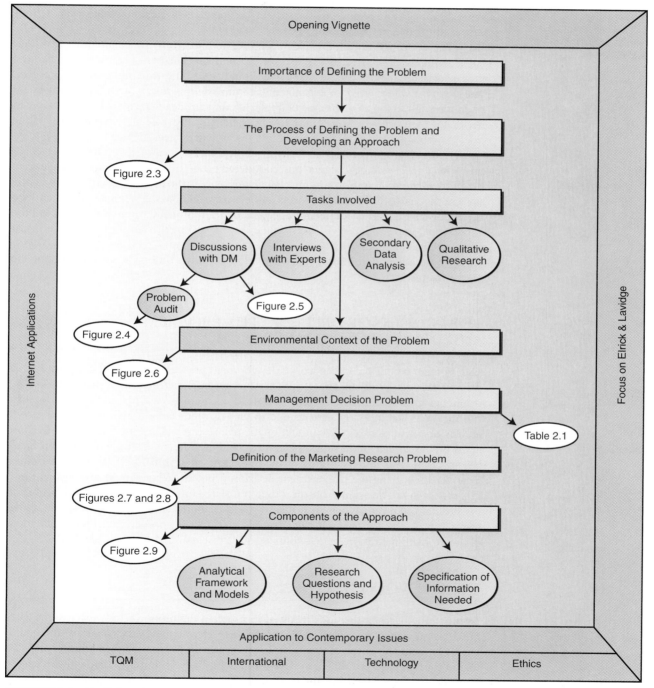

FIGURE 2.2   Defining the Marketing Research Process and Developing an Approach: An Overview

THE IMPORTANCE OF DEFINING THE PROBLEM

problem definition
A broad statement of the general problem and identification of the specific components of the marketing research problem.

While every step in a marketing research project is important, problem definition is the most important step. As mentioned in Chapter 1, marketing researchers consider problems and opportunities confronting management as interchangeable since an investigation of both follows the same research process. **Problem definition** involves stating the general problem and identifying the specific components of the marketing research problem, as illustrated in the opening vignette.

The opening vignette provided a broad statement of the problem confronting Subaru and also identified its five specific components. Furthermore, the researcher and the key decision makers on the client side should agree on the definition of the problem. The client is the individual or organization commissioning the research. The client might be an internal person as in the case of a research director dealing with a decision maker in her or his own organization. Alternatively, the client might be an external entity if the research is being conducted by a marketing research firm (see Chapter 1).

Only when both parties have clearly defined and agreed on the marketing research problem can research be designed and conducted properly. Mistakes made at this level of the process can only mushroom into larger mistakes as the project progresses. Of all the steps in the marketing research process, none is more vital to the ultimate fulfillment of a client's needs than an accurate and adequate definition of the research problem. All the effort, time, and money spent from this point on will be wasted if the problem is not properly defined.

The problem definition process provides guidelines on how to correctly define the marketing research problem.

THE PROCESS OF DEFINING THE PROBLEM AND DEVELOPING AN APPROACH

The problem definition and approach development process is illustrated in Figure 2.3. To define a research problem correctly, the researcher must perform a number of tasks. The researcher must discuss the problem with the decision makers (DMs) in the client organization, interview industry experts and other knowledgeable individuals, analyze secondary data, and sometimes conduct qualitative research. This informal data collection helps the researcher understand the context or environment within which the problem has arisen. A clear understanding of the marketing environment also provides a framework for identifying the management decision problem: What should management do? The management decision problem is then translated into a marketing research problem: the problem that researcher must investigate. Based on the definition of the marketing research problem, the researcher develops an appropriate approach. Further explanation of the problem definition process follows with a discussion of the tasks involved.

TASKS INVOLVED

As mentioned earlier, the tasks involved in problem definition include discussions with the decision makers, interviews with industry experts, secondary data analysis, and qualitative research. The purpose of performing these tasks is to obtain information on the factors of the environment that are relevant to the problem and to help define the management decision problem and the corresponding marketing research problem. We will discuss and illustrate each of these tasks.

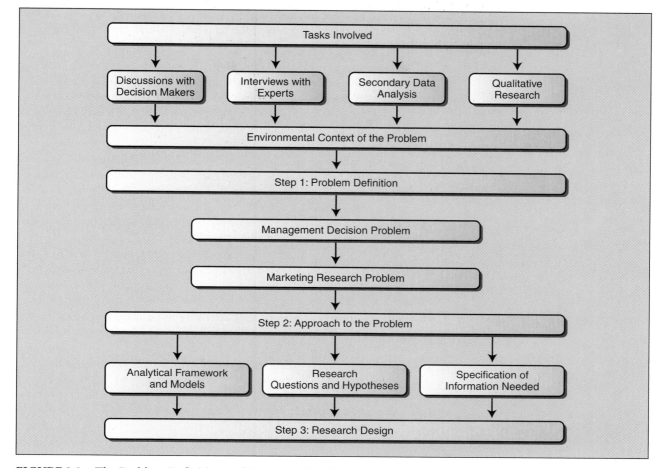

FIGURE 2.3   The Problem Definition and Approach Development Process

Discussions with Decision Makers

It is essential that the researcher understand the nature of the decision the managers face—the management decision problem—as well as management's expectations of the research. This discussion gives the researcher an opportunity to establish achievable expectations. The decision maker needs to understand the capabilities as well as the limitations of research. Research does not provide automatic solutions to problems; rather, it serves as an additional source of information that the manager should consider in the decision-making process.

To identify the management problem, the researcher must possess considerable skill in interacting with the decision maker and maneuvering through the organization. When the ultimate decision maker is a senior executive, the researcher may have difficulty gaining access to that individual. To complicate the situation even further, several individuals may be involved in the final decision. All individuals responsible for resolving the marketing problem should be consulted in this early phase of the project. The quality of the project will be dramatically improved when the researcher is given the opportunity to interact directly with the key decision makers.

Discussions with the decision maker can be structured around the **problem audit** that helps identify the underlying causes of the problem. The problem audit, like any other type of audit, is a comprehensive examination of a marketing problem with the

problem audit
A comprehensive examination of a marketing problem to understand its origin and nature.

purpose of understanding its origin and nature (Figure 2.4). The problem audit involves discussions with the decision maker on the following issues, which are illustrated with a problem facing M&M/Mars.

1. **The history of the problem.** The events that led to the decision to act. M&M/Mars would like to maintain and increase its share of the market at the start of the new century. This problem has come into focus due to recent introductions by Hershey Chocolates. Recently, Hershey's Hugs, Hershey's Hugs with Almonds, and Hershey's Nuggets Chocolates were introduced, threatening M&M/Mars.

2. **The alternative courses of action available to the decision maker.** The set of alternatives may be incomplete at this stage, and qualitative research may be needed to identify the more innovative courses of action. The alternatives available to the management of M&M/Mars include introducing new brands of chocolates, reducing the prices of existing brands, expanding channels of distribution, and increasing advertising expenditures.

3. **The criteria that will be used to evaluate the alternative courses of action.** For example, new product offerings might be evaluated on the basis of sales, market share, profitability, return on investment, and so forth. M&M/Mars will evaluate the alternatives based on contributions to market share and profits.

4. **The nature of potential actions that are likely to be suggested based on the research findings.** The research findings will likely call for a strategic marketing response by M&M/Mars.

5. **The information that is needed to answer the decision maker's questions.** The information needed includes a comparison of Hershey's and M&M/Mars on all the elements of the marketing mix (product, pricing, promotion, and distribution) in order to determine relative strengths and weaknesses.

FIGURE 2.4   Conducting a Problem Audit

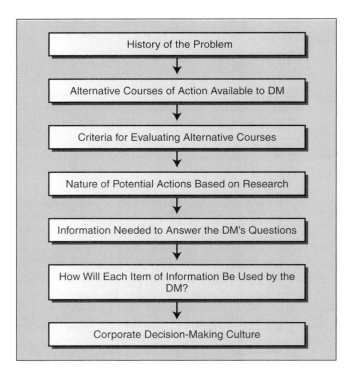

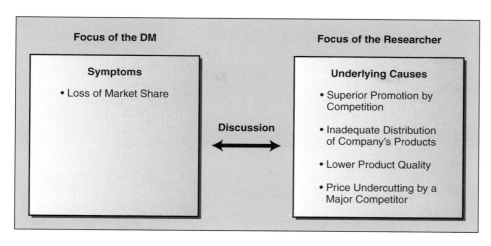

FIGURE 2.5 Discussion Between the Researcher and the DM

6. **The manner in which the decision maker will use each item of information in making the decision.** The key decision makers will devise a strategy for M&M/Mars based on the research findings and their intuition and judgment.

7. **The corporate culture as it relates to decision making.** In some firms, the decision-making process is dominant; in others, the personality of the decision maker is more important. A sensitivity to corporate culture in order to identify the individuals who are either responsible for the decision or who have a significant influence over the decision process is essential. In this case, the corporate culture at M&M/Mars calls for a committee approach in which key decision makers make the critical decisions.

Conducting a problem audit is essential to clarify the problem for the researcher. Not surprisingly, it may serve the same function for the decision maker. Often, the decision maker has only a vague idea of the real problem. For example, the decision maker may know that the firm is losing market share but may not know why. This is because most decision makers focus on the symptoms of a problem rather than its causes. An inability to meet sales forecasts, loss of market share, and a decline in profits are all symptoms. Research that adds value goes beyond the symptoms to address the underlying causes. For example, loss of market share may be caused by a superior promotion by the competition, inadequate distribution of the company's products, lower product quality, price undercutting by a major competitor, or any number of factors (Figure 2.5). Only when the underlying causes are identified can the problem be successfully addressed, as exemplified by the effort of BellSouth to stop the loss of market share and revenues in its call collect business.

EXAMPLE

"FORGET THE CODE," NOT PHONE WAR, RINGS THE BELLS FOR BELLSOUTH

In the 1990s, BellSouth, headquartered in Atlanta, was losing sales and market share in the collect calling business. Declining sales and market share resulted in management's attention being placed on those two symptoms. Unable to find an easy solution, the management commissioned marketing research. The researcher firm conducted a problem audit that examined all of the possible underlying causes and looked at each aspect of the marketing mix in order to identify alternative courses of action. The problem audit did not reveal any specific criticism of BellSouth's collect calling services. It was found that as a southern phone company, BellSouth was perceived as customer friendly, civil, and trustworthy.

The real cause of the problem was intense competition from AT&T and MCI WorldCom. AT&T and MCI WorldCom had spent $15 million in BellSouth's territory with their 1 800 CALL ATT and 1 800 COLLECT campaigns, respectively. Their goal was to convince consumers to call them directly and bypass the BellSouth operators. These two companies used the traditional "phone wars" language of "savings." Their efforts had paid off.

Once the underlying causes were identified, the problem was broadly defined as how to enhance the comparative appeal of BellSouth's collect calling services, rather than narrowly as retaliating with price cuts and counter savings claims. Subsequent research revealed that for many consumers the promise of "savings" had proved empty once they found out how many conditions were attached. Furthermore, consumers were willing to pay a premium for simplicity. This led BellSouth to develop a campaign based on the strategic focus of "the simplest way to call collect." Consumers had to simply dial "0" rather than an 11-digit code. BellSouth's new slogan was "Forget the Code," a jab at AT&T's "Know the Code." The campaign was very successful. Determining the underlying causes and appropriately defining the problem enabled BellSouth to avoid the trappings of the phone wars and focus on what consumers really wanted. This approach led to increased sales and market share.[2]

Interviews with Industry Experts

In addition to discussions with the decision maker, interviews with industry experts—individuals knowledgeable about the firm and the industry—may help researchers formulate the marketing research problem. Experts may be found both inside and outside the firm. While formal questionnaires are normally not used, a prepared list of topics to be covered during the interview is often helpful. The order in which these topics are covered and the questions to ask should not be predetermined but decided as the interview progresses. This allows greater flexibility in capturing the insights of the experts. The purpose of interviews with experts is to help define the marketing research problem rather than to develop a conclusive solution. Expert interviews are more commonly used in industrial rather than consumer research applications. In industrial or highly technical environments, the experts are often more easily identified than they would be in consumer research settings. This is because consumer settings are broader and more diffused than industrial or technical environments. Expert interviews are also helpful in situations in which little information is available from other sources, as in the case of radically new products. Experts can provide valuable insights in modifying or repositioning existing products, as illustrated by the repositioning of Sears.

For years, the sales at this giant retailer floundered and it lost its status as America's number one retailer to Wal-Mart in 1989. When industry experts were consulted, researchers were able to identify the real problem: lack of image. Traditionally a discount store, Sears had unsuccessfully tried to upgrade its image to a prestigious department store, thereby alienating its loyal customers. Sears finally gave up its attempt to upgrade and re-embraced the image of a discount chain store. Since then, sales and profitability have improved.

Secondary Data Analysis

The information that researchers obtain from the decision maker and the industry experts should be supplemented with available secondary data. **Secondary data** are data collected for some purpose other than the problem at hand, such as data available from trade organizations, the Bureau of Census, and the Internet. **Primary data,** on the other hand, are originated by the researcher for the specific problem under study, such as survey data. Secondary data include information made available by business and government sources, commercial marketing research firms, and computerized databases. Secondary data are an economical and quick source of background information.

secondary data
Data collected for some purpose other than the problem at hand.

primary data
Data originated by the researcher specifically to address the research problem.

Analyzing available secondary data is an essential step in the problem-definition process and should always precede primary data collection. Secondary data can provide valuable insights into the problem situation and lead to the identification of innovative courses of action. For example, the U.S. Department of Labor says that the average age of the American workforce will increase from 35 to 39 by the year 2002. This is in part the result of the maturation of the "baby bust" generation (those born between 1965 and 1976), which will cause a decline in the number of young (age 16 to 24) workers available to fill entry-level positions. This potential shortage of young workers has caused many marketers, particularly those in the service industries, to investigate the problem of consumer response to self-service. Some companies, such as Arby's, have switched from a "high-touch" to a "high-tech" service orientation. By using high-tech equipment, consumers now perform many of the services formerly done by workers, such as placing their own orders by entering them directly into the electronic terminal. Given the tremendous importance of secondary data, this topic will be discussed in detail in Chapters 4 and 5, including a further discussion of the differences between them.

Qualitative Research

Information obtained from the decision maker, industry experts, and secondary data may not be sufficient to define the research problem. Sometimes qualitative research must be undertaken to gain a clear understanding of the factors underlying a research problem. **Qualitative research** is unstructured in that the questions asked are formulated as the research proceeds. It is exploratory in nature, and based on small samples, and may use popular qualitative techniques such as focus groups (group interviews) or in-depth interviews (one-on-one interviews that probe the respondents' thoughts in detail). Other exploratory research techniques, such as pilot surveys with small samples of respondents, may also be undertaken.

qualitative research
An unstructured, exploratory research methodology based on small samples intended to provide insight and understanding of the problem setting.

Once the leader in the Caribbean cruise market, Norwegian Cruise Lines, Coral Gables, Florida, had slipped to fourth position. To identify the underlying causes and appropriately define the problem, focus group and pilot (small-scale) surveys were conducted. This qualitative research revealed that one worry that kept people from cruising was the fear of being confined to a boat for a week or more with little to do. This concern was particularly acute among young people. Addressing this concern became a major component of the problem and, therefore, a large survey was conducted. The survey verified the findings of qualitative research. Based on these research findings, Norwegian Cruise Lines' advertising fought this myth by emphasizing that passengers have the flexibility to make their cruise vacation whatever they want it to be. Its provocative, award-winning print and TV campaigns featured close-ups of young people, often on land, having lots of fun. The campaign helped Norwegian attract new and younger customers and improve its market share and penetration. This success was achieved despite the fact that Norwegian was outspent in advertising two to one by Carnival Cruise Lines and one and one-half to one by Royal Caribbean Cruises.[3] (Exploratory research is discussed in more detail in Chapter 3, and qualitative research techniques are discussed in detail in Chapter 6.)

While research undertaken at this stage may not be conducted in a formal way, it can provide valuable insights. These insights, together with information obtained from discussions with the decision makers and industry experts and analysis of secondary data, guide the researcher to an appropriate definition of the problem, as illustrated by the Century City Hospital in Los Angeles.

EXAMPLE

CENTURY CITY HOSPITAL MOVES INTO NEW CENTURY OF HEALTH CARE

Like most hospitals across the country were doing in the late 1990s, the Century City Hospital in Los Angeles was considering a course of action that emphasized cost cutting to improve profitability. An external marketing research firm was hired to suggest areas where costs could be cut without alienating consumers. However, the research firm realized that lower profitability was merely a symptom. Based on discussions with key decision makers and industry experts, the underlying cause of low profitability was identified as lack of a clear focus and market positioning by the hospital. Specifically, the hospital did not understand who its target customers were and what their unique needs were.

Secondary data from the Bureau of Census indicated that nearly 50 percent of the local residents had high incomes. Qualitative research in the form of focus groups revealed that this group valued the best in food, accommodation, privacy, and exclusiveness. These people were not price sensitive and were willing to pay for added benefits.

As an outcome of this process, the problem was redefined to how the Century City Hospital could best meet the medical needs of its high-income residents. Based on the findings of the research undertaken subsequently, the Century City Hospital opened its deluxe Century Pavilion, offering luxurious private accommodations at a premium price. Thus, the Century City Hospital was able to carve a profitable niche and entered the twenty-first century in a strong position.[4]

environmental context of the problem
Consists of the factors that have an impact on the definition of the marketing research problem, including past information and forecasts, resources and constraints of the firm, objectives of the decision maker, buyer behavior, legal environment, economic environment, and marketing and technological skills of the firm.

ENVIRONMENTAL CONTEXT OF THE PROBLEM

The insights gained from qualitative research, along with discussions with decision makers, interviews with industry experts, and analysis of secondary data, help the researcher understand the environmental context of the problem. The researcher must have a full understanding of the client's firm and industry. Several factors that comprise the **environmental context of the problem** can play an important role in defining the marketing research problem. These factors consist of past information and forecasts pertaining to the industry and the firm, resources and constraints of the firm, objectives of the decision maker, buyer behavior, legal environment, economic environment, and marketing and technological skills of the firm (Figure 2.6). Each of these factors is discussed briefly below.

Past Information and Forecasts

Past information and forecasts of trends with respect to sales, market share, profitability, technology, population, demographics, and lifestyle combine to provide the researcher with a fuller picture of the underlying marketing research problem. Not only should the firm's performance and projections be analyzed, but the firm's performance relative to the overall industry should be examined as well. For example, if a firm's sales have decreased but industry sales have increased, the problems will be very different than if the industry sales have also decreased. In the former case, the problems are likely to be specific to the firm.

Past information, forecasts, and trends can be valuable in uncovering potential opportunities and problems. For example, pizza restaurants have sought to exploit potential opportunities in the recent trend toward takeout food and home delivery. Pizza Hut has successfully capitalized on this trend by emphasizing takeout and home delivery services. It opened several takeout-only (with no dine-in service) outlets to better serve this market. As another illustration, in the Subaru vignette, forecasts of future sales of station wagons and sports utility vehicles indicated to management that both these types of automobiles were not tapping the full market potential.

Past information and forecasts can be especially valuable if resources are limited and there are other constraints on the organization.

Resources and Constraints

To formulate a marketing research problem of appropriate scope, it is necessary to take into account the resources available, such as money, research skills, and operational capabilities, as well as operational and time constraints. While adjustments in proposed

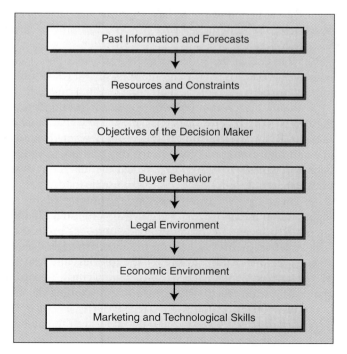

FIGURE 2.6 Factors to Be Considered in the Environment Context of the Problem

research expenditure levels are common, proposing a large-scale $100,000 project when only $40,000 has been budgeted will put the research firm at a serious competitive disadvantage. Time constraints are also an important factor in many research projects. A project for Fisher-Price, a major toy manufacturer, involving mall-intercept interviews (conducted with shoppers in malls) in six major cities (Chicago, Fresno, Kansas City, New York, Philadelphia, and San Diego) had to be completed in six weeks. Why the rush? The results had to be presented at an upcoming board meeting where a major (go/no go) decision was to be made about a new product introduction. Time constraint was a major factor that guided the problem definition and the approach adopted in this case.

Objectives of the Decision Maker

objectives
Goals of the organization and of the decision maker must be considered in order to conduct successful marketing research.

In formulating the management decision problem, the researcher must also have a clear understanding of two types of **objectives:** (1) the organizational objectives (the goals of the organization), and (2) the personal objectives of the decision maker. For the project to be successful, it must serve the objectives of the organization and of the decision maker. This may become a challenge when the two are not complementary. For example, the decision maker may wish to undertake research to postpone an awkward decision, to lend credibility to a decision that has already been made, or to get promoted.

It may take skill to get the decision maker to think in terms of objectives that management can act upon (actionable objectives). One effective technique may be to confront the decision maker with a number of possible solutions to a problem and ask whether he or she would follow that course of action. If the answer is no, further probing may be needed to uncover any deeper objectives as to why this solution is unsatisfactory.

Buyer Behavior

buyer behavior
A body of knowledge that tries to understand and predict consumers' reactions based on an individual's specific characteristics.

Buyer behavior is a central component of environment. It includes the underlying motives, perceptions, attitudes, buying habits, and demographic and psychographic (psychological and lifestyle) profiles of buyers and potential buyers. Most marketing decisions involve a prediction of the buyers' response to a particular marketing action. An understanding of the underlying buyer behavior can provide valuable insights into the problem.

Note that in the Subaru vignette, information on the demographic and psychographic characteristic of the automobile segment whose needs were not being met was an important component of the marketing research problem.

In another case, buyer behavior research told ConAgra Frozen Foods that more than 55 percent of Americans pack a lunch and that more and more meals are eaten on the run. But while consumers increasingly want their food to be portable, they still demand high flavor and good nutrition. Wanting to capitalize on this aspect of buyer behavior, ConAgra further investigated the marketing research problem of consumer preferences for healthy, delicious, and portable food.

The company's answer, based on the findings of this research, was a new entry into the premium meals category, Healthy Choice Hearty Handfuls frozen sandwiches. As an alternative to many frozen convenience foods, the product targeted an adult taste profile with bakery-style breads, lean meats, and crisp vegetables. True to the name, the sandwiches are both healthy (low in fat and calories) and hearty (at six ounces, an estimated 35 percent larger than most frozen sandwiches). According to ConAgra, the Hearty Handfuls line exceeded sales expectations, becoming the number three frozen sandwich brand in its first six months.

The increased preference for portable, healthy, and hearty food could be attributed to changes in the sociocultural environment, which includes demographic trends and consumer tastes. The legal, economic, and marketing environment also has a significant impact in some industries.

Legal Environment

The **legal environment** includes public policies, laws, government agencies, and pressure groups that influence and regulate various organizations and individuals in society. Important areas of law include patents, trademarks, royalties, trade agreements, taxes, and tariffs. Federal regulation and deregulation has had a huge impact on the marketing process in many industries, such as the airline, banking, and telecommunication industries. The legal and regulatory considerations relevant to a business must be taken into account by the researcher.

legal environment
Regulatory policies and norms within which organizations must operate.

In the opening vignette, it was explained that cars are subject to regulations in terms of emissions control and Corporate Average Fuel Economy (CAFE). The Outback did not negatively influence its CAFE ratings because Subaru makes primarily high-mileage economy cars. However, the big automakers could not respond to the Outback because such an introduction would have negatively affected their CAFE ratings.

Economic Environment

Another important component of the environmental context is the economic environment, which is composed of purchasing power, gross income, disposable income, discretionary income, prices, savings, credit availability, and general economic conditions. The general state of the economy (rapid growth, slow growth, recession, or stagflation) influences the willingness of consumers and businesses to take on credit and spend on big-ticket items. Thus, the economic environment can have important implications for marketing research problems.

JCPenney is one of the largest and most well-known department stores in the United States. In the 1980s, Penney suffered due to inconsistent sales growth and a drop in company image. In the early 1990s, JCPenney began a massive overhaul of its image toward a higher quality image to counter these problems. The company courted famous name brands such as Oshkosh B'Gosh, Levis, and Charles of the Ritz. Unfortunately, Penney decided to raise prices and go for the high-end fashion line at a bad time. Price increases coincided with the recession and the Gulf War, and people did not have sufficient money to spend.

Its most recent attempt in 2001 to recover its image has been to stick with good brand names, to control prices, and market itself as the store for "middle America." JCPenney's lost image has been found through keeping prices competitive and carrying good brand names.

Marketing and Technological Skills

A firm's marketing and technological skills greatly influence which marketing programs and strategies can be implemented. A company's expertise with each element of the marketing mix as well as its general levels of marketing and production skills affect the nature and scope of the marketing research project. For example, the introduction of a new product that requires retooling of a manufacturing process or presumes sophisticated marketing skills may not be a viable alternative if the firm lacks the skills to manufacture or market such a product. On the other hand, if the company can capitalize on its marketing and technological skills, its products and new introductions are likely to succeed, as illustrated in the Subaru vignette.

A good understanding of the environmental context of the problem enables the researcher to appropriately define the problem, as illustrated by the Gillette Company.

SATIN CARE FOR WOMEN PROVIDES A SATIN TOUCH FOR GILLETTE

Analysis of past information indicated that most women continued to pamper themselves with products for their beauty regimen and that this trend is likely to continue. The Gillette Company was willing to devote its tremendous financial resources and its marketing expertise with the objective of capturing a larger share of the women's shaving products market. An examination of the underlying buyer behavior revealed that women had a strong preference for personal care products that were rich in moisturizers. Economic and marketing analysis indicated that a substantial segment was not price sensitive and was willing to pay a premium for such products. Accordingly, the marketing research problem was formulated as the investigation of women's preferences and purchase intentions for a shaving preparation rich in moisturizers.

Based on the affirmative findings of this research, Gillette introduced Satin Care for Women. The product brought innovation to the category with the first non-soap-based shaving preparation with seven moisturizers. The product introduction was so successful that Satin Care for Women exceeded all expectations in the launch markets of the United States, Canada, and northern Europe. This success reinforced Gillette's understanding of the shaving environmental factors.[5]

Gaining an adequate understanding of the environmental context of the problem allows the researcher to define both the management decision problem and the marketing research problem.

MANAGEMENT DECISION PROBLEM AND MARKETING RESEARCH PROBLEM

management decision problem
The problem confronting the decision maker. It asks what the decision maker needs to do.

marketing research problem
The marketing research problem asks what information is needed and how it can best be obtained.

The **management decision problem** asks what the decision maker needs to do, whereas the **marketing research problem** asks what information is needed and how it can best be obtained (Table 2.1). Research is directed at providing the information necessary to make a sound decision. The management decision problem is action oriented, framed from the perspective of what should be done. How should the loss of market share be arrested? Should the market be segmented differently? Should a new product be introduced? Should the promotional budget be increased?

In contrast, the marketing research problem is information oriented. Research is directed at providing the information necessary to make a sound decision. The management decision problem focuses on the symptoms, whereas the marketing research problem is concerned with the underlying causes.

In the opening vignette, the management decision problem was "What can Subaru do to expand its share of the automobile market?" The marketing research problem

TABLE 2.1   **Management Decision Problem Versus the Marketing Research Problem**

MANAGEMENT DECISION PROBLEM	MARKETING RESEARCH PROBLEM
Asks what the decision maker needs to do	Asks what information is needed and how it should be obtained
Action oriented	Information oriented
Focuses on symptoms	Focuses on the underlying causes

focused on information about the needs of the buyers of passenger cars, station wagons, and sports utility vehicles, and on identifying a segment whose needs were not being met. Also, information was to be obtained on the automobile features desired by the identified segment, and on the demographic and psychographic characteristics of this segment.

To further illustrate the distinction between the two orientations, we will consider an illustrative problem: loss of market share for the Old Spice product line (aftershave, cologne, deodorant). The decision maker is faced with the problem of how to recover this loss. Possible responses include modifying existing products, introducing new products, reducing prices, changing other elements in the marketing mix, and segmenting the market. Suppose the decision maker and the researcher believe that the problem can be traced to market segmentation in that Old Spice should be targeted at a specific segment. They decide to conduct research to explore that issue. The research problem would then become the identification and evaluation of different ways to segment or group the market. As the research process progresses, problem definition may be modified to reflect emerging information. The distinction between the management decision problem and the marketing research problem may be further clarified by the following table that gives additional examples, including that of Subaru in the opening vignette.

MANAGEMENT DECISION PROBLEM	MARKETING RESEARCH PROBLEM
Should the advertising campaign be changed?	To determine the effectiveness of the current advertising campaign.
Should the price of the product be changed?	To determine the impact on sales and profits of various levels of price changes.
What can Subaru do to expand its share of the automobile market?	To determine the various needs of automobile users and the extent to which those needs were being satisfied by the current product offerings.

DEFINING THE MARKETING RESEARCH PROBLEM

A general guideline for defining the research problem is that the definition should (1) allow the researcher to obtain all the information needed to address the management decision problem and (2) guide the researcher in proceeding with the project. Researchers can make two common errors by defining the research problem either too broadly or too narrowly (Figure 2.7). A broad definition fails to provide clear guidelines for the subsequent steps involved in the project. Examples of overly broad marketing research problem

FIGURE 2.7   Errors in Defining the Market Research Problem

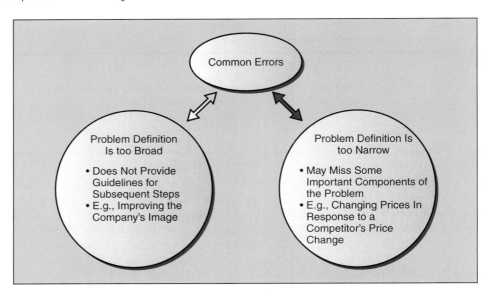

definition include developing a marketing strategy for the brand, improving the competitive position of the firm, and improving the company's image. These definitions are not specific enough to suggest an approach to the problem or a research design.

Focusing the problem definition too narrowly can also be a serious flaw. A narrow focus may inhibit a full examination of plausible options, particularly innovative options. It may also prevent the researcher from addressing important components of the management decision problem. For example, a problem will be too narrowly defined if it is confined to how a company should adjust its pricing, given that a major competitor has initiated price changes. The narrow focus on pricing alone overlooks other possible responses (alternative courses of action), such as introducing new brands, changing advertising, or adding new distribution channels.

A narrow definition of the problem could also lead to restrictive sampling, resulting in erroneous conclusions. If Revlon is targeting females age 16 to 29 for its cosmetics line, that's fine for guiding media placement. However, the problem would be too narrowly defined for research measuring advertising effectiveness if the study is restricted to females 16 to 29 years old. The reason is that TV advertising has a much larger reach. Suppose the advertising turns out to be really effective among women age 34 to 54 instead of 16 to 29. Revlon might have canceled a very effective campaign because it appeared to be failing among the target audience. On the other hand, it is possible that Revlon's commercials are working among 16 to 29 year olds but driving all other age groups away. If we were sampling only the 16 to 29 segment, we would have overlooked this critical failing.

Remember: Always define the problem broadly enough so as not to overlook any relevant aspects, a mistake Quaker Oats made.

EXAMPLE

SNAPPLE LEFT A BAD AFTERTASTE FOR QUAKER OATS

In 1995, analysts and media pundits sneered when Quaker paid $1.7 billion for Snapple, the tea-and-juice-blends company. After the purchase, Snapple and Gatorade made up 40 percent of Quaker's sales, making it the third-largest beverage company in the United States, behind Coke and Pepsi, and the largest vendor of noncarbonated drinks. But Quaker Oats saw its earnings slide after the acquisition of Snapple Beverage. Several marketing problems arose, and in two years Quaker Oats was forced to sell Snapple for a mere $300 million, incurring a huge loss. Where did the company go wrong?

According to industry insiders, Quaker defined the marketing research problem too narrowly when considering the acquisition of Snapple. In particular, three aspects of the problem were overlooked.

First, the ease with which Gatorade had succeeded in the past made Quaker complacent, and they overlooked competition. Initially, both Snapple and Gatorade were able to grow because there was no direct competition when they were introduced. Later, both PepsiCo and Coca-Cola Company entered into direct competition with Quaker's Snapple and Gatorade product lines, which further hurt growth.

Second, Quaker did not adequately consider the marketing synergy between Gatorade and Snapple. In particular, Quaker failed to consider the impact that Gatorade and Snapple would have on distributors. Plans to distribute the two lines together fell apart when Snapple distributors did not want to deal with Gatorade, as it offered notoriously low profit margins. By not taking into consideration all of its stakeholders—in this case, the distributors—Quaker failed to properly research the impact of acquiring Snapple.

Third, Quaker took a very narrow view of Gatorade, thinking of it as merely a sports drink rather than a general beverage, thus limiting its market. According to one industry expert, "The key for Gatorade is to go beyond being a sports drink to a lifestyle drink so accessible that every kid has to have it in his lunchbox."

Defining the problem too narrowly led to limited research and an incorrect marketing decision. Quaker Oats and PepsiCo merged on August 2, 2001.[6]

To minimize the possibility of a wrong decision due to an incorrect definition of the marketing research problem, it's a good idea for the researcher to adopt a two-stage process. First, the marketing research problem is stated in broad, general terms; then it is reduced to its specific components (Figure 2.8). The **broad statement of the problem** provides perspective on the problem and acts as a safeguard against committing the second type of error. The **specific components of the problem** focus on the key aspects and provide clear guidelines on how to proceed further, avoiding the first type of error.

This process was illustrated in the opening vignette. The broad statement of the problem was to determine the various needs of automobile users and the extent to which current product offerings were satisfying those needs. In addition, five specific components were identified. Another example of an appropriate marketing research problem definition follows.

broad statement of the problem
The initial statement of the marketing research problem that provides an appropriate perspective on the problem.

specific components of the problem
The second part of the marketing research problem definition. The specific components focus on the key aspects of the problem and provide clear guidelines on how to proceed.

EXAMPLE

RESEARCH SERVES *TENNIS* MAGAZINE

Tennis magazine, a publication of the New York Times Company, wanted to obtain information about its readers. The magazine hired Signet Research, an independent research company in Cliffside Park, New Jersey, to conduct marketing research.

The management of *Tennis* magazine needed to learn more about its subscribers, and so the broad marketing research problem was defined as gathering information about them. The specific components of the problem were as follows:

1. **Demographics.** Who are the men and women that subscribe to the magazine?
2. **Psychological characteristics and lifestyles.** How do subscribers spend their money and their free time? Lifestyle indicators to be examined were fitness, travel, car rental, apparel, consumer electronics, credit cards, and financial investments.
3. **Tennis activity.** Where and how often do subscribers play tennis? What are their skill levels?
4. **Relationship to *Tennis* magazine.** How much time do subscribers spend with the issues? How long do they keep them? Do they share the magazine with other tennis players?

Because the questions were so clearly defined, the information provided by this research helped management design specific features on tennis instruction, equipment, famous tennis players, and locations to play tennis to meet readers' specific needs. These changes made *Tennis* magazine more appealing to its readers and resulted in increased circulation.

Once the marketing research problem has been broadly stated and its specific components identified, as in the case of *Tennis* magazine, the researcher is in a position to develop a suitable approach.

FIGURE 2.8 Proper Definition of the Marketing Research Problem

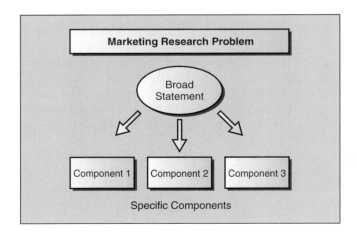

COMPONENTS OF THE APPROACH

An approach to a marketing research problem should include the following components: analytical framework and models, research questions and hypotheses, and a specification of the information needed (see Figure 2.3). Each of these components is discussed in the following sections.

Analytical Framework and Models

In general, research should be based on objective evidence and supported by theory. **Objective evidence** (evidence that is unbiased and supported by empirical findings) is gathered by compiling relevant findings from secondary sources. A **theory** guides the collection of this data. It is a conceptual framework based on foundational statements, which are assumed to be true. Theory may come from academic literature contained in books, journals, and monographs. For example, according to attitude theory, attitude toward a brand, such as Nike sneakers, is determined by an evaluation of the brand on salient attributes (price, comfort, durability, and style). Relevant theory provides insight regarding which variables should be investigated and which should be treated as dependent variables (those whose values depend on the values of other variables) and which as independent variables (those whose values affect the values of other variables). Thus, attitude toward Nike will be the dependent variable; price, comfort, durability, and style will be independent variables. The approach should be based on some kind of working theory or framework. This is also helpful in developing an appropriate model.

An **analytical model** consists of a set of variables related in a specified manner to represent all or a part of some real system or process. Models can take many forms. The most common are verbal, graphical, and mathematical structures. In **verbal models,** the variables and their relationships are stated in prose form. These models are often a summary or restatement of the main points of the theory. **Graphical models** are visual and pictorially represent the theory. They are used to isolate variables and to suggest directions of relationships but are not designed to provide numerical results. They are logical, preliminary steps to developing mathematical models. **Mathematical models** explicitly specify the strength and direction of relationships among variables, usually in equation form. Graphical models are particularly helpful in conceptualizing an approach to the problem, as the following jeans purchase model illustrates.

objective evidence
Unbiased evidence that is supported by empirical findings.

theory
A conceptual scheme based on foundational statements, which are assumed to be true.

analytical model
An explicit specification of a set of variables and their interrelationships designed to represent some real system or process in whole or in part.

verbal model
Analytical models that provide a written representation of the relationships between variables.

graphical model
Analytical models that provide a visual picture of the relationships between variables.

mathematical model
Analytical models that explicitly describe the relationships between variables, usually in equation form.

EXAMPLE

LEE RIVETED RIVETS YOUNG CONSUMERS WITH "THE BRAND THAT FITS"

According to consumer decision-making theory, the consumer first decides whether to purchase jeans or other casual clothes. If jeans are to be purchased, the consumer will form selection criteria for evaluating alternative brands. The selection criteria consist of factors such as color, price, fit, cut, comfort, and quality. The competing brands of jeans are then evaluated based on the selection criteria to purchase one or more brands. The follow-

ing graphical model illustrates the decision process for jeans for a consumer considering the purchase of casual clothing. Lee Riveted jeans are targeted at young people who buy jeans based primarily on fit and cut. Therefore, the marketing themes of Lee Riveted with tag lines "the brand that fits," "cut to be noticed," and "that unstoppable spirit" were based on this model.

Graphical Model

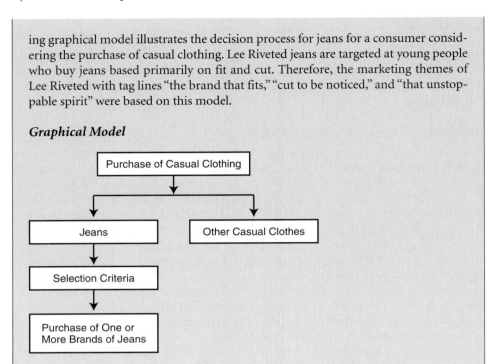

In the opening vignette, the analytical model postulated that buyers first decide on the type of car they want (station wagon, sports utility vehicle, passenger car) and then they decide on a specific brand. The verbal, graphical, and mathematical models complement each other and help the researcher identify relevant research questions and hypotheses, as shown in Figure 2.9.

FIGURE 2.9
Development of Research
Questions and Hypotheses

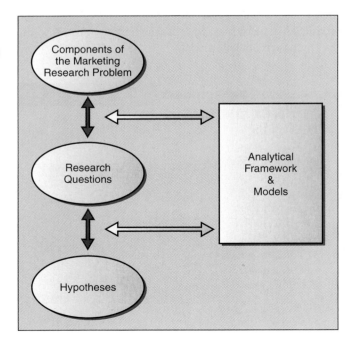

Research Questions and Hypotheses

Research questions (RQs) are refined statements of the specific components of the problem. A problem component may break into several research questions. Research questions are designed to ask the specific information required to address each problem component. Research questions that successfully address the problem components will provide valuable information for the decision maker.

research questions
Refined statements of the specific components of the problem.

   The formulation of the research questions should be guided, not only by the problem definition, but also by the analytical framework and the model adopted. In the Lee Riveted jeans example, the factors of the choice criteria were postulated based on theoretical framework as color, price, fit, cut, comfort, and quality. Several research questions can be posed related to these factors: What is the relative importance of these factors in influencing consumers' selection of jeans? What factor is the most important? What is the least important factor? Does the relative importance of these factors vary across consumers?

   A **hypothesis** (H) is an unproven statement or proposition about a factor or phenomenon that is of interest to the researcher. It may be a tentative statement about the relationships discussed in the theoretical framework or represented in the analytic model. The hypothesis may also be stated as a possible answer to the research question. Hypotheses are statements about proposed relationships rather than merely questions to be answered. They reflect the researchers' expectation and can be tested empirically (see Chapter 16). Hypotheses also play the important role of suggesting variables to be included in the research design. The relationship between the marketing research problem, research questions, and hypotheses, along with the influence of the objective/theoretical framework and analytical models, is described in Figure 2.9.

hypothesis
An unproven statement or proposition about a factor or phenomenon that is of interest to the researcher.

   In commercial marketing research, the hypotheses are not formulated as rigorously as they are in academic research. An interesting research question and related hypotheses that could be posed about the need for a hybrid product in the Subaru vignette are as follows.

RQ: Is there an overlap between the features sought by station wagon buyers and buyers of sports utility vehicles (SUVs)?

H1: The buyers of station wagons rate certain features of SUVs as important.

H2: The buyers of SUVs rate certain features of station wagons as important.

The following example further illustrates research questions and hypotheses.

EXAMPLE

"GOT MILK?"

Milk consumption had steadily declined for 20 years until 1993. Qualitative research indicated that people had misconceptions about milk. Hence, survey research was undertaken to address the following research question (RQ) and hypotheses (H):

RQ: Do people have misconceptions about milk?

H1: Milk is perceived as fat-laden and unhealthy.

H2: Milk is perceived as an old-fashioned drink.

H3: People believe that milk is meant only for kids.

   When the survey data supported these hypotheses, the Milk Processor Education Program launched the well-known "milk mustache" campaign. This creative advertising was a real attention-getter, showing celebrities from Joan Lunden to Rhea Perlman and Danny DeVito sporting the famous white mustache. The result? Humble milk, until a few years before an also-ran in the advertising race behind soft drinks and juices, catapulted into a key beverage-industry player. The decline in milk consumption was arrested and consumption continued to be stable through 2000.[7]

Specification of Information Needed

By focusing on each component of the problem and the analytical framework and models, research questions, and hypotheses, the researcher can determine what information should be obtained. It is helpful to carry out this exercise for each component of the problem and make a list specifying all the information that should be collected. We illustrate this process with respect to the opening vignette.

COMPONENT 1

- Needs of buyers of passenger cars operationalized in terms of the attributes or features desired in an automobile.
- Needs of buyers of station wagons operationalized in terms of the attributes or features desired in an automobile.
- Needs of buyers of SUVs operationalized in terms of the attributes or features desired in an automobile.

COMPONENT 2

- Evaluation of passenger cars on the desired attributes.
- Evaluation of station wagons on the desired attributes.
- Evaluation of SUVs on the desired attributes.

COMPONENT 3

- No new information to be collected. The segment can be identified based on information obtained for the first two components.

COMPONENT 4

- No new information to be collected. The desired features can be identified based on information obtained for the first two components.

COMPONENT 5

- Standard demographic characteristics (gender, marital status, household size, age, education, occupation, income). Type and number of automobiles owned. Psychographic characteristics include outdoor and recreational activities, family orientation, and attitude toward daily commuting.

SUMMARY ILLUSTRATION USING THE OPENING VIGNETTE

We can summarize and illustrate the major concepts discussed in this chapter by return-ing to the opening vignette. The Subaru vignette illustrates the importance of correctly defining the problem and showing how a problem audit can help in the process. The tasks involved in formulating the marketing research problem should lead to an understanding of the environmental context of the problem. In the case of Subaru, forecasts of future sales of station wagons and SUVs indicated that these two types of automobiles were not tapping the market potential. Subaru undertook research to understand the underlying behavior of the consumers, their needs and desires. It capitalized on its marketing and technological skill to achieve the successful introduction of "the world's first sports utility wagon."

Analysis of the environmental context should help identify the management deci-sion problem, which should then be translated into a marketing research problem. The management decision problem focuses on what the decision maker should do, while the marketing research problem asks what information is needed and how it can be obtained effectively and efficiently. In the opening vignette, the management decision problem was "What can Subaru do to expand its share of the automobile market?" The marketing research problem focused on information about the needs of the buyers of passenger cars, station wagons, and SUVs, and identifying a segment whose needs were not being met. Also, information was to be obtained on the automobile features desired by the members of this segment and on their demographic and psychographic characteristics. A broad statement of the problem was given, and specific components were identified.

Developing an approach to the problem is the second step in the marketing research process. The components of an approach consist of analytical framework and models, research questions, hypotheses, and specification of the information needed. The analytical model postulated that buyers first decide on the type of car (station wagon, sports utility vehicle, passenger car) and then decide on a specific brand. Research ques-tions and hypotheses related to the overlap between the features sought by station wagon buyers and buyers of SUVs were formulated. In specifying the information required, the researcher operationalized the needs of automobile buyers in terms of the attributes or features desired. Evaluations of passenger cars, station wagons, and SUVs on the desired attributes had to be obtained. Information on standard demographic characteristics and the identified psychographic characteristics was also needed.

MARKETING RESEARCH AND TQM

Problem definition is the most important step not only in marketing research but also in total quality management (TQM). TQM begins by asking how the customer defines value, in other words, what the customer value package (CVP) is.

The largest of all AT&T units, AT&T Consumer Communications Services (CCS) provides long-distance telephone services to over 80 million, primarily residential, cus-tomers. CCS measures its progress against the company's chief goal of achieving a perfect connection and contact for each customer, every time. On the basis of customer surveys, extensive marketing research, and competitive benchmarking, CCS has defined five key components of the customer value package: call quality, customer service, billing, price, and company reputation. With emphasis on these elements of the CVP, levels of customer satisfaction are moving steadily upward, with more than 90 percent of customers rating the overall quality of the company's services as good or excellent.

For companies new to TQM, the management decision problem could be "How do we improve quality for our customers?" The marketing research problem derived from

FOCUS ON

ELRICK & LAVIDGE

Elrick & Lavidge (E&L) performs both problem identification and problem-solving research. For problem-solving research, the marketing research problem has been more or less defined when the client comes to E&L with a request for proposal (RFP) for a marketing research project. However, some clients do seek input from E&L in defining the problem or developing an approach. On the other hand, problem identification research is usually not well defined when the RFP is brought to E&L. In fact, sometimes the RFP is actually a phone call from a client to one of the research directors asking for ideas to address ill-defined concerns on the part of the client. In these cases, the client will look to E&L for paid consulting help in order to define the problem further. Perhaps E&L will help develop a valid approach to the problem and the broad research design before an RFP has been created. The project will then be sent out to competing research firms (including E&L) for bids.

The research director at E&L does much of the problem definition, developing of the approach to the problem, and research design formulation for the client; and the tasks performed are similar to those discussed earlier.

■ TASKS INVOLVED IN PROBLEM DEFINITION

Discussions with Decision Makers

From the perspective of E&L, there are two sets of decision makers. The first set is the people who have brought the project to E&L and who will decide if E&L wins the project in a competitive bidding environment. They will also decide whether E&L has performed its services in a satisfactory manner. Often, these people are the marketers and/or market researchers from the client company. The second set of decision makers is those who will use the results of the research to make marketing decisions. Often, these are two entirely different sets of people. E&L must have discussions with both sets of decision makers in order to become fully familiar with the environmental context of the problem. The discussion process involves a "problem audit" format.

Interviews with Industry Experts

E&L has many industry-specific consultants on staff. These people have done projects with companies in various industries and have developed an understanding of those industries as a result. E&L will also consult with outside industry experts as the need arises. An example of the latter type is provided by the telecommunications industry for which E&L has done several projects.

Secondary Data Analysis

E&L uses the internal secondary data the client supplies, as well as other secondary data such as the results of past research projects, if they are available. In addition, the company obtains industry, company, and product data from computerized business databases.

Qualitative Research

E&L does not use much qualitative research in the problem-definition stage before a proposal has been submitted to the client, unless the client is paying for development of the RFP. Once a proposal has been developed and presented to the client and the client has initiated the project, E&L often conducts qualitative research to explore the research issues and define the data to be gathered for quantitative research.

■ STATING THE PROBLEM

After the research director has completed the tasks above, he or she is ready to create a formal statement of the client's problem. E&L incorporates this statement of the problem into the "objectives" section of the RFP that will be returned to the client. The research director begins by stating a general objective that incorporates a statement of the general problem, then lists specific objectives or components that include the elements of the marketing research problem.

■ DEVELOPING AN APPROACH

Some of E&L's research directors have PhDs. They take the lead in specifying an appropriate theoretical framework and developing a suitable model. Most projects also involve specific research questions that are investigated. However, not all projects involve the formulation of hypotheses. The information needed is specified in each project and approved by the client.

The close involvement of the client in defining the problem and developing an approach goes a long way in ensuring the success of projects E&L undertakes.

this could be to determine what aspects of a company's products and services and their acquisition does the customer value, and what aspects do not add value for the customer. Once the CVP has been defined, the management decision problem may focus on a particular quality improvement to see if it was effective. The driving force behind any company implementing quality improvement should be increasing value for the customer by improving the quality of the customer value package, as illustrated by Pizza Hut.

EXAMPLE

PIZZA HUT: BUILDING A HUT BASED ON CUSTOMER VALUE

Stiff competition from Domino's and Papa John's was hurting Pizza Hut, and the company was losing market share. The management decision problem was identified as "What can Pizza Hut do to fight competition from other pizza restaurants and improve its market share?" A problem audit identified lower levels of customer value as the underlying cause for loss of market share. The marketing research problem was to identify the factors that determine customer value and to compare Pizza Hut and its competitors on these factors. The specific components of the problem were as follows:

1. What factors determine consumers' perception of value associated with pizza restaurants?
2. How do consumers evaluate Pizza Hut and its competitors based on the value determinants?
3. What are the demographic and psychographic differences between customers who rate Pizza Hut high and those who rate it low on customer value?

Marketing research revealed that service, product freshness, waiting time, price, and unit cleanliness were the primary determinants of customer value. Pizza Hut launched a chainwide effort to improve quality on all these factors, resulting in increased customer value, satisfaction, and market share.[8]

INTERNATIONAL MARKETING RESEARCH

Conducting research in international markets often means working within unfamiliar environments. This lack of familiarity with the environmental factors of the country in which the research is being conducted can greatly increase the difficulty of appropriately defining the problem, as illustrated by the Heinz Company in Brazil.

HEINZ KETCHUP COULDN'T CATCH UP IN BRAZIL

Despite good track records domestically and overseas, H. J. Heinz failed in its initial attempts to penetrate South America's biggest and most promising market. As an entry strategy into Brazil, Heinz entered into a joint venture with Citrosuco Paulista, a giant orange juice exporter, with the future possibility of buying the profitable company. The sales of Heinz products, including ketchup, did not take off, however. Where was the problem?

A post-entry problem audit revealed that the company lacked a strong local distribution system. Heinz had also attempted to duplicate a strategy, which had been successful in Mexico: distribution through neighborhood shops. However, the problem audit revealed that 75 percent of the grocery shopping in São Paulo is done in supermarkets, not the smaller shops. Although Mexico and Brazil may appear to have similar cultural and demographic characteristics, consumer behavior was found to vary greatly. A problem audit and an examination of the environmental context of the problem prior to entry in Brazil could have prevented this failure.[9]

Many international marketing efforts fail because a problem audit is not conducted prior to entering the foreign market, and the relevant environmental factors are not taken into account. This leads to an incorrect definition of the marketing research problem and an inappropriate approach, as illustrated in the case of Heinz. While developing theoretical frameworks, models, research questions, and hypotheses, remember that differences in the environmental factors, especially the sociocultural environment, may lead to differences in the formation of perceptions, attitudes, preferences, and choice behavior.

For example, orientation toward time varies considerably across cultures. In Asia, Latin America, and the Middle East, people are not as time conscious as Westerners, which can influence perceptions and preferences for convenience foods such as frozen foods and prepared dinners. In defining the problem and developing an approach, the researcher must be sensitive to the underlying factors that influence consumption and purchase behavior.

TECHNOLOGY AND MARKETING RESEARCH

Technological advances have produced software that can process and analyze facts and ideas, restructuring them to facilitate problem definition and the development of an approach. Such software comes in two formats: text or idea processors, and outline processors. Text processors create electronic index cards that the user can search by using key words. Outline processors allow the user to list ideas in the order they come to mind and subsequently sort them into outline format. The ideas can be arranged in a hierarchy, from general to particular. The ideas can be moved around until the thinking related to the problem has been represented fully and logically. Acta, Idea Generator, Freestyle, Fact Cruncher, Maxthink, and Think Tank are some of the more popular outline processing software.

Decision support and expert systems (see Chapter 1) can also help identify alternative courses of action and define the marketing research problem and development of an approach. Other specialized software enables the researcher to use a systematic approach to organizing problems in components, resulting in logical problem formulation. These programs can portray graphically the relationship between the many facets of a complex problem and incorporate both quantitative and qualitative information, including managerial experience and intuition. This type of software allows the researcher to structure complex problems into manageable forms and to develop suitable approaches, as illustrated by Marriott.

The Marriott Corporation is faced with the problem of developing an effective marketing strategy for its resorts. Data obtained from depth interviews with potential customers are analyzed with an outline processor such as Idea Generator. This analysis reveals that different ideas are associated with different regions of the United States. West Coast cities, such as San Diego, are associated with sand, surf, sun, and palm trees. Midwest cities, such as Chicago, are considered exciting, fun, and big. East Coast cities, such as Buffalo elicit ideas such as Niagara Falls, friendliness, and neighbors. This suggests an approach that considers different marketing strategies for resorts in different regions. Furthermore, decision support systems can be used to conduct "what if" analysis and determine the demand for resorts in different regions based on assumed levels of marketing expenditures. Regions can be combined or split so that the demand potential for each region lies in a predetermined range.

ETHICS IN MARKETING RESEARCH

The stakeholders involved in ethical conflicts during the process of defining the problem and developing an approach are likely to be the marketing researcher and the client. Personal interests or hidden agendas of either stakeholder may lead to ethical dilemmas. Ethical issues arise when the personal objectives of the decision maker (e.g., defending a decision already made) are at variance with the objectives of the client firm. The client should be forthright in disclosing the relevant objectives and the purpose for which the research is being undertaken. Likewise, the researcher should have the best interest of the client at heart.

Suppose, for example, that while conducting the problem definition tasks, a researcher discovers that the problem is a lot simpler than both parties originally thought. While the reduced scope of the problem will result in substantial savings for the client, it will also cut the revenues for the research firm. Does the researcher continue with the problem definition given in the proposal? Codes of ethics suggest that this situation should be fully discussed with the client.

Sometimes a client wants to conduct research that, in the opinion of the researcher, is not warranted or needed. Again, the researcher is faced with the ethical dilemma of what to do. Codes of ethics indicate that the researcher should communicate to the client that the research is not necessary. If the client is still insistent, the researcher should feel free to undertake the research.[10]

Likewise, ethical issues may also arise in developing an approach to the problem. Such issues include using models and approaches developed for specific projects for other clients. Researchers who conduct studies for different clients in related industries (e.g., banks and brokerage firms) or in similar research areas (e.g., measuring company image) may be tempted to reuse client-specific models or findings from other projects. However, unless the researcher has obtained client permission, this practice may be unethical.

INTERNET APPLICATIONS

The Internet can help define the problem and develop an approach and add value to the traditional methods. It can greatly facilitate discussions with the decision maker and industry experts.

Discussions with the Decision Makers

The Internet provides several mechanisms that can help the researcher communicate with decision makers. The first and most obvious is Internet e-mail. This makes it possible to reach the decision makers at any place or time. Chat rooms can provide good forums for discussion with the decision makers. For instance, a discussion could be developed around a problem audit with multiple decision makers. The researcher could introduce the audit issues in the chat, and then the decision makers could respond to the issue and to each other's responses. Chat rooms can be secured with a password should proprietary information be included in the discussion.

Interviews with Industry Experts

Researchers can also use the Internet to enhance their ability to obtain information from experts in a specific industry. One approach to finding experts is to use Usenet newsgroups. Due to the large amount of information available, searching through the newsgroups for specific information can be an arduous task. A good place to start is with AltaVista *(www.altavista.com),* Deja.com *(www.deja.com)* and Google *(www.google.com),* free sites that provide categorized lists of newsgroups. Also, you may have access to newsgroups through your ISP (Internet service provider). After finding a relevant newsgroup, access the newsgroup and search for postings about the topics you are interested in. If, for example, you were interested in finding experts in the pulp and paper industry, you would begin by subscribing to "misc.industry.pulp-and-paper." Surveying the postings in this newsgroup would provide a good starting point for making contacts with the experts in this industry.

Environmental Context of the Problem

Many of the factors to be considered in the environmental context of the problem can be researched via the Internet. Past information and forecasts of trends can be found by searching for the appropriate information with the search engines.

For company-specific information pertaining to the client or a competitor, the researcher can go to the company home page. After clicking on the Netsearch icon on the browser, simply type the company's name, and get the information from there.

EXAMPLE

THE AMERICAN WAY TO GEN Y

American Demographics' Web site *(www.demographics.com)* is an excellent source for obtaining information on consumer and business trends. It contains publications such as:

- *American Demographics* (consumer trends for business leaders)
- *Marketing Tools* (tactics and techniques for information-based marketers)
- *Forecast* (a newsletter of demographic trends and business forecasts)

The November 1999 issue of *American Demographics* posted at this Web site carried information on trends affecting Gen Y, the youth segment. A large market, 70 million strong and ranging from 5 to 22 years old, Gen Y spent $94 billion of their own money in 1998. The Shooting Gallery, an independent film company best known for producing the award-winning *Sling Blade,* was able to use such information to successfully launch its movie *Minus Man* by targeting Gen Y.

SPSS

In defining the problem and developing an approach, the researcher can make use of Decision Time and What If? distributed by SPSS. Forecasts of industry and company sales, and other relevant variables, can be aided by the use of Decision Time. Once the data are loaded onto Decision Time, the program's interactive wizard asks you three simple questions. Based on the answers, Decision Time selects the best forecasting method and creates a forecast.

What If? uses the forecast by Decision Time to enable the researcher to explore different options to get a better understanding of the problem situation. The researcher can generate answers to questions such as: How will an increase in advertising affect the sales of the product? How will a decrease (increase) in price affect the demand? How will an increase in the sales force affect the sales by region? and so on.

Forecasts and what if analyses can help the researcher to isolate the underlying causes, identify the relevant variables that should be investigated, and formulate appropriate research questions and hypotheses.

SUMMARY

The most important step in a research project is defining the marketing research problem. It is frequently made difficult by the tendency of managers to focus on symptoms rather than underlying causes. The researcher's role is to help management identify and isolate the problem.

The tasks involved in formulating the marketing research problem include discussions with management, including the key decision makers; interviews with industry experts; analysis of secondary data; and qualitative research. This data-gathering process should lead to an understanding of the environmental context of the problem. Within the environmental context, a number of factors should be analyzed and evaluated. These factors include past information and forecasts about the industry and the firm, objectives of the decision maker, buyer behavior, resources and constraints of the firm, the legal and economic environment, and marketing and technological skills of the firm.

Analysis of the environmental context should help identify the management decision problem, which should then be translated into a marketing research problem. The management decision problem focuses on what the decision maker should do, while the marketing research problem asks what information is needed and how it can be obtained effectively and efficiently. The researcher should avoid defining the marketing research problem either too broadly or too narrowly. The researcher can avoid these errors by first defining the research problem using a broad statement and then breaking it down into specific components.

The second step in the marketing research process is to develop an approach to the problem. The components of an approach are the analytical framework and models, research questions, and hypotheses. In addition, all the information that needs to be obtained in the marketing research project should be specified. The approach developed should be based on objective or empirical evidence and be grounded in theory. Models are useful for portraying the relationships among variables. The most common kinds of models are verbal, graphical, and mathematical. The research questions are refined statements of the components of the problem that ask what specific information is required with respect to each component. Research questions may be further refined into hypotheses. By focusing on each component of the problem and the analytical framework and models, research questions, and hypotheses, the researcher can determine what information should be obtained.

TQM companies need to know what the customer values, in other words what the elements of the customer value package (CVP) are. When defining the problem and developing an approach in international marketing research, the researcher must isolate and examine the impact of cultural factors. Technological advances have produced software in the form of text or idea processors, and outline processors that can process and analyze facts and ideas, restructuring them to facilitate problem definition and the development of an approach. Several ethical issues that have an impact on the client and the researcher can arise at this stage but can be resolved by open and honest communication. The Internet can be useful in the process of defining the problem and developing an approach.

KEY TERMS AND CONCEPTS

Problem definition, 38
Problem audit, 39
Secondary data, 43
Primary data, 43
Qualitative research, 43
Environmental context of
   the problem, 44
Objectives, 46
Buyer behavior, 46
Legal environment, 47

Management decision
   problem, 48
Marketing research
   problem, 48
Broad statement of the
   problem, 51
Specific components of
   the problem, 51
Objective evidence, 53
Theory, 53

Analytical model, 53
Verbal model, 53
Graphical model, 53
Mathematical model, 53
Research questions, 55
Hypothesis, 55

ACRONYMS

The factors to be considered while analyzing the environmental context of the problem may be summed up by the acronym PROBLEM:

P ast information and forecasts

R esources and constraints

O bjectives of the decision maker

B uyer behavior

L egal environment

E conomic environment

M arketing and technological skills

EXERCISES

1. What is the first step in conducting a marketing research project?
2. Why is it important to correctly define the marketing research problem?
3. What are some reasons that management is often not clear about the real problem?
4. What is the role of the researcher in the problem-definition process?

5. What is a problem audit?

6. What is the difference between a symptom and a problem? How can a skillful researcher differentiate between the two and identify a true problem?

7. What are some differences between a management decision problem and a marketing research problem?

8. What are the common types of errors encountered in defining a marketing research problem? What can be done to reduce the incidence of such errors?

9. How are the research questions related to components of the problem?

10. What are the differences between research questions and hypotheses?

11. What are the most common forms of analytical models?

PROBLEMS

1. State the research problems for each of the following management decision problems.
   a. Should a new product be introduced?
   b. Should an advertising campaign, which has run for three years, be changed?
   c. Should the in-store promotion for an existing product line be increased?
   d. What pricing strategy should be adopted for a new product?
   e. Should the compensation package be changed to motivate the sales force better?

2. State the management decision problems for which the following research problems might provide useful information.
   a. Estimate the sales and market share of department stores in a certain metropolitan area.
   b. Determine the design features for a new product, which would result in maximum market share.
   c. Evaluate the effectiveness of alternative TV commercials.
   d. Assess current and proposed sales territories with respect to their sales potential and workload.
   e. Determine the prices for each item in a product line so as to maximize total sales for the product line.

3. Identify five symptoms and a plausible cause for each one.

4. Suppose you are doing a project for American Airlines. Identify, from secondary sources, the attributes or factors passengers consider when selecting an airline.

5. You are a consultant to PepsiCo, Inc. working on a marketing research project for Pepsi-Cola. Use the online databases in your library to compile a list of articles published during the past year related to the PepsiCo, Pepsi-Cola, and the soft drink industry.

INTERNET AND COMPUTER EXERCISES

1. You are a consultant to Coca-Cola USA working on a marketing research project for Diet Coke.
   a. Use the online databases in your library to compile a list of articles related to the Coca-Cola Company, Diet Coke, and the soft drink industry published during the past year.

b. Visit the Coca-Cola *(www.cocacola.com)* and PepsiCo *(www.pepsico.com)* Web sites and compare the information available at each.

c. Based on the information collected from the Internet, write a report on the environmental context surrounding Diet Coke.

2. Select any firm. Using secondary sources, obtain information on the annual sales of the firm and the industry for the last 10 years. Use a spreadsheet package, such as Lotus 1-2-3 or Excel, or any microcomputer or mainframe statistical package, to develop a graphical model relating the firm's sales to the industry sales.

3. Visit the Web sites of competing sneaker brands (Nike, Reebok, Adidas). The URLs are *www.nike.com, www.reebok.com,* and *www.adidas.com.* From an analysis of information available at these sites, determine the factors of the choice criteria used by consumers in selecting a sneaker brand.

4. Bank of America Corp. wants to know how it can increase its market share and has hired you as a consultant. Read the 10-K reports for Bank of America and three competing banks at *www.sec.gov/edgar.shtml* and analyze the environmental context of the problem.

ACTIVITIES

ROLE PLAYING

1. Ask a fellow student to play the role of a decision maker for a local soft drink firm contemplating the introduction of a lemon-lime soft drink. This product would be positioned as a "change of pace" soft drink to be consumed by all soft drink users, including heavy cola drinkers. You play the role of a researcher. Hold discussions with the decision maker and identify the management decision problem. Translate the management problem into a written statement of the research problem. Does the decision maker agree with your definition? Develop an approach to the research problem that you have identified.

2. You are vice president of marketing for Delta Airlines and would like to increase your share of the business market. Make a list of relevant objectives for Delta Airlines. As the decision maker, what are your personal objectives?

FIELD WORK

1. Set up an appointment and visit a bookstore, restaurant, or any other business located on or near the university campus. Hold discussions with the decision maker. Can you identify a marketing research problem that could be fruitfully addressed?

2. Consider the field trip described above. For the problem you have defined, develop an analytical model, research question, and the appropriate hypotheses. Discuss these with the decision maker you visited earlier.

GROUP DISCUSSION

1. Form a group of five or six people to discuss the following statement: "Correct definition of the marketing research problem is more important to the success of a marketing research project than sophisticated research techniques." Did your group arrive at a consensus?

2. We are all aware that the Coca-Cola Company changed its flagship brand of 99 years to New Coke and subsequently returned to the old favorite, Coca-Cola Classic. Working in a group of four, read as much material as you can on this marketing bungle. Identify the decision problem the Coke management faced. As a team of researchers, define the marketing research problem and its specific components.

NOTES

1. Based on Jim Henry Edison, "Subaru Gives the Market Just What It Wants: A Six," *Automotive News,* 74 (5886) (July 31, 2000): 16; *www.subaru.com:* Subaru Debuts New 6-Cylinder Outback Wagons, April 20, 2000; and "American Marketing Association, Best New Product Awards," *Marketing News,* 31(6) (March 17, 1997): E11.

2. Chuck Moozakis, "BellSouth Expands Services," *Internetweek* (817) (June 12, 2000): 14; Brian Quinton, "BellSouth Open to IntraLATA Parity," *Telephony,* 236(8) (February 22, 1999): 7; and "Forget the Code—BellSouth," *Adweek,* Special Planning Section (August 5, 1996): 13.

3. "Norwegian Cruise Line," *Successful Meetings,* 49 (1) (January 2000): 84; David Goetzl, "Luxury Cruise Lines Woo Boomers to Sea," *Advertising Age,* 70(11) (March 15, 1999): 26; and "It's Different Out Here—Norwegian Cruises," *Adweek,* Special Planning Section (August 5, 1996): 7.

4. Erin Murphy, "The Patient Room of the Future," *Nursing Management,* 31 (3) (March 2000): 38–39; David Gordon, "Redefining Processes to Create a More Humane Patient Environment," *Health Care Strategic Management,* 17(3) (March 1999): 14–16; Rachel Zoll, "Hospitals Offer Hotel-Style Perks to Fill Maternity Beds," *Marketing News,* 31(10) (May 12, 1997): 11; and "Hospital Puttin' on the Ritz to Target High-End Market," *Marketing News,* (January 17, 1986): 14.

5. Holly Acland, "Gillette Sensitive Takes to the Road," *Marketing* (April 27, 2000): 27–28; "A Woman's Touch," *Discount Merchandiser,* 39(5) (May 1999): 104; Sean Mehegan, "Gillette Big on Body Wash," *Brandweek,* 38(5) (February 3, 1997): 5; and *Marketing News,* 30(10) (May 6, 1996).

6. Rose Geller, "Snapple Pumps $30M into New Image," *Long Island Business News,* 47 (20) (May 19, 2000): 5A; Gerry Khermouch, "Snapple Looks to Surmount Plastic-Bottle Hurdle with Hydro," *Brandweek,* 40(13) (March 29, 1999): 16; and "At Quaker Oats, Snapple Is Leaving a Bad Aftertaste," *Wall Street Journal* (August 7, 1995).

7. Jennifer Sabe, "Advertising Agency of the Year 2000," *MC Technology Marketing Intelligence,* 20 (4) (April 2000): 44; Hillary Chura and Stephanie Thompson, "Bozell Moving Beyond Mustaches in Milk Ads," *Advertising Age,* 70(43) (October 18, 1999): 81.

8. James Fink, "Changes at Pizza Hut Focus on Market Share," *Business First,* 16 (26) (March 20, 2000): 8; Ed Rubenstein, "Research Prompts Pizza Hut to Listen to Its Customers," *Nation's Restaurant News,* 32(14) (April 6, 1998): 8.

9. Ellen Loft, "Heinz Boldly Goes Where No Ketchup Has Gone Before," *Pittsburgh Business Times,* 19 (52) (July 14, 2000): 17; and Judann Dagnoli, "Why Heinz Went Sour in Brazil," *Advertising Age* (December 5, 1988).

10. Ishmael P. Akaah, "Influence of Deontological and Teleological Factors on Research Ethics Evaluations," *Journal of Business Research,* 39(2) (June 1997): 71–80; and G. R. Laczniak, and P. E. Murphy, *Ethical Marketing Decisions, the Higher Road.* Boston, MA: Allyn and Bacon, 1993.

CASES

CASE 1.1 ■ WHEN THE GOING GETS TOUGH, THE TOUGH GET GOING FOR UPSCALE GYMS

Imagine cocktails, fine dining, shopping, massage therapy, and beautifying luxuries all found in a work-out gym. Sounds like a five-star resort for some, but for others, it's a part of everyday life. Considered an "upscale gym," Chicago's East Bank Club offered a trendy array of exercise facilities, hair and nail salons, a full-service bar and restaurant, and child-care services for its members in 2001. Members at the East Bank Club were also entertained by the occasional appearance of celebrities such as Michael Jordan, Oprah Winfrey, and Heather Graham. Those who were not members called the East Bank Club a "snobby haven for beautiful people." East Bank's management didn't mind that title at all.

Despite the 2001 economic slowdown, many upscale gyms were not worried about membership or profits declining. East Bank's Managing General Partner, Daniel Levin, looked at the economic slowdown like it was "almost as recession-proof as cigarettes used to be." To further illustrate how unconcerned most luxury gyms were about the declining economy, East Bank member Jeanine Meola said that if money became tight for her, her car would be the first to go, followed by her membership at East Bank.

Nearly all luxury gyms market to families with such amenities as child-care services, playrooms, swimming pools, and dance classes. With these convenient amenities, many families have kept their memberships even when "times are tight." Throughout the 1990s and continuing today, less luxurious and less expensive gyms primarily made their profits from new membership. During recession times, their profits tended to experience a sharp decline. However, upscale gyms pulled their revenues from sources other than new memberships, such as food, clothing, salons, and personal trainers. In fact, of East Bank's $42 million revenues in 1999, only 53 percent accounted for dues, while the remaining 47 percent of revenues came directly from other sources.

Many upscale members of luxury gyms viewed their membership as a direct representation of their character, status, and personality. To withdraw one's membership would display to the public that either problems may exist financially or working out and staying healthy is no longer a number one priority. Many people were members simply for status reasons and socializing, while others were mainly concerned with staying healthy. Perhaps there are additional reasons why people join upscale gyms. The management of East Bank Club was wondering what it should do to attract new members and increase the revenues during the challenging economic environment of the early 2000s.

Questions

1. What is the role of marketing research in attracting new members to upscale gyms?
2. What is the role of marketing research in ensuring the satisfaction of existing members of upscale gyms?
3. What is the management decision problem facing the management of East Bank Club?

4. Define the marketing research problem corresponding to the management decision problem you have identified in question 3.
5. Formulate one research question and two hypotheses.

References

1. Kevin Helliker, "How Hardy Are Upscale Gyms?" *Wall Street Journal* (February 9, 2001): B1.

CASE 1.2 ■ SEARS: MEETING THE CHALLENGE OF THE FUTURE

Right behind Wal-Mart, Sears Roebuck and Company holds the title of the nation's second largest retailer of apparel, home furnishings, electronics, and automotive products. Sears operates approximately 860 department stores and over 2,000 retail locations throughout the United States. In addition, Sears provides a full line of products through online shopping at the company's Web site, *www.sears.com*. For many years, consumers have relied on Sears as a one-stop-shop for home, auto, and clothing needs.

Despite Sears' success and consumer popularity, they have experienced a recent decline in net income. Due to store closings and disappointing sales from the 2000 holiday season, Sears reported a 40 percent drop in net income for fourth-quarter 2000 earnings. Reports indicated that net income for the fourth quarter was $442 million, down from $740 million. These reports did not include a $197 million charge, which was a result of closing 89 retail stores. In addition, bad weather in December 2000 kept people away from stores, and uncertainties in the economy made consumers hesitant to spend money. Such uncertainties included the 2000 presidential election, stock market fluctuations, and increased interest rates.

Due to the economic slow down, Sears' CEO, Alan Lacy, predicted that Sears would face a challenging environment in the early 2000s. As Sears looked to the future, it was clear that in order to experience continued growth, the company would have to adopt sound marketing strategies based on extensive marketing research. Mr. Lacy realized that Sears' marketing strategies should be based on an understanding of how consumers select department stores while shopping for specific needs. He looked to his marketing research department to provide him with this information.

Questions

1. What role can marketing research play in helping Sears continue to grow sales?
2. Visit *www.sears.com* and write a report about Sears' marketing program.
3. What is the management decision problem facing Sears' CEO, Alan Lacy?
4. Give an appropriate definition of the marketing research problem in this case.
5. Develop a graphical model explaining how consumers select a department store for shopping.

References

1. Calmetta Coleman, "Sears Net Falls 40% After Charges and Disappointing Holiday Sales," *Wall Street Journal* (January 19, 2001): B5.
2. *www.sears.com*.

CASE 1.3 ■ EASTMAN KODAK: FROM HIGH TOUCH TO HIGH TECH

Eastman Kodak primarily develops, manufactures, and markets consumer, professional, health, and other imaging products and services. For the fiscal year ended December 31, 2000, revenues fell 1 percent to $13.99 billion. Revenues reflected a technology and economic slowdown and adverse currency movements. Kodak realized that it was necessary to produce new innovative products in order to reestablish itself in the new high-tech market. Recently, Kodak unveiled ideas for a new line of digital products and imaging solutions. Kodak's management promised that new products and services would be produced and made available to the public as soon as possible.

Through customer research, Kodak realized that its customers were looking for new high-tech ways to view, share, and order photographs. In this high-tech world, consumers are not willing to go out of their way to develop their pictures. These facts led to an agreement between Kodak and Scientific-Atlanta to jointly develop a photo-sharing service for interactive television. The new service was connected to Kodak's digital infrastructure and became part of the company's comprehensive online photo services. "By combining Scientific-Atlanta's Explorer set-top boxes and interactive digital network with Kodak's leadership in photography and world-class photo finishing infrastructure, consumers are able to have their film images scanned and share them via the cable TV medium." Said Dan Palumbo, president of Kodak. "This new service will make picture sharing as easy to use as the TV set, backed by the trust consumers place in the Kodak brand."

This service offered many benefits to its users, such as the ability to upload pictures from digital cameras, create electronic photo albums, order photographic prints through Kodak's Internet site, and share pictures through e-mail. "By eliminating the need to start a computer, log onto a service, and wait for the photographs to download, we can use cable's large bandwidth to streamline the experience and provide outstanding value to subscribers, a factor that may play a significant role in reducing churn for the cable operators," said Jim McDonald, president and CEO at Scientific-Atlanta. Kodak hoped this new agreement would put it back on the road to success and allow it to compete better in the new high-tech market.

Questions

1. How can marketing research help Kodak better penetrate the photography market?
2. Dan Palumbo, president of Kodak, would like to undertake marketing research to determine consumers' response to the new photo-sharing service. Define the marketing research problem.
3. Based on your problem definition in question 2, develop two research questions and two hypotheses for each research question.

References

1. www.kodak.com.

CASE 1.4 ■ A BREEZE FOR DARDEN RESTAURANTS

Bill Darden created the Red Lobster chain of restaurants in the late 1960s. At the time, the new chain was a much-appreciated casual dining concept geared toward families. Darden Restaurants' pioneering move led to a boom of new restaurants in the same segment throughout the 1970s and 1980s. The family restaurant boom continued to be fueled by changing demographics in the United States. More and more women were going back to work, divorce rates were on the rise, and the number of dual-income families was increasing. This translated into fewer prepared meals and more dining out.

Today, Darden Restaurants is composed of three major national chains, with varying concepts to serve the casual dining market: Red Lobster, Olive Garden, and the newly created, Caribbean-themed Bahama Breeze. With these three chains, Darden racks up $3.3 billion in sales and has a 10 percent market share. Darden's ability to keep its chains ahead of the competition is a result of being more in tune with its customers.

To accomplish this, Darden relied on a strong vision and a hefty amount of marketing research. Research became a key focus in the early 1980s when Darden formed a development team to investigate the potential for creating an Italian restaurant in the casual dining segment. During this development, Darden used a wide variety of research techniques, ranging from field work, data analysis, reviewing social and demographic trends, and focus groups. The objective of the research was to find out what connections consumers made with Italian restaurants. The result: People expected a warm, homey place for family gatherings with lots of food.

Darden soon began making plans to unveil its new chain, Olive Garden. The marketing strategy behind the rollout directly reflected the attitudes and demographic trends the development team uncovered during their marketing research. Olive Garden ads depicted large Italian families laughing and eating together at large tables overflowing with pasta and wine. The research and marketing efforts definitely paid off. Olive Garden is now patronized by over 150 million customers a year and comprises 41 percent of Darden's total sales.

Shortly after the successful launch of the Olive Garden chain, Darden began a new initiative to save the Red Lobster chain, which had been experiencing lagging sales for quite some time. Again, Darden relied heavily on marketing research to gain a better understanding of what customers expected in a seafood restaurant. Revitalizing Red Lobster posed more of a challenge than developing Olive Garden, in that it had to overcome an already tired image. Red Lobster was quick to change the menu, adding fresh-catch-of-the-day specials and began offering regional dishes such as baked fish with a cracker crumb crust in New England. Management also revamped the physical appearance of the restaurants: adding bars, changing the wardrobe of the staff to a more casual look, and even adding new colorful dinnerware instead of the traditional white. In Red Lobster's case, the research was not limited to just customers. Executives held "town hall" meetings and sent out surveys to employees. Some of the employee input surveys led to the lifting of the ban on beards and earrings for staff and allowed chefs to test new recipes for a month in order to get real customer feedback. The result of the new efforts was an entirely new Red Lobster, and store sales have slowly been recovering since.

Darden's most recent experiment is the new chain of Bahama Breeze restaurants. These restaurants focus on creating a true Caribbean atmosphere. Each restaurant provides frozen drinks, tropical fruit, and a fun outdoor atmosphere. The rollout of the Bahama Breeze chain has been slow so that Darden managers can truly assess the performance of the new chain and determine if new marketing approaches need to be implemented. To date, Bahama Breeze has been a huge success in each of the markets.

Darden Restaurants' success can largely be attributed to its focus on customers and its understanding of the demographic trends in the industry through better marketing research. Darden's success prompted new efforts by other restaurants like Outback Steakhouse, Applebee's, and Chili's Bar and Grill. Darden's competitors will continue to try to emulate its strategy, but Darden will still remain a step ahead because of its reliance on marketing research.

Questions

1. What role does marketing research play in helping Darden Restaurants remain a step ahead of competition?
2. Define the management decision problem facing Darden Restaurants when it was thinking of launching a new initiative to save the Red Lobster chain.
3. Define an appropriate marketing research problem corresponding to the management decision problem you have identified in question 2.
4. Based on the definition of the marketing research problem, develop two research questions and two hypotheses for each.

References

1. Richard Papiernik, "Darden Opens Year Strong with Earnings Rising 20%," *Nation's Restaurant News,* 34(40) (October 2, 2000): 16.
2. Paul King, "Family Dining Chains Launch Redesign to Change Image, Reach New Customers," *Nation's Restaurant News,* 35(3) (January 15, 2001): 51–54.

CASE 1.5 ■ GILLETTE HAS A RAZOR-SHARP EDGE OVER ITS COMPETITORS

Founded in 1901, Gillette is the world leader in male grooming products. This category includes blades, razors, and shaving preparations. Gillette also holds the number one position worldwide in selected female grooming products, such as wet-shaving products and hair epilating devices. The company is the world's top seller of writing instruments and correction products, toothbrushes, and oral care appliances under the brands of Papermate, Waterman, Parker, and Oral-B. In addition, this company is the world leader in alkaline batteries with the Duracell brand.

Manufacturing operations are conducted at 57 facilities in 23 countries, and products are distributed in over 200 countries and territories around the world. Gillette's sales in 2000 amounted to $9.3 billion. The company employs more than 40,000 people, and nearly three-quarters of them are outside the United States.

As shown by the above statistics, Gillette has been a very successful consumer products company. However, its current status was not achieved without some ups and downs along the way. In the late 1980s, Gillette found itself in the precarious position of being a victim of a market it helped create. In the 1970s and 1980s, inexpensive disposable razors became the razor of choice. Gillette helped to foster this by participating in a strategy that deemphasized brand quality and focused on price. Marketing dollars went to promotions, not to its then premium shaving system, the Atra Plus. Gillette was guilty of teaching consumers how to not be loyal and how the best razor was the cheapest one at the moment. By employing this strategy, the disposable razor market grew to over 60 percent of total razor sales. Gillette lost some of its quality image and saw its margins shrink, which led to three failed hostile takeover attempts.

Gillette managers were forced to examine their position in the market or risk losing control of their company. Gillette compiled and analyzed past sales information that uncovered the flaws in its marketing strategy. Marketing research in the form of focus groups and surveys revealed that Gillette could reform its approach to the market by reemphasizing quality and brand equity in the hopes of reversing the trend. To accomplish this, Gillette discontinued all advertising for its disposable razors and began to heavily market its shaving systems. This effort led to the well-known Gillette catchphrase, "The Best a Man Can Get." Marketing research also revealed the critical importance of developing and introducing new products. Therefore, Gillette began making significant investments in research and development, developing new shaving systems over the coming years (Sensor, Sensor Excel, Mach III, Venus, etc.). In addition to changing its advertising focus, Gillette has undertaken numerous direct mail campaigns giving away free razors in order to further develop its brands. Gillette believes that once men and women try its products and experience the superior quality, they will be willing to pay the premium.

Through its refocused marketing strategy, Gillette was very successful at reversing the trend. Since the launch of its Sensor razor system, 10 percent of men switched from using disposables to refillable razors. This shift gave refillable razors over 50 percent of the entire razor market. Gillette has continued this aggressive approach to marketing the premium shaving systems and has clearly become the market leader.

In addition to the men's and women's razor markets, Gillette has refocused its marketing efforts in other personal care segments. In each one, the focus is on creating a distinctive brand and differentiating its products. Currently, 1.2 billion people around the world use one or more of Gillette's products. About 700 million consumers use Gillette razor blades. Across the consumer products industry, Gillette is considered to be one of the most effective companies at translating brand muscle into revenues and profits, with the likes of Coca-Cola and Procter & Gamble.

Gillette's success can be attributed to its willingness to rethink its overall strategy based on marketing research findings. By simply examining internal historical sales information, Gillette realized that the current trends would lead it further away from profit growth and closer to the inevitable hostile takeover. The changes made based on marketing research results throughout the past decade have made Gillette what it is today, much to the delight of its stockholders. The market value of Gillette's outstanding stock increased from $6 billion to $53 billion from year-end 1990 to year-end 1998.

Questions

1. Discuss the role of marketing research in determining consumer preferences for personal care products.
2. What was the management decision problem facing Gillette when it realized that its brand equity had eroded?
3. Define the marketing research problem corresponding to the management decision problem you have identified in question 2.
4. Develop a graphical model explaining men's choice of a shaving razor.
5. Develop a research question and a corresponding hypothesis about the role of brand loyalty and price in consumers' selection of personal care products.

References

1. www.gillette.com/company.
2. Ian Darby, "Razor Wars Force Gillette Shake-up," Marketing (July 8, 1999): 1.
3. Tara Rummell, "What's New at Gillette?" Global Cosmetic Industry, 165(4) (October 1999): 16–18.
4. Holly Acland, "Gillette Sensitive Takes to the Road," Marketing (April 27, 2000): 27.

VIDEO CASES

VIDEO CASE 1.1 ■ RITZ CARLTON: "PUTTING ON THE RITZ" FOR CUSTOMERS

Among the grand hotels of the world, Ritz Carlton Hotels and Resorts are renowned for indulgent luxury. The Ritz Carlton Hotel Company was founded on principles of groundbreaking levels of customer service. This video case emphasizes the importance of customer service focus and how to develop this value in employees, and how the Ritz Carlton used employee empowerment to achieve these goals. Through the use of marketing research, the Ritz Carlton was able to improve its strategies and remain successful in the luxury hotel industry.

The "gold standard" is central to Ritz Carlton customer service and is built on its credo, motto, and 20 basics. Through research, Ritz Carlton found the different aspects that it believes make a successful employee. The selection process is very important to Ritz Carlton's success, as employees are chosen for a caring attitude and the right behavioral characteristics and then are trained to be successful. There is an intensive two-day orientation supported by continual training in the 20 basics of superior service. Once trained, employees are empowered to adjust a customer's bill or call in other employees to help them.

Problem solving includes follow-up calls to guests to ensure satisfaction and a proactive approach to dealing with problems before they arise through the use of customer databases and the training of employees in process management. Ritz Carlton maintains a database of 240,000 customers. This database is used to update customer preferences and to track customer visits. This detailed information is used not only to satisfy the customers during their stay, but also to market the Ritz Carlton prior to a customer's visits. TQM and self-directed work teams are key to their success. Detailed planning meetings occur from top management down through all levels, reviewing quality, setting goals, and implementing actions. Relationship marketing is central to the Ritz Carlton's success: A lot of marketing emphasis is placed on guest recognition. Ritz Carlton employees are expected to learn customer names and to use them as often as possible. Marketing research has shown that customer recognition leads to a more favorable experience for the customer and a higher retention rate.

In managing quality, the hotel chain is striving to reach six sigma in quality, a goal unachieved by any other chain or service industry. Some think Ritz Carlton is going too far and will spend too much money to make marginal improvements. It is attempting to reach this goal because it understands that keeping an old customer is much less expensive than obtaining a new customer. It will have to rely on marketing research to achieve this goal. First, Ritz Carlton will have to conduct research to get a firm grasp on what it will take to reach six sigma. Then, it will have to determine the amount of extra money that will be needed in different areas in order to reach this goal. Once Ritz Carlton figures out how much it will cost, it will need to conduct marketing research in order to learn whether customers will be willing to pay the extra cost for an already pricey hotel room. These are all really important questions that should be answered before Ritz Carlton makes any drastic moves.

QUESTIONS

1. What role can marketing research play in helping Ritz Carlton enhance its share of the upscale hotel market?
2. Using the Internet, determine possible sources of secondary data pertaining to upscale hotels.
3. The management of Ritz Carlton would like to enhance its share of the upscale hotel market. Define the management decision problem.
4. Define an appropriate marketing research problem corresponding to the management decision problem you have identified in question 3.
5. Develop a graphical model explaining how a top executive on a business trip would select an upscale hotel.
6. Develop two research questions, each with two hypotheses, based on the marketing research problem you have defined in question 4.

REFERENCES

1. *http://www.ritzcarlton.com/*.

2. Barbara A. Worcester, "On-the-Job Training Nurtures IT Career," *Hotel and Motel Management,* 214(19) (November 1, 1999): 118.

3. Lauren Capotosto, "You Rang, Sir?" *CIO,* 14(3) (November 1, 2000): 260.

VIDEO CASE 1.2 ■ WNBA: A FAST START

The Women's National Basketball Association (WNBA) defied odds and has grown considerably, with 10,000 fans per game and a viewing audience of 2 million. The WNBA started fast in 1997 and grew to 14 teams in its third season and has very respectable attendance and TV audiences. Cheryl Miller, head coach of the Phoenix Mercury, feels that the passion and life of the fans fostered this growth. Rick Welts, chief marketing officer, thinks it's the freshness that the WNBA brings to competition in sports. He feels that the league taps into fun, entertainment, family, and affordability for its target markets. By conducting market research, the WNBA has been able to determine its target market and the best new cities to originate teams. Marketing research helps the WNBA learn which markets to tap into and will ultimately be the main driver of its success.

Val Ackerman, WNBA's president, thinks it is the relationship the players have with the fans that contributes to the WNBA's success. Fans are brought closer to the players and are allowed to interact with players on a much different level than the NBA. Also, the WNBA avoids the crowded winter schedule by playing in the summer. This does not mean that fans are merely watching the games because the NBA season has ended. Marketing research showed that 70 percent of the fans are women, not diehard sports enthusiasts passing the time between seasons. Part of their success is related to timing—they started the league immediately after the Olympics. Marketing researchers studied the growth of women's athletics in colleges, which in turn helped to energize the start of the WNBA. Sponsors see the WNBA as a way to reach women consumers in a way other sports don't.

Considerable planning went into launching the WNBA, showing the detail of thought given to the start of the league. Lots of time and money were spent researching all the different aspects of the product in order to market it effectively to the public. Marketing research showed the WNBA that families and children were its target. Therefore, in an effort to please this market, marketing researchers used surveys to determine exactly what the consumer looked for in a sporting experience. From these data, arenas were chosen and tickets were priced affordably.

The WNBA strived to sell the players as real people, as role models. The teams and players also strive to give back to the communities in different ways. This is where they tie in their mission with marketing. The WNBA supports selected causes that fit who it is, such as physical fitness, and domestic violence prevention and intervention. The teams and the players also get involved in local and national causes. Marketing research indicated that this involvement has a positive impact on fan loyalty. Therefore, the players stay in touch with the fans personally and through community involvement.

Marketing research will be a vital aspect in the future growth of the WNBA. First, it must continue to research the different cities across the country. The WNBA plans to continue to grow the number of teams in the league, and knowing where the largest WNBA fan bases are will help decide what cities should be used in the opening of new teams. The league must also continuously conduct research on its main consumers/target markets. The WNBA has overcome many large obstacles and has done an exceptional job marketing its product to consumers. The only way it will be able to continue this success is by continuously researching its consumers in order to keep up-to-date with what the consumers want and expect out of a WNBA experience. Hence, marketing research has a crucial role in the future of WNBA.

QUESTIONS

1. Discuss the role of marketing research in helping WNBA expand its franchise.
2. Discuss the environmental context relevant to the WNBA.
3. The WNBA is considering expanding to other major cities in the United States. Define the management decision problem.
4. Define an appropriate marketing research problem corresponding to the management decision problem you have identified.
5. Develop a plausible graphical model explaining consumers' selection of a sporting event for TV viewing.

REFERENCES

1. *www.wnba.com/.*
2. John Greenwald, "One for the Team," *Time,* 155(25) June 19, 2000: 138.
3. Laura Petrecca, "WNBA Hands the Ball to Aspiring Creatives in Do-It-Yourself Ads," *Advertising Age,* 71(23) (May 29, 2000): 4.

VIDEO CASE 1.3 ■ CELEBRATING CELEBRITY MARKETING

This case deals with talent agencies negotiating salaries and other perks for celebrities. Such agencies find and secure the best roles, money, and other benefits for actors. The major factors affecting salaries are popularity, position in career, and whether or not the actor/actress has just made a blockbuster film. Salaries are typically lower for more serious films and art films. Marketing research plays a very important role in determining the demand for a new film, which ultimately determines a celebrity's salary.

Although stars receive high salaries, they have high costs for publicists, agents, managers, and lawyers. Their salaries are negotiated along with billing, poster positioning, and other perks such as trailers, makeup rooms, per diems, and provisions for families. Sometimes, stars take risks with pet film projects. Often, flops can ruin a career, as they tend to stick longer than successes.

There are external factors that make up the demand for a movie. It is important to undertake marketing research to study external factors in order to determine how much demand the movie is expected to generate. If a movie's predicted demand is very high, that can affect the movie's budget, celebrity's salary, and many other factors involved. Through the use of surveys, marketing researchers can find the public's opinion about celebrity popularity, and the public's movie preference for future films (drama, comedy, action, or romance types of films). Marketing research shows if the film will appeal to popular tastes or to more serious tastes, which in turn helps agencies set estimated salaries for the clients they represent.

Value-based pricing applies specifically to the pricing of celebrities. Marketing researchers investigate the elements found in previous blockbuster movies in order to determine the success and popularity of new films. In addition, researchers investigate the market to figure out what types of movies will meet the needs of moviegoers. If a movie meets the needs of its viewers, it's clear that the movie will be a popular hit. The market determined that *Forrest Gump* and *Titanic* were major hits. Therefore, producers and studios were willing to spend more on these types of films. The same is true of Richard Gere and Julia Roberts movies. *Pretty Woman* was a smash hit, so the studio was willing to pay more to put them in another movie together such as *Runaway Bride*. After marketing research is conducted and a movie is expected to be a blockbuster hit, studios and filmmakers can set a large celebrity salary and budget to produce the film. Thus, marketing research plays a crucial role in investigating, predicting, and celebrating celebrity success in movies.

QUESTIONS

1. Why is marketing research significant in the process of determining a celebrity's salary?

2. Give an example of a movie that was expected to be a hit but resulted in a flop. Do you think that marketing research was conducted properly or at all?

3. The producer of *Titanic* is thinking about producing *Titanic II,* but wonders what the audience response would be to the sequel. Define the management decision problem.

4. Define the marketing research problem corresponding to the management decision problem you have identified.

5. Based on your problem definition, identify two research questions and develop two hypotheses for each question.

REFERENCES

1. Anthony Breznican, "Hollywood Writers, Directors Spar Over Movie Credits," *Marketing News,* 35(5) (February 26, 2001): 48.

2. Anonymous, "FTC Won't Sue Over Movie Marketing," *Broadcasting & Cable,* 130(49) (November 27, 2000): 18.

VIDEO CASE 1.4 ■ MARKETING RESEARCH SUPPLIES ERICSSON WITH SUPPLIER INFORMATION

Ericsson is the world's leading supplier in telecommunications and has the largest customer base, which also includes the world's top 10 operators. Ericsson provides telecommunication solutions from systems and applications to mobile phones and other communication tools. Beginning in 1876 and continuing through today, Ericsson operates worldwide in more than 140 countries.

Cellular phones only make up 20 percent of Ericsson's business, while the other 80 percent constitutes heavy-duty business-to-business (B2B) products that support the cellular industry. Technical development investments contribute to Ericsson's leadership in mobile infrastructure and mobile Internet. With 23 research and development (R&D) centers worldwide, and 23,000 R&D engineers and technicians, Ericsson is nearly twice the size of its closest competitor.

The Ericsson case illustrates the strength of B2B relationships. The case begins by indicating the large number of specifications that any component in a mobile phone must meet. This alone indicates the need for good relationships with suppliers. The case shows that Ericsson has four factors in mind when selecting suppliers: (1) technical performance (can they make the part?), (2) commercial performance (do they own the proper patents?), (3) suppliers' capabilities (do they have the production capacity?), and (4) timing (can they meet Ericsson's timetable?). Based on these four criteria, Ericsson has chosen Naloto, a global company in Sweden to supply its component parts.

In order to keep relationships with suppliers working, companies should aim for long-term relationships. Ericsson tends to stick with suppliers over the long haul, as it needs them to work on R&D for components. Furthermore, Ericsson must build trust with suppliers in order to decrease the chances of risk associated in conducting business. Trust among suppliers eventually turns into a personal as well as business relationship, which is useful in sending a consistent message through the layers of management in a supplier business.

Because Ericsson is an assembler rather than a manufacturer, it needs to forecast supplier needs for as much as five to seven years in advance. Extensive marketing research must be conducted on a particular company before Ericsson would even begin to think about conducting supplier business with them. Since having a good supplier relationship is crucial for business success, Ericsson must thoroughly research any new supplier. In addition, by conducting marketing research on the newest technologies available in the field, Ericsson is better able to determine if a new supplier will deliver new technologies to the needs of Ericsson. Through the use of consumer and business surveys for cellular phone preference, Ericsson is able to better meet the needs of its customer market. Surveys can reveal certain features that customers look for in cellular phones such as size, weight, voice mail, reliability, and other convenience options. If marketing researchers can gather such important information about their customers, then Ericsson can develop cellular phones that meet the needs of cellular phone consumers.

QUESTIONS

1. What are the major drivers that determine the nature of the relationship between Ericsson and its suppliers? What role can marketing research play in discovering these drivers?
2. Why is it so crucial for marketing researchers to investigate potential supplier companies and new technologies for Ericsson?
3. What are the environmental factors affecting Ericsson?
4. Ericsson is seeking to develop long-term relationships with its suppliers. Define the management decision problem.
5. Define the marketing research problem corresponding to the management decision problem you have identified.

REFERENCES

1. *www.ericsson.com/*.
2. Toby Elkin, "Ericsson Seeks Innovative Spin," *Advertising Age,* 12 (March 19, 2001): 6.
3. Joanna Witt, "Is Outsourcing the Way Forward for Ericsson? *Marketing* (March 1, 2001): 19.

Research Design Formulation

II

3

RESEARCH DESIGN

A RESEARCH DESIGN
IS THE HEART AND
SOUL OF A
MARKETING
RESEARCH PROJECT.
IT OUTLINES HOW
THE MARKETING
RESEARCH PROJECT
WILL BE CONDUCTED
AND GUIDES DATA
COLLECTION,
ANALYSIS, AND
REPORT
PREPARATION.

*Robert F. Klein, Managing Director / Sr. Vice
President, Elrick & Lavidge.*
*Robert Klein is responsible for Research Service
and Project Direction. He has a broad base of
strategic market research experience. He has
worked with various packaged goods, healthcare,
and service based clients.*

Opening Questions

1. What is a research design?
2. What are the kinds of basic research designs?
3. How can the basic research designs be compared and contrasted?
4. What are the major sources of errors in a research design?
5. How does the researcher coordinate the budgeting and scheduling aspects of a research project?
6. What elements make up the marketing research proposal?
7. What role does research design play in total quality management?
8. What factors should the researcher consider while formulating a research design in international marketing research?
9. How can technology facilitate the research design process?
10. What ethical issues arise when selecting a research design?
11. How can the Internet be used in the research design process?

MARKETING RESEARCH HELPS SPIEGEL DESIGN THE EDDIE BAUER LINE

Spiegel is one of the leading direct marketers, offering the benefits of home-based shopping via the catalog and the Internet. From 1995 to 1998, Spiegel's catalog sales decreased an overwhelming 50 percent and catalog circulation dropped by 45 percent. Spiegel's catalog CEO, John Irvin, realized a turnaround had to happen to regain profits and customer growth. To achieve this turnaround, the company lowered expenses, reduced inventory, and concentrated on creating an improved Web site to draw in new customers and ultimately boost revenues. In February 2001, the Spiegel Group announced that it achieved a 46 percent increase in earnings for the year 2000 with a 9 percent increase in revenue. This was the company's second consecutive year of record earnings in a challenging economy. Although the overall company has fared much better than it had in the past, Spiegel's Eddie Bauer division had some shortfalls that needed to be addressed.

Eddie Bauer sales had not seen the large market growth that the rest of the Spiegel Company had over the past few years. After Spiegel spent time studying this underperforming division, it realized that Eddie Bauer had some major problems in its performance, management team, and apparel offerings. In order to address this problem, Spiegel conducted extensive marketing research. The marketing research problem was to understand the shopping behavior of Eddie Bauer's potential and current consumers. The approach Spiegel adopted treated this group of consumers as a distinct segment; several research questions and hypotheses were formulated to examine the unique aspects of the buying behavior of this group.

The research design Spiegel used consisted of two phases. The first, exploratory phase, consisted of analysis of secondary data plus six focus groups with Eddie Bauer consumers. Secondary data provided good background information on current and potential catalog shoppers and vital statistics such as the size of this segment. Focus groups helped Spiegel understand the values, attitudes, and behavior of this segment related to clothing and shopping. The focus groups revealed that these customers wanted variety and quality. They also felt appreciated when a company designed special promotions directed at this segment. Eddie Bauer came up short on both dimensions.

In the second, descriptive phase, the findings of the exploratory phase were tested with a telephone survey of a sample of 1,000 Eddie Bauer consumers. The sample was randomly selected from a list of Eddie Bauer consumers, that is, selected based on chance, to measure and control random sampling error. Efforts were also undertaken to control the various sources of nonsampling error. For example, the interviewers were carefully selected and thoroughly trained, and close supervision was exercised to minimize interviewing errors. The results of the survey confirmed the demand for more Eddie Bauer product offerings, and also showed that the Eddie Bauer line needed more promotion.

Spiegel chairman Michael R. Moran stated, "We made significant progress in the first half of year 2000, further enhancing the competitive positioning of our business." One major flaw found in the Eddie Bauer division was lack of product offerings and promotional campaigns. The research results led to the production of more product offerings and an increased amount of promotions across the Eddie Bauer division. Since then, Spiegel has witnessed an increased growth rate of the Eddie Bauer line, and they believe these changes will lead to continued success.[1]

OVERVIEW

As we saw in Chapter 2, defining a marketing research problem and developing a suitable approach are both critical to the success of the entire marketing research project. The next step is to formulate a detailed research design to achieve the defined goals. Figure 3.1 gives the relationship of research design to previous chapters and to the marketing research process.

This chapter classifies and describes the basic research designs. At the broad level, there are two major types of research designs: exploratory and conclusive. Conclusive research designs can be further classified as descriptive or causal. Thus, this classification results in three basic designs—exploratory, descriptive, and causal. These three basic designs are used in different combinations and sequences.

We consider the value of marketing research information within the context of controlling research design errors. We discuss budgeting and scheduling of a proposed research project and present guidelines for writing research proposals. As applications, we consider research design concepts in the context of contemporary issues such as total quality management (TQM), international marketing research, technology, ethics in marketing research, and the Internet. Figure 3.2 presents an overview.

WHAT IS A RESEARCH DESIGN?

research design
A framework or blueprint for conducting the marketing research project that specifies the procedures necessary to obtain the information needed to structure and/or solve the marketing research problem.

The **research design** is a road map for conducting the marketing research project. It provides details of each step in the marketing research project. Implementation of the research design should result in all the information needed to structure or solve the man-

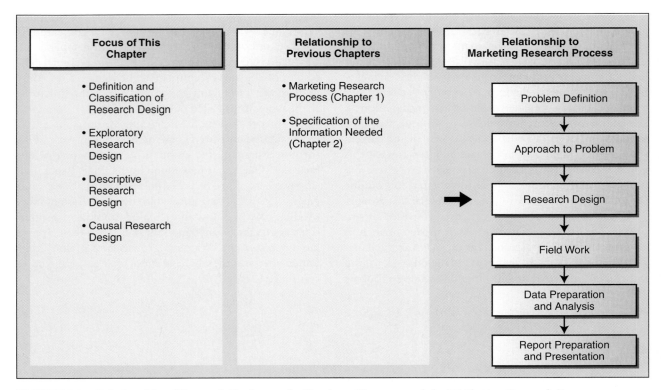

Focus of This Chapter	Relationship to Previous Chapters	Relationship to Marketing Research Process
• Definition and Classification of Research Design • Exploratory Research Design • Descriptive Research Design • Causal Research Design	• Marketing Research Process (Chapter 1) • Specification of the Information Needed (Chapter 2)	Problem Definition → Approach to Problem → Research Design → Field Work → Data Preparation and Analysis → Report Preparation and Presentation

FIGURE 3.1   Relationship of Research Design to the Previous Chapters and the Marketing Research Process

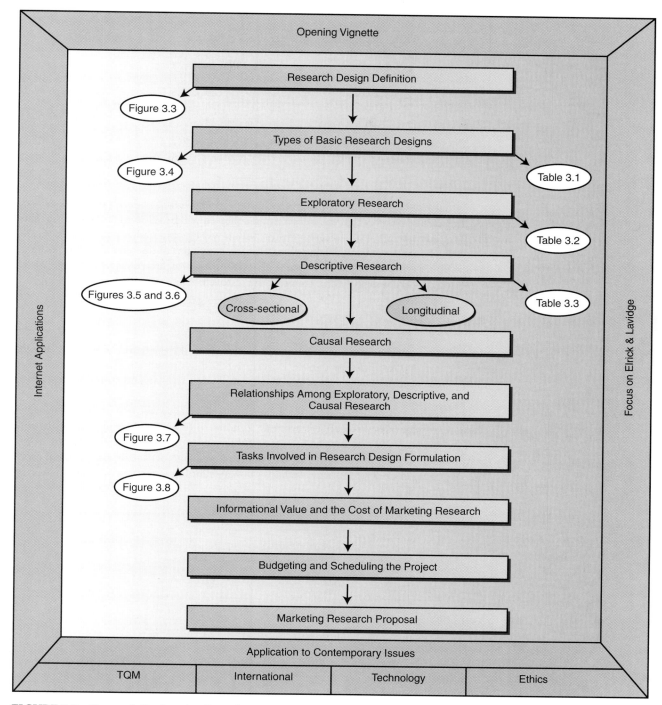

FIGURE 3.2   Research Design: An Overview

agement decision problem. The design process begins by defining the marketing research problem. Next comes the approach: a conceptual framework, research questions, hypotheses, and the information needed (see Chapter 2). The research design is based on the results of these first two steps: the problem definition and the approach (Figure 3.3).

FIGURE 3.3
Steps Leading
to the Formulation
of a Research Design

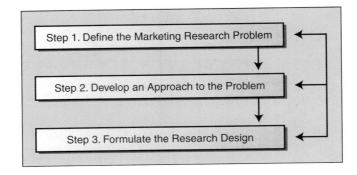

Many designs may be appropriate for a given marketing research problem. A good research design ensures that the information collected will be relevant and useful to management and that all of the necessary information will be obtained. A good design should also help ensure that the marketing research project will be conducted effectively and efficiently. In this chapter, we will consider the basic types of research designs available. These basic designs can be classified in terms of the research objectives.

BASIC RESEARCH DESIGNS

Research designs are of two broad types: exploratory and conclusive. Conclusive designs may be either descriptive or causal. Descriptive designs may be further categorized as either cross-sectional or longitudinal. Exploratory, descriptive, and causal are the basic research designs we examine in this chapter (see Figure 3.4).

exploratory research
A type of research design that has as its primary objective the provision of insights into and comprehension of the problem situation confronting the researcher.

The differences between the exploratory and conclusive research are summarized in Table 3.1. **Exploratory research** is research conducted to explore the problem situation, that is, to gain ideas and insight into the problem confronting the management or the researcher. Exploratory research may be used when management realizes a problem exists but does not yet understand why. Perhaps sales are slipping in a particular region, or cus-

FIGURE 3.4
A Classification of Market
Research Designs

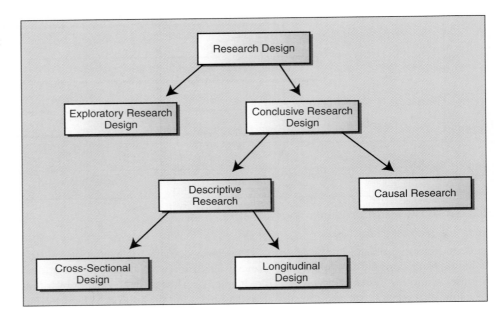

TABLE 3.1 DIFFERENCES BETWEEN EXPLORATORY AND CONCLUSIVE RESEARCH

	EXPLORATORY	CONCLUSIVE
Objective	To provide insights and understanding	To test specific hypotheses and examine relationships
Characteristics	Information needed is defined only loosely	Information needed is clearly defined
	Research process flexible and unstructured	Research process is formal and structured
	Sample is small and nonrepresentative	Sample is large and representative
	Analysis of primary data is qualitative	Data analysis is quantitative
Findings/Results	Tentative	Conclusive
Outcome	Generally followed by further exploratory or conclusive research	Findings used as input into decision making

tomer service complaints have increased sharply. As a first step, the problem must be defined and alternate courses of action identified.

Because the information needs are only loosely defined at this stage, exploratory research must be flexible and unstructured. For example, exploratory research investigating why some customers are dissatisfied with Ivory bath soap may begin with an analysis of calls recorded on the consumer hot line regarding the nature of complaints. Then, depending on the nature of the findings, the researcher may decide to conduct focus groups with users of Ivory soap. Suppose six focus groups, each involving 10 respondents, reveal that users are dissatisfied with the lack of lather and moisturizing ability. Should Procter & Gamble immediately change the Ivory formula?

No! Exploratory research is conducted on a small and nonrepresentative sample, so the findings should be regarded as tentative and should be used as building blocks for further research. Typically, more formally defined exploratory research or conclusive research follows. There is a danger when exploratory research is the only step taken toward developing a solution. The tendency to overlook the limited usefulness of the information, particularly if it confirms preconceived ideas about a problem, can lead management in the wrong direction. Despite these risks, exploratory research can be valuable when researchers are faced with a problem that is not fully understood, for example, why some customers are dissatisfied with a specific brand of bath soap. Exploratory research in the form of focus groups could provide valuable insights.

Conclusive research is research designed to assist the decision maker in determining, evaluating, and selecting the best course of action in a given situation. Conclusive research can be used to verify the insights gained from exploratory research. As illustrated in the opening vignette, the findings from secondary data and focus groups (exploratory research) were further tested in a telephone survey (conclusive research). Conclusive research is based on the assumption that the researcher has an accurate understanding of the problem at hand. The information needed for addressing the management decision problem has been clearly specified. The objective of conclusive research is to test specific hypotheses and examine specific relationships.

Conclusive research is typically more formal and structured than exploratory research. The researcher specifies the detailed steps in the research to be conducted prior

conclusive research
Research designed to assist the decision maker in determining, evaluating, and selecting the best course of action for a given situation.

to initiating the project. Large, representative samples are used to collect data that are analyzed with statistical techniques. In the Ivory soap example, a large national survey involving 1,000 randomly selected respondents could be conducted to verify the findings of the focus groups. The survey could be used to obtain consumer evaluations of Ivory soap and competing brands on the important attributes such as mildness, lather, shrinkage, price, fragrance, packaging, moisturizing, and cleaning power.

Performance Monitoring

Research designs, regardless of whether they are exploratory or conclusive, often include a performance-monitoring component. The purpose of performance monitoring is to track and report changes in performance measures such as sales levels, market share, or marketing program results. This type of research may be conducted informally and as needed, or it may be embedded in a formal, ongoing research effort. The data used for performance monitoring can range from secondary data generated either externally or as a function of day-to-day operations (see Chapter 2) to quantitative data generated via surveys. Analysis of consumer complaints is one example of performance-monitoring research, as the following example illustrates.

EXAMPLE

SNAP-ON LID SNAPS CUSTOMER COMPLAINTS

Exploratory research by Kraft Foods into customer complaints revealed that the packaging for a recently introduced brand of salad dressing was causing problems. Because the opening of the bottle was too large, users were "drowning their salad," to quote one irate customer. Complaints also indicated a perception that the design was intended to cause the user to "go through the bottle" faster. Several customers had demanded their money back.

These comments led to more formal exploratory research, in the form of six focus groups, to assess the reaction to a new snap-on lid with a narrower opening than the bottle. The new lid was designed to better control the flow of dressing. Focus group results were all positive, and Kraft decided to further examine consumer reaction to a snap-on lid via a mall intercept survey.

Mall intercept interviews were conducted with 500 female heads of households in 10 major cities across the country. Respondents were asked to use the new packaging of salad dressing with the snap-on lid and then respond to a questionnaire. The survey results were also favorable, and the snap-on lid was introduced.

In the three months following the introduction of the modified package, customers were again surveyed. Feedback on the new lid was positive. Additional evidence of its effectiveness was provided by calls to the customer service center: Complaints related to the packaging had disappeared. This example illustrates the usefulness of analyzing consumer complaints, which is an essential element of performance monitoring research at Kraft Foods.

The packaging example relied on qualitative feedback from the focus groups (exploratory research) as well as quantitative information collected from a mall intercept survey (conclusive research) for performance monitoring. Both exploratory and conclusive techniques were used, as in the Spiegel vignette.

EXPLORATORY RESEARCH

As its name implies, the objective of exploratory research is to explore or search through a problem or situation to provide insights and understanding (Tables 3.1 and 3.2). For example, Adidas could make use of exploratory research to understand the reasons for its lower market share in the United States as compared to Nike. Exploratory research could be used for any of the following purposes, which are illustrated using the Adidas example.

1. **To formulate a problem or define a problem more precisely.** Exploratory research may reveal that Adidas has a lower market share because its brand image is not as strong as Nike.

2. **To identify alternative courses of action.** Alternative courses of action to boost the image of Adidas might include improving product quality, increasing the television advertising budget, distributing the product through upscale company-owned stores, increasing the prices of its athletic shoes and apparel, and so on.

3. **To develop hypotheses.** An interesting hypothesis is that heavy users of athletic shoes are more brand conscious than light users. Another is that heavy users have a weaker image of Adidas as compared to light users.

4. **To isolate key variables and relationships for further examination.** Celebrity endorsements can have a positive influence on the image of Adidas.

5. **To gain insights for developing an approach to the problem.** Brand image is a composite variable that is influenced by the quality of the product, pricing strategy, image of the outlets through which the product is distributed, and the quality and intensity of advertising and promotion.

6. **To establish priorities for further research.** Adidas might want to examine the purchase and consumption behavior of heavy users of athletic shoes.

Exploratory research is often conducted in the beginning stages of a project, as illustrated in the Spiegel vignette. Secondary data provided good background information on Eddie Bauer consumers, while focus groups helped Spiegel understand the values, attitudes, and behavior of this segment concerning clothing and shopping. The results

TABLE 3.2   A COMPARISON OF BASIC RESEARCH DESIGNS

	EXPLORATORY	DESCRIPTIVE	CAUSAL
Objective	Discovery of ideas and insights	Describe market characteristics or functions	Determine cause-and-effect relationships
Characteristics	Flexible Versatile Often the front end of total research design	Marked by the prior formulation of specific hypotheses Preplanned and structured design	Manipulation of one or more independent variables Control of other mediating variables
Methods	Expert surveys Pilot surveys Case studies Secondary data Qualitative research	Secondary data Surveys Panels Observational and other data	Experiments

indicated that Eddie Bauer current and potential customers wanted variety and quality and also appreciated special promotions. However, exploratory research can be used at any point in the research process when the researcher is unclear about the problem situation.

Exploratory research relies heavily on the curiosity and insight of the researcher. It is more like a process of informal discovery. Yet the abilities of the researcher are not the sole determinants of good exploratory research. While the process is highly flexible and relatively informal, exploratory research can benefit from use of the following methods (see Table 3.2):

- Survey of experts (discussed in Chapter 2)
- Pilot surveys (discussed in Chapter 2)
- Analysis of secondary data, including literature review (discussed in Chapters 4 and 5)
- Qualitative research, such as focus groups and one-on-one depth interviews (discussed in Chapter 6)

Spiegel analyzed secondary data and conducted six focus groups as part of its exploratory research to understand the clothing preferences and shopping behavior of Eddie Bauer customers. The use of exploratory research in defining the problem and developing an approach was discussed in Chapter 2. The following example provides another application of exploratory research.

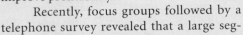

EXAMPLE

BANKING ON EXPLORATORY RESEARCH

Bank of America (BOA), formed by merging NationsBank and BankAmerica, is the largest bank in the United States *(www.bankofamerica.com)*. Assets in 2001 exceeded $600 billion. In order to increase its share of a very competitive market, BOA conducted exploratory research using focus groups of current and potential customers to find out where new branches should be located and what new products to introduce. Many new product ideas were generated through exploratory research. These ideas were further investigated using descriptive research in the form of customer and noncustomer surveys. The research enabled BOA to successfully introduce new products, such as innovative checking, savings, and institutional accounts, and to improve profitability.

Recently, focus groups followed by a telephone survey revealed that a large segment of households wanted interest payment on their checking account balances but were very sensitive to any checking account fees. These consumers maintained large balances in their checking account and were therefore open to a reasonable minimum balance requirement. Accordingly, BOA introduced an interest-paying checking account with no fees (monthly or per check) but with a minimum balance requirement of $1,000. Exploratory and descriptive research helped Bank of America to become the largest bank in the country.

Note that Bank of America, like Spiegel, did not rely exclusively on exploratory research. Once new product ideas were identified, they were further tested by descriptive research in the form of surveys.

DESCRIPTIVE RESEARCH

Descriptive research is a type of conclusive research that has as its major objective the description of something—usually market characteristics or functions. Most commercial market research is descriptive in nature. Descriptive research is particularly useful whenever research questions relate to describing a market phenomenon, such as frequency of purchase, identifying relationships, or making predictions (see Table 3.2). Here are some examples of descriptive research goals:

descriptive research
A type of conclusive research that has as its major objective the description of something—usually market characteristics or functions.

1. **To develop a profile of a target market.** Levi Strauss would like to know the age, educational level, income, and media habits of heavy users of jeans in order to make advertising placement decisions.
2. **To estimate the frequency of product use as a basis for sales forecasts.** Knowing that a "heavy" perfume user buys 1.8 bottles of perfumes per month can help Mary Kay Cosmetics predict potential sales for a new perfume brand.
3. **To determine the relationship between product use and perception of product characteristics.** In developing its marketing platform, Motorola would like to determine if and how heavy users of cellular phones differ from nonusers, in terms of the importance they attach to performance and ease of use.
4. **To determine the degree to which marketing variables are associated.** Microsoft would like to know to what extent Internet usage is related to age, income, and education level.

Descriptive research assumes that the researcher has prior knowledge about the problem situation. This is one of the major differences between descriptive and exploratory research. Thus, descriptive research, in contrast to exploratory research, is based on a clear statement of the problem, specific hypotheses, and specification of the information needed (see Chapter 2). The data are collected in a structured fashion, typically using large, representative samples. The findings are then used to make generalizations about an entire customer group or market. Microsoft, for example, could survey a representative sample of Internet users to determine Internet use and project the findings to the population of Internet users.

Descriptive studies are used to portray market variables. They describe the customer and the market and measure the frequency of behaviors such as purchasing. Among the major types of descriptive studies are internally or externally focused sales studies, consumer perception and behavior studies, and market characteristic studies (Figure 3.5).

- Sales studies include market potential studies, which describe the size of the market, the buying power of consumers, and historic growth rates; market share studies, which determine the proportion of total sales a company and its competitors receive; and sales analysis studies, which describe sales by geographic region, product line, and type and size of the account.
- Consumer perception and behavior studies include image studies, which determine consumer perceptions of the firm and its products; product usage studies, which describe consumption patterns; advertising studies, which describe media consumption habits and audience profiles for specific television programs and magazines; and pricing studies, which describe the range and frequency of price changes and probable consumer response to proposed price changes.

FIGURE 3.5 Major Types of Descriptive Studies

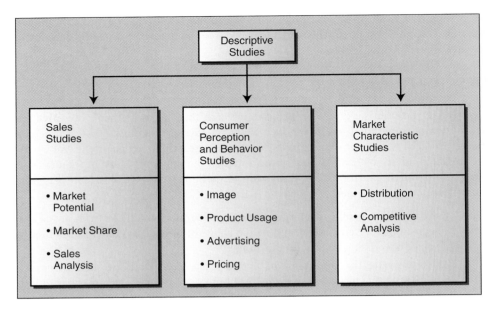

- Market characteristic studies include distribution studies, which determine traffic flow patterns and the number and location of distributors; and competitive analyses, which compare strengths and weaknesses of industry participants.

Say that Swatch would like to determine the size of the market for sports watches, at what rate the market is growing, and the market shares of the leading brands. It might do an analysis of its own sales of Swatch sport watches by type of outlet—jewelry stores, department stores, sporting goods stores, specialty stores, catalog, Internet operations, and other outlets. The management might ask: How do consumers perceive Swatch? Does the image of Swatch vary between owners and nonowners? Which TV programs do people who buy premium sports watches watch? How much of a premium are consumers willing to pay for a high-quality sports watch? Swatch would have to undertake consumer perception and behavior studies to provide management with answers to these questions.

Finally, market characteristic studies may examine questions such as: How many distributors does Swatch have for each type of outlet, and how does this compare with other competing brands?

These examples demonstrate the range and diversity of descriptive research studies. Descriptive research also uses a variety of data-collection techniques, which we discuss in the following chapters. They include:

- Secondary data (Chapters 4 and 5)
- Surveys (Chapter 7)
- Panels (Chapters 5 and 7)
- Observational and other data (Chapter 7)

The survey Spiegel conducted in the opening vignette is an example of descriptive research. Descriptive research using these methods can be further classified into cross-sectional and longitudinal research (Figure 3.4).

Cross-Sectional Designs

cross-sectional design
A type of research design involving the one-time collection of information from any given sample of population elements.

A **cross-sectional design,** sometimes called a sample survey, can be thought of as a snapshot of the marketplace taken at a specific point in time. In this design, the selected group of respondents is measured only once. The cross-sectional survey is the most frequently used descriptive design in marketing research. Spiegel's survey of 1,000 Eddie Bauer consumers is a cross-sectional design, and so is the Jergens Body Shampoo example that follows.

E X A M P L E

JERGENS BODY SHAMPOO WASHES AWAY CONSUMER GRIPES

The Andrew Jergens Company periodically conducts surveys to measure consumers' perceptions, attitudes, and use of soap bars and related personal care products. A cross-sectional survey involving 600 mall intercept interviews in six major cities showed that many consumers had complaints about the standard soap bar: They didn't like having to pick a mushy bar out of the dish. They didn't like the nasty film it left in their shower or bath. They didn't like the way it dried out their skin. These findings led to the development of an innovative new product. Jergens Body Shampoo was designed to eliminate those woes by providing what the company calls "a creamy lather that rinses away easily for a clean that never felt so good." The product was introduced in 1995 and met with instant success.

The company credits the product for revolutionizing its category, noting it has spawned more than 10 competitors. Jergens reports that the brand is the number one seller among body shampoos in food stores and that it helped the category grow to over $500 million—almost a quarter of the soap category—by 2000.[2]

Longitudinal Design

The typical cross-sectional design gives us a snapshot at a single point in time. In contrast, a **longitudinal design** provides a series of pictures, which track the changes that take place over time. In longitudinal designs, a fixed sample from the population is measured repeatedly on the same variables. In other words, two or more measurements on the same variables are obtained from a given group of respondents at different points in time (see Figure 3.6). A cross-sectional design would be used to ask the question, "How did the American people rate the performance of Bill Clinton immediately following the vote on

longitudinal design
A type of research design involving a fixed sample of population elements that is measured repeatedly. The sample remains the same over time, providing a series of pictures which, when viewed together, portray both the situation and the changes that are taking place.

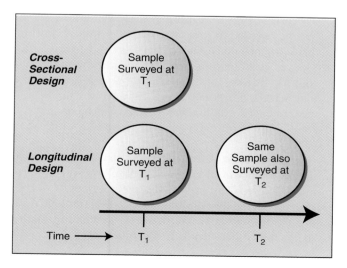

FIGURE 3.6
Cross-Sectional Versus Longitudinal Designs

his impeachment?" A longitudinal design would be used to address the question, "How did the American people change their view of Clinton's performance before and after his last State of the Union address?"

Sometimes, the term *panel* is used interchangeably with the term *longitudinal design*. A **panel** consists of a sample of respondents, generally households that have agreed to provide information at specified intervals over an extended period. Because of the long-term commitment needed for participation on a panel, its members are compensated with gifts, coupons, information, or cash. Panel data are typically collected by commercial research organizations known as syndicated firms. The National Purchase Diary (NPD) is one such firm. The NPD tracks changes in consumer purchase patterns and then sells the data to other businesses or interested groups for a flat subscription price. The example that follows illustrates longitudinal design. The application is discussed in more detail in Chapters 5 and 7.

panel
A panel consists of a sample of respondents, generally households, that have agreed to provide information over an extended period.

EXAMPLE

WOW! NO FAT, REDUCED CALORIES, AND A GREAT TASTE!

Longitudinal tracking studies using mail panels indicated that Frito-Lay chips had developed strong brand loyalty. Many consumers were repeatedly purchasing Frito-Lay chips. Given a loyal army of users, Frito-Lay saw an opportunity to capitalize on this success. Thus, in 1998, PepsiCo's $11 billion snack food division, Frito-Lay, introduced Wow! chips. Marketing research showed that consumers were looking for a tasty, flavorful snack without the fat and calories of regular chips. Wow! chips are made with Procter & Gamble's fat-free and calorie-free cooking oil, Olean. The launch of Wow! Chips in 1998 was one of the biggest new food product launches during the 1990s. The new line of Wow! chips included Lay's, Ruffles, Doritos, and Tostitos. During the first eight weeks of introduction, Wow! racked up $58 million in sales. Company spokeswoman Lynn Markley said that Wow! has been "meeting every expectation" since its February 1998 launch. She also said that Frito-Lay was very confident in the taste but they needed to raise the awareness level of consumers by letting them know that Wow! had no fat, reduced calories, and a great taste.

In 1998, Doritos Wow! tortilla chips were the number 7 tortilla chip in the country and sales for that same year were $51.5 million with a 2.2 percent share of that market. For potato chips, Lay's Wow! chips were the number 6 brand with more than $87.1 million in sales and a 3 percent market share. Such high sales were attributed to consumers' repeat purchases, which were tracked through a mail panel.

As of 2000, research showed that most Americans today are seeking out intense and flavorful salty snacks. While Wow! chips provide a very flavorful, low-fat, and low-calorie snack, consumers are not so worried about calories anymore and are buying more full-fat snacks. Even though Wow! chips remains the most popular low-fat chip, Frito-Lay has placed more emphasis on taste-filled, full-fat snacks rather than their healthier products.[3]

Cross-Sectional Versus Longitudinal Designs

The relative advantages and disadvantages of longitudinal versus cross-sectional designs are summarized in Table 3.3. Since in most situations the researcher is interested in obtaining a picture of the marketplace at one point in time, cross-sectional designs are far more commonly used than longitudinal designs. Cross-sectional studies cost less. It is relatively simple to select a representative sample, that is, to select a group of respondents whose characteristics of interest are a reflection of the entire population. Because different respondents are selected each time a survey is conducted, bias due to the same set of respondents' answering multiple surveys is eliminated.

A major advantage of longitudinal designs is the ability to detect change as a result of repeated measurements of the same variables on the same respondents. This is illustrated in the Wow! example. Since the same individuals provide data on the same variables repeatedly, it is possible to compare the brand of chips an individual purchases at any given time with the brand purchased in the preceding time period. Thus, we can determine whether an individual is engaging in repeat purchase or brand switching.

Panel research also has an advantage over cross-sectional research in terms of the amount of data that can be collected as well as the accuracy of that data. A typical cross-sectional survey requires recall of past purchases and behavior. Panel data, which rely on continuous recording of purchases in a diary, place less reliance on the respondent's memory. A comparison of panel and cross-sectional survey estimates of retail sales indicates that panel data give more accurate estimates.

The main disadvantage of panels is that they may not be representative of the population of interest. This may happen because of refusals to participate and because of high dropout rates for panel participants. Bias is also introduced when participants try to give the "right" answer or become bored or fatigued and make incomplete diary entries. In addition, longitudinal designs are more expensive to implement given the expenses associated with maintaining a panel. In light of these limitations, longitudinal designs are used only when it is necessary to examine changes over time, such as in studies of repeat purchases, brand switching, and brand loyalty.

CAUSAL RESEARCH

Like descriptive research, causal research requires a planned and structured design. While descriptive research can determine the degree of association between variables, it is generally not very appropriate for examining causal relationships. Causal relations are those that involve cause-and-effect variables.

The hypothesis that a promotional campaign will lead to (cause) an increase in sales is an example. To examine this hypothesis, a researcher would need a **causal design**—a design

causal design
A type of conclusive research whose major objective is to obtain evidence regarding cause-and-effect (causal) relationships.

TABLE 3.3 RELATIVE ADVANTAGES AND DISADVANTAGES OF LONGITUDINAL AND CROSS-SECTIONAL DESIGNS

EVALUATION CRITERIA	CROSS-SECTIONAL DESIGN	LONGITUDINAL DESIGN
Detecting change	−	+
Large amount of data collection	−	+
Accuracy	−	+
Representative sampling	+	−
Response bias	+	−

Note: A + indicates a relative advantage over the other design. A − indicates a relative disadvantage.

in which the causal or independent variables are manipulated in a relatively controlled environment. A relatively controlled environment is one in which the other variables that may affect the dependent variable are controlled or checked as much as possible. The effect of this manipulation on one or more dependent variables is then measured to infer causality.

The main method of causal research is an experiment. Experiments can take place either in a laboratory or in a natural setting. An experiment can be designed to test the causal relationship that promotion causes brand sales. Here, the independent variable that will be manipulated is promotion and the dependent variable is brand sales. Participants in a laboratory study may be told to imagine they are on a shopping trip. Various promotional offers, as manipulated by the researcher, will be displayed, with each group of respondents seeing only one offer. The purchases of the respondents in this simulated shopping experience would be measured and compared across groups. The experimenter creates and controls the setting. In a field experiment, the same study would occur in a natural setting, such as retail stores. Various promotional offers would be displayed in stores, with each group of respondents seeing only one offer. The resulting brand sales would be monitored.

Causal research can help BMW to assess the effect of a promotional campaign on sales.

Causal research is appropriate for the following purposes, illustrated in the context of examining the effect of a promotional campaign on the sales of BMW cars:

1. **To understand which variables are the causes (independent variables) and which variables are the effects (dependent variables) of a phenomenon.** The independent variables will be the dollar amount spent on advertising and the dollar amount spent on sales promotion during a given time period. The dependent variable will be the sales of BMW (measured in units and dollars).

2. **To determine the extent of the relationship between the predicted effect and the causal variables.** The relationship between sales promotion and advertising expenditures and the sales of BMW is likely to be nonlinear: As more and more is spent on advertising, sales of BMW will increase less and less due to the saturation effect.

The implementation of a causal design is further illustrated by Microsoft's experiment with Windows 2000.

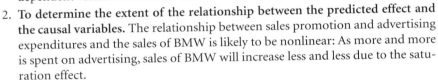

EXAMPLE

WINDOWS 2000: A WINDOW TO THE HEARTS OF COMPUTER USERS

The key to the success (high awareness and high sales) of Windows 2000 was that the product was carefully designed and tested. In a controlled experiment, one group of computer users was asked to work with Windows 2000. Two other carefully matched groups worked with the previous versions of Windows: one with Windows 98 and the other with Windows NT. All three groups rated the operating system on ease of use, power, capabilities, and the ability to enhance a computer user's experience. Windows 2000 was rated significantly better than the previous versions on all factors.[4]

In this experiment, the causal (independent) variable was the operating system, which was manipulated to have three levels: Windows 2000, Windows 98, and Windows NT. The effect (dependent) variables were ease of use, power, capabilities, and ability to enhance a computer user's experience. The influence of the user's background was controlled by carefully matching the three groups.

Due to its complexity and importance, the topic of causal designs and experimental research will be fully explained in a separate chapter (Chapter 8). In that chapter, we discuss the conditions for causality, validity in experimentation, and specific types of experimental designs.

RELATIONSHIPS AMONG EXPLORATORY, DESCRIPTIVE, AND CAUSAL RESEARCH

While the preceding example distinguished causal research from other types of research and showed the benefits of causal research, causal research should not be viewed in isolation. Rather, exploratory, descriptive, and causal designs should be used to complement each other. As mentioned earlier, a given project may incorporate more than one basic research design, depending on the nature of the problem and the approach. We offer the following general guidelines for choosing research designs:

1. When little is known about the problem situation, it is desirable to begin with exploratory research. For example, exploratory research is suitable for generating alternative courses of action, research questions, or hypotheses. Exploratory research can then be followed by descriptive or causal research, as in the Spiegel vignette (Figure 3.7(a)).

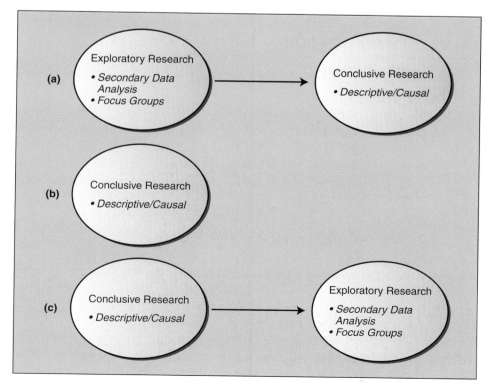

FIGURE 3.7
Some Alternative Research Designs

2. It is not necessary to begin every research design with exploratory research. If the researcher has a good understanding of the problem situation, descriptive or causal research may be a more appropriate initial step (Figure 3.7(b)). Annual consumer satisfaction surveys are an example of research that need not begin with or include an exploratory phase.

3. Exploratory research can be used at any point in a study. For example, when descriptive or causal research leads to results that are unexpected or difficult to interpret, the researcher may turn to exploratory research for insight (Figure 3.7(c)).

Suppose an image study is conducted for a supermarket chain to identify its strengths and weaknesses relative to competing supermarkets. Exploratory research, including secondary data analysis and focus groups, is first conducted to define the problem and develop a suitable approach. This is followed by a descriptive study consisting of a survey in which a questionnaire is constructed and administered by telephone interviews.

Suppose the image study is to be repeated after two years to determine if any changes have taken place. At that point, exploratory research would probably be unnecessary, and the research design could begin with the descriptive study.

Assume that the survey is repeated two years later and that some unexpected findings are obtained. Management wonders why supermarket's ratings on in-store service have declined when the supermarket staff has increased. Exploratory research in the form of focus groups might be undertaken to probe these unexpected findings. The focus groups might reveal that while the store clerks are present, they are not very helpful. This would suggest the need for training the store clerks.

This example illustrates how exploratory and descriptive research can be integrated. Exploratory and descriptive designs are frequently used in commercial marketing research; causal research is not as popular.

TASKS INVOLVED IN FORMULATING A RESEARCH DESIGN

In formulating a research design, typically the researcher must perform the following tasks (Figure 3.8):

1. Specify the information needed (Chapter 2).
2. Design the exploratory, descriptive, and/or causal phases of the research (Chapters 4 through 8).
3. Specify the measurement and scaling procedures (Chapters 9 and 10).
4. Construct and pretest a questionnaire (interview form) or an appropriate form for data collection (Chapter 11).
5. Specify the sampling process and sample size (Chapters 12 and 13).
6. Develop a plan of data analysis (Chapter 15).

Chapter 2 described how to specify the necessary information. As noted, we will discuss the rest of the tasks involved in a research design in detail in subsequent chapters.

RESEARCH DESIGN AND THE VALUE OF MARKETING RESEARCH

Research is conducted to help reduce management error in decision making. The key word here is *reduce*. Research is not designed to "prove" assumptions, but rather to pro-

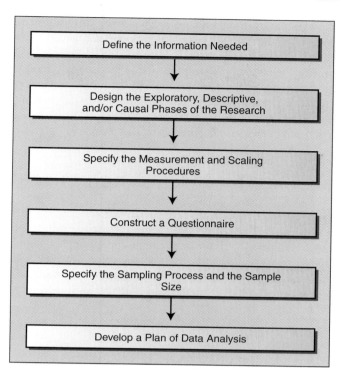

FIGURE 3.8

Tasks Involved in a Research Design

vide management with an assessment of the degree of risk associated with making decisions based on tested assumptions. As the cost of making the wrong decision increases, typically the formality and structure of a study design increases as well. The research design has a major impact on the cost and value of the marketing research project. Ultimately, the cost of any project must be weighted against the reduced risk of making the decision with additional information.

Before committing funds to a study, management must assess, either formally or informally, the value of the additional information obtained by marketing research. For example, suppose the brand manager for Cap'n Crunch cereal is faced with a proposal to spend $50,000 to conduct a causal study regarding the effect of using various promotional offers. The manager must decide whether or not the value of a decision based on current knowledge could be improved by more than $50,000 with the help of research. If the various promotional offers involved couponing versus free trials, the difference in expenses associated with the two approaches (not to mention the difference in consumer response) could far exceed the $50,000 cost of research. In that case, the high cost of making the wrong decision makes it easier to justify the cost of the research.

The information value of research must also be discounted by the degree of error inherent in a study. No research design, no matter how sophisticated, can eliminate all risk from a decision because no research is completely error free. Several potential sources of error can affect a research design. Estimating the level of error in a study is complicated by the fact that typically only random sampling error is quantified. **Random sampling error** is the error due to the particular sample selected being an imperfect representation of the population of interest. Total error is made up of both sampling and nonsampling error.

Nonsampling errors, as would be expected, can be attributed to sources other than sampling. They result from a variety of causes, including errors in problem definition, approach, scales, questionnaire design, survey methods, interviewing techniques, and

random sampling error
The error due to the particular sample selected being an imperfect representation of the population of interest.

nonsampling error
Errors that can be attributed to sources other than sampling; they can be random or nonrandom.

data preparation and analysis. These nonsampling errors can be attributed to the researcher, the interviewer, or the respondent. A good research design attempts to control the various sources of error, as illustrated in the opening vignette, in which Spiegel made an effort to control the sampling and nonsampling errors. Random sampling errors were controlled by having a large sample (1,000) that was randomly selected. Spiegel also controlled various sources of nonsampling errors, including interviewer and respondent errors, by careful selection, training, and supervision of the interviewers. These errors are discussed in greater detail in subsequent chapters.

BUDGETING AND SCHEDULING THE PROJECT

budgeting and scheduling
Management tools needed to help ensure that the marketing research project is completed within the available resources.

Once a research design has been specified, the researcher should prepare a detailed budget and schedule. **Budgeting and scheduling** help to ensure that the marketing research project is completed with the available resources: financial, time, personnel, and others. The budget process allows the researcher and the decision maker to compare the estimated value of the information with the projected costs. Additionally, the project schedule will help ensure that the information is obtained in time to address the management decision problem.

MARKETING RESEARCH PROPOSAL

marketing research proposal
It contains the essence of the project and serves as a contract between the researcher and management.

Once the research design has been formulated and budgeting and scheduling of the project has been accomplished, the researcher should prepare a written **marketing research proposal**. It contains the essence of the project and serves as a contract between the researcher and management. The proposal covers all phases of the marketing research process including cost and time schedules. The format of a research proposal may vary considerably depending on the nature of the problem and the relationship of the client to the research supplier. Most proposals present a detailed research design and contain some or all of the following elements:

1. **Executive Summary.** The proposal should begin with an overview of the entire proposal, a summary of the major points from each of the other sections.
2. **Background.** The background to the problem, including the environmental context, should be described.
3. **Problem Definition/Research Objectives.** Normally, a statement of the problem should be presented. If this statement has not been developed (as in the case of exploratory research), the objectives of the marketing research project should be clearly specified.
4. **Approach to the Problem.** A review of the relevant academic and trade literature, along with some kind of an analytical model, should be included. If research questions and hypotheses have been identified, these should be included in the proposal.
5. **Research Design.** The type of research design, whether exploratory, descriptive, causal, or a combination, should be specified. Information should be provided on the following components: (a) kind of information to be obtained, (b) method of administering the questionnaire (mail, telephone, personal, or electronic interviews), (c) scaling techniques, (d) nature of the questionnaire (type of questions asked, length, average interviewing time),

and (e) sampling plan and sample size. This section often forms the heart of the proposal.

6. **Field Work/Data Collection.** The proposal should discuss how the data will be collected and who will collect it. If the fieldwork is to be subcontracted to another supplier, this should be stated. Control mechanisms to ensure the quality of data collected should be described.

7. **Data Analysis.** The kind of data analysis that will be conducted and how the results will be interpreted should be described.

8. **Reporting.** The proposal should specify the nature and number of intermediate reports. The form of the final report, including whether a formal presentation of the results will be made, should also be stated.

9. **Cost and Time.** The cost of the project and a time schedule, broken down by phases, should be presented. A payment schedule should also be worked out in advance, especially for large projects.

10. **Appendices.** Any statistical or other information that is of interest to only a few people should be presented in appendices.

The research proposal represents the contract between management and the researcher. It ensures that there is agreement regarding the objectives of the project, and it helps sell the project to management. Therefore, a research proposal should always be prepared, even when repeating a project for a previous client.

SUMMARY ILLUSTRATION USING THE OPENING VIGNETTE

The research design in the opening vignette described how a project was conducted for Spiegel. Research designs may be broadly classified as exploratory or conclusive, while conclusive research may be either descriptive or causal. Typically, the project begins with exploratory research, which is followed by descriptive (or causal) research. As seen in the opening vignette, in order to understand the problem situation, Spiegel analyzed secondary data and conducted six focus groups. This exploratory research helped Spiegel to identify and understand the unique aspects of the shopping behavior and clothing needs of Eddie Bauer consumers. The findings of exploratory research were treated as tentative and further verified by descriptive research consisting of telephone interviews with a randomly selected sample of 1,000 Eddie Bauer consumers.

Typically, as in the case of Spiegel, a research project begins with exploratory research. However, other combinations of the basic designs are possible. Exploratory research may be conducted at any point in the project or may not be undertaken at all. A well-formulated research design will attempt to control the random sampling as well as the nonsampling errors, as in the opening vignette. A large and randomly selected sample was used to measure and control random sampling error. Efforts were also made to control the various sources of nonsampling error. For example, the interviewers were carefully selected and thoroughly trained, and close supervision was exercised to minimize interviewing errors attributed to the interviewers and respondents.

MARKETING RESEARCH AND TQM

Exploratory research helps managers better understand quality and its components and can also help define what quality means to the customer. Conclusive research can be used to test specific hypotheses about the customer value package.

FOCUS ON

ELRICK & LAVIDGE

A good example of a research design that is formulated for the purpose of a competitive bid can be found in the proposal generated by Elrick & Lavidge (E&L) for a national operator of roadside truck stops. The marketing research problem was to define the typical customer segments found in truck stop patrons and to define a complete set of attributes relevant to the patronage decision.

■ RESEARCH DESIGN

In its proposal to the truck stop operator, E&L specified that exploratory research would be conducted first, followed by descriptive research:

> Elrick & Lavidge proposes conducting qualitative research among truck stop customers prior to any quantitative measurement of customer wants and needs, prioritization of those wants and needs, measurement of customer expectations, or demographic profiling of customers. Given that we would be working at truck stops in an uncontrolled environment, we propose using a combination of techniques—one-on-one interviews and focus groups. The use of one-on-one interviews will allow more detailed discussion with individual respondents who are unable or unwilling to participate in a focus group discussion. Focus groups will provide interaction, which is often valuable in spawning new ideas and sparking opinions about what is and what is not important with respect to various products and services.

The results of the qualitative research would be used to develop a questionnaire that would be administered in person at the truck stops. In addition, the proposal stated that, "The interview is expected to average no longer than 15 minutes in length and contain no more than 6 open-ended questions." E&L also generally defines the sampling procedures at this time:

> A number of sampling approaches might be taken, depending on budgetary constraints and requirements for statistical precision. For the purpose of this proposal and as the foundation for further discussion, we propose that 400 customers be interviewed in person at (the operator's) truck stops. This many interviews will yield data that are, overall, statistically reliable.

E&L proposed that the interviews be dispersed over 10 geographically different facilities in order to develop a better sample mix.

Because the questionnaire had not been developed, E&L could only indicate the general type of data analysis that would be done:

> Once the data have been collected, Elrick & Lavidge will code the open-ended questions and tabulate the data. Elrick & Lavidge will also analyze and draw conclusions from the data and provide the findings to (the operator) in a written summary report including, where appropriate, charts and graphs.

Descriptive research can be used to define the customer value package. Cross-sectional designs can be used to obtain respondents' perceptions of quality and its components. Hewlett-Packard (HP) might, for example, send a mail survey to 1,000 owners of printers to find out how they evaluate printers on various quality attributes. This would help HP identify attributes on which its printers are not rated competitively and make the needed improvements. Longitudinal designs can be used to measure changes in customers' perceptions of quality and value. Finally, causal research can be used to test the effect of product modification on customers' perceptions of quality and value. A firm can experimentally manipulate price levels to examine whether the perceived product quality increases as price increases. Thus, marketing research can help in designing quality products, as illustrated by Keebler.

EXAMPLE

QUALITY'S SWEET SPOTS

Over 20 percent of Keebler's cookie and cracker sales come from new products introduced in the five years from 1996 through 2000. Although the failure rate for new products is high, Keebler enjoys a high success rate. The main reason is that its marketing research and subsequent launch of its new products are guided by TQM principles, as in the case of Sweet Spots.

Typically, Keebler adopts an exploratory research design followed by descriptive research in assessing the consumers' response to its new products. Attention is paid to every detail, and the focus is on the quality of research. While developing Sweet Spots, focus groups revealed that consumers were looking for a quality confection that bridged the gap between cookies and candy. In forming quality perceptions, the taste, ingredients, and look of the product and the package were important. However, they indicated that the product should not be high priced or it would be perceived as a luxury rather than an everyday item.

This exploratory research was followed by a descriptive survey involving mall intercept interviews. The respondents were recruited and taken to a special facility in the mall. They tasted a prototype of the new product and then answered a questionnaire administered by an interviewer.

Based on this research, Keebler developed Sweet Spots, shortbread cookies with a chocolate drop on top. The product was targeted at upscale women and positioned as a quality product that bridged the market from cookies to candy. The focus on quality helped Keebler launch another successful product. Keebler is well aware that quality has its own sweet spots.[5]

INTERNATIONAL MARKETING RESEARCH

The various methods associated with implementing each step of the research design discussed in this chapter must be reassessed within the context of cultural differences before they can be used internationally. Given environmental and cultural differences, a research design appropriate for one country may not be suitable for another. Consider the problem of determining household attitudes toward major appliances in the United States and Saudi Arabia. When conducting exploratory research in the United States, it is appropriate to conduct focus groups jointly with male and female heads of household. It would not be appropriate to conduct such focus groups in Saudi Arabia. Given the traditional culture, wives are unlikely to participate freely in the presence of their husbands. It would be more useful to conduct one-on-one depth interviews with both male and female heads of households included in the sample. Procter & Gamble (P&G) encountered a similar situation in Japan.

P&G Exploring and Wooing Japanese Women

The consumer market in Japan is one of the toughest, most competitive, fastest-moving markets in the world. Japan represents the cutting edge of worldwide technology in many product categories. When P&G started business in Japan, it conducted a detailed study of market characteristics and market profile. The target market for P&G was housewives, who were largely responsible for the consumption of several products, such as diapers, household cleaners, soaps, and detergents. Exploratory research followed by descriptive research was undertaken for this purpose. While focus groups are most popular in the United States, one-on-one in-depth interviews were preferred given the Japanese cultural tendency to not disagree openly in group settings. The descriptive surveys used in-home personal interviews.

Results showed that the average Japanese homemaker was uncompromising in her demands for high quality, value, and service. She was a paragon of conservation and efficiency in the management of her household. About half the adult women in Japan were employed, but they generally worked outside of the home before marriage and after their children were raised. Child rearing was the number one priority for Japanese mothers.

When it came to foreign versus domestic brands, Japanese women preferred foreign name brand products that had style and status, such as fashionable clothing, French perfumes, wines, liquors, and designer bags. They did not prefer functional products made in foreign countries since these products usually did not meet their exacting and demanding quality standards.

Japanese women greatly preferred commercials that conserved traditional social and family values and roles rather than the typical Western examples. P&G made a few mistakes initially in misjudging nuances of the Japanese culture before this study was conducted. For example, the introduction of Camay bath soap and Pampers diapers were supported with Western-style advertising that was not well received by Japanese women. However, based on the market profile study, the advertising was changed to stress traditional social and family values, thereby increasing its effectiveness.[6]

In developing countries, there are no consumer panels, which makes it difficult to conduct descriptive longitudinal research. In many countries, such as Sierra Leone in Africa, the marketing support infrastructure—retailing, wholesaling, advertising, and promotion development—is often lacking, which makes it difficult to implement a causal design involving a field experiment. In formulating a research design, considerable effort is required to ensure the equivalence and comparability of secondary and primary data obtained from different countries. In the context of collecting primary data, qualitative research, survey methods, scaling techniques, questionnaire design, and sampling considerations are particularly important. We discuss these topics in more detail in subsequent chapters.

TECHNOLOGY AND MARKETING RESEARCH

"Smart" products have been around for years. Coffeemakers and VCRs can be told when to perform their respective duties. Automobiles tell the driver when the lights have been left on or when the door is not fully closed. In the very near future, these products, and others, will become even more "intelligent." Networking subsystems will soon be embedded into numerous products, both hardware and software, giving them the ability to "talk" and to remember.[7]

These networking subsystems could be added to the production process for new products or easily added to existing products. The necessary technology already exists; it is just a matter of applying it. When triggered, or turned on, by a preprogrammed event, the product would "speak" with the user and record the conversation. The conversation (or data) could then be transmitted to the producer instantly or stored and gathered in batches and transmitted at a later date. Such data would be invaluable to marketing managers. Smart products could be used to collect not only exploratory data but also cross-sectional or longitudinal descriptive data.

These subsystems could prove very useful to companies, including software developers such as Microsoft. When added to a software application like Microsoft Office, they could be programmed to activate when the user encounters an error message. After conversing with the user, the subsystem would store all the relevant data. Then the developer could determine what happened and what could be done to prevent that error from recurring. Any user observations or opinions could also be stored for analysis. This information would assist Microsoft when producing new products or upgrading versions of Microsoft Office.

ETHICS IN MARKETING RESEARCH

The choice of a research design has ethical overtones for both the client and the research firm. If Maxwell House is interested in examining brand switching in coffee purchases, for example, a longitudinal design is the only appropriate way to assess changes in an individual respondent's choice of coffee brands. A research firm that justifies the use of a cross-sectional design simply because it has no experience in conducting longitudinal studies is behaving unethically.

Researchers must ensure that the research design will provide the information needed to address the marketing research problem. The client should have the integrity not to misrepresent the project and should describe the constraints under which the researcher must operate and not make unreasonable demands. If customer contact has to be restricted or if time is an issue, the client should make these constraints known at the start of the project. It would be unethical for a client to extract details from a proposal submitted by one research firm and pass them on to another. A proposal is the property of the research firm that prepared it, unless the client has paid for it. The client should not take advantage of the research firm by making false promises of future research contracts in order to solicit concessions for the current project.

EXAMPLE

JUST BUSINESS VERSUS UNETHICAL CONCESSIONS

Ethical dilemmas may arise due to the strong desire of marketing research firms to become suppliers to large business firms who are heavy users of marketing research. Take, for example, Visa, Delta Airlines, Coca-Cola, or Ford Motor Company. Such firms have large marketing research budgets and regularly hire external marketing research suppliers. These large clients can manipulate the price for the current study or demand unreasonable concessions in the research design (e.g., more focus groups, a larger sample, or additional data analyses) by suggesting the potential for the marketing research firm to become a regular supplier. This may be considered just business, but it becomes unethical when there is no intention to follow up with a larger study or to use the research firm in the future. Marketing research firms should be aware of such unethical practices and must discern the intent of the client firms before offering concessions to gain future business.[8]

It is equally important that responsibilities to respondents not be overlooked. The researcher should design the study so as not to violate the respondents' right to safety, privacy, or choice. Furthermore, the client must not violate the anonymity of the respondents. (Respondent-related issues are discussed in more detail in Chapters 4, 5, 6, and 7).

INTERNET APPLICATIONS

The Internet can facilitate the implementation of various types of research designs.

Exploratory Research

As discussed in Chapter 2, the Internet can provide many resources for marketing research. Newsgroups list servers and other bulletin board–type services can be very useful in the exploratory phase of research. Messages posted to newsgroups can often direct you to other valid sources of information. Newsgroups can be used to set up more formal focus groups with experts or individuals representing the target audience in order to obtain initial information on a subject. In Chapter 6, we discuss the use of the Internet for conducting focus groups in more detail.

Conclusive Research

Many descriptive studies use secondary data, which we describe in Chapters 4 and 5; surveys, which are discussed in Chapter 7; and panels, which are discussed in Chapters 5 and 7. The use of the Internet for causal research designs is discussed in Chapter 8. The Internet, in its capacity as a source of information, can be useful in uncovering secondary data and collecting primary data needed in conclusive research, as illustrated by E-Valuations.com.

EXAMPLE

E-Valuations.com *(www.e-valuations.com)*, based in Seattle, is a full-service marketing research firm specializing in online marketing research services. E-Valuations.com manages a research site called Questions.net. Questions.net assembles groups of willing research participants by offering them incentives to answer survey questions. Participants are selected from a target group defined by the client and are best suited for providing the specific information required. E-Valuations.com uses a variety of electronic options when conducting exploratory research, including newsgroup discussions and electronic focus groups. Conclusive research is conducted mainly by using Internet surveys posted at its Web site. The company has conducted exploratory and conclusive research for a wide range of clients and has helped them make successful marketing decisions.

SUMMARY

A research design is the road map for conducting the marketing research project. It specifies the details of how the project should be conducted. Research designs may be broadly classified as exploratory or conclusive. The primary purpose of exploratory research is to provide insights into the problem. Conclusive research is used to test hypotheses and examine specific relationships. Conclusive research may be either descriptive or causal and is used as input into managerial decision making.

The major objective of descriptive research is to describe market characteristics or functions. Descriptive research can be further classified into cross-sectional and longitudinal designs. Cross-sectional designs involve the collection of information from a sample drawn from a population at a single point in time. In contrast, longitudinal designs entail repeated measurements on a fixed sample at different points in time. Causal research is designed to obtain evidence about cause-and-effect (causal) relationships via an experiment.

In evaluating a research proposal, management must discount the value of the information by the level of error inherent in the study. Error can be associated with any of the six components of the research design. Managers should prepare a written marketing research proposal that includes all the elements of the marketing research process.

In the context of TQM, exploratory research helps managers to better understand quality and its components. Conclusive research can be used to test hypotheses about the customer value package and the price–quality–value relationship. The various methods associated with implementing each step of the research design must be reassessed within the context of cultural differences before they can be used internationally. In addition to ethical aspects that concern researcher and client, the rights of respondents must be respected when formulating the research design. Technology and the Internet can facilitate the implementation of exploratory, descriptive, or causal research.

KEY TERMS AND CONCEPTS

Research design, 82
Exploratory research, 84
Conclusive research, 85
Descriptive research, 89
Cross-sectional
   design, 90

Longitudinal design, 91
Panel, 92
Causal design, 93
Random sampling
   error, 97

Nonsampling error, 97
Budgeting and
   scheduling, 98
Marketing research
   proposal, 98

ACRONYMS

The components of a research design may be summarized by the acronym DESIGN:

   D ata analysis plan

   E xploratory, descriptive, causal design

   S caling and measurement

   I nterviewing forms: questionnaire design

   G enerating the needed information

   N umber: sample size and plan

EXERCISES

1. Define *research design* in your own words.

2. How does formulating a research design differ from developing an approach to a problem?

3. Differentiate between exploratory and conclusive research.
4. What are the major purposes for which descriptive research is conducted?
5. Compare and contrast cross-sectional and longitudinal designs.
6. Discuss the advantages and disadvantages of panels.
7. What is a causal research design? What is its purpose?
8. What is the relationship between exploratory, descriptive, and causal research?
9. List the major components of a research design.

PROBLEMS

1. Sweet Cookies is planning to launch a new line of cookies and wants to assess the market size. The cookies have a mixed chocolate–pineapple flavor and will be targeted at the premium end of the market. Discuss the type of research design that may be used.

2. Welcome Inc. is a chain of fast-food restaurants located in major metropolitan areas in the South. Sales have been growing very slowly for the last two years. Management has decided to add some new items to the menu, but first they want to know more about their customers and their preferences.
   a. List two hypotheses.
   b. What kind of research design is appropriate? Why?

INTERNET AND COMPUTER EXERCISES

1. Visit the Greenfield Online Research Center (www.greenfieldonline.com).
   a. What are the surveys currently being conducted by Greenfield?
   b. How are the respondents being recruited for these surveys?
   c. Discuss the different type of errors likely to arise given the way the respondents are being recruited.
2. Visit the Web page of three of the marketing research firms listed in Table 1.2. What types of research designs have these firms implemented recently?
3. You are conducting an image study for Carnival Cruise Lines. As part of exploratory research, analyze the messages posted to the newsgroup: rec.travel.cruises to determine the factors that consumers use in evaluating cruise companies. This newsgroup can be located at www.dejanews.com or groups.google.com.

ACTIVITIES

ROLE PLAYING

1. Assume the role of marketing manager of Sweet Cookies and have your partner assume the role of a researcher hired by the firm (see problem 1). Discuss the issue and formulate the appropriate:
   a. Management decision problem
   b. Marketing research problem
   c. Research design
2. You are a manager in charge of a marketing research project. Your goal is to determine what effects different levels of advertising have on consumption behavior. Based on the results of the project, you will recommend the amount of money to be

budgeted for advertising various products next year. Your supervisor will require strong justification for your recommendations, so your research design has to be as sound as possible. However, your resources (time, money, and labor) are limited. Develop a research project to address this problem. Focus on the kind of research designs you would use, why you would use them, and how you would conduct the research.

FIELD WORK

1. Contact a few marketing research organizations and ask them about the research designs they have used during the last year and the nature of the problems addressed. Write a report on your findings.

GROUP DISCUSSION

1. Discuss the following statement: "If the research budget is limited, exploratory research can be dispensed with."

2. Discuss the following statement: "The researcher should always attempt to develop an optimal design for every marketing research project."

3. "There are many potential sources of error in a research project. It is impossible to control all of them. Hence, marketing research contains many errors and we cannot be confident of the findings." Discuss these statements as a group. Did your group arrive at a consensus?

NOTES

1. Adapted from "The Spiegel Group Reports 46 Percent Increase in Earnings for 2000," *www.thespiegelgroup.com/news/20010215-32670.htm;* and "Spiegel, Inc. Reports Significant Earnings Improvement and 10 Percent Sales Increase in Second Quarter," *www.thespiegelgroup.com/news/19990722-13042.htm.*

2. Adapted from Faye Brookman, "Study Sheds Light on Inspiration," *Discount Stores News,* 38(18) (September 20, 1999) 25; "Bath Boom Rah!" *Discount Merchandiser,* 39(6) (June 1999): 52; Rick Klein; and "1995 Edison Best New Products Awards Winners," *Marketing News,* 30(10) (May 6, 1996): E4–E11.

3. Debbie Howell, "Snack Food Resurgence Puts Kibosh on Health Trend," *DSN Retailing Today,* 39(19) (October 2, 2000): 48–50; Laura Liebeck, "Salty Snacks Battle Rages On," *Discount Store News,* 37(19) (October 5, 1998): 31–32.

4. Adapted from Scott Spanbaur, "Windows 2000: The First 100 Days," *PC World,* 18(7) (July 2000): 54; Cara Cunningham, "Microsoft Talks Windows Futures," *InfoWorld,* 19(11) (March 17, 1997): 26; and "1995 Edison Best New Products Awards Winners," *Marketing News,* 30(10) (May 6, 1996): E4–E11.

5. Deborah Cohen, "Keebler Spin-off Takes Root for Flowers," *Crain's Chicago Business,* 23(17) (April 24, 2000): 2; Juadann Pollack, "Famous Amos Gets 1st Nat'l Push from Keebler," *Advertising Age,* 70(12): (March 22, 1999): 6; and Chad Rubel, "Keebler Learns to Pay Attention to Research Right from the Start," *Marketing News,* 30(12) (June 3, 1996): H33.

6. Adapted from Andrew Mollet, "Japan's Washday Blues," *Chemical Week,* 162(4) (January 26, 2000): 36; Steve Bell, "P&G Forced by Rivals to Change Old Habits," *Marketing* (June 17, 1999): 15; and Catherine Becker, "Hair and Cosmetic Products in the Japanese Market," *Marketing and Research Today,* 25(1) (February 1997): 31–37.

7. Robin Layland, "QOS: Moving Beyond the Marketing Hype," *Data Communications,* 28(6) (April 21, 1999): 17–18; and Daniel Abelow, "Networking Subsystems: Products that Talk," *Data Communications* (March 21, 1993): 90.

8. John R. Sparks and Shelby D. Hunt, "Marketing Researcher Ethical Sensitivity: Conceptualization, Measurement, and Exploratory Investigation," *Journal of Marketing,* 62(2) (April 1998): 92–109; and Betsy Peterson, "Ethics Revisited," *Marketing Research: A Magazine of Management & Applications,* 8(4) (Winter 1996): 47–48.

4

EXPLORATORY RESEARCH DESIGN: SECONDARY DATA

SECONDARY DATA
CAN PROVIDE USEFUL
BACKGROUND
INFORMATION TO THE
MARKETING
RESEARCH PROBLEM.
THEY CAN HELP THE
RESEARCHER IN
FORMULATING ALL
THE STEPS OF THE
PROJECT.

Marsha White, Vice President/Sr. Research Director (Retired), Elrick & Lavidge. Marsha White joined E&L in 1996. She was responsible for management of the research needs of several clients as well as supervision of the Research Services in Atlanta.

Opening Questions

1. Why are secondary data important? How do we distinguish secondary data from primary data?
2. What are the advantages and disadvantages of secondary data?
3. How should secondary data be evaluated to determine their usefulness?
4. What are the different sources of secondary data, including internal sources and external sources?
5. What is database marketing? How does it make use of secondary data?
6. How can published secondary data be classified?
7. How can computerized databases be classified?
8. Do secondary data play a role in total quality management?
9. How do we identify and classify the sources of secondary data useful in international marketing research?
10. How can technology enhance the usefulness of secondary data?
11. What ethical issues are involved in the use of secondary data?
12. How can the use of the Internet enhance secondary data analysis?

SECONDARY DATA VINDICATE THE *VINDICATOR*!

The *Vindicator (www.vindy.com* or *www.vindicator.com),* a medium-sized Youngstown, Ohio, newspaper, wanted to increase its revenues from advertising. Management set forth a one-year goal for its 14 retail and four classified salespeople to substantially raise the number of advertisers and thus total ad revenue. To be able to increase ad revenues, the sales force needed to pinpoint what specifically could help them recruit more advertisers to the newspaper or increase the amount that existing advertisers were spending. From past experience, many on the sales force knew that to recruit advertisers required proving to these advertisers, with hard facts, that their money spent in the *Vindicator* would be an excellent investment. For this purpose, the internally available data routinely collected by the *Vindicator* on the number of customers, duration of subscription, renewals/nonrenewals, and so on would not be sufficient. Additional data would have to be obtained by conducting marketing research.

In this case, the *Vindicator* decided that it needed information on the potential in advertising readership and how these numbers compared to the potential of other advertising media that the advertisers could use instead of the *Vindicator.* While the sales force could commission marketing research to obtain primary data, this project would be quite expensive and time consuming. Hence, this course of action was not taken. Instead, the *Vindicator* decided to search for secondary research that could be used to obtain the answers they sought. Because the *Vindicator* is a medium-sized newspaper with limited staff resources, they turned to an outside supplier, Inland Research Corporation, a small sized Erie, Pennsylvania–based company, to conduct a secondary research study.

The Inland Research Corporation compiles data developed from interviews from about 40 different sources. Half of their data comes from general business sources, such as the Audit Bureau of Circulations *(www.accessabc.com),* and the other half comes from state and federal agencies, such as the U.S. Census Bureau *(www.census.gov)* and the Bureau of Labor Statistics *(www.bls.gov).* In addition to printed publications, Inland Research also searches several online and Internet databases. Inland Research evaluates all secondary data by examining the methodology, accuracy, timeliness, and nature of the data. Only data from dependable sources are used.

Inland Research receives requests from its clients concerning the clients' needs for data to solve a specific problem the client is faced with. Inland Research then begins an exhaustive search through its data warehouse to obtain information that is pertinent to the needs of the client. The corporation produces reports useful to solving the clients' problem(s) in about four to six weeks, which, in the case of smaller firms like the *Vindicator,* is a fraction of the time it would take for the client to do the research. Inland's biggest selling point is the low price they charge for their research services. The prices range from $3,595 for a newspaper with circulation up to 14,900 to $8,445 for a newspaper with circulation of 60,000 or more. According to Inland Research president and chief executive officer (CEO), Jerry Szorek, "No other company produces similar reports for newspapers," which makes the information they provide to firms like the *Vindicator* extremely valuable.

For the *Vindicator,* Inland Research focused on obtaining data reports on topics such as the amount of advertising effectiveness and penetration for different forms of media. For example, information like data on the relationship between advertising frequency in different media and the resulting effectiveness were collected. Using Inland research results and secondary data available internally within the organization, the *Vindicator* sales respresentatives were able to persuade some current advertisers to increase the frequency at which their ads were run. They accomplished this in a number of ways utilizing the Inland reports. For instance, one Inland chart demonstrated that advertisement readership grows from 53.5 percent with one ad a week to 81.3 percent with five ads per week. This gave advertisers a reason to increase the frequency of advertising.

In attempting to wean advertisers' dollars away from radio, the Inland data provided information that each of the city's seven biggest radio stations had less than 8,000 listeners during an average quarter hour. In contrast, internal secondary data showed that the *Vindicator* had a circulation of 200,000. To reduce advertising spending on TV, the reps used the following statistics on viewer activity during commercials: 33.6 percent got up and left the viewing room, 29.6 percent talked with others, 9.2 percent switched channels, and 5.9 percent muted the set. It was discovered that only 21.7 percent listened to the TV commercial. Such selling tactics by the sales force were successful. Thus, the *Vindicator* management discovered that using secondary research on sales calls could help back up the sales pitches with hard data that could sway advertisers toward spending more on print advertising.[1]

OVERVIEW

As mentioned in Chapter 2, analysis of secondary data helps to first define the marketing research problem and then develop an approach to that problem. Also, as part of formulating the research design (Chapter 3), the researcher should analyze the relevant secondary data, as illustrated by the *Vindicator*. The relationship of secondary data to the previous chapters is shown in Figure 4.1. This chapter discusses the distinction between primary and secondary data as well as the advantages, disadvantages, and criteria for evaluating secondary data, which can be generated both internally and externally. The chapter concludes with a discussion of the practice of merging internal and external secondary data. Additionally, we will discuss applications of secondary data in total quality management, collecting international secondary data, the impact of technology, ethical questions related to secondary data, and Internet applications. Figure 4.2 presents an overview of this chapter.

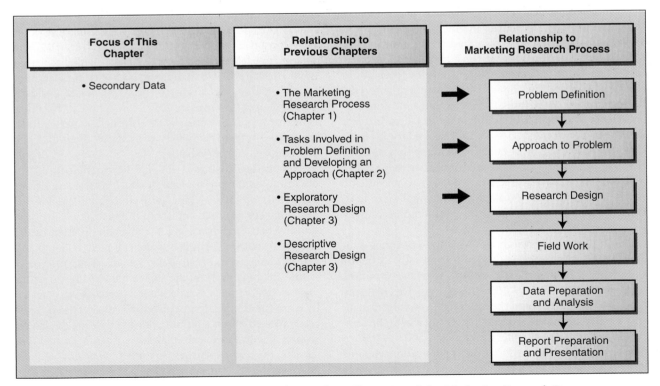

FIGURE 4.1   Relationship of Secondary Data to the Previous Chapters and the Marketing Research Process

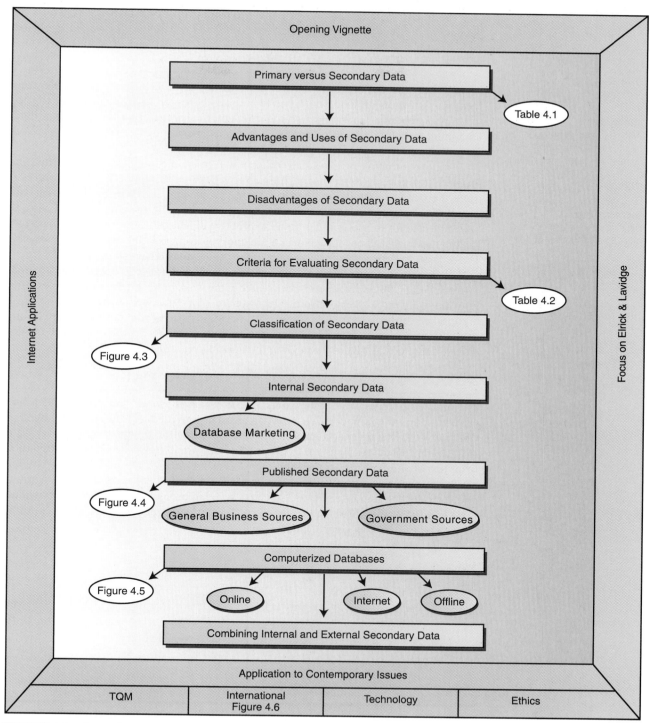

FIGURE 4.2 Secondary Data: An Overview

Secondary data can best be distinguished from primary data when we consider the purpose of the original data collection.

PRIMARY VERSUS SECONDARY DATA

primary data
Data originated by the researcher for the specific purpose of addressing the research problem.

An early outcome of the research process is to define the marketing research problem and identify specific research questions and hypotheses (Chapter 2). When data are collected to address a specific marketing research problem, they are referred to as **primary data.** Obtaining primary data can be expensive and time consuming because it involves all six steps of the marketing research process (Figure 4.1).

Before initiating primary data collection, a researcher should remember that the problem under study might not be unique. It is possible that someone else has investigated the same or a similar marketing research problem. A search through existing data may lead to relevant information. **Secondary data** represent any data that have already been collected for purposes other than the problem at hand. Relative to primary data collection, these data can be located quickly and inexpensively, as in the case of the *Vindicator*. The differences between primary and secondary data are summarized in Table 4.1.

secondary data
Data collected for some purpose other than the problem at hand.

It is easy to overlook many sources of secondary data while developing a formal research design. Once a secondary data search is initiated, however, the volume of existing information can be overwhelming. In order to cost-effectively browse through this mountain of information, it is important that the researcher be familiar with various sources of secondary data, including marketing research firms that specialize in secondary data, such as Inland Research in the opening vignette.

ADVANTAGES AND USES OF SECONDARY DATA

The main advantages of secondary data are the time and money they can save. This was evident from the low-cost secondary research provided by the Inland Research Corporation in the opening vignette. Additionally, the collection of some secondary data, such as those provided by the U.S. Census Bureau, would not be feasible for individual firms like Inland Research or the *Vindicator*. While it is rare for secondary data to provide all the answers to a nonroutine research problem, analysis of secondary data should always be the first step taken toward solving a research problem. Secondary data provided the *Vindicator* with a better understanding of advertising effectiveness and penetration for different forms of media. Such data can help you:

1. Identify the problem.
2. Better understand and define the problem.
3. Develop an approach to the problem.
4. Formulate an appropriate research design (for example, by identifying the key variables).
5. Answer certain research questions and test some hypotheses.
6. Interpret primary data with more insight.

TABLE 4.1   A Comparison of Primary and Secondary Data

	PRIMARY DATA	SECONDARY DATA
Collection purpose	For the problem at hand	For other problems
Collection process	Very involved	Rapid and easy
Collection cost	High	Relatively low
Collection time	Long	Short

Given these advantages and uses of secondary data, we state a basic rule of research: Examine available secondary data first. The research project should proceed to primary data collection only when the secondary data sources have been exhausted or yield marginal returns.

The *Vindicator* exemplifies the rich dividends obtained by following this rule in the opening vignette. Another example is Frost National Bank.

EXAMPLE

BANK "ZIPS" UP THE MARKET

Frost National Bank was considering modifying its Young Leaders Club (YLC) account to enhance its appeal to San Antonians between the ages of 21 and 35. The YLC offered members a checking account with enhancements such as life insurance, discount movie tickets, store coupons, tours, and social events, all for a monthly membership fee. Extensive analysis of secondary data was conducted. Using internal secondary data on transactions and addresses, club members were evaluated by zip code and account activity. The results of zip code analysis helped attract advertising and discount coupons from merchants in areas of San Antonio where large numbers of YLC members lived. External secondary data available on this age group provided additional insights in redeveloping the YLC package. Census information related to population, age, and income allowed Frost National Bank to estimate the size of the potential market for YLC. This secondary data analysis was followed by focus groups and survey research. After completing their marketing research, which began with the examination of secondary data, Frost National Bank was able to significantly increase the number of YLC accounts in the target market.[2]

This example shows that analysis of secondary data can provide valuable insights and lay the foundation for conducting more formal research, such as focus groups and surveys. However, the researcher should be cautious when using secondary data because there are some disadvantages.

DISADVANTAGES OF SECONDARY DATA

The value of secondary data is typically limited by their degree of fit to the current research problem and by concerns regarding data accuracy. The objectives, nature, and methods used to collect secondary data may not be compatible with the present situation. Also, secondary data may be lacking in terms of its accuracy, compatibility of units of measurement, or time frame. Before using secondary data, it is important to evaluate them using the criteria in Table 4.2. The Inland Research Corporation used similar criteria in the opening vignette.

CRITERIA FOR EVALUATING SECONDARY DATA

Specifications: Methodology Used to Collect the Data

The research design specifications, that is, the methodology used to collect the data, should be critically examined to identify possible sources of bias. Factors such as the

TABLE 4.2 Criteria for Evaluating Secondary Data

CRITERIA	ISSUES	REMARKS
Specifications/ Methodology	Data collection method Response rate Quality of data Sampling technique Sample size Questionnaire design Field work Data analysis	Data should be reliable, valid, and generalizable to the problem at hand.
Error/Accuracy	Examine errors in: Approach, research design, sampling, data collection, data analysis, reporting	Assess accuracy by comparing data from different sources.
Currency	Time lag between collection and publication Frequency of updates	Census data are periodically updated by syndicated firms.
Objective	Why were the data collected?	The objective will determine the relevance of data.
Nature	Definition of key variables Units of measurement Categories used Relationships examined	Reconfigure the data to increase their usefulness, if possible.
Dependability	Expertise, credibility, reputation, and trustworthiness of the source	Data should be obtained from an original rather than an acquired source.

size and nature of the sample, response rate and quality, questionnaire design and administration, procedures used for field work, and data analysis and reporting procedures are all important in identifying potential error as well as relevance of the data. One reason it is advantageous to use data from the originating source is that a description of the research design is typically provided as a part of the original published study.

Error: Accuracy of the Data

Both secondary and primary data can have errors, stemming from the research approach, research design, sampling, data collection, analysis, and reporting stages of the project. Moreover, it is difficult to evaluate the accuracy of secondary data when the researcher has not directly participated in the research.

Secondary data can be obtained either directly from the source that originated the data or from a secondary source that secured the data from someone else. The further removed you are from the originating data source, the greater the possibility of problems with accuracy. An original source is likely to be more accurate and complete than a non-originating source. Always use the originating source if it is available.

One approach to controlling accuracy problems is to find multiple sources of data and compare them using standard statistical procedures. The accuracy of secondary data can also be verified by conducting field investigations, as recommended by the International Council of Shopping Centers.

EXAMPLE

POPULATION DYNAMICS AND THE ACCURACY OF SECONDARY DATA

The International Council of Shopping Centers conducted a study to evaluate the consistency of market profiles provided by private vendors of secondary demographic information. Six vendors (CACI, Claritas, Donnelley Marketing Information Services, National Decision Systems, National Planning Data Corporation, and Urban Decision Systems) participated in the research. Three market areas were analyzed: Baltimore, Detroit, and Phoenix. The vendors supplied the Council with statistics and demographic data for each market area. The Council then analyzed the differences among the vendors' reports using standard statistical procedures.

The results indicated that there was little variation in the data from different sources when the population was relatively stable. However, the vendor-supplied demographic data varied considerably in areas with rapidly changing population. In such cases, the Council recommended that users verify vendor data findings with field investigations of their own.[3]

As this example indicates, the accuracy of secondary data can vary, particularly if it relates to highly volatile market conditions. Moreover, data obtained from different sources may not agree. In these cases, the researcher should verify the accuracy of secondary data by conducting pilot studies or by other appropriate methods. With a little creativity, this can often be accomplished with little expense and effort.

Currency: When the Data Were Collected

Secondary data may not be current. There may be a time lag between data collection and publication, as is the case with census data. Additionally, the data may not be updated frequently enough to answer questions related to the problem at hand. Marketing research requires current data; therefore, the value of secondary data is diminished as they become dated. For instance, while the 2000 Census of Population data are comprehensive, they may not be applicable to a metropolitan area whose population has changed rapidly in recent years. Thus, such data may not be current enough for use by Home Depot in planning new store locations for 2005. Fortunately, several marketing research firms update census data periodically and make the current information available for a fee.

Objective(s): The Purpose for the Study

Understanding why secondary data were originally collected can sensitize the researcher to the limitations of using them for the current marketing problem. Suppose *Sports Illustrated* surveyed its renewing subscriber base regarding readership of its articles and recall of its advertising. One objective of this study was to use the information to sell advertising space. With that in mind, the results of the study would be made available to advertising managers who were likely to be making decisions regarding advertising placement. This type of secondary information may be relevant to the question of where to place future advertising. However, the results of this survey from *Sports Illustrated* would be biased in that they would reflect the behavior of *Sports Illustrated* renewing subscribers, a group that may be more involved with the magazine than the general subscribers. To accurately interpret this secondary data, the advertising manager would have to understand how closely the *Sports Illustrated* renewing segment represented its total subscribing population.

Nature: The Content of the Data

The nature, or content, of the data should be examined with special attention to the definition of key variables, the units of measurement, categories used, and the relationships examined. One of the most frustrating limitations of secondary data comes from differences in definition, units of measurement, time frame examined, or questionable assumptions regarding the relationships of key variables. If the key variables have not been defined or are defined in a manner inconsistent with the researcher's definition, then the usefulness of the data is limited.

For secondary data on retail sales to be useful to Visa, retail sales should be defined precisely.

Consider, for example, secondary data related to retail sales. While interpreting the information, questions may arise regarding whether the sales are defined net of returned items or whether they represent cash and credit sales. For example, if Visa decides to investigate the sales of credit card services, this level of distinction becomes critical. Visa spends millions of dollars in marketing the card to retailers and in advertising the card to consumers with the theme "It's everywhere you want to be."

Secondary data may be measured in units that are not appropriate for the current problem. For example, income can be measured by individual, family, household, or spending unit, and can be reported gross or net after taxes and deductions. If income categories reported in secondary sources are different from those required by the research, the information may not be usable. If Mercedes is interested in high-income consumers with gross annual household incomes over $90,000, secondary data with income categories less than $15,000, $15,001 to $35,000, $35,001 to $50,000, and more than $50,000 will not be of much use.

Finally, we must consider the variables of interest to the researcher. For example, if the researcher is interested in actual purchase behavior, then information on attitudes that only implies behavior may have limited usefulness.

Dependability: Overall, How Dependable Are the Data?

An overall indication of the dependability of the data may be obtained by examining the expertise, credibility, reputation, and trustworthiness of the source. This information can be obtained by checking with others who have used information this source provides. Data published to promote sales, to advance specific interests, or to carry on propaganda should be viewed with suspicion. The same may be said of data published anonymously or in a form that attempts to hide the details of the data collection methodology and process. On the other hand, secondary data published by reputable organizations, such as the U.S. Census Bureau, are very dependable and of high quality.

CLASSIFICATION OF SECONDARY DATA

internal data
Data available within the organization for which the research is being conducted.

external data
Data that originate external to the client organization.

As represented in Figure 4.3 and discussed earlier in this chapter, there are two primary sources of secondary data: internal and external. **Internal data** are data generated within the organization for which the research is being conducted. **External data** are data generated by sources outside the client organization. In the opening vignette, data on circulation obtained from the records of the *Vindicator* were internal data. However, data obtained on advertising effectiveness and penetration for different forms of media from Inland Research were external data.

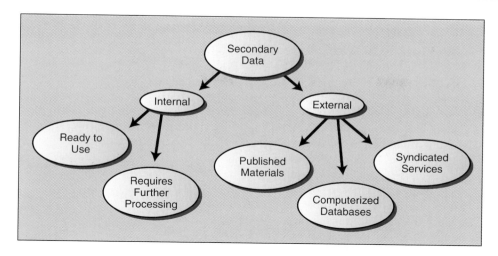

FIGURE 4.3
A Classification of
Secondary Data

INTERNAL SECONDARY DATA AND DATABASE MARKETING

Before collecting external secondary data, it is always useful to analyze internal secondary data. Internal data are typically generated as part of the ongoing process of doing business. These data can come from accounting records, sales reports, production or operation reports, or internal experts. In the opening vignette, the *Vindicator* routinely collects data on the number of customers, duration each customer has been a subscriber, renewals/nonrenewals, and so on. Although it is possible that internal secondary data may be available in usable form, it is more typical that considerable processing effort will be required before such data can be used. For example, cash register receipts of a department store may contain a wealth of information, such as sales by product line, sales by specific stores, sales by geographic region, sales by cash versus credit purchases, sales in specific time periods, sales by size of purchase, and so on. However, to derive this information, data have to be transcribed from the paper-based sales receipts to a computer database and analyzed extensively. Many organizations are building sophisticated internal databases as platforms for their marketing effort.

Database marketing involves using computers to capture and track customer profiles and purchase detail. For many companies, the first step in creating a database is to transfer raw sales information, such as that found on sales call reports or invoices, to a microcomputer. This is augmented with demographic and psychographic information about the customers obtained from secondary sources. Several companies in this business, including R. R. Donnelley *(www.rrdonnelley.com)*, Experian *(www.experian.com)*, R. L. Polk *(www.polk.com)*, and others, have compiled household lists, which include names, addresses, and a great deal of individual-specific data.

This augmented information can then be analyzed in terms of a customer's activity over the life of the business relationship. Signs of change in the usage relationships (e.g., a heavy user decreases usage) or significant "customer life cycle" events such as anniversaries can be identified and acted upon. These databases provide the essential tool needed to nurture, expand, and protect the customer relationship and can also serve as a foundation for developing marketing programs.

Organizations that bill their customers for services or provide statements of customer activities are in a particularly strong position to use their internal secondary data. Utilities, cable television systems, banks, department stores, and health care providers are all examples of organizations that use database marketing.

database marketing
Marketing that involves using computers to capture and track customer profiles and purchase detail.

GENERAL ELECTRIC: ELECTRIFYING MARKETING WITH A CUSTOMER DATABASE

General Electric (GE) has built a huge customer database, which it uses effectively for target marketing. GE has combined demographic, psychographic, media consumption, and purchasing data available externally with internal customer transaction records to pinpoint a customer's appliance ownership and history.

Using this database, GE can determine, for example, which customers are ready to replace their washing machines: those who bought the washing machine six years ago and have large families. The company can then direct marketing efforts in the form of gift certificates, discounts, and special deals for washing machines at these customers. The database has electrified GE's marketing resulting in increased market share and profitability.[4]

As the GE example illustrates, database marketing can lead to quite sophisticated and targeted marketing programs.

EXTERNAL SECONDARY DATA: PUBLISHED SOURCES

Secondary data sources have grown dramatically over the past 20 years. This growth has been stimulated, in part, by the introduction of personal computers into the workplace, which give employees easy access to commercial databases. The following section will provide an overview of some of the sources of published external secondary data. Nonprofit organizations (e.g., Chambers of Commerce), trade and professional organizations, commercial publishers, investment brokerage firms, and professional marketing research firms are just a few of the nongovernmental sources available. To enable you to sort through the overwhelming amount of secondary data, we will begin our discussion with a classification of published secondary data (see Figure 4.4).

Published external sources may be broadly classified as general business data or government data. General business sources include guides, directories, indexes, and statistical data. Government sources may be broadly categorized as census data and other publications.

General Business Data

Businesses publish a great deal of information in the form of books, periodicals, journals, newspapers, magazines, reports, and trade literature. The Audit Bureau of Circulations, cited in the opening vignette, is a general business source that provides data on audits of media such as newspapers, consumer magazines, trade shows, and the Web. Guides, directories, and indexes can help locate information available from general business sources. Sources are also available for identifying statistical data. A brief description of each of these resource categories follows.

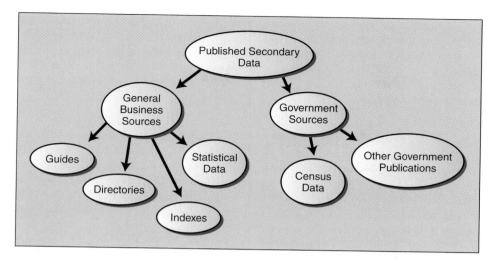

FIGURE 4.4
A Classification of
Published Secondary
Sources

GUIDES Standard or recurring information is summarized in guides. Guides provide a path to other sources of secondary data contained in directories or published by professional or trade associations. Because guides can open the door to other sources of data, they are one of the first sources a researcher should consult. Some of the most useful are *Business Information Sources, Data Sources for Business and Market Analysis,* and *Encyclopedia of Business Information Sources.*

INDEXES AND BIBLIOGRAPHIES Bibliographies, which are organized alphabetically by topic, are another good place to start external secondary research. Current or historic discussion of a particular topic of interest will be indexed in these references, leading you to a number of authors.

Several indexes are available for referencing both academic and business topics. Some of the more useful business indexes are *Business Periodical Index, Business Index, Predicasts F & S Index: United States, Social Sciences Citation Index,* and the *Wall Street Journal Index.*

DIRECTORIES Directories provide brief descriptions of companies, organizations, or individuals. They are helpful for identifying manufacturers operating in your market, for compiling names and addresses of associations in your sales territory, or for verifying names and addresses of prospective customers who carry a specific job title. Some of the important directories include *Directories in Print; Consultants and Consulting Organizations Directory; Encyclopedia of Associations; FINDEX: The Directory of Market Research Reports, Studies and Surveys;* and *Research Services Directory.*

NONGOVERNMENTAL STATISTICAL DATA Business research often involves compilation of statistical data reflecting market or industry factors. A historic perspective of industry participation and growth rates can provide a context for market share analysis. Market statistics related to population demographics, purchasing levels, television viewership, and product usage are just some of the types of nongovernmental statistics available from secondary sources. Important sources of nongovernmental statistical data include *A Guide to Consumer Markets, Predicasts Forecasts, Sales and Marketing Management Survey of Buying Power, Standard & Poor's Statistical Service,* and *Standard Rate and Data Service.*

Government Sources

The U.S. government is the largest source of secondary data in this country, indeed in the world. The data the government collects could not feasibly be collected by private industry. Its value ranges from developing sales forecasts and market potential estimates to simply locating specific retailers, wholesalers, or manufacturers. The breadth and accuracy of government sources makes it a rich source of secondary data. In the opening vignette, Inland Research obtained data from government sources such as the U.S. Census Bureau and the Bureau of Labor Statistics. Government publications can be divided into census data and other types.

CENSUS DATA Census data are useful in a variety of marketing research projects. The demographic data collected by the Census Bureau includes information about household types, sex, age, marital status, and race. Consumption detail related to automobile ownership, housing characteristics, work status, and practices as well as occupations are just a few of the categories of information available. What makes this demographic information particularly valuable to marketers is that these data can be geographically categorized at various levels of detail. These data can be summarized at the zip code or city block level, or they can be aggregated for the nation as a whole.

In general, the quality of census data is quite high, and the data are often extremely detailed. To facilitate business analysis, this information is available in multiple forms. One can purchase computer tapes, diskettes, or CD-ROMs from the Census Bureau for a nominal fee and recast this information into the desired format. Important census data include Census of Housing, Census of Manufacturers, Census of Population, Census of Retail Trade, Census of Service Industries, and Census of Wholesale Trade. Claritas is a secondary research company that has created a number of research tools using census and other lifestyle data. Integrating enhanced census data with internal company databases is a useful application of multiple secondary sources. This integration of secondary data will be discussed later in the chapter.

OTHER GOVERNMENT PUBLICATIONS In addition to the census, the federal government collects and publishes a great deal of statistical data, much of it relevant to business. The government developed the Standard Industrial Classification Code (SIC) as the classification scheme used for its Census of Manufacturers. The SIC system classified manufacturing into 20 major groups. Each group was further classified into industry groups and then product categories. The United States, Mexico, and Canada have created a new common classification system to replace the previous classification of each country. The four-digit SIC of the United States has been replaced by the six-digit North American Industry Classification System (NAICS), which was phased in beginning in 1999.

Why was NAICS needed? According to statements from the U.S. Department of Commerce, the SIC didn't keep up with rapid changes in U.S. and world economics. The two extra digits in NAICS accommodate the larger number of sectors and allow more flexibility in designating subsections. NAICS is organized in a hierarchical structure, much like the SIC. The new codes will be reviewed every five years. You can obtain more information on NAICS at *www.ntis.gov*.

Other useful government publications include *Business America, Business Conditions Digest, Business Statistics, Index to Publications, Statistical Abstract of the United States,* and *Survey of Current Business.*

Most published information is also available in computerized databases.

COMPUTERIZED DATABASES

Computerized databases, accessed directly online or available over the Internet, have made secondary data easily available for organizations of all sizes, as in the opening vignette. A microcomputer equipped with a modem linked to relevant telecommunication networks can connect a researcher to vast libraries of information, accessible at any time, from any place. Marketing researchers no longer need to leave their office to monitor changes in their industry, technology, or regulatory environments.

Today, there are thousands of databases. Their phenomenal growth is a result of the advantages of electronic dissemination of data over printed data:

1. **Current information.** Because printing is no longer an essential step in information dissemination, data can be updated continuously. Publishers who use computers to edit and publish their periodicals can now electronically transfer those documents to relevant databases, making them available with remarkable speed, as compared to the traditional methods of print production and physical distribution.

2. **Faster data search.** Online vendors provide increasing uniformity in the search process, enabling even a relative novice at secondary research to access data more quickly and completely.

3. **Low cost.** The relative cost of accessing computerized databases is low.

4. **Convenience.** This has become perhaps one of the greatest benefits computerized databases have delivered. Information providers now have a direct link to the end user equipped with a microcomputer and modem. They are no longer forced to distribute their products through libraries or retail outlets.

Conducting secondary research via computerized databases, however, is not without limitations. A researcher who doesn't know how to conduct a focused key word search or is unsure whether a particular database provides abstracts or articles in their entirety can be buried under a mountain of irrelevant data. However, researchers can overcome these limitations as they gain experience in the computerized search process.

Knowing how computerized databases are classified can help the researcher narrow the search. Database vendors provide a wide array of public information, available to anyone who has computer access to a telecommunications network. Computerized databases are classified in terms of how they are distributed as online, Internet, or offline, as shown in Figure 4.5.

Online Databases

Online databases provide direct, interactive access to data stored remotely on a mainframe computer. A microcomputer linked to these mainframes via modem and a telecommunication network is all that is required to initiate a data search and retrieval process. Usage fees are typically based on minutes spent searching a computer file (time online) and data requests made. A flat monthly access fee may also be charged.

online databases
Databases stored in computers that require a telecommunications network to access.

The online database provides an advantage in terms of its currency. Data can be updated and made available for distribution almost simultaneously.

Internet Databases

Internet databases are a special form of online database. All knowledge workers, and especially market researchers, can benefit from **Internet databases,** which are information sources available on the World Wide Web (WWW). In addition to worldwide e-mail access, the Internet can provide a variety of marketing research documents, as well as both primary and secondary research data. Document access and retrieval via keyword search are of particular interest for secondary data search.

Internet databases
Databases that can be searched, accessed, or analyzed on the Internet.

Numerous search utilities and search services can be launched from Internet browsers such as Netscape or Internet Explorer. These packages are general, user-friendly, all-purpose Internet navigation tools that provide access to the WWW, including down-

FIGURE 4.5
A Classification of
Computerized Databases

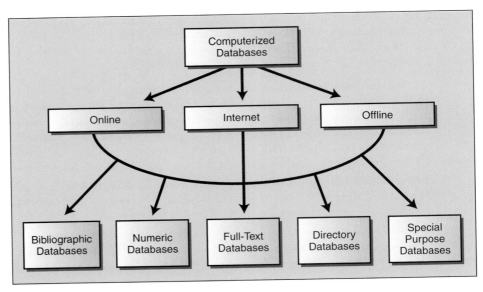

load and document browsing services. Some of the many Internet search services are the popular Lycos, Yahoo!, and Webcrawler. The following example illustrates that the Internet is a very popular option in searching for secondary data, and its use is growing daily.[5]

EXAMPLE

TOP BUSINESS INTERNET TRENDS

- 83% use the Internet for communications: e-mail and file sharing
- 78% use the Internet for research: accessing secondary data
- 55% access the Internet several times a day, most spending 5 to 30 minutes per session
- 54% worry about the security of information they exchange on the Internet[6]

Offline Databases

offline databases
Databases that are available on
diskette or CD-ROM.

Another way of making information available to users is via **offline databases** that are physically distributed on diskettes or CD-ROM disks. This type of database service transfers information from the mainframe environment to a microcomputer. Access to a telecommunication network is not necessary if the researcher is using offline databases. Thus, the usage fees associated with database access are eliminated. However, the potential cost savings have to be offset against the time lag inherent in updating offline data. Nevertheless, there is a market for offline databases. The U.S. Census Bureau makes data files available on CD-ROM disks. These disks contain detailed information organized by census tract or zip code.

As a further classification, databases, whether they are online, Internet, or offline, can vary in terms of nature and content. As shown in Figure 4.5, there are five major types of databases: bibliographic, numeric, full-text, directory, or special-purpose databases.

BIBLIOGRAPHIC DATABASES **Bibliographic databases** are indexes of studies and reports published in journals, magazines, and newspapers. They can be on any subject, ranging from marketing research to technical reports and government documents. Summaries of the report findings, known as abstracts, are often provided. For marketers, one of the largest bibliographic databases is the FIND/SVP. It reflects the work of over 500 research firms on subjects such as consumer and product studies, store audit reports, subscription research services, and surveys of 55 industries worldwide. Copies of these studies are provided on request.

Other examples of bibliographic databases include ABI/Inform and the Predicasts Terminal System. ABI/Inform contains 200-word abstracts of articles published in more than 750 journals. Management Contents, which is accessed through the Dialog Corporation (also the source for FIND/SVP), is another rich bibliographic database.

NUMERIC DATABASES **Numeric databases** specialize in disseminating statistical information, such as survey and time series data. Economic and industry data lend themselves to time series presentations, which are developed when the same variables are repeatedly measured over time. This type of data is particularly relevant for assessing market potential, making sales forecasts, or setting sales quotas. Vendors such as Boeing Computer Services, Data Resources, Evans Economics, and the Office of Economic Coordination and Development all provide time series data.

Commercially updated census data are another example of numeric databases. Donnelley Demographics provides updated, current-year and five-year projections on population statistics collected in the latest census. A variety of geographic categorization schemes including census tract, zip code, and AC Nielsen's Designated Market Areas or Selling Areas can be used as keys for searching in this database. The U.S. Census Bureau, CACI, and National Decision Systems provide similar services.

FULL-TEXT DATABASES As the name implies, **full-text databases** contain the complete text of the source documents contained in the database. Vu/Text Information Systems provides electronic full-text delivery and search capabilities for a number of newspapers (*Washington Post, Boston Globe, Miami Herald*). One of the most useful full-text business databases can be accessed through Nexis. Mead Data Central's Nexis service provides full-text access to hundreds of business data sources, including selected newspapers, periodicals, company annual reports, and investment firm reports.

DIRECTORY DATABASES **Directory databases** provide information on individuals, organizations, and services. Standard & Poor's Corporate Descriptions is an example of a directory database that provides summary data on publicly held U.S. corporations. A secondary researcher wanting to compile information on a competitor or prospective customer can obtain data related to the growth of that organization, the size of its workforce, and its financial performance.

Firmographics are the business equivalent of demographics. They include variables such as market share, corporate location, SIC classification, and employment size. Economic Information Systems (EIS) collects this type of data on more than 200,000 nonmanufacturing firms that employ more than 20 people.

The largest database of companies in this country is contained in the national Electronic Yellow Pages. This database contains more than 10 million records compiled from the nation's 4,800 telephone books. The names, addresses, phone numbers, and SIC codes for manufacturers, wholesalers, retailers, professionals, and service organizations are available through this source.

bibliographic databases
Databases composed of citations to articles in journals, magazines, newspapers, marketing research studies, technical reports, government documents, and the like. They often provide summaries or abstracts of the material cited.

numeric databases
Databases that contain numerical and statistical information that may be important sources of secondary data.

full-text databases
Databases containing the complete text of secondary source documents comprising the database.

directory databases
Directory databases provide information on individuals, organizations, and services.

special-purpose databases
Databases that contain information of a specific nature, for example, data on a specialized industry.

SPECIAL-PURPOSE DATABASES **Special-purpose databases** are more focused in their scope, such as the Profit Impact of Market Strategies (PIMS). The Strategic Planning Institute in Cambridge, Massachusetts, maintains PIMS, which reflects its research and analysis on business strategies from more than 250 companies, representing over 2,000 businesses. Another relevant database is the Market Research Library by LEXIS-NEXIS.

EXAMPLE

MARKET RESEARCH LIBRARY

In the LEXIS-NEXIS Market Research Library, customers can purchase report information online by subsection, eliminating the cost of buying an entire report. Users may browse the entire table of contents and study the methodology of most reports, as well as view actual tables, minus the data, before purchasing the information. The subsections of the market research reports on the NEXIS Market Research Product have been formatted by the market research providers as complete, stand-alone units of information. The product offers research data from such sources as AC Nielsen, Business Trend Analysts, Datamonitor, Euromonitor, FIND/SVP, The Freedonia Group, Leading Edge, and Packaged Facts. For more information, call 1-800-227-4908 or visit the company's Web site at *www.lexis-nexis.com/marketing/*.[7]

The process of locating the database relevant to your specific research problem may seem overwhelming at first. Fortunately, directories of databases have been developed to assist the researcher in narrowing the database search.

Directories of Databases

To avoid being buried under mountains of irrelevant data and to make the process efficient, a search of database directories may be a useful early step in the research process. The following are some useful directories that are periodically updated:

> *Directory of On-Line Databases*
> Santa Monica, California: Cuadra Associates, Inc.
>
> *Encyclopedia of Information System and Services*
> Detroit: Gale Research Company
>
> *Information Industry Marketplace*
> New York: R. R. Bowker

COMBINING INTERNAL AND EXTERNAL SECONDARY DATA

The usefulness of secondary data can be greatly enhanced when internally generated data are merged with data obtained from external sources. By using both internal and external secondary sources, marketing researchers can overlay demographic, economic, or business statistics on proprietary customer files. These data can then be used to develop market assessments or profiles of various customer groups, or simply to educate the sales force. The combination of internal and external data results in inexpensive and valuable information that can be used for a variety of purposes, including database marketing, discussed earlier. In the following sections, we illustrate the merging of internal and external secondary data with applications to geo-demographic coding and geo-visual mapping.

Geo-Demographic Coding

Geo-demographic coding involves merging internal customer data with external geographic, demographic, and lifestyle data on the same customers. Some **syndicated services** have developed demographic and **psychographic** databases at the household level, along with many products based on these data.

Consider a local cable television operator who maintains a computerized database of its cable subscribers. This internal database contains customer information on the number of cable services subscribed to, the length of time on service, the changes in subscribed services over time, and the billing history for the past three years. Imagine that the president of the cable company has ambitious plans to increase penetration and market share over the next year. He is looking for a recommendation regarding which geographic markets to target. He wants the geographic market potential, profitability of various customer segments, and current cable operating restrictions to be incorporated in this analysis.

In response to this request, the director of market research decides to supplement the internal customer database with external secondary data. To expand the internal customer file, the director reviews several outside sources of geographic, demographic, and lifestyle data and then selects the Claritas Corporation.

Claritas *(www.claritas.com)* combines data from a number of sources including the U.S. Census, and commercial marketing research firms such as Arbitron, Simmons Marketing Research Bureau, and Mediamark. One of its products, PRIZM (Potential Rating Index for Zip Markets), seems highly appropriate for this research problem. PRIZM is a target marketing system that describes every U.S. neighborhood in terms of 62 distinct lifestyle types, called clusters. Geographic matching of the internal customer database with PRIZM files begins with a zip code match, followed by street address.

These external data are overlaid on the customer file, in a process called geo-coding. The researcher can use the geo-coded information to develop demographic and lifestyle profiles of customer types in terms of cable subscription levels or any other relevant variable. For example, the analysis of geo-coded data may reveal that heavy cable television users may be described as midscale families with children at home, who fall into the lifestyle cluster PRIZM has named "pools and patios." The PRIZM profiles provide a colorful description of customer segments in terms of income, education, and family size as well as lifestyles. Combining profiles with customer profit history helps the researcher formulate the cable company's expansion plans. Based on this information, the cable company can target direct-selling efforts and direct-mail campaigns and also design an appropriate advertising campaign to reach the heavy cable television users.

Geo-Visual Databases

Another factor to consider before beginning a marketing campaign is the physical coverage of the cable system's wire. There is no point in launching a full-scale effort in geographic areas where cable services are not currently available. This pitfall can be avoided by making use of geo-visual databases. Geo-visual databases are created by combining internal customer databases with geographic data from the Census Bureau and making use of appropriate **computer mapping** software.

The Census Bureau has introduced a geo-visual product called TIGER (Topologically Integrated Geographic Encoding and Referencing), which provides a digital street map of the entire United States. These mapping files contain data on street locations, highways, railroads, pipeline, power lines, and airports. Overlaying the maps of current neighborhoods wired for cable with customer geo-demographic information results in a powerful targeting tool. Such information is very useful in target market selection and the development of direct selling, direct mail, advertising, and sales promotion efforts.

syndicated services (sources)
Information services offered by marketing research organizations that provide information from a common database to firms that subscribe to their services.

psychographics
Quantified psychological profiles of individuals.

computer mapping
Maps that solve marketing problems are called thematic maps. They combine geography with demographic information and a company's sales data or other proprietary information and are generated by a computer.

SUMMARY ILLUSTRATION USING THE OPENING VIGNETTE

We summarize and illustrate secondary data by returning to the opening vignette. In contrast to primary data, which are collected for a specific research problem, secondary data have been generated for reasons other than the current research problem. The data on advertising effectiveness and penetration for different forms of media provided by the Inland Research Corporation and used by the *Vindicator* are an example of secondary data. The cost and speed advantages of secondary data must be weighed against their limited applicability and accuracy. In evaluating secondary data, factors such as specifications, error, currency, objectivity, nature, and dependability should be considered, as done by Inland Research.

Internally generated information can represent a gold mine for a market researcher. Any department that touches the final consumer in some way may be a source of valuable market data. The *Vindicator* generates data on the number of customers, duration of subscription, and renewals/nonrenewals as a normal business operation. The internally generated data can be supplemented with data available from external sources to produce a rich database that can target customers and guide marketing efforts. In the opening vignette, external data on advertising effectiveness and penetration for different forms of media were combined with internal data on circulation to stress the comparative advantages of the *Vindicator* over other media (i.e., radio and television).

External data are generated by sources outside the organization. These data exist in the form of published (printed) material, online, Internet, and offline databases, or information made available by syndicated services. The Inland Research Corporation obtains secondary data from all of these sources.

MARKETING RESEARCH AND TQM

External sources of data can also be used to define product quality. For example, *Consumer Reports* rates competing brands on quality in a wide range of product categories and identifies the relevant attributes used in calculating quality ratings. Many companies are building internal databases based on augmented sales records (see section on database marketing). Marketing research can help to analyze internal data in order to better pinpoint the customer's needs.

Marketing research at Lands' End uses customer purchase records to divide consumers into groups based on the type of articles they purchase. They also use customer complaints as warning flags for areas that need improvement. The Gap collects daily data on store sales. These data are used for inventory purposes to help prevent stock outs (items not available on the store shelf for purchase) and to indicate when sales or markdowns are necessary to move products more quickly. These data could also be used to assess the benefits of adding an additional credit card for acceptance as payment. The data could be analyzed for use of the card and increased sales. Thus, both internal and external databases yield information that can help TQM companies better define their markets, understand customer needs, and target their marketing effort.

EXAMPLE

MASTERCARD DEVELOPS A MASTER DATABASE

MasterCard, a company committed to the TQM concept and one of the primary credit card providers in the world, has developed a new product that uses a massive

FOCUS ON

ELRICK & LAVIDGE

The use of secondary data in the problem definition phase or for developing approaches to research problems varies greatly from one research project to another. Some projects involve well-defined issues that are very familiar to both the research director and to the client. These projects typically use very little, if any, secondary data. Other projects involve issues that are new to Elrick & Lavidge (E&L) or new to the client. In these cases, secondary data can help to better identify important issues related to the problems at hand. Some projects have very little data available, regardless of the level of knowledge of those doing the research. This is true for many of the business-to-business research projects E&L undertakes. The types of secondary data used in E&L's research projects run the full gamut of available sources of secondary data.

In a recent project for an insurance company interested in diversifying into other financial products, the purpose was to "develop an understanding about the retirement savings market." E&L researchers searched indexes and guides to find information in a number of external secondary sources: trade journals, trade group reports, and government sources. Using about 32 sources of published and computerized data-

bases, E&L put together a report on the past performance and future trends in the retirement savings market.

This report included some very interesting information about the retirement savings market. For instance, the report pointed out that the market size would increase dramatically with the aging of the baby boomer generation. In addition, the report predicted that future retirees would have twice the assets saved by retirement age compared to retirees in the past. This implies that these retirees will require a wider variety of retirement savings options. In the area of company image, consumers viewed insurance companies more favorably than mutual fund companies. However, insurance companies lagged behind banks. The report offered several dimensions along which the retirement savings market could be segmented, including the investor's level of investment risk tolerance and the investor's current product portfolio composition.

E&L and the client used the results of this research to better frame questions and to ask more relevant questions about retirement savings in the next round of satisfaction research.

database of information about credit card holders. The new product, Merchant Advisor, is a quality database that consists of details about MasterCard purchases shaped into consumer buying patterns. Retailers now have access to a high-quality database and the ability to efficiently track consumer spending, compare sales to competitors, and scrutinize the habits of target customers.

With Merchant Advisor, a large national department store such as Dillard's can study the types of makeup and clothes being purchased by the demographic group consisting of women 25 to 45 years old. Dillard's could use the database to find which brands they are buying, what media to use to reach them, and where its advertising dollars should be spent. For example, women in this age group purchase national brands such as Chaus, Liz Claiborne, and Sag Harbor and are heavy readers of magazines such as *Self*. Thus, Dillard's stocks these brands and advertises in *Self* to reach women in this group and to better meet their needs. This focus on

> TQM has paid big dividends for Dillard's and has resulted in a loyal following of women 25 to 45.
>
> It appears that MasterCard, through its dedication to TQM, will be able to generate a large amount of surplus revenue by selling Merchant Advisor to retailers.[8]

INTERNATIONAL MARKETING RESEARCH

Secondary international data are available from both domestic government and nongovernment sources (Figure 4.6). The most important government sources are the Department of Commerce, the Agency for International Development, the Small Business Administration, the Export–Import Bank of the United States, the Department of Agriculture, the Department of State, the Department of Labor, and the Port Authority of New York and New Jersey. The Department of Commerce offers not only a number of publications but also a variety of other services, such as the foreign buyer program, matchmaker events, trade missions, export contact list service, the foreign commercial service, and custom statistical service for exporters.

Nongovernment organizations, including international organizations located in the United States, can also provide information about international markets. These data sources include the United Nations, the Organization for Economic Cooperation and Development (OECD), the International Monetary Fund (IMF), the World Bank, the International Chambers of Commerce, the Commission of the European Community to the United States, and the Japanese External Trade Organization (JETRO). Finally, locally

FIGURE 4.6
Sources of Secondary Data for International Marketing Research

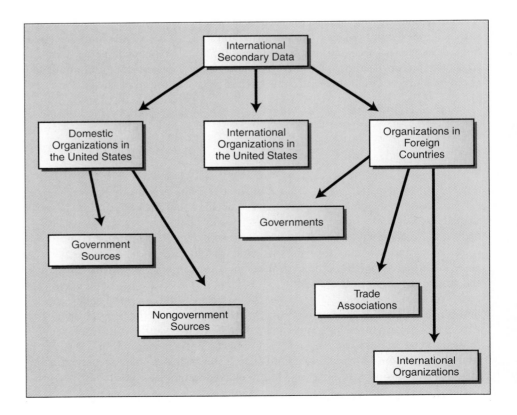

sourced secondary data are available from foreign governments, international organizations located abroad, trade associations, and private services, such as syndicated firms.

The problems with data compatibility are even more pronounced when dealing with secondary data from international sources. Differences in units of measurement for such common economic statistics as personal disposable income make comparisons between two countries difficult. The accuracy of secondary data may also vary with the level of industrialization in a country. Data from countries such as the United States are likely to be more accurate than those from developing countries. The taxation structure and the extent of tax evasion affect reported business and income statistics. The measurement frequency of population census data varies considerably. An extreme example is the comparison of the U.S. census, conducted every 10 years, to the census conducted in the People's Republic of China, where a 29-year gap occurred between the census of 1953 and 1982.

Broad demographic data related to population, age, income, occupation, and educational levels, particularly when evaluated over time, can be very useful in providing insight into trends in international markets. The following example illustrates the value of this kind of basic statistical data that are available from international secondary sources.

EXAMPLE

OXYCUTE 'EM

It is a rare opportunity to seize a market with an entire line of products. This is exactly what SmithKline Beecham did. As the first Western marketer in Eastern Europe with an acne remedy, SmithKline used the Oxy name as its global brand for medicated facial care products such as lotions, creams, and washing gels. Based on secondary data, SmithKline estimated the female teenage market for its product line at 3 million. Because of foreign regulatory restrictions, advertising for the entire product line had to be limited to one brand. The Oxy pad brand was chosen.

The company chose Poland as the entry market. Secondary data revealed that teenage girls in Poland were heavy readers of *Popcorn* magazine and also spent a lot of time watching soap operas on TV. Therefore, SmithKline Beecham directed the advertising placement toward the teen magazine *Popcorn* followed by a TV campaign airing commercials in popular soap operas. This early entry into Poland guided by secondary data analysis helped SmithKline secure a leadership position for its Oxy product line.[9]

TECHNOLOGY AND MARKETING RESEARCH

New information technologies have begun and will continue to revolutionize the ways in which marketing research is undertaken. Innovations will change the way in which both secondary and primary research is conducted. Technological advances have not only facilitated the establishment of sophisticated internal databases, they have enabled firms to collect primary data using creative promotions and automated systems, as illustrated by Pepsi Cola.

"PEPSI PUTS CALLERS IN TOUCH WITH RAY"

Recently, Pepsi Cola mailed 1 million cases of Diet Pepsi to Diet Coke consumers drawn from its internal database, in a one-time effort to promote its product. Pepsi then decided to follow up its initial promotion with a research-oriented one.

Pepsi wanted an interactive marketing tool, and its direct marketing agency, Tracy-Locke Direct, consulted Modern Media for suggestions on the best available options. The result was an 800-number hotline called "Convert a Million."

Pepsi sent a direct-mail promotion to the same 1 million households to which it had mailed the Diet Pepsi cases, and invited them to "talk" to Ray Charles, the Diet Pepsi pitchman, and potentially win an assortment of prizes. Consumers were required to answer a select group of marketing research questions before they were able to speak to Ray Charles and find out if they had won a prize.

West Interactive, an inbound telemarketing company, was contracted to manage the 800 number, and set up the 3½-minute, touch-tone automated telephone response survey. Pepsi wanted information on the types of soft drinks the consumers drank, how much they purchased, and so on in an effort to probe the mind of the Diet Coke drinker, and possibly find how to best market Diet Pepsi in an effort to convert Diet Coke drinkers.

Pepsi was surprised by the enormity of the response: More than 50 percent of the 1 million consumers targeted responded to the promotion. The respondents provided information concerning "brand preference, consumption rates, and lifestyle activities." The "Convert a Million" survey was so successful, it won a Gold Echo award from the Direct Marketing Association.

According to Jerry Winter, manager of database marketing at Pepsi, the success of the interactive survey convinced Pepsi of the value of technology in marketing research. The company has plans for other interactive survey/promotions using the database in the future.[10]

ETHICS IN MARKETING RESEARCH

Researchers can overlook the disadvantages and advantages of secondary data that we discussed earlier, which raises ethical issues. The research firm has the ethical responsibility to use only secondary data that are relevant and appropriate to the problem. The data used should be critically evaluated, using the criteria described in this chapter. The researcher should discuss issues surrounding the relevance and accuracy of secondary data with the client.

After a detailed analysis of secondary data has been conducted, the researcher should reexamine the collection of primary data stipulated in the proposal to see if it is still appropriate. Any needed changes in the primary data collection methodology should be discussed with the client. In the extreme case, if primary data are no longer needed, then it is the ethical responsibility of the researcher to disclose this to the client.

In addition to evaluating their quality and completeness, secondary data should also be evaluated in terms of moral appropriateness. Data collection may be unethical if the data are generated without the respondents' knowledge or consent, and their use raises ethical questions. While generating secondary data, researchers and syndicate firms should not engage in any questionable or unethical practices, such as abuse of respondents' privacy. Privacy has, indeed, become a burning issue, as illustrated by the following example.

EXAMPLE

PRIVACY ISSUE GOES PUBLIC

The legal environment is becoming increasingly hostile toward marketing research. Government is considering more legislation that will cover a list of alleged privacy abuses in marketing research. Some 500 bills that cover a list of privacy abuses and protections have been introduced around the United States. The privacy issue has gone public with a wave of consumer complaints against many forms of marketing research.

Two main issues are involved. First, consumers feel they should not have to cope with unsolicited sales pitches that flood their mailboxes, phones, and e-mail addresses. The second issue concerns the sophisticated databases that maintain enormous amounts of information about consumers, ranging from their names to specifics about their lifestyles and product consumption habits. In a privacy survey conducted by Equifax, 78 percent of the respondents said they were concerned about the personal privacy issue. A majority of the respondents said they thought it was reasonable for companies to check public record information such as credit checks, auto insurance checks, or job checks but that consumers should be able to opt out of all other transactions.[11]

INTERNET APPLICATIONS

The Web is an important source of secondary data for the marketing researcher. As mentioned in Chapter 1, the general search engines provide the best starting point for performing any kind of research. In addition, the researcher can visit one of the many sites of companies that directly provide marketing research data.

Internal Secondary Data

Most large organizations have intranets, which greatly facilitate the search for and access to internal secondary data. Procter & Gamble, for example, has developed powerful intranet applications that enable its managers worldwide to search for past and current research studies and a wide variety of marketing-related information on the basis of key words. Once located, the information can be accessed online. Sensitive information can be secured electronically with user names and passwords.

General Business Sources

A variety of business-related sites can provide sales leads, mailing lists, business profiles, and credit ratings for American businesses. Many sites supply information on many businesses within a specific industry. For example, *www.truckinginfo.com* provides information on companies and trends in the trucking industry. Another good source is USAData.com.

EXAMPLE

CONSUMER INFORMATION TO GO: USADATA.COM

USAData.com *(www.usadata.com)* combines business and marketing information from its comprehensive database and distributes it over the Internet. It assembles marketing research information from respected data providers into a searchable format to be purchased by other businesses requiring quick access to information. Using demographic information that has been previously collected, USAData.com can quickly assemble mailing lists that target specific customers. In addition to mailing lists, it provides reports on various industries and companies containing information such as market share, consumer habits, and geographic penetration.

For example, USAData.com can quickly assemble an Internet mailing list targeting middle-aged professionals on the West Coast for a high-class resort seeking to geographically expand its customer base. This approach allows client firms fast access to up-to-date information about consumers and competitors. Thus, USAData.com is a valuable source of secondary data available on the Internet.

Government Data

One of the major sources of secondary data is the U.S. government. Several sites administered by the government are very useful:

1. FedWorld *(www.fedworld.gov)* is an online locator service for a comprehensive inventory of information disseminated by the federal government.
2. Global Information Location Service *(www.gils.net)* makes it easy for people to find information of all kinds, in all media, in all languages, and over time.
3. The U.S. Department of State International Information Programs Web site *(www.usinfo.state.gov)* provides information on current policy and global issues.
4. United States Department of Commerce *(www.doc.gov)* provides a wealth of information related to commerce and the economy.
5. United States Business Statistics *(www.stat-usa.gov)* delivers vital economic, business, and international trade information produced by the U.S. government.
6. New Products and Service Announcements *(www.access.gpo.gov)* provides library services, an online bookstore, and aids for locating specific information.

These government sites can provide valuable information to the marketing researcher.

SPSS

SPSS Maps integrates seamlessly with SPSS base menus, enabling you to map a variety of data. You can choose from six base thematic maps, or create other maps by combining map options. Maps can be further customized using the SPSS Syntax Editor. Such maps can be used for a variety of purposes including interpreting sales and other data geographically to determine where the biggest customers are located, displaying sales trend for specific geographic locations, using buying trend information to determine the ideal location for new company stores, and so on.

SUMMARY

In contrast to primary data that are collected for a specific research problem, secondary data have been generated for reasons other than the current research problem. The cost advantage and speed with which secondary data can be obtained must be weighed against their limited fit to the current research problem and concerns regarding data accuracy. In evaluating secondary data, the researcher should consider factors such as specifications, error, currency, objectivity, nature, and dependability.

Internally generated information can represent a gold mine for a researcher. Any department that touches the final consumer in some way may be a source of valuable market data. The internally generated data can be supplemented with demographic and lifestyle data available from external sources to produce a rich database that can target customers and guide marketing effort.

External data are generated by sources outside the organization. These data exist in the form of published (printed) material, online, Internet, and offline databases, or information made available by syndicated services. Published external sources may be broadly classified as general business data or government data. General business sources comprise guides, directories, indexes, and statistical data. Government sources may be broadly categorized as census data and other data. Computerized databases may be online, Internet, or offline, and may be further classified as bibliographic, numeric, full-text, directory, or specialized databases.

Both internal and external databases yield information that can help TQM companies better define their markets, understand customer needs, and target their marketing efforts. When conducting international research, problems of data quality become even more pronounced, and thus these data should be carefully evaluated. Technological advances are facilitating the establishment of sophisticated internal databases. The researcher has the ethical responsibility to use only secondary data that are relevant and appropriate to the problem. The Internet is a valuable source of secondary data.

KEY TERMS AND CONCEPTS

Primary data, 112
Secondary data, 112
Internal data, 116
External data, 116
Database marketing, 117
Online databases, 121

Internet databases, 121
Offline databases, 122
Bibliographic
    databases, 123
Numeric databases, 123
Full-text databases, 123

Directory databases, 123
Special-purpose
    databases, 124
Syndicated services, 125
Psychographic, 125
Computer mapping, 125

ACRONYMS

The criteria used for evaluating secondary data may be described by the acronym SECOND:

S pecifications: methodology used to collect the data

E rror: accuracy of the data

C urrency: when the data were collected

O bjective: purpose for which data were collected

N ature: content of the data

D ependability: overall, how dependable are the data

EXERCISES

1. What are the differences between primary and secondary data?
2. Why is it important to obtain secondary data before primary data?
3. What are the advantages of secondary data?
4. What are the disadvantages of secondary data?
5. What are the criteria to be used when evaluating secondary data?
6. What is the difference between internal and external secondary data?
7. What are the various sources of published secondary data?
8. What are the different forms of computerized databases?
9. What are the advantages of computerized databases?
10. Is it useful to combine internal and external secondary data? Why?
11. What does geo-coding mean? Give an example.
12. Explain a geo-visual database.
13. What is database marketing?

PROBLEM

1. Select an industry of your choice. Using external published sources, obtain industry sales and the sales of the major firms in that industry for the past year. Estimate the market shares of each major firm. Use a computerized database to obtain information on the market shares of these same firms. Do the two estimates agree? Was it easier to obtain the information from published sources or from a computerized database?

INTERNET AND COMPUTER EXERCISES

1. Conduct an online data search to obtain background information on an industry of your choice (e.g., sporting goods). Your search should encompass both qualitative and quantitative information.
2. Visit the Web site of a company of your choice. Suppose the management decision problem facing this company was to expand its share of the market. Obtain as much secondary data from the Web site of this company and other sources on the Internet as are relevant to this problem. Discuss the relevance of your data to the management decision problem.
3. Visit the Web site of the U.S. Census Bureau (*www.census.gov*). Write a report about the secondary data available from the Bureau that would be useful to a fast food firm such as McDonald's for the purpose of formulating a domestic marketing strategy.
4. Visit *www.census.gov/statab.* Use State Rankings and Vital Statitics to identify the top six states for marketing products to the elderly.
5. Macy's would like you to summarize the retail sales in the United States by visiting *www.census.gov/ftp/pub/indicator/www/indicat.html.*

ACTIVITIES

ROLE PLAYING

1. You are the marketing research manager of a local bank. Management has asked you to assess the demand potential for checking accounts in your metropolitan area. What sources of secondary data should you consult? What kind of information would you expect to obtain from each source? Ask a group of fellow students to play the role of management. Explain to them the role of secondary data in this project.

FIELD WORK

1. Make a trip to your local library. Write a report explaining how you would use the library to collect secondary data for a marketing research project assessing the demand potential for Cross soft-tip pens. Be specific.

GROUP DISCUSSION

1. Discuss the significance and limitations of the government census data as a major source of secondary data.
2. Discuss the growing use of computerized databases.

NOTES

1. Joe Nicholson, "Pa. Firm Arms Small Papers With Low-Cost Research," *Editor & Publisher,* 132(38) (September 18, 1999): 38–39; Anonymous, "Secondary Source Materials," *Database,* 21(5) (October/November 1998): 20; and Joe Nicholson, "Report for the *Vindicator,*" *Editor & Publisher,* 132(38) (September 18, 1999): 38.

2. Sebastian Weiss, "Frost Laying Groundwork for Banking Internet Strategy," *San Antonio Business Journal,* 14(4) (February 2, 2000): 6; Jennifer L. Baljko, "Texas Banks Attract Customers with Imaging," *Bank Systems & Technology,* 34(4) (April 1997): 40; and Bill Stoneman, "Banking on Customers," *American Demographics,* 19(2) (February 1997): 36–41.

3. John T. Riordan, "Not Yet and Not Likely," *Chain Store Age,* 73(5) (May 1997): 120; and John Chapman, "Cast a Critical Eye: Small Area Estimates and Projections Sometimes Can Be Dramatically Different," *American Demographics,* 9 (February 1987): 30.

4. Pamela L. Moore, "GE Catches Online Fever," *Business Week* (3694) (August 14, 2000): 122; and Andy Cohen, "General Electric," *Sales & Marketing Management* 149(11) (October 1997): 57.

5. Yue-Shan Chang, "A New Multi-Search Engine for Querying Data Through and Internet Search Service on CORBA," *Computer Networks,* 34(3) (September 2000): 467; and Diane K. Bowers, "The New Research Tool," *Marketing Research: A Magazine of Management & Applications,* 10(3) (Fall 1998): 34, 38.

6. "Research: Some Internet Uses Already Entrenched," *Logistics Management and Distribution Report* (April 2000): E29; Nanette Byrnes and Paul C. Judge, "Internet Anxiety," *Business Week* (3635) (June 28, 1999): 78–88; and 1996 Network World 500 Survey, Advertising Supplement to the *Wall Street Journal* (July 31, 1996): 2.

7. Deanne Barmakian, "Lexis-Nexis Academic Universe," *Library Journal,* 125(3) (February 15, 2000): 207–209; and "No Fees on NEXIS Market Research Reports Through December," *Quirk's Marketing Research,* 10(10) (December 1996): 39–40.

8. "Mastercard Offers Free E-Wallets," *American Banker,* 165(139) (July 21, 2000): 8; and Jennifer Kingson Bloom, "MasterCard Dips into Its Data to Paint Pictures of Buying Patterns for Retailers," *American Banker,* 164(15) (January 25,1999): 1.

9. David Goetzl, "Pimple-Fighter Returns to TV with Slick Ads," *Advertising Age,* 71(9) (February 28, 2000): 4; Tanya Gazdik, "Oxy Balance Gets 'N Sync with Teens," *Brandweek,* 40(7) (February 15, 1999): 12; and Dagmar Mussey, "SmithKline brings Oxy Acne Remedy to Poland," *Advertising Age* (January 18, 1993).

10. Todd Wasserman, "Soft Drinks," *Adweek,* 41(17) (April 24, 2000): U38; Larry Light, "Now That's a Pepsi Challenge," *Business Week* (3627) (May 3, 1999): 151; and Peter J. DePaulo and Rick Weitzer, "Interactive Phone Technology Delivers Survey Data Quickly," *Marketing News* (June 6, 1994): H33–34.

11. "Survey Results Show Consumers Want Privacy," *Direct Marketing,* 61(11) (March 1999): 10; and Carol Kroll, "Consumers Reach the Boiling Point over Privacy Issues," *Advertising Age,* 70(13) (March 29, 1999): 22.

5

EXPLORATORY RESEARCH DESIGN: SYNDICATED SOURCES OF SECONDARY DATA

As they serve multiple clients, syndicate firms are able to collect and provide data which could not be collected by individual users in a feasible way.

Opening Questions

1. How are syndicated data different from other secondary data? How can such data be classified?

2. What are the major methods of obtaining syndicated data from households/consumers?

3. How are syndicated data collected from institutions?

4. Why should multiple sources of secondary data be used? What is meant by single-source data?

5. Do syndicated data play a role in total quality management?

6. What syndicated data are available for conducting international marketing research?

7. How does technology enhance the usefulness of syndicated data?

8. What ethical issues are involved in the use of syndicated data?

9. What are the applications of the Internet for syndicated data?

Frank Bossu, PhD, Sr. Vice President, Elrick & Lavidge.
Dr. Frank Bossu is responsible for New Product Consulting Services and assists a variety of clients on the design and implementation of their research programs. He has a wealth of experience in the packaged goods industry, having spent 17 years with Procter & Gamble.

A CASUAL AFFAIR

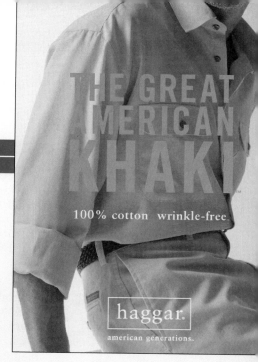

THE GREAT AMERICAN KHAKI

100% cotton wrinkle-free

haggar.
american generations.

Even though clothing designers seem to be defining fashion as dressy, most Americans seem to be opting for a more casual approach to their fashion needs. Today, companies are saying goodbye to three-piece suits, wingtips, and high heels and are welcoming a more casual dress style. The West Coast dot-com companies have definitely contributed to the casual dress trend. More recently, consulting firms, law firms, and investment companies on the East Coast are joining this trend as well. A survey conducted in April 2000 reported that a remarkable 87 percent of responding companies had a casual Friday or an everyday casual policy at their place of business. Such companies as Coca-Cola, Ford, J. P. Morgan, and Accenture have implemented full-time casual dress policies. At many companies today, when someone wears a suit to work, the question asked immediately is "Are you going on a job interview?"

According to data available from syndicated marketing research firms, there is a growing "business casual" segment. As discussed in Chapter 1, syndicated data are made available for purchase by multiple clients on a subscription basis. For example, according to a recent survey by the NPD Group *(www.npd.com)*, a well-known source of syndicated services, almost 90 percent of U.S. workers said they were dressing down at least some of the time. The NPD study revealed that while sales in many categories of tailored clothing, including dresses and men's suits, were down, sales of casual apparel, such as no-iron cotton slacks and sweaters, were on the rise. Several marketers of casual clothing have built their strategies based on these findings.

Haggar Apparel is out to convince its male customers that the company can do everything from tailored to casual. Based on such syndicated data, Haggar realized that the trend is not in the direction of tailored suits, where for years it has been the market leader. The company responded by introducing its "City Casuals" line. The wrinkle-free cotton trousers have been the biggest success in this line. Haggar supported all its lines, formal to casual, with its slogan, "Haggar. stuff You Can Wear," which was developed by Goodby, Silverstein & Partners.

Haggar is not the only company offering fashion tips for a more casual appearance. Marshall Field's, one of the premier department stores in the United States, has also tailored its efforts toward the corporate market. Its customer newsletter featured an article on workday dressing down, and offered a one-hour seminar, complete with free lunch.

In an effort to capitalize on this trend toward casual clothing, Levi Strauss is pushing both its Dockers and jeans lines. There is some reluctance by employees to sport jeans to work as they are considered too casual, even though 87 percent of U.S. offices permit employees to wear jeans. However, the company has had huge success with the Dockers line that has become standard wear for the casual business dresser. As part of its marketing strategy, Levi Strauss has promoted "dress down" days. The company developed a four-page newsletter, full of reasons that casual dress codes should be adopted. The newsletter was sent to 42,000 human resources managers. About 20 percent of the companies responded, including 81 of the *Fortune* 100 companies.[1] As this vignette illustrates, even competing firms such as Haggar, Marshall Field's, and Levi Strauss are able to make use of the same data available from syndicate firms such as the NPD Group to formulate their marketing strategies.

OVERVIEW

Chapters 1 and 4 introduced the concept of syndicated sources of information. In this chapter, we explain syndicated data in detail and distinguish them from other external sources of secondary data.

As shown in Figure 5.1, this chapter relates to marketing research suppliers and services discussed in Chapter 1, the tasks involved in problem definition and developing an approach covered in Chapter 2, and exploratory and descriptive research designs of Chapter 3. Thus, it is related to the first three steps of the marketing research process. The three major methods of collecting syndicated data related to consumers and households are surveys, diary panels, and electronic scanner services. Syndicated data are also collected from institutions. The chapter will also describe retail and wholesale audits and industrial services used to collect such data. This is followed by a discussion of single-source data. As the name indicates, single-source data combine data from various sources to create a unified database that contains information on consumer purchases, demographic and psychographic variables, and marketing management variables. Finally, the chapter will discuss the applications of syndicated data to total quality management (TQM), international marketing research, the impact of technology, ethics, and the use of the Internet. Figure 5.2 gives an overview of the topics discussed in this chapter and how they flow from one to the next.

THE NATURE OF SYNDICATED DATA

In addition to published data or data available in the form of computerized databases, syndicated sources constitute the other major source of external secondary data.

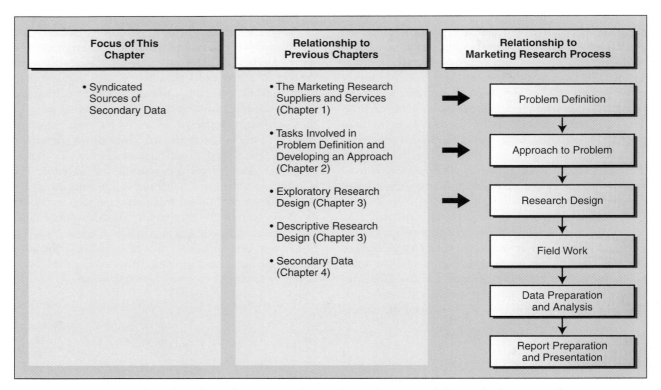

FIGURE 5.1   Relationship of Syndicated Sources to the Previous Chapters and the Marketing Research Process

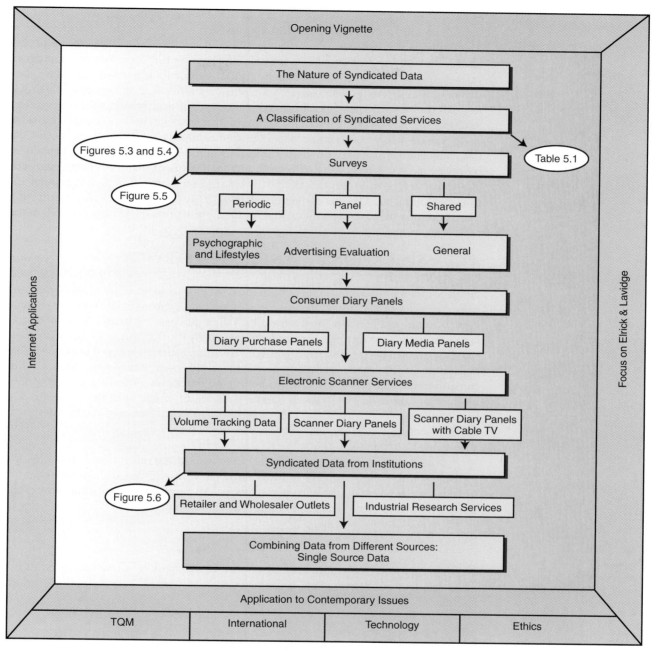

FIGURE 5.2   Syndicate Sources of Secondary Data: An Overview

Syndicated sources (also referred to as **syndicated services**) are companies that collect and sell common pools of data designed to serve information needs shared by a number of clients, including competing firms in the same industry. This was illustrated in the opening vignette. Survey data the NPD Group collected were useful to Haggar, Marshall Field's, and Levi Strauss. These data differ from primary data in that the research objective guiding the study is common to several client firms. Syndicated firms make their money by collecting data and designing research products that fit the information needs

syndicated services (sources)
Companies that collect and sell common pools of data designed to serve information needs shared by a number of clients, including competing firms in the same industry.

of more than one organization. Often, syndicated data and services are designed for use by multiple clients from multiple industries.

Although classified as secondary, syndicated data differ from other sources of secondary data in that syndicated data are collected because they have known commercial value to marketers. Both census data and other externally generated secondary data (Chapter 4) are general data collected for purposes other than the specific marketing research problems a client faces. In contrast, the types of data syndicated services collect have very specific marketing research applications that are of interest to a number of clients.

Any client, even two competitors in the same industry, for example, the Coca-Cola Company and PepsiCo, can purchase the same syndicated data, typically through a subscription process. This process reflects the ongoing nature of many syndicated projects. These proj-ects provide data that enable tracking of change over time as well as point-in-time measurements. The data and reports that syndicate firms supply to client companies can be personalized to fit specific needs. For example, reports could be organized on the basis of the client's sales territories or product lines.

A CLASSIFICATION OF SYNDICATED SERVICES

Figure 5.3 presents a classification of syndicated sources based on either a household/consumer or institutional unit of measurement. Household/consumer data typically relate to general values and lifestyles, media use, or product purchase patterns. Data may be collected through a survey process, recorded manually by the respondent in diaries, or captured electronically via scanners (Figure 5.4). Consumer surveys are used to obtain information on beliefs, values, attitudes, preferences, and intentions. Diary panels used in consumer research emphasize information on purchases or media consumption. Electronic scanner services track purchases at the point of sale or in the home through handheld scanners (Figure 5.4). These data collection techniques may also be integrated, linking electronic scanner data with diary panels, survey data, or targeted television advertising through cable.

When syndicated services obtain data from institutions rather than households, the primary subjects they track are product movement through the distribution channel (retailers and wholesalers) or corporate statistics. An overview of the various syndicated sources is given in Table 5.1. Each of these sources will be discussed.

SURVEYS

surveys
Interviews with a large number of respondents using a predesigned questionnaire.

We will begin our discussion with general **surveys.** The NPD survey reported in the opening vignette is an example. There are three types of general surveys: periodic, panel, and shared (Figure 5.5).

FIGURE 5.3
A Classification of
Syndicated Services

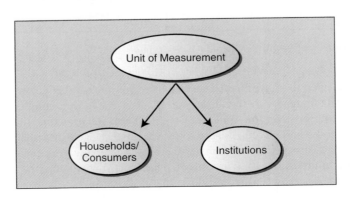

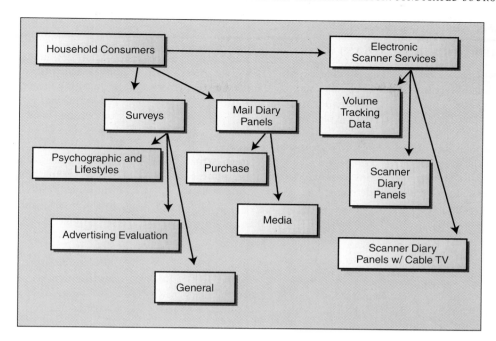

FIGURE 5.4
A Classification of
Syndicated Services:
Household/Consumers

Periodic Surveys

Periodic surveys collect data on the same set of variables at regular intervals, each time sampling a new group of respondents. Like longitudinal research, periodic surveys track change over time. However, the changes due to variation in the respondent pool is not controlled in the way it is for true longitudinal studies. A new sample of respondents is chosen, with each survey taken by the syndicate firm. Once analyzed, the data are made available to subscribers.

periodic surveys
Periodic surveys collect data on the same set of variables at regular intervals, each time sampling from a new group of respondents.

Panel Surveys

Syndicated **panel surveys** measure the same group of respondents over time but not necessarily on the same variables. A large pool of respondents is recruited to participate on the panel. From this pool, different subsamples of respondents may be drawn for different surveys. Any of the survey techniques may be used, including mail, telephone, or personal or electronic interviewing. The content and topics of the surveys vary and cover a wide range. Also known as omnibus panels, these panels are different from the panels using longitudinal designs discussed in Chapter 3. It may be recalled that in a longitudinal design, repeated measurements on the same variables are made on the same sample.

panel surveys
Panel surveys measure the same group of respondents over time but not necessarily on the same variables.

Panel surveys are used primarily because of their lower cost compared to random sampling. These savings result due to streamlining of the data collection process, enhanced response rates, and readily available sample frames, which can be precisely targeted. Comprehensive demographic, lifestyle, and product-ownership data are collected only once, as each respondent is admitted into the panel. The panel is used as a respondent pool, from which the research organization can draw either representative or targeted samples, based on the relevant background characteristics of the panel members. Response rates to panel surveys, including mail panels, are substantially improved over the random sampling processes because of the commitment panel members make to participate in surveys.

TABLE 5.1   Overview of Syndicated Services

TYPE	CHARACTERISTICS	ADVANTAGES	DISADVANTAGES	USES
Surveys	Surveys conducted at regular intervals	Most flexible way of obtaining data; information on underlying motives	Interviewer errors; respondent errors	Market segmentation, advertising theme selection, and advertising effectiveness
Diary purchase panels	Households provide specific information regularly over an extended period of time; respondents asked to record specific behaviors as they occur	Recorded purchase behavior can be linked to the demographic/psychographic characteristics	Lack of representativeness; response bias; maturation	Forecasting sales, market share, and trends; establishing consumer profiles, brand loyalty, and switching; evaluating test markets, advertising, and distribution
Diary media panels	Electronic devices automatically recording behavior, supplemented by a diary	Same as diary purchase panel	Same as diary purchase panel	Establishing advertising rates; selecting media program or air time; establishing viewer profiles
Scanner volume tracking data	Household purchases are recorded through electronic scanners in supermarkets	Data reflect actual purchases; timely data less expensive	Data may not be representative; errors in recording purchases; difficult to link purchases to elements of marketing mix other than price	Price tracking, modeling, effectiveness of in-store modeling
Scanner diary panels with cable TV	Scanner panels of households that subscribe to cable TV	Data reflect actual purchases; sample control; ability to link panel data to household characteristics	Data may not be representative; quality of data limited	Promotional mix analyses, copy testing, new-product testing, positioning
Audit services	Verification of product movement by examining physical records or performing inventory analysis	Relatively precise information at the retail and wholesale levels	Coverage may be incomplete; matching of data on competitive activity may be difficult	Measurement of consumer sales and market share, competitive activity, analyzing distribution patterns: tracking of new products
Industrial product syndicated services	Data banks on industrial establishments created through direct inquiries of companies, clipping services, and corporate reports	Important source of information on industrial firms, particularly useful in initial phases of the projects	Data are lacking in terms of content, quantity, and quality	Determining market potential by geographic area, defining sales territories, allocating advertising budget

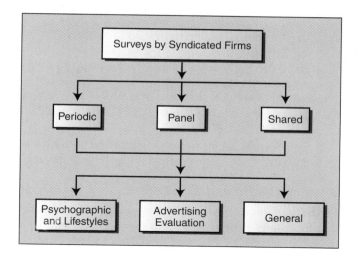

FIGURE 5.5
Classification of Syndicated Survey Research

Shared Surveys

As the name implies, **shared surveys** are developed and executed for multiple clients, each of whom shares the expenses. The bulk of a shared survey will deal with questions of general interest to the client group. These general questions are also typically supplemented with proprietary questions from each participating client. Responses to the general interest questions are available to the entire group, while the answers to proprietary questions are held in confidence and provided only to the appropriate client. This survey may be repeated at regular intervals, or it may be a one-time study. The sample may be drawn from an omnibus panel or randomly from the population of interest. Shared surveys are one way for syndicated research organizations to offer customized reports to their clients.

The primary advantage of shared surveys, as with all forms of secondary research, is lower cost. The fixed cost of research design and the variable cost of data collection are shared across the participants, making the cost per question relatively low for each client. Popular ongoing shared surveys include TeleNation and Data Gage from Marketfacts, the Multicard Survey by NFO, and Insta-Vue from the Home Testing Institute. Although a number of clients share these surveys, a certain degree of customization is offered, as illustrated by Roper Reports.

shared surveys
Shared surveys are developed and executed for multiple clients, each of whom shares the expenses.

EXAMPLE

CUSTOMIZATION VIA SYNDICATION

The Roper Reports, prepared by RoperASW *(www.roper.com)*, is a syndicated service that offers customization. This public opinion research service collects data on a broad range of social, economic, political, and consumer issues every five weeks. The organization conducts in-home interviews with a national sample of 2,000 adults aged 18 and older. In addition to the standard questions that are common across clients, clients can add customized questions that are proprietary. Thus, Ford Motor Company can purchase the general survey results related to automobiles. Ford can also request proprietary questions about its models, such as Taurus, to determine why sales are lagging behind major competitors such as Toyota Camry and Honda Accord.

According to the Roper organization, the ability to add proprietary questions along with customized report generation offers a unique combination of frequency, speed of report delivery, quality, low cost, large sample size, and extensive demographic breaks. This ability to customize surveys and reports has been a major factor in the popularity of the Roper Reports.

Surveys may also be broadly classified on the basis of their content as psychographics and lifestyles, advertising evaluation, or general surveys (Figures 5.4 and 5.5).

Psychographics and Lifestyles

psychographics
Quantified psychological profiles of individuals.

lifestyle
A distinctive pattern of living that is described by the activities people engage in, the interests they have, and the opinions they hold of themselves and the world around them (AIOs).

Psychographics refer to the psychological profiles of individuals and to psychologically based measures of lifestyle, such as brand loyalty and risk taking. **Lifestyles** refer to the distinctive modes of living of a society or some of its segments, such as the DINKs (Double Income No Kids) lifestyle, characterized as being money rich and time poor. Together, these measures are generally referred to as Activities, Interests, and Opinions, or simply as AIOs. The Yankelovich Monitor provides an application.

EXAMPLE

FREE AT LAST

The firm of Yankelovich and Partners provides the Yankelovich Monitor (*www.yankelovich.com*), a survey that contains data on lifestyles and social trends. The survey is conducted at the same time each year among a nationally projectable sample of 2,500 adults, 16 and older, including a special sample of 300 college students living on campus. The sample is based on the most recent updates of census data. All interviews are conducted in person at the respondent's home and take approximately 2.5 hours to complete.

The Yankelovich Monitor indicated that Americans were becoming more and more health and nutrition conscious. Concerned with health and nutrition, many consumers were giving up hot dogs. Based on these findings, Kraft created a fat-free frank that the company claimed would still offer the expected taste and texture. This marked the introduction of Oscar Mayer FREE Hot Dogs. This little doggie was big news. As the first one to market, the product had news value that generated a lot of coverage.

The company reported that the trial exceeded expectations, with almost 10 percent of households giving the product a shot in the first year. Based on volume, velocity, and distribution, Oscar Mayer FREE is the number one selling brand among "ultra-healthy" products, which the company believes helped fuel that segment's growth of more than 60 percent.[2]

Another example of a psychographics and lifestyles survey is the Needham, Harper & Steers Lifestyle Study, which has been tracking consumer attitudes and behaviors for a number of years. The Stanford Research Institute conducts an annual survey of consumers that is used to classify persons into VALS-2 (Values and Lifestyles) types for seg-mentation purposes. Information on specific aspects of consumers' lifestyles is also avail-able. Audits and Surveys conducts an annual survey of 5,000 consumers who participate in leisure sports and recreational activities. Several syndicate firms conduct surveys to compile demographic and psychographic information at the household, sub–zip code (e.g., 30306-3035), and zip code level, which is then made available on a subscription basis. Such information is particularly valuable for client firms seeking to enhance inter-nally generated customer data for database marketing.

Advertising Evaluation

The purpose of these surveys is to measure the size and profile of the advertising audience and to assess the effectiveness of advertising using print and broadcast media. Two well-known surveys are the Gallup and Robinson Magazine Impact Studies, and the Starch Readership Survey. The following example shows how Starch is used.

EXAMPLE

STARCH STIFFENS AD EFFECTIVENESS EVALUATIONS

The Starch Ad Readership Survey *(www.roper.com)* specializes in measuring audi-ence levels for print media. Starch annually measures exposure and readership lev-els for nearly 1,000 issues of consumer, business, and industrial publications. Personal interviews are conducted with a sample of 100 to 200 respondents for each ad tested.

A recognition method is used in which the respondents are shown advertise-ments in recently published magazines. Each individual is questioned about each ad. Based on the response to an ad, the individual is classified into one of the fol-lowing four levels of recognition: (1) Noted: The individual remembers seeing any part of the advertisement in this issue; (2) Associated: The individual has seen the advertisement and recognizes the brand or advertiser's name; (3) Read Some: The individual who read any of the copy; and (4) Read most: The individual read 50 percent or more of the written material in the advertisement.

These data are summarized for each advertisement in each magazine. From these statistics, Starch can generate overall readership percentages, readership per advertising dollar (based on current advertising rates), and advertisement rank within product categories. This type of data can be used to compare advertisements across current or past issues as well as against averages for the product category. This information is very useful to companies that advertise heavily in print media, such as American Airlines, Gucci, and GM, for evaluating the effectiveness of their advertising.[3]

Evaluation of effectiveness is even more critical in the case of television advertising. Television commercials are evaluated using either the recruited audience method or the in-home viewing method. In the recruited audience method, respondents are brought to a theater or mobile viewing laboratory. After viewing a series of advertisements, they are surveyed regarding related product knowledge, attitudes, and preferences as well as re-action to the advertisements.

With the in-home viewing method, consumers evaluate commercials in their normal viewing environment. New commercials can be pretested at the network level or in local markets. Audience reaction to the advertisements is recorded along with respondent demographics.

General Surveys

Surveys are also conducted for a variety of other purposes, including examination of purchase and consumption behavior. The Gallup Organization surveys 15,000 households annually about their purchase of consumer products. The National Menu Census conducted by Marketing Research Corporation of America asks about consumption of food products in the home. Data are provided about meals, snack items, carryout foods, and so forth. Trendex surveys 15,000 households quarterly about ownership and acquisition of consumer durables.

EXAMPLE

COLOR COLORS CONSUMER CHOICE

Predictions of consumer color preferences are traditionally based on past sales trends. Cooper Marketing Group in Oak Park, Illinois, has developed a new method of predicting consumer preference. Working with Market Facts in Arlington Heights, Illinois, Cooper Marketing conducts a nationwide consumer color preference survey each year and sells the results to manufacturers and retailers of home furnishings and apparel, as well as to major automakers.

Participants in the study are from the 400,000 member households in Market Facts' Consumer Mail Panel. Market Facts maintains the demographic profiles of the 400,000 panelists, who represent a cross-section of the U.S. population. A sample of 5,000 of these consumer panelists are surveyed by mail each year to gauge their color preferences for automotive, home, and apparel products. Along with a questionnaire, the respondents receive two color cards. One has 37 automotive colors, the other 100 colors for clothing and home furnishings. The colors are carefully selected to represent past best sellers, current best sellers, and forecasted colors of the future.

For consumer products, wherein color selection is an important part of the purchase decision, respondents are asked to identify their most and least favorite colors, colors of products they currently own, and the colors of products they anticipate buying in the future. For automotive colors, the questionnaire is divided by vehicle type: economy, midpriced, luxury, vans, sports utility vehicles, small pickups, and large pickups. Respondents are instructed to answer only for types of vehicles they already own or are likely to buy soon.

With over 30 car companies worldwide striving to catch the consumer's eye, a striking new paint color is a relatively inexpensive way to differentiate a new model or bring new life to an old one. Car manufacturers try to use color to establish brand character and distinguish themselves from their cousins or competition. Thus, Ford has used color as a tool to distinguish the Taurus and Sable lines, which share a number of features.[4]

Uses of Surveys

Surveys that are designed to collect psychographic and lifestyle data can be used for market segmentation, developing consumer profiles, or determining consumer preferences, as for casual clothing in the opening vignette. Surveys are also useful for determining product image or positioning, and for conducting price perception analysis and advertising research.

Advantages and Disadvantages of Surveys

Surveys are the primary means of obtaining information about consumers' motives, attitudes, and preferences. The flexibility of surveys is reflected in the variety of questions that can be asked, and the visual aids, packages, products, or other props that can be used during the interviews. Additionally, the sampling process enables targeting of respondents with very specific characteristics.

Because survey researchers have to rely primarily on the respondents' self-reports, there can be serious limitations to data gathered in this way. What people say is not always what they actually do. Errors may occur because respondents remember incorrectly or feel pressured to give the "right" answer. Furthermore, samples may be biased, questions poorly phrased, interviewers not properly instructed or supervised, and results misinterpreted.

Although surveys remain popular for both primary and secondary research, diary panels do a much better job of tracking consumer behavior.

CONSUMER DIARY PANELS

A diary panel is made up of a group of individuals, households, or organizations that record their purchases and behavior in a diary over time. Households are continually being recruited and added to the panel as respondents drop out of the study or are removed in order to rotate the panel. The makeup of the panel is designed to be representative of the U.S. population in terms of demographics.

Panel diaries are different from survey research in that the respondents are asked to record behavior as it occurs rather than being asked to recall past behavior or speculate on future behavior. This makes the information more accurate. Panel members are compensated for their participation with gifts, coupons, information, or cash. Media usage (e.g., television viewership or newspaper readership) can be measured using this same diary format.

The primary suppliers of diary panel data in this country are Nielsen Household Services, National Purchase Diary (NPD), National Family Opinion (NFO), and Market Research Corporation of America (MRCA). Based on the content of information recorded, diary panels can be classified as diary purchase panels or diary media panels.

Diary Purchase Panels

Often, survey data can be complemented with data obtained from **diary purchase panels** in which respondents record their purchases in a diary. The National Purchase Diary Panel maintained by the NPD Group (see opening vignette) was the largest diary panel in the United States. More than 14,500 households used preprinted diaries to record their monthly purchases in about 50 product categories. Respondents provided detailed information regarding the brand and amount purchased, price paid, whether any special deals were involved, the store where purchased, and intended use. The total panel included 29 miniature panels, each representative of a local market. The composition of the panel was representative of the U.S. population as a whole. While the NPD group still maintains some of its diary purchase panels, these are being rapidly replaced by online panels. Information provided by the National Purchase Diary Panel is used by soft drink firms

diary purchase panels
A data-gathering technique in which respondents record their purchases in a diary.

such as the Coca-Cola Company to determine brand loyalty and brand switching and to profile heavy users of various brands.

Special-purpose panels, focusing on specific product categories are also maintained. NFO World Group *(www.nfow.com)* maintains a beverage panel called Share of Intake Panel (SIP), that provide quarterly information on beverage consumption. NFO is also replacing its diary panels with online panels.

Diary Media Panels

In **diary media panels,** electronic devices automatically record viewing behavior, thus supplementing a diary. Perhaps the most familiar diary media panel is Nielsen Television Index (NTI) by Nielsen Media Research. The Index consists of a representative sample of approximately 5,000 households. Each of these households has an electronic device called a storage instantaneous peoplemeter attached to its television sets. The peoplemeter continuously monitors television viewing behavior, including when the set is turned on, what channels are viewed, and for how long. These data are stored in the peoplemeter and transmitted via telephone lines to a central computer. The data collected by the peoplemeter are supplemented with diary panel records, called audilogs. The audilog contains information on who was watching each program, so that audience size and demographic characteristics can be calculated.[5] The NTI *(www.nielsenmedia.com)* is useful to firms such as AT&T, Kellogg, JCPenney, Pillsbury, and Unilever, who are looking for advertising media that are reaching their target markets.

Another index by the same company is the Nielsen Homevideo Index® (NHI). The NHI was established in 1980 and provides a measurement of cable, pay cable, VCRs, DVD players, satellite dishes, and other new television technologies. The data are collected through the use of peoplemeters, set-tuning meters, and paper diaries.

Given the growing popularity of the Internet, syndicated services are also geared to this medium. NetRatings, Inc. *(www.netratings.com),* tracks and collects Internet usage in real time from over 50,000 home and work users. It reports site and e-commerce activity: number of visits to properties, domains, and unique sites; rankings by site and by category; time and frequency statistics; traffic patterns; and e-commerce transactions. It also reports banner advertising; audience response to banners, creative content, frequency, and site placement. This service has been launched in collaboration with AC Nielsen. The latter firm has launched this service internationally as ACNielsen eRatings.com *(www.acnielsen.com).*

Syndicated services also collect the same type of audience data for radio. Radio audience statistics are typically collected using diaries two to four times per year. An example of this service is The Arbitron Radio Listening Diary *(www.arbitron.com).*

Uses of Diary Panels

Diary purchase panels provide information useful for forecasting sales, estimating market shares, assessing brand loyalty and brand switching behavior, establishing profiles of specific user groups, measuring promotional effectiveness, and conducting controlled store tests. Diary media panels yield information helpful for establishing advertising rates by radio and TV networks, selecting appropriate programming, and profiling viewer or listener subgroups. Advertisers, media planners, and buyers find panel information to be particularly useful.

Advantages and Disadvantages of Diary Panels

The advantages of panel data over survey data relate to data accuracy and the generation of longitudinal data. Repeated measurement of the same variables from the same group of respondents classifies this as a form of longitudinal data. Longitudinal data enables manufacturers to measure changes in brand loyalty, usage, and price sensitivity over time.

Involvement in a diary panel represents a commitment on the part of the respondent. That commitment is thought to enhance the accuracy and therefore the quality of panel data. Diary panels, which record information at the time of purchase, also eliminate recall errors. Information recorded by electronic devices is even more accurate because the devices eliminate human errors.

The disadvantage of panel data can be traced to the nonrepresentativeness of panel members and to increased response errors uniquely associated with the process of maintaining a diary. Recruiters for diary panels attempt to mirror the population in the panel makeup. However, they tend to underrepresent certain groups, such as minorities and those with low education levels. The time commitment necessary to participate on panels contributes to the relatively high level of refusal and dropout rates. Additionally, response biases may occur since simply being on the panel may alter behavior. Since purchase or media data are entered by hand, recording errors are also possible.

ELECTRONIC SCANNER SERVICES

Scanner data are obtained by using electronic scanners at the cash register that read the Universal Product Code (UPC) from consumer purchases. Among the largest syndicated firms specializing in this type of data collection are Nielsen, IMS, and Information Resources. These companies compile and sell data that tell subscribers how well their products are selling relative to the competition. This analysis can be conducted for each item with a unique UPC, that is, brand, flavor, and package size. Scanner-based companies represent formidable competition for both diary panels and physical audit services. The accuracy and speed with which product movement at the retail level can be recorded using electronic scanners have reshaped the marketing research industry.

Three types of scanner data are available: volume-tracking data, scanner diary panels, and scanner diary panels with cable TV. **Volume-tracking data** are data routinely collected by supermarkets and other outlets with electronic checkout counters. When the consumer purchases are scanned, the data are automatically entered into a computer. These data provide information on purchases by brand, size, price, and flavor or formulation, based on sales data collected from the checkout scanner tapes. However, this information cannot be linked to background characteristics of consumers since their identities are not recorded when their purchases are scanned. This information is collected nationally from a sample of supermarkets with electronic scanners. Scanner services providing volume-tracking data include SCANTRACK (AC Nielsen) and InfoScan (Information Resources, Inc.). The InfoScan tracking service monitors 266 supermarket categories, 207 drugstore categories, 199 mass merchandise categories, and 199 multi-channel categories.

scanner data
Data obtained by passing merchandise over a laser scanner that reads the UPC code from the packages.

volume-tracking data
Scanner data that provides information on purchases by brand, size, price, and flavor or formulation.

EXAMPLE

PEPSI ONE IS NUMBER ONE

The Top 10 Best Selling New Consumer Packaged Goods (CPG) Products list is one of the services that Information Resources, Inc. (IRI) provides. These data are collected by IRI's InfoScan tracking service and Shoppers' Hotline household panel.

"Only three percent of the 1,000 or so new CPG products introduced annually clear the $50 million sales hurdle in their first year," according to Ed Kuehnle, group president of IRI North America. The ranking shows that suppliers are addressing two of consumers' most pressing needs and wants, quick and easy cleaning products and convenient foods, snacks, and beverages. The number one product or line extension introduced between late 1998 and July 2000 was Pepsi One, PepsiCo Inc.'s low-calorie soft drink, with sales topping $225 million. Convenient meal options also made the list with Nestlé's Stouffer's Skillet Sensations and Mars, Inc.'s Uncle Ben's Rice Bowls, which were fifth and sixth, respectively (see Table 5.2).

TABLE 5.2   IRI's Top 10 CPG Products 1999–2000

PRODUCT	COMPANY	SALES (FIRST 52 WEEKS OF BROAD DISTRIBUTION)
Pepsi One (diet cola)	PepsiCo, Inc.	$225.3 million
Swiffer (cleaning system)	Procter & Gamble	193.8 million
Post Selects (cereals)	Kraft Foods	169.9 million
Iam's Premium Dog & Cat Foods	Procter & Gamble	138.6 million
Stouffer's Skillet Sensations	Nestlé	121.7 million
Uncle Ben's Rice Bowls	Mars, Inc.	98.4 million
Dryel (home dry cleaner)	Procter & Gamble	97.8 million
Starbucks Ground Coffee & Beans	Kraft Foods	97.6 million
Pampers Rash Guard	Procter & Gamble	97.2 million
Hershey's Bites	Hershey's Foods	92.4 million

Source: Information Resources, Inc., January 31, 2001.

The ranking also shows that innovations in cleaning floors and clothes are bringing life to more mature areas of the consumer-packaged products. Procter & Gamble has been very successful in this area with Swiffer, a cleaning system that uses charged fibers to trap dust, dirt, and hair. Another P&G product, Dryel, a home dry cleaning product also made the list, bringing P&G's total to four CPG leading products. CPG manufacturers such as P&G can use IRI's Top CPG Products list as secondary data for insights into consumer behaviors.

P&G and other CPG companies can also use IRI's list to identify the fastest expanding product lines. For instance, P&G does not currently have a large presence in the convenience foods markets, but scanner volume tracking data show that there is large potential for growth in this area. P&G has been successful with its Pringles snacks and has the opportunity to expand more into the food market.[6]

scanner diary panels
Scanner data wherein panel members are issued an ID card allowing panel members' purchases to be linked to their identities.

In **scanner diary panels,** each household member is given an ID card that can be read by the electronic scanner at the cash register. The scanner panel members simply present the ID card at the checkout counter each time they shop. In this way, consumer identity is linked to products purchased as well as the time and day of the shopping trip, and the firm can build a shopping record for that individual.

Alternatively, some firms provide handheld scanners to panel members. These members scan their purchases once they are home. The AC Nielsen Consumer Panel called Homescan is used to record the purchases of approximately 125,000 households throughout the world *(www.acnielsen.com)*. The consumer scans the bar codes on purchases with a handheld scanner, which records the price, promotions, and quantity of each item. The information in the handheld scanner is then transmitted to AC Nielsen through telephone lines. AC Nielsen uses the information from the scanner and additional information gathered from the consumer to determine such things as consumer demographics, quantity and frequency of purchases, percentage of households purchasing, shopping trips and expenditures, price paid, and usage information. Manufacturers and retailers use this information to better understand the purchasing habits of consumers.

An even more advanced use of scanning technology, **scanner diary panels with cable TV,** combines diary panels with new technologies growing out of the cable TV industry. Households on these panels subscribe to one of the cable TV systems in their market. By means of a cable TV "split," the researcher targets various commercials into the homes of the panel members. For example, half the households may see test commercial A during the 6 o'clock newscast while the other half see test commercial B. These panels allow researchers to conduct fairly controlled experiments in a relatively natural environment.

Technology has been developed that allows transmission of advertising into participating households without the use of a cable TV system. Because the panels can be selected from all available TV households, not just those with cable TV, the bias of cable-only testing is eliminated. Using this type of system, General Mills, for example, can test which one of four test commercials for Total cereal results in the highest sales. Four groups of panel members are selected, and each receives a different test commercial. These households are monitored via scanner data to determine which group purchased the most Total cereal. As can be seen, scanner services incorporate advanced marketing research technology, which results in some advantages over survey and diary panel data.

scanner diary panels with cable TV
The combination of a scanner diary panel with manipulations of the advertising that is being broadcast by cable television companies.

Uses of Scanner Data

Scanner data are useful for a variety of purposes. National volume-tracking data can be used for tracking sales, prices, distribution, modeling, and analyzing early warning signals. Scanner diary panels with cable TV can be used for testing new products, repositioning products, analyzing promotional mix, and making advertising and pricing decisions. These panels provide marketing researchers with a unique controlled environment for the manipulation of marketing variables.

Advantages and Disadvantages of Scanner Data

Given that the large grocery chains have largely completed the conversion to electronic scanning and drug stores are following suit, electronic data collection is likely to continue to grow. The prompt feedback about point-of-sale product activity enables managers to evaluate existing marketing programs as well as formulate new ones.

Scanner data are not only available more quickly, they are also typically more accurate than data collected through either surveys or diary panels. The response bias that plagues manual data collection is lessened because the respondents are much less conscious of their role as a member of a scanner panel. Errors due to failures in recall are also eliminated with electronic data collection.

Another advantage is that in-store variables such as pricing, promotions, and displays are also recorded. Finally, a scanner panel with cable TV provides a highly controlled test environment for alternate promotional messages.

A major weakness of scanner data is found in its lack of representativeness. Only retailers equipped with scanners are included in the research. Entire retail categories, such as food warehouses and mass merchandisers, may be excluded. Likewise, the availability of scanners may be lacking in certain geographic areas.

The quality of scanner data is only as good as the scanning process itself and may be limited by several factors. All products may not be scanned. For example, a clerk may use the register to ring up a heavy item to avoid lifting it. If an item does not scan on the first try, the clerk may key in the price and ignore the bar code. Sometimes a consumer purchases many flavors of the same item, but the clerk scans only one package and then rings in the number of purchases. Thus, the transaction is recorded inaccurately.

With respect to scanner panels, the available technology permits the monitoring of only one TV set per household. Hence, there is a built-in bias if the household has a second or third TV set because the viewing of these additional sets is not considered. Also, the system provides information on TV sets in use rather than actual viewing behavior. Thus, the set may be turned on but the people may not be really paying any attention to it. While scanner data provide behavioral and sales information, they do not provide information on underlying attitudes, preferences, and reasons for specific choices.

SYNDICATED DATA FROM INSTITUTIONS

We have already discussed syndicated data collected from consumers and households. Parallel electronic and manual systems are also used to collect institutional and industrial data. As Figure 5.6 shows, syndicated data are available for retailers and wholesalers as well as industrial firms.

Retailer and Wholesaler Audits

Collecting product movement data for wholesalers and retailers is referred to as an audit. These periodic audits may be a physical count of the inventory, or they may be managed through a link to the scanning process.

A physical **audit** is a formal examination and verification of product movement carried out by examining physical records or analyzing inventory. These audits track inventory flow, current inventory levels, and the impact of both promotional and pricing programs on inventory levels.

A major provider of such services is Audits and Surveys Worldwide (ASW) (*www.surveys.com*). ASW's National Retail Census is a comprehensive source of information on the number and kind of stores in the U.S. selling various product categories and specific brands. This census provides manufacturers with measures of penetration of their brands and that of their competitors in every type of retail outlet that carries their

audit
The collection of product movement data for wholesalers and retailers. These periodic audits may be a physical count of inventory, or they may be managed through a link to the scanning process.

FIGURE 5.6
Classification of Syndicated Services: Institutions

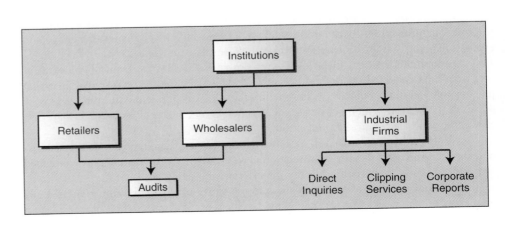

product category. The National Retail Census is based on a national probability sample of 35,000 outlets of all kinds in more than 800 geographic areas throughout the country. Data are gathered through on-site, personal store visits. For example, imagine that Colgate Palmolive is contemplating introducing a new toothpaste brand. A retail audit can help determine the size of the total market and distribution of sales by type of outlet and by different regions.

Wholesale audit services, the counterpart of retail audits, monitor warehouse withdrawals. Participating operators, including supermarket chains, wholesalers, and frozen-food warehouses, typically account for over 80 percent of the volume in the area.

USES OF AUDIT DATA Standardized as well as customized reports are available to help subscribers manage their brands. These reports provide information that can be used to (1) determine market size and share for both categories and brands by type of outlet, region, or city; (2) assess competitive activity; (3) identify distribution problems including shelf space allocation and inventory issues; (4) develop sales potentials and forecasts; and (5) develop and monitor promotional allocations based on sales volume. Scanners are now used to collect data that crosses the wholesale, retail, and customer levels. The information they offer has had a profound impact on the marketing process.

EXAMPLE

AUDITS & SURVEYS WORLDWIDE'S AUDIT REVEALS POTENTIAL FOR WORLDWIDE EXPANSION

Audits & Surveys Worldwide's National Retail Census recently revealed that 13 percent of all U.S. retail establishments are automotive related, compared to only 4.5 percent elsewhere in the world. Despite the relative prominence of automotive retailers in the United States (13 percent versus 4.5 percent), the sector now has 29 percent fewer outlets in the United States than it did in 1970. This indicates that the U.S. market is becoming saturated and automotive stores such as Pep Boys should look overseas for continued expansion. Retailers such as Pep Boys can make use of the Audits & Surveys Worldwide's National Retail Census to plot their expansion strategies on a global basis.[7]

ADVANTAGES AND DISADVANTAGES OF AUDIT DATA Audits provide relatively accurate information on the movement of many products at the wholesale and retail levels. Furthermore, this information can be broken down by a number of important variables, such as brand, type of outlet, and size of market.

However, a major disadvantage of physical audits is the limited retail coverage and delay associated with compiling and reporting inventory data. Typically, there is a two-month gap between the completion of the audit cycle and the publication of reports. Another disadvantage of physical audits is that, unlike scanner data, audit data cannot be linked to consumer characteristics. In fact, there may even be a problem in relating audit data to advertising expenditures and other marketing efforts.

Industrial Research Services

industry services
Secondary data derived from industrial sources and intended for industrial use.

Industry services provide syndicated data about industrial firms, businesses, and other institutions. Financial, operating, and employment data are also collected by these syndicated research services for almost every North American Industry Classification System (NAICS) industrial category. These data are collected by making direct inquiries; from clipping services that monitor newspapers, the trade press, or broadcasts; and from corporate reports. The range and sources of syndicated data available for industrial goods firms are more limited than those available to consumer goods firms. Services available include those provided by Dun and Bradstreet (D&B®).

The D&B® International Business Locator *(www.dnb.com)* provides you one-click access to over 28 million public/private companies in over 200 countries. After locating a business, the Locator will provide key business data including full address information, NAIC/line of business details, business size (sales, net worth, employees), names of key principals and identification of this location's headquarters, domestic parent company, and/or global parent company.

These data are very useful in developing business-to-business sales plans and direct marketing lists, estimating market potential and share within industries, and developing overall market strategies. Business statistics related to annual sales, geographic coverage, supplier relationships, and distribution channels are just a few of the categories of information available to business-to-business market planners. These secondary sources also serve as a source for sampling frames when conducting business-to-business research.

USES OF INDUSTRIAL RESEARCH SERVICES Information provided by industrial services is useful for sales management decisions, including identifying prospects, defining territories, setting quotas, and measuring market potential by geographic areas. It can also aid in advertising decisions such as targeting prospects, allocating advertising budgets, selecting media, and measuring advertising effectiveness. In addition, this kind of information is useful for segmenting the market and designing custom products and services for segments in the target markets.

ADVANTAGES AND DISADVANTAGES OF INDUSTRIAL RESEARCH SERVICES Published industrial information provides a valuable first step in business-to-business marketing. However, the information is typically limited to publicly traded firms, and dissemination of that data is typically controlled by the reporting firm itself. A researcher has to be wary of the completeness of reported data, as well as the bias introduced by this form of respondent self-report. These data are limited in the nature, content, quantity, and quality of information.

COMBINING INFORMATION FROM A VARIETY OF SOURCES: SINGLE-SOURCE DATA

single-source data
An effort to combine data from different sources by gathering integrated information on household and marketing variables applicable to the same set of respondents.

As we discussed in Chapter 4, combining data from different sources can enhance the value of secondary data. This practice in syndicated services is referred to as single-source research. Single-source research tracks the full marketing process from initial advertising communication through product purchase. The process links a person's demographic and psychographic information with TV, reading, and shopping habits. A combination of surveys, diaries, and electronic scanners is used to integrate such information. Manufacturer pricing and promotional activities are overlaid on this consumer data as well. Thus, **single-source data** provides integrated information on household variables, including media consumption and purchases, and marketing variables, such as product sales, price, advertising, promotion, and in-store marketing effort. The following example illustrates Campbell Soup Company's application of single-source data.

EXAMPLE

SOAPS SHED A "GUIDING LIGHT" ON V8 CONSUMPTION

The Campbell Soup Company used single-source data to restructure its advertising for V8 juice. It found that demographically similar TV audiences consume vastly different amounts of V8 juice. For example, the dominant segment of viewers of *General Hospital* had the same demographic profile as heavy V8 users (female, 25 to 54 years of age). However, single-source data indicated that V8 consumption among this audience was below average. On the other hand, the *Guiding Light* audience had above-average consumption. Based on these data, Campbell switched its TV advertising from *General Hospital* to *Guiding Light*. Thus, using such information from single-source data, Campbell Soup was able to supplement the known demographics of consumers with viewership patterns to improve its advertising effectiveness in reaching the users and potential users of V8 juice.[8]

SUMMARY ILLUSTRATION USING THE OPENING VIGNETTE

Syndicated research firms specialize in designing research systems that collect data of commercial interest to multiple users. This was seen in the opening vignette, where the results of the NPD survey were used by multiple firms in the same industry: Haggar, Marshall Field's, and Levi Strauss.

Syndicated sources can be classified based on the unit of measurement (households/consumers or institutions). Syndicated data from households may be obtained via surveys, diary panels, or electronic scanner systems. Although a survey was used in the opening vignette, data on purchases of business casual clothing can also be collected using diary panels and electronic scanners (or similar systems) installed in department stores. When institutions are the unit of measurement, the data may be obtained from retailers, wholesalers, or industrial firms. For example, data obtained from consumers on business casual clothing could be complemented by data obtained from marketers of these products, such as Haggar, Marshall Field's, and Levi Strauss. It is desirable to combine information obtained from different secondary sources to get a more complete picture of the marketplace. Thus, one could combine data on casual clothing obtained from consumers with data from retailers (Macy's, Sears, etc.) and manufacturers (Haggar and Levi Strauss) to get a better understanding of the casual clothing market.

MARKETING RESEARCH AND TQM

Syndicated data are directly connected to the total quality management concept. Syndicated data can aid a firm in continuous improvement and can help a firm put quality first. Firms will realize increased profits and reduced costs, and can continually make improvements in the quality of the products and services they offer consumers.

FOCUS ON
ELRICK & LAVIDGE

Elrick & Lavidge specializes in custom marketing research involving primary data collection. One of E&L's research directors noted that E&L rarely uses syndicated data sources such as diary panels or electronic scanner services. Sometimes a client that has already contracted with the syndicator of such data will provide the data to be incorporated in the results of an E&L study. However, E&L often purchases external demographic and psychographic data supplied by syndicated services.

As an example, one of E&L's recent projects used internal secondary data combined with demographic and psychographic syndicated data. The client, a service company, wanted to gain a better understanding of its customers. The client provided E&L with an internally generated list of recent users of its services, compiled from a number of its facilities. E&L created a database from this list and used the addresses on the list to overlay external secondary data, in the form of household demographic and psychographic information, onto each name on the list. A syndicated geo-coding product provided this overlay of demographic and psychographic information. The specific product used was Microvision 50 by Claritas (*claritas.com*). In geo-coding, the country is divided into geographic units by the sub–zip code level (nine-digit level such as 30332-0520). Geo-coding algorithm assigns an average set of characteristics common to all households in that unit. It is possible to analyze all of the households in the United States, and through "clustering" of demographic and psychographic characteristics many of these households across the country can be placed into common groupings. These groupings are given names that reflect the households' dominant demographic and psychographic characteristics, such as "Great Beginnings," which defines young, affluent people who are just starting their careers; "Trying Metro Times," which refers to less affluent families living in cities; and "White Picket Fences," which includes suburban families.

By applying the geo-coding to the client's customer list, E&L was able to describe the list in terms of 50 Microvision groupings and to analyze the customer list for dominant psychographic or demographic characteristics. This resulted in information on the percentage of the client's customers who were represented by each Microvision cluster (e.g., Great Beginnings, Trying Metro Times, and White Picket Fences). Using this analysis, the client was able to better understand the type of customer that was currently attracted to its facilities. With the aid of the geo-coded database of the entire country, the client was able to better define other cities (and locations within those cities) where a new facility would have the greatest probability of attracting the core user segments.

Syndicated services offer psychographic and lifestyle data that can help marketing researchers determine what constitutes quality to different market segments. These marketing segments may define quality differently based on what they value. Similarly, information from diary purchase panels and scanner panels can be very helpful in determining the differences between buyers of high-quality and low-quality brands and in identifying the characteristics of the heavy users of quality brands. Single source data can provide information on the media consumption habits of quality conscious consumers, enabling management to effectively target them.

EXAMPLE

AT HOME WITH QUALITY VIA HOMESCAN

The Kellogg Company uses AC Nielsen's Homescan scanner panel, discussed earlier in this chapter, to answer a variety of questions:

- In what areas of the country are Kellogg's cereals purchased most frequently?
- What promotions were offered at the time of purchase?
- What is the number and size of the cereal boxes the typical consumer purchases?
- What are the demographic characteristics of the heavy cereal users?

Kellogg uses this information to better target its products to consumers. The information is also used to design sales promotions, such as coupons and point-of-sale displays, to better meet the needs of consumers. For example, larger families of Hispanic origin in California tend to be heavy users of Kellogg's Corn Flakes. Kellogg has attempted to cultivate and retain the patronage of these users by directing coupons and promotional offers to them. Thus, the quality of Kellogg's marketing is greatly increased by achieving a greater focus on consumer needs through Homescan.[9]

INTERNATIONAL MARKETING RESEARCH

U.S. syndicated research firms are an important source of information on overseas consumer and industrial markets. For companies considering expansion internationally, or managing existing international ventures, one of the first steps toward understanding and monitoring these markets may be through syndicated sources. The need for relatively inexpensive, comprehensive data related to international markets, consumer and social trends, as well as existing market structures, creates a built-in demand for international syndicated services. Many of the same major syndicated firms operating in the United States have invested heavily in creating data collection systems to support their internationally operating clients. Gallup International is just one of the U.S. syndicated firms that have expanded their services to include international research.

EXAMPLE

EUROCONSUMERS GO FOR SPENDING SPLASH

The Gallup organization, which specializes in survey research obtaining both lifestyle and psychographic data, recently conducted interviews with over 22,500 adults across the European Community. Their results point to an exploding consumer durable market, particularly for convenience items, such as remote control TVs, microwave ovens, VCRs, and cellular phones. The educational level and the standard of living among this consumer group are generally improving. Europeans are also displaying higher levels of discretionary purchasing demonstrated in growing demand for travel packages that continued to be strong through the year 2000, despite the weakness in the Euro. In the personal care market, the number of European women using perfume is declining, offset by growing demand for deodorants.

> This type of syndicated data is useful to marketers such as Motorola, GE, AT&T, and RCA, which are looking to develop European markets. For example, when renting an apartment in Germany, the renter must install all the major appliances and lighting fixtures. GE has developed value packages offering significant savings on appliances and lighting fixtures that are carefully targeted at apartment renters.[10]

Like the Gallup organization, AC Nielsen has made huge investments in European markets over the past 30-plus years, introducing scanner and tracking services at the retail level. With international operations much larger than that of the United States, about 70 percent of Nielsen's business is outside the United States. Fifty percent of that overseas business is in Europe.

TECHNOLOGY AND MARKETING RESEARCH

As technology develops, syndicated firms will establish newer types of panels using sophisticated data collection methods. One distinct possibility in the near future is panels based on two-way TV, and interactive TV and video services. In fact, such technology has been developed and is being refined and tested.

As early as 1995, Verizon Communications conducted two market trials of interactive video services: Stargazer video-on-demand system in northern Virginia and Toms River, New Jersey. Marketers that participated in the first phase of the Stargazer test included Lands' End, Nordstrom, JCPenney, Nissan Motor Cars USA, and Visa International. Verizon's Video Services spokesman Mr. Smith told marketing researchers to be prepared because interactive TV will be here much sooner than people expect. "The leaders will establish themselves very fast," he said. "The rest will have trouble ever catching up."[11]

In addition, technology used in existing panels, such as scanner and media panels, is being continuously refined. In 1987, Nielsen Media Research introduced the original "peoplemeter." This system keeps track of which family member is watching television at a given time. It will also keep a record of which program is being watched. The problem with the original system is that viewers must enter the information manually via a keypad whenever they begin and finish watching television. Many viewers do not always log in or log out because the system can become very tedious. Others, especially children, simply forget to do it.

To deal with this problem, both Nielsen and their main competitor, Arbitron, have developed new "passive peoplemeters." All that is required of viewers under this system is to turn their TV set on or off. Using "computer image recognition" technology, which is a more advanced version of the scanner technology used in supermarkets, the "passive peoplemeter" scans the room to identify all preprogrammed viewers. The new system also detects whether or not the viewers are looking at the TV set or are looking at something else in the room.

The new passive systems allow researchers to monitor families at a much cheaper rate than possible with the previous technology. Using the older meters, it costs in the thousands of dollars to monitor a single family. The cost is expected to decrease to somewhere in the hundreds. With this dramatic reduction in the average cost per household, researchers are able to increase the size of the samples, and hence the accuracy of the data, while keeping overall costs at a constant level.[12]

ETHICS IN MARKETING RESEARCH

Ethical issues in formulating a research design, discussed in Chapter 3, are also relevant in collecting syndicated data. Respondents' rights, particularly their privacy, are another salient issue. Obtaining data from the respondents without their full knowledge or consent is an invasion of privacy. Consider, for example, the frequent shopper cards that supermarkets issue. These cards provide a variety of services, such as check cashing, special notification of sales, and cash discounts or rebates, at no apparent cost to the cardholders. While this may sound like a good deal, many cardholders are unaware of the hidden costs involved.

While applying for a card, each shopper provides data on demographic and shopping-related variables and is assigned a UPC code. The shopper's UPC code is scanned first, before the grocery purchases are scanned. Thus, a shopper's purchases are linked to that shopper's demographic and shopping-related data collected at the time of application for the card. This information results in a database that contains rich information on shoppers, including a complete demographic profile, when they shop, how much they spend, how they pay for purchases, and what products they buy. As discussed in Chapter 4, this database can be used to target consumers and formulate effective marketing strategies. Often, these data are sold to syndicated firms, who in turn sell them to multiple clients, resulting in much wider dissemination and use. However, most consumers are unaware that the supermarket has all this information about them simply because they are cardholders.

The supermarkets and other firms engaging in this practice of collecting data without the respondent's knowledge or consent are violating the ethical principle of informed consent. According to this principle, researchers have the ethical responsibility to avoid both uninformed and misinformed participation by respondents in marketing research projects. On a positive note, syndicate firms are playing a significant role in researching ethical issues and sensitizing marketing firms, the marketing research industry, and the general public about these concerns.

EXAMPLE

REACHING KIDS BUT ALIENATING ADULTS: ETHICAL REPERCUSSIONS

According to a recent survey by RoperASW, a syndicated marketing research firm, the general public is skeptical about advertising aimed at kids. Eight in ten adults agree that business marketing and advertising exploit children by convincing them to buy things that are bad for them or that they don't need.

But adults don't necessarily object to all advertising, only to advertising they perceive as harmful to kids. Eight in ten adults say it is "all right" to advertise products such as toys, cereal, and clothing on television during children's programming. But adults are more likely to object to commercials that "sell" sex and poor nutrition with products such as PG-13 movies and candy bars. Thus, marketers who engage in such practices in an attempt to reach kids run the risk of alienating adults. Several syndicated firms, such as RoperASW, are playing a significant role in addressing ethical issues in marketing research by sensitizing researchers, clients, and the general public to such issues.[13]

INTERNET APPLICATIONS

For syndicated sources of information, one can visit the home pages of the various market research companies and providers of syndicated information. The AC Nielsen home page *(www.acnielsen.com)* is a very good source. Further, at the Dunn and Bradstreet home page *(www.dnb.com)*, business services and syndicated information are available, such as D&B Business Reference CD-ROMs and Directories.

Information Resources (IRI) is the largest provider of UPC scanner-based solutions to the U.S. consumer packaged goods (CPG) industry. IRI obtains data from point-of-sale scanners, integrates them with other proprietary data, and stores them in massive data warehouses. The data are then used to provide CPG manufacturers, brokers, retailers, and wholesalers with a variety of services critical to their sales, marketing, and logistics operations. An example of the type of information available from IRI follows.

EXAMPLE

FOOD, FOOD, ANYWHERE

Information Resources' *(www.infores.com) Times & Trends,* available at the company's Web site, highlights the consumer packaged goods (CPG) industry's year-end review. *Times & Trends* is a valuable report for busy executives who need a summary insight into today's economic and general business conditions but who also need a detailed insight into CPG trends and retail marketing conditions.

For example, the 1999 year-end review stated that food consumption for 1999 reached a peak for the decade, increasing 3.7 percent over 1998, peaking at a 9.3 percent increase the final quarter of 1999. Food-away-from-home recorded a hot 12.4 percent gain, and food-at-home spending recorded a buoyant 7.6 percent increase in the final quarter of 1999. Such information is useful not only for restaurants such as McDonald's that emphasize food-away-from-home but also for supermarkets such as Kroger that make their marketing plans by taking into account food-at-home spending.

SUMMARY

Syndicated research firms specialize in designing research systems that collect data of commercial interest to multiple users. Collecting data to serve a known commercial purpose is one of the primary differentiators when comparing syndicated services to other types of secondary data (discussed in Chapter 4). Syndicated data are timely and cost effective. Given the need for an impartial monitor of marketwide trends, as well as consumer reactions or behaviors, syndicated researchers provide a unique and valuable service.

Syndicated sources can be classified based on the unit of measurement (households/consumers or institutions). Syndicated data from households may be obtained via surveys, diary panels, or electronic scanner systems. When institutions are the unit of measurement, the data may be obtained from retailers, wholesalers, or industrial firms. It is desirable to combine information from different sources.

Syndicated services offer psychographic and lifestyle data that can help TQM companies determine what constitutes quality to different market segments. U.S. syndicated research firms are an important source of information on overseas consumer and industrial markets. As technology develops, syndicated firms will establish newer types of panels that collect data from panel members using sophisticated methods. One distinct possibility in the near future is panels based on two-way TV and interactive TV and video services. A major ethical issue in collecting syndicated data is the invasion of privacy of the respondents by obtaining data without their full knowledge or consent. The Internet serves as an important source of information about syndicated firms and their services.

KEY TERMS AND CONCEPTS

Syndicated sources, 139
Surveys, 140
Periodic surveys, 141
Panel surveys, 141
Shared surveys, 143
Psychographics, 144

Lifestyles, 144
Diary purchase
    panels, 147
Diary media panels, 148
Scanner data, 149
Volume-tracking data, 149

Scanner diary panels, 150
Scanner diary panels with
    cable TV, 151
Audit, 152
Industry services, 154
Single-source data, 154

ACRONYMS

The salient characteristics of syndicated data may be described by the acronym SYNDICATED:

S urveys
Y ields data of known commercial value
N umber of clients use the data
D iary panels
I ndustrial services
C ost is low
A udits
T imely and current
E lectronic scanner services
D ata combined from different sources: single-source data

EXERCISES

1. What are the differences between syndicated data and data available from other secondary sources?
2. List and describe the various syndicated sources of secondary data.
3. What is the nature of information collected by surveys?
4. How can surveys be classified?
5. Explain what a diary panel is. What is the difference between diary purchase panels and diary media panels?
6. What are the relative advantages of diary panels over surveys?
7. What kinds of data can be gathered through electronic scanner services?
8. Describe the uses of scanner data.
9. What is an audit? Discuss the uses, advantages, and disadvantages of audits.

10. Describe the information provided by industrial services.

11. Why is it desirable to use multiple sources of secondary data?

12. Explain what is meant by single-source data.

PROBLEM

1. Select an industry of your choice. Contact one of the syndicated firms to obtain industry sales and the sales of the major firms in that industry for the past year. Estimate the market shares of each major firm. From a published source, obtain information on the market shares of these same firms. Do the two estimates agree?

INTERNET AND COMPUTER EXERCISES

1. Visit *www.npd.com* and write a description of the panel maintained by NPD.

2. Visit *www.acnielsen.com* and write a report about the various services offered by AC Nielsen.

3. Visit *www.infores.com* and write a report about the products and services offered by Information Resources, Inc.

4. Visit *www.gallup.com* and write a report about the syndicated services offered by the Gallup Organization.

5. Visit *www.arbitron.com* and write a report about the syndicated services offered by Arbitron.

ACTIVITIES

ROLE PLAYING

1. You are the group product manager for Procter & Gamble in charge of laundry detergents. How would you make use of information available from a store audit? Ask another student to play the role of vice president of marketing. Explain to your boss the value of store audit information related to laundry detergents.

FIELD WORK

1. Make a trip to your local supermarket. Ask the store manager to explain how the scanner data collected at checkout counters are processed. Write a report explaining how you would use the scanner data for a marketing research project assessing the market share for different brands of peanut butter. Please be specific.

GROUP DISCUSSION

1. Discuss how the Nielsen TV ratings can affect the price that advertisers pay for a commercial broadcast during a particular time.

NOTES

1. Jennifer Boyde, "Casual Day Goes Every Day," *Business Journal Serving Charlotte and the Metropolitan Area*, 15(13) (June 30, 2000): 29; *news.cnet.com*, "Casual Wear: Dressing for Success or for Stress?" (June 10, 2000); Elisa Biecher, Paul N. Keaton, and A. William Pollman, "Casual Dress at Work," *SAM Advanced*

Management Journal, 64(1) (Winter 1999): 17–20; and Cyndee Miller, "A Casual Affair: Clothesmakers respond to dress-down trend with new lines, consumer education programs," *Marketing News,* 29(6) (March 13, 1995): 1–2.

2. Stephanie Thompson, "Oscar Mayer Hams It Up for New Lunch Meat Line," *Advertising Age,* 71(32) (July 31, 2000): 14; Richard Merli, "Top Five Meatless Brands See Sales Rise by 53.4%," *Frozen Food Age,* 47(11) (June 1999): 24; and "1995 Edison Best New Products Awards Winners," *Marketing News,* 30(10) (May 6, 1996): E4–E11.

3. *Starch Readership Report: Scope, Method, and Use.* Mamaroneck, NY: Starch INRA Hooper, undated; and *www.roper.com.*

4. Arrol Gellner, "Bias Tints Debates Over Color," *San Francisco Chronicle* (March 22, 2000): Home 1; Joan H. Walker, "Forecasters See 'Boom Time' 1998 Colors," *Modern Paint & Coatings,* 88(1) (January 1998): 64; and "Research Probes How Consumers Rely on Color for Their Purchases," *Marketing News,* 29(18) (August 28, 1995): 1, 39.

5. Rick Wartzman, "Nielson Ratings Spark a Battle Over Just Who Speaks Spanish," *Wall Street Journal* (February 25, 2000): B1; Megan Larson, "Nielsen Does Full Cable Book," *Mediaweek,* 9(15) (April 12, 1999): 16; Steve McClellan, "Nielsen's Digital Display," *Broadcasting & Cable,* 127(17) (April 21, 1997): 37–38.

6. George Zouvelos, "Consumers Speak, Manufacturers Listen," *Business Wire* (January 31, 2001), online. Lexis-Nexis Academic Universe 5 February 2001.

7. Joanna Lowenstein, "The Shift to Specialty Distribution," *Folio: The Magazine for Magazine Management,* 28(7) (June 1999): 65–72; "U.S. Retail Census Finds Fewer Retail Outlets, Bigger Stores," *Survey Monitor, Marketing Research,* X(10) (December 1996): 37–38.

8. Stephanie Thompson, "Diet V8 Splash Carves Niche in Juice Category for Adults," *Advertising Age,* 71(13) (March 27, 2000): 24; Judann Pollack, "V8, Tropicana Pump Spending for Juices," *Advertising Age,* 68(33) (August 18, 1997): 30; and Joanne Lipman, "Single-Source Ad Research Heralds Detailed Look at Household Habits," *Wall Street Journal* (February 16, 1988): 39.

9. *www.acnielsen.com.*

10. David Smith, "A Deficit of Consumer Loyalty," *Management Today* (July 1996): 22; and "Europeans More Active as Consumers," *Marketing News* (October 6, 1991).

11. Tim Greene, "Bell Atlantic Expands Beyond Local Data Market," *Network World,* 17(25) (June 19, 2000): 48; "Bell Atlantic TV, Mail Push Backs DirecTV," *Advertising Age,* 70(13) (March 29, 1999): 31; Richard Tedesco, "Bell Atlantic's ITV Scorecard," *Broadcasting & Cable,* 126(9) (February 26, 1996): 52; and Williamson, Debra Aho, "Two-Way, Interactive TV Panels," *Advertising Age* (May 1, 1995): 26.

12. Katy Bachman, "U.S. Advertisers Following Arbitron," *Mediaweek,* 9(7) (February 15, 1999): 16; Donna Petrozzello, "Arbitron Moves to Offer Audio Measuring," *Broadcasting & Cable,* 126(36) (August 26, 1996): 38; and Steve McClellan, "New Nielsen System Is Turning Heads," *Broadcasting* (May 18, 1992): 8.

13. Rob Gray, "Perils of Sending Brands to School," *Marketing* (April 22, 1999): 30–31; and Kevin Heubusch, "Is It OK to Sell to Kids?", *American Demographics,* 19(1) (January 1997): 55.

6

EXPLORATORY RESEARCH DESIGN: QUALITATIVE RESEARCH

QUALITATIVE RESEARCH PROVIDES RICH INSIGHTS INTO THE UNDERLYING NEEDS, MOTIVES, BELIEFS, PREFERENCES, AND BEHAVIORS OF CONSUMERS AND CUSTOMERS.

Anita Watkins, Vice President-Qualitative Research, Elrick & Lavidge.
Anita Watkins is responsible for qualitative research. She joined E&L in 1996. She and her staff moderate and analyze hundreds of focus groups and in-depth interviews each year.

Opening Questions

1. How is qualitative research different from quantitative research in terms of the objectives, sampling, data collection, data analysis, and outcomes?

2. What are the various forms of qualitative research, including direct and indirect procedures?

3. How are focus groups conducted? What are their applications? Their advantages and disadvantages?

4. In what way are depth interviews different from focus groups? What are their applications? Their advantages and disadvantages?

5. What is meant by *projective techniques*? What are their uses?

6. What role does qualitative research play in total quality management?

7. How is conducting qualitative research in an international setting different than doing this research domestically?

8. How can technology facilitate qualitative research?

9. What ethical issues are involved in conducting qualitative research?

10. How can the Internet be used to conduct qualitative research?

GILLETTE SUPPORTS EQUAL RIGHTS FOR WOMEN: A CLOSE SHAVE

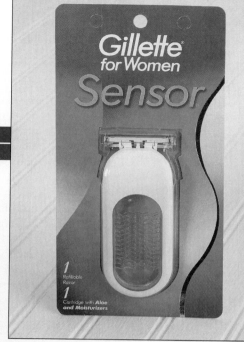

In October 2000, Gillette announced the introduction of a new women's razor that would contain special features found in the popular Mach3 men's razor. The name of the razor, Venus, was disclosed at a New York press conference and became available to consumers in April 2001. While Gillette's sales have steadily declined over the past few years, the company is confident that their new triple-blade women's razor ("with a funky handle") will help to recover sales growth and customers. The sales from Gillette's women's products are expected to increase to a whopping $1 billion dollars by the year 2003. This new product idea was inspired by the earlier successful introduction of Sensor for Women.

How was Sensor for Women developed? After being given the job of redesigning Gillette's feminine razor, Jill Shurtleff relied heavily on qualitative research. She used one-on-one or individual depth interviews with 30 women chosen on the basis of her judgment from different segments of the potential target market. Individual depth interviews were selected over focus groups because shaving is a rather personal experience for women. This technique allows for extensive probing of the respondent's feelings in a more personal setting, and thus provided deeper insights into the shaving experience.

The depth interviews showed that women shave very differently from men. The American woman shaves much more surface area than a man but only shaves two or three times a week. She changes the blade about once a month. While men usually shave in front of a well-lit mirror, women generally prefer to shave in the shower, which is often dimly lit, and must shave areas that they can't see well, such as underarms or backs of legs. The research indicated that shaving was a personal experience for women that evoked feelings of anticipation and acceptance.

This research also showed that most women did not like so-called women's razors and opted instead for men's razors or cheap disposables. Women preferred razors with a firm grip and those that gave a clean, smooth shave. Typically, men's razors have a much sharper blade than women's. While the chances of a woman nicking herself greatly increase with the use of a man's razor, the shaving quality was better than traditional women's razors. These findings were substantiated in a survey of women using in-home personal interviews. A representative sample of 500 women was selected for this purpose.

With information on the current state of affairs under her belt, Shurtleff began her product design. She first tossed out the T-shaped design used for men's razors that gives men the sensitive control they need but puts women at risk due to shifting blade angles. Shurtleff settled on a wafer-like design for the handle, white with an aqua insert in the center. The colors were different from the typical pink for women's razors and evoked a clean, watery feeling. The aqua insert was clear plastic and had wavy ridges to help prevent slippage. The razor head was nearly the same as that used by the Sensor (men's razor) and was angled at 46 degrees, which was a compromise between the ideal underarm and leg shaving angles.

The finishing touch was the name. Lady Sensor was declined because it seemed almost condescending and many women didn't like it. The company settled on the name Sensor for Women because it seemed straightforward, honest, and elicited the most favorable response in a word association test examining several possible names.

Qualitative research helped to develop a truly successful product. The Sensor for Women quickly and easily displaced the market leader, Personal Touch, and garnered 60 percent of the market share.[1]

OVERVIEW

In Chapter 3, we classified marketing research as exploratory or conclusive. Secondary data analysis, discussed in Chapters 4 and 5, is one aspect of exploratory research. The other major exploratory technique, qualitative research, is the subject of this chapter. Figure 6.1 briefly explains the focus of the chapter, the relationship of this chapter to the previous ones, and the steps of the marketing research process on which this chapter concentrates. As can be seen from this figure, qualitative research is part of the marketing research process presented in Chapter 1, is one of the tasks involved in problem definition and developing an approach covered in Chapter 2, and is one of the techniques of exploratory research design discussed in Chapter 3.

Often, qualitative research follows a review of internal and external sources of secondary data. It is typically used to define the problem more precisely, formulate hypotheses, or identify or clarify key variables to be investigated in the quantitative phase. Our opening vignette illustrated these concepts. The findings of depth interviews regarding how women shaved were further investigated by conducting an in-home personal survey (quantitative research).

Unlike secondary data, which are generated for purposes other than the specific marketing research problem at hand, qualitative research generates primary data. The definition of the marketing research problem and the approach guide qualitative data collection.

In this chapter, we discuss the differences between qualitative and quantitative research and the role of each in the marketing research project. We present a classification of qualitative research techniques and provide an overview of the major qualitative techniques used in the industry. They include focus groups, depth interviews with individu-

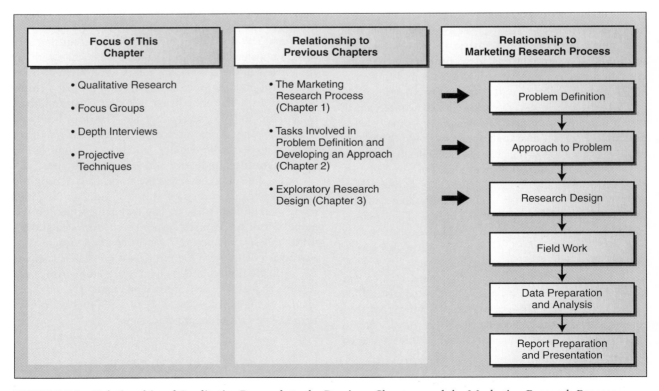

FIGURE 6.1   Relationship of Qualitative Research to the Previous Chapters and the Marketing Research Process

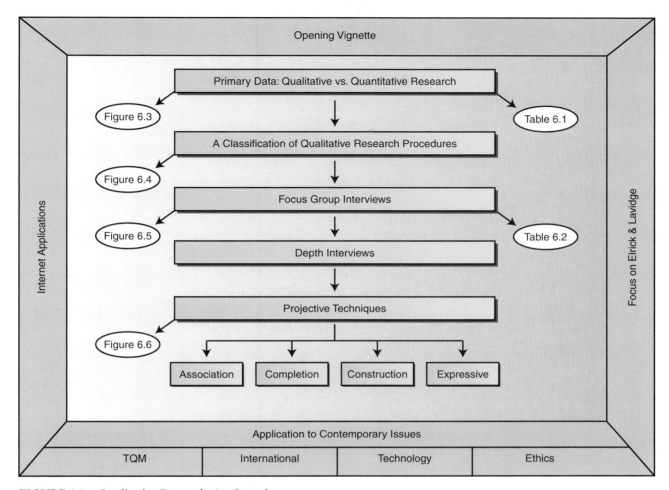

FIGURE 6.2   Qualitative Research: An Overview

als, and projective techniques. In keeping with the pervasive emphasis of this book, we discuss the application of qualitative research to total quality management (TQM) and international marketing research, as well as the impact of technology, ethics, and the use of the Internet. Figure 6.2 gives an overview of the topics discussed in this chapter and how they flow from one to the next.

PRIMARY DATA: QUALITATIVE VERSUS QUANTITATIVE RESEARCH

As mentioned before, even though qualitative research is exploratory in nature, it results in primary data because the research is carried out for the specific purpose of addressing the problem at hand. Therefore, both qualitative and quantitative research may generate primary data, as shown in Figure 6.3. The distinction between qualitative and quantitative research closely parallels the distinction between exploratory and conclusive research discussed in Chapter 3. The differences between the two research methodologies are summarized in Table 6.1.

Qualitative research provides insights and understanding of the problem setting. It explores the problem with few preconceived notions about the outcome of that explo-

qualitative research
An unstructured, exploratory research methodology based on small samples, which provides insights and understanding of the problem setting.

FIGURE 6.3

A Classification of
Marketing Research Data

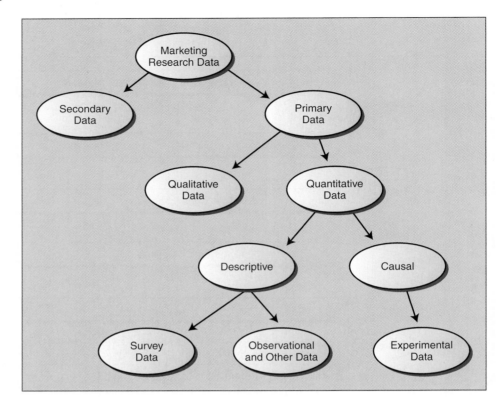

ration. In addition to defining the problem and developing an approach, qualitative research is also appropriate when facing a situation of uncertainty, such as when conclusive results differ from expectations. It can provide insight before or after the fact. In the opening vignette, Gillette used qualitative research at the beginning of the project to better understand the shaving needs of women. Qualitative research is based on small, nonrepresentative samples, and the data are analyzed in a nonstatistical way. In the Gillette vignette, the researcher chose a sample size of 30 so as to interview women from various segments of the target market.

On the other hand, **quantitative research** seeks to quantify the data. It seeks conclusive evidence, which is based on large, representative samples and typically applies some

quantitative research
A research methodology that
seeks to quantify the data and,
typically, applies some form of
statistical analysis.

T A B L E   6 . 1   Qualitative Versus Quantitative Research

	QUALITATIVE RESEARCH	**QUANTITATIVE RESEARCH**
Objective	To gain a qualitative understanding of the underlying reasons and motivations	To quantify the data and generalize the results from the sample to the population of interest
Sample	Small number of nonrepresentative cases	Large number of representative cases
Data collection	Unstructured	Structured
Data analysis	Nonstatistical	Statistical
Outcome	Develop an initial understanding	Recommend a final course of action

form of statistical analysis. In contrast to qualitative research, the findings of quantitative research can be treated as conclusive and used to recommend a final course of action. This was seen in the opening vignette where Gillette used quantitative (survey) research to substantiate the findings of qualitative research (depth interviews).

The approach to data collection can vary along a continuum from highly structured to completely unstructured. In a highly structured approach, the researcher predetermines the wording of the questions asked and the range of responses available. Thus, the researcher assumes full understanding of the range of possible response options. A multiple-choice question is an example of a highly structured question. Typically, a formal questionnaire is used. This is in contrast to an unstructured data collection approach in which neither the questions nor the possible responses are predetermined. The respondent is encouraged to talk freely about the subject of interest. Qualitative or exploratory research lies at the unstructured end of this continuum, while quantitative research is highly structured.

Whenever a new marketing research problem is addressed, quantitative research must be preceded by appropriate qualitative research, as Gillette did. Sometimes qualitative research is undertaken to explain the findings obtained from quantitative research. However, the findings of qualitative research are misused when they are regarded as conclusive and are used to make generalizations to the population of interest. For example, if 20 of the 30 women in the depth interviews said that they preferred men's razors to women's razors, it would not be appropriate to conclude that 66.7 percent of the women in the general population have the same preference. Quantitative data should be collected using a survey, as in the opening vignette, if the sample results are to be projected to the population. It is a sound principle of marketing research to view qualitative and quantitative research as complementary rather than competitive parts of the research process.

The danger of ignoring qualitative research when the research problem is not fully understood and directly proceeding to quantitative research is illustrated by Coca-Cola's decision to change Coke to New Coke in 1985. The decision to change the formulation of the flagship soft drink brand was based on extensive quantitative taste tests, without the benefit of appropriate qualitative research. The results clearly indicated that consumers preferred the taste of the new formulation. However, when the change was made and New Coke replaced Coke, there was a strong consumer backlash. The loyal users of Coke reacted because their favorite soft drink had been tampered with. The quantitative research conducted was misguided as it was asking the wrong questions. The researchers were focusing on taste, rather than the emotional attachment consumers had forged with the brand, which was actually a more significant variable guiding brand preference and loyalty than taste.

These types of mistakes can be avoided by conducting qualitative research. Had the researchers first used qualitative techniques to explore why people purchased Coke, rather than assuming they knew why, the quantitative research conducted would have been different, leading management to a different decision. This classic marketing mistake also points out that the researcher must obtain an adequate understanding of the problem situation before formulating a research design.

A CLASSIFICATION OF QUALITATIVE RESEARCH PROCEDURES

A classification of qualitative research procedures is presented in Figure 6.4. These procedures are classified as either direct or indirect, based on whether the respondents know the true purpose of the project. A **direct approach** is not disguised. The purpose of the project is disclosed to the respondents or is otherwise obvious from the questions asked.

direct approach
One type of qualitative research in which the purposes of the project are disclosed to the respondent or are obvious given the nature of the interview.

FIGURE 6.4
A Classification of
Qualitative Research
Procedures

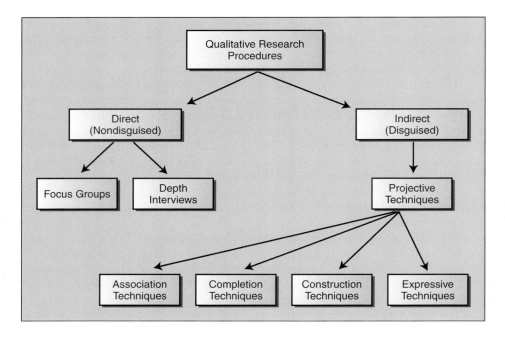

Focus groups and depth interviews are the major direct techniques. In contrast, research that takes an **indirect approach** disguises the true purpose of the project. Projective techniques are the most commonly used indirect approach. A discussion of each of these techniques follows, beginning with focus groups.

indirect approach
A type of qualitative research in which the purposes of the project are disguised from the respondents.

FOCUS GROUP INTERVIEWS

A **focus group** is an interview with a small group of respondents conducted by a trained moderator who leads the discussion in a nonstructured and natural manner. The main purpose of a focus group is to gain insights on issues of interest to the researcher by listening to a group of people from the appropriate target market. The value of the technique lies in the rich findings that can be obtained from a free-flowing group discussion.

focus group
An interview conducted by a trained moderator among a small group of respondents in an unstructured and natural manner.

Focus groups are the most important qualitative research procedure. They are so popular that many marketing research practitioners consider this technique synonymous with qualitative research. Several hundred facilities around the country now conduct focus groups several times a week. The typical focus group costs the client about $4,000. Given their importance and popularity, we describe the procedure for conducting focus groups in detail.

Conducting a Focus Group

The process of conducting a focus group, as with any research effort, involves careful planning. We will be discussing considerations related to the environment for focus groups, the selection of participants, and the moderator. We will also cover the development of a discussion guide, conducting the group interview, and the format for summarizing the results (Figure 6.5).

DESIGNING THE ENVIRONMENT Focus group sessions are typically held in facilities specially equipped to comfortably accommodate and record a group discussion. The setting is typically an informal conference room equipped with a one-way mirror and micro-

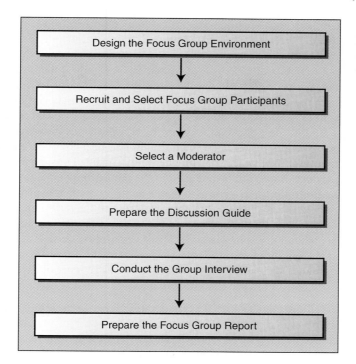

FIGURE 6.5
Procedure for Conducting a Focus Group

phones throughout the room. Behind the one-way mirror is a viewing room for management.

Most focus groups are scheduled to last one to three hours. This amount of time is needed to establish rapport with the participants and to explore, in depth, their beliefs, feelings, ideas, attitudes, and insights regarding the topics of concern. Focus groups will be either audio-recorded or videotaped to preserve the comments for analysis later. Videotaping has the advantage of recording facial expressions and body movements, but it can increase the costs significantly. Frequently, clients observe the session from an adjacent room using a one-way mirror. Video transmission technology can also allow the clients to observe the focus group session live from a remote location.

RECRUITING AND SELECTING FOCUS GROUP PARTICIPANTS The major characteristics of a focus group are summarized in Table 6.2. A focus group is generally made up of 8 to 12 members. The advantages that come from the group dynamics are often lost to groups larger than this. Minigroups of four or five respondents may sometimes be used if the session is highly exploratory and if extensive, unstructured probing is necessary.

A focus group should be homogeneous in terms of demographic and socioeconomic characteristics. This commonality among group members avoids interactions and

T A B L E 6 . 2   Characteristics of Focus Groups

Group size	8–12
Group composition	Homogeneous; respondents prescreened
Physical setting	Relaxed, informal atmosphere
Time duration	1–3 hours
Recording	Use of audiocassettes and videotapes
Moderator	Observational, interpersonal, and communication skills of the moderator are critical

conflicts on side issues. Suppose a focus group is conducted to evaluate the appeal of a line of frozen foods. It may not be desirable to include professional women and home-makers in the same group. It is clear that these two subgroups have strong differences of opinion regarding the role of women in the family. If they are included in the same group, the conversation could deviate into a discussion of the role of women in the family rather than the appeal of the frozen foods. If so, the researcher would not gain any insights relevant to the objective of assessing the basic appeal of the product.

Not only should the group be homogeneous in terms of demographic and socio-economic characteristics, there should also be a common base of experience or involvement with the object or issue being discussed. Thus, heavy users and nonusers of the product should not be included in the same group. Finally, people who have participated in multiple focus groups become familiar with the process to the point that their responses may be biased by their exposure to the technique. These so-called professional respondents should be screened out of the group. To ensure that the focus group respondents are homogeneous in terms of experience, demographic, and other relevant variables, potential respondents are prescreened. A questionnaire covering demographic characteristics, attitudes, product use, and experience of the respondent is typically developed and administered to potential respondents.

SELECTING A MODERATOR The moderator plays a key role and must be well trained. General group management skills as well as background in psychology and marketing typically suffice in most focus group situations. The moderator must be able to establish rapport with the participants, keep the discussion moving forward, and probe the respondents to elicit insights. In addition, this individual may also play a central role in the analysis and interpretation of the data. Therefore, the moderator should possess knowledge of the discussion topic and an understanding of the nature of group dynamics in order to appropriately interpret focus group responses.

Despite the importance of the moderator, there is no central body that certifies or trains focus group moderators. This lack of standardization in qualifications is one of the problems to be overcome in this type of research. This limitation can be minimized by preparing a detailed moderator discussion guide.

PREPARING THE DISCUSSION GUIDE Regardless of the skills or qualifications of the moderator, any focus group will flounder without an outline of the topics to be covered. The discussion guide should reflect the objectives of qualitative research. The objectives, in turn, should be derived from the definition of the marketing research problem, approach, and the research design adopted. A moderator's discussion guide can reduce some of the reliability problems inherent in focus groups, such as the lack of consistency in topics covered from group to group.

Most group discussions can be broken into three phases, the first being an introduction to establish rapport, relax the group, and describe the process. The bulk of the group session revolves around discussion of the research topic. In the closing phase, the moderator summarizes the comments and attempts to get a final read on the strength of the group's commitment to the statements made. This is done by having the respondents express their degree of agreement or disagreement to the statements. The questions are typically kept fairly general to allow the moderator to pursue important ideas when participants mention them. To be effective, the moderator must understand the client's business, the focus group objectives, and how the findings will be used.

CONDUCTING THE GROUP INTERVIEW During the interview, the moderator must (1) establish rapport with the group; (2) state the rules of group interaction; (3) set objectives; (4) probe the respondents and provoke intense discussion in the relevant areas; and (5) attempt to summarize the group's response to determine the extent of agreement.

The number of focus groups conducted depends on (1) the nature of the issue, (2) the number of distinct market segments, (3) the number of new ideas generated by each successive group, and (4) time and cost. Ideally, groups should be conducted until the moderator becomes familiar enough with the range of responses and can anticipate what will be said. This usually happens after three or four groups. It is recommended that a minimum of two groups be conducted.[2]

PREPARING THE FOCUS GROUP REPORT Following the focus group session, the moderator and the managers who viewed the session often engage in an instant interpretation. There is value in this free exchange in that it captures the impressions of the group and may be a good source of information for additional brainstorming. However, the danger is that the emotional power of the group's comments can cloud important points, which may be lost unless a detailed review of the focus group tapes is conducted. Hence, no conclusions should be drawn until either the moderator or an analyst reviews and analyzes the results and a complete report has been prepared.

Due to the small number of participants, frequencies and percentages are not usually reported in a focus group summary. Instead, reports typically include expressions such as "most participants thought" or "participants were divided on this issue." The report should not only present the findings based on the verbal comments but should also analyze consistent responses, new ideas, and concerns suggested by facial expressions and body language. Meticulous documentation and interpretation of the session lays the groundwork for the final step: taking action. This usually means doing additional research.

EXAMPLE

ENTER THE WIDE WORLD WITH LEVI'S WIDE LEG JEANS

Levi's conducted focus groups with young jean wearers, who revealed they often were "sizing up" in the waist to create a wide leg look. These youth were buying loose-fitting, large-size jeans that were tightened at the waist by wearing a belt. Some respondents remarked that they were doing the "stovepipe test," a quick measurement comparison done by laying the pants flat and flipping the pant leg up so that the leg opening lines up directly with the knee area.

These findings formed the basis of survey research, which confirmed a preference for wide leg jeans. Accordingly, Levi's designed the wide leg jeans, which are worn to fit at the waist and hips but have a wide leg from the knee to the ankle: a stovepipe look. "The wide leg trend represents the most important shift in jeans-wearing since the loose fit trend of the early 1990s," said John Fernandes, ad manager for Levi's Wide Leg jeans. "It's a cool, up-to-date look."

The "It's Wide Open" ad campaign, created to reach men and women 18 to 34, introduced the Levi's expanded line featuring Levi's Red Tab and Silver Tab jeans. The campaign featured three 30- and 60-second TV spots that showed target consumers that Levi's Wide Leg jeans enable them to enter "the wide world," a hypothetical zone where the impossible becomes possible. Each spot incorporated the Levi's Wide Leg jeans logo to mark the transformation from the real world to the Wide World.

Both the Wide Leg jeans and the advertising campaign were designed based on focus group and survey findings, resulting in a notable success.[3]

Advantages and Disadvantages of Focus Groups

Focus groups are popular because of their many advantages. The immediacy and the richness of the comments, which come from real customers, make this technique highly useful. The group interaction produces a wider range of information, insights, and ideas than individual interviews. The comments of one person can trigger unexpected reactions from others, leading to snowballing, with participants responding to each other's comments. The responses are generally spontaneous and candid, providing rich insights. Ideas are more likely to arise out of the blue in a group than in an individual interview, and are likely to be unique and potentially creative.[4]

However, some of the qualities that make focus groups so strong also create some of their more serious limitations. The disadvantages of focus groups should not be overlooked. The clarity and conviction with which group members often speak leads to a tendency for researchers and managers to regard findings as conclusive rather than as exploratory. Focus groups are also difficult to moderate. The quality of the results depends heavily on the skills of the moderator; unfortunately, moderators who possess all of the desirable skills are rare. Further, the unstructured nature of the responses makes coding, analysis, and interpretation difficult.

Applications of Focus Groups

Focus groups can be used in almost any situation that requires preliminary understanding or insight into the problem. The range of research topics relevant for focus group investigation include research designed to do any of the following:

1. Understand consumer perceptions, preferences, and behavior concerning a product category (how consumers select a long distance telephone company and their perceptions of AT&T, MCI/World Com, and Sprint).
2. Obtain impressions of new product concepts (consumer response to the Advantix Photo System by Kodak).
3. Generate new ideas about older products (new packaging and positioning for Cheer detergent).
4. Develop creative concepts and copy material for advertisements (a new campaign for Diet Pepsi).
5. Secure price impressions (the role of price in consumer selection of luxury cars such as Cadillac, Lexus, Mercedes, BMW, and Infinity).
6. Obtain preliminary consumer reaction to specific marketing programs (General Mills' instant coupons for Cheerios).
7. Interpret previously obtained quantitative results (the reasons for the 5.6 percent sales decline of Vanderbilt perfume).

Despite broad applicability, focus groups are only one of the personal interviewing techniques used to collect qualitative data. We will now turn our discussion to one-on-one depth interviews.

DEPTH INTERVIEWS

depth interview
An unstructured, direct, personal interview in which a single respondent is probed by a highly skilled interviewer to uncover underlying motivations, beliefs, attitudes, and feelings on a topic.

Depth interviews are loosely structured conversations with individuals drawn from the target audience. Like focus groups, depth interviews are an unstructured and direct way of obtaining information. Unlike focus groups, however, depth interviews are conducted on a one-on-one basis. These interviews typically last from 30 minutes to more than an hour. They attempt to uncover underlying motives, prejudices, or attitudes toward sensitive issues.

Conducting Depth Interviews

As with focus groups, the interviewer prepares a discussion outline to guide the interview. However, the purpose of depth interviews is to uncover hidden issues that may not be shared in a group setting. Therefore, substantial probing is done to surface underlying motives, beliefs, and attitudes. This was illustrated in the opening vignette when Gillette used depth interviews to understand the underlying motives and attitudes of women toward shaving. The depth interviews showed that women shave much more surface area than men but do this only two or three times a week, and that they often shave in a dimly lit shower and must shave areas they can't see well. Furthermore, shaving tends to be a personal experience for women that evokes feelings of anticipation and acceptance. Probing is necessary to understand these findings and feelings. Probing is done by asking such questions as "Why do you say that?" "That's interesting, can you tell me more?" or "Would you like to add anything else?" (Probing is further discussed in Chapter 14.) As the interview progresses, the type of questions asked, the probes used, and the wording of the questions depends on the answers received.

After asking the initial question, the direction of the interview is determined by the respondent's initial reply. To illustrate the technique, suppose an interviewer is conducting depth interviews with working men and women who are frequent catalog shoppers. The objective is to understand how these shoppers view the catalog shopping experience. The interview may go something like this:

Interviewer: "How do you feel about shopping through catalogs?" The interviewer then encourages the subject to talk freely about attitudes and feelings about catalog shopping.

Respondent: "I sometimes like to relax with a cup of coffee, flipping through a catalog at the end of the day. It's fun and relaxing."

Interviewer: "Why is it fun and relaxing?" If the answer is not very revealing ("It lets my mind wander?"), the interviewer may ask further probing questions, such as "Why is it fun to let your mind wander?"

Respondent: "I have to think logically all day long. When I sit down with a catalog, I can fantasize about how I will look in certain clothing or how my living room will look with a piece of furniture. And there is no pressure to do anything!"

Interviewer: "Why is it important to have no pressure to do anything?"

Respondent: "My whole day is pressure. In my job, I have to constantly react to pressure someone else is putting on me. Home is the one place where I can control the pressure, even eliminate it."

As this example indicates, probing is effective in uncovering underlying or hidden information. In this case, the respondent finds catalog shopping relaxing and a form of low-stress escape (the need to feel "no pressure to do anything").

As with focus groups, the success of depth interviews rests with the skill of the interviewer. The interviewer should (1) avoid appearing superior and put the respondent at ease; (2) be detached and objective, yet personable; (3) ask questions in an informative manner; (4) not accept brief yes or no answers; and (5) probe the respondent.

Depth interviews can be used to create an environment that fosters a more candid and comprehensive discussion of an issue than can be done in a group. The resulting data provides insight into motivation, beliefs, attitudes, and perceived consequences of behavior. Also, because depth interviews are conducted one-on-one, the comments can be traced directly to individual respondents. This may be particularly relevant in business-to-business research where a decision maker's comments can be evaluated within the context of that individual's personal and corporate background.

Advantages of Depth Interviews

Depth interviews can uncover deeper insights than focus groups. Also, depth interviews attribute the responses directly to the respondent, unlike focus groups, where it is often difficult to determine which respondent made a particular response. Depth interviews result in a free exchange of information that may not be possible in focus groups in which there is sometimes social pressure to conform. As a result of probing, it is possible to get at real issues when the topic is complex. This was illustrated in the opening vignette in which Gillette used depth interviews to understand the shaving needs of women.

Disadvantages of Depth Interviews

The disadvantages of focus groups are magnified in individual depth interviews. Skilled interviewers capable of conducting depth interviews are expensive and difficult to find. The lack of structure makes the results susceptible to the interviewer's influence, and the quality and completeness of the results depend heavily on the interviewer's skills. The data obtained are difficult to analyze and interpret; the services of skilled psychologists are typically required for this purpose. The length of the interview combined with high costs means that only a small number of depth interviews can be conducted in a project.

Despite these disadvantages, depth interviews do have applications, particularly in business-to-business marketing in which it is often difficult to assemble a group of executives for a focus group session. They are also useful in advertising research in which it is important to understand the feelings and emotions the advertisement evokes.

Applications of Depth Interviews

As with focus groups, the primary use of depth interviews is for exploratory research to gain insight and understanding. However, unlike focus groups, depth interviews are used infrequently in marketing research. Nevertheless, depth interviews can be effectively employed in special problem situations, such as those requiring:

1. Detailed probing of the respondent (automobile purchase).
2. Discussion of confidential, sensitive, or embarrassing topics (personal finances, loose dentures).
3. Situations in which strong social norms exist and the respondent may be easily swayed by the group's response (attitude of college students toward sports).
4. Detailed understanding of complicated behavior (department store shopping).
5. Interviews with professional people (industrial marketing research).
6. Interviews with competitors, who are unlikely to reveal the information in a group setting (travel agents' perceptions of airline package travel programs).
7. Situations in which the product consumption experience is sensory in nature, affecting mood states and emotions (shaving experience, as in the opening vignette).

Research with children is an example in which depth interviews may be productive. M&M/Mars used depth interviews to uncover an effective advertising approach.

EXAMPLE

MISSION FROM MARS

Most children have a very active and colorful fantasy life. Recognizing this characteristic in their target audience, M&M/Mars decided to use depth interviews to uncover childhood fantasies that might be relevant to the company's promotional efforts. Mars conducted depth interviews with schoolchildren and found that a majority of these fantasies revolve around extraterrestrial beings, wars, and exciting action. Previously, the candy manufacturer had never fully developed its extraterrestrial images, although they seemed natural, given product names like Mars and Milky Way. However, in response to the depth interview findings, they decided to introduce extraterrestrial characters from the planet Mars.

The company developed an imaginative story involving the Mars' Minister of Candy. He directed four Martians to bring back the "best candy in the universe," in order to eliminate the suffering Martians had endured for many years. Moreover, this advertising was linked to a promotional campaign that included back-to-school sweepstakes offering a grand prize of $100,000, 50 trips to Disney World, and other prizes. The four extraterrestrial heroes made appearances at malls and children's hospitals across the country. This successful multimillion-dollar campaign was shaped by the fantasies of children, uncovered by using depth interviews.[5]

This example illustrates the value of depth interviews in uncovering the hidden responses that underlie the clichés (for example, "It's good; I like it") elicited in ordinary questioning.

PROJECTIVE TECHNIQUES

Both focus groups and depth interviews are direct approaches in which the true purpose of the research is disclosed to the respondents or is otherwise obvious to them. **Projective techniques** are different from these techniques in that they attempt to disguise the purpose of the research. They are used in market research situations in which the respondent is unable or unwilling to answer a question directly. To get around this problem, the interviewer presents the respondent with a series of vague or incomplete pictures, statements, or scenarios. The underlying assumption is that when asked to respond to these prompts, the individual will be revealing personal information that is perhaps held subconsciously.

Projective techniques are unstructured, indirect forms of questioning that encourage respondents to project their underlying motivations, beliefs, attitudes, or feelings regarding the issues of concern by responding to vague and ambiguous stimulus situations. In describing these situations, respondents indirectly project their own motivations, beliefs, attitudes, or feelings into the situation. The underlying information about respondents is uncovered by analyzing their responses.

As an example, respondents may be asked to interpret the behavior of others rather than describe their own behavior. In interpreting the behavior of others, respondents indirectly project their own motivations, beliefs, attitudes, or feelings into the situation. In a landmark study, the United States Postal Service (USPS) made use of this technique to determine why most boys aged 8 to 13 years did not collect stamps as a hobby. A sample of boys was shown a picture on a screen of a 10-year-old boy fixing stamps in his album

projective technique
An unstructured and indirect form of questioning that encourages respondents to project their underlying motivations, beliefs, attitudes, or feelings regarding the issues of concern.

and asked to describe the scene and characterize the boy. Most respondents described the boy in the picture as a "sissy." Thereafter, the Postal Service undertook a successful advertising campaign directed at 8 to 13 year olds to dispel the belief that stamp collecting was for "sissies."

Projective techniques used in marketing research may be classified as association, completion, construction, and expressive techniques.

Association Techniques

association technique
A type of projective technique in which the respondent is presented with a stimulus and asked to respond with the first thing that comes to mind.

In **association techniques,** the individual is presented with a list of words or images and asked to respond with the first thing that comes to mind. Word association is the best known of these techniques. In **word association**, respondents are presented with a list of words, one at a time, and asked to respond to each with the first word that comes to mind. The words of interest, called test words, are interspersed throughout the list that also contains some neutral, or filler, words to disguise the purpose of the study. For example, in a retailing study, some of the test words might be: *location, parking, shopping, quality,* and *price.* The subject's response to each word is recorded verbatim and responses are timed. Respondents who hesitate or reason out (defined as taking longer than three seconds to reply) are identified. In analyzing these data, the researcher looks at the frequency with which a response is given, the amount of hesitation before responding, and the number of instances when no response is given. Patterns in responses are analyzed, as are the response times. It is often possible to classify the associations as favorable, unfavorable, or neutral. The longer an individual hesitates before answering, the higher the assumed level of involvement with the subject. A nonresponse is thought to indicate the highest level of emotional involvement, as these people are too involved to be able to respond in a short time. Gillette used word association to help them name the Sensor for Women shaver (see opening vignette). A sample of women was presented with several different names for the new feminine razor, including Sensor for Women and Lady Sensor, and asked to write down the first word that came to mind. Because Sensor for Women elicited the most favorable responses, the company selected this name.

word association
A projective technique in which respondents are presented with a list of words, one at a time. After each word, they are asked to give the first word that comes to mind.

Completion Techniques

completion technique
A projective technique that requires the respondent to complete an incomplete stimulus situation.

Completion techniques are a natural extension of association techniques, generating more detail about the individual's underlying feelings and beliefs. The respondent is asked to complete a sentence, a paragraph, or a story. In **sentence completion**, respondents are given incomplete sentences and asked to complete them. Generally, they are asked to use the first word or phrase that comes to mind, as in the following example.

sentence completion
A projective technique in which respondents are presented with a number of incomplete sentences and asked to complete them.

EXAMPLE

TOMMY HILFIGER IS A HIGH FLYER IN MEN'S SHIRTS

In order to determine men's underlying attitudes towards Tommy Hilfiger shirts, sentence completion could be used as follows:

A person who wears Tommy Hilfiger shirts is

_____

As compared to Polo, Gant, and Eddie Bauer, Tommy Hilfiger shirts are

_____

Tommy Hilfiger shirts are most liked by

_____

When I think of Tommy Hilfiger shirts, I

_____

Using such techniques, Tommy Hilfiger discovered that men preferred shirts that were less formal with a nontraditional cut. Men preferred to buy these shirts at upscale department stores such as Macy's. These findings, after they were confirmed by survey research, formed the platform for Tommy Hilfiger's successful marketing strategy.

A variation of sentence completion is paragraph completion, in which the respondent completes a paragraph beginning with the stimulus phrase. A further expanded version of sentence completion and paragraph completion is story completion. In **story completion,** respondents are given part of a story, enough to direct attention to a particular topic but not enough to hint at the ending. They are required to give the conclusion in their own words.

story completion
A projective technique in which respondents are provided with part of a story and required to give the conclusion in their own words.

Construction Techniques

Construction techniques follow the same logic as other projective techniques, requiring the respondent to construct a response to a picture or cartoon. These techniques provide even less initial structure than verbally oriented association or completion techniques. In **picture response techniques,** persons or objects are depicted in pictures, and respondents are asked to write a descriptive story, dialog, or description. The analysis of the responses attempts to identify themes reflecting the individual's perceptual interpretation of the pictures. In a variation of this technique recently proposed by Professor Gerald Zaltman of Harvard University, the respondents are asked to bring 12 to 15 pictures of their choice to the interview and then asked to describe the salient content of each picture. The picture descriptions reveal the underlying values, attitudes, and beliefs of the respondents.

construction technique
A projective technique in which the respondent is required to construct a response in the form of a story, dialogue, or description.

picture response technique
A projective technique in which the respondent is shown a picture and asked to tell a story describing it.

In **cartoon tests,** highly stylized stick characters are used to eliminate references to clothing, facial expressions, and even gender. The respondents are asked to complete the conversation they would attribute to the cartoon characters. These techniques typically ask both for verbal responses from the cartoon characters and for unspoken thoughts. This tends to maximize the candid nature of the response. Because cartoon tests are simpler to administer and analyze than picture response techniques, they are the most commonly used construction technique. An example is shown in Figure 6.6.

cartoon tests
Cartoon characters are shown in a specific situation related to the problem. The respondents are asked to indicate the dialogue that one cartoon character might make in response to the comment(s) of another character.

In marketing research applications, construction techniques are used to evaluate attitudes toward the topic under study and to build psychological profiles of the respondents, as illustrated by Porsche.

FIGURE 6.6   A Cartoon Test

TAXONOMY OF A PORSCHE BUYER

Porsche sells sports cars, the lowest price unit costing over $40,000. The demographics of the Porsche owner are well known: male, mid-40s, college graduate, with average earnings over $200,000 per year.

Traditional advertising had focused on the car's performance and how good the car makes the owner look.

Not knowing their motivations and psychological profile, Porsche hired a group of researchers to find out why its buyers bought the car. Among other techniques, the researchers used picture responses. Current and potential buyers were shown pictures of

Porsche owners with their cars and were asked to describe the owners. The results were surprising and revealed that Porsche had been using the wrong advertising approach.

According to the results, most of the Porsche owners couldn't care less if people saw them in their Porsche. So that advertising could be better directed to potential buyers, researchers produced five psychographic profiles: (1)"Top Guns." Driven, ambitious types. Power and control matter to these people, and they expect to be noticed. (2)"Elitists." Old money, blue bloods. To them a car is just a car, not an extension of their personality. (3)"Proud Patrons." Their car is a trophy earned for hard work, and they are not concerned with whether they are seen in it or not. (4) "Bon Vivants." Worldly jet setters and thrill seekers. Their car adds excitement to their passionate lives. (5)"Fantasists." Their car is a fantasy escape. They are not trying to impress anyone, and in fact are a little embarrassed about owning a Porsche.

After survey research confirmed these findings, marketing and advertising were directed at these psychographic segments. As a result of this research, after years of poor sales, Porsche's sales in the United States increased by 48 percent and continued to be strong through 2000.[6]

Expressive Techniques

In **expressive techniques,** respondents are presented with a verbal or visual situation and asked to relate, not their own feelings or attitudes, but those of others. The two main expressive techniques are role playing and the third-person technique. In **role playing,** respondents are asked to play the role or assume the behavior of someone else. The researcher assumes that the respondents will project their own feelings into the role.

In the **third-person technique,** the respondent is presented with a verbal or visual situation and asked to relate the beliefs and attitudes of a third person rather than directly expressing personal beliefs and attitudes. This third person may be a friend, a neighbor, a colleague, or a "typical" person. Again, the researcher assumes that the respondent will reveal personal beliefs and attitudes while describing the reactions of a third party. Asking the individual to respond in the third person reduces the social pressure to give an acceptable answer, as the following example shows.

expressive techniques
Projective techniques in which the respondent is presented with a verbal or visual situation and asked to relate the feelings and attitudes of other people to the situation.

role playing
A projective technique in which respondents are asked to play the role or assume the behavior of someone else.

third-person technique
A projective technique in which the respondent is presented with a verbal or visual situation and asked to relate the beliefs and attitudes of a third person to the situation.

EXAMPLE

WHAT WILL THE NEIGHBORS SAY?

A study was performed for a commercial airline to understand why some people do not fly. When the respondents were asked, "Are you afraid to fly?", very few people said yes. The major reasons given for not flying were cost, inconvenience, and delays caused by bad weather. However, it was suspected that the answers were heavily influenced by the need to give socially desirable responses. Therefore, a follow-up study was done in which the third-person technique was used. In the second study, the respondents were asked, "Do you think your neighbor is afraid to fly?" The answers indicated that most of the neighbors who traveled by some other means of transportation were afraid to fly. Thus, the third-person technique was able to uncover the true reason for not flying: fear of flying.[7]

Note that asking the question in the first person (Are you afraid to fly?) did not elicit the true response. Phrasing the same question in the third person (Do you think your neighbor is afraid to fly?) lowered the respondent's defenses and resulted in truthful answers. In another popular version of the third-person technique, the researcher presents the respondent with a description of a shopping list and asks for a characterization of the purchaser, thus gaining data on shopping behavior.

Suppose the researcher is interested in determining attitudes toward prepared dinners. Two otherwise identical grocery shopping lists will be prepared except that one list will contain prepared dinners. Respondents would be asked to characterize the purchaser identified with each list. The differences in the characteristics of the two purchasers will then reveal attitudes toward prepared dinners. For example, as compared to the other purchaser, the purchaser of prepared dinners may be described as lazy and disorganized. This would reveal that respondents think that lazy and disorganized people purchase prepared dinners.

We conclude our discussion of projective techniques by describing their advantages, disadvantages, and applications.

Advantages of Projective Techniques

Projective techniques have a major advantage over the unstructured direct techniques (focus groups and depth interviews): They may elicit responses that subjects would be unwilling or unable to give if they knew the purpose of the study. At times, in direct questioning, the respondent may intentionally or unintentionally misunderstand, misinterpret, or mislead the researcher. In these cases, projective techniques can increase the validity of responses by disguising the purpose. This is particularly true when the issues to be addressed are personal, sensitive, or subject to strong social norms. Projective techniques are also helpful when underlying motivations, beliefs, and attitudes are operating at a subconscious level.

Disadvantages of Projective Techniques

Projective techniques suffer from many of the disadvantages of unstructured direct techniques, but to a greater extent. These techniques generally require personal interviews with highly trained interviewers and require skilled interpreters to analyze the responses. Hence, they tend to be expensive. Furthermore, there is a serious risk of interpretation bias. With the exception of word association, all techniques are open-ended, making analysis and interpretation difficult and subjective.

Some projective techniques, such as role playing, require respondents to engage in unusual behavior. For example, to assess a company's image, respondents may be asked to play the role of a person that best describes the company. It is possible that respondents who agree to participate are themselves unusual in some way. Therefore, they may not be representative of the population of interest. As a result, it is desirable to compare findings generated by projective techniques with the findings of the other techniques that permit a more representative sample.

Application of Projective Techniques

With the exception of word association, projective techniques are used much less frequently than either focus groups or depth interviews. Word association is commonly used for testing brand names and occasionally to measure attitudes about particular products, brands, packages, or advertisements. As the examples have shown, projective techniques can be used in a variety of situations. The usefulness of these techniques is enhanced when the following guidelines are observed:

1. Projective techniques are used when the sensitivity of the subject matter is such that respondents may not be willing or able to answer direct questions honestly.

2. Projective techniques are used to uncover subconscious motives, beliefs, or values, providing deeper insights and understanding as part of exploratory research.

3. Projective techniques are administered and interpreted by trained interviewers who understand their advantages and limitations.

Given these guidelines, projective techniques, along with other qualitative techniques, can yield valuable information.

SUMMARY ILLUSTRATION USING THE OPENING VIGNETTE

Qualitative research is appropriate when a company is faced with an uncertain situation or is presented with conclusive results that differ from expectations. This type of research can provide insight either before or after the fact. Qualitative research methods tend to be much less structured than quantitative methods and are based on small, nonrepresentative samples. In the opening vignette, Gillette used qualitative research at the beginning of the project to understand the shaving needs of women.

On the other hand, quantitative research seeks conclusive evidence that is based on large, representative samples and typically applies some form of statistical analysis. This was seen in the opening vignette in which Gillette used quantitative research involving a survey of a representative sample of 500 women to substantiate the findings of qualitative research (depth interviews).

Focus groups, the most frequently used qualitative technique, are conducted in a group setting, whereas depth interviews are conducted one-on-one. In the opening vignette, Gillette choose depth interviews over focus groups because shaving is a rather personal experience for women, and their personal feelings could be tapped much better in a one-on-one setting than in a group environment.

Projective techniques aim to project the respondent's motivations, beliefs, attitudes, and feelings onto ambiguous situations. The projective techniques may be classified as association, completion, construction, and expressive techniques. Gillette used word association to select an appropriate name for the new razor. Using word association to select names for new products is quite common.

MARKETING RESEARCH AND TQM

Qualitative research can help determine what features customers value and how customers form quality perceptions. Focus groups and depth interviews can help define the components of the customer value package and gauge quality expectations. The San Francisco Symphony Orchestra, for example, used focus groups to discover what major donors value about their relationship with the orchestra. This qualitative research revealed that major donors wanted more opportunities to interact with orchestra members so that they could feel a part of the extended orchestra family. The donors measured the quality of their experience in terms of the opportunity to relate to orchestra members in a family atmosphere. This led the San Francisco Symphony Orchestra to invite major donors to spend time with the orchestra members backstage after selected performances in an informal, family-type setting.

The ABC Television Network further illustrates the role of qualitative research in improving the quality of a firm's product and service offerings.

FOCUS ON ELRICK & LAVIDGE

One of the most common methods of qualitative research at E&L involves focus groups. For example, E&L recently proposed performing a research project involving menu development at a major restaurant chain. The restaurant chain wanted to understand the factors that prompt people to go to a casual dining restaurant. They wanted to know how customers view the expected variety and value of menu choices from such a restaurant. They also wanted customers to compare menus from the restaurant chain along with a number of competitors and to make comments about what is good on each menu and what is not. E&L's proposal included four focus groups, two to be run in Richmond, Virginia, and two in Atlanta, Georgia. Since the first step in a successful focus group involves recruiting and screening the participants, having the right screener is very important. Potential subjects can be recruited from databases that are available internally to E&L, or they can come from lists the client provides.

E&L and the client will jointly develop a moderator's guide to help lead the discussion and to make sure that all relevant points are covered. The moderators usually start with very broad questions and work toward more specific ones. Generally, each focus group includes about 8 to 10 participants, and lasts from an hour and a half to two hours. The focus groups are usually audio-recorded or videotaped, and take place in a room with a one-way mirror that observers sit behind. Moderators inform the respondents that other members of the research team are viewing the session and that the session is being recorded so that the researchers do not miss any information. Using a matter-of-fact tone, the moderator attempts to increase the respondents' comfort level from the start of the session. One moderator noted that most respondents soon forget about the mirror, the observers behind it, and the recording equipment.

The moderator prepares the focus group report, usually soon after the completion of the group interview, and the results are summarized in qualitative rather than in quantitative terms. E&L often cautions clients that they should not expect definitive answers from the qualitative research and that quite often these projects will result in more questions being asked, and thus will lead to quantitative projects.

EXAMPLE

FOCUS (GROUPS) ON QUALITY: THE ABC OF TV PROGRAMMING

ABC television relies heavily on qualitative research to determine how consumers define quality TV programming. Focus groups conducted by the company have revealed that the characters, plots, and punch lines determine the quality of most TV programs. Therefore, ABC pays close attention to these features while developing its shows. Once the pilot shows are developed, focus groups are conducted to assess consumer reaction and to undertake refinement. ABC has recently decided to only schedule the shows that test well.

ABC applies the information obtained from focus groups to a total quality management goal. By conducting this research, they can capture the customers' perceptions of the program, which allows ABC to improve the quality of television programming by tailoring the programs to the consumers' perceptions of quality and their preferences.

ABC applied the total quality management concept with the TV show *Dharma & Greg*. The show aired on ABC at 8 P.M. Eastern time and was a hit with the TV viewers. Because of the consistently high ratings, the show remained at the top of the lineup. Other ABC programs that had successful ratings are *The Drew Carey Show* and *Two Guys, a Girl, and a Pizza Place*. These shows have remained in the lineup because of viewer demand. ABC's customer focus and involvement, achieved via focus groups and other marketing research techniques, demonstrates the network's commitment to quality. The whole organization is run for the customer.[8]

INTERNATIONAL MARKETING RESEARCH

When a company is unfamiliar with the nuances of foreign markets, decisions that on the surface appear harmless and logical from a strategic business perspective may fail because the company did not fully understand the culture. This is why qualitative research is crucial in international marketing research. In the initial stages, qualitative research can provide insights into the problem and help in developing an approach by generating relevant models, research questions, and hypotheses. Thus, qualitative research may reveal the differences between foreign and domestic markets.

Focus groups can be used in many settings, particularly in industrialized countries. The moderator should not only be trained in focus group methodology, but should also be familiar with the language, culture, and patterns of social interaction prevailing in that country. The focus group findings should be derived not only from the verbal contents but also from nonverbal cues, such as voice intonations, inflections, expressions, and gestures. In some countries, such as in the Middle or Far East, people are hesitant to discuss their feelings in a group setting. In these cases, depth interviews should be used. The use of projective techniques should be carefully considered, as the responses that these techniques generate may reflect deeply rooted cultural influences. However, when used appropriately, as in the following example, qualitative techniques can play a crucial role in the success of the marketing research project.

EXAMPLE

SPANISH EXPANSION

The Spanish airline, Iberia, was faced with the problem of expanding the number of routes from Europe to South and Central America in the late 1990s. Amidst a multitude of airliners operating over the Atlantic, the question was how to differentiate Iberia from its many competitors. Focus groups provided some initial answers by revealing several insights: (1) International travelers saw Iberia as "the gateway to South America," (2) providing several days' layover in Miami would attract a number of passengers, particularly tourists, and (3) the pairing of destinations such as Miami and Cancun in travel

packages would promote more business. When subsequent survey research confirmed the focus group findings, Iberia chose to make Miami a hub for its flights to South America. These findings were also used to design travel packages, make changes in services, and differentiate the airline.[9]

TECHNOLOGY AND MARKETING RESEARCH

Researchers are using remote data collection techniques for qualitative research. The availability of videoconferencing links, remote control cameras, and digital transmission equipment has boosted the amount of research that can be conducted long distance. The videoconferencing industry has reported growing revenues for the last seven years, a market that could exceed $10 billion by 2002. While videoconferencing may never replace direct interaction with focus groups, it does offer a cost-saving alternative for conducting qualitative research.

Another interesting development is AT&T's multimedia 800 service. A financial services prospect could call a firm's 800 number and see and talk to the agents he or she may wish to do business with. The agent could act as if he or she was in an in-person, face-to-face conversation, pointing to graphs and charts as appropriate, perhaps showing the analytical and financial services resources the company could make available to serve the client. Such systems can also be used to conduct focus groups and depth interviews long distance.

ETHICS IN MARKETING RESEARCH

Respondents' rights and privileges must be respected when conducting qualitative research. Some of the salient ethical issues relate to misleading or deceiving respondents, not maintaining their anonymity, and embarrassing or harming the respondents. An additional issue with wider ramifications relates to the use of research results in an unethical manner.

Some qualitative researchers allow their clients to be present at focus group discussions by introducing them as co-researchers. However, many participants are able to discern that the co-researcher is in fact the client. This deception raises ethical concerns and generates mistrust that has an adverse impact on the quality of the data and the integrity of marketing research.

As mentioned earlier, focus group discussions are often recorded using hidden video cameras. Whether or not they have been told of the hidden camera at the beginning, at the end of the meeting the respondents should be informed about the recording. The purpose of the video, including who will be able to view it, should be disclosed. In particular, if the client will have access to it, this should be made known as well. Each respondent should be asked to sign a written statement granting permission to use the recording. Participants should be given the opportunity to refuse signing, in which case the tapes should be edited to completely omit the identity and comments of the respondents who refuse.

The researcher has an obligation to make the respondents feel comfortable. If a respondent is experiencing discomfort or stress, the interviewer should show restraint and should not aggressively probe any further. At the end of the interview, respondents should be allowed to reflect on all they have said and be allowed to ask questions. This helps reduce their stress and return them to their preinterview emotional state. A final issue relates to the ethics of using qualitative research results for questionable purposes, as in the Bush campaign profiled below.

EXAMPLE

FOCUS (GROUPS) ON MUDSLINGING

The ethics of negative or "attack" ads has been debated for some time. The focus, however, has shifted from the ads themselves to the ethics of employing marketing research techniques to design the ad message. Nowhere is this phenomenon more prevalent than in political "mudslinging" campaigns. The Bush campaign against Dukakis in the 1988 U.S. presidential election is one example.

Before designing negative ads about Dukakis, Bush campaign leaders tested negative information about Dukakis in focus groups. The idea was to develop some insight into how the American public would react if this negative information were released in the form of advertisements. Negative issues that elicited very negative emotions from the focus groups were chosen for Bush's political advertising. The result? Partly because he was painted "as an ineffectual, weak, liberal, do-gooder lacking in common sense," Dukakis lost the election by a wide margin.

Similar misuse of qualitative research was observed in the 1992 and 1996 presidential elections that Bill Clinton won in part by negatively attacking the Republicans. In the 2000 presidential election, Gore unfairly attacked Bush as lacking in experience when focus groups revealed that experience was an important criterion for voters.[10]

INTERNET APPLICATIONS

The Internet is especially useful in assembling a homogeneous group in terms of demographic and socioeconomic characteristics. For example, the Internet allows individuals who live too far away to participate in a focus group. The Internet also enables focus group interaction to be recorded immediately, with the help of electronic emotion indicators, such as :-) and :-(. Using and recording electronic emotions reduces the cost of the focus group because videotaping is not required. However, electronic emotions obviously do not capture as full a breadth of emotion as videotaping.

Many Internet marketing research providers, such as SurveySite, conduct online focus group research.

EXAMPLE

ONLINE FOCUS: E*TRADE CANADA

E*TRADE Canada *(www.canada.etrade.com)* is a premiere online securities trading company. Due to the growing number of firms participating in online trading, E*TRADE Canada recently developed a comprehensive research plan to evaluate and improve its trading Web site to maintain market leadership. E*TRADE Canada decided to partner with SurveySite *(www.surveysite.com),* a marketing research firm specializing in online research, to conduct this project.

The research began with online focus groups with current E*TRADE Canada customers. The objective of the focus groups was to develop insights into key areas of satisfaction, including reactions to customer service, product fees, product quality, technical support, and so on. The focus groups were followed up by a quantitative online survey using respondents recruited through various Internet resources and e-mail invitations. The result of the focus groups and survey information was a new and improved E*TRADE Canada Web site that improved customer satisfaction and provided a significant boost in subscriptions.

As compared to their conventional counterparts, online focus groups are faster, less costly, and give access to individuals who otherwise might be difficult to recruit (e.g., business executives) or who are geographically dispersed. Yet the respondent base is limited to those who use the Internet. Also, the effectiveness of Internet focus groups to stimulate group dynamics and to generate valid findings has not been fully established.

Like focus groups, depth interviews can also be conducted over the Internet. Virtually all the projective techniques we have discussed can be implemented over the Internet. For example, various companies and market researchers are using the picture response technique effectively. Coca-Cola can provide a picture on a Web site and ask respondents to write a story about it. The demographic data of the person coupled with the story can provide valuable insights into the psychographic profile and the consumption pattern of the respondent. The success of conducting qualitative research over the Internet lies in the respondents' having access to and being comfortable with the Internet.

SUMMARY

Qualitative and quantitative research should be viewed as complementary. Qualitative research methods tend to be much less structured and are based on small, nonrepresentative samples. The various qualitative options vary in terms of how directly they ask questions of the respondent. Direct methods, such as focus groups and depth interviews, do not attempt to disguise the purpose of the research. Focus groups, the most frequently used qualitative technique, are conducted in a group setting, whereas depth interviews are done one-on-one.

The indirect techniques make a deliberate attempt to disguise the true purpose of the research. They are called projective techniques, as they aim to project the respondent's motivations, beliefs, attitudes, and feelings onto ambiguous situations. The projective techniques may be classified as association, completion, construction, and expressive techniques. Projective techniques are particularly useful when respondents are unwilling or unable to provide the required information by direct methods.

Focus groups and depth interviews can help define the components of the customer value package. In the international context, qualitative research may reveal the differences between the foreign and domestic markets. Technological advances, such as the availability of videoconferencing links, remote control cameras, and digital transmission equipment have boosted the amount of research that can be conducted long distance. Ethical issues in qualitative research relate to respecting respondents' rights and privileges. Focus groups and other qualitative procedures can be conducted using the Internet.

KEY TERMS AND CONCEPTS

Qualitative research, 167
Quantitative research, 168
Direct approach, 169
Indirect approach, 170
Focus group, 170
Depth interviews, 174
Projective techniques, 177
Association
    techniques, 178

Word association, 178
Completion
    techniques, 178
Sentence completion, 178
Story completion, 179
Construction
    techniques, 179

Picture response
    techniques, 179
Cartoon tests, 179
Expressive techniques, 181
Role playing, 181
Third-person
    technique, 181

ACRONYMS

The key characteristics of a focus group may be described by the acronym FOCUS GROUPS:

    F ocused (on a particular topic)
    O utline prepared for discussion
    C haracteristics of the moderator
    U nstructured
    S ize: 8 to 12
    G roup composition: homogeneous
    R ecorded: audiocassettes and videotapes
    O bservation: one-way mirror
    U ndisguised
    P hysical setting: relaxed
    S everal sessions needed: One to three hours each

The main features of a depth interview may be summarized by the acronym DEPTH:

    D epth of coverage
    E ach respondent individually interviewed
    P robe the respondent
    T alented interviewer required
    H idden motives may be uncovered

EXERCISES

1. What are the primary differences between qualitative and quantitative research techniques?
2. What is qualitative research and how is it conducted?
3. What are the differences between direct and indirect qualitative research? Give an example of each.
4. Why is the focus group the most popular qualitative research technique?
5. Why is the focus group moderator so important in obtaining quality results?
6. What are some key qualifications of focus group moderators?
7. Why should one safeguard against professional respondents?

8. What are two ways in which focus groups can be misused?

9. What is a depth interview? Under what circumstances is it preferable to focus groups?

10. What are the major advantages of depth interviews?

11. What are projective techniques? What are the four types of projective techniques?

12. What is the word-association technique? Give an example of a situation in which this technique is especially useful.

13. When should projective techniques be employed?

PROBLEMS

1. Following the methods outlined in the text, develop a plan for conducting a focus group to determine consumers' attitudes toward and preferences for imported automobiles. Specify the objectives of the focus group and write a screening questionnaire.

2. Suppose Baskin Robbins wants to know why some people do not eat ice cream regularly. Develop a cartoon test for this purpose.

INTERNET AND COMPUTER EXERCISES

1. The Coca-Cola Company has asked you to conduct Internet focus groups with heavy users of soft drinks. Explain how you would identify and recruit such respondents.

2. Could a depth interview be conducted via the Internet? What are the advantages and disadvantages of this procedure over conventional depth interviews?

3. Visit the Web site of Qualitative Research Consultants Association *(www.qrca.org)*. Write a report about the current state of the art in qualitative research.

4. *Tennis* magazine would like to recruit participants for online focus groups. How would you make use of a newsgroup to recruit participants? Visit *http://groups. google.com* and then select rec.sport.tennis.

ACTIVITIES

ROLE PLAYING

1. You are a marketing research consultant hired to organize focus groups for an innovative German-style fast food restaurant. What kind of people would you select to participate in focus groups? What screening criteria would you use? What questions would you ask?

2. As a marketing researcher, persuade your boss (a fellow student) not to bypass quantitative research once the qualitative research has been conducted in a project seeking to determine how consumers select a hotel for a personal stay.

FIELD WORK

1. The campus athletic center is trying to determine why more students do not use its facilities. Conduct a series of focus groups to determine what could be done to attract more students to the athletic center. Based on the focus group results, generate relevant hypotheses.

2. A cosmetics firm would like to increase its share of the female college student market. The firm hires you as a consultant to obtain an understanding and preliminary

insights into the students' attitudes, purchases, and use of cosmetics. Conduct at least five depth interviews. Prepare a report that summarizes your findings.

GROUP DISCUSSION

1. In a group of five or six, discuss whether qualitative research is scientific.
2. Discuss this statement in a small group: If the focus group findings confirm prior expectations, the client should dispense with quantitative research.
3. Discuss this statement in a small group: Quantitative research is more important than qualitative research because it results in statistical information and conclusive findings.

NOTES

1. *www.cnetinvestor.com*, "Gillette CEO Looks to Women's Razor for Sales," *Bloomberg Forum*, October 24, 2000; "A Woman's Touch," *Discount Merchandiser*, 39(5) (May 1999): 104; Suzanne Oliver, "Happy Birthday From Gillette," *Forbes*, 157(8) (April 22, 1996): 37–38; and M. Maremont, "A New Equal Right: The Close Shave," *Business Week* (March 29, 1993): 58.

2. Judith Langer, "'On' and 'Offline' Focus Groups: Claims, Questions," *Marketing News*, 34(12) (June 5, 2000): H38; Richard Cook, "Focus Groups Have to Evolve if They Are to Survive," *Campaign-London* (July 9, 1999): 14; Howard Furmansky, "Debunking the Myths About Focus Groups," *Marketing News*, 31(13) (June 23, 1997): 22.

3. Louise Lee, "Can Levi's Be Cool Again? It's Trying to Woo Kids—Without Turning Off Grown-ups," *Business Week* (3672) (March 13, 2000): 144; "Edison, American Marketing Association, Best New Product Awards," *Marketing News*, 31(6) (March 17, 1997): E6.

4. Janis Mara, "Staying in Focus," *Adweek*, 41(30) (July 24, 2000): 40–41; Lynn Vincent, "7 Deadly Sins of Focus Groups," *Bank Marketing*, 31(5) (May 1999): 36–39; and John M. Hess and R. L. King, eds., "Group Interviewing," *New Science of Planning* (Chicago: American Marketing Association: 1968): 4.

5. Stephanie Thompson, "M&M/Mars Gives New Snickers $40 Mil Kickoff," *Advertising Age*, 71(34) (August 14, 2000): 1–2; "M&M's Aims for the Millennium," *Retail World*, 52(4) (March 1–March 12, 1999): 24; Carol Kennedy, "The Chocolate Wars: Inside the Secret Worlds of Mars and Hershey," *Director*, 52(9) (April 1999): 80; and Judann Pollack, "Mars Says Milky Way Lite Eating Up the Competition," *Advertising Age*, 67(40) (September 30, 1996): 28.

6. "Porsche Boxster," *Consumer Reports*, 65(4) (April 2000): 58; Lucy Barrett, "Porsche Looks to Agencies to Fulfill Integrated Strategy," *Marketing* (June 3, 1999): 3; and Alex Taylor III, "Porsche Slices Up Its Buyers," *Fortune*, 131(1) (January 16, 1995): 24.

7. Debbie Seaman, "Conquer Your Fear of Flying," *Success*, 46(2) (February 1999): 27; and "Fear of Flying," *Economist*, 339(7966) (May 18, 1996): 30.

8. Wayne Friedman, "ABC Holds High Cards, but Each Net Is Vulnerable," *Advertising Age*, 71(21) (May 15, 2000): S20–S21; and T. L. Stanley, "Fate by Focus Group," *Mediaweek*, 6 (July 8, 1996): 22–23.

9. "Innovative Iberia Pleases Market," *Airfinance Journal* (224) (January 2000): 15; "Sepi Allows Iberia Ties with AA/BA," *Airfinance Journal* (215) (March 1999): 12; and John Pollack, "Iberia Eyes Americas," *Advertising Age International* (April 27, 1992).

10. Ira Teinowitz, "Presidential Ad Duels Go Easy on the Negative," *Advertising Age*, 71(1) (January 3, 2000): 3–4; Debra Goldman, "Simple Politics," *Adweek* (Eastern Edition) 37(20) (May 13, 1996): 34–36; and S. Banker, "The Ethics of Political Marketing Practices, The Rhetorical Perspective," *Journal of Business Ethics*, 11 (1992): 843–848.

7

DESCRIPTIVE RESEARCH DESIGN: SURVEY AND OBSERVATION

SURVEY RESEARCH IS THE MOST POPULAR METHOD FOR COLLECTING QUANTITATIVE DATA. AS MORE HOUSEHOLDS GAIN ACCESS TO THE WEB, THE USE OF INTERNET SURVEYS WILL BECOME INCREASINGLY POPULAR.

Fran Basso, Vice President/Sr. Research Director, Elrick & Lavidge.
Fran Basso is responsible for directing specialized package good quantitative research programs. She is based in Elrick & Lavidge's Chicago office.

Opening Questions

1. What survey methods are available to marketing researchers, and how can these methods be classified?

2. What are the criteria for evaluating survey methods and comparing them to determine which is best suited for a particular research project?

3. How can survey response rates be improved?

4. How is observation different than the survey method? What procedures are available for observing people and objects?

5. What are the relative advantages and disadvantages of observational methods as compared to the survey methods?

6. How can survey methods be used in implementing total quality management programs?

7. How can survey and observation methods be implemented in an international setting?

8. How can technology improve survey and observation methods?

9. What ethical issues are involved in conducting survey and observation research?

10. What is the role of the Internet in implementing survey and observation methods?

P&G's New Marketing Platform: EDLP and BE

As part of its ongoing marketing research, Procter & Gamble (P&G) routinely analyzes scanner data and conducts consumer surveys. Scanner panel data from AC Nielsen revealed that a typical family that was brand loyal spent $725 for a year's worth of P&G products. In comparison, a family that bought similar products as private label or low-priced brands spent less than $500. In a time when value consciousness dominated, this premium pricing strategy presented a problem to P&G. This led P&G to create a new marketing platform for its products.

At the base of the new platform was the concept of value. The platform was designed to fully recognize that P&G had been overcharging for many of its products, including Tide detergent, Crest toothpaste, Pampers disposable diapers, Vick's cough syrup, and Head & Shoulders shampoo. Focus groups and depth interviews conducted by Procter & Gamble revealed that customers were no longer willing to pay for non–value-added costs. Furthermore, surveys using mail panels indicated that customers who were loyal to P&G preferred prices that were consistently low rather than price discounts and special deals. A computer-assisted telephone survey of a randomly selected representative sample resulted in similar findings for the general population. The concept developed from these findings is known as EDLP: Every Day Low Pricing. This concept was the exact opposite of P&G's previous platform of maintaining high list prices offset by frequent and irregular discounts.

Another problem that led Procter & Gamble to reformulate its platform had to do with new product development. Previous research indicated that P&G brands enjoyed considerable equity in that they were well known and preferred by a large segment of the market. This led to the strategy of brand extensions (BE), the practice of using a successful brand name to launch a new or modified product, for example, Oil of Olay Beauty Bar, which is a brand extension of Oil of Olay lotion. The beauty bar was developed as a response to the growing consumer demand for a product that would keep skin feeling soft and young, not only on the face but all over. The bar was specially engineered with a synthetic cleansing system and light Oil of Olay moisturizers that help the skin to hold moisture better than soap. In addition to the special formulation, the bar was designed to stay firm during use and not to melt away like most other beauty bars.

Prior to introduction, the Oil of Olay Beauty Bar was tested in mall intercept interviews. In these interviews, respondents actually washed their hands and face with the bar in a test area located in the mall before responding to a survey. Because the results of these mall intercept interviews were quite positive, three types of bars were introduced: pink and white with different scents, and an unscented hypoallergenic version for sensitive skin. The beauty bar has been a great success and won one of Marketing News' Edison Best New Products Awards.

Procter & Gamble is gaining momentum in the U.S. market and abroad. Domestic unit volumes and market shares are once again increasing in 22 out of 32 categories. The strategies of EDLP and BE continue to pay dividends for the company. In March 1999, P&G made another brand extension by launching the Olay cosmetics line.[1]

OVERVIEW

The marketing research process begins by defining the research problem and then formulating an approach and a research design. As we discussed in Chapter 3, the major types of research designs are exploratory and conclusive. Exploratory designs rely primarily on secondary data analysis (Chapters 4 and 5) and qualitative research (Chapter 6). Conclusive research designs may be classified as causal or descriptive. Causal designs will be explained in Chapter 8. This chapter discusses survey and observation methods, the quantitative techniques typically used to collect descriptive research data. Figure 7.1 briefly explains the focus of the chapter, the relationship of this chapter to the previous ones, and the steps of the marketing research process on which this chapter concentrates.

Survey data do much more than merely report behavior. Surveys can provide insights into who the consumers are, how they behave, and why they behave in certain ways. Respondents' reports of their conscious motives, values, or beliefs provide some insight into consumer behavior. This was illustrated in the opening vignette, where P&G used different types of surveys to understand consumer's preferences for everyday low prices versus discounts and special sales. (Qualitative techniques, discussed in Chapter 6, are more useful in understanding behaviors driven by unconscious motives.)

Surveys can be classified in terms of how the data are collected: telephone interviews, computer-assisted telephone interviews, in-home interviews, mall intercept interviews, computer-assisted personal interviews, mail interviews, mail panels, and electronic surveys (e-mail and Internet). In this chapter, we will describe each of these methods and discuss the criteria used to select an appropriate method for a particular project.

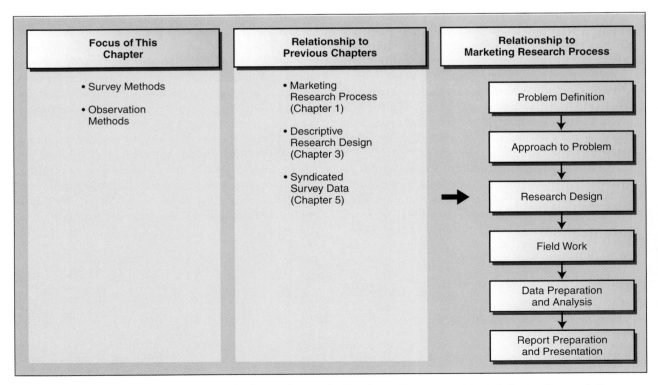

FIGURE 7.1   Relationship of Survey and Observation to the Previous Chapters and the Marketing Research Process

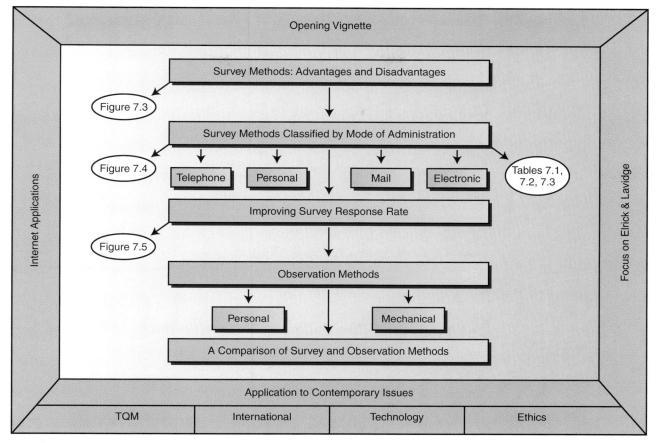

FIGURE 7.2   Survey and Observation: An Overview

We will consider the major observational methods—personal observation and mechanical observation—and discuss the advantages and disadvantages of observation over survey methods as well as the role of survey and observation methods in TQM and international marketing research. We will also discuss the impact of technology and Internet applications, and identify several ethical issues that arise in survey research and observation methods. Figure 7.2 gives an overview of the topics discussed in this chapter and how they flow from one to the next.

SURVEY METHODS

The **survey method** of obtaining information is based on questioning respondents. Surveys are used when the research involves sampling a large number of people and asking them a series of questions (Figure 7.3). Surveys may be conducted in person, by telephone, through a mailed questionnaire, or electronically via the computer. Perhaps the biggest issue researchers face is how to motivate respondents to candidly answer their questions. The uninvited intrusion of telemarketers and direct marketers into the home has resulted in an increasing number of consumers shutting the door to anyone trying to make contact. We will discuss the challenges of controlling this nonresponse problem later in the chapter.

survey method
A structured questionnaire given to a sample of a population, designed to elicit specific information from respondents.

FIGURE 7.3
Methods of Obtaining
Quantitative Data in
Descriptive Research

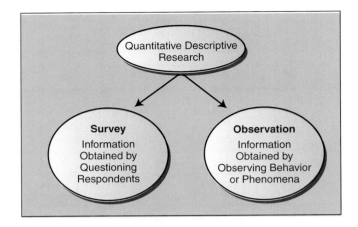

The range of topics that can be investigated using surveys is as varied as the research problems business face. Questions regarding behavior, intentions, attitudes, awareness, motivations, and demographic and lifestyle characteristics all lend themselves to survey research.

Advantages and Disadvantages of Survey Research

The survey method has the advantages of ease, reliability, and simplicity. Questionnaires are relatively easy to administer. Using fixed-response (multiple-choice) questions reduces variability in the results that may be caused by differences in interviewers, and enhances reliability of the responses. It also simplifies coding, analysis, and interpretation of data.

Disadvantages of the survey method are that respondents may be unable or unwilling to provide the desired information. For example, consider questions about motivational factors. Respondents may not be consciously aware of the real reasons they prefer one brand to another. The subconscious nature of their motives may make it impossible for them to answer questions accurately. Respondents may be unwilling to respond if the information requested is sensitive or personal. For example, consider questions about religious beliefs. Respondents may view this topic as very personal and may be unwilling to answer any questions related to it.

structured data collection
Use of a formal questionnaire that presents questions in a prearranged order.

Also, **structured data collection** involving a questionnaire with fixed-response choices may result in loss of validity for certain types of data, such as beliefs and feelings. Finally, properly wording questions is not easy (see Chapter 11 on questionnaire design). Yet, despite these disadvantages, the survey approach is by far the most common method of primary data collection in marketing research.

SURVEY METHODS CLASSIFIED BY MODE OF ADMINISTRATION

Figure 7.4 illustrates the various methods of collecting survey data, broadly classified as telephone, personal, mail, or electronic interviews. Telephone interviewing can be further broken down in terms of whether or not computers are being used in the interviewing process. Personal interviews may be conducted in-home, as mall intercept interviews, or as computer-assisted personal interviews (CAPIs). The third major method, mail interviewing, takes the form of ordinary mail surveys or surveys conducted using mail panels. Electronic interviews are generally administered over the Internet or by using e-mail. Of

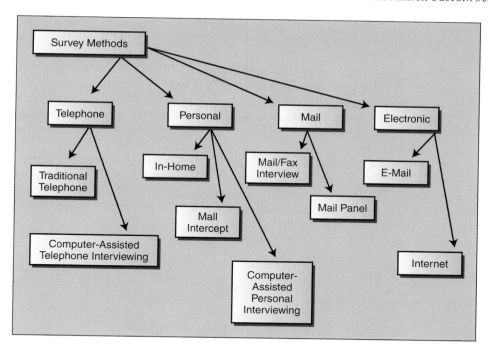

FIGURE 7.4
Classification of Survey Methods

these methods, telephone interviews are the most popular, followed by personal interviews. The popularity of electronic surveys is increasing quickly. Mail interviews are the least popular.

Telephone Methods

As stated earlier, telephone interviews vary in terms of the degree of computer assistance supporting the interview.

TRADITIONAL TELEPHONE INTERVIEWS Traditional telephone interviews involve phoning a sample of respondents and asking them a series of questions. The interviewer uses a paper questionnaire and records the responses with a pencil. Telephone interviews are generally conducted from centrally located research facilities. Telephone research centers are specifically equipped to accommodate large groups of interviewers. These facilities have proliferated because of the cost and control advantages they offer. Low-priced WATS (wide area telephone service) lines have made nationwide telephone interviewing from a central location practical.

Additionally, field service supervisors can closely monitor the telephone conversations. This monitoring helps to control interviewer bias that results from variation in the way in which the questions are asked and the responses are recorded. Data quality is also enhanced with on-the-spot review of completed questionnaires. Finally, the research budget, both in terms of labor costs and time restrictions, can be more easily managed when the interviewers are assembled in one location.

COMPUTER-ASSISTED TELEPHONE INTERVIEWING Computer-assisted telephone interviewing (CATI) from a central location is now more popular than the traditional telephone method. More than 90 percent of all telephone interviews are conducted using a CATI system. Computer-assisted telephone interviewing uses a computerized questionnaire administered to respondents over the telephone. A computerized questionnaire may be generated using a mainframe computer, a minicomputer, or a personal computer. The interviewer sits in front of a computer screen and wears a mini-headset. The computer screen replaces a paper and pencil questionnaire, and the mini-headset substitutes for a telephone.

Upon command, the computer dials the telephone number to be called. When contact is made, the interviewer reads the questions posed on the CRT screen and records the respondent's answers directly into the computer memory bank. CATI combines the interview with the editing and data entry steps to produce a highly efficient and accurate survey process. Because the responses are entered directly into the computer, interim and update reports can be compiled instantaneously as the data are being collected.

CATI software has built-in logic, which also enhances data accuracy. The program will personalize questions and control for logically incorrect answers, such as percentage answers that don't add up to 100 percent. The software has built-in branching logic, which will skip questions that are not applicable or will probe for more detail when warranted. For example, if a respondent answered yes to the question, "Have you ever purchased Nike athletic shoes?", an entire series of questions related to the experience with Nike shoes would follow. If, however, the respondent answered no, that line of questioning would be skipped. An application of CATI was illustrated in the opening vignette in which P&G used this method to survey a randomly selected sample, asking questions related to pricing preferences.

Advantages and Disadvantages of Telephone Interviewing

Telephone interviewing, whether conducted with pen and paper or in a computer-assisted format, remains one of the most popular survey methods. This popularity can be traced to several factors. Interviews can be completed quickly since the travel time associated with personal interviews is completely eliminated. **Sample control,** or the ability to reach the units specified in the sample, is high when proper sampling and callback procedures are followed. The control of field force is good because the interviewers can be supervised from a central location. The control is even better in CATI, as these systems allow the supervisor to monitor an interview without the interviewer or the respondent being aware of it. The **response rate**—the percentage of total attempted interviews that are completed—is good. Moreover, telephone surveys are not very expensive.

There are some inherent disadvantages, however (see Table 7.1 on page 200). The questioning is restricted to the spoken word. Interviewers cannot use physical stimuli such as visual illustrations or product demonstrations. Moreover, they cannot ask complex questions. This limits the applicability of telephone techniques for certain types of research, such as new product or advertising research.

Personal rapport and commitment are difficult to establish due to lack of face-to-face interaction between the interviewer and the respondent. Respondents can easily escape the interview process, either by cutting the interview short or simply hanging up the phone. This results in less tolerance for lengthy interviews over the phone and limits the quantity of data that can be collected.

sample control
The ability of the survey mode to reach the units specified in the sample effectively and efficiently.

response rate
The percentage of the total attempted interviews that are completed.

EXAMPLE

TELEPHONE CALLING MAKES PIZZA HUT THE ONE TO CALL ON

Pizza Hut, which initiated the customer satisfaction survey in January 1995, currently conducts 50,000 interviews a week. Data are collected through an outbound telephone survey (which means that Pizza Hut initiates the telephone call). Selected customers in Pizza Hut's delivery and carryout database are called within 24 hours of their purchase. The outbound interviews are limited to four minutes, and customers are given a 60-day breather before they are called again.

The company also has an interactive 800 number inbound survey of randomly selected dine-in customers (the customer initiates the call). One of every 20 to 30 dine-in customers receives a coupon at the bottom of the receipt and a toll-free number to call to participate in the interactive survey. Tracking results show that 67 percent of the surveys are completed within one day of the visit, fulfilling a desire by management for the inbound survey results to be fresh.

The survey focuses only on issues that unit managers can control. The questions deal with service, food, and problems during the customer's latest visit. The survey results have been very useful. For example, customers rushed to buy the new Stuffed Crust Pizza, but there was no subsequent rise in loyalty. Survey results showed that because of service problems, new customers were not making return trips. The survey helped Pizza Hut identify problems, and it now has a better understanding of how to handle the next major product launch. Half of the unit manager's quarterly bonus is linked to the survey results. As a result, customer satisfaction is at an all-time high.[2]

Personal Methods

Personal interviewing methods may be categorized as in-home, mall intercept, or computer-assisted.

PERSONAL IN-HOME INTERVIEWS In personal in-home interviews, respondents are interviewed face-to-face in their homes. The interviewer's task is to contact the respondents, ask the questions, and record the responses. In recent years, the use of personal in-home interviews has declined. Nevertheless, they are still used, particularly by syndicated firms (see Chapter 5).

ADVANTAGES AND DISADVANTAGES OF IN-HOME INTERVIEWING In-home interviewing offers many advantages. It enables the interviewer to provide clarifications to the respondent, allowing for complex questions. It permits the use of physical stimuli such as visual aids, charts, and maps, and allows the interviewer to display or demonstrate the product. It provides very good sample control as well since homes can be selected without generating a list of all the homes in a given area. The homes can be selected by instructing the interviewer to start at a given location, travel in a certain direction, and select every nth (for example eighth) home. A large quantity of data can be collected because the respondents are interviewed in their own homes and, therefore, they're more willing to participate for a longer period of time. The response rate is very good, particularly if the respondents have been prenotified.

In-home interviewing has lost favor due to social, labor, and control factors. Change in the family, particularly related to the dominance of two-income earners, leaves few people at home during the day. Interviewer supervision and control is difficult, as the

TABLE 7.1   Relative Advantages of Different Survey Methods

METHOD	ADVANTAGES	DISADVANTAGES
Telephone	Fast High sample control Good control of field force Good response rate Moderate cost	No use of physical stimuli Limited to simple questions Low quantity of data
In-Home	Complex questions can be asked Good for physical stimuli Very good sample control High quantity of data Very good response rate	Low control of field force High social desirability Potential for interviewer bias Most expensive
Mall Intercept	Complex questions can be asked Very good for physical stimuli Very good control of environment Very good response rate	High social desirability Potential for interviewer bias Moderate quantity of data High cost
CAPI	Complex questions can be asked Very good for physical stimuli Very good control of environment Very good response rate Low potential for interviewer bias	High social desirability Moderate quantity of data High cost
Mail	No field force problems No interviewer bias Moderate/high quantity of data Low social desirability Low/moderate cost	Limited to simple questions Low sample control for cold mail No control of environment Low response rate for cold mail Low speed
Electronic	No field force problems No interviewer bias Low cost Low social desirability High speed	Limited to simple questions Low sample control No control of environment Low response rate Moderate quantity of data

social desirability
The tendency of the respondents to give answers that may not be accurate but that may be desirable from a social standpoint.

interviewer bias
The error due to the interviewer's not following the correct interviewing procedures.

interviewers are traveling door-to-door. Consequently, problems with the questionnaire or with the style of the interviewer become more difficult to detect and correct. **Social desirability,** the tendency of respondents to give answers that are socially desirable but incorrect, is high when there is face-to-face contact between the interviewer and the respondent. This factor also leads to a high potential for **interviewer bias.** Interviewers can influence the answers by facial expressions, intonations, or simply by the way they ask the questions. This method is also the most expensive.

Despite their value, personal in-home interviews are being replaced by mall intercepts.

MALL INTERCEPT PERSONAL INTERVIEWS In mall intercept personal interviews, respondents are intercepted in shopping malls. The process involves stopping the shoppers, screening them for appropriateness, and either administering the survey on the spot or inviting them to a research facility located in the mall to complete the interview. For example, in a survey for a cellular phone manufacturer, a shopper is intercepted and asked about age, education, and income. If these characteristics match the client's target population, the individual is then questioned on product usage. Some usage of cellular phones is a prerequisite for inclusion in the sample. Only those who have experience with cellular phones are invited to a test facility located in the mall to evaluate several new prototype designs under consideration.

Although the sample is composed only of individuals who shop in that retail mall, this is not a serious limitation. While not representative of the population in general, shopping mall customers do constitute a major share of the market for many products.

ADVANTAGES AND DISADVANTAGES OF MALL INTERCEPTS A major advantage of mall intercept interviews is that it is more efficient for the respondent to come to the interviewer than for the interviewer to go to the respondent. The popularity of this method is evidenced by the several hundred permanent mall research facilities located across the country. Complex questions can be asked when there is face-to-face contact. Mall intercepts are especially appropriate when the respondents need to see, handle, or consume the product before they can provide meaningful information. This was illustrated in the opening vignette when P&G used this technique to determine consumers' responses to Oil of Olay Beauty Bar prior to introduction. Mall intercept interviewing was chosen because it conveniently allowed the respondents to use the beauty bar in a test area in the mall before they responded to the survey. The researcher has very good control of the environment in which the data are being collected, and the response rate is very good.

The main disadvantages are the potential for social desirability and interviewer bias due to face-to-face contact in the interviewing process. The quantity of data that can be collected is only moderate, as people are generally in a hurry while shopping. The cost of mall intercept interviewing is high.

EXAMPLE

OH! OREO O'S

In July 1998, Post cereal introduced Oreo O's cereal as round speckled rings with the same taste of Oreo's that Americans have loved for years. The development of Oreo O's cereal was guided by the fact that Americans love Oreo cookies and Post believed that this cereal would be a big hit among families. Post conducted mall intercept surveys to determine the consumer taste appeal and probability of purchase for this new product. Shoppers recruited in specified locations in malls were taken to an interviewing facility located in the mall, where they could taste the Oreo O's cereal and then respond to a questionnaire administered by an interviewer. Survey results revealed that 9 out of 10 people who tried the cereal said it tasted like the original cookies, and three-quarters of those people said they would buy the new product. Based on these results, Post made the decision to launch Oreo O's cereal nationally. Post spent nearly $45 million on network TV and print ads to introduce their new cereal product, which has been a great success.[3]

COMPUTER-ASSISTED PERSONAL INTERVIEWING (CAPI) In computer-assisted personal interviewing (CAPI), the third form of personal interviewing, the respondent sits in front of a computer terminal and answers a questionnaire on the screen by using the keyboard or a mouse. Several user-friendly, electronic packages can aid in designing easy and understandable questions. Help screens and courteous error messages are also provided. The colorful screens and on- and off-screen stimuli add to the respondent's interest and involvement in the task. This method has been classified as a personal interview technique since an interviewer is usually present to serve as a host and to guide the respondent as needed.

This approach is used in shopping malls, preceded by the intercept and screening process described earlier. It is also used to conduct business-to-business research at trade shows or conventions. For example, UPS could measure its image and test the effectiveness of its slogan, "Moving at the speed of business," by administering a CAPI survey at the expedited package delivery trade show. The process of interacting with the computer is simplified to minimize respondent effort and stress. Thus, the use of open-ended questions that require typing is minimized.

ADVANTAGES AND DISADVANTAGES OF CAPI CAPI seems to hold respondent interest and has several advantages. Complex questions can be asked, and the computer automatically performs skip patterns and conducts logic checks. Interviewer bias is reduced since the computer administers the interview. Like mall-intercepts, CAPI can be useful when the survey requires the use of physical stimuli. It also offers very good control of the data collection environment and results in a very good response rate.

Its main disadvantages, which are shared with mall intercept, are high social desirability, moderate quantity of data, and high cost.

Mail Methods

Mail interviews, the third major form of survey administration, can be conducted with independently compiled mailing lists or by using a mail panel.

MAIL INTERVIEWS The traditional mail interview is a "cold" mail survey, which is sent to individuals who meet a specified demographic profile, but who have not been precontacted to participate in the survey. A typical mail interview package consists of the outgoing envelope, cover letter, questionnaire, postage-paid return envelope, and possibly an incentive. Those individuals motivated to do so complete and return the questionnaire through the mail. There is no verbal interaction between the researcher and the respondent. Individuals are selected for cold surveys through mailing lists the client maintains internally or has purchased commercially. Commercial mailing lists typically contain some demographic and psychographic information that assists in the targeting process.

Table 7.2 illustrates the variety of mailing lists offered by one firm, the approximate number of names per list, and the respective prices. Regardless of its source, a mailing list should be current and closely related to the population of interest.

TABLE 7.2 Sample Mailing Lists

LIST TITLE	NUMBER ON LIST	PRICE[a]
Advertising Agencies	3,892	$62/M
Banks, Main Offices	11,089	$85/M
Boat Owners	4,289,601	$100/M
Chambers of Commerce	6,959	$62/M
Personal Computer Owners	2,218,672	Inquire
Families	76,000,000	Inquire
Hardware Wholesalers	7,378	$62/M
Magazines, Consumer	4,119	Inquire
Photographic, Portrait	33,742	$62/M

[a] Price shown is per 1,000 names (/M), except where noted.
Source: Best Mailing Lists, Inc., Catalog 2001 (800-692-2378).

The researcher must also make decisions about the various elements of the mail interview package (see Table 7.3). The type of envelope, the cover letter, the length of the questionnaire, and the incentive, if one is offered, all affect response rates.

The time involved and the response rate can be improved by faxing the questionnaire instead of mailing it. This option is attractive when surveying business and institutional respondents.

MAIL PANELS In contrast to cold mail interviews, **mail panels** consist of a large and nationally representative sample of individuals who have agreed to participate in periodic survey research (see Chapters 3 and 5). Incentives in the form of cash or gifts are often offered to the individuals who agree to participate. Once the individuals have been admitted to the panel, detailed demographic and lifestyle data are collected on each household. The researcher uses this information to select targeted mailing lists within the panel based on client needs.

NFO World Group (*www.nfow.com*) and the NPD group (*www.npd.com*) are organizations that maintain mail panels. Mail panels can be used to reach a general as well as a targeted sample. In the opening vignette, P&G used mail panel surveys to target consumers loyal to P&G and determine their pricing preferences. In a longitudinal design, the purchases of these customers for P&G and competing brands were monitored over time to identify the loyal customers.

ADVANTAGES AND DISADVANTAGES OF MAIL SURVEYS Mail surveys are an economical and efficient way to reach consumers. The problems of interviewer bias and the expense of field staff management are eliminated. Cold mail surveys have a low cost, and the cost of mail panels is only moderately higher. Social desirability is low, as there is no personal contact with the respondent during data collection. A moderate amount of data can be collected through cold mail surveys, while mail panels permit the collection of large quantities of data.

mail panels
A large and nationally representative sample of households who have agreed to periodically participate in mail questionnaires, product tests, and telephone surveys.

T A B L E 7 . 3   Some Decisions Related to the Mail Interview Package

OUTGOING ENVELOPE

Outgoing Envelope: size, color, return address
Postage
Method of Addressing

COVER LETTER

Sponsorship	Signature
Personalization	Postscript
Type of appeal	

QUESTIONNAIRE

Length	Layout
Content	Color
Size	Format
Reproduction	Respondent anonymity

RETURN ENVELOPE

Type of envelope
Postage

INCENTIVES

Monetary vs. nonmonetary
Prepaid vs. promised amount

However, these clear advantages are offset by problems of lack of control of the interviewing process. Unlike telephone and personal interviewing, there is no personal contact, and the respondent may feel less compelled to either participate or candidly complete the questionnaire. This problem is particularly acute with cold mail interviews. There is little control over who answers the questionnaire, how they answer it, and how quickly they return it. This results in low sample control, low speed, and no control over the data collection environment. Thus, it is difficult to assess the quality and validity of the data.

Finally, response rates to cold mail surveys are low, and nonresponse introduces a serious bias in the data. Those individuals who choose not to participate in mail interviews may have very different demographic and psychographic profiles than responders, resulting in **nonresponse bias.** Individuals with higher income and educational levels, or individuals inexperienced or uninterested in the research topic all tend to have lower response rates. Mail panels are successful in boosting response rates, and the problem of nonresponse bias is also reduced.

nonresponse bias
Bias that arises when actual respondents differ from those who refuse to participate in ways that affect the survey results.

Despite its shortcomings, the relative ease and low cost of mail interviews continue to make this a viable research option.

EXAMPLE

KICK THE CAN—CANNED SOUP, THAT IS

In a mail survey, respondents were asked to make canned or dry soups at home and then respond to a questionnaire. The findings indicated a strong desire for a fresh alternative to canned and dry soups. Guided by these results, Redmond, Washington–based Stockpot Soups developed Stockpot Classic Soups Soup Concentrate. Packed in resealable pouches, these soups are sold in the refrigerated dairy case as an alternative to canned and dry soups. Each 10-ounce pouch makes four bowls of hearty home-style soup with ingredients like fresh-cut vegetables, real dairy products, and premium meats and seafoods. This new product has been a success as it was born of consumer desire discovered via a mail survey.[4]

Electronic Methods

Electronic surveys can be conducted via electronic mail (e-mail) if the respondents' addresses are known or by posting the survey to a Web site. If the addresses are known, the survey can simply be mailed electronically to respondents included in the sample. E-mail usage in the United States is very high, particularly in business firms in which virtually everyone has access to e-mail. Using batch-type electronic mail, researchers send e-mail surveys to potential respondents who use electronic mail. Respondents key in their answers and send an e-mail reply. Alternatively, using interactive e-mail, researchers can send potential respondents e-mail prompting them to access an Internet address that contains an interactive survey. Respondents access the survey and enter their answers. Otherwise, the survey can be posted to an Internet site. Visitors to the site will then have the option of participating.

Both methods suffer from respondent selection bias in that only people with access to electronic mail or the Internet can be included in the sampling frame. This bias is further accentuated by the fact that heavy users of these media will have a higher probability of being actually included in the sample. These individuals may differ from the target population in ways that can seriously bias the results. Until usage of electronic media becomes more widespread, these methods may be more appropriate for specialized applications, such as IBM surveying heavy computer users.

The electronic method shares many of the advantages of the mail method: no field force problems, no interviewer bias, low social desirability, and low cost. In addition, data can be collected and analyzed at high speeds due to the use of computers.

The method also shares many of the disadvantages of mail surveys: Only simple questions can be asked, there is low sample control and no control of the data collection environment, and there is a low response rate. Only moderate quantities of data can be obtained. Even though these disadvantages exist, the Internet holds tremendous promise.

EXAMPLE

ON THE PROMISE OF INTERNET

Michael Naples, President, Advertising Research Foundation (ARF), thinks the Internet holds a lot of promise:

"There's a lot happening now. We're in a transition period. There's going to be a lot of opportunity for research with the Internet approach. We old-time researchers are skeptical about the extent you can use a self-selected sample and make something of it. But we're all attuned to the fact that any new capability carries with it less than complete satisfaction, like the telephone interview when it first started. But over time, the telephone interview became not just important but dominant because of its inherent capabilities. The Internet has the potential to, once it reaches critical mass, be a vehicle for certain types of research."[5]

Criteria for Selecting a Survey Method

When evaluating the various survey methods within the context of a specific research project, one has to consider the salient factors relevant to data collection. Often, certain factors dominate, leading to a particular survey method as the natural choice. For example, if a new perishable food product has to be tested, respondents would have to taste the product before answering the questionnaire. This would involve interviewing at central locations, leading to mall intercept or CAPI as the natural choices. If no method is clearly superior, the choice must be based on an overall consideration of the advantages and disadvantages of the various methods.

Often, these methods are combined to enhance the quality of data in a cost-effective manner. This is likely when the research project is large in scope, as in the case of P&G's formulating its new marketing platform (opening vignette). Note that P&G used scanner panels to monitor household expenses of P&G and competing brands, and used mail panels to target consumers loyal to P&G. It used CATI to reach a representative sample of all households, and used mall intercepts to determine consumer response to the Oil of Olay Beauty Bar prior to introduction. The following examples illustrate the selection of survey modes.

EXAMPLE

GOOD THINGS COME IN SMALL PACKAGES—AND DISKETTES

Compaq Computer Corporation was sorting through survey options, attempting to identify the best method for conducting product research. The complexity of the questions eliminated telephone interviewing as an option. Personal interviews would have been ideal, but costs were prohibitive. Historically low response rates associated with mail surveys also raised concerns about that technique. Compaq knew they could boost response rates with incentives, but the response bias associated with that technique, as well as the cost, was a concern. As the sample was composed entirely of computer users, they adopted the innovative option of computer interviewing by mail, mailing the questionnaire on a diskette. The electronic option was not used because the e-mail addresses were not available and it was believed that respondents' access to the Internet would be limited.

Using a computer interviewing system, the researchers converted the survey to a series of questions related to various product scenarios, which displayed various product benefits. They mailed the questionnaire, in diskette form, to the respondent group. The researchers thought that the uniqueness of a questionnaire on diskette would motivate this targeted group, eliminating the need for costly monetary incentives. Instead, a plastic diskette holder served as an inexpensive incentive.

To the researchers' pleasant surprise, the response rate exceeded 55 percent, higher than any mail survey Compaq had ever conducted. Compaq obtained the relevant information at a low cost and was able to design a successful new product.[6]

Improving Survey Response Rates

Regardless of the survey method chosen, researchers should attempt to improve response rates. This can be done by prior notification, incentives, follow-up, and implementing other facilitators of response (Figure 7.5).

PRIOR NOTIFICATION Prior notification consists of sending a letter or e-mail, or making a telephone call to potential respondents, notifying them of the imminent mail, telephone, personal, or electronic survey. Prior notification increases response rates for samples of the general public because it reduces surprise and uncertainty and creates a more cooperative atmosphere.

FIGURE 7.5
Improving Response Rates

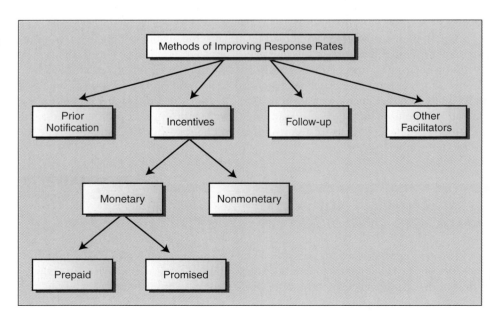

INCENTIVES Offering monetary as well as nonmonetary incentives to potential respondents can increase response rates. Monetary incentives can be prepaid or promised. The **prepaid incentive** is included with the survey or questionnaire. The **promised incentive** is sent to only those respondents who complete the survey. The most commonly used nonmonetary incentives are premiums and rewards, such as pens, pencils, books, and offers of survey results.

Prepaid incentives have been shown to increase response rates to a greater extent than promised incentives. The amount of incentive can vary from 25 cents to $50 or more. The amount of incentive has a positive relationship with response rate, but the cost of large monetary incentives may outweigh the value of the additional information obtained.

FOLLOW-UP Follow-up, or contacting the nonrespondents periodically after the initial contact, is particularly effective in decreasing refusals in mail surveys. The researcher might send a postcard or letter to remind nonrespondents to complete and return the questionnaire. Two or three mailings are needed, in addition to the original one. With proper follow-up, the response rate in mail surveys can be increased to 80 percent or more. Follow-up can also be done by telephone, e-mail, or personal contact.

OTHER FACILITATORS OF RESPONSE Personalization, or sending letters addressed to specific individuals, is effective in increasing response rates. The example that follows describes the procedure that *Bicycling* magazine uses to increase its response rate.

prepaid incentive
The prepaid incentive is included with the survey or questionnaire.

promised incentive
The promised incentive is sent to only those respondents who complete the survey.

EXAMPLE

BICYCLING MAGAZINE'S PROCEDURE FOR INCREASING RESPONSE TO MAIL SURVEYS

Bicycling magazine conducts a semiannual survey of individual bicycle dealers throughout the United States. The following procedure is used to increase the response to the survey:

1. An "alert" letter is sent to advise the respondent that a questionnaire is coming.
2. A questionnaire package is mailed five days after the alert letter. The package contains a cover letter, a five-page questionnaire, a new $1 bill, and a stamped return envelope.
3. A second package, containing a reminder letter, a questionnaire, and a stamped return envelope, is mailed five days after the first package.
4. A follow-up postcard is mailed a week after the second package.
5. A second follow-up postcard is mailed a week after the first.

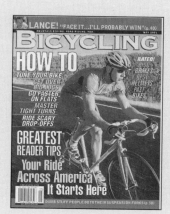

In a recent survey, 1,000 questionnaires were mailed to bicycle dealers, and 68 percent of these were returned after follow-up. This represents a good response rate for a mail survey.

OBSERVATION METHODS

observation
The recording of behavioral patterns of people, objects, and events in a systematic manner to obtain information about the phenomenon of interest.

Observation methods are the second type of methodology used in descriptive research. **Observation** involves recording the behavioral patterns of people, as well as data on objects and events in a systematic manner to obtain information about the phenomenon of interest. The observer does not question or communicate with the people being observed. Information may be recorded as the events occur or from records of past events. The major methods are personal observation and mechanical observation.

Personal Observation

personal observation
An observational research strategy in which human observers record the phenomenon being observed as it occurs.

In **personal observation,** a trained observer collects the data by recording behavior exactly as it occurs. The observer does not attempt to control or manipulate the phenomenon being observed but simply records what takes place. For example, a researcher might record traffic counts and observe traffic flows in a department store. This information could aid in determining store layouts, location of individual departments, shelf locations, and merchandise displays.

The main advantage of personal observation is that it is a highly flexible method, as the observer can record a wide variety of phenomena (Table 7.4). It is also highly suitable for use in natural settings. For example, the sales manager of General Motors can observe the attitudes of dealers toward a new inventory policy at one of the regular sales meetings.

The main disadvantage is that the method is unstructured in that an observation form is generally not used for recording the behavior as it occurs. Rather, the observer will record the phenomenon after completing the observation in a free, unstructured format. This leads to high observation bias. Also the data and their interpretation are highly subjective, leading to high analysis bias.

EXAMPLE

A STAMP OF APPROVAL FOR THE POSTAL SERVICE: "WE DELIVER"

Researchers from Young & Rubicam utilized personal observation to develop a successful marketing campaign for the U.S. Postal Service. This method was used since researchers felt that they had to overcome the stigma of the U.S. Post Office, which was historically perceived as an uncaring government organization. Researchers followed individual mail carriers along their routes for days at a time to observe consumer sentiment toward the Post Office. Although viewed poorly as an organization, the research showed that people related very positively to their individual mail carriers since they know them personally and come into direct contact with them on a daily basis. Margaret Mark, director of consumer insights, said, "That guy was their friend, a member of the community."

Young & Rubicam used this information to devise their successful "We Deliver" marketing campaign. The campaign presented the U.S. Post Office as a conglomeration of individual community members working for the Post Office and collectively serving the community. This campaign resulted in a marked improvement in the public's attitude toward the U.S. Postal Service.[7]

TABLE 7.4   **Relative Advantages of Observation Methods**

METHOD	ADVANTAGES	DISADVANTAGES
Personal observation	Most flexible Highly suitable in natural settings	High observation bias High analysis bias
Mechanical observation	Low observation bias Low to medium analysis bias	Can be intrusive Not always suitable in natural settings

Mechanical Observation

Mechanical observation, as one would expect, involves the use of a mechanical device to record behavior. These devices may or may not require the respondents' direct participation. They are particularly useful for recording continuous behavior, such as traffic flow in a grocery store. AC Nielsen's peoplemeter (Chapter 5) is an example of indirect observational devices in use today. The respondent does not need to change his or her behavior in any way to be involved in this type of observational study. The peoplemeter is attached to a television set to continually record not only the channels a set is tuned to but also who is watching.

Other common examples of indirect mechanical observation include turnstiles that record the number of people entering or leaving a building and traffic counters placed across streets to determine the number of vehicles passing certain locations. On-site cameras (still, motion picture, or video) are increasingly used by retailers to assess the impact of package designs, counter space, floor displays, and traffic flow patterns. The universal product code (UPC) is also a built-in source for mechanical observation. For those retailers equipped with optical scanners, the UPC system allows for the automatic collection of consumer purchase information, classifying it by product category, brand, store type, price, and quantity (see Chapter 5).

The scanner data that P&G used in the opening vignette is an example of mechanical observation. These data revealed that a typical family that was brand-loyal spent $725 for a year's worth of P&G products. In comparison, a family that bought similar products as private label or low-priced brands spent less than $500.

When it comes to developing new products, some smart companies like Compaq, Motorola, and Steelcase are observing their customers rather than just listening to what they say. Traditional research, relying exclusively on questioning, can produce bland products. New Coke test marketed well, yet was a dismal failure. People wanted low-cal burgers but wouldn't buy McDonald's McLean. The movie *Junior* did great in screenings but made only $36 million. Baseball players loved the pump baseball glove but wouldn't pay the increased cost. This is why it is important to combine questioning with observation methods and why mechanical observation is gaining ground.

mechanical observation
An observational research strategy in which mechanical devices, rather than human observers, record the phenomenon being observed.

> ## EXAMPLE
>
> ### STEELCASE MAKES THE CASE FOR MECHANICAL OBSERVATION
>
> Steelcase, a major national furniture manufacturer, used mechanical observation when it designed a furniture line for work teams. It set up hidden video cameras at various companies to observe what really goes on during the workday, looking for

information on behavior and routines people might not even know they exhibited.

The company found that teams function best when members can work collectively some of the time and independently at other times. The results of this study led to the very successful introduction of modular office furniture called Personal Harbor. This furniture can be quickly and easily assembled or reassembled to allow office workers to work in a large team area or in individual work spaces.[8]

Although this study did not require direct involvement of the participants, many mechanical observation devices do. Physical responses to sights, sounds, smells, or any sensory stimuli are an important area of observational research. Advertising or other promotional changes such as special sales can elicit a physical response in consumers that cannot be observed by merely looking at them. Specialized equipment designed to monitor heart and breathing rates, skin temperature, and other physiological changes is used in these situations. Because these measurements cost more than verbal reports of the respondent's reaction, they are used only when it is assumed that the respondent cannot or will not respond accurately to questioning. All of the physiological measurement devices operate on the assumption that the cognitive and emotional responses to stimuli elicit predictable differences in physical response. However, this assumption has not yet been clearly demonstrated.

The main advantage of mechanical observation is low observation bias, as the behavior is recorded mechanically, not by an observer. Likewise, the data are analyzed according to prespecified norms and guidelines, resulting in low to medium analysis bias. The main disadvantages are that some of these methods can be intrusive or expensive and may not be suitable in natural settings such as the marketplace.

A COMPARISON OF SURVEY AND OBSERVATION METHODS

With the exception of scanner data, marketing research is seldom conducted solely with observational methods. There are some unique advantages, however, to collecting data in this fashion. When combined with survey techniques, observation can deliver excellent results.

Relative Advantages of Observation

There are several advantages to using observational data collection methods. First, they do not require conscious respondent participation, which minimizes nonresponse errors. Although ethical questions surround the practice of observation without consent, even conscious participation requires less effort from the respondent than that required with other research techniques.

Interviewer bias resulting from interaction with the respondent or subjective interpretation of the questionnaire is minimized because the observer only has to record what is occurring. Additionally, the errors inherent in self-reported behavior are eliminated given that the observer records only actual behavior without asking any questions of the respondent.

Data regarding product preferences or reactions to marketing materials from children or pets can best be collected using observational techniques. Observation is also useful in situations investigating unconscious behavior patterns or behaviors that individuals may be unwilling to discuss honestly.

Observational techniques are best applied to phenomena that occur frequently or are of short duration. In these types of applications, observational methods may cost less and be faster than survey methods.

Relative Disadvantages of Observation

Observational data provides insight into what behavior is occurring, but not why. Attitudes, motivations, and values are all lost to the observational method. Additionally, highly personal behaviors related to personal hygiene or intimate family interactions are not available for observation.

Individuals have a tendency to only observe what they want to, and that may cause an observer to overlook important aspects of behavior. This perceptual difference among observers threatens the integrity of the approach.

Finally, observational techniques can be adopted for only frequent behaviors of short duration. Behaviors occurring infrequently or spanning a long period of time are too expensive to record using this technique.

To sum up, observation can potentially provide valuable information when properly used. From a practical standpoint, it is best to view observation as a complement to survey methods, rather than as being in competition with them.

EXAMPLE

HEFTY ONEZIP BAG: CUSTOMER SATISFACTION IS IN THE BAG

Mechanical observation coupled with mall intercept interviewing provided rich information on consumers' needs for food storage bags. Shoppers intercepted in malls were led to an observation facility in the mall. They were asked to use food storage bags, and their behavior was recorded using video cameras. They were then administered a survey in an adjoining room. This methodology provided rich insights into needs of consumers, such as the desire for bags that can be closed easily and more securely.

This finding was the impetus behind the development of Hefty OneZip food storage and freezer bags. Looking more like an actual zipper than the closures on most zipper bags, the OneZip Slider promised to eliminate the bothersome tasks of alignment, pinching, and double-checking needed to close conventional zipper bags.

In first quarter 1995 rollout, Hefty OneZip averaged a 21 percent dollar share of the storage and freezer segments of the zipper-bag market, where available. With

Hefty name recognition, broader distribution, and an aggressive advertising and sampling campaign, OneZip's popularity grew into the peak food bag months of summer.

The product became America's number two zipper bag in June 1995 and has since held on to that position. Hundreds of customer compliments thanking the company for making their lives "a little easier" have made Hefty feel as if the OneZip customer satisfaction is securely in the bag.[9]

SUMMARY ILLUSTRATION USING THE OPENING VIGNETTE

Surveys involve the administration of a questionnaire and may be classified as traditional telephone interviews, computer-assisted telephone interviews, in-home personal interviews, mall intercept interviews, computer-assisted personal interviews, mail surveys, mail panels, and electronic surveys administered by e-mail or Internet. These data collection methods should not be considered mutually exclusive. Often, it is possible to employ them productively in combination, as illustrated in the opening vignette. P&G used the CATI method to survey the general population, a mail panel to determine the pricing preferences of consumers loyal to P&G brands, and mall intercept interviews to assess reaction to the Oil of Olay Beauty Bar prior to introduction.

CATI is very suitable for surveying a representative sample of household, as telephone numbers can be randomly generated using efficient computer programs. A mail panel allows repeated measurements on the same respondents; thus, brand loyal users can be identified (respondents who purchased P&G brands repeatedly). Mall intercept interviews are very conducive to showing a new product to respondents before questioning them. Thus, this method was appropriate for assessing consumer response to P&G's brand extension (Oil of Olay Beauty Bar).

In contrast to direct questioning in surveys, observation methods simply observe people and objects. The major observational methods are personal observation and mechanical observation. Certain types of data can be obtained best by observation. An example would be consumers' purchases of various brands in supermarkets. P&G used scanner data (mechanical observation) to determine that a typical family that was brand-loyal spent $725 for a year's worth of P&G products. In comparison, a family that bought similar products as private label or low-priced brands spent less than $500.

MARKETING RESEARCH AND TQM

The Malcolm Baldrige Award for quality has a section for rating firms on Customer Focus and Satisfaction. This section carries more weight than any other category, representing 30 percent of the total points. It is through descriptive research that a firm can determine the extent to which its product offerings are meeting customers' needs. Firms that are focused on quality improvement use many traditional survey and observation methods to collect data, as well as some innovative ways of defining the customer and his or her needs.

Great Plains Software conducts telephone surveys with firms that purchase their accounting software packages. In order to increase response rates (and to ensure that all products are registered), the accounting program has a code that blocks usage after 50 transactions are entered. In order for the software to work again, the customer must call Great Plains to get a "key." When the customer calls, Great Plains asks them 20 marketing

FOCUS ON ELRICK & LAVIDGE

When performing survey research, Elrick & Lavidge (E&L) can use any of the nine major interviewing methods, because E&L has a full complement of personnel who are familiar with administering surveys using each method. However, E&L does have a preferred method of administering surveys in each of the major modes of administration.

For instance, though E&L telephone interviewers are proficient in traditional paper-and-pencil telephone survey administration, the vice president in charge of data collection estimated that over 90 percent of E&L's telephone surveys are implemented using computer-assisted telephone interviewing. E&L has a number of telephone centers around the country that are linked together over a wide area network that use state of the art equipment and software. E&L believes that CATI provides superior results over traditional telephone methods due to increased efficiency.

For personal interviewing methods, E&L prefers the mall intercept type of implementation. Along with the true mall intercept that occurs in an actual mall, E&L includes in this category interviewing that takes place at a central location to which the respondents are prerecruited (and prequalified) via the telephone. In fact, one E&L research director stated that the prerecruited interviews at a central location are preferable to the actual intercept at a mall because the people who frequent malls may not be representative of the target population. Because of security concerns, E&L rarely uses the personal in-home interviewing method. They also rarely use CAPI. A project manager cited logistical issues involved in CAPI, such as leasing computers for the duration of the study, as the main reason the company does not use this method much.

E&L uses traditional mail interviews much more frequently than it uses mail panels. They do not maintain their own mail panels, but will use other marketing research organization's panels when the survey is expected to have an extremely low response rate. The response rate can be improved by preceding the survey with a post card telling the potential respondents to look for the survey, and also by following up the survey with a post card reminding them about the survey. E&L is putting a lot of emphasis on electronic surveys, especially Internet surveys that are posted to a Web site, because these methods are gaining in importance.

research questions and some questions about the company, including location, size, and industry. Great Plains has used this information to create a database of company profiles that helps them to better determine their customers' needs. The use of surveys to make quality improvements is illustrated in the following example.

EXAMPLE

BANKING ON QUALITY

Stillwater National Bank decided to use some of its retail customers to help improve the quality of products and services. The bank first conducted focus groups to determine which characteristics of the bank were most important in customers' quality perceptions. The characteristics identified included responsiveness, trust, reliability, empathy, and information availability. Stillwater National Bank then conducted a survey to determine the relative importance of these characteristics in customers' evaluation of the bank's quality. The survey was mailed to 700 randomly selected customers, with a cover letter from the bank president, a postage-paid business reply envelope, and a $1 incentive.

After careful review of the survey findings, Stillwater Bank determined several areas that needed to receive the most attention if they were to provide customers with service quality. The survey indicated that the bank should focus on providing consistent, dependable service and on providing customers with access to information. The bank then decided it needed to undertake reengineering and reorganize itself in order to meet the needs and exceed the expectations of customers. These efforts demonstrate the bank's commitment to continuous quality improvement (CQI).[10]

Quality firms are finding various ways to increase response rates while collecting data. It is often hard for consumers to articulate their experiences and what is important to them, so observational methods are used to help researchers go beyond words and see people's actions.

To help them better define their market, Bugle Boy hired the Chilton research firm to collect observation data. Using a new observation methodology, participants used an 8-mm video camera to record what they do at home, school, work, while shopping, and in their free time. These tapes allowed Bugle Boy to understand their teenage consumers better by giving the company insights into which clothes the teenagers wore for which occasions.

INTERNATIONAL MARKETING RESEARCH

Selecting appropriate interviewing methods is much more difficult internationally because of the challenges of conducting research in foreign countries. Given the differences in the economic, structural, informational and technological, and sociocultural environments, the feasibility and popularity of the different interviewing methods vary widely. In the United States and Canada, nearly all households have telephones. As a result, telephone interviewing is the dominant mode of administering questionnaires. This is also true in some European countries, such as Sweden. However, in many other European countries, not all households have telephones. In developing countries only a few households have them.

In-home personal interviews are the dominant mode of collecting survey data in many European countries, such as Switzerland, and in newly industrialized countries (NICs) or developing countries. While mall intercepts are being conducted in some European countries, such as Sweden, they are not popular in other European countries or in developing countries. In contrast, central location/street interviews constitute the dominant method of collecting survey data in France and the Netherlands.

Due to their low cost, mail interviews continue to be used in most developed countries where literacy is high and the postal system is well developed: the United States, Canada, Denmark, Finland, Iceland, Norway, Sweden, and the Netherlands, for example. In Africa, Asia, and South America, however, the use of mail surveys and mail panels is low because of illiteracy and the large proportion of the population living in rural areas. Mail panels are used extensively only in a few countries outside the United States, such as Canada, the United Kingdom, France, Germany, and the Netherlands. However, the use of panels may increase with the advent of new technology. Likewise, although a Web site can be accessed from anywhere in the world, access to the Web or e-mail is limited in many countries, particularly developing countries. Hence, the use of electronic surveys is not feasible, especially for interviewing households.

Various methods may be reliable in some countries but not others. When collecting data from different countries, it is desirable to use survey methods with equivalent levels of reliability, rather than necessarily using the identical method, as illustrated in the following example.

EXAMPLE

USING DOMINANT SURVEY METHODS TO GAIN DOMINANT MARKET SHARE

Nike, with a 42 percent share of the athletic shoe market in the United States in 2000, is seeking to expand in Europe with the goal of significantly improving its competitive position by 2003. Europe is a market with vast potential, with sales of athletic shoes amounting to more than $8 billion in 2000. Nike would like to strengthen its marketing programs to sell athletic shoes to the large European market. A survey of consumer preferences for athletic shoes is to be undertaken in three countries: Sweden, France, and Switzerland. Comparability of results can best be achieved by using the dominant mode of interviewing in each country: telephone interviews in Sweden, central location/street interviews in France, and in-home personal interviews in Switzerland.

The findings of this survey would help Nike to understand the factors that Europeans consider important while purchasing athletic shoes (for example, comfort, style, and performance) and whether the importance attached to these factors varies across Sweden, France, and Switzerland. Nike will then be able to determine whether a uniform marketing strategy should be adopted across Sweden, France, and Switzerland or whether marketing efforts should be customized for each of these countries.[11]

As in the case of surveys, the selection of an appropriate observation method in international marketing research should also take into account the differences in the economic, structural, informational and technological, and sociocultural environment.

TECHNOLOGY AND MARKETING RESEARCH

New information technologies will continue to revolutionize the ways in which both primary and secondary data are collected. In earlier chapters, we talked about the role of automated databases in secondary research. Primary data collection and analysis is also changing due to advances in information technology. The researcher can use a computer to automatically dial the telephone numbers of potential respondent's fax machines and electronically send a survey. New software allows fax machines to read and store incoming text and data using "optical character recognition" technology. This makes it possible to conduct and tabulate surveys on a computer. This technology could replace the traditional mail survey, especially in researching business customers since it can gather the same type of information with much greater speed. Field workers in the near future will gather information in various locations with the aid of notebook computers. These computers will have built-in, wireless modems, allowing for transmission of data to and from virtually anywhere in the world. Another technological innovation is the use of interactive kiosks to collect data in central location interviews conducted in malls and trade shows.

Marketing researchers now have access to a new form of survey data: interactive phone technology. These systems are called Completely Automated Telephone Surveys (CATS) and circumvent the need for the human interviewer. The CATS system uses interactive voice response technology to conduct interviews. The recorded voice of a professional interviewer asks the questions. The individual simply keys in the corresponding push button to log her or his answer. For surveys requiring more detailed consumer responses, individual answers can be recorded and later transcribed. This can be very beneficial because managers can not only learn what customers said, but also hear how they said it.

CATS systems can be of the outbound or inbound format. With the outbound format, a computer dials from a sample of phone numbers, the interactive voice asks questions, and the responses are automatically recorded. This method is not very successful because it is very easy for the respondent to hang up, even before the human interviewer has a chance to say hello. The inbound format has better results because the consumer initiates the call, so the likelihood of a completed call is far greater. Generally, some added incentive is attached to influence the individual to participate. ID codes can help limit multiple call-ins (to hoard the incentives). These codes can also help to determine the characteristics of the individual who calls in (if the incentive card/letter is mailed, the code can be used as a tag for the person's location, sex, income, and so on), which aids in the examination of the data.[12]

All of these innovations, as well as future advances in information technology, will continue to improve the way in which researchers collect data.

ETHICS IN MARKETING RESEARCH

Surveys are often used as a cover for a targeted sales effort. The real purpose is not to obtain information to address a marketing research problem but to sell a product. This practice—called "sugging" in the trade language—is unethical. A similar unethical practice is "frugging" and involves fund raising under the guise of research. To illustrate, you get a call from a company stating that they are conducting research on consumer attitudes. After asking a few diagnostic questions, the company tries to sell you one of its products (sugging) or asks for a donation (frugging).

Respondents' anonymity, discussed in the context of qualitative research in Chapter 6, is an important issue in both survey and observational research. Researchers have an ethical obligation to not disclose the identities of respondents to anyone outside the research organization, including the client. Only when researchers notify respondents in advance and obtain their consent prior to administering the survey can an exception be made and the respondents' identities revealed to the client. Even in such cases, prior to disclosing identification information the researcher should obtain an assurance from the client that the respondents' trust will be kept and their identities will not be used for sales effort or misused in other ways. Ethical lapses in this respect by unscrupulous researchers and marketers have resulted in a serious backlash for marketing research.

The researcher has the responsibility to use an appropriate survey method in an ethical and legal way. For instance, federal legislation prohibits unsolicited faxed surveys. In many states, totally automated outgoing (initiated by the researcher) telephoning is illegal.

Often, researchers observe people's behavior without their consent, arguing that informing the respondents may alter their behavior. However, this can be considered an invasion of the respondents' privacy. One guideline proposed to resolve this problem is that research observation should be conducted only in places where people would expect to be observed by the public. Public places such as malls or grocery aisles, places where people observe other people routinely, are fair game. However, notices stating that these areas are under observation for marketing research purposes should be posted at the sites. And after observing their behavior, the researcher is still obligated to obtain the necessary permission from the respondents.[13]

It should also be mentioned that the common practice of serving cookies on the Internet raises ethical concerns. Many users do not realize it, but they have been served a cookie or two while on the Internet. A "cookie" is not a culinary delight in this case. It is a sophisticated means by which a Web site can collect information on visitors. Often, this process takes place without the knowledge of Web surfers and is an invasion of their privacy and right to consent.

EXAMPLE

HAVE A COOKIE

Hotwired.com offers dynamic online tools such as search engines, which provide people with important information. Hotwired's *Packet* uses cookies to collect information about Web site traffic by tracking an individual's preference for hotel choice, airline travel, and other interests. Hotwired uses this information to target customers with advertisements by promoting discounts and specials using the individual's preferred choice. In addition, the information helps marketing personnel at the electronic and print magazine collect demographics on the reader. Also, the company can monitor "hits" on particular topics and gain valuable feedback on user interest.

For example, using cookies, Hotwired may find out that after visiting its Web site, a particular respondent then visits travelocity.com for flight and hotel information pertaining to Jamaica. Then next time that visitor visits Hotwired.com, a pop-up Web advertisement will alert that visitor of special airfare and hotel packages to Jamaica offered by Hotwired.

Data collection is based on visitor behavior. This disguised technique enables Hotwired to monitor use patterns and to eliminate socially acceptable response bias. Information collected in this manner has been used to modify editorial content and format to make the magazine more appealing. While this information is helpful to Hotwired, the use of cookies in this manner raises several ethical issues.[14]

INTERNET APPLICATIONS

The use of Internet surveys has been discussed throughout the chapter. Internet or Web-based surveys are gaining in popularity. One reason is that the cost, in most cases, is less than phone and mail surveys or personal interviews. Also, the Internet survey is not as inconvenient as the phone call in the middle of dinner. The online survey can be completed in one's own time and place. Quick response time is also an advantage cited by those using online surveys. Another advantage of Internet market research is the ability to target specific populations. For example, a survey of high-tech individuals or technology buffs can be efficiently conducted on the Internet. Several hundred qualified respondents can be located quickly.

Electronic surveys do have limitations, however. Internet or e-mail users are not representative of the general population. It is difficult to verify who is actually responding to the survey. Security and privacy are also areas of concern. The research company can receive "flame" messages—messages that express anger or rage—from recipients who consider receiving an online survey an invasion of their privacy.

The following example shows how CompuServe conducted an Internet survey in the United Kingdom to find out what business professionals looked for in an Internet service.

EXAMPLE

INTERNET SURVEYS HELP COMPUSERVE SERVE THE U.K. MARKET

Prior to the rollout of its Internet service in the United Kingdom, CompuServe (*www.compuserve.com*) partnered with Nua (*www.nua.ie*) to help research and develop its interactive strategy. Nua is an Internet research and consulting firm headquartered in Ireland.

The first step in this project involved secondary data analysis to develop an extensive knowledge base of Web usage in the United Kingdom. This was followed by an Internet survey. The primary objective of the survey was to help CompuServe research the target group—business professionals—and determine what features they desired in an Internet service. The business respondents were recruited via mail, telephone, and Internet banner ads and directed to a survey posted at a password-protected Web site. The Internet survey revealed that basic service-related features, such as no disconnects without warning, high-speed connections, quick response to questions, and antivirus protection, were considered fundamental requirements.

Based on these results, CompuServe was able to develop the appropriate level of service to build a strong presence in the new market. Shortly after rollout, CompuServe became the leading Internet service provider in the United Kingdom. Since then, CompuServe has continued to use Internet surveys to keep abreast of the needs of the marketplace.

The Internet can be a very good source for observation and can provide valuable information. Observations can be made of the number of times a Web page is visited and the time spent on that page. The analysis of the links from where the company site is being approached by the individuals will provide important information regarding the consumers' related interests. Suppose an individual visits a financial services Web site, *www.fidelity.com,* for example, before visiting an insurance company's site. Clearly, this individual is interested in financial services besides insurance. Further, the researcher can provide various other links on the Web page and can observe which links are accessed more often.

SUMMARY

Surveys and observations are the two primary methods of conducting quantitative, descriptive research. Surveys involve the direct questioning of respondents, while respondent behavior is simply recorded in observation.

Surveys involve the administration of a questionnaire and may be classified, based on the method or mode of administration, as traditional telephone interviews, computer-assisted telephone interviews (CATI), in-home personal interviews, mall intercept interviews, computer-assisted personal interviews (CAPI), mail surveys, mail panels, and electronic surveys administered by e-mail or Internet. Of these methods, traditional tele-phone interviews and CATI are the most popular. However, each method has some gen-eral advantages and disadvantages. Although these data collection methods are usually thought of as distinct and competitive, they should not be considered mutually exclusive. It is possible to employ them productively in combination.

The major observational methods are personal observation and mechanical obser-vation. As compared to surveys, the relative advantages of observational methods are (1) they permit measurement of actual behavior, (2) there is no reporting bias, and (3) there is less potential for interviewer bias. Also, certain types of data can be obtained best, or only, by observation. The relative disadvantages of observation are (1) very little can be inferred about motives, beliefs, attitudes, and preferences, (2) there is potential for observer bias, (3) most methods are time consuming and expensive, (4) it is difficult to observe some forms of behavior, (5) and there is potential for unethical behavior. With the exception of scanner data, observation is rarely used as the sole method of obtaining primary data, but it can be usefully employed in conjunction with survey methods.

Data on customer focus and satisfaction required for quality enhancements and by the Baldrige Award could best be obtained by surveys and observation methods. An impor-tant consideration in selecting the methods of administering surveys internationally is to ensure equivalence and comparability across countries. New technologies such as comput-erized fax machines and Completely Automated Telephone Surveys (CATS) are revolution-izing survey administration. Misuse of surveys as a guise for selling, failing to maintain the anonymity of respondents, and observing behavior without respondents' knowledge or consent are major ethical issues in implementing survey and observation methods. Finally, Internet surveys are becoming more popular—a trend that is likely to continue.

KEY TERMS AND CONCEPTS

Survey method, 195	Social desirability, 200	Promised incentive, 207
Structured data collection, 196	Interviewer bias, 200	Observation, 208
	Mail panels, 203	Personal observation, 208
Sample control, 198	Nonresponse bias, 204	Mechanical observation, 209
Response rate, 198	Prepaid incentive, 207	

ACRONYMS

The classification of survey methods by mode of administration may be described by the acronym METHODS:

M ail panels

E lectronic interviews

T elephone interviews

H ome (in-home personal) interviewing

O n-site mall interviews

D irect mail interviews

S oftware for CATI/CAPI

EXERCISES

1. Explain briefly how the topics covered in this chapter fit into the framework of the marketing research process.

2. Name the major modes for obtaining information via a survey.

3. What are the relevant factors for evaluating which survey method is best suited to a particular research project?
4. What would be the most appropriate survey method for a project in which control of field force and cost are critical factors?
5. Name the types of mechanical observation, and explain how they work.
6. What are the relative advantages and disadvantages of observation?

PROBLEMS

1. Describe a marketing research problem in which both survey and observation methods could be used for obtaining the information needed.
2. The campus food service would like to determine how many people eat in the student cafeteria. List the ways in which this information could be obtained. Which method is best?

INTERNET AND COMPUTER EXERCISES

1. Ask your instructor or other faculty members if you could serve as a respondent in a computer-assisted personal interview. Then answer the same questionnaire in a pencil-and-paper format. Compare the two experiences.
2. Locate and answer an Internet survey for which you would qualify as a respondent. How would you evaluate this survey based on the discussion in this chapter?
3. Locate an Internet survey and examine the content of the questionnaire carefully. What are relative advantages and disadvantages of administering the same survey using CATI or mall intercept interviewing?
4. Design an e-mail survey to measure students' attitudes toward credit cards. E-mail the survey to 10 students. Summarize, in a qualitative way, the responses received. Are students' attitudes toward credit cards positive or negative?
5. Visit the Gallup organization's Web site at *www.gallup.com*. What survey methods has Gallup used in some of the recent surveys posted at this site? Why were these survey methods selected?

ACTIVITIES

ROLE PLAYING

1. You work for a high-tech company and are asked to do a study of people's responses to your advertising. Specifically, your boss wants to know which ads in a series are especially appealing or interesting to consumers. Your recommendations will be used to determine the product's copy mix. Explain how you will obtain this information. Which methods will you use and why? Be specific.
2. You have been hired by the campus bookstore to determine how students make purchase decisions while shopping. You are to use the method of personal observation. Disguise yourself as a shopper and observe the behavior of other students in the bookstore. Write a report about your findings.

FIELD WORK

1. Visit a local marketing research firm engaged in survey research. Tour their CATI facilities. Write a report describing how this firm conducts CATI.

2. Contact a marketing research firm with mall intercept interviewing facilities. Arrange to visit these facilities when mall intercept interviews are being conducted. Write a report about your experience.

GROUP DISCUSSION

1. As a small group, discuss the ethical issues involved in disguised observation. How can such issues be addressed?
2. With advances in technology, observation methods are likely to become popular. Discuss this statement as a small group.

NOTES

1. Based on Jack Neff, "P&G Steps Up Licensing For Brands, Technology," *Advertising Age,* 71(30) (July 17, 2000): 16–17; Mercedes Cardona, "P&G Ads Support Oil of Olay Brand Extension," *Advertising Age,* 70(10) (March 8, 1999): 22; Bill Saporito, "Behind the Tumult at P&G," *Fortune* (March 7, 1994): 74–82; "1993 Edison Best New Products Awards Winners," *Marketing News* (April 25, 1994): E5.

2. Jennifer Waters, "Better Strategies Better Pizza Hut," *Restaurants & Institutions,* 110(5) (February 15, 2000): 47–49; Amy Zuber, "Large Pizza Players Slice Growing Pie While Keeping Eyes on Hot 'Take-and-Bake' Rival," *Nation's Restaurant News,* 33(26) (June 28, 1999): 124–128; and Chad Ruben, "Pizza Hut Explores Customer Satisfaction," *Marketing News,* 30(7) (March 25, 1997): 15.

3. Stephanie Thompson, "The O's Have It," *Brandweek,* 39(13) (March 30, 1998): 1, 6; Stephanie Thompson, "A Buyer's Market: Cereal," *Brandweek,* 39(20) (May 18, 1998): U28; *www.postcereal.com.*

4. Based on Stephanie Thompson, "Campbell Can Latest Soup Effort," *Advertising Age,* 71(32) (July 31, 2000): 1–2; "Campbell Soup's Stockpot Makes Appointments to Its Sales Teams," *Nation's Restaurant News,* 33(5) (February 1, 1999): 48; and "1996 Saw Record Number of New Products," *Quirk's Marketing Research,* 11(2) (February 1997): 27–30.

5. Diane K. Bowers, "The New Research Tool," *Marketing Research: A Magazine of Management & Applications,* 10(3) (Fall 1998): 34, 38; "Marketing research: On the threshold of opportunity? A roundtable discussion on the past, present and future of research," *Quirk's Marketing Research* (March 1996).

6. Paul Edwards, "Can Internet Sales Save Compaq UK?" *Marketing Week,* 22(14) (May 6, 1999): 25–26; John Longwell, "Compaq Earns Crown," *Computer Reseller News* (Channel Champions Supplement) (June 17, 1996): 17–21; and *Quirk's Marketing Research Review* (April, 1988): 20.

7. Leslie Beyer, "A Stamp of Approval for the Post Office," *Credit Card Management,* 12(1) (April 1999): 121–124; and Rebecca Piirto, "Socks, Ties, and Videotape," *American Demographics* (September 1991).

8. Lillian Chaney, "Making U.S. Teams Work," *SuperVision,* 61(1) (January 2000): 6–8; Anne Marie Moss, "The Challenges of the Future," *FDM, Furniture Design & Manufacturing,* 71(5) (April 1999): 108–115; Anne Marie Moss, "The Office of the Future," *FDM, Furniture Design & Manufacturing,* 69(8) (August 1997): 36–42; and "Ignore your Customers," *Fortune* (May 1, 1995): 121–122, 124, 126.

9. Based on "1998 Edison Best New Product Winners," *Marketing News,* 33(7) (March 29, 1999): E4, E13+; and "1995 Edison Best New Products Awards Winners," *Marketing News,* 30(10) (May 6, 1996): E4–E11.

10. Jane W. Licata, "Get your customers to help with your budget decisions," *Bank Marketing,* 27 (September 1995): 27–31.

11. Charles McKelvey, "UEFA Engages Nike in Guerilla Warfare," *Marketing Week (UK),* 23(17) (May 25, 2000): 20; Terry Lefton, "Nike Bulls Ahead," *Brandweek,* 40(7) (February 15, 1999): 3; Roger Baird, "Game, Set and Match," *Marketing Week,* 20(22) (August 28, 1997): 28–31.

12. Gordon A. Wyner, "Collaborative Filtering: Research or IT?" *Marketing Research: A Magazine of Management & Applications,* 10(3) (Fall 1998): 35–37; Tim Powell, "Information Technology Helps Reengineer Research," *Marketing News* (February 28, 1994): 11, 14; Peter J. DePaulo and Rick Weitzer, "Interactive Phone Technology Delivers Survey Data Quickly," *Marketing News* (June 6, 1994): H33–H34.

13. Diane K. Bowers, "Connecting With Consumers," *Marketing Research,* 11(4) (Winter 1999/Spring 2000): 36–37; Lou E. Pelton, Jhinuk Chowdhry, and Scott J. Vitell, Jr., "A Framework for the Examination of Relational Ethics: An Interactionist Perspective," *Journal of Business Ethics,* 19(3) (Part 2) (April 1999): 241–253; Betsy Peterson, "Ethics Revisited," *Marketing Research: A Magazine of Management & Applications,* 8(4) (Winter 1996): 47–48; and Marla Royne Stafford and Thomas F. Stafford, "Participant Observation and the Pursuit of Truth: Methodological and Ethical Considerations," *Journal of the Market Research Society,* 35 (January 1993): 63–76.

14. Based on Ellen Messmer, "ISP Software Tack Customers' Every Move," *Network World,* 14(39) (September 29, 1997): 17.

8

CAUSAL RESEARCH DESIGN: EXPERIMENTATION

WHILE EXPERIMENTS CANNOT PROVE CAUSALITY, EXPERIMENTATION IS THE BEST METHOD FOR MAKING CAUSAL INFERENCES.

Sheri Bretan, Vice President/Managing Director, Elrick & Lavidge.
Sheri Bretan is based in Elrick & Lavidge's New York area office. She is responsible for designing and managing the research needs for several clients in a variety of industries. She has several years of full-service marketing research experience.

Opening Questions

1. How is the concept of causality defined in marketing research, and how do we distinguish between the ordinary meaning and the scientific meaning of causality?

2. What are the conditions for causality? Can a causal relationship be demonstrated conclusively?

3. How do we define and differentiate the two types of validity: internal and external?

4. What are the various types of experimental designs, and what are the differences among preexperimental, true experimental, quasi-experimental, and statistical designs?

5. How can we compare and contrast the use of laboratory versus field experimentation and experimental versus nonexperimental designs in marketing research?

6. What is test marketing, and how does it involve experimentation?

7. Can experimentation play a role in total quality management?

8. Why is the internal and external validity of field experiments that are conducted overseas generally lower than in the United States?

9. How does technology facilitate causal research?

10. What ethical issues are involved in conducting causal research, and how can debriefing address some of these issues?

11. How can the Internet be used to conduct causal research?

MUZAK: AN UNCOMMON REMEDY FOR THE COMMON COLD

Once referred to as "background music," Muzak is now referred to as "audio architecture" in the business world. Muzak has provided products to more than 300,000 businesses and currently generates close to $200 million in revenues. The company offers music, sound systems, videos, and messaging at 200 sales and service locations across the United States.

Muzak is now moving into audio marketing in supermarkets. In a time of increasing competition, more store advertising at the point of purchase may be just what is needed. Research shows that few customers come to the grocery store with a specific brand in mind. Most consumers know what items they need and choose brands or sizes when they reach the store. So audio advertising, such as Muzak provides, seems to hold promise.

An experiment was designed to test the effectiveness of Muzak advertising. Twenty randomly selected supermarkets were assigned to one of two groups, each group containing 10 supermarkets. One group of supermarkets, randomly selected, was the experimental group and the other the control group. Muzak ads for selected products were run in the experimental group supermarkets for a period of 10 weeks. These ads were informational, informing consumers of the benefits of the advertised products. The price and other factors (e.g., shelf space) affecting the sale of these items were kept the same in both the experimental and control group stores. The sales of the advertised products were monitored for both the experimental and control groups. The results showed an increase in the sales of advertised items, with cold/allergy/sinus products recording the highest increase of 29.8 percent (see table). Thus, there may be an expanding market for Muzak in the near future.[1]

PRODUCT	PERCENTAGE OF SALES INCREASE IN EXPERIMENTAL STORES
Potato chips	3.5
Condensed milk	7.1
Tea bags	13.7
Cold cereal	12.2
Juice	14.5
Laundry detergent	27.4
Toothpaste	28.9
Cold/allergy/ sinus relief	29.8

OVERVIEW

In Chapter 3, we introduced the two broad categories of conclusive research: causal and descriptive research designs. We discussed descriptive designs in Chapter 7. In this chapter, we will concentrate our discussion on causal research designs. Figure 8.1 briefly explains the focus of the chapter, the relationship of this chapter to the previous ones, and the steps of the marketing research process on which this chapter concentrates. Experimentation is the primary method employed to collect data in causal research designs. The opening vignette illustrates an experiment conducted to determine the effect of in-store Muzak advertising on the sales of selected items.

We will discuss experimentation in detail in this chapter. We will explain the concept of research validity and threats to that validity. We will present a classification of experimental designs and consider specific designs, along with the relative merits of laboratory versus field experiments. We will consider applications in test marketing, total quality management (TQM), and international marketing research. Finally, we will discuss the impact of technology and ethical issues in experimentation, as well as Internet applications. Figure 8.2 gives an overview of the different topics discussed in this chapter and how they flow from one to the next.

CONCEPT OF CAUSALITY

A causal inference relates to whether a change in one marketing variable produces a change in another variable. Marketing managers are often faced with decisions in which they attempt to infer causal relationships. For example, will a 10 percent price reduction

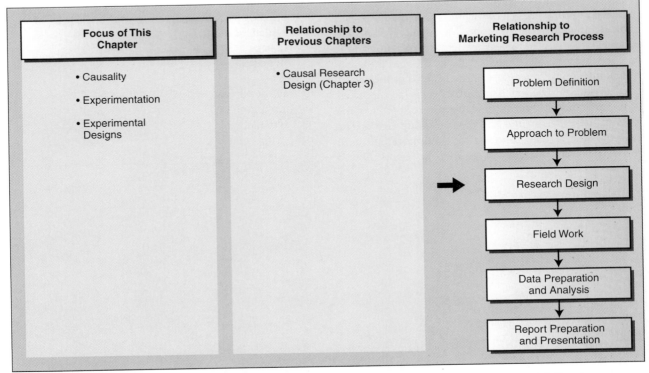

FIGURE 8.1   Relationship of Experimentation to the Previous Chapters and the Marketing Research Process

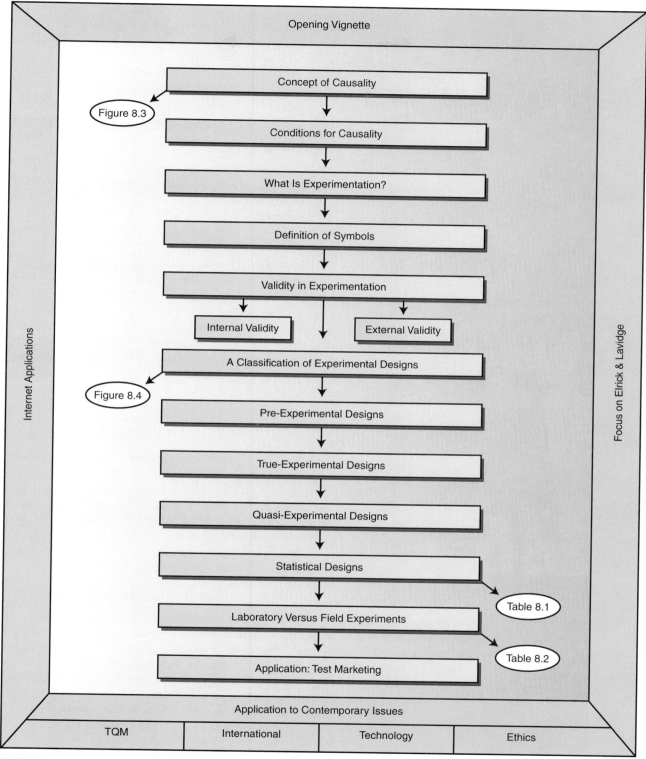

FIGURE 8.2 Experimentation: An Overview

causality
When the occurrence of X increases the probability of the occurrence of Y.

in Maxwell House coffee result in an increase in sales to a level that will at least cover the revenues lost due to the price reduction? In evaluating this question, the marketing manager is drawing a causal inference that price influences the sales of Maxwell House coffee. In the opening vignette, the inference was that Muzak advertising leads to (causes) increased sales. **Causality** means something very different to the average person on the street than it means to a scientist. Take, for example, the statement "X causes Y."

ORDINARY MEANING	SCIENTIFIC MEANING
X is the only cause of Y.	X is only one of a number of possible causes of Y.
X must always lead to Y.	The occurrence of X makes the occurrence of Y more probable.
(X is a deterministic cause of Y.)	(X is a probabilistic cause of Y.)
It is possible to prove that X is a cause of Y.	We can never prove that X is a cause of Y. At best, we can infer that X is a cause of Y.

To identify the cause of variation in fast food sales, all three conditions for causality must be satisfied.

concomitant variation
A condition for inferring causality that requires that the extent to which a cause, X, and an effect, Y, occur together or vary together is predicted by the hypothesis under consideration.

The scientific meaning of causality is more appropriate to marketing research because it is sensitive to the limitations that surround our data collection process and the causal inferences we can legitimately draw. In the opening vignette, experimenters realized that in-store advertising was only one cause of sales. There were other causes, such as prices and shelf displays, which affected sales and consequently had to be controlled.

CONDITIONS FOR CAUSALITY

At least three conditions must be satisfied in order to justify the inference of a causal relationship between two variables: (1) concomitant variation, (2) time order of occurrence of variables, and (3) absence of other possible causal factors. These conditions are necessary but not sufficient to demonstrate causality. By that we mean that they must be satisfied to justify drawing a causal inference; however, their presence does not guarantee that we have isolated the true variables responsible for the effects we are observing. These conditions are explained in more detail in the following sections.

Concomitant Variation

Concomitant variation occurs when the presumed cause (X) and presumed effect (Y) are both present and both vary in a manner our hypothesis predicted. Suppose a regional marketing manager for a fast-food outlet wants to identify the causes of variation in food sales across the 20 outlets in her region. After visiting all 20 sites, she has concluded that the monthly outlet performance scores (X)—which reflect factors such as average wait time during peak hours, cleanliness, and food quality—directly impact sales (Y). Given that hypothesis, outlets that are scoring high on performance measurements should be recording the highest sales levels. Her analysis indicates that this relationship does, in fact, hold. Can she conclude that high performance scores "cause" high sales?

The answer to that question is no. Many other factors may be affecting sales. For example, the outlet location, the presence of competition, and the concentration of the surrounding residential area may all have an impact on sales even though they are not included in the outlet performance score. This example illustrates the limitations associated with drawing causal inferences. We cannot conclude that we have identified the cause of fast-food outlet sales from this research. All we can say is that an association exists between performance scores and sales.

Time Order of Occurrence of Variables

Another requirement in determining a causal relationship relates to when the variables occur, that is, the occurrence in time of the presumed cause relative to the presumed effect. For one variable to hypothetically cause another, it must precede or occur simultaneously with the effect. This is referred to as the time order of variables.

Although time order of variables seems like an intuitively obvious requirement, it is not always easy to determine time order in a marketing situation. For example, customers who shop frequently in a department store are more likely to have the credit card for that store. Also, customers who have a department store charge card are likely to shop there frequently. The time order of these variables—charge card ownership and frequent shopping—is not obvious. Did charge card ownership precede frequent shopping or did frequent shopping precede charge card ownership? An understanding of the underlying phenomena associated with department store shopping may be necessary to accurately identify time order.

Absence of Other Possible Causal Factors

As can be seen in the above examples, both time order and concurrent variation conditions may be satisfied, yet we may not have identified the relevant cause–effect relationship. The presence of additional or extraneous variables that impact the effect (dependent) variable must be controlled in order to draw causal inferences. In-store service may be a cause of sales if we can be sure that changes in all other factors affecting sales, such as pricing, advertising, level of distribution, product quality, competition, and so on, were held constant or otherwise controlled. Ruling out other possible causal factors is seldom an easy task. The following example illustrates the difficulty of establishing a causal relationship.

EXAMPLE

POP BUYS

Recent statistical data show that consumers make as much as 80 percent of their buying decisions at the point-of-purchase (POP). POP buying decisions have increased concurrently with increased advertising efforts in stores. These include radio advertisements, ads on shopping carts, floor space, and grocery bags, ceiling signs, and shelf displays. It is difficult to separate the cause from the effect of POP advertising and POP buying. It is possible that these variables may be both causes and effects in this relationship. In other words, there is more POP advertising because there is more POP buying, and there is more POP buying because there is more POP advertising.[2]

If, as the preceding example indicates, it is difficult to establish cause–effect relationships, what is the role of evidence obtained in experimentation?

Role of Evidence

The combination of evidence of causality in the form of concomitant variation, time order of occurrence of variables, and elimination of other possible causal factors does not guarantee that a causal relationship exists. However, an accumulation of consistent evidence increases our confidence that a causal relationship exists. Controlled experiments can provide strong evidence on all the three conditions.

WHAT IS EXPERIMENTATION?

Experimentation is the research technique used in causal research (Figure 8.3). Experiments can be described in terms of independent, dependent, and extraneous variables, test units, and random assignment to experimental and control groups. To conduct an **experiment,** the researcher manipulates and controls one or more independent variables and then observes the effects those manipulated variables have on the dependent variables, while controlling the influence of outside or extraneous variables. In this section, we define these concepts and illustrate them using the example in the opening vignette.

Independent Variables

Independent variables are variables or alternatives that are manipulated (i.e., the researcher changes the levels of these variables) and whose effects are measured and compared. These variables, also known as treatments, may include price levels, package designs, and advertising themes. In the opening vignette, the independent variable was Muzak advertising, and the treatments consisted of Muzak advertising versus no advertising.

Test Units

Test units are individuals, organizations, or other entities whose response to the independent variables or treatments is being examined. Test units may include consumers, stores, or geographic areas. The test units were supermarkets in the opening vignette.

Dependent Variables

Dependent variables are the variables that measure the effect of the independent variables on the test units. These variables may include sales, profits, and market shares. The dependent variables in the opening vignette were the sales of specific products.

experiment
The process of manipulating one or more independent variables and measuring their effect on one or more dependent variables, while controlling for the extraneous variables.

independent variables
Variables that are manipulated by the researcher and whose effects are measured and compared.

test units
Individuals, organizations, or other entities whose response to independent variables or treatments is being studied.

dependent variables
Variables that measure the effect of the independent variables on the test units.

FIGURE 8.3
Experimentation as
Conclusive Research

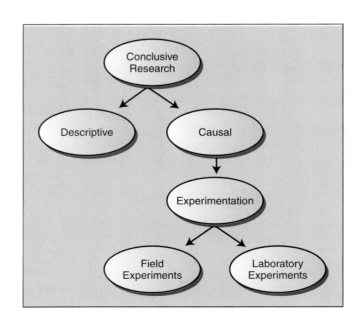

Extraneous Variables

Extraneous variables are all variables other than the independent variables that affect the response of the test units. These variables can confound the dependent variable measures in a way that weakens or invalidates the results of the experiment. Extraneous variables include store size, store location, and competitive effort. In the Muzak vignette, the extraneous variables would be other variables, such as price, amount of shelf space, and so on, that would affect the sales of the selected products.

extraneous variables
Variables, other than the independent variables, that influence the response of the test units.

Random Assignment to Experimental and Control Groups

Random assignment is one of the most common techniques used to control for the effect of extraneous variables on the dependent variable. Random assignment to experimental and control groups attempts to minimize the influence of extraneous factors such as age, income, or brand preference by spreading them equally across the groups under study.

When an experiment is being conducted, at least one group will be exposed to the manipulated independent variable. This is called the **experimental group.** The results of this experimental group may be compared to another experimental group at a differing level of manipulation or to a control group. The **control group** is not exposed to the independent variable manipulation. It provides a point of comparison when examining the effects of these manipulations on the dependent variable. In the opening vignette, the supermarket stores were randomly assigned to the two groups. One of the groups was randomly chosen to be the experimental group (that was exposed to Muzak advertising), and the other served as the control group (that received no advertising).

experimental group
The group exposed to the manipulated independent variable.

control group
The control group is not exposed to the independent variable manipulation. It provides a point of comparison when examining the effects of these manipulations on the dependent variable.

Experimental Design

An **experimental design** is a set of procedures specifying (1) the test units and how these units are to be divided into homogeneous subsamples, (2) what independent variables or treatments are to be manipulated, (3) what dependent variables are to be measured, and (4) how the extraneous variables are to be controlled.

In the Muzak vignette, the test units were stores that were randomly assigned to two groups. The independent variable to be manipulated was Muzak advertising versus no advertising, and the dependent variables were the sales of specific products. Extraneous variables such as price and shelf space were kept at the same levels in both the experimental group and the control group supermarkets by exercising managerial control.

As a further illustration of these definitions, consider the following example.

experimental design
The set of experimental procedures specifying (1) the test units and sampling procedures, (2) independent variables, (3) dependent variables, and (4) how to control the extraneous variables.

EXAMPLE

TAKING COUPONS AT FACE VALUE

An experiment was conducted to test the effects of coupon value on redemption. Personal interviews were conducted in New York with 280 shoppers who were entering or leaving a supermarket. Two levels of the independent variable (coupon value) were used, one offering 15 cents off and the other 50 cents off. Shoppers were randomly assigned to these two coupon-value levels.

Brand usage was presumed to be an extraneous variable. Four brands—Tide detergent, Kellogg's corn flakes, Aim toothpaste, and Joy liquid dishwashing detergent—were used. The respondents answered questions about which brands they used so that the effect of this extraneous variable could be controlled during analysis. Respondents were also asked how likely they were to cash coupons of the given face value the next time they shopped. An interesting finding was that higher face-value coupons produced a higher likelihood of redemption among infrequent or nonbuyers of the promoted brand but had little effect on regular buyers.[3]

In the preceding experiment, the independent variable that was manipulated was the value of the coupon (15 cents versus 50 cents). The dependent variable was the likelihood of cashing the coupon. The extraneous variable that was controlled was brand usage. The experimental design required the random assignment of shoppers to two experimental groups. A control group was not used in this design.

DEFINITION OF SYMBOLS

To help in our discussion of extraneous variables and specific experimental designs, we will use a set of symbols commonly used in marketing research:

> X = The exposure of a group to an independent variable, treatment, or event, the effects of which are to be determined
>
> O = The process of observation or measurement of the dependent variable on the test units or group of units
>
> R = The random assignment of test units or groups to separate treatments

In addition, the following conventions are adopted:

- Movement from left to right indicates movement through time.
- Horizontal alignment of symbols implies that those symbols refer to a specific treatment group.
- Vertical alignment of symbols implies that those symbols refer to activities or events that occur simultaneously.

For example, the symbolic arrangement

> X O_1 O_2

means that a given group of test units was exposed to the treatment variable (X), and the response was measured at two different points in time O_1 and O_2.

Likewise, the symbolic arrangement

> R X_1 O_1
> R X_2 O_2

means that two groups of test units were randomly assigned (R) to two different treatment groups at the same time (X_1 and X_2), and the dependent variable was measured in the two groups simultaneously (O_1 and O_2).

VALIDITY IN EXPERIMENTATION

In conducting an experiment, a researcher has two goals. The first is to draw valid conclusions about the effect of the independent variables on the dependent variables. This is referred to as internal validity. The second goal is to make valid generalizations from the specific experimental environment to a larger population. This goal is satisfied when external validity is achieved.

Internal Validity

Internal validity refers to whether the manipulation of the independent variables or treatments actually caused the observed effects on the dependent variables. Internal validity is threatened when the influences of extraneous variables are mixed with the independent variables. Without proper control of the extraneous variables, the researcher is unable to isolate the effect of the independent variable and thus cannot establish internal validity. In the opening vignette, to claim internal validity the researcher had to show that the increase in sales of the products in the experimental group supermarkets was in fact due to (caused by) Muzak advertising. Thus, the researcher had to show that price and other extraneous variables (e.g., shelf space) affecting the sale of these products were kept the same in both the experimental and control group stores.

internal validity
A measure of accuracy of an experiment. It measures if the manipulation of the independent variables, or treatments, actually caused the effects on the dependent variable(s).

External Validity

External validity refers to whether the cause–effect relationships found in the experiment remain the same when replicated in a larger population. In other words, can the results be generalized beyond the experimental situation? If so, to what populations, settings, times, independent variables, and dependent variables can the results be projected? In the opening vignette, to claim external validity the researcher must show that the sample of 20 supermarkets was representative, no peculiar conditions were encountered, and the results are generalizable to all supermarkets.

external validity
A determination of whether the cause–effect relationships found in the experiment can be generalized.

Threats to external validity arise when the experiment is conducted in an unrealistic manner, limiting the ability to generalize. This occurs when the experimental conditions do not account for factors likely to be encountered in the real world. Experiments conducted in a laboratory environment are more likely to lack external validity than field experiments. This is because laboratory experiments are conducted in artificial, highly controlled environments.

Market researchers often have to make decisions to trade off one form of validity in order to gain another. However, internal validity must be protected in order to produce results that are meaningful enough to generalize, as illustrated in the following example.

E X A M P L E

EXPERIMENTING WITH NEW PRODUCTS

Controlled-distribution electronic test markets are used increasingly to conduct experimental research on new products. The entire test marketing project is handled by an external research supplier. The research company distributes the actual new product in stores that represent a predetermined percentage of the market. The arrangement with the selected stores allows the research company a high degree of control over how the product is sold in these stores. Thus, this method makes it possible to control for several extraneous factors that affect new product performance and manipulate the variables of interest. It is possible to ensure that a new product: (1) obtains the right level of store acceptance and distribution, (2) is positioned in the correct aisle in each store, (3) receives the right number of facings on the shelf,

(4) has the correct everyday price, (5) never has out-of-stock problems, and (6) obtains the planned level of trade promotion, display, and price features on the desired time schedule. Thus, a high degree of internal validity can be achieved.

Procter & Gamble (P&G) uses this method to test new products before introducing them to the national market. For example, Oil of Olay Beauty Bar was test marketed in this manner. The results of electronic test marketing indicated a favorable consumer response to Oil of Olay Beauty Bar and, as a result, this new product was introduced nationally.

While we will consider test marketing in more detail later in the chapter, the preceding example shows that controlled-distribution electronic test markets can be effective in controlling for specific extraneous variables. Extraneous variables can also be controlled by adopting specific experimental designs, as described in the next section.

A CLASSIFICATION OF EXPERIMENTAL DESIGNS

preexperimental designs
Designs that do not control for extraneous factors by randomization.

There are four broad categories of experimental designs: preexperimental, true experimental, quasi-experimental, and statistical designs (Figure 8.4). **Preexperimental designs** do not use randomization to control for extraneous factors. Thus, they suffer from many threats to internal and external validity. However, with a proper note of their limitations, they can add value when used in an exploratory fashion. Three examples of this design are the one-shot case study, the one-group pretest–posttest design, and the static group. These designs, along with the others that follow, are discussed in detail later.

FIGURE 8.4
A Classification of Experimental Designs

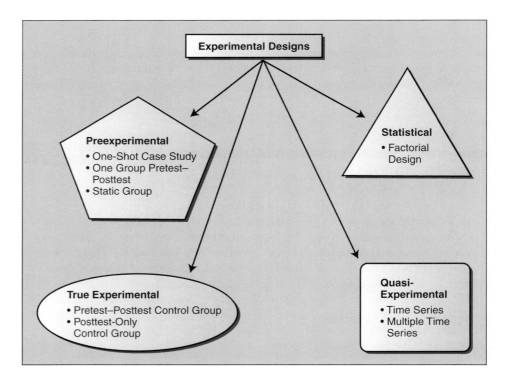

In **true experimental designs,** the researcher can randomly assign subjects and experimental groups. Therefore, these designs provide a larger degree of control over extraneous variables. Included in this category are the pretest–posttest control group design and the posttest-only control group design.

Quasi-experimental designs result when the researcher is unable to fully manipulate the independent variables or treatments but can still apply part of the apparatus of true experimentation. These designs are typically employed in natural environments, enabling some degree of experimental control in a natural setting. Two such designs are time series and multiple time series designs.

A **statistical design** is a series of basic experiments that allows for statistical control and analysis of external variables. Statistical designs are classified on the basis of their characteristics and use. The important statistical designs include factorial designs.

We will illustrate the various experimental designs in the context of measuring the effectiveness of PepsiCo advertising. Pepsi makes heavy use of celebrities in its advertising. To capture the teenage market, Pepsi ads highlighted superstars Michael Jackson and Lionel Richie with the theme, "Choice of a New Generation." Other "New Generation" stars featured in Pepsi ads included Don Johnson (of *Miami Vice* fame), Michael J. Fox (star of *Back to the Future*), and comedian Billy Crystal. The "You've Got the Right One Baby, Uh Huh!" campaign for Diet Pepsi featured star singer Ray Charles. In March 1999, Pepsi struck the right chord when it launched the much-lauded "Joy of Cola" campaign, featuring appearances by dimpled Hallie Eisenberg and the ironic, iconic television show host Tom Green.

Should Pepsi continue to feature celebrities in its advertising? Is this advertising effective? Experimental research measuring advertising effectiveness can provide useful information. We begin our discussion with the preexperimental designs.

PepsiCo can make use of the various experimental designs to examine the effectiveness of its advertising.

true experimental designs
Experimental designs are distinguished by the fact that the researcher can randomly assign test units to experimental groups and also randomly assign treatments to experimental groups.

quasi-experimental designs
Designs that apply part of the procedures of true experimentation, while lacking full experimental control.

statistical design
Designs that allow for the statistical control and analysis of external variables.

PREEXPERIMENTAL DESIGNS

Preexperimental designs are characterized by an absence of randomization. We will describe three specific designs: the one-shot case study, the one-group pretest–posttest design, and the static group.

One-Shot Case Study

Also known as the after-only design, the **one-shot case study** may be symbolically represented as

$$X \quad O_1$$

A single group of subjects is exposed to a treatment (X), and then a single measurement on the dependent variable is taken (O_1). This type of design is constructed using a nonrandom sampling process in which the subjects are self-selected or selected arbitrarily by the researcher. Without randomization, the observed dependent variables are subject to the influences of several extraneous variables.

Additionally, the design lacks a control group. Without a control group, there is no point of comparison for the results. Due to lack of randomization and the absence of a control group, this design is clearly weak in terms of internal validity. For these reasons, the one-shot case study is more appropriate for exploratory rather than conclusive research.

one-shot case study
A preexperimental design in which a single group of test units is exposed to a treatment X, and then a single measurement on the dependent variable is taken.

ONE SHOT AT PEPSI ADVERTISING

To assess the effectiveness of Pepsi advertising featuring celebrities, telephone interviews would be conducted with respondents who report watching the particular TV program on which the commercial was aired the previous night (X). The dependent variables (Os) are unaided and aided recall, attitudes toward the advertisement, the brand, and the celebrity. First, unaided recall would be measured by asking the respondents whether they recall seeing a commercial for a soft drink. If they recall the Pepsi commercial, details about commercial content and execution would be solicited. Respondents who do not recall the test commercial would be asked if they saw a Pepsi commercial (aided recall). For those who have an unaided or aided recall of the commercial, attitudes toward the commercial, the brand advertised, and the celebrity featured would be measured. The results of these experimental measures can be compared with normal scores for these types of questions in order to assess the effectiveness of the advertising and the celebrity featured.

One-Group Pretest–Posttest Design

one-group pretest–posttest design
A preexperimental design in which a group of test units is measured before and after exposure to the treatment.

The **one-group pretest–posttest design** may be symbolized as

$$O_1 \quad X \quad O_2$$

In this design, a group of subjects is measured once before the experimental treatment (O_1) and once after (O_2). Again, there is no control group for comparison. The treatment effect is computed as $O_2 - O_1$. Although this design is considered better than a case study, the validity of conclusions is questionable since extraneous variables are largely uncontrolled due to lack of randomization and a control group. The following example shows how this design is used.

CAN PEPSI PERFORM IN A THEATER?

In the one-group pretest–posttest design to measure the effectiveness of test commercials, respondents are recruited to central theater locations in various test cities. The respondents are interviewed, and their attitudes toward Pepsi advertising, brand, and celebrity (O_1) are measured. Then they watch a TV program containing the Pepsi commercial (X) and other filler commercials. After viewing the TV program, the respondents are again interviewed regarding their attitudes toward Pepsi advertising, brand, and celebrity (O_2). The effectiveness of the test commercial is determined by the difference between O_2 and O_1.

static group
A preexperimental design in which there are two groups: the experimental group (EG), which is exposed to the treatment, and the control group (CG). Measurements on both groups are made only after the treatment, and test units are not assigned at random.

Static Group Design

The **static group** is a two-group experimental design in which one of the groups acts as a control group (CG). Only one group, the experimental group (EG), receives the experimental treatment. The subjects are not assigned randomly, and measurements are made on both groups following the treatment (posttest). This design is expressed symbolically as:

EG: X O_1

CG: O_2

The treatment effect would be measured as the difference between the control and experimental group $(O_1 - O_2)$. The lack of randomization leaves the experiment open to some extraneous effects. The two groups may differ before the treatment, leading to selection bias.

In practice, the control group is often defined as the group receiving the current level of marketing activity, rather than as a group that receives no treatment at all. In many cases, it is impossible to reduce marketing input to zero.

EXAMPLE

IS PEPSI ADVERTISING STATIC?

A static group comparison to measure the effectiveness of a Pepsi commercial would be conducted as follows. Two groups of respondents would be recruited on the basis of convenience. Only the experimental group would be exposed to the TV program containing the Pepsi commercial (X). Attitudes toward Pepsi advertising, brand, and celebrity would then be measured in both the experimental (O_1) and the control group (O_2). The effectiveness of the Pepsi commercial would be measured as the difference between the test and control group $(O_1 - O_2)$.

TRUE EXPERIMENTAL DESIGNS

True experimental designs are differentiated from preexperimental designs by the fact that subjects are randomly assigned to groups. Treatment conditions are also randomly assigned to groups. For example, respondents are randomly assigned to one of three experimental groups. One of the three versions of a test commercial, selected at random, is administered to each group. As a result of random assignment, extraneous factors can be represented equally in each group or treatment condition. **Randomization** is the preferred procedure for ensuring the prior equality of experimental groups. However, randomization may not be effective when the sample size is small because it merely produces groups that are equal on average. It is possible, though, to check whether randomization has been effective by measuring the possible extraneous variables and comparing them across the experimental and control groups.

True experimental designs include the pretest–posttest control group design and the posttest-only control group design.

randomization
One method of controlling extraneous variables that involves randomly assigning test units to experimental groups by using random numbers. Treatment conditions are also randomly assigned to experimental groups.

Pretest–Posttest Control Group Design

In the **pretest–posttest control group design,** subjects are randomly assigned to either the experimental or the control group. A pretreatment measure is taken on each group. Thus, each group is measured prior to administering the treatment to the experimental group. This design is symbolized as:

EG: R O_1 X O_2

CG: R O_3 O_4

pretest–posttest control group design
An experimental design in which the experimental group is exposed to the treatment but the control group is not. Pretest and posttest measures are taken on both groups. Test units are randomly assigned.

The treatment effect (TE) is measured as:

$$(O_2 - O_1) - (O_4 - O_3)$$

The randomization of this design controls for most extraneous variables. The extraneous effects are presumed to be equally represented in both the control and experimental groups. The difference between the control and experimental groups is thought to reflect only the treatment. With the use of a pretest measure in this design, the posttest measurement is susceptible to **interactive testing effects,** which means that a prior measurement affects the test unit's response to the independent variable.

interactive testing effect
An effect in which a prior measurement affects the test unit's response to the independent variable.

EXAMPLE

PEPSI PRE- AND POSTMORTEM

An experiment for measuring the effectiveness of Pepsi's advertising using a pretest–posttest control group design would be designed as follows. A random sample of respondents would be distributed randomly into two equal groups. One group, selected randomly, will be the experimental group and the other the control group. A pretest questionnaire would be administered to the respondents in both groups to obtain a measurement on attitudes toward Pepsi advertising, brand, and celebrity. Only the respondents in the experimental group would be exposed to the TV program containing the Pepsi commercial. Then a questionnaire would be administered to respondents in both groups to obtain posttest measures on attitudes toward Pepsi advertising, brand, and celebrity.

As this example shows, the pretest–posttest control group design involves two groups and two measurements on each group. A simpler design is the posttest-only control group design.

Posttest-Only Control Group Design

The **posttest-only control group design** does not involve any premeasurement. It may be symbolized as:

posttest-only control group design
Experimental design in which the experimental group is exposed to the treatment but the control group is not and no pretest measure is taken. Test units are randomly assigned.

$$\text{EG:} \quad R \quad X \quad O_1$$
$$\text{CG:} \quad R \qquad\quad O_2$$

The treatment effect is the difference between the experimental and control group measurements.

$$TE = O_1 - O_2$$

One significant advantage of this design over the pretest–posttest control is the elimination of the interactive testing effect that comes with pretesting. Additionally, the simplicity of this design offers time, cost, and sample size advantages. For these reasons, it is the most popular experimental design in marketing research.

However, this design is not without limitations. Although randomization is used to equalize groups, without a pretest, there is no way to verify group similarity. Without a pretest, researchers are also unable to examine changes in individual subjects over the course of the study. Note that, except for premeasurement, the implementation of this design is very similar to that of the pretest–posttest control group design. The opening vignette provided an application. The supermarket stores were randomly assigned to the experimental group and the control group. No premeasurements were taken. Only the stores in the experimental group were exposed to Muzak advertising. Measurements on the sales of advertised items were obtained in the experimental group (O_1) and control group (O_2) stores. The increase in sales due to Muzak advertising was determined as ($O_1 - O_2$).

QUASI-EXPERIMENTAL DESIGNS

Quasi-experimental designs are appropriate when researchers are faced with situations in which they are unable to randomize or control the scheduling of experimental treatments. The experimenters may, however, be able to control when and on whom experimental measurements are taken. Quasi-experimental designs are faster and less expensive than other experimental designs and in some natural research settings may be the only avenue open for data collection. However, because full experimental control is lacking, researchers must take into account the specific variables that are not controlled. Popular forms of quasi-experimental designs are time series and multiple time series designs.

Time Series Design

The **time series design** involves the use of periodic measurements of a group or individuals. At some point during the measurement, an experimental manipulation occurs naturally or is artificially introduced. Additional measurement follows. A time series experiment may be symbolized as:

$$O_1 \, O_2 \, O_3 \, O_4 \, O_5 \, X \, O_6 \, O_7 \, O_8 \, O_9 \, O_{10}$$

This is a quasi experiment because of the lack of control the researcher has in terms of randomization of the subjects to treatments. Additionally, the researcher may have no control over the timing of treatment presentation, as well as which subjects are exposed to the treatment. Multiple measurement may create an interactive testing effect, causing a change in measured behavior simply because the respondents know they are being measured. Nevertheless, time series designs are useful, particularly when evaluating behavior occurring in a natural setting.

time series design
A quasi-experimental design that involves periodic measurements on the dependent variable for a group of test units. Then, the treatment is administered by the researcher or occurs naturally. After the treatment, periodic measurements are continued in order to determine the treatment effect.

EXAMPLE

TIME WILL TELL THE EFFECTIVENESS OF PEPSI ADVERTISING: TIME SERIES DESIGN

The effectiveness of a Pepsi commercial (X) may be examined by broadcasting the commercial into a series of markets a predetermined number of times. The test units or respondents are members of a panel. Although the marketer can control the scheduling of the test commercial, it is not possible to control when or if panel members are exposed to it. The marketer will examine panel members' attitudes toward Pepsi advertising, brand, and the celebrity as well as purchases before, during, and after the campaign to determine whether the test commercial had a short-term effect, a long-term effect, or no effect.

multiple time series design
A time series design that includes another group of test units to serve as a control group.

The **multiple time series design** is similar to time series except that it adds a control group that is also repeatedly measured. This group is not subject to the experimental treatment. If the control group is carefully selected, this design can be an improvement over the simple time series experiment.

STATISTICAL DESIGNS

Statistical designs consist of a series of basic experiments that allow for statistical control and analysis of external variables. In other words, several basic experiments are conducted simultaneously. Thus, statistical designs are influenced by the same sources of invalidity that affect the basic designs being used. Statistical designs offer the following advantages:

1. The effects of more than one independent variable can be measured.
2. Specific extraneous variables can be statistically controlled.
3. Economical designs can be formulated when each subject is measured more than once.

The most common statistical designs are the factorial designs.

Factorial Design

factorial design
A statistical experimental design used to measure the effects of two or more independent variables at various levels and to allow for interactions between variables.

A **factorial design** is used to measure the effects of two or more independent variables at various levels. It allows for the measurement of interactions between variables. An interaction is said to take place when the simultaneous effect of two or more variables is different from the sum of their separate effects. For example, an individual's favorite drink might be coffee and her favorite temperature level might be cold, but this individual might not prefer cold coffee, leading to an interaction.

A factorial design may also be thought of as a table. In a two-factor design, each level of one variable represents a row, and each level of another variable represents a column. Factorial designs involve a cell for every possible combination of treatment variables, as in the example that follows.

EXAMPLE

FACTORING HUMOR AND INFORMATION IN PEPSI COMMERCIALS

Suppose that in the Pepsi case the researcher is interested in examining the effect of humor and the effect of various levels of brand information on advertising effectiveness. Three levels of humor (no humor, medium humor, and high humor) are to be examined. Likewise, brand information is to be manipulated at three levels (low, medium, and high). The resulting table would be three rows (levels of information) by three columns (levels of humor), producing nine possible combinations or cells, as laid out in Table 8.1.

The respondents would be randomly assigned to one of the nine cells. Respondents in each cell would receive a specific treatment combination. For example, respondents in the upper left-hand corner cell would view a commercial that had no humor and low brand information. After exposure to a treatment combination, measures would be obtained on attitudes toward Pepsi advertising, brand, and the celebrity from respondents in each cell.

TABLE 8.1   An Example of a Factorial Design

AMOUNT OF BRAND INFORMATION	AMOUNT OF HUMOR		
	No Humor	Medium Humor	High Humor
Low			
Medium			
High			

Statistical procedures such as analysis of variance (discussed in Chapter 17) are used to analyze the treatment effects and interactions. The main disadvantage of a factorial design is that the number of treatment combinations increases multiplicatively with an increase in the number of variables or levels. However, this is often not a serious limitation as the researcher can control both the number of variables and the levels.

SELECTING AN EXPERIMENTAL DESIGN

Selecting an experimental design often involves a tradeoff in terms of control. Designs that offer the greatest degree of internal validity typically are conducted in highly artificial environments that can threaten the generalizability or external validity of the experimental results.

One solution to finding the optimum combination of internal and external validity may be to use differing experimental designs at differing points in the study. For example, designs that offer tight internal validity may be used during the early stages of the research effort. In this way, a more reliable measure of the true treatment effect may be secured. During later stages of the study, more natural settings may be used to enable generalization of results.

In the following section, we will discuss the distinction between laboratory and field experimentation in more detail.

LABORATORY VERSUS FIELD EXPERIMENTS

A **laboratory environment** is an artificial one, which affords the greatest amount of control over the crucial factors involved in the study. Advertising testing in central location theaters and test kitchens are examples of laboratory experiments used in marketing research. Because the environments are highly contrived, questions of external validity are raised. Compared to field experiments, the artificial nature of laboratory environments may cause reactive error, in that the respondents react to the situation itself rather than to the independent variable. Also, laboratory environments may cause **demand artifacts**, a phenomenon in which the respondents attempt to guess the purpose of the experiment, modifying their responses accordingly. On the positive side, laboratory experiments do allow for more complex designs than field experiments. Hence, the researcher can control for more factors or variables in the laboratory setting, which increases internal validity.

laboratory environment
An artificial setting for experimentation in which the researcher constructs the desired conditions.

demand artifacts
Responses given because the respondents attempt to guess the purpose of the experiment and respond accordingly.

TABLE 8.2   **Laboratory Versus Field Experiments**

FACTOR	LABORATORY	FIELD
Environment	Artificial	Realistic
Control	High	Low
Reactive error	High	Low
Demand artifacts	High	Low
Internal validity	High	Low
External validity	Low	High
Time	Short	Long
Number of units	Small	Large
Ease of implementation	High	Low
Cost	Low	High

field environment
An experimental location set in actual market conditions.

A **field environment** involves measurement of behavior, attitudes, or perceptions in the environment in which they occur. The researcher has much less control over extraneous variables that may affect internal validity. However, if internal validity can be maintained, the results may generalize more easily than those obtained in a laboratory setting. The opening vignette presents an example of a field experiment. The differences between the two environments are summarized in Table 8.2.

LIMITATIONS OF EXPERIMENTATION

Although experimentation is becoming increasingly important in marketing research, it does have limitations: time, cost, and administration of an experiment.

Time

Many types of field experiments become increasingly accurate with time. To observe the long-term effect of a promotional campaign or a new product introduction, for example, purchase behavior must be observed over multiple purchase cycles. The accuracy of such behavioral information tends to increase with the passage of time. This added precision must be weighed against the costs of delaying a product rollout or the launch of a new advertising campaign.

Cost

New product research in field environments can be extremely expensive. It is much more expensive than laboratory experiments, which typically occur on a small scale and use a limited number of subjects. In order to field test a new product, management must consider more than just the direct costs of data collection and analysis. Production must be initiated on a limited scale; point-of-sale promotional campaigns as well as advertising must be developed and introduced on a limited basis. Limited distribution channels may also have to be opened. Test market experiments can easily cost millions of dollars.

Administration

Controlling the effects of extraneous variables is an essential aspect of experimental research. Achieving the desired level of control becomes increasingly difficult as the research moves from the laboratory to the field. Field experiments often interfere with a company's ongoing operations, and obtaining cooperation from the retailers, wholesalers, and others involved can be difficult. Finally, competitors may deliberately contaminate the results of a field experiment.

APPLICATION: TEST MARKETING

Test marketing is an example of a controlled field experiment conducted in limited but representative parts of a market. The research sites are called **test markets.** In a test market experiment, a national marketing program is replicated on a small scale. The two major objectives of test marketing are (1) to determine market acceptance of the product, and (2) to test alternative levels of marketing mix variables. The independent variables being manipulated in such studies typically include elements of the marketing mix. Promotional investments, pricing, product modifications, or distribution elements are all factors that the researcher can manipulate. Observed consumer reactions represent the dependent variables, measured in terms of purchase behavior (sales) and/or attitudes or reactions to the marketing manipulations being studied.

Designing a standard market test involves deciding what criteria to use for selecting test markets, how many test markets to use, and the duration of the test. Among all of the criteria considered in selecting a test market, representativeness of that market is perhaps the most important. Information gathered from a new product test, for example, can be used to predict ultimate market acceptance of that product and will govern the "go/no-go" decision regarding full market rollout. The test market must also be self-contained in terms of media coverage if mass-market advertising is planned to support the test. This prevents wasting promotional dollars. Additionally, the promotion of new products that are available in only a limited area can create negative consumer reaction toward future rollouts.

Test marketing runs the risk of revealing strategies, new product developments, or modified product positioning to the competition. Therefore, the strength of competition in a particular test site is another important consideration. Some commonly used test markets are Charlotte, North Carolina; Fort Wayne, Indiana; Kansas City, Missouri; Knoxville, Tennessee; Rochester, New York; and Sacramento–Stockton, California. These cities are desirable test markets because each is considered to be fairly representative of a large segment of the U.S. population.

In general, the more test markets that can be used, the better. If resources are limited, at least two test markets should be used for each program variation to be tested. However, where external validity is important, at least four test markets should be used.

Despite its limitations in terms of time demands, costs, and competitive responses, test marketing can be very beneficial to a product's successful introduction, as the following example demonstrates.

test marketing
An application of a controlled experiment done in limited, but carefully selected, test markets. It involves replicating the planned national marketing program for a product in the test markets.

test markets
A carefully selected part of the marketplace that is particularly suitable for test marketing.

EXAMPLE

CHRYSLER SHOWCASE: THE SHOWPLACE FOR CAR BUYERS

Research by Plymouth indicated that many customers were unhappy with the process of purchasing a car. In response to this finding, the company created Plymouth Place, a site where people could learn about Plymouth without sales pressure. The concept of Plymouth Place was simple: Why not provide a place for people to visit that is comfortable, convenient, accessible, and stress-free while providing the information they need? Why not take Plymouth outside the dealership to where the target market already is: regional shopping malls?

Physically, Plymouth Place is typically a 1,000-square-foot space in a regional shopping mall that is open whenever the mall is open. It houses the Voyager, Breeze, and Neon models, with doors, trunks, hoods, and so on open and accessible at all times, communicating to the visitor that he or she is invited to explore. An advisor answers questions, talks about Plymouth Place, and generally tries to be helpful to consumers, but cannot sell a car.

The Plymouth Place concept was tested in two test markets: Portland, Oregon, and Milwaukee, Wisconsin. The results were encouraging. Significant sales signaled a major improvement in the shopping process. Compared to the national norm, which served as a control level, Portland's sales increased by 16 percent, and Milwaukee's increased by an astounding 36 percent. These results only confirmed what marketers have known for years: Making the customer happy results in improved sales, increased profits, and, perhaps even more important, enduring customer relationships.[4]

Based on the results of test marketing, the concept of Plymouth Place was expanded to include other models and was renamed Chrysler Showcase. Chrysler Showcase has been operating since 1995 and is currently in 35 markets nationwide.

SUMMARY ILLUSTRATION USING THE OPENING VIGNETTE

Three conditions must be satisfied before causal inferences can be made that X is a cause of Y: (1) concomitant variation, which implies that X and Y must vary together in a hypothesized way; (2) time order of occurrence of variables, which implies that X must precede or occur simultaneously with Y; and (3) elimination of other possible causal factors, which implies that competing explanations must be ruled out. Thus, for Muzak advertising to be a cause of sales, sales of advertised products must be higher in stores with Muzak than in stores without Muzak, Muzak advertising must occur before or simultaneously with an increase in sales (it cannot occur afterwards), and the sales increase must not be attributable to other factors such as price, shelf space, and so on.

Experiments provide the most convincing evidence of all three conditions. An experiment is formed when the researcher manipulates one or more independent variables (presence or absence of Muzak advertising) and measures their effect on one or more dependent variables (sales of advertised products), controlling for the effect of extraneous variables (price, shelf space, and so on).

In designing an experiment, it is important to consider internal and external validity. Internal validity refers to whether the manipulation of the independent variables actually caused the effects on the dependent variables. External validity refers to the generalizability of experimental results. In the opening vignette, to claim internal validity the researcher must show that the increase in sales of the products in the experimental group of supermarkets was in fact due to (caused by) Muzak advertising. Thus, the researcher must show that price and other extraneous variables (e.g., shelf space) affecting the sale of these products were kept the same in both the experimental and control group stores. To claim external validity, the researcher must show that the sample of 20 supermarkets selected was representative, that no peculiar conditions were encountered, and that the results are generalizable to all supermarkets.

Experimental designs may be classified as preexperimental, true experimental, quasi-experimental, and statistical designs. The design selected in the opening vignette was a true experimental design because the supermarkets were randomly selected and assigned to the two groups, and one of the groups was randomly chosen as the experimental group. The specific design adopted was the posttest-only control group. An experiment may be conducted in a laboratory environment or under actual market conditions in a real-life setting, as in the opening vignette.

MARKETING RESEARCH AND TQM

Experiments can be performed to determine which product characteristics have an impact on the quality of the product in the customer's eyes. We can manipulate several variables using a factorial design. CitiBank may want to measure the effect of changing the checking account levels for the minimum balance, interest rate, and monthly fee. A high, medium, and low amount could be picked for each, and a three-by-three-by-three factorial design could be used. There would be three factors (minimum balance, interest rate, and monthly fee) and three levels (high, medium, low). This experiment will help determine which combination of levels and factors has the highest quality rating for the consumer. This would help CitiBank determine at what levels it should set these factors in order to be perceived by their customers as delivering a quality product.

As the following example illustrates, companies have used test marketing to test the perceived quality of their products before nationwide rollout.

EXAMPLE

QUALITY RESULTS IN GREEN SIGNAL FOR YELLOW PAGES

Yellow Pages directories reach 98 percent of American households. In its continuous quality improvement (CQI) efforts, the Yellow Pages Publishers Association conducted a laboratory experiment to determine why people choose one ad over another in the Yellow Pages. Eye movement data were collected while consumers chose businesses from telephone directories.

The color, graphics, types of information, fonts, and ad size were systematically varied according to a complex statistical design. Thirty-two directory pages were recreated to control layout and design effects, while at the same time maintaining realism. Each page represented a typical assortment of advertisements and was mounted on a special holder on the computer screen in front of the subject. The Eyegaze System then recorded the subject's eye movements.

The results of the experiment indicated that Yellow Pages users were more likely to notice color ads before any other type of advertisement. The users also noticed larger ads and ads with graphics. Viewing time increased as the number of types of information (price, location, etc.) increased from zero to three, and then decreased with any additional increase in information.

The Yellow Pages Publishers Association used these results to improve the effectiveness of advertising in the Yellow Pages by formulating guidelines for advertisers. Through such quality-enhancing techniques, the Yellow Pages Publishers Association has gained an edge over the competition in attracting advertising dollars.[5]

FOCUS ON ELRICK & LAVIDGE

Most of the research Elrick & Lavidge (E&L) performs for clients is of the conclusive, descriptive variety. However, from time to time E&L does undertake conclusive, causal research. E&L performed one such research project for a major producer of greeting cards. This producer was interested in determining how important selected characteristics of greeting cards were in the consumer's decision to purchase a specific card. In addition, the producer wanted to determine whether different characteristics of greeting cards were important to different segments of consumers. For instance, do young men use different criteria for selecting a greeting card than older women do?

The experimental design that E&L implemented was a one-shot case study and included the following features. The major independent variables manipulated in this experiment were the tone of the message within the card (humorous, emotional, or no message), whether or not the card had a picture, and size of the card (three levels). Thus, $(3 \times 2 \times 3 =)$ 18 different types of cards or treatments were created by considering all possible combinations of the independent variables.

These 18 cards were identified by randomly assigned numbers. The test units were consumers in four geographically dispersed cities who were prerecruited by telephone and who were selected based on quotas that covered the full range of age, sex, and other demographic characteristics. These consumers were asked to come to a central location in each city where E&L had set up a mock card shop. Once they arrived at the facility, the respondents were asked to browse through the shop and to "purchase" cards for whomever they would normally purchase cards. Since this test was implemented prior to one of the biggest card shopping holidays, Valentine's Day, most consumers selected one or more cards and brought them to the register.

At this point, the consumer filled out a questionnaire that included demographic and psychographic questions. The field worker noted which cards the consumer had selected, for whom the consumer had selected each card (wife, husband, mother, son, etc.), and the consumer's stated reasons for selecting each card (humorous message, beautiful design, size, etc.). The field worker also noted the card's test number, which identified the combination of treatment (independent) variables.

The primary dependent variable in this experiment was the purchase of a card. This dependent variable could be further classified by the recipient of the card. For instance, this experiment could also test which of the independent variables were important to the purchase of a card for one's mother. This experiment would provide other information, such as the demographics of respondents who purchased specific types of cards.

The brand of the card was considered an extraneous variable. In fact, the experiment was designed to hide the brand from the consumer. E&L placed a masking sticker on the back of each card where the brand is located. Another extraneous variable was price. The sticker that masked the brand also masked the price.

By designing a mock shop, E&L could control other extraneous variables, such as the effects of in-store promotions, sales, sold-out cards, noncard products, and the card shop staff. By controlling these extraneous effects, E&L tried to ensure the internal validity of this experiment. These tight controls risked making the environment somewhat artificial and thereby undermining external validity. One might question the applicability of the results of the experiment to real-world situations. However, note that the primary issues being tested in this experiment dealt with the influence of the independent variables on card purchase. The results of this experiment provided useful information from that standpoint.

INTERNATIONAL MARKETING RESEARCH

Field experiments pose even greater challenges in international markets than those faced in the United States. The researcher may be faced with market differences in terms of marketing support systems, economic, structural, information, and technological environment. For example, in many countries, television stations are owned and operated by the government, with severe restrictions on television advertising. This makes field experiments manipulating advertising levels extremely difficult because the researcher may lack the flexibility to vary advertising content and expenditures.

Consider, for example, M&M/Mars. They have established manufacturing facilities in Russia and promote their candy bars on government-controlled television. Their products, however, have not achieved their estimated potential. Without the ability to manipulate advertising levels and message content in a controlled field experiment, M&M/Mars is unable to determine the optimum level and content of their advertising messages.

Differential levels of infrastructure development and differing practices associated with retailing also plague test market feasibility. In the Baltic States, for example, the lack of supermarkets makes it difficult for P&G to conduct experiments to determine the effect of in-store promotions on the sales of its detergents. In emerging countries in Asia, Africa, and South America, achieving adequate distribution of products to the rural populations is difficult because of the lack of basic infrastructures, such as roads, transportation, and warehouse facilities.

Thus, the internal and external validity of field experiments conducted overseas is generally lower than in the United States. While pointing to the difficulties of conducting field experiments in other countries, we do not wish to imply that such causal research cannot or should not be conducted. To the contrary, as the following example indicates, creatively designed field experiments can result in rich findings.

EXAMPLE

FRENCH COLA WARS

When putting together their strategy to fight Coca-Cola in France, PepsiCo abandoned a strategy of using singers and celebrities such as Rod Stewart, Tina Turner, Gloria Estefan, and M. C. Hammer in their commercials. Marketing research in France had revealed that overplaying American celebrities could be detrimental in that market. Coca-Cola had used a similar strategy, and PepsiCo felt they had an opportunity to attack this weakness. Research had told them that Europeans in  general considered Coca-Cola's marketing effort as "too American." Pepsi, therefore, decided to use taste as a competitive tool. The French, however, prohibited direct competitive advertising. PepsiCo responded by communicating their taste advantage through music. How did this work?

PepsiCo used sweet and melodious music as the backdrop for their product. They found that the music transferred good feelings to the Pepsi brand. As an indirect, competitive attack, they used repugnant and undesirable music as a backdrop for a visual of Coke, with the hope that a negative connotation would also transfer from the music to the brand Coke. This mechanism is called classical conditioning. Test market experimentation confirmed that positive attitudes were transferred from good music, negative attitudes from bad music. Pepsi designed its advertising based on these findings. Subsequently, retail sales in France increased although they still lag behind Coke.[6]

TECHNOLOGY AND MARKETING RESEARCH

Virtual Reality (VR) is a real-time, 3D environment made to represent either reality or an environment out of someone's imagination. These environments are created by high-powered computer systems. As with many of the technological innovations used in marketing research, VR was not developed specifically with research in mind. But VR is finding its way into the field of marketing research nonetheless and holds great promise for conducting causal research. Using VR, the researcher can create an environment that represents the field (marketplace) and yet exercise the degree of control possible only in a laboratory setting.

MarketWare Simulation Services, a company based in Norcross, Georgia, has developed a program, Visionary Shopper, that allows respondents to shop in a VR store. The goal of the program is to give the user as real, or as close to lifelike, a shopping experience as possible. It does not use all of the "space-age" gadgetry normally associated with VR. The respondents do not have to wear helmets or gloves, and they are not hooked up to a machine with an inordinate number of wires. The system uses a video screen that has high resolution, color, and 3D images. The screen shows the user a shelf filled with products, just as they would see in the actual store. The image is complete with brand names, price tags, and special displays.

The respondents use either a track-ball or more advanced touch screen technology to go "shopping" in the VR store. They are able to choose the aisle and the product category. For example, the user can "walk" to the cereal aisle and see the multitude of choices that would be stocked in any grocery store, including Cap'n Crunch, Cheerios, and Frosted Flakes. The shopper can then select a specific item, which is then displayed more prominently on the screen. The shopper can turn the box and read any of the labels on the product. The price of an item is also displayed when that item is selected. After the shopper is done looking at the item, he or she can put it back on the shelf or place it in the cart to be "purchased."

Visionary Shopper allows marketing researchers to manipulate almost any variable that they would be able to change in the store in the real world. They can experiment with prices, special displays, labeling, shelf location, and/or packaging. The system even allows researchers to test new product concepts. These new items can be placed near goods that researchers believe will be the main competition if and when the item is introduced. Again, the "Four P's" of marketing—product, price, promotion, and place—can be tested to come up with the best alternative for the concept.

The system is being used at malls throughout the United States. Respondents are selected as they are in any other mall intercept survey. Each volunteer participates in a session that lasts 20 minutes. In contrast to the typical questionnaire survey, which is often quite daunting, this new method of researching consumer goods is described as enjoyable or fun. In addition, it is much more realistic.[7]

ETHICS IN MARKETING RESEARCH

In experimentation, often there is a deliberate attempt by the researcher to disguise the purpose of the research, arguing that disguise is needed to produce valid results. Consider the earlier example of determining the effectiveness of Pepsi commercials. The respondents are recruited and brought to a central facility. They are told that they will be watching a television program on food and then will be asked some questions. Interspersed in the program is the commercial for Pepsi (test commercial) as well as commercials for some other products (filler commercials). After viewing the program and the commercials, the respondents are administered a questionnaire. The questionnaire obtains evaluations on the program content, the test commercial, and some of the filler commercials. Note, the evaluations of the program content and the filler commercials are not of interest but are obtained to reinforce the nature of the disguise. If the respondents knew the true purpose was to determine the effectiveness of the Pepsi commercial, their responses might be biased. However, disguising the purpose of the research does not have to, and should not, lead to deception.

One solution to this problem would be to tell respondents about the possible existence of deception at the start of the experiment and allow them to inquire about it at the conclusion of the experiment. Thus, at the beginning, the researcher should explain the general nature of the experiment, that the purpose of the experiment will be disguised but will be fully explained at the end, and the role of the respondents. The respondents should know that they are free to discontinue the experiment at any time and withdraw the information they have provided.

Explaining the purpose and details at the conclusion of the experiment is called **debriefing.** Debriefing should include procedures for reducing experimental stress. In the Pepsi example, the respondents could find it discouraging that they'd spent their time evaluating a soft drink commercial. The researcher should address this issue and ease the respondents' discomfort by explaining the true purpose and importance of the experiment as well as the experimental procedures.

Finally, it is the researcher's responsibility to use the most appropriate experimental design for the problem at hand. The researcher should disclose to the client any problems that arise during the course of the experiment, and the research firm and the client should jointly work out a solution, as in the following example.

debriefing
After the experiment, the process of informing test subjects what the experiment was about and how the experimental manipulations were performed.

EXAMPLE

DIET PEPSI ADVERTISING: SHOOTING THE STAR

Suppose the effectiveness of Diet Pepsi advertising featuring singer Ray Charles is investigated using a one-group pretest–posttest design. Respondents' attitudes toward Pepsi advertising, Diet Pepsi, and Ray Charles are obtained prior to respondents being exposed to a food program and several commercials, including the one for Diet Pepsi. Attitudes are again measured after respondents have viewed the program and the commercials. By observing the first few subjects, it is discovered that strongly held prior attitudes about Ray Charles are affecting the measurement of attitudes toward Pepsi and Diet Pepsi advertising. This problem should be disclosed immediately to the client and corrective action should be taken jointly. For example, the client and the researcher may decide a more sophisticated statistical design is needed that explicitly controls for attitude toward Ray Charles. If the researcher chooses to ignore this problem and continue with the experiment, a serious ethical breach takes place. In this case, the researcher discovers that the research design adopted is inadequate but this knowledge is withheld from the client.

INTERNET APPLICATIONS

The Internet can provide a mechanism for controlled experimentation in a laboratory type of environment. Let us continue with the example of testing the effectiveness of Pepsi's advertising. Various Pepsi advertisements or commercials can be posted at various Web sites. Matched or randomly selected respondents can be recruited to visit these sites, with each group visiting only one site. If any pretreatment measures have to be obtained, the respondents answer a questionnaire posted on the site. They are then exposed to a particular Pepsi advertisement or a commercial at that site. After viewing the advertisement or commercial, the respondents answer additional questions providing posttreatment measures. Control groups can be implemented in a similar way. Thus, all types of experimental designs that we have considered can be implemented in this manner.

EXAMPLE

COOLSAVINGS.COM: A COOL WAY TO INTERNET EXPERIMENTATION

ADVO's subsidiary Super Coups, the leading direct-mail coupon company, and CoolSavings®, a leading destination for consumer savings and a pioneering direct-marketing service for advertisers, launched a co-branded, targeted local coupon Web site. This site *(www.coolsavings.com)* provides consumers with convenient online access to coupons from neighborhood merchants and service providers throughout the country.

The objective of the site is to link the existing traffic of CoolSavings and the businesses served by Super Coups. This gives the businesses access to an extensive member database of potential shoppers, and the tracking capabilities to accurately measure the success of the offers they have posted. CoolSavings makes extensive use of posttest-only control group designs to measure the effectiveness of various coupons for demographically different users.

In one experiment, randomly selected households of different sizes (1, 2, 3, 4, 5, and 6+) served as experimental groups, and a representative sample of households served as a control group. Cereal coupons were electronically distributed to the experimental group members. Coupon redemption for all groups was tracked electronically. The results showed that larger households were more likely to redeem electronic coupons. This information can be very useful for cereal marketers, such as General Mills, who can target large families for distributing cereal coupons.

SUMMARY

The scientific notion of causality implies that we can never prove that X causes Y. At best, we can only infer that X is one of the causes of Y in that it makes the occurrence of Y probable. Three conditions must be satisfied before causal inferences can be made: (1) concomitant variation, which implies that X and Y must vary together in a hypothesized way; (2) time order of occurrence of variables, which implies that X must precede Y; and (3) elimination of other possible causal factors, which implies that competing explanations must be ruled out. Experiments provide the most convincing evidence of all three conditions. An experiment is formed when the researcher manipulates or controls one or more independent variables and measures their effect on one or more dependent variables.

In designing an experiment, it is important to consider internal and external validity. Internal validity refers to whether the manipulation of the independent variables actually caused the effects on the dependent variables. External validity refers to the generalizability of experimental results. For the experiment to be valid, the researcher must control the threats that extraneous variables pose.

Experimental designs may be classified as preexperimental, true experimental, quasi-experimental, and statistical designs. An experiment may be conducted in a laboratory environment or under actual market conditions in a real-life setting.

While experiments have limitations in terms of time, cost, and administration, they are becoming increasingly popular in marketing. Test marketing is an important application of experimental design. Causal research can be used to test whether changes in a product's attributes increase the quality of the product in the eyes of the consumer. Field experiments pose even greater challenges in international markets than those faced in the United States. Using technological advances such as virtual reality, the researcher can create an environment that represents the field (marketplace) and yet exercise the degree of control possible only in a laboratory setting. Disguising the purpose of the research should not lead to deception, and debriefing should be used to reduce experimental stress. The Internet provides a convenient medium for conducting experiments with certain type of stimuli, such as ads or TV commercials.

KEY TERMS AND CONCEPTS

Causality, 226
Concomitant
  variation, 226
Experiment, 228
Independent
  variables, 228
Test units, 228
Dependent variables, 228
Extraneous variables, 229
Experimental group, 229
Control group, 229
Experimental design, 229
Internal validity, 231
External validity, 231
Preexperimental
  designs, 232

True experimental
  designs, 233
Quasi-experimental
  designs, 233
Statistical design, 233
One-shot case study, 233
One-group pretest–
  posttest design, 234
Static group, 234
Randomization, 235
Pretest–posttest control
  group design, 235
Interactive testing
  effects, 236
Posttest-only control
  group design, 236

Time series design, 237
Multiple time series
  design, 238
Factorial design, 238
Laboratory
  environment, 239
Demand artifacts, 239
Field environment, 240
Test marketing, 241
Test markets, 241
Debriefing, 247

ACRONYMS

The salient characteristics of experiments may be described by the acronym EXPERI-MENT:

E xtraneous variables

X independent variable or treatment

P reexperimental, true experimental, quasi-experimental, and statistical designs

E ffect or dependent variable

R andom assignment

I nternal validity

M easurement or observation

E xternal validity

N eutral or control group

T est units

EXERCISES

1. What are the requirements for inferring a causal relationship between two variables?
2. Differentiate between internal and external validity.
3. What key characteristic distinguishes true experimental designs from preexperimental designs?
4. List the steps involved in implementing the posttest-only control group design. Describe the design symbolically.
5. What is a time series experiment? When is it used?
6. How is a multiple time series design different from a basic time series design?
7. What advantages do statistical designs have over basic designs?
8. Compare laboratory and field experimentation.
9. What is test marketing?

PROBLEMS

1. A pro-life group wants to test the effectiveness of an anti-abortion commercial. Two random samples, each of 250 respondents, are recruited in Chicago. One group is shown the anti-abortion commercial. Then, attitudes toward abortion are measured for respondents in both groups.
   a. Identify the independent and dependent variables in this experiment.
   b. What type of design was used?
2. In the experiment just described, suppose the respondents had been selected by convenience rather than randomly. What type of design would result?
3. State the type of experiment being conducted in the following situations.
   a. A major distributor of office equipment is considering a new sales presentation program for its salespersons. The largest sales territory is selected, the new program is implemented, and the effect on sales is measured.
   b. Procter & Gamble wants to determine if a new package design for Tide detergent is more effective than the current design. Twelve supermarkets are randomly selected in Denver. In six of them, randomly selected, Tide is sold in the new packaging. In the other six, the detergent is sold in the old package. Sales for both groups of supermarkets are monitored for three months.
4. Describe a specific situation for which each of the following experimental designs is appropriate. Defend your reasoning.
   a. One-group pretest–posttest design
   b. Pretest–posttest control group design
   c. Posttest-only control group design
   d. Time series design
   e. Factorial design

INTERNET AND COMPUTER EXERCISES

1. Survey the relevant literature and write a short paper on the role of the Internet and computers in controlled experiments in marketing research.
2. Design an experiment for determining the effectiveness of online coupons based on relevant information obtained from *www.coupons-online.com*.
3. Coca-Cola has developed three alternative package designs for its flagship product, Coke. Design an Internet-based experiment to determine which, if any, of these new package designs is superior to the current one.

4. Microsoft has developed a new version of its spreadsheet EXCEL, but is not sure what the user reaction will be. Design an Internet-based experiment to determine user reaction to the new and the previous versions of EXCEL.

5. Explain how you would implement a posttest-only control group design on the Internet to measure the effectiveness of a new print ad for Toyota Camry.

ACTIVITIES

ROLE PLAYING

1. You are a marketing research manager for the Coca-Cola Company. The company would like to determine whether it should increase, decrease, or maintain the current level of advertising dollars spent on Coke Classic. Design a field experiment to address this issue.

2. What potential difficulties do you see in conducting the experiment just described? What assistance would you require from Coca-Cola management to overcome these difficulties?

FIELD WORK

1. Select two different perfume advertisements for any brand of perfume. Design and conduct an experiment to determine which ad is more effective. Use a student sample with 10 students being exposed to each ad (treatment condition). Develop your own measures of advertising effectiveness in this context.

GROUP DISCUSSION

1. "Since one cannot prove a causal relationship by conducting an experiment, experimentation is unscientific for examining cause-and-effect relationships." Discuss this statement as a small group.

NOTES

1. *www.muzak.com*: Muzak History and Corporate Profile 2000; Rebecca Ganzel, Michele Picard, and David Stamps, "Muzak to Their Ears," *Training*, 35(4) (April 1998): 14; Ed Rubinstein, "New System Puts Snap, Crackle and Pop into Static Menus," *Nation's Restaurant News*, 31(20) (May 19, 1997): 112; and D. Yang, "Hear the Muzak Buy the Ketchup," *Business Week* (June 28, 1993): 70–72.

2. David Murphy, "Taking Your Ads In-Store," *Marketing* (March 18, 1999): 35–36; Ken Gofton, "POP Moves Up the Charts," *Marketing* (POP & Field Marketing Supplement) (April 17, 1997): XI.

3. Alisa Priddle, "King of Coupons," *Printing Impressions*, 42(11) (April 2000): 26–28; John Yarbrough, "Still Clipping Away," *Sales & Marketing Management*, 149(3) (March 1997): 74–75; and Robert W. Shoemaker and Vikas Tibrewala, "Relating Coupon Redemption Rates to Past Purchasing of the Brand," *Journal of Advertising Research*, 25 (October–November 1985): 40–47.

4. Joan Muller, David Welch, and Kathleen Kerwin, "The Merger That Can't Get in Gear; Daimler Chrysler Must Now Trim Costs, Just When Chrysler Needs to Spiff Up Its Fleet," *Business Week* (3692) (July 31, 2000): 46; Jean Halliday, "Chrysler Gives Prospects 3 Avenues for Response," *Advertising Age*, 70(3) (January 18, 1999): 40; Steven D. Bruyn, "The Plymouth Renaissance," *Marketing Management*, 5(2) (Summer 1996): 56–59.

5. Adams Hudson, "How to Make Yellow Pages Ads Pull More Leads," *Air Conditioning*, 210(13) (July 24, 2000): 14–15; and Gerald L. Lohse, "Consumer eye movement patterns on yellow pages advertising," *Journal of Advertising*, 26 (Spring 1997): 61–73.

6. Bruce Gilley, "Pepsi Gets Street Smart," *Far Eastern Economic Review*, 163(22) (June 1, 2000): 37; Natalie Cheary, "All in the best possible taste," *Marketing Week*, 20(6) (May 8, 1997): 26–29; and Bruce Crumley (1990), "French Cola Wars," *Advertising Age*, 61(52) (December 17): 22.

7. "Business: Virtual Advertising," *The Economist*, 354(8153) (January 15, 2000): 68; Robyn Lawrence, "Virtual Advertising Becomes a Reality," *Campaign-London* (July 2, 1999): 26; Laurence N. Gold, "Virtual Reality Now a Research Reality," *Marketing Research* (Fall 1993): 50–51; and Howard Schlossberg, "Shoppers Virtually Stroll Through Store Aisles to Examine Packages," *Marketing News* (June 7, 1993): 2.

9

MEASUREMENT AND SCALING: FUNDAMENTALS AND COMPARATIVE SCALING

THE PRIMARY SCALES FORM THE FOUNDATION OF HOW WE MEASURE PEOPLE AND OBJECTS. IT IS ESSENTIAL THAT WE USE APPROPRIATE SCALES.

Opening Questions

1. What is meant by measurement and scaling? Can scaling be considered a part of measurement?

2. What are the primary scales of measurement, and how do we differentiate among them?

3. How can scaling techniques be classified, and what are the various comparative scaling techniques?

4. How do measurement and scaling relate to the various steps of the marketing research process?

5. Why are scaling and measurement important to total quality management?

6. What considerations are involved in implementing the primary scales of measurement in an international setting?

7. How does technology improve measurement and scaling?

8. What ethical issues are involved in selecting scales of measurement?

9. How can the Internet be used to construct primary scales of measurement?

Roger Bacik, Executive Vice President, Elrick & Lavidge.
Roger Bacik is based in the Atlanta office of Elrick & Lavidge. He is responsible for working with clients in many areas including financial services, telecommunications, utilities, and other service-related organizations. He also provides expertise in customer and employee satisfaction programs.

SCALING THE OLYMPICS

The Olympic games are quite popular among teen watchers. In fact, the games are the single most popular televised sporting venue (ranked number one) among teenage boys (71 percent) and girls (62 percent), according to The New World Teen Study. The BrainWaves Group, a New York global consulting and trends company conducted this survey of 6,500 teens in 26 countries. Elissa Moses, managing director of The BrainWaves Group, says, "The Olympics are young people's favorite athletic package because in the global teen culture sport is a dominant theme, with both boys and girls being active participants and spectators."

Globally, the Olympics enjoys its highest popularity rating in the Middle East where it is the favorite televised sporting event of 85 percent of both teen boys and girls. Australia, host of the 2000 Olympic games, is third, where the games are the favorite of 84 percent of teen males and 80 percent of teen females. The United States is lower in the ranking: Only 71 percent of teen girls and 68 percent of teen boys named the Olympics their favorite televised sports competition.

However, any similarity between the tastes of teen boys and girls ends with the Olympics. A majority of teen boys (63 percent) cite basketball as their favorite sport, followed by soccer (58 percent). Teen girls voted gymnastics their most popular sport (57 percent), followed by basketball (51 percent). Only 17 percent of the boys voted gymnastics their favorite spectator sport. In fact, on a global basis, teens' favorite spectator sport is basketball.

The BrainWaves Group developed a complete ranking of the popularity of all sports in terms of the percentage of teenagers who indicated each sport as their favorite. Information of this type can be used by marketers of global brands, such as Levi's, in their attempts to penetrate the teenage segment. For example, Levi's would do well to air its commercials on televised basketball and soccer games in order to reach teenage boys. However, to reach teenage girls, Levi's should replace soccer with gymnastics.[1]

OVERVIEW

After developing the type of research design (Chapters 3 through 8), the researcher is ready to move on to the next phase of the research design. The researcher must decide how to measure information and which types of scales to use. In the opening vignette, scales had to be designed to measure the popularity of various sports and sporting events.

This chapter describes the concepts of scaling and measurement. Figure 9.1 briefly explains the focus of the chapter, the relationship of this chapter to the previous ones, and the steps of the marketing research process on which this chapter concentrates. In this chapter, we review four primary scales of measurement: nominal, ordinal, interval, and ratio. We then discuss both comparative and noncomparative scaling techniques and explain comparative techniques in detail. (Noncomparative techniques are discussed in more depth in Chapter 10.) We discuss the applications of primary scales and comparative scaling in total quality management and international marketing research, as well as the impact of technology on scaling and ethical issues that arise in measurement and scaling. Figure 9.2 gives an overview of the topics discussed in this chapter and how they flow from one to the next.

MEASUREMENT AND SCALING

measurement
The assignment of numbers or other symbols to characteristics of objects according to certain prespecified rules.

Measurement means assigning numbers or other symbols to characteristics of objects being measured, according to predetermined rules. We are measuring characteristics of the item, rather than the item directly. Thus, we do not measure consumers—only their

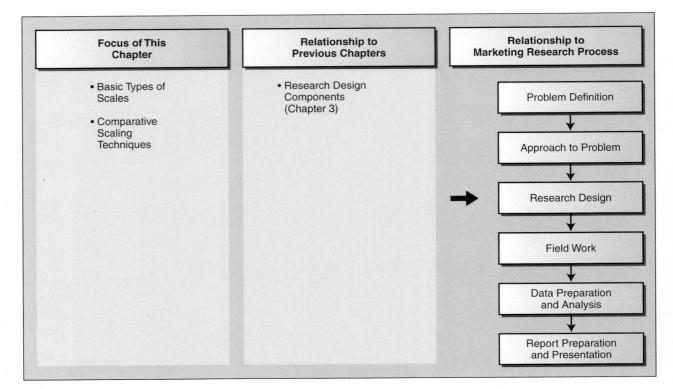

Focus of This Chapter	Relationship to Previous Chapters	Relationship to Marketing Research Process
• Basic Types of Scales • Comparative Scaling Techniques	• Research Design Components (Chapter 3)	Problem Definition ↓ Approach to Problem ↓ Research Design ↓ Field Work ↓ Data Preparation and Analysis ↓ Report Preparation and Presentation

FIGURE 9.1   Relationship of Comparative Scaling to the Previous Chapters and the Marketing Research Process

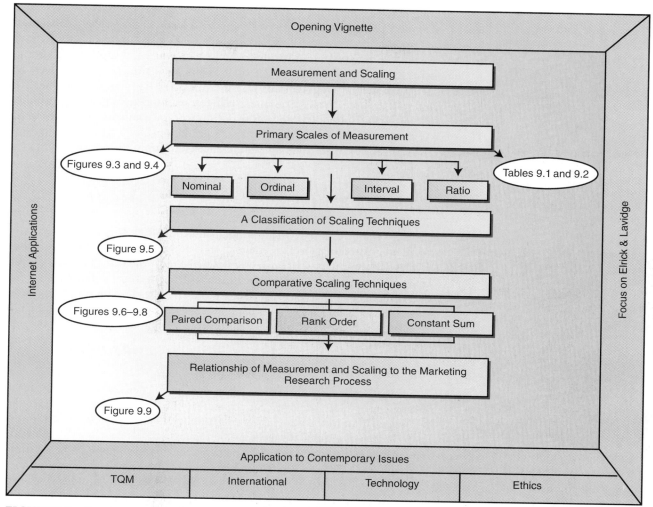

FIGURE 9.2 Fundamentals and Comparative Scaling: An Overview

perceptions, attitudes, preferences, or other relevant characteristics. In the opening vignette, we measured teenagers' preferences for various sports and sporting events.

In marketing research, numbers are usually assigned for one of two reasons:

1. Numbers permit statistical analysis of the generated data.
2. Numbers help communicate information about the results.

The most important aspect of measurement is deciding how to assign numbers to the characteristics being studied. In the opening vignette, numbers had to be assigned to measure the popularity of different sports in terms of the percentage of respondents who mentioned each sport as their favorite (most preferred). In developing the assignment process, there must be a one-to-one correspondence between the numbers and the characteristics being measured. Only then can the numbers be associated with specific characteristics of the object being measured. For example, the same dollar figures are assigned to products that are priced the same. In addition, the rules for assigning numbers should be applied in a standard way. They must not change over objects or time.

scaling
The generation of a continuum upon which measured objects are located.

Scaling may be considered a part of measurement. Scales place the objects being measured along a continuum. To illustrate, suppose we wanted to measure consumers in terms of their attitude toward Wrigley chewing gum. Based on the response, each consumer would be assigned a number indicating an unfavorable attitude (measured as 1), a neutral attitude (measured as 2), or a favorable attitude (measured as 3). Measurement is the actual assignment of 1, 2, or 3 to each respondent using a scale that ranged from one to three. In this example, scaling is the process of placing consumer response along an attitudinal continuum from unfavorable, to neutral, to favorable. The scale is the set of values ranging from 1 to 3. In the opening vignette, scaling was the process of placing each sport along a preference continuum from zero to 100 percent.

PRIMARY SCALES AND LEVELS OF MEASUREMENT

nominal scale
A scale whose numbers serve only as labels or tags for identifying and classifying objects with a strict one-to-one correspondence between the numbers and the objects.

The word *primary* means basic or fundamental. The four primary scales of measurement are nominal, ordinal, interval, and ratio scales (Figure 9.3). The nominal scale is the most basic or limited, followed by the ordinal, the interval, and the ratio scale. As the measurement level increases from nominal to ratio, scale complexity increases. For the respondents, nominal scales are the simplest to use, whereas ratio scales are the most complex. These scales are illustrated in Figure 9.4. Their properties are summarized in Table 9.1 and are discussed in the following sections.

Nominal Scale

A **nominal scale** uses numbers as labels or tags for identifying and classifying objects. For example, teenagers participating in the sports survey discussed in the opening vignette may each be assigned a number. This number would be a nominal scale. When a nominal scale is used for identification, there is a strict one-to-one correspondence between the numbers being assigned and the objects being measured. Each number is assigned to only one object, and each object has only one number assigned to it. Common examples include Social Security numbers and numbers assigned to football players and worn on their jerseys. In marketing research, nominal scales are

A common example of a nominal scale is numbers assigned to football players.

FIGURE 9.3
Primary Scales of Measurement

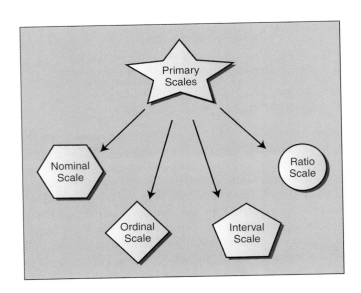

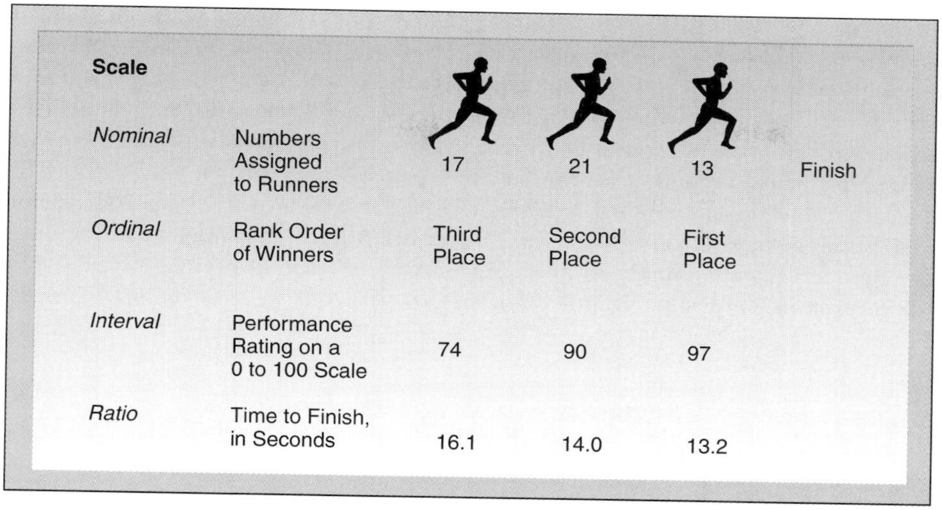

FIGURE 9.4
Primary Scales
Measurement

used for identifying participants in a study, brands, attributes, stores, and other objects. In the opening vignette, numbers could be used to denote the various spectator sports: 1. Tennis, 2. Hockey, 3. Soccer, 4. Basketball, and so on, resulting in a nominal scale.

Nominal scales are used for classification purposes. They serve as labels for classes or categories. The classes are mutually exclusive and collectively exhaustive. *Mutually exclusive* means that there is no overlap between classes; every object being measured falls into only one class. The objects in each class are viewed as equivalent in terms of the characteristic represented by the nominal scale. All objects in the same class have the same number, and no two classes have the same number. *Collectively exhaustive* means that all the objects fall into one of the classes. For example, the numbers 1 and 2 can be used to classify survey respondents based on sex or gender, with 1 denoting female and 2 denoting male. Each respondent will fall into one of these two categories.

TABLE 9.1   Primary Scales of Measurement

PRIMARY SCALE	BASIC CHARACTERISTICS	COMMON EXAMPLES	MARKETING EXAMPLES	PERMISSIBLE STATISTICS
Nominal	Numbers identify and classify objects	Social Security numbers, numbering of football players	Brand numbers, store types, sex classification	Percentages, mode
Ordinal	Numbers indicate the relative positions of the objects but not the magnitude of differences between them	Quality rankings, rankings of teams in a tournament	Preference rankings, market position, social class	Percentile, median
Interval	Differences between objects can be compared; zero point is arbitrary	Temperature (Fahrenheit, Celsius)	Attitudes, opinions, index numbers	Range, mean, standard deviation
Ratio	Zero point is fixed; ratios of scale values can be computed	Length, weight	Age, income, costs, sales, market shares	Geometric mean (All)

The numbers assigned in a nominal scale do not reflect relative amounts of the characteristic being measured. For example, a high Social Security number does not imply that the person is in some way superior to those with lower Social Security numbers or vice versa. The same applies to numbers assigned to classes. By assigning 1 to female and 2 to male, we do not imply that either sex is superior to the other in any way. The numbers in a nominal scale can only be counted. Therefore, the only statistics that are useful when using a nominal scale are those based on frequency counts. These include percentage, mode, and chi-square (see Chapter 16). It is not meaningful to compute an average Social Security number or the average sex of the respondents in a survey. The following example illustrates this limitation.

E X A M P L E

NOMINAL SCALE

In a study to measure consumer preferences for jeans, numbers 1 through 10 were assigned to the ten brands being considered (see Table 9.2). Thus, brand number 9 referred to Old Navy. Brand number 6 was assigned to Jordache. This did not imply that Old Navy was in any way superior or inferior to Jordache. Any reassignment of the numbers, such as switching the numbers assigned to Old Navy and Jordache, would have no effect on the results. The numbers did not reflect any characteristics of the brands.

It is meaningful to make statements such as "Thirty-five percent of the respondents had purchased Levi jeans." The mode, defined as the number with the highest frequency, denotes the brand preferred by the largest number of respondents, for example, Guess?. However, while the average of all the assigned numbers, 1 to 10, is 5.5, it is not meaningful to state that the number of the average brand of jeans is 5.5.

Ordinal Scale

ordinal scale
A ranking scale in which numbers are assigned to objects to indicate the relative extent to which some characteristic is possessed. Thus, it is possible to determine whether an object has more or less of a characteristic than some other object.

An **ordinal scale** is a ranking scale. In an ordinal scale, numbers are assigned to objects, which allows researchers to determine whether an object has more or less of a characteristic than some other object. However, we cannot determine how much more or less from this type of scale. Objects ranked first have more of the characteristic being measured than objects ranked second, but we have no way of knowing whether the object ranked second is a close second or a distant second. Common examples of ordinal scales include quality rankings, rankings of teams in a tournament, and educational levels (less than high school, high school, some college, and so on).

In marketing research, ordinal scales are used to measure relative attitudes, opinions, perceptions, and preferences. Measurements of this type ask the respondent to make "greater than" or "less than" judgments. Asking respondents to rank order the various sports in terms of their preference, as in the opening vignette, is an example of an ordinal scale.

Ordinal scales are like nominal scales in that equivalent objects receive the same rank. Any series of numbers can be assigned as long as they preserve the ordered relationships between the objects. Because of this quality, ordinal scales can be transformed in any way as long as the basic ordering of the objects is maintained. In ordinal scales, numbers differ only in terms of their order, not in terms of their magnitude (see the following

T A B L E   9 . 2   **Illustration of Primary Scales of Measurement**

No.	NOMINAL SCALE Jeans Brand	ORDINAL RATIO SCALE Preference Rankings	INTERVAL SCALE Preference Ratings 1–7	11–17	RATIO SCALE Price in Dollars
1	Bugle Boy	7	79	5	15	30
2	Calvin Klein	2	25	7	17	48
3	Diesel	8	82	7	17	27
4	Gap	3	30	6	16	32
5	Guess?	1	10	7	17	34
6	Jordache	5	53	5	15	35
7	Lee	9	95	4	14	30
8	Levi	6	61	5	15	33
9	Old Navy	4	45	6	16	29
10	Wrangler	10	115	2	12	24

example). For these reasons, in addition to the counting operation allowable for nominal scale data, ordinal scales also permit the use of statistics based on centiles. This means that it is meaningful to calculate percentile, median, or other summary statistics from ordinal data (see Chapter 16).

E X A M P L E

ORDINAL SCALE

Table 9.2 gives one respondent's preference rankings. Respondents ranked ten brands of jeans in order of preference by assigning a 1 to the most preferred brand, a 2 to the second most preferred brand, and so on. Note that Guess? (ranked 1), is preferred to Calvin Klein (ranked 2). However, we have no way of knowing how much more it is preferred. Also, it is not necessary that we assign numbers from 1 to 10 to obtain a preference ranking. The second ordinal scale, which assigns a number 10 to Guess?, 25 to Calvin Klein, 30 to Gap, and so on, is an equivalent scale. The two scales result in the same ordering of the brands according to preference. This illustrates an important property of ordinal scales: Any series of numbers can be assigned as long as they preserve the ordered relationships between the objects.

Note that the ordinal scale does not replace the nominal scale but merely supplements it. We could say that brand number 5 receives the highest preference ranking—rank 1 on the first ordinal scale—and identify it as Guess?.

Interval Scale

In an **interval scale,** numerically equal distances on the scale represent equal values in the characteristic being measured. An interval scale contains all the information of an ordinal scale. In addition, it allows you to compare the differences between objects. The difference between 1 and 2 is the same as the difference between 2 and 3, which is the same as the difference between 5 and 6. In marketing research, data on attitudes (for example, attitude toward sports) obtained from rating scales (1= Do not like at all, 7 = Like very much) are often treated as interval data. In the opening vignette, interval data would be obtained if

interval scale
A scale in which the numbers are used to rank objects such that numerically equal distances on the scale represent equal distances in the characteristic being measured.

All the four primary scales can be used in marketing research related to jeans.

the respondents were asked to rate each sport in terms of preference using a seven-point scale with 1 = Not at all preferred, and 7 = Greatly preferred. Note that in an interval scale two objects can be assigned the same number if they each contain the characteristic being measured to the same extent. Scales of this type are discussed further in Chapter 10 on noncomparative scaling.

In an interval scale, the location of the zero point is not fixed. Both the zero point and the units of measurement are arbitrary. This is illustrated in the measurement of temperature. The Fahrenheit scale uses different zero points and smaller units of measurement than the Celsius scale. However, both are used to measure the same quality: temperature. Any positive linear transformation of the form y = a + bx will preserve the properties of the scale. Here, x is the original scale value, y is the transformed scale value, b is a positive constant, and a is any constant. Two interval scales that rate women's handbag brands Coach, Dooney and Bourke, Vende, and Gucci as 1, 3, 3, and 5, or as 22, 26, 26, and 30 are equivalent. Note that the latter scale can be derived from the former by using a = 20 and b = 2 in the transforming equation. Their equivalence can also be seen as follows.

Poor	1	2	3	4	5	Excellent
	22	24	26	28	30	

Because the zero point is not fixed, it is not meaningful to take ratios of scale values. Thus, it is not meaningful to say that it is 1.5 times as hot in Phoenix (temperature = 90 degrees Fahrenheit) as it is in Buffalo (temperature = 60 degrees Fahrenheit). Note, this ratio changes on the Celsius scale. In the handbag example, the ratio of Gucci to Dooney and Bourke is 5:3 using the first scale. It becomes 15:13 when the scale is transformed.

All the statistical techniques and measures of central tendency (mode and median) that apply to nominal and ordinal data can also be applied to interval scale data. In addition, the arithmetic mean, standard deviation (Chapter 16), and other statistics commonly used in marketing research are permitted. However, certain specialized statistics, such as geometric means, are not meaningful on interval scale data. The jeans example gives a further illustration of an interval scale.

EXAMPLE

INTERVAL SCALE

In Table 9.2, a respondent's preferences for the 10 brands in the jeans study are expressed on a seven-point rating scale. We can see that, although Gap received a preference rating of 6 and Wrangler a rating of 2, this does not mean that Gap is preferred three times as much as Wrangler. When the ratings are transformed to an equivalent 11 to 17 scale (next column), the ratings for these brands become 16 and 12, and the ratio is no longer 3 to 1. This example becomes clearer when you realize that an interval scale has an arbitrary origin or zero point.

Ratio Scale

ratio scale
The highest level of measurement. It allows the researcher to identify or classify objects, rank order the objects, and compare intervals or differences. It is also meaningful to compute ratios of scale values.

A **ratio scale** possesses all the properties of the nominal, ordinal, and interval scales. In addition, an absolute zero point is specified; that is, the origin of the scale is fixed. When measurement is taken using ratio scales, we can identify or classify objects, rank the objects, and compare intervals or differences. Unlike interval data, it is meaningful to compute ratios of scale values. Not only is the difference between 2 and 5 the same as the difference between 14 and 17, but 14 is seven times as large as 2 in an absolute sense. Common examples of ratio scales include height, weight, age, and income. In marketing, sales, costs, market share, and number of customers are variables measured on a ratio scale. In the opening vignette, ratio data would be obtained if the teenagers were asked to state the amount of time they spent watching each sport on TV during the Olympics.

Ratio scales can be transformed using proportions. The transformation formula is $y = bx$, where b is a positive constant. Note, that the a of the interval scale transformation formula is missing here. One cannot transform a ratio scale by adding an arbitrary constant (a), as in the case of an interval scale. An example of a ratio transformation is provided by the conversion of yards to feet ($b = 3$). Comparisons between measurements are identical, whether made in yards or feet.

All statistical techniques can be applied to ratio data. These include specialized statistics, such as the geometric mean. An illustration of the use of a ratio scale in the context of the jeans example follows.

EXAMPLE

RATIO SCALE

The ratio scale illustrated in Table 9.2 gives the prices of the 10 brands of jeans. Note that since the price of Calvin Klein is $48 and the price of Wrangler is $24, Calvin Klein costs the buyer twice as much as Wrangler. In dollar terms, the zero point is fixed. A price of zero dollars means that the item is free. Additionally, multiplying these prices by 100 to convert dollars to cents results in an equivalent scale, thus illustrating the fact that the ratio scale has an absolute zero or a fixed origin.

A CLASSIFICATION OF SCALING TECHNIQUES

The scaling techniques commonly used in marketing research can be classified into comparative and noncomparative scales (see Figure 9.5). **Comparative scales** involve the direct comparison of two or more objects. For example, respondents might be asked whether they prefer Coke or Pepsi. A comparative scale gives the marketer data that measure relative differences. It has only ordinal or rank order properties.

Comparative scaling is sometimes referred to as nonmetric scaling. The opening vignette presented an example of comparative scaling when the different sports were ranked in terms of the percentage of respondents mentioning each sport as their favorite. The resulting scale presented a relative comparison of all the sports. As Figure 9.5 illustrates, comparative scales include paired comparisons, rank order, and constant sum scales.

The major benefit of comparative scaling is that small differences between objects under study can be detected. The comparison process forces respondents to choose between two objects. Respondents asked to perform a ranking task bring the same point of reference to the task. This makes comparative scales easy to understand and apply. They also tend to reduce halo or carryover effects in which early judgments influence later judgments. The major disadvantage of comparative scales is the limitation in terms of analyzing ordinal data. We are also unable to generalize beyond the objects under study. For instance, say a study was done to compare Coke and Pepsi. If later these brands were to be compared to RC Cola, the researcher would have to do a new study. These disadvantages are substantially overcome by the noncomparative scaling techniques.

comparative scales
One of two types of scaling techniques in which there is direct comparison of stimulus objects with one another.

FIGURE 9.5
A Classification of Scaling Techniques

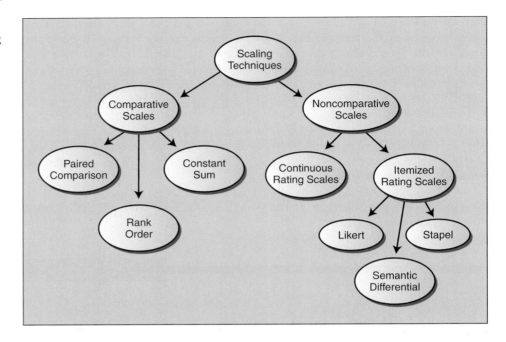

noncomparative scales
One of two types of scaling techniques in which each stimulus object is scaled independently of the others.

In **noncomparative scales,** also referred to as monadic or metric scales, objects are scaled independently of each other. The resulting data are generally assumed to be interval scaled. For example, respondents may be asked to evaluate Coke on a 1 to 7 preference scale (1 = not at all preferred, 7 = greatly preferred). Similar evaluations would be obtained for Pepsi and RC Cola. In the opening vignette, the use of noncomparative scaling would involve respondents rating each sport, taken by itself, on a 1 to 7 preference scale. As Figure 9.5 illustrates, noncomparative scales comprise continuous rating or itemized rating scales. The itemized rating scales can be further classified as Likert, semantic differential, or Stapel scales.

Noncomparative scaling is the most widely used scaling technique in marketing research. Given its importance, Chapter 10 is devoted entirely to noncomparative scaling. The rest of this chapter focuses on comparative scaling techniques.

COMPARATIVE SCALING TECHNIQUES

Paired Comparison Scaling

paired comparison scaling
A comparative scaling technique in which a respondent is presented with two objects at a time and asked to select one object in the pair according to some criterion. The data obtained are ordinal in nature.

As its name implies, in **paired comparison scaling** a respondent is presented with a pair of alternatives and asked to select one according to some criterion. Data obtained in this way are ordinal in nature. A consumer involved in a paired comparison study may state that she shops in JCPenney more than in Sears, likes Total cereal better than Kellogg's Product 19, or likes Crest toothpaste more than Colgate. Paired comparison scales are frequently used when the research involves physical products. Coca-Cola is reported to have conducted more than 190,000 paired comparisons before introducing New Coke. Paired comparison scaling is the most widely used comparative scaling technique (see Figure 9.6).

Paired comparison scaling is useful when the number of brands under consideration is limited to no more than five. When a large number of brands are involved, the number of comparisons becomes unwieldy. For example, to evaluate the 10 brands of jeans in Table 9.2, 45 paired comparisons would be involved. The order in which the alter-

Instructions

We are going to present you with ten pairs of shampoo brands. For each pair, please indicate which one of the two brands of shampoo in the pair you would prefer for personal use.

Recording Form

	Jhirmack	Finesse	Vidal Sassoon	Head & Shoulders	Pert
Jhirmack		0	0	1	0
Finesse	1[a]		0	1	0
Vidal Sassoon	1	1		1	0
Head & Shoulders	0	0	0		0
Pert	1	1	0	1	
Number of times preferred	3[b]	2	0	4	1

[a] A 1 in a particular box means that the brand in that column was preferred over the brand in the corresponding row. A 0 means the row brand was preferred over the column brand.
[b] The number of times a brand was preferred is obtained by summing the 1s in each column.

FIGURE 9.6   Paired Comparison Scaling

natives are presented may bias the results. Also problematic is the fact that paired comparisons bear little resemblance to the marketplace situation, which involves selection from multiple alternatives. Respondents may prefer one alternative to another; however, that does not imply that they like it in an absolute sense. The following example provides further insights into paired comparison scaling.

EXAMPLE

PAIRED COMPARISON TASTE TEST: LACKING IN TASTE FOR THE MARKETPLACE?

The most common method of taste testing is paired comparison. The consumer is asked to sample two products and select the one with the most appealing taste. The test is blind in that the brands being compared are not identified. This type of test is done in private, either in homes or at convenient centralized sites. A minimum of 1,000 responses is considered an adequate sample size.

However, a blind taste test for a soft drink may not be a good indicator of performance in the marketplace. Imagery, loyalty, and brand reputation are very impor-

tant factors in the consumer's purchasing decision, but these are not captured in a blind paired comparison test. The introduction of New Coke illustrates this point. New Coke was heavily favored in blind paired comparison taste tests. Its introduction was less than successful, however, because image and loyalty play a major role in the purchase of Coke.[2]

Rank Order Scaling

rank order scaling
A comparative scaling technique in which respondents are presented with several objects simultaneously and asked to order or rank them according to some criterion.

After paired comparisons, the most popular comparative scaling technique is rank order scaling. In **rank order scaling,** respondents are presented with several alternatives simultaneously and are asked to rank them according to some criterion (Figure 9.7). For example, consumers may be asked to rank brands of jeans according to overall preference, as in Table 9.2. These rankings are typically obtained by asking the respondents to assign a rank of 1 to the most preferred brand, 2 to the second most preferred, and so on, until each alternative is ranked down to the least preferred brand. Like paired comparison, this approach is also comparative in nature. However it is possible that even the brand ranked 1 is not liked in an absolute sense; that is, it may be the least disliked. Rank order scaling also results in ordinal data. See Table 9.2, which uses rank order data to derive an ordinal scale.

Rank order scaling is commonly used to measure preferences among brands as well as among brand attributes. Rank order scaling forces the respondent to discriminate among alternatives. This type of scaling process comes closer to resembling the shopping environment. It also takes less time than paired comparisons. Another advantage is that it is easily understood, and the results are easy to communicate. The opening vignette showed that the Olympic games is the single most popular (ranked number one) sporting venue among teenage boys and girls, and basketball is teenagers' overall favorite spectator sport. These results are easy to communicate. The major disadvantage of this technique is that it produces only ordinal level data.

FIGURE 9.7   Rank Order Scaling

Instructions
Rank the various brands of toothpaste in order of preference. Begin by picking out the one brand that you like most and assign it a number 1. Then find the second most preferred brand and assign it a number 2. Continue this procedure until you have ranked all the brands of toothpaste in order of preference. The least preferred brand should be assigned a rank of 10.

No two brands should receive the same rank number.

The criterion of preference is entirely up to you. There is no right or wrong answer. Just try to be consistent.

Brand	Rank Order
1. Crest	_____
2. Colgate	_____
3. Aim	_____
4. Mentadent	_____
5. Macleans	_____
6. Ultra Brite	_____
7. Close Up	_____
8. Pepsodent	_____
9. Plus White	_____
10. Stripe	_____

EXAMPLE

WINNING VOTES WITH MARKETING RESEARCH

Since its birth in 1939, The Gallup Organization has been asking Americans what they believe is the most important problem facing this country today. Gallup based its most recent results on telephone interviews of over 1,000 national adults over the age of 18. This straightforward question had no predefined answers (open-ended), which means that the participants state whatever answers come to mind. After collecting all of the results, Gallup places similar answers into broad categories. According to the 2000 survey, the five most important issues, in order of importance, are (1) ethics/dishonesty, (2) education, (3) crime/violence, (4) dissatisfaction with government, and (5) drug enforcement. This order of importance reflects a rank order scale. These issues turned out to be crucial in the 2000 presidential election and were hotly debated by the Democratic and Republican candidates. By focusing on past Democratic presidential ethics and by developing what was seen as a strong education bill and a platform for a safer America, George W. Bush was able to win over enough votes to make it to the White House.[3]

Constant Sum Scaling

In **constant sum scaling,** respondents allocate a constant sum of units, such as points, dollars, or chips, among a set of alternatives according to some specified criterion. Respondents may be asked, for example, to allocate 100 points to eight attributes of a bath soap (Figure 9.8). The points are allocated to represent the importance attached to each attribute. If an attribute is unimportant, the respondent assigns it zero points. If an attribute is twice as important as some other attribute, the respondent assigns it twice as many points. All the points a respondent assigns must total 100. Hence, the name of the scale: constant sum. A constant sum scale also results whenever percentages are calculated, as in the opening vignette.

> **constant sum scaling**
> A comparative scaling technique in which respondents are required to allocate a constant sum of units, such as points, dollars, chits, stickers, or chips, among a set of stimulus objects with respect to some criterion.

Note that the constant sum scale has an absolute zero—10 points are twice as many as 5 points, and the difference between 5 and 2 points is the same as the difference between 57 and 54 points. For this reason, constant sum scale data are sometimes treated as metric. While this may be appropriate in the limited context of the objects scaled, these results are not generalizable or applicable to other objects not included in the study. Hence, strictly speaking, the constant sum should be considered an ordinal scale.

The main advantages of the constant sum scale are that it allows for fine discrimination among alternatives and does not require too much time. However, it has one major disadvantage. Respondents may allocate more or fewer units than those specified. For example, a respondent may allocate 108 or 94 points. If this occurs, the researcher must adjust the data to sum to 100 points or eliminate that respondent from analysis.

Constant sum scales in the form of percentages are often used to present research results. In the opening vignette, the popularity of a spectator sport was measured in terms of the percentage of respondents who reported it as their favorite. As another example, consider the following.

Constant sum scaling can be used to determine the relative importance of attributes of bathing soaps.

THE MALLING OF AMERICA

According to a recent Maritz Ameri-Poll, visiting the local mall has become part of the American lifestyle. The results of this poll indicated that, on average, 40 percent of adults shop at a mall one or two times per month. Another 20 percent shop three or four times per month, while 10 percent make five to seven trips. "Born to shop" is the description applied to people who average eight or more trips each month. According to this poll, seven percent of the population is "born to shop."

Information conveyed as percentages is an illustration of a constant sum scale. Department store chains use this type of information in planning the number of store locations in malls. The 23 percent who shop less than once per month represent a segment that needs to be penetrated.[4]

RELATIONSHIP OF MEASUREMENT AND SCALING TO THE MARKETING RESEARCH PROCESS

The relationship of measurement and scaling to the previous and subsequent steps of the marketing research process is described in Figure 9.9. The marketing research problem is defined in step 1. Based on this definition, an approach to the problem is developed (step 2). An important component of the approach is specifying the information needed to address the marketing research problem. Measurement and scaling are part of the

FIGURE 9.8   Constant Sum Scaling

Instructions
Below are eight attributes of bathing soaps. Please allocate 100 points among the attributes so that your allocation reflects the relative importance you attach to each attribute. The more points an attribute receives, the more important the attribute is. If an attribute is not at all important, assign it zero points. If an attribute is twice as important as some other attribute, it should receive twice as many points.

Form

AVERAGE RESPONSES OF THREE SEGMENTS

Attribute	Segment I	Segment II	Segment III
1. Mildness	8	2	4
2. Lather	2	4	17
3. Shrinkage	3	9	7
4. Price	53	17	9
5. Fragrance	9	0	19
6. Packaging	7	5	9
7. Moisturizing	5	3	20
8. Cleaning Power	13	60	15
Sum	100	100	100

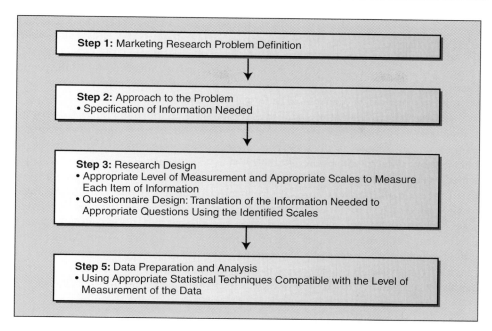

FIGURE 9.9
Relationship of Measurement and Scaling to the Marketing Research Process

research design (step 3). The researcher must identify an appropriate level of measurement (nominal, ordinal, interval, or ratio) for each item of information needed. If the measurement level is ordinal, the researcher generally selects one of the comparative techniques (paired comparison, rank order, or constant sum). If the data are interval, the researcher selects one of the noncomparative techniques (continuous or itemized rating scale: Likert, semantic differential, or Stapel).

Likewise, the researcher must select an appropriate scale for an information item that is to be measured on a nominal or ratio level. When designing a questionnaire, also part of the research design, the researcher must translate the information needed to appropriate questions using the identified scales. When analyzing the data (step 5), the researcher should only use those statistical techniques that are compatible with the measurement level of the data. For example, regression analysis, discussed in Chapter 18, assumes that the dependent variable is measured using an interval or ratio scale. Thus, regression analysis should not be used when the data have been measured on an ordinal level.

SUMMARY ILLUSTRATION USING THE OPENING VIGNETTE

The four primary scales of measurement are nominal, ordinal, interval, and ratio. Of these, the nominal scale is the most basic. The numbers are used only for identifying or classifying objects under study. In the opening vignette, numbers could be used to denote the various spectator sports: 1. Tennis, 2. Hockey, 3. Soccer, 4. Basketball, and so on. The fact that soccer is identified by the number 3 and basketball by the number 4 does not mean that soccer is either more or less preferred to basketball. In the ordinal scale, the numbers indicate the relative position of the objects but not the magnitude of difference between them. The ranking of the various sports, with basketball at the top, constitutes an ordinal scale. The interval scale permits a comparison of the differences between the objects. However, it has an arbitrary zero point. Therefore, it is not meaningful to calculate ratios of scale values on an interval scale. Preference ratings for the various spectator sports on a seven-point scale (1 = not so preferred, 7 = greatly preferred) would be an interval scale.

Alternatively, this preference scale could go from −3 to +3. The latter scale can be derived from the former by subtracting 4 from each scale unit. The ratio scale in which the zero point is fixed represents the highest level of measurement. The researcher can compute ratios of scale values using this scale. The ratio scale incorporates all the properties of the lower-level scales: nominal, ordinal, and interval. Time or money spent watching each sport would be examples of ratio scales.

Scaling techniques can be classified as comparative or noncomparative. Comparative scaling involves a direct comparison of alternatives. The opening vignette presented an example of comparative scaling when the different sports were ranked in terms of the percentage of respondents mentioning each sport as their favorite. The resulting scale presented a relative comparison of all the sports. In noncomparative scaling, objects are evaluated individually, one at a time. In the opening vignette, the use of noncomparative scaling would involve respondents rating each sport, taken by itself, on a 1 to 7 preference scale. Comparative scales include paired comparisons, rank order, and constant sum. The data obtained by these procedures have only ordinal properties. The opening vignette illustrates the use of rank order scaling by ranking basketball at the top. The respondents indicate which sport is their favorite. From these data, we can derive the percentage of respondents indicating each sport as their favorite, which would be a constant sum scale.

MARKETING RESEARCH AND TQM

Steak and Ale can make use of rank order scaling and constant sum scaling to determine consumers' perceptions of restaurant quality.

Comparative scaling can yield information vital to improving quality. Companies can determine how they stand relative to the competition, and which attributes are the most important to customers. The simplest of the comparison scales, the paired comparison, yields information about how a company stands relative to the competition. If Wendy's wants to find out where it stands relative to Burger King, it can conduct paired comparisons.

A rank order also yields information for quality companies. Consumers can be asked to rank products in order of quality; for example, they can rank a selection of fast-food restaurants in this way. Steak and Ale, which competes nationally with Longhorn Steaks, Outback Steakhouse, and Sizzler, may want to determine how they are ranked compared to their competition. Respondents could be asked to rank order these four restaurants based on quality to help Steak and Ale determine their quality relative to the competition.

The constant sum comparative scale method can also be used to determine what attributes are important when making quality judgments. Respondents could be asked to delegate 100 points to attributes such as quick service, friendly service, quality of food, atmosphere, and availability of a nonsmoking section based on their importance in determining quality for a steak restaurant. This would help to determine which attributes are important in determining quality for Steak and Ale.

A company must be committed to TQM in order to dominate its markets, as illustrated by Coca-Cola.

EXAMPLE

QUALITY FIRST MAKES COKE NUMBER ONE

Every company wants to be ranked number one. This is especially important in the fiercely competitive beverage industry. The top 100 beverage companies of 1998

FOCUS ON ELRICK & LAVIDGE

While Elrick & Lavidge makes use of all four types of primary scales, they prefer to use interval scales because of their flexibility: The data obtained can be analyzed using all the commonly used statistical procedures. The specific types of scales used are described in the next chapter.

However, E&L also uses rank order scales. These scales are used for a variety of purposes, such as obtaining preference rankings of competing brands, quality rankings of service operations, and image rankings of firms. E&L also uses paired comparison scaling, mainly to conduct taste tests, as shown.

were ranked in terms of dollar sales. They were then placed in slots ranging from number 1 (the top-most dollar sales) to number 100 (the 100th highest dollar sales). The top five companies in the beverage industry are (1) Coca-Cola, (2) Nestlé, (3) Diageo, (4) PepsiCo, and (5) Anheuser-Busch.

As the world's largest beverage company, Coca-Cola is committed to creating value for the company, its bottling partners, shareowners, and the consumers it serves. A consistent focus on the various customer groups and an intense desire to meet their needs has formed the backbone of Coca-Cola's TQM program. Marketing research has played a central role in monitoring and identifying the needs in the marketplace. Quality is measured using ordinal (e.g., quality rankings), interval (e.g., quality index), as well as ratio scales (e.g., number of service defects). For instance, Coca-Cola has developed a quality index for rating all of its bottlers on an interval scale from 0 to 100. This index allows the company to continuously monitor the quality of its bottlers and to implement continuous quality improvements (CQI). Due to the total quality management that Coke implements, it has the world's most recognized trademark and the world's most effective distribution system. Coke is proud of its devotion to all-around quality measured via marketing research, and it is this commitment that has made it the dominant figure in the beverage industry.[5]

INTERNATIONAL MARKETING RESEARCH

The higher levels of education and product experience of respondents in many developed countries enable them to provide responses on interval and ratio scales. In some developing countries, the respondents may have difficulty expressing their opinions in a fashion required by interval and ratio scales. Therefore, consumer preferences in these types of countries are best measured with ordinal scales. In particular, dichotomous scales (such as preferred/not preferred), the simplest type of ordinal scale, are recommended. For example, while measuring preferences for jeans in the United States, Levi Strauss could ask consumers to rate their preferences for wearing jeans on specified occasions using a seven-point interval scale. Consumers in the United States have experience with jeans, which should lead to a wide range of preference levels. However, consumers in Papua, New Guinea, could be shown a pair of jeans and simply asked whether or not they would prefer to wear it for a specific occasion (when shopping, working, relaxing on a holiday, etc.). The advantage of matching the primary scales to the profile of the target respondents is well illustrated by the Japanese survey of automobile preferences in Europe.

EXAMPLE

CAR WAR—JAPAN MAKING A SPEARHEAD

For the first time, European journalists gave their car-of-the-year award to a Japanese model—Nissan's new British-made Micra, a $10,000 subcompact. This came as a blow to European automakers, who had have been trying to keep the Japanese off the continent. "They will change the competitive balance," warned Bruce Blythe, Ford of Europe's head of business strategy.

How did the Japanese do it?

Nissan conducted a survey of European consumers' preferences for automobiles. They used interval scales to capture the range of differences in preference. For instance, consumers were asked to rate the popular automobile brands and features in terms of preference, using a seven-point scale, with 1 = not at all preferred, and 7 = greatly preferred. The data derived from these interval scales enabled Nissan to compare the differences between automobile brands and features and determine which features were preferred for what brands. The findings revealed distinct consumer preferences. The cars were redesigned to meet consumer preferences and needs.

The Japanese also benefited by setting up production plants in Europe to customize their cars to local styling tastes and preferences. By 2001, the Japanese were producing about one million cars a year in Europe, 75 percent of them in Britain. With a strong focus on consumer preferences measured via interval scales, the Japanese are taking away market share from Renault in the French, Italian, and Spanish markets.[6]

TECHNOLOGY AND MARKETING RESEARCH

Database managers allow researchers to develop and test several different scales to determine their appropriateness for a particular application. For example, the author has developed and tested ordinal, interval, and ratio scale configurations using dBASE. Several programs are available for designing and administering paired comparison scales. EzPair by Barry Cohen can design paired comparison scale and paired comparison product tests using statistical quality control techniques. It allows testing to end early, without compromising test reliability, if one product is clearly winning. Pulse/MPC by Pulse Analytics enables multiple paired comparison analysis. It projects pairwise comparison data onto a share-of-preference scale. Up to 30 brands or variables can be analyzed simultaneously. Computers can also be used to construct and administer rank order, constant sum, and ratio scales to determine consumer preferences among competing alternatives.

Using ratio scales administered by a computer, the International Data Group (IDG) has found a way to calculate the percentage of information technology consumers that are "fence riders," a group or category of consumers who appear to use a product loyally, but in reality do not have a high degree of loyalty for that product. These consumers would be vulnerable to competitive brands. The research also indicated the product types that were likely to exhibit a high probability for "fence riders."

Purchasers of presentation graphics software were the least brand loyal, as only 33 percent indicated they would purchase the same brand again. Portable notebook PC consumers also exhibited a low brand loyalty, as only 36 percent of those polled indicated they would purchase the same brand again. Purchasers of network operating systems and laser printers were the most loyal, as 61 percent of the respondents indicated that they would purchase the brand merchandise again. The research can be very useful for those companies that are ambitious and trying to gain market share in technology markets.[7]

ETHICS IN MARKETING RESEARCH

It is the researcher's responsibility to use the appropriate scales to obtain the necessary data to answer the research questions and test the hypotheses. Take, for example, a study IBM initiated to measure and explain consumer preferences for different brands of computers (IBM, Packard Bell, Acer, Gateway, NEC, Apple, Compaq, and Dell). One way to gain information on the preferences of these consumers would be to give each respondent several cards, each listing one computer brand. The respondent rank orders the brands (cards) in order of preference. The respondent selects the card for the most preferred brand first, followed by the card for the second most preferred brand, third most preferred brand, and so on until, last of all, the card for the least preferred brand is selected. This results in ordinal data. Although it will provide rich insight into brand preference by allowing respondents to compare the cards, shuffle them, compare again, and reshuffle, these data cannot be analyzed using popular statistical techniques. To explain preferences for computer brands in terms of the relevant attributes, interval scale data are needed.

Knowingly using inappropriate scales raises ethical questions. It is the obligation of the researcher to obtain the data that are most appropriate given the research questions, as the following example illustrates.

EXAMPLE

SCALING ETHICAL DILEMMAS

In a study designed to measure ethical judgments of male and female marketing researchers, scale items from a previously developed and tested scale were used. However, after a pretest was conducted on a convenience sample of 65 marketing professionals, it became apparent that some original scale items were worded in a way that did not reflect current usage. Therefore, these items were updated. For example, an item that was gender-specific, such as, "He pointed out that . . ." was altered to read, "The project manager pointed out that . . ."

Respondents were asked to show their approval or disapproval of the stated action of a marketing research director with regard to specific scenarios. Realizing that a binary or dichotomous scale would be too restrictive, approval or disapproval was indicated by having respondents supply interval level data via five-point scales with descriptive labels of 1 = disapprove, 2 = disapprove somewhat, 3 = neither approve or disapprove, 4 = approve somewhat, and 5 = approve. The results revealed some differences, one of which was that female marketing researchers were found to be more ethical than their male counterparts. These differences probably would not have been discovered if the original dichotomous scale (approve, disapprove) had been used. However, the finer discrimination afforded by the five-point interval scale enabled the researcher to discover these differences. This example illustrates the use of appropriate scaling techniques in examining ethical issues in marketing research.[8]

INTERNET APPLICATIONS

All the primary scales of measurement that we have considered can be implemented on the Internet. The same is true for the commonly used comparative scales. Paired comparisons involving verbal, visual, or auditory comparisons can be implemented with ease. However, taste, smell, and touch comparisons are difficult to implement. Searching the Internet for similar scales that have been implemented by other researchers may facilitate the process of implementing comparative scales.

EXAMPLE

PRIMARY SCALES IN ONLINE SURVEYS

Custominsight.com (*www.custominsight.com*) is a host service and provider of software used to create online surveys. Its service is provided to anyone who needs to administer a survey through the Internet. The company's software, the Survey Administrator, guides users through the creation of surveys and allows for the use of all of the scales of measurement. Surveys can easily be designed for employee or customer satisfaction, group feedback, organizational effectiveness, and various other applications.

A sample employee satisfaction survey includes questions using the following measurement scales:

1. Job function—nominal scale

2. Employee level—nominal scale

3. Years of service—ratio scale

4. Empowerment assessment—interval scale

5. Compensation assessment—interval scale

6. Ranking of management efficiency—ordinal scale

Surveys of this type have been used to develop better human resource programs to attract and retain the best employees.

SPSS

Using SPSS Data Entry, the researcher can design any of the primary types of scales: nominal, ordinal, interval, or ratio. Either the question library can be used or customized scales can be designed. Moreover, paired comparison, rank order, and constant sum scales can be easily implemented. We show the use of SPSS Data Entry to design ordinal scales to measure education and income. This software is not included but may be purchased separately from SPSS.

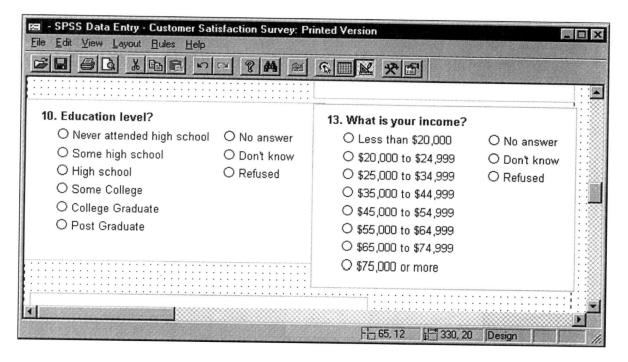

SUMMARY

Measurement is the assignment of numbers or other symbols to characteristics of objects according to set rules. Scaling involves the generation of a continuum upon which measured objects are located. The four primary scales of measurement are nominal, ordinal, interval, and ratio. Of these, the nominal scale is the most basic. The numbers are used only for identifying or classifying objects under study. In the ordinal scale, the numbers indicate the relative position of the objects but not the magnitude of difference between them. The interval scale permits a comparison of the differences between the objects. However, because it has an arbitrary zero point, it is not meaningful to calculate ratios of scale values on an interval scale. The ratio scale in which the zero point is fixed represents the highest level of measurement. The researcher can compute ratios of scale values using this scale. The ratio scale incorporates all the properties of the lower-level scales.

Scaling techniques can be classified as comparative or noncomparative. Comparative scaling involves a direct comparison of alternatives. Comparative scales include paired comparisons, rank order, and constant sum. The data obtained by these procedures have only ordinal properties.

Comparative scaling can yield information vital to improving quality and determining which attributes have the greatest impact on quality. In developed countries, respondents are quite used to providing responses on interval and ratio scales. However, in developing countries responses can be best measured by using simple ordinal scales. Software is available to enable researchers to construct a variety of comparative scales. Ethical considerations require that the appropriate type of scales be used in order to get the data needed to answer the research questions and test the hypotheses. All of the primary scales can be implemented on the Internet.

KEY TERMS AND CONCEPTS

Measurement, 254	Interval scale, 259	Paired comparison scaling, 262
Scaling, 256	Ratio scale, 260	Rank order scaling, 264
Nominal scale, 256	Comparative scales, 261	Constant sum scaling, 265
Ordinal scale, 258	Noncomparative scales, 262	

ACRONYMS

The four primary types of scales may be described by the acronym FOUR:

F igurative: nominal scale

O rdinal scale

U nconstrained zero point: interval scale

R atio scale

The different comparative and noncomparative itemized scales may be represented by the acronym SCALES:

S emantic differential scale

C onstant sum scale

A rranged in order: rank order scale

L ikert scale

E ngaged: paired comparison scale

S tapel scale

EXERCISES

1. What is measurement?
2. What are the primary scales of measurement?
3. Describe the differences between a nominal and an ordinal scale.

4. What are the implications of having an arbitrary zero point in an interval scale?

5. What are the advantages of a ratio scale over an interval scale? Are these advantages significant?

6. What is a comparative rating scale?

7. What is a paired comparison?

8. What are the advantages and disadvantages of paired comparison scaling?

9. Describe the constant sum scale. How is it different from the other comparative rating scales?

PROBLEMS

1. Identify the type of scale (nominal, ordinal, interval, or ratio) being used in each of the following. Please explain your reasoning.

   a. I like to solve crossword puzzles.

      Disagree   Agree

          1   2   3   4   5

   b. How old are you? _____

   c. Please rank the following activities in terms of your preference by assigning ranks 1 to 5.

      i.   Reading magazines   _____

      ii. Watching television   _____

      iii. Dating   _____

      iv. Shopping   _____

      v.   Eating out   _____

   d. What is your Social Security number? _____

   e. On an average weekday, how much time do you spend doing your homework and class assignments?

      i.   Less than 15 minutes   _____

      ii. 15 to 30 minutes   _____

      iii. 31 to 60 minutes   _____

      iv. 61 to 120 minutes   _____

      v.   More than 120 minutes _____

   f. How much money did you spend last month on entertainment? _____

2. Show how intentions to purchase four brands of soft drinks (Coke, Pepsi, Dr. Pepper, and 7-Up) can be measured using ordinal, interval, and ratio scales.

INTERNET AND COMPUTER EXERCISES

1. Visit the Web sites of two marketing research firms conducting surveys. Analyze one survey of each firm to critically evaluate the primary type of scales being used.

2. Surf the Net to find two examples of each of the four primary types of scales. Write a report describing the context in which these scales are being used.

3. Search the Internet to identify the five top-selling automobile brands during the last calendar year. Rank order these brands according to sales.

4. Target and Wal-Mart are two of the major department stores. Develop a series of paired comparison scales comparing these two stores on store image characteristics. Identify the relevant store image characteristics by visiting the Web sites of these two stores *(www.target.com, www.walmart.com).*

ACTIVITIES

ROLE PLAYING

1. You are a marketing research analyst with the Coca-Cola Company. After missing the mark in changing the formulation of Coke, management has become wary of taste tests. You are asked to write a technical report on the uses and limitations of taste tests and to make a recommendation about whether taste tests should be used in the future research conducted by the Coca-Cola Company. Present your report to a group of students representing Coca-Cola management.

FIELD WORK

1. Develop three comparative (paired comparison, rank order, and constant sum) scales to measure attitude toward five popular brands of toothpaste (Crest, Colgate, Aim, Pepsodent, and Ultra Brite). Administer each scale to five students. No student should be administered more than one scale. Note the time it takes each student to respond. Which scale was the easiest to administer? Which scale took the shortest amount of time?

2. Develop a constant sum scale to determine preferences for restaurants. Administer this scale to a pilot sample of 20 students to determine their preferences for some of the popular restaurants in your city. Based on your pilot study, which restaurant is most preferred?

GROUP DISCUSSION

1. "A brand could receive the highest median rank on a rank order scale of all the brands considered and still have poor sales." Discuss.

2. Select one of the readings from the notes in this chapter and lead a class discussion.

NOTES

1. *www.nbcolympics.com,* U.S. Women Claim Fourth Olympic Hoops Gold, September 30, 2000; Marianne Bhonslay, "Gender Gap," *Sporting Goods Business,* 30(3) (February 10, 1997): 56; and "Olympics Big With Teens Around the World," *Quirk's Marketing Research* (March 1996).

2. Gerry Khermouch, "New Coke Gets Ready to Enter a New Age," *Brandweek,* 41(10) (March 6, 2000): 28; Joan Voight, "Coke to Break First Ads for Citra," *Brandweek,* 38(13) (March 31, 1997): 6; and Noreen O Leary, "Taste Test," *Adweek* (Eastern Ed.), 34(10) (March 8, 1993): 20–24.

3. Frank Newport, "Morality, Education, Crime, Dissatisfaction with Government Head List of Most Important Problems Facing Country Today," *www.gallup.com/poll/releases/pr010205.asp* (February 5, 2001).

4. Tony Seideman, "Retailers, Malls Place Growing Importance on Store Traffic Statistics," *Stores,* 82(4) (April 2000): 96; Stephanie Thompson, "Tired of Shopping? ESPN Gives Men Mallside Sports Op," *Brandweek,* 40(16) (April 19, 1999): 28; Warren Shoulberg, "Mall People," *Home Textiles Today,* 18(49) (August 18, 1997): 16; and "The Malling of America," *Quirk's Marketing Research Review* (May 1990): 15.

5. Kent Steinriede, "Beverage Industry Top 100," *Beverage Industry,* 91(6) (June 2000): 32–36; and Kent Steinriede, "Top 100 Beverage Companies of 1998," *Beverage Industry,* 89 (June 1998): 31–36.

6. Cordella Brabbs, "Renault and Nissan in Joint Initiatives," *Marketing* (May 18, 2000): 4; Gail Edmondson, "Dangerous Liaison: Renault and Nissan," *Business Week* (3622) (March 29, 1999): 48–49; Michele Martin, "Why Nissan Cars Are Sporty in the US but Sensible in Europe," *Campaign-London* (July 4, 1997): 21.

7. Deborah Schwab, "International Data Group," *Folio: The Magazine for Magazine Management,* 29(5) (April 15, 2000): 55; Bradley Johnson, "IDG to Launch Giant Tech Site," *Advertising Age,* 68(23) (June 9, 1997): 38; and Tim Clark, "IDG Research Helps Identify Key Prospects," *Business Marketing,* 78(11) (November 1993): 18.

8. Diana J. Wong-Mingji, "Women's Studies and Business Ethics: Toward a New Conversation," *Journal of Organizational Behavior,* 21(1) (February 2000): 119; James Hoffman, "Are Woman Really More Ethical Than Men? Maybe It Depends on the Situation," *Journal of Managerial Issues,* 10(1) (Spring 1998): 60–73; Cheryl MacLellan and John Dobson, "Women, Ethics, and MBAs," *Journal of Business Ethics,* 16(11) (August 1997): 1201–1209; and Ishmael Akaah, "Differences in Research Ethics Judgments Between Male and Female Marketing Professionals," *Journal of Business Ethics,* 8(1989): 375–381.

OVERVIEW

As we discussed in Chapter 9, scaling techniques are classified as comparative or noncomparative. The comparative techniques discussed in the last chapter consisted of paired comparison, rank order, and constant sum scaling. The subject of this chapter is noncomparative techniques. Figure 10.1 briefly explains the focus of the chapter, the relationship of this chapter to the previous ones, and the steps of the marketing research process on which this chapter concentrates.

As discussed in Chapter 9, noncomparative scales are broadly classified as either continuous or itemized. The most popular itemized scales are Likert, semantic differential, and Stapel (see Figure 9.5). The opening vignette illustrated the use of both continuous and itemized rating scales to measure audience response to movies prior to release. Continuous scaling was illustrated by the use of handheld dials that the respondents turn continuously while watching the movie. The five-point Likert scale measuring response to the ending of the movie was an example of an itemized rating scale.

In this chapter, we will briefly describe multi-item rating scales and the importance and meaning of a scale's reliability and validity. We will discuss applications of these scaling techniques in total quality management and international marketing research, we will identify the impact of technology and several ethical issues that arise in rating scale construction, and we will discuss Internet applications. Figure 10.2 gives an overview of the topics discussed in this chapter and how they flow from one to the next.

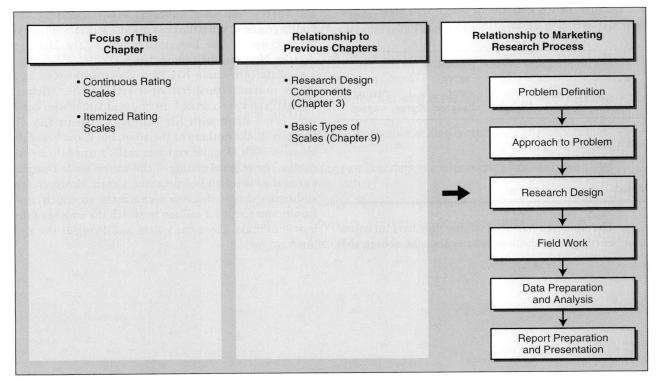

Focus of This Chapter	Relationship to Previous Chapters	Relationship to Marketing Research Process
• Continuous Rating Scales • Itemized Rating Scales	• Research Design Components (Chapter 3) • Basic Types of Scales (Chapter 9)	Problem Definition → Approach to Problem → Research Design → Field Work → Data Preparation and Analysis → Report Preparation and Presentation

FIGURE 10.1   Relationship of Noncomparative Scaling to the Previous Chapters and the Marketing Research Process

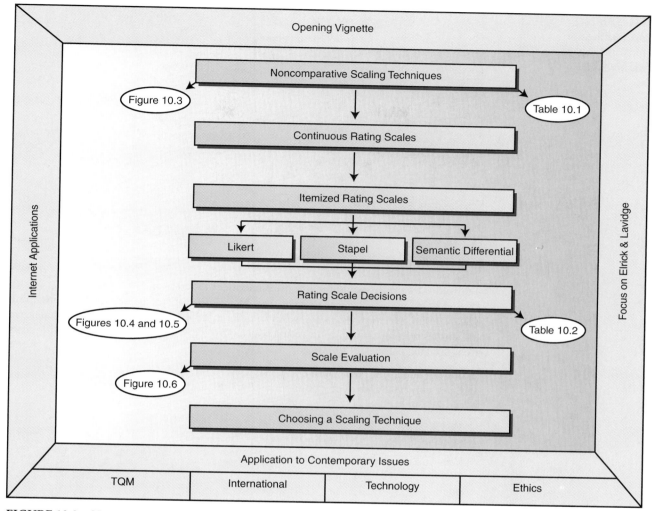

FIGURE 10.2 Noncomparative Scaling Techniques: An Overview

NONCOMPARATIVE SCALING TECHNIQUES

Noncomparative scales are often called *monadic scales* because only one object is evaluated at a time. There is no comparison to another object or to some specified ideal, such as "the perfect brand." Respondents using a noncomparative scale apply their own rating standard. This was illustrated in the opening vignette in which the movie *Fatal Attraction* was evaluated by itself, without comparison to any other movie. The range of noncomparative techniques and their relationship to each other is illustrated in Figure 10.3. The basic characteristics of each scale are summarized in Table 10.1 and will be discussed in the following sections.

Continuous Rating Scale

A **continuous rating scale** allows the respondent to place a mark at any point along a line running between two extreme points rather than selecting from among a set of predetermined response categories. Thus, a score on a continuous scale could be 28.637, while an

noncomparative scales
One of two types of scaling techniques in which each stimulus object is scaled independently of the other objects in the stimulus set.

continuous rating scale
A measurement scale in which respondents rate the objects by placing a mark at the appropriate position on a line that runs from one extreme of the criterion variable to the other.

FIGURE 10.3
A Classification
of Noncomparative
Rating Scales

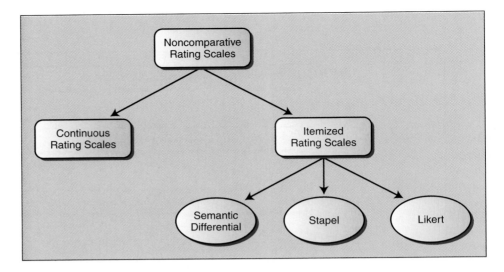

itemized rating scale would require the respondent to circle one of the numbers (1, 5, 10, 15, and so on up to 100). The form of the continuous scale may be vertical or horizontal. The scale points may be brief descriptions or numbers. Continuous rating scales are sometimes referred to as graphic rating scales. Three versions of a continuous rating scale are illustrated below.

Survey question: How would you rate Dial brand of bath soap? The cursor/tick mark may be placed at any point along the line.

Version 1
Very   Very
poor - - - - - - - - - -I -good

Version 2
Very   Very
poor - - - - - - - - - -I -good
　　　　　　　　0　　10　20　30　40　50　60　70　80　90　100

T A B L E   1 0 . 1   Basic Noncomparative Scales

SCALE	BASIC CHARACTERISTICS	EXAMPLES	ADVANTAGES	DISADVANTAGES
Continuous Rating Scale	Place a mark on a continuous line	Reaction to TV commercials	Easy to construct	Scoring can be cumbersome unless computerized
ITEMIZED RATING SCALES				
Likert Scale	Degree of agreement on a 1 (strongly disagree) to 5 (strongly agree) scale	Measurement of attitudes	Easy to construct, administer, and understand	More time consuming
Semantic Differential	Seven-point scale with bipolar labels	Brand, product, and company images	Versatile	Difficult to construct appropriate bipolar adjectives
Stapel Scale	Unipolar ten-point scale, −5 to +5, without a neutral point (zero)	Measurement of attitudes and images	Easy to construct Administered over telephone	Confusing and difficult to apply

Version 3

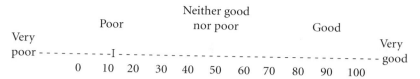

Once the respondent has provided the ratings or markings on the continuous line, the researcher divides the line into as many categories as desired and assigns scores based on the categories into which the ratings fall. Because the distance between categories is constant, and the zero point is arbitrary, this type of scale would produce interval data.

Continuous scales are easy to construct. However, scoring them can be difficult and unreliable unless they are presented on a computer screen, as in computer-assisted personal interviewing discussed in Chapter 7, or using computerized equipment, as in the opening vignette (Table 10.1). However, they are being used more frequently as computers and other technologies are used more often in surveys, as illustrated by the opening vignette. Continuous scales are particularly useful for evaluating movies and TV commercials continuously over time. You've already seen an example of evaluating a movie; an example of a commercial follows.

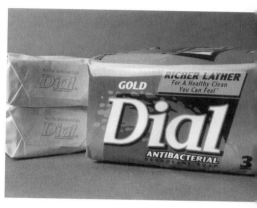

Continuous rating scales may be used to measure consumers' evaluations of Dial soap.

EXAMPLE

CONTINUOUS LIKEABILITY MEASUREMENT

The Perception Analyzer *(www.perceptionanalyzer.com)* by MSInteractive is a computer-supported, interactive feedback system composed of wireless or wired handheld dials for each participant, a console (computer interface), and special software that edits questions, collects data, and analyzes participant responses. Members of focus groups use it to record their emotional response to television commercials instantly and continuously. Each participant is given a dial and instructed to continuously record his or her reaction to the material being tested. As the respondents turn the dials, the information is fed to a computer. Thus, the researcher can determine the second-by-second response of the respondents as the commercial is run. Furthermore, this response can be superimposed on the commercial to see the respondents' reactions to the various frames and parts of the commercial.

The Analyzer was recently used to measure responses to a series of "slice of life" commercials for McDonald's. The researchers found that mothers and daughters had different responses to different aspects of the commercial. Using the emotional response data, the researchers could determine which commercial had the greatest emotional appeal across mother–daughter segments.[2]

ITEMIZED RATING SCALES

itemized rating scale
A measurement scale having numbers and/or brief descriptions associated with each category. The categories are ordered in terms of scale position.

An **itemized rating scale** has a number or brief description associated with each response category. The categories are typically arranged in some logical order, and the respondents are required to select the categories that best describe their reactions to whatever is being rated, as illustrated in the opening vignette. Itemized rating scales are the most widely used scales in marketing. We will begin by describing the commonly used itemized rating scales—the Likert, semantic differential, and Stapel scales—and then examine the major issues surrounding the use of itemized rating scales.

Likert Scale

Likert scale
A measurement scale with five response categories ranging from "strongly disagree" to "strongly agree," which requires the respondents to indicate a degree of agreement or disagreement with each of a series of statements related to the stimulus object.

Named after its developer, Rensis Likert, the Likert scale is one of the most widely used itemized scales. The end-points of a **Likert scale** are typically "strongly disagree" and "strongly agree." The respondents are asked to indicate their degree of agreement by checking one of five response categories. The following example shows how a Likert scale was used in a retailing study.

INSTRUCTIONS Listed below are different opinions about Macy's. Please indicate how strongly you agree or disagree with each statement by placing an X beside a number from 1 to 5, where:

1 = Strongly disagree
2 = Disagree
3 = Neither agree nor disagree
4 = Agree
5 = Strongly agree

FORM

	Strongly disagree	Disagree	Neither agree nor disagree	Agree	Strongly agree
1. Macy's sells high quality merchandise.	1	2X	3	4	5
2. Macy's has poor in-store service.	1	2X	3	4	5
3. I like to shop at Macy's.	1	2	3X	4	5
4. Macy's does not offer a good mix of different brands within a product category.	1	2	3	4X	5
5. The credit policies at Macy's are terrible.	1	2	3	4X	5
6. Macy's is where America shops.	1X	2	3	4	5
7. I do not like the advertising done by Macy's.	1	2	3	4X	5
8. Macy's sells a wide variety of merchandise.	1	2	3	4X	5
9. Macy's charges fair prices.	1	2X	3	4	5

When using this approach to determine the total score for each respondent on each store, it is important to use a consistent scoring procedure so that a high (or low) score consistently reflects a favorable response. This requires that the categories assigned to the negative statements by the respondents be scored by reversing the scale. Note that for a negative statement, an agreement reflects an unfavorable response, whereas for a positive statement, agreement represents a favorable response. Accordingly, a "strongly agree" response to a favorable statement and a "strongly disagree" response to an unfavorable statement would both receive scores of five.

In the scale shown above, if a higher score is to denote a more favorable attitude, the scoring of items 2, 4, 5, and 7 will be reversed. This can be easily done by subtracting the original scale value from a number that is the highest scale value plus one. Thus, the second item will be scored as $(5 + 1) - 2 = 4$. The respondent in our example has an attitude score of 22. This equals the sum of all the nine item scores after scores for the negative items are reversed. Each respondent's total score for each store is calculated. A respondent will have the most favorable attitude toward the store with the highest score.

The Likert scale has several advantages (Table 10.1). It is easy for the researcher to construct and administer this scale, and it is easy for the respondent to understand. Therefore, it is suitable for mail, telephone, personal, or electronic interviews. Several variants of the Likert scale are commonly used in marketing that vary the number of scale points (for example, 7 or 9 points) as well as the descriptors (for example, importance, familiarity) and other characteristics discussed later. Consider, for example, a seven-point scale designed to measure the importance of attributes, where 1 = Not at all important, and 7 = Very important.

The major disadvantage of the Likert scale is that it takes longer to complete than other itemized rating scales. Respondents have to read the entire statement rather than a short phrase. The following example shows another use of a Likert scale in marketing research.

EXAMPLE

HAPPINESS IS A BMW?

J. D. Power and Associates has announced a new measure that gauges customer satisfaction: owner happiness. This measure stresses what went right, instead of what went wrong. The company that made itself famous by ranking cars based on driver irritation with flaws has taken a decidedly different approach with its newest measurement creation.

The company's "Automotive Performance, Execution and Layout" study ranks about 200 new cars and trucks in seven categories based on 100 different responses. The survey is conducted using 28,000 new car owners. Selection is based on registration for new cars. Carmakers use the results of the J. D. Power survey in advertisements and to check their own results of consumer satisfaction surveys as well as those of competitors. Thus, they can benchmark their performance.

The seven categories include topics such as styling, comfort and convenience, transmission, ride and handling, seats, sound system, and cockpit layout and instrument clusters. In a recent survey, the top scorer in the luxury model class was the BMW 7-series. In the sports car class, the top scorer was the Chevrolet Corvette. In the midsize class, the BMW 325 was top scorer. The Volkswagen Golf was top scorer among small cars. The Chevy Tahoe was the top scorer in the sports utility class. The Dodge Ram led the pickup class. The Honda Odyssey led in vans.

Owner happiness is measured using Likert-type scales. The top scorer, the BMW 7-series, scored 841 out of a possible 1,000 points. The average for all the vehicles in the survey was 682, with the lowest score being a 544. The message that J. D. Power wants to send is that there is plenty of room for improvement in car design and "enhancements to make cars and trucks more appealing to own and operate."[3]

semantic differential
A seven-point rating scale with end points associated with bipolar labels that have semantic meaning.

Semantic Differential Scale

The **semantic differential** is a seven-point rating scale on which the end points are adjectives representing opposites. When using a semantic differential, the respondent is typically asked to rate a brand, store, or some other object in terms of these bipolar adjectives, such as *cold* and *warm*. We illustrate this scale by presenting a respondent's evaluation of Macy's on five attributes.

INSTRUCTIONS This part of the study measures what certain department stores mean to you. We want you to judge the department stores in terms of the following questions. Each question is bounded by bipolar adjectives, which are opposite in meaning. Please mark (X) at the point along the scale which best describes what the store means to you. Please be sure to mark every scale; do not omit any scale.

FORM Macy's is:

Powerful —:—:—:—:-X-:—:—: Weak
Unreliable —:—:—:—:—:-X-:—: Reliable
Modern —:—:—:—:—:—:-X-: Old-fashioned
Cold —:—:—:—:—:-X-:—: Warm
Careful —:-X-:—:—:—:—:—: Careless

All three itemized rating scales may be used to measure consumers' evaluations of Macy's.

The respondents mark the blanks that best indicate how they would describe the object being rated. Thus, in our example Macy's is evaluated as somewhat weak, reliable, very old-fashioned, warm, and careful. To encourage careful consideration of each question, the negative adjective or phrase sometimes appears on the left side of the scale and sometimes on the right. This helps to control the tendency of some respondents, particularly those with very positive or very negative attitudes, to mark the right- or left-hand sides without reading the labels. For an expanded discussion of how to select labels for semantic differential scales, see the referenced work by the author, describing the application of this scaling technique to the measurement of self-concepts, person concepts, and product concepts. That scale is described in the following example.[4]

EXAMPLE

A SEMANTIC DIFFERENTIAL SCALE FOR MEASURING SELF-CONCEPTS, PERSON CONCEPTS, AND PRODUCT CONCEPTS

1. Rugged:—:—:—:—:—:—:—:Delicate
2. Excitable:—:—:—:—:—:—:—:Calm

  3. Uncomfortable:—:—:—:—:—:—:—:Comfortable
  4. Dominating:—:—:—:—:—:—:—:Submissive
  5. Thrifty:—:—:—:—:—:—:—:Indulgent
  6. Pleasant:—:—:—:—:—:—:—:Unpleasant
  7. Contemporary:—:—:—:—:—:—:—:Noncontemporary
  8. Organized:—:—:—:—:—:—:—:Unorganized
  9. Rational:—:—:—:—:—:—:—:Emotional
 10. Youthful:—:—:—:—:—:—:—:Mature
 11. Formal:—:—:—:—:—:—:—:Informal
 12. Orthodox:—:—:—:—:—:—:—:Liberal
 13. Complex:—:—:—:—:—:—:—:Simple
 14. Colorless:—:—:—:—:—:—:—:Colorful
 15. Modest:—:—:—:—:—:—:—:Vain

PepsiCo, for example, can make use of such a scale for measuring the self-concept of target consumers, the concept or image of selected celebrities, as well as the concept or image of the Pepsi brand (see Chapter 8 examples). This analysis will help Pepsi determine the brand image that will have the greatest appeal to target consumers. It will also help Pepsi select the right celebrities to endorse the brand so as to achieve the desired image and positioning.

Individual items on a semantic differential scale may be scored on either a −3 to +3 or a 1 to 7 scale. The resulting data are typically treated as interval data, and analyzed using profile analysis. In profile analysis, means or median values for each item are calculated, plotted, and statistically analyzed. By plotting the results, the researcher can see overall differences and similarities among the objects measured. Differences across respondent groups can also be compared. When the researcher requires an overall comparison of objects, such as to determine store preference, the individual item scores can also be summed to arrive at a total score.

The semantic differential is a highly popular scale in market research because of its versatility (Table 10.1). It is used to compare brand, product, and company images to develop advertising and promotion strategies, and in new product development studies. The major disadvantage is the difficulty in determining the appropriate bipolar adjectives required to construct the scale. Several modifications of the basic scale have been proposed.

Stapel Scale

The **Stapel scale,** named after its developer, Jan Stapel, is typically presented vertically, with one adjective appearing at the midpoint of a scale ranging from plus five to minus five. The respondent is not allowed a neutral response, as no zero point is offered. Respondents are asked to indicate how accurately or inaccurately each term describes the object by selecting the appropriate number. The higher the number, the more accurately the adjective describes the object. In the retailing study, evaluations of Macy's would be obtained as follows.

Stapel scale
A scale for measuring attitudes that consists of a single adjective in the middle of an even-numbered range of values.

INSTRUCTIONS Please evaluate how accurately each word or phrase describes each of the department stores. Select a plus number by placing an X beside it for the phrases you think describe the store accurately. The more accurately you think the phrase describes the store, the larger the positive number you should choose. You should select a negative number for phrases you think do not describe the store accurately. A large negative number indicates that the phrase does not describe the store at all. You can select any number, from +5 for phrases you think are very accurate, to −5 for phrases you think are very inaccurate.

FORM

	Macy's	
+5	+5	+5
+4	+4	+4X
+3	+3	+3
+2	+2	+2
+1	+1	+1
High Quality	**Poor Service**	**Wide Variety**
−1	−1X	−1
−2X	−2	−2
−3	−3	−3
−4	−4	−4
−5	−5	−5

The data obtained by using a Stapel scale are also treated as interval data, analyzed in much the same way as semantic differential data. Using only one adjective in the Stapel scale has an advantage over semantic differentials, in that no pretest is needed to ensure that the adjectives chosen are indeed opposites. The simplicity of the scale also lends itself to telephone interviewing. However, some researchers believe the Stapel scale is confusing and difficult to apply. It is therefore used the least of the three itemized rating scales discussed here (Table 10.1). The advantages of this scale warrant wider applications than have been made in the past. For instance, it could be used more widely in telephone interviewing, which is currently the most popular method of administering consumer surveys.

NONCOMPARATIVE ITEMIZED RATING SCALE DECISIONS

One of the advantages of using noncomparative scales is the flexibility of adapting them to a specific research project. When constructing itemized scales discussed in this chapter, six factors can be adjusted. These factors, along with recommended guidelines, are described in Table 10.2. We briefly review them here.

T A B L E 1 0 . 2   Summary of Itemized Rating Scale Decisions

1. Number of categories	While there is no single, optimal number, traditional guidelines suggest that there should be between five and nine categories.
2. Balanced versus unbalanced	In general, the scale should be balanced to obtain objective data.
3. Odd or even number of categories	If a neutral or indifferent scale response is possible for at least some of the respondents, an odd number of categories should be used.
4. Forced versus nonforced	In situations in which the respondents are expected to have no opinion, the accuracy of data may be improved by a non-forced scale.
5. Verbal description	An argument can be made for labeling all or many scale categories. The category descriptions should be located as close to the response categories as possible.
6. Physical form	A number of options should be tried and the best one selected.

Number of Scale Categories

From the researcher's perspective, the larger the number of categories contained in a scale, the finer the discrimination between the brands, alternatives, or other objects under study. However, the larger the number of categories, the greater the information-processing demands imposed on the respondents. Thus, the desire for more information must be balanced against the demands on the respondent. There is a limit to how much information a respondent can process when answering a question.

Another important factor is the mode of data collection. Telephone interviews, in which the respondent cannot see the questionnaire, can become very confusing if the number of scale categories becomes too large. Space limitations on the survey form itself represent another constraint.

While there is no optimal number, the researcher should strive to balance the need for information with consideration of the demands placed on the respondent and the nature of the data-collection task. Traditional guidelines suggest that no fewer than five and no more than nine categories of information should be used. With fewer than five scale categories, we do not get enough information to make the research useful. Beyond nine scale categories, the respondents become confused and fatigued, and the quality of data suffers. The opening vignette illustrated the use of five-point scales to measure reaction to new films.

Balanced Versus Unbalanced Scale

In a **balanced scale,** the number of favorable and unfavorable categories or scale points is equal; in an unbalanced scale they are unequal. Examples of balanced and unbalanced scales are given in Figure 10.4. Generally, balanced scales are desirable, ensuring the data collected are objective, as in the opening vignette. However, if the researcher suspects that the responses are likely to skew either negatively (i.e., most of the responses will be negative or unfavorable) or positively, an unbalanced scale may be appropriate. Under these conditions, more categories are included in the direction of the skew. For example, customer satisfaction is typically positively skewed because most of the customers are satisfied with the company and its products. Therefore, many researchers prefer to use an unbalanced scale with a larger number of satisfied categories and fewer unsatisfied categories when measuring customer satisfaction. When unbalanced scales are used, the nature and degree of unbalance in the scale should be taken into account in data analysis.

balanced scale
A scale with an equal number of favorable and unfavorable categories.

Odd or Even Numbers of Categories

When an odd number of categories are used in a scale, the mid-point typically represents a neutral category. The decision to use a neutral category and its labeling will have a sig-

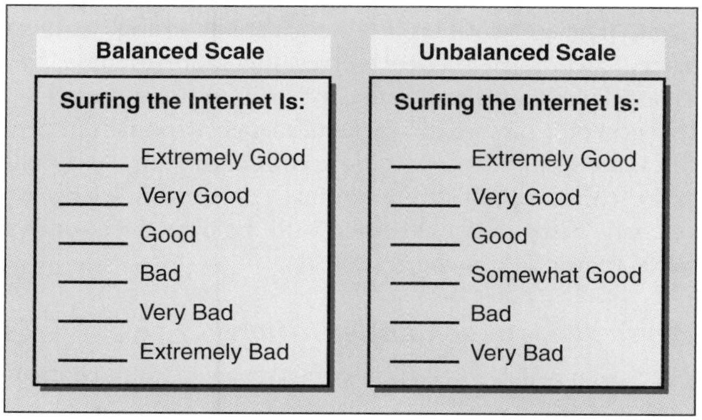

Balanced Scale	Unbalanced Scale
Surfing the Internet Is:	**Surfing the Internet Is:**
_____ Extremely Good	_____ Extremely Good
_____ Very Good	_____ Very Good
_____ Good	_____ Good
_____ Bad	_____ Somewhat Good
_____ Very Bad	_____ Bad
_____ Extremely Bad	_____ Very Bad

FIGURE 10.4
Balanced and Unbalanced Scales

nificant influence on the response. The Likert scale is an example of a balanced rating scale with an odd number of categories and a neutral point.

The scale should have an odd number of categories if the researcher has reason to believe that a portion of the respondent population is actually neutral on a particular subject. This was illustrated in the opening vignette in which a neutral response was allowed for measuring audience response. It was recognized that many respondents may not like or dislike specific scenes in movies. On the other hand, if the researcher wants to force a response or believes that no neutral or indifferent response exists, a rating scale with an even number of categories should be used. A related issue is whether the choice should be forced or nonforced.

Forced or Nonforced Choice

In a **forced rating scale,** the respondents are forced or required to express an opinion, because a "no opinion" option is not provided. When forced rating scales are applied to situations in which a significant portion of the response population holds no opinion, the respondents will tend to select an option at the midpoint of the scale. Marking a middle position when in fact "no opinion" is the desired response will distort measures of central tendency and variance. In situations in which the respondent holds no opinion rather than simply being reluctant to disclose that opinion, a nonforced scale that includes a "no opinion" category may improve the accuracy of data. Otherwise, the use of a "no opinion" category should be avoided, as in the opening vignette. While the neutral point would be the midpoint of the scale, a "no opinion" option may be better placed at the far right or left of the scale, as shown below:

Strongly disagree				Strongly agree	
1	2	3	4	5	No opinion

Nature and Degree of Verbal Description

The way in which a scale category is described can have a considerable effect on the response. Scale categories may have verbal, numerical, or even pictorial descriptions. They may be provided for each category or only at the end points of the scale. Surprisingly, providing a verbal description for each category may not improve the accuracy or reliability of the data. Yet, an argument can be made for labeling all or many scale categories to reduce scale ambiguity. The category descriptions or labels should be located as close to the response categories (i.e., the scale point numbers) as possible, as illustrated by the Likert scale in the opening vignette.

The strength of the adjectives used to anchor the scale also influences the responses. Suppose respondents are asked to indicate their degree of (dis)agreement with the statement, "The moral values in America are declining," Strong anchors (1 = completely disagree, 7 = completely agree) will result in more responses toward the midpoint of the scale as respondents are hesitant to check extreme responses (1 or 7). By contrast, weak anchors (1 = generally disagree, 7 = generally agree) produce uniform or flat distributions. In such cases, the respondents feel more comfortable in checking the scale end points (1 or 7) because these responses are not that extreme. Knowledge of the distribution of the characteristic being measured along with the objectives of the study can help the researcher select appropriate anchors.

Physical Form or Configuration

The way in which a scale is presented can vary quite dramatically. Scales can be presented vertically or horizontally. Categories can be expressed by boxes, discrete lines, or units on

A variety of scale configurations may be employed to measure the comfort of Nike shoes. Some examples include:

Nike shoes are;
1) Place an "X" on one of the blank spaces . . .
   Very Uncomfortable _____ _____ _____ _____ _____ _____ _____ _____ Very Comfortable

2) Circle the number . . .
   Very Uncomfortable   1   2   3   4   5   6   7   Very Comfortable

3) Place an "X" on one of the blank spaces . . .
   _____ Very Uncomfortable

   _____

   _____ Neither Uncomfortable nor Comfortable

   _____

   _____ Comfortable

4)
   _____   _____   _____   _____   _____   _____   _____
   Very   Uncomfortable Somewhat   Neither   Somewhat   Comfortable   Very
   Uncomfortable   Uncomfortable Comfortable nor Comfortable   Comfortable
                                                Uncomfortable

5) −3   −2   −1   0   1   2   3
    Very   Neither   Very
    Uncomfortable   Comfortable nor   Comfortable
                                                 Uncomfortable

FIGURE 10.5   Rating Scale Configurations

a continuum and may or may not have numbers assigned to them. If numerical values are used, they may be positive, negative, or both. Several possible configurations are presented in Figure 10.5. Before selecting a configuration, the researcher should try a number of options.

MULTI-ITEM SCALES

A **multi-item scale** consists of multiple items, where an item is a single question or statement to be evaluated. Developing multi-item rating scales requires considerable technical expertise. The researcher begins by generating a set of scale items based on theory, analysis of secondary data, and qualitative research. This initial pool is repeatedly reduced using input from experts and the researcher's qualitative judgment. If the reduced set of items is still too large, quantitative techniques are available for further reduction and "purification." As a final step, the researcher evaluates the purified scale for reliability and validity and selects a final set of scale items. The Likert, semantic differential, and Stapel scales presented earlier to measure attitudes toward Macy's are examples of multi-item scales. Note that each of these scales has multiple items.

SCALE EVALUATION

A multi-item scale should be evaluated for reliability and validity, as shown in Figure 10.6. To understand these concepts, it is useful to think of total measurement error as the sum of systematic error and random error. **Systematic error** affects the measurement in a constant way, that is, in the same way each time the measurement is made. **Random error,** on

multi-item scale
A scale consisting of multiple items, in which an item is a single question or statement to be evaluated.

systematic error
Systematic error affects the measurement in a constant way and represents stable factors that affect the observed score in the same way each time the measurement is made.

random error
Measurement error that arises from random changes that have a different effect each time the measurement is made.

FIGURE 10.6   Scale
Evaluation

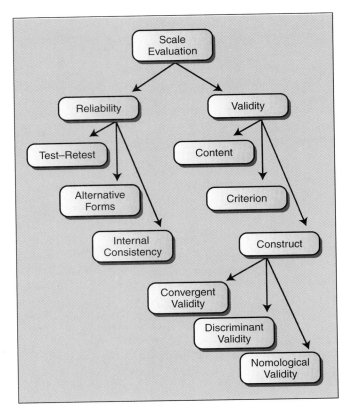

the other hand, arises from random changes and has a different effect each time the measurement is made. Thus,

Total measurement error = Systematic error + Random error

Reliability

reliability
The extent to which a scale produces consistent results if repeated measurements are made on the characteristic.

Reliability refers to the extent to which a scale produces consistent results if repeated measurements are made. Therefore, reliability can be defined as the extent to which measures are free from random error.

Reliability is determined by repeatedly measuring the construct or variable of interest. The higher the degree of association between the scores derived through this repeated measurement, the more reliable the scale. Popular approaches for assessing reliability are test–retest, alternative-forms, and internal consistency methods.

Test–Retest Reliability

test–retest reliability
An approach for assessing reliability in which respondents are administered identical sets of scale items at two different times under as nearly equivalent conditions as possible.

In **test–retest reliability,** respondents are administered scales at two different times under as nearly equivalent conditions as possible. The retest typically follows the original measurement by two to four weeks. The degree of similarity between the two measurements is determined by computing a correlation coefficient (see Chapter 18). The higher the correlation coefficient, the greater the reliability.

Alternative-Form Reliability

alternative-form reliability
An approach for assessing reliability, which requires two equivalent forms of the scale to be constructed, and then measures the same respondents at two different times using the alternate forms.

In order to test **alternative-form reliability,** two equivalent forms of the scale are constructed. The same respondents are measured at two different times using alternative scale forms. Correlation between the responses to the two equivalent forms of the scale provides a measure of reliability.

Internal Consistency Reliability

Internal consistency reliability is used to assess the reliability of a summated scale, or subscale, where scores for several items are summed to form a total score for a construct (for example, attitude). In a scale of this type, each item measures some aspect of the construct measured by the entire scale. The items should be consistent in what they indicate about the characteristic. This measure of reliability refers to the consistency with which each item represents the construct of interest. Consider the nine-item Likert scale used to measure attitude toward Macy's discussed earlier. How consistently do items, such as "Macy's sells high-quality merchandise" or "I like to shop at Macy's," measure attitude toward Macy's?

The simplest measure of internal consistency is **split-half reliability.** In applying this procedure, the scale items are randomly divided into halves, and the resulting half scores are correlated. High correlations between the halves indicate high internal consistency. The correlation between the halves will be affected by how the groups are split.

A popular approach to overcoming this problem is to use the coefficient alpha. The **coefficient alpha,** or Cronbach's alpha, is calculated by averaging the coefficients that result from all possible combinations of split halves.[5] This coefficient varies from 0 to 1, and a value of 0.6 or less generally indicates unsatisfactory internal consistency reliability. The Beaumont Emotion Battery provides an illustration.

internal consistency reliability
Internal consistency reliability is used to assess the reliability of a summated scale and refers to the consistency with which each item represents the construct of interest.

split-half reliability
A form of internal consistency reliability in which the items constituting the scale are divided into two halves, and the resulting half scores are correlated.

coefficient alpha
A measure of internal consistency reliability that is the average of all possible split-half coefficients resulting from different splittings of the scale items.

EXAMPLE

EMOTIONALLY CHARGED BATTERY

The Beaumont Emotion Battery, developed by the Beaumont Organization, Ltd., is designed to measure an individual's emotional response to advertising. After watching an advertisement, a respondent is asked a battery of questions that cover the range of emotions she or he may have experienced. Eight primary emotions are included: acceptance, fear, surprise, sadness, disgust, anger, anticipation, and joy. Internal consistency, measured in terms of Cronbach's alpha, is computed for each of the eight emotions. For the emotions listed, reliability coefficients have been found to be 0.73, 0.66, 0.63, 0.75, 0.72, 0.81, 0.79, and 0.85. As values of alpha above 0.6 are considered satisfactory, these results indicate satisfactory internal consistency reliability for the Beaumont emotion battery.[6]

Validity

The **validity** of a scale may be defined as the extent to which differences in observed scale scores reflect true differences in what is being measured, rather than systematic or random error. A scale with perfect validity would contain no measurement error, that is, no systematic error and no random error. Researchers may assess validity in different ways: content validity, criterion validity, or construct validity.

CONTENT VALIDITY **Content validity** involves a systematic but subjective assessment of how well a scale measures the construct or variable of interest. For a scale to be content valid, it must address all dimensions of the construct. This is a commonsense evaluation of the scale. For example, a scale designed to measure the construct store image would be considered inadequate if it omitted any of the major dimensions of image (quality, variety,

validity
The extent to which differences in observed scale scores reflect true differences among objects on the characteristic being measured, rather than systematic or random errors.

content validity
A type of validity, sometimes called face validity, which consists of a subjective but systematic evaluation of the representativeness of the content of a scale for the measuring task at hand.

and assortment of merchandise, and so on). Content validity alone is not a sufficient measure of the validity of a scale. It must be supplemented with a more formal evaluation of the scale's validity, namely, criterion validity and construct validity.

criterion validity
A type of validity that examines whether the measurement scale performs as expected in relation to other variables selected as meaningful criteria.

CRITERION VALIDITY   **Criterion validity** reflects whether a scale performs as expected given other variables considered relevant to the construct. These variables are called criterion variables. They may include demographic and psychographic characteristics, attitudinal and behavioral measures, or scores obtained from other scales. For example, the researcher may measure attitudes toward cereal brands using a multi-item scale administered to members of a scanner panel. Based on attitude levels, future purchases of cereal (criterion variable) are predicted. Scanner data are used to track the actual cereal purchases of the panel members. The predicted and actual purchases are compared to assess criterion validity of the attitudinal scale.

construct validity
A type of validity that addresses the question of what construct or characteristic the scale is measuring. An attempt is made to answer theoretical questions of why a scale works and what deductions can be made concerning the theory underlying the scale.

CONSTRUCT VALIDITY   **Construct validity** addresses the question of what construct or characteristic the scale is, in fact, measuring. In order to assess construct validity, the researcher must have a strong understanding of the theory that provided the basis for constructing the scale. The researcher uses theory to explain why the scale works and what deductions can be drawn from it. As Figure 10.6 shows, construct validity includes convergent, discriminant, and nomological validity. **Convergent validity** is the extent to which the scale correlates positively with other measures of the same construct. **Discriminant validity** is the extent to which a measure does not correlate with other constructs from which it is supposed to differ. **Nomological validity** is the extent to which the scale correlates in theoretically predicted ways with measures of different but related constructs.

convergent validity
A measure of construct validity that measures the extent to which the scale correlates positively with other measures of the same construct.

In the opening vignette, construct validity is assessed by measuring audience reaction via continuous measurement using a dial and Likert scales, and correlating the measures to examine convergent validity. We illustrate construct validity in the context of a multi-item scale designed to measure self-concept, the image that consumers have of themselves. This construct is of interest to marketers because consumers prefer products and brands that are consistent with and reinforce their self-concept.

discriminant validity
A type of construct validity that assesses the extent to which a measure does not correlate with other constructs from which it is supposed to differ.

nomological validity
A type of validity that assesses the relationship between theoretical constructs. It seeks to confirm significant correlations between the constructs as predicted by a theory.

EXAMPLE

TO THINE OWN SELF BE TRUE

Following are findings that provide evidence of validity for a multi-item scale to measure self-concept.

- Three experts agree that all the items in the scale are relevant for measuring self-concept (content validity).
- High correlations between scales designed to measure self-concept and personality assessments of the same person by their friends (criterion validity).
- High correlations with other scales designed to measure self-concepts (convergent validity).
- Low correlations with unrelated constructs of brand loyalty and variety seeking (discriminant validity).
- Brands that are congruent with the individual's self-concept are more preferred, as postulated by the theory (nomological validity).
- A high level of reliability.

Notice that a high level of reliability was included as evidence of construct validity in this example. This illustrates the relationship between reliability and validity.

Relationship Between Reliability and Validity

If a measure is perfectly valid, it is also perfectly reliable. In this case, neither systematic nor random error is present. Thus, perfect validity implies perfect reliability. (No measurement error implies no random error.) If a measure is unreliable, it cannot be perfectly valid since at a minimum random error is present. (If random error is present, measurement error is present.) Furthermore, systematic error may also be present. Thus, unreliability implies invalidity. If a measure is perfectly reliable, it may or may not be perfectly valid, because systematic error may still be present. (If there is no random error, measurement error may still be present due to systematic error). While lack of reliability constitutes negative evidence for validity, reliability does not in itself imply validity. Reliability is a necessary, but not sufficient, condition for validity.

CHOOSING A SCALING TECHNIQUE

In addition to theoretical considerations and evaluation of reliability and validity, the researcher should consider certain practical factors in selecting scaling techniques for a particular marketing research problem. These include the level of measurement desired (nominal, ordinal, interval, or ratio), the experience of the respondents with the research topic, the difficulty of administering the scales, and the context.

As a general rule, the scaling technique used should be the one that will yield the highest level of measurement feasible. Such a scaling technique will permit the greatest flexibility in statistical analysis of the data. Additionally, using multiple scale items to measure the same characteristic will improve the accuracy of results. In many situations, it is desirable to use more than one scaling technique, as illustrated in the opening vignette.

SUMMARY ILLUSTRATION USING THE OPENING VIGNETTE

Noncomparative rating scales can be either continuous or itemized. Both types were illustrated in the opening vignette. Audience members viewing a movie are each given a dial and are told to continuously rate their reaction to the film from positive to negative by turning the dial in the desired direction, thus recording their response on a continuous scale. The itemized rating scales are further classified as Likert, semantic differential, or Stapel scales. Large-scale surveys conducted to assess respondents' reactions to movies make use of Likert scales.

When using noncomparative itemized rating scales, the researcher must decide on the number of scale categories, balanced versus unbalanced scales, odd or even number of categories, forced versus nonforced scales, nature and degree of verbal description, and the physical form or configuration. The Likert scale in the opening vignette made use of five categories following the traditional guidelines and is balanced to avoid bias in any direction. A neutral response (3) is allowed as it is recognized that many respondents may not like or dislike specific scenes in movies. All the scale categories are labeled in order to reduce ambiguity. A forced scale is used, without a "no opinion" category, as people generally express opinions on movies they have seen.

Multi-item scales consist of a number of rating scale items. These scales should be evaluated in terms of reliability and validity. Reliability refers to the extent to which a scale produces consistent results if repeated measurements are made. Approaches to assessing reliability include test–retest, alternative-form, and internal consistency. Validity, or accuracy of measurement, may be assessed by evaluating content validity, criterion validity, and construct validity. In the opening vignette, construct validity is assessed by measuring audience reaction using different methods—continuous measurement using a dial and Likert scales—and then correlating the measures to examine convergent validity.

The choice of particular scaling techniques in a given situation should be based on theoretical and practical considerations. As a general rule, the scaling technique used should be the one that will yield the highest level of measurement feasible. Also, multiple measures should be obtained, as in the opening vignette.

MARKETING RESEARCH AND TQM

The scaling techniques discussed in this chapter have been used to develop several scales for measuring quality. For example, SERVQUAL, a multi-item, noncomparative scale, was developed to measure service quality. The original SERVQUAL proposed 10 dimensions on which service quality was rated: reliability, responsiveness, competence, access, courtesy, communication, credibility, security, understanding/knowing the customer, and tangibles. These 10 dimensions were later combined into five: tangibles, reliability, responsiveness, assurance, and empathy. SERVQUAL can be divided into two sections. The first section collects data about respondents' feelings toward quality firms possessing certain features or attributes. The second section asks respondents to rate to what extent they believe a firm has certain attributes. The answers from the first section give a measure of a consumer's expectations for certain attributes for a quality firm. The second section measures the consumers' perceptions for a given firm on the same attributes. SERVQUAL uses the difference between the perception and expectation measures as a measure of quality.[7] Similar instruments can be developed to measure quality for products in a noncomparative form, as illustrated by Winn-Dixie.

EXAMPLE

QUALITY IS ALWAYS IN BLOOM

Winn-Dixie, the supermarket chain, wanted to improve the quality of its floral department. The floral departments in the competitor stores ranged from limited service with no custom work or deliveries to full-service capable of special orders, catering events, and deliveries. Only about half of Winn-Dixie's floral departments had the resources to handle special events such as weddings. Winn-Dixie used Likert scales, such as the one below, to better understand how their customers felt about the floral department.

Listed below are statements about Winn-Dixie's floral center. Please circle the number that best describes how you feel about each statement.

FOCUS ON
ELRICK AND LAVIDGE

Elrick & Lavidge (E&L) predominantly uses 5-point scales with the end points anchored, but sometimes uses a 10-point scale with the end points anchored. The anchored scales use descriptors for only the extreme scale categories. When the anchored scales are used, the results are reported in terms of the means as well as the "top 2 box" scores that indicate the percentage of respondents checking the top two categories, that is, four or five on a five-point scale.

Project managers typically use a scale with which they are comfortable or one that the client requests based on the need to be consistent with other research that has been performed in the past. For instance, much of E&L's customer satisfaction measurement uses a 10-point scale to match the standard set by the American Customer Satisfaction Index. In addition, broad measures of overall satisfaction may be recorded with a five-point scale in the same survey if that is what the client has used in the past. The use of five-point scales would enable a comparison of the results of the present study with those obtained in the past.

	STRONGLY DISAGREE	DISAGREE	NEITHER AGREE NOR DISAGREE	AGREE	STRONGLY AGREE
1. Winn-Dixie's floral center has high quality.	1	2	3	4	5
2. The floral center does not have a wide variety of flowers.	1	2	3	4	5
3. The floral center provides every service I have needed.	1	2	3	4	5
4. The floral center charges fair prices.	1	2	3	4	5
5. The floral center personnel are not helpful.	1	2	3	4	5

The results of this survey showed that the floral departments in several stores were not evaluated favorably. Consequently, Winn-Dixie prepared a plan for upgrading its floral departments nationwide. Quality is vital for Winn-Dixie's survival in the competitive grocery industry. Its commitment to finding out what the customers want has helped achieve total quality management in the floral departments and throughout the stores.[8]

INTERNATIONAL MARKETING RESEARCH

Pan-cultural scales, designed to be free of cultural biases, are used in international research. In addition to eliminating cultural biases, accommodating differing levels of education and experience are also essential. Of the scaling techniques we have considered, the semantic differential has been applied with the greatest consistency in results across countries.

EXAMPLE

COPYING THE NAME XEROX

For nearly 30 years, Xerox had been building a solid reputation and market in the Soviet Union. The name Xerox had become synonymous with the act of copying documents and was a brand name people equated with quality. However, with the disintegration of the Soviet Union into the Commonwealth of Independent States (CIS), sales of Xerox began to fall. The problem was initially attributed to competition from Canon, Ricoh Company, Mitsubishi Electric Corporation, and Minolta Camera Company. However, when Xerox's attempts to improve the competitiveness of its product failed, the company undertook marketing research.

The researchers used semantic differential scales to measure Xerox's image. The bipolar labels used were carefully tested to eliminate cultural bias. For example, good–bad was used as a scale item, as these concepts were well understood in the CIS.

The results of the study revealed that the real problem was a growing negative perception of Russian customers toward Xerox products. Xerox management finally traced the explanation for this negative perception to growing trademark infringement by illegal counterfeiters. Some dealers were selling machines with counterfeit Xerox labels. With the disintegration of the Soviet Union, government protection from trademark infringement was going unchecked. The low quality of the counterfeits was damaging the entire Xerox image. After registering its trademark separately in each republic, Xerox began an extensive corporate image campaign emphasizing its commitment to quality. This was a definite step in removing some of the misconceptions Russian consumers had begun to develop about Xerox.[9]

An alternative approach to developing pan cultural scales is to use descriptors the respondents create themselves. For example, respondents may be asked to indicate the verbal descriptors for the extreme scale categories (anchors) before positioning an object along the scale. This approach is useful when conducting attitude research related to cultural norms (e.g., attitude toward friends). Suppose the researcher is interested in measuring the influence of friends on the purchase of personal clothing in a cross-cultural study involving students in the United States and India. The question asked is "To what extent should your friends influence your purchase of personal clothing?". The responses are obtained on a seven-point scale. Respondents in India may provide the anchors as 1 = little, 7 = much. Respondents in the United States may provide different anchors: 1 = not at all, 7 = a great deal. Such scales have proven to be universally adaptable because they are relatively insensitive to differences in educational levels across countries. On the other hand, if the researchers specify the anchors, they should pay special attention to determining equivalent verbal descriptors in different languages and cultures. The end descriptors used to anchor the scale are particularly prone to different interpretations.

Additionally, the scale numbering may have different meanings. In some cultures, 1 may be interpreted as best, while in others it may be interpreted as worst, regardless of how it is scaled (1 = best, 7 = worst, or 1 = worst, 7 = best). In such cases, it may be desirable to avoid numbers and to just use boxes that respondent can check (worst ❏ ❏ ❏ ❏ ❏ ❏ best). It is important that the scale end points and the verbal descriptors be employed in a manner that is consistent with the culture. Finally, in international marketing research it is critical to establish the equivalence of scales and measures used to obtain data from different countries. This topic is complex and is discussed elsewhere by the author.[10]

TECHNOLOGY AND MARKETING RESEARCH

Database managers, such as dBASE, allow researchers to develop scales and test their appropriateness for a particular application. Specialized programs, such as ATTITUDE SCALES by Persimmon Software, construct a variety of rating scales for measuring attitudes in marketing and opinion research. EZWRITER by Computers for Marketing Corporation (CfMC) of San Francisco can customize scales for printed questionnaires or for use by telephone interviewers at computer screens in a fraction of the time this would take without automation.

For each new scale, the researcher would be presented a screen asking for information about the intended scale. For example, if the question is a noncomparatively scaled question, the researcher would indicate that a "number" response is sought. The researcher would then indicate the valid range of the numbers. After this, a second screen would allow formatting of the scale on the screen as interviewers would see it during data collection.

Another technological development is "smart" instruments that can constantly monitor their own condition and the quality of the information they provide. They can also "talk" directly to the other components of the measurement process, making the integration and processing of information quick and reliable. One such instrument is from Option Technologies of Minnesota and is called Option Finder. This system allows for instantaneous feedback. It is designed for use in gathering information from groups rather than single individuals and can be used on groups as large as 250 persons. The respondent reads a question, then inputs his or her response into the system using a keypad. Since the keypad is the method of data entry, questions are limited to fixed response, including paired comparisons, Likert-type scales, and discrete labeled points. The feedback from Option Finder is immediate. The answers to the questions are tallied and processed into graphical form as the respondents enter them.

ETHICS IN MARKETING RESEARCH

The use of inappropriate scale descriptors can bias the evaluations of Lexus raising ethical issues.

Since scale construction can influence scale responses and hence the results of the study, several ethical issues are pertinent. Of particular concern is the researcher's attempt to deliberately bias the results by building that bias into noncomparative scales. This can be done, for example, by using scale descriptors that can be manipulated to bias results in a desired direction, for example, to generate a positive view of the client's brand or a negative view of a competitor's brand. To project the client's brand favorably, the respondents can be asked to indicate their opinion of the brand on several attributes using seven-point scales anchored by the descriptors "extremely poor" to "good." Note that this scale has a strongly negative descriptor with only a mildly positive one. Respondents will be reluctant to rate the product extremely negatively by rating it as "extremely poor." In fact, respondents who believe the product to be only mediocre will end up responding favorably. Try this yourself. How would you rate Lexus automobiles on the following attributes?

Reliability:	Horrible	1	2	3	4	5	6	7	Good
Performance:	Very poor	1	2	3	4	5	6	7	Good
Quality:	One of the worst	1	2	3	4	5	6	7	Good
Prestige:	Very low	1	2	3	4	5	6	7	Good

Did you find yourself rating Lexus cars positively? The same technique can also be used to negatively bias evaluations of competitors' products by providing a mildly negative descriptor against a strongly positive descriptor.

Thus, we see how important it is to use scales with comparable positive and negative descriptors. This problem emphasizes the need to adequately establish the reliability and validity of scales so that we can be confident that the variables have been accurately measured. The researcher has a responsibility to both the client and respondents to ensure the applicability and usefulness of the scale, as we see in the following example.

EXAMPLE

AN ETHICAL SCALE FOR MEASURING ETHICS

The theory of moral philosophy was used to develop a scale for measuring ethical evaluations of marketing activities. The resulting scale had 29 seven-point bipolar items ranging from fair to unfair and efficient to inefficient. Evaluations of this scale, through use in evaluating various ethical scenarios, indicated high internal consistency reliability (measured via Cronbach's alpha), and a strong degree of construct (convergent, discriminant, and nomological) validity. Accordingly, this scale has been useful in a variety of contexts for investigating ethical issues in marketing. In a recent study, this scale was used to classify the firms as ethical or unethical and to examine the variables that differentiated the two groups. It was found that in ethical firms ethics were considered more important, the leadership was committed to ethical practices, and codes of ethical conduct were enforced. Also, smaller firms tended to be more ethical than larger firms.[11]

INTERNET APPLICATIONS

Continuous rating scales may be easily implemented on the Internet. The cursor can be moved on the screen in a continuous fashion to select the exact position on the scale that best describes the respondent's evaluation. The computer can automatically score the scale values, increasing the speed and accuracy of processing the data.

Similarly, it is also easy to implement all three itemized rating scales (Likert, semantic differential, and Stapel) on the Internet. Moreover, using the Internet one can search for and locate similar scales used by other researchers. It is also possible that other researchers have reported reliability and validity assessments for multi-item scales. Before generating new scales, a researcher should first examine similar scales used by other researchers and use them if they meet the measurement objectives.

EXAMPLE

UNBALANCED SCALES HELP ADVANCED MICRO DEVICES ACHIEVE BALANCE IN CUSTOMER SATISFACTION

CustomerSat.com *(www.customersat.com)* is a premier provider of Internet survey research services. It conducted an Internet-based customer satisfaction survey for Advanced Micro Devices (AMD), a leading manufacturer of integrated circuits. Various types of itemized rating scales were employed. The importance of attributes used to evaluate AMD was measured on five-point balanced scales (Very Important, Important, Neutral, Unimportant, Very Unimportant). However, satisfaction was measured using five-point unbalanced scales (Excellent, Very Good, Good, Fair, Poor). The use of unbalanced scales to measure satisfaction was justified as satisfaction levels tend to be positively skewed.

Furthermore, a "Not Applicable (N/A)" option was also allowed when measuring satisfaction with AMD on specific attributes, as not all attributes may be relevant for a particular respondent. The results of this survey helped AMD identify customer concerns affecting satisfaction levels and take corrective actions. For example, filling the orders accurately and in a timely manner had a very important impact on customer satisfaction. Yet, this was an area where AMD was not up to par. Accordingly, AMD reorganized this function, resulting in improved performance and increased customer satisfaction.

SPSS

Using SPSS Data Entry, the researcher can design any of the three noncomparative scales: Likert, semantic differential, or Stapel. Moreover, multi-item scales can be easily accommodated. Either the question library can be used or customized scales can be designed. We show the use of SPSS Data Entry to design Likert-type scales for rating salespeople and product characteristics.

SUMMARY

In noncomparative scaling, each object is scaled independently of the other objects in the stimulus set. Noncomparative rating scales can be either continuous or itemized. The

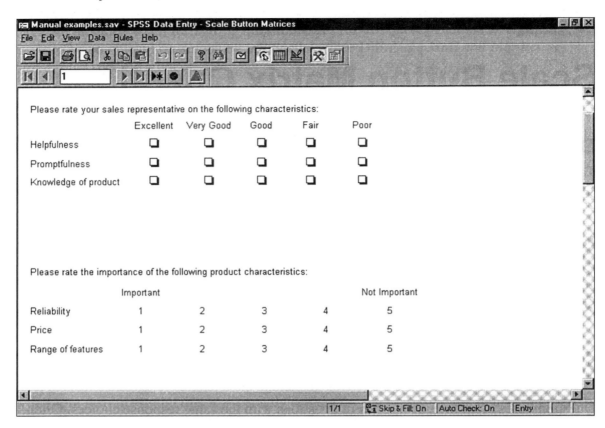

itemized rating scales are further classified as Likert, semantic differential, or Stapel scales. When using noncomparative itemized rating scales, the researcher must decide on the number of scale categories, balanced versus unbalanced scales, odd or even number of categories, forced versus nonforced scales, nature and degree of verbal description, and the physical form or configuration.

Multi-item scales consist of a number of rating scale items. These scales should be evaluated in terms of reliability and validity. Reliability refers to the extent to which a scale produces consistent results if repeated measurements are made. Approaches to assessing reliability include test–retest, alternative-form, and internal consistency. Validity, or accuracy of measurement, may be assessed by evaluating content validity, criterion validity, and construct validity.

The choice of particular scaling techniques in a given situation should be based on theoretical and practical considerations. As a general rule, multiple measures should be taken, and the techniques used should be the ones that provide the highest level of information feasible.

Specialized scales, such as SERVQUAL, have been developed for measuring service quality. In international marketing research, special attention should be devoted to determining equivalent verbal descriptors in different languages and cultures. Software is available for developing and testing continuous and itemized rating scales, particularly multi-item scales. The misuse of scale descriptors also raises serious ethical concerns. Ethically, the researcher has the responsibility to both the client and respondents to ensure the applicability, usefulness, and honesty of the scales. Continuous and itemized rating scales can be easily implemented on the Internet.

KEY TERMS AND CONCEPTS

Noncomparative
  scales, 281
Continuous rating
  scale, 281
Itemized rating scale, 284
Likert scale, 284
Semantic differential, 286
Stapel scale, 287
Balanced scale, 289
Forced rating scale, 290

Multi-item scale, 291
Systematic error, 291
Random error, 291
Reliability, 292
Test–retest reliability, 292
Alternative-form
  reliability, 292
Internal consistency
  reliability, 293
Split-half reliability, 293

Coefficient alpha, 293
Validity, 293
Content validity, 293
Criterion validity, 294
Construct validity, 294
Convergent validity, 294
Discriminant validity, 294
Nomological validity, 294

ACRONYMS

The rating scale decisions may be described by the acronym RATING:

R esponse option: forced versus nonforced

A ttractive versus unattractive number of categories: balanced versus unbalanced

T otal number of categories

I mpartial or neutral category: odd versus even number of categories

N ature and degree of verbal description

G raphics: physical form and configuration

EXERCISES

1. What is a semantic differential scale? For what purposes is this scale used? Give an example.
2. Describe the Likert scale. Give an example.
3. What are the differences between the Stapel scale and the semantic differential? Which scale is more popular?
4. What are the major decisions involved in constructing an itemized rating scale?
5. How many scale categories should be used in an itemized rating scale? Why?
6. What is the difference between balanced and unbalanced scales? Give an example of each.
7. Should an odd or even number of categories be used in an itemized rating scale? Why? When?
8. What is the difference between forced and nonforced scales? Give an example of each.
9. How does the nature and degree of verbal description affect the response to itemized rating scales?
10. What are multi-item scales? Give an example.
11. What is reliability?
12. What are the differences between test–retest and alternative-form reliability?
13. Describe the notion of internal consistency reliability.
14. What is validity?
15. What is criterion validity? How is it assessed?

16. What is the relationship between reliability and validity?

17. How would you select a particular scaling technique?

PROBLEMS

1. Develop a Likert, semantic differential, and a Stapel scale for measuring store loyalty.

2. Develop a multi-item scale to measure students' attitudes toward internationalization of the management curriculum. How would you assess the reliability and validity of this scale?

3. Construct a Likert scale for measuring Internet usage. Show how the rating scale decisions were made.

INTERNET AND COMPUTER EXERCISES

1. Design Likert scales to measure the usefulness of Ford Motor Company's Web site. Visit the site at *www.ford.com* and rate it on the scales that you have developed.

2. Design semantic differential scales to measure the perception of FedEx overnight delivery service and compare it to that offered by UPS. Relevant information may be obtained by visiting the Web sites of these two companies *(www.fedex.com, www.ups.com)*

3. Visit the Office of Scales Research Web site *(www.siu.edu/departments/coba/mktg/osr)*. Identify one application of the Likert scale and one application of the semantic differential. Write a report describing the context in which these scales have been used.

4. Visit the Web sites of two marketing research firms conducting surveys. Analyze one survey of each firm to critically evaluate the itemized rating scales being used.

5. Surf the Net to find two examples each of Likert, semantic differential, and Stapel scales. Write a report describing the context in which these scales are being used.

ACTIVITIES

ROLE PLAYING

1. You work in the marketing research department of a firm specializing in developing decision support systems (DSSs) for the health care industry. Your firm would like to measure the attitudes of hospital administrators toward DSSs. The interviews would be conducted by telephone. You have been asked to develop an appropriate scale for this purpose. Management would like you to explain and justify your reasoning in constructing this scale.

FIELD WORK

1. Develop a semantic differential scale to measure the images of two major airlines that fly to your city. Administer this scale to a pilot sample of 20 students. Based on your pilot study, which airline has a more favorable image?

2. Develop a Likert scale to measure the images of two major banks in your city. Administer this scale to a pilot sample of 20 students. Based on your pilot study, which bank has a more favorable image?

3. Develop a Stapel scale to measure the images of two supermarkets in your city. Administer this scale to a pilot sample of 20 students. Based on your pilot study, which supermarket has a more favorable image?

GROUP DISCUSSION

1. "It really does not matter which scaling technique you use. As long as your measure is reliable, you will get the right results." Discuss this statement as a small group.

2. "One need not be concerned with reliability and validity in applied marketing research." Discuss this statement as a small group.

3. As a small group or as a class, discuss one of the articles listed in the notes to this chapter.

NOTES

1. Matthew Gwyther, "The Big Box Office Bet," *Management Today* (March 1999): 48–54; Shannon Dortch, "Going to the Movies," *American Demographics*, 18(12) (December 1996): 4–7; and Joe Rapolla, "Music Finds an Audience if You Know How to Look," *Marketing News*, 29(18) (August 28, 1995): 17.

2. William Murphy and Sidney Tang, "Continuous Likeability Measurement," *Marketing Research: A Magazine of Management & Applications*, 10(2) (Summer 1998): 28–35; and Ian Fenwick and Marshal D. Rice, "Reliability of Continuous Measurement Copy-Testing Methods," *Journal of Advertising Research*, 31(1) (February/March 1991): 23–29.

3. David Zoia, "Wanna Buy BMW?" *Ward's Auto World*, 35(4) (April 1999): 28–33; and "J. D. Power Releases New Ranking: Owner Happiness," *Marketing News* (November 6, 1995).

4. Naresh K. Malhotra, "A Scale to Measure Self-Concepts, Person Concepts and Product Concepts," *Journal of Marketing Research*, 18 (November 1981): 456–464. See also A. Ben Oumil and Orhan Erddem, "Self-Concept by Gender: A Focus on Male–Female Consumers," *Journal of Marketing Theory & Practice*, 5(1) (Winter 1997): 7–14.

5. Kenneth O. Doyle, "Research Note: Reliability and Dimensionality of Stimulus Ratings," *Journal of Advertising Research*, 38(2) (March/April 1998): 45–50; and Robert A. Peterson, "A Meta-Analysis of Chronbach's Coefficient Alpha," *Journal of Consumer Research*, 21 (September 1994): 381–391.

6. Joanna S. Bers, "Forge an Emotional Bond," *Success*, 46(4) (April 1999): 6; Martha L. Stone, "Survey Finds Increasing Emphasis on Emotion in Ads," *Advertising Age's Business Marketing*, 82(8) (September 1997): 3, 65; and David J. Moore, William D. Harris, and Hong C. Chen, "Affects Intensity: An Individual Difference Response to Advertising Appeals," *Journal of Consumer Research*, 22(2) (September 1995): 154–164; and David M. Zeitlin and Richard A. Westwood, "Measuring Emotional Response," *Journal of Advertising Research* (October– November 1986): 34–44.

7. Alison M. Dean, "The Applicability of SERVQUAL in Different Health Care Environments," *Health Marketing Quarterly*, 16(3) (1999): 1–21; Simon S. K. Lam, "Measuring Service Quality: A Test–Retest Reliability Investigation of SERVQUAL," *Journal of Market Research Society*, 39(2) (April 1997): 381–396.

8. "Service Industries Mustn't Take Customers for Granted," *Marketing News*, 33(10) (May 10, 1999): 29–30; and Stephen Bennett, "Flower Power," *Progressive Grocer*, 73(11) (November 1994) 105–110.

9. Larry Pace and Eileen Kelly, "TQM at Xerox: Lessons Worth Duplicating," *International Journal of Technology Management*, 16(4–6) (1998): 326–335; Sam M. Malone, "The Baldrige Award: One Step in Xerox's Quest for Excellence," *Quality Progress*, 30(6) (June 1997): 39–42; and Betsy Mckay, "Xerox Fights Trademark Battle," *Advertising Age International* (April 27,1992).

10. Naresh K. Malhotra, *Marketing Research: An Applied Orientation*, 3rd ed. Upper Saddle River, NJ: Prentice Hall, 1999.

11. Saul Klein, "Marketing Norms Measurement: An International Validation and Comparison," *Journal of Business Ethics*, 18(1) (January 1999) 65–72; Anusorn Singhapakdi, Scott J. Vitell, Kumar C. Rallapalli, and Kenneth L. Kraft, "The Perceived Role of Ethics and Social Responsibility: A Scale Development," *Journal of Business Ethics*, 15(11) (November 1996): 1131–1140; and Reidenbach, R. Eric and Donald P. Robin, A Response to "On Measuring Ethical Judgments," *Journal of Business Ethics*, 14 (February 1995): 159–162.

11

QUESTIONNAIRE AND FORM DESIGN

A GOOD QUESTIONNAIRE MUST MOTIVATE THE RESPONDENTS TO PROVIDE COMPLETE AND UNBIASED ANSWERS. EVERY QUESTIONNAIRE SHOULD BE PRETESTED.

Opening Questions

1. What is the purpose of a questionnaire, and what are its objectives?
2. What is the process of designing a questionnaire, what steps are involved, and what are the guidelines for each step?
3. How are observational forms designed to most effectively observe behavior?
4. What role does questionnaire design play in implementing total quality management?
5. What considerations are involved in designing questionnaires for international marketing research?
6. How does technology interface with questionnaire design?
7. What ethical issues are involved in questionnaire design?
8. What role can the Internet play in the questionnaire design process?

Susan Lipske, Vice President/Sr. Research Director, Elrick & Lavidge.
Susan Lipske is responsible for designing and managing research programs for several clients. She supervises the Research Services in Elrick & Lavidge's Chicago office.

WORLD VISION IMPARTS DONORS A VISION FOR CARING

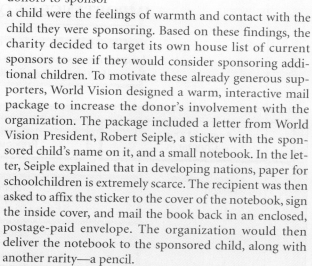

World Vision (WV), one of the top 100 charities in 2001, is a Christian-based organization that helps relief victims and needy children in nearly 100 countries around the world. WV needed at least $800,000 to continue caring for unsponsored children in developing countries. The children, who needed food, shelter, and medical care, had either never been sponsored or had lost their sponsors for various reasons. World Vision designed a questionnaire to determine donors' motivations for giving. The information obtained and the order in which it was obtained were as follows:

1. Priorities and motivations for giving
2. Awareness of the organization (WV)
3. Perceptions of the organization
4. Communication with donors
5. Demographic information

To increase the willingness of the donors and potential donors to participate and complete the questionnaire, the researchers made the context of the survey clear and minimized the effort required of the respondents by asking them questions that were easy to answer. Only necessary questions were asked, and combined questions were avoided. Most of the questions were structured; the respondents simply had to circle a number on the scale. However, a few unstructured or open-ended questions were included where it was felt that the respondents needed the freedom to express underlying motivations for giving.

In deciding on question wording, words with unequivocal meaning but familiar to the donors were used. Special effort was made to be objective so as not to bias the responses in any direction. The questionnaire was kept simple and detailed, and clear instructions were given since it had to be administered by mail. The questionnaire was divided into parts, with a separate part devoted to each type of information sought. The name and address of the respondents was optional and obtained at the end of the questionnaire. The questionnaire was professionally reproduced to have a neat appearance and was thoroughly pretested.

The results of the mail survey showed that the most important factors motivating donors to sponsor a child were the feelings of warmth and contact with the child they were sponsoring. Based on these findings, the charity decided to target its own house list of current sponsors to see if they would consider sponsoring additional children. To motivate these already generous supporters, World Vision designed a warm, interactive mail package to increase the donor's involvement with the organization. The package included a letter from World Vision President, Robert Seiple, a sticker with the sponsored child's name on it, and a small notebook. In the letter, Seiple explained that in developing nations, paper for schoolchildren is extremely scarce. The recipient was then asked to affix the sticker to the cover of the notebook, sign the inside cover, and mail the book back in an enclosed, postage-paid envelope. The organization would then deliver the notebook to the sponsored child, along with another rarity—a pencil.

With a total budget of $105,500, World Vision sent 240,893 pieces of direct mail. The response rate in terms of donations received was 46.1 percent, beating the previous campaign by 25.95 percent. The cost per response was a low $0.95. The total income exceeded the goal by $197,000 (23 percent). Beyond the 46.1 percent who responded by making a donation, more than 80 percent of the respondents returned their notebooks, signifying a much higher level of donor involvement than suggested by the donations.[1]

processing. As illustrated in the opening vignette, a questionnaire also enables the researcher to collect the relevant information necessary to address the management decision problem.

Questionnaire Definition

questionnaire
A structured technique for data collection that consists of a series of questions, written or verbal, that a respondent answers.

A **questionnaire** is a formalized set of questions for obtaining information from respondents. It has three specific objectives. First, the overriding objective is to translate the researcher's information needs into a set of specific questions that respondents are willing and able to answer. While this may seem straightforward, questions may yield very different and unanticipated responses. For example, how would you answer the following question: "Which State is larger, New York or Texas?" Would you answer based on population or area?

Second, a questionnaire should be written to minimize demands imposed on respondents. It should encourage them to participate in the entire interview, without biasing their responses. Incomplete interviews have limited usefulness, at best. In order to keep a respondent involved throughout a questionnaire, the researcher should attempt to minimize fatigue and boredom.

Third, a questionnaire should minimize response error. These errors can arise from respondents who give inaccurate answers or from misrecording or misanalyzing their answers. Minimizing the error introduced by the questionnaire itself is an important objective of questionnaire design. The following is an example of how questionnaires can be designed to achieve these objectives.

EXAMPLE

AN OLD-FASHIONED APPROACH WITH YOUNG RESPONDENTS

Youth Research (YR) (*www.youthresearch.com*) of Teenage Research Unlimited (*www.teenresearch.com*) surveys two age categories of children—6 to 8 year olds and 9 to 12 year olds—on a quarterly basis. The objective is to record children's views on favorite snack foods, television shows, commercials, radio, magazines, buzzwords, and movies. The one-on-one interviews conducted in malls are kept short, typically lasting only eight minutes.

YR attempts to make questions as clear and meaningful as possible so that kids can understand and answer them. This is done by establishing a context for questions. YR president Karen Forcade says, "For example, when asking about their radio listening habits we said, 'What about when you're in Mom's car, do you listen to radio?' rather than, 'How often do you listen to radio? More than once a day, once a day, more than once a week?' Those are kind of big questions for little children."

A trade-off is made between attempting to cover all possible areas of interest in one study and ensuring that the most important information is of high quality. Given children's limited attention span, minimizing boredom and being sensitive to fatigue becomes more important than asking all possible questions. Thus, YR motivates the kids to complete the questionnaire.

Forcade further notes that some clients attempt to meet all of their research objectives with one study. "The questionnaires keep going through the approval process and people keep adding questions, 'Well, let's ask this question, let's add that question, and why don't we talk about this also?' And so you end up keeping children 25 minutes in a central mall location and they get kind of itchy." The response error increases and the quality of data suffers. By keeping the questionnaire short and clear, YR also tries to reduce response error. While conducting research on children is not easy, YR has been successful in designing questionnaires that meet their stated objectives.[2]

QUESTIONNAIRE DESIGN PROCESS

No scientific principles guarantee an optimal or ideal questionnaire. Questionnaire design is as much an art as a science. The creativity, skill, and experience of the researcher play a major role in the end design. However, several guidelines are available to assist researchers in the questionnaire development process and to help them avoid major mistakes.

The guidelines to support questionnaire design are shown as a series of 10 steps (see Figure 11.3): (1) specify the information needed, (2) specify the type of interviewing method, (3) determine the content of individual questions, (4) design the questions to overcome the respondent's inability and unwillingness to answer, (5) decide on the question structure, (6) determine the question wording, (7) arrange the questions in proper order, (8) choose the form and layout, (9) reproduce the questionnaire, and (10) pretest the questionnaire. In practice, questionnaire design is an iterative rather than a sequential process. For example, pretesting of a question may reveal that respondents misunderstand the wording, sending the designer back to an earlier step.

SPECIFY THE INFORMATION NEEDED

The first step in questionnaire design is to specify the information needed. A continual review of the earlier stages of the research project, particularly the specific components of the problem, the research questions, and the hypotheses, will help keep the questionnaire focused. This was illustrated in the World Vision study in the opening vignette, which clearly specified the information the questionnaire was to obtain.

Questionnaires should also be designed with the target respondents in mind, taking into account their educational level and experience. The language used and the context of the questions must all be familiar to the respondents. Questions that are appropriate for college students may not be appropriate for those with only a high school education. Questionnaires that fail to keep in mind the characteristics of the respondents, particularly their educational level and experience, lead to a high incidence of "uncertain" or "no opinion" responses.

SPECIFY THE TYPE OF INTERVIEWING METHOD

Another important consideration in questionnaire design relates to how the data will be collected. An understanding of the various methods of conducting interviews provides guidance for questionnaire design (see Chapter 7). For example, personal interviews use face-to-face interaction. Due to the opportunity for feedback and clarification, questionnaires can be lengthy and complex and incorporate visual aids. Because a respondent cannot see the questionnaire in telephone interviews, the questions must be short and simple.

FIGURE 11.3
Questionnaire Design
Process

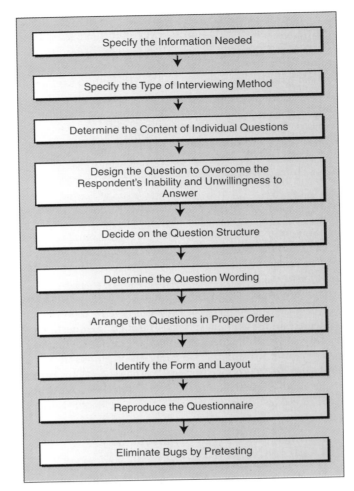

Any type of personally administered questionnaire should be written in a conversational style. Mail and electronic questionnaires are self-administered, involving no personal interaction between the researcher and the respondent. Therefore, both questions and instructions must be kept simple and thorough, as in the World Vision study in the opening vignette. In computer-assisted interviewing (CAPI, CATI, or Internet; see Chapter 7), the computer guides the respondent through complex skip patterns and can incorporate randomization of questions to eliminate order bias. The impact of the type of interviewing method on the nature of questions is illustrated in the context of obtaining consumer preferences for luxury cars.

EXAMPLE

EFFECT OF INTERVIEWING METHOD ON QUESTIONNAIRE DESIGN

Mail, E-Mail, or Web Site Questionnaire

Please rank the following luxury cars in order of your preference. Begin by picking out the one car brand that you like most and assign it a number 1. Then find the second most preferred car brand and assign it a number 2. Continue this procedure until you have ranked all the cars in order of preference. The least preferred car brand should be assigned a rank of 7. No two brands should receive the same rank number. The criterion of preference is entirely up to you. There is no right or wrong answer. Just try to be consistent.

CAR BRAND	RANK ORDER
1. Acura	_____
2. Cadillac	_____
3. Lexus	_____
4. Lincoln	_____
5. Infiniti	_____
6. Mercedes	_____
7. BMW	_____

Telephone Questionnaire

I will read to you the names of some luxury cars. Please rate them in terms of your preference. Use a six-point scale, where 1 denotes not so preferred and 6 denotes greatly preferred. Numbers between 1 and 6 reflect intermediate degrees of preference. Again, please remember that the higher the number, the greater the degree of preference. Now, please tell me your preference for . . . (READ ONE CAR BRAND AT A TIME.)

CAR BRAND	NOT SO PREFERRED				GREATLY PREFERRED	
1. Acura	1	2	3	4	5	6
2. Cadillac	1	2	3	4	5	6
3. Lexus	1	2	3	4	5	6
4. Lincoln	1	2	3	4	5	6
5. Infiniti	1	2	3	4	5	6
6. Mercedes	1	2	3	4	5	6
7. BMW	1	2	3	4	5	6

Personal Questionnaire

(HAND CAR BRAND CARDS TO THE RESPONDENT.) Here is a set of luxury car names, each written on a separate card. Please examine these cards carefully. (GIVE RESPONDENT TIME.) Now, please examine these cards again and pull out the card that has the name of the car brand you like the most, that is, your most preferred car. (RECORD THE CAR NAME AND KEEP THIS CARD WITH YOU.) Now, please examine the remaining six cards. Of these remaining six names, what is your most preferred car brand? (REPEAT THIS PROCEDURE SEQUENTIALLY UNTIL THE RESPONDENT HAS ONLY ONE CARD LEFT.)

	CAR RANK	NAME OF THE CAR
1.	1	
2.	2	
3.	3	
4.	4	
5.	5	
6.	6	
7.	7	

In the luxury car example, you can see how a ranking question changes as the method of interviewing changes. Ranking seven car brands is too complex a task to be administered over the telephone. Therefore, the simpler rating task in which brands are rated one at a time was used. In personal interviewing, the ranking task can be simplified by giving the respondent cards imprinted with the car brand name, and the interviewer is provided with special instructions (in capital letters). The type of interviewing method also influences the content of individual questions.

DETERMINE THE CONTENT OF INDIVIDUAL QUESTIONS

Once the information needed is specified and the type of interviewing method is decided, the next step is to determine question content. In other words, the researcher must determine what should be included in each question. Two types of questions should be asked at this step.

Is the Question Necessary?

Before including a question, the researcher should ask, "How will I use these data?" Questions that may be nice to know but that don't directly address the research problem should be eliminated. There are exceptions to this rule. Filler questions may be added to disguise the purpose or sponsorship of the project. For example, in brand studies, a researcher may include questions about the full range of competing brands so the respondents won't know who is sponsoring the study. Early in the interviewing process when the researcher is attempting to build a relationship with respondents and capture their attention, a few easy-to-answer neutral questions may be helpful. At times, certain questions may also be repeated for the purpose of assessing reliability or validity.

More than one question may be needed to measure the respondents' evaluations of Nike Town.

Are Several Questions Needed Instead of One?

In some cases, two questions are better than one. However, asking two questions in one is not the solution. Consider the following question:

Do you think Nike Town offers better variety and prices than other Nike stores?

(Incorrect)

double-barreled question
A single question that attempts to cover two issues. Such questions can be confusing to respondents and can result in ambiguous responses.

A "yes" answer will presumably be clear, but what if the answer is "no"? Does this mean that the respondent thinks that Nike Town does not offer better variety, that it does not offer better prices, or that it offers neither better variety nor better prices? Such a question is called a **double-barreled question** because two or more questions are combined into one. To avoid confusion, these questions should be asked separately,

Do you think Nike Town offers better variety than other Nike stores?
Do you think Nike Town offers better prices than other Nike stores?

(Correct)

DESIGN THE QUESTION TO OVERCOME THE RESPONDENT'S INABILITY TO ANSWER

Respondents may not always be able to answer the questions posed to them. Researchers can help them overcome this limitation by keeping in mind the reasons people typically cannot answer a question: They may not be informed, may not remember, or may be unable to articulate certain types of responses.

Is the Respondent Informed?

Respondents are often asked to answer questions they are uninformed about. A husband may not be informed about monthly expenses for groceries and department store purchases if it is the wife who makes these purchases, or vice versa. Despite the fact that they are uninformed, respondents may provide answers, as the following example shows.

EXAMPLE

UNKNOWN QUESTION ELICITS KNOWN ANSWERS

In one study, respondents were asked to express their degree of agreement or disagreement with the following statement: "The National Bureau of Consumer Complaints provides an effective means for consumers who have purchased a defective product to obtain relief." Even with a "don't know" option available, 51.9 percent of the lawyers and 75.0 percent of the public still expressed an opinion about the National Bureau of Consumer Complaints. Why should this high response rate be problematic? Because there is no such entity as the National Bureau of Consumer Complaints![3]

When the research topic requires specialized experience or knowledge, **filter questions** measuring familiarity, product use, and past experience should be asked before questions about the topics themselves. Filter questions enable the researcher to eliminate from the analysis those respondents who are not adequately informed.

In addition to filter questions, a "don't know" option to a question is helpful. This option has been found to reduce the number of uninformed responses without reducing overall response rate. If it is suspected that many respondents may be uninformed about the topic, "don't know" should be added to the list of response alternatives.

filter questions
An initial question in a questionnaire that screens potential respondents to ensure they meet the requirements of the sample.

Can the Respondent Remember?

Many common experiences or practices are difficult to remember. Can you remember the brand name of the shirt you are wearing, what you had for lunch a week ago, or what you were doing a month ago today? Further, do you know how many gallons of soft drinks you consumed during the last four weeks? When making estimates about product consumption levels, in particular, research has found that consumers dramatically overestimate usage.

We tend to remember events that are personally relevant or unusual or that occur frequently. People remember their wedding anniversary and birthday or the day Princess Diana was killed. Likewise, the more recently the event occurred, the more readily an event will be recalled. For example, you are more likely to remember the purchases you made on your last trip to the grocery store than the purchases you made three shopping trips ago.

Questions can be designed to aid recall or they can be unaided, depending on the research objectives. For example, unaided recall of soft drink commercials could be measured by questions such as, "What brands of soft drinks do you remember being advertised last night on TV?" A question that employs aided recall attempts to stimulate the respondent's memory by providing cues related to the event of interest. The aided recall approach would list a number of soft drink brands and then ask, "Which of these brands were advertised last night on TV?" One of the risks of presenting cues is that they may bias responses and make respondents unduly sensitive to a topic, thus distorting their answers.

Can the Respondent Articulate?

Respondents may be unable to articulate certain types of responses. This does not mean, however, that they do not have an opinion on that topic. For example, it is difficult to describe the ideal atmosphere of a department store. On the other hand, if the respondents are provided with alternative descriptions of store atmosphere, they will be able to indicate the one they like best. When asked to provide answers that are difficult to articulate, respondents are likely to ignore that question and may refuse to complete the questionnaire. Visual aids in the form of pictures, diagrams, or maps as well as verbal descriptions can help respondents articulate responses.

DESIGN THE QUESTIONNAIRE TO OVERCOME THE RESPONDENT'S UNWILLINGNESS TO ANSWER

Even if respondents are able to answer a particular question, they may be unwilling to do so. Refusal to answer a question may be due to a variety of circumstances. The respondent may feel there's simply too much effort involved, that the question serves no legitimate purpose, or that the information requested is too sensitive.

Effort Required of the Respondent

While most individuals are willing to participate in a survey, this sense of cooperation may vanish if the questions require too much effort to answer. Suppose the researcher is interested in determining from which departments in a store the respondent purchased merchandise on the most recent shopping trip. This information can be obtained in at least two ways. The researcher could ask the respondent to list all the items purchased on her most recent shopping trip, or the researcher could provide a list of departments and ask the respondent to check the applicable ones.

Please list all the departments from which you purchased merchandise on your most recent shopping trip to a department store.

(Incorrect)

In the list that follows, please check all the departments from which you purchased merchandise on your most recent shopping trip to a department store.

1. Women's dresses   _____
2. Men's apparel   _____
3. Children's apparel   _____
4. Cosmetics   _____
5. Jewelry   _____
6. Other (please specify)   _____

(Correct)

The second option is preferable because it requires less effort from respondents. In the World Vision questionnaire in the opening vignette, the effort required of the respondents was reduced by asking easy questions for which the respondents merely had to check one of the response options.

Legitimate Purpose

Respondents also object to questions that do not seem to serve a legitimate purpose. Why should a firm marketing cereals want to know their age, income, and occupation? The researcher should anticipate these types of objections and attempt to overcome them by explaining why the data are needed. A statement such as, "To determine how the consumption of cereal and preferences for cereal brands vary among people of different ages, incomes, and occupations, we need information on . . ." can make the request for information seem legitimate. Moreover, the context of the survey should be clearly explained, as in the World Vision project.

Sensitive Information

Information of a personal or highly sensitive nature may be difficult to obtain from respondents. Examples of sensitive topics include money, family life, political and religious beliefs, and involvement in accidents or crimes. The respondents may be embarrassed to answer such questions because accurate responses may threaten their prestige or self-image. To increase the likelihood of obtaining sensitive information, such topics should be placed at the end of the questionnaire. By then, rapport has been created and legitimacy of the project established, making respondents more willing to give information. Where appropriate, sensitive information should be obtained in the form of response categories rather than asking for specific figures. While respondents may refuse to answer the question,

What is your household's exact annual income?

(Incorrect)

they may be willing to check the appropriate income category. A better way of obtaining information on income is to ask:

Which one of the following categories best describes your household's annual income?

1. under $25,000 _____   3. $50,001–$75,000 _____
2. $25,001–$50,000 _____   4. over $75,000 _____

(Correct)

DECIDE ON THE QUESTION STRUCTURE

A question may be unstructured or structured. In the following sections, we define unstructured questions and discuss their advantages and limitations. This is followed by a

FIGURE 11.4
Types of Questions

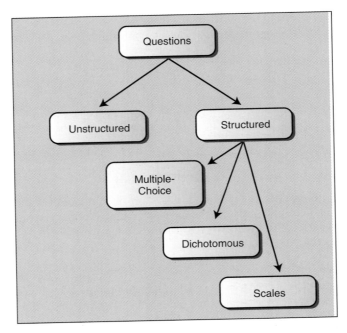

discussion of the popular forms of structured questions: multiple-choice, dichotomous, and scales (see Figure 11.4).

Unstructured Questions

unstructured questions
Open-ended questions that respondents answer in their own words.

Unstructured questions are open-ended questions that respondents answer in their own words. They are also referred to as free-response or free-answer questions. The following are examples of unstructured questions:

- What is your favorite pastime?
- How would you describe the typical user of Land Rover sports utility vehicles?

Open-ended questions are good as first questions on a topic. They enable the respondents to express general attitudes and opinions that can help the researcher interpret their responses to structured questions. Open-ended questions allow the respondent to express their attitudes or opinions without the bias associated with restricting responses to predefined alternatives. Thus, they can be useful in identifying underlying motivations, beliefs, and attitudes, as in the World Vision vignette. Analysis of the verbatim comments provides a rich context for interpreting later questions. Unstructured questions are useful in exploratory research.

EXAMPLE

OPEN-ENDED QUESTIONS OPEN THE WAY TO A NEW OPPORTUNITY FOR NABISCO

In an exploratory survey, Nabisco Biscuit Company asked a series of open-ended questions related to cookies with a view to identifying any consumer needs they were not satisfactorily meeting. Included in the survey were questions such as these: What do you like about cookies? What do you dislike about cookies? What are the health benefits of cookies? What are health disadvantages of cookies?

The findings revealed that the needs of a subset of specialty cookie consumers were not being met by existing "wellness specialty offerings," cookies that offered health benefits. These consumers wanted great taste combined with health benefits, so that they could enjoy the cookies without feeling guilty. Seeing this opportunity, Nabisco and ConAgra joined to create and market Healthy Choice, an adult specialty cookie with an indulgent yet healthful profile. Healthy Choice cookies rank among the top 100 specialty cookie/cracker category. The Raspberry Tart ranks 33, the Apricot Tart 92. According to Nabisco, both were outselling all of key competitor Pepperidge Farms' wellness cookies shortly after introduction. This success is attributed to a focus on unsatisfied consumer needs identified through open-ended questions.[4]

The disadvantages of unstructured questions relate to recording error, data coding, and the added complexity of analysis. In personal or telephone interviews, successfully recording verbatim comments depends entirely on the recording skills of the interviewer. Interviewer bias is introduced as decisions are made regarding whether to record answers verbatim or write down only the main points. Tape recorders should be used if verbatim reporting is important.

Categorizing the recorded comments to open-ended questions introduces the second source of bias and another major disadvantage. Implicitly, unstructured or open-ended questions give extra weight to respondents who are more talkative or articulate. The process of summarizing comments into a format that can be analyzed is both time consuming and expensive. Unstructured questions are also of limited value in self-administered questionnaires (mail, CAPI, or electronic) because respondents tend to be more brief in writing than in speaking.

In general, open-ended questions are useful in exploratory research and as opening questions. However, in a large survey, the complexity of recording, tabulation, and analysis outweighs their advantages.

Structured Questions

Structured questions specify the set of responses as well as their format. A structured question may offer multiple choices, only two choices (dichotomous question), or a scale (Figure 11.4).

MULTIPLE-CHOICE QUESTIONS In multiple-choice questions, the researcher provides a choice of answers, and respondents are asked to select one or more of the alternatives given. Consider the following question:

Do you intend to travel overseas within the next six months?
1. Definitely will not travel _____
2. Probably will not travel _____
3. Undecided _____
4. Probably will travel _____
5. Definitely will travel _____

structured questions
Questions that prespecify the set of response alternatives and the response format. A structured question could be multiple choice, dichotomous, or a scale.

Many of the issues associated with constructing itemized rating scales (Chapter 10) also apply to multiple-choice answers. Two additional concerns in designing multiple-choice questions are (1) the number of alternatives that should be included and (2) order or position bias.

Multiple-choice questions should include choices that cover the full range of possible alternatives. The alternatives should be mutually exclusive and collectively exhaustive. An "other (please specify)" category should be included where appropriate. Instructions should clearly indicate whether the respondent is to choose only one alternative or select all that apply. (For example, "Please indicate all the brands of soft drinks that you have consumed in the past week.") As the list of choices increases, the questions become more difficult to answer. When the alternative list becomes long, the researcher should consider using more than one question to simplify the workload for respondents.

order bias (position bias)
A respondent's tendency to choose an alternative merely because it occupies a certain position on the page or in a list.

Order or **position bias** is the respondents' tendency to check an alternative merely because it occupies a certain position in a list. Alternatives that appear at the beginning and, to a lesser degree, at the end of a list have a tendency to be selected most often. When questions relate to numeric values (quantities or prices), there is a tendency to select the central value on the list. Order bias can be controlled by preparing several forms of the questionnaire with changes in the order of the alternatives from form to form. Each alternative should appear once in each of the extreme positions, once in the middle, and once somewhere in between.

Multiple-choice questions are easier for respondents to answer. They are also easier to analyze and tabulate than open-ended questions. Interviewer bias is also reduced, given that these types of questions work very well in self-administered conditions. Respondent cooperation in general is improved if the majority of the questions are structured.

Multiple-choice questions are not without disadvantages. It is difficult to develop effective multiple-choice options. Often, exploratory research must be conducted using open-ended questions to identify the appropriate response options. Large numbers of respondents checking the "other (please specify)" category indicate that the alternative list may be seriously flawed. The list of options itself also introduces bias.

DICHOTOMOUS QUESTIONS A **dichotomous question** has only two response alternatives: yes or no, agree or disagree, and so on. Sometimes, multiple-choice questions can alternatively be framed as dichotomous, as in the overseas travel question asked earlier:

dichotomous question
A structured question with only two response alternatives, such as yes and no.

Do you intend to travel overseas within the next six months?

1. Yes _____
2. No _____

Dichotomous questions should be used when the researcher has reason to believe that the respondent thinks of the topic in yes/no terms. When the respondent is highly involved in a subject or has a great deal of knowledge related to the topic, a multiple-choice question or scale may be more appropriate.

Dichotomous questions have many of the same strengths and weaknesses of multiple-choice questions. They are among the easiest types of questions to code and analyze. They have one serious flaw, however. The direction of question wording can have a significant effect on the responses given. To illustrate, the statement, "Individuals are more to blame than social conditions for crime and lawlessness in this country," produced agreement from 59.6 percent of the respondents. However, on a matched sample that responded to the opposite statement, "Social conditions are more to blame than individuals for crime and lawlessness in this country," 43.2 percent (as opposed to 40.4 percent) agreed. To overcome this problem, the question should be framed in one way on one-half of the questionnaires and in the opposite way on the other half. This is referred to as the split-ballot technique.

SCALES Scales were discussed in detail in Chapters 9 and 10. Sometimes, multiple-choice questions can alternatively be framed as scales, as in the overseas travel question asked earlier:

Do you intend to travel overseas within the next six months?

Definitely will not travel	Probably will not travel	Undecided	Probably will travel	Definitely will travel
1	2	3	4	5

Questions making use of scales are easy to answer and are therefore popular, as in the World Vision vignette.

DETERMINE THE QUESTION WORDING

Translating the information needed into clearly worded questions that are easily understood is the most difficult aspect of questionnaire development. Poorly worded questions can confuse or mislead respondents, leading to nonresponse or response error. Such questions can also frustrate the respondents to the point that they refuse to answer those questions or items. This is referred to as item nonresponse and leads to nonresponse error. If respondents interpret questions differently than intended by the researcher, serious bias can occur, leading to response error.

To avoid problems in question wording, we offer five guidelines: (1) define the issue, (2) use ordinary words, (3) avoid ambiguous words, (4) avoid leading questions, and (5) use positive and negative statements.

Define the Issue

Questions should always clearly define the issue being addressed. Beginning journalists are told to define the issue in terms of who, what, when, where, why, and way (the six Ws). These—particularly who, what, when, and where—can also serve as guidelines for defining the issue in a question. Consider the following question:

A well-defined question is needed to determine which brand of toothpaste a person uses.

Which brand of toothpaste do you use?

(Incorrect)

On the surface, this may seem to be a well-defined question, but we may reach a different conclusion when we examine it under the microscope of who, what, when, and where.

THE W'S	DEFINING THE QUESTION
Who	The Respondent
	It is not clear whether this question relates to the individual respondent or the respondent's total household.
What	The Brand of Toothpaste
	It is unclear how the respondent is to answer this question if more than one brand is used.
When	Unclear
	The time frame is not specified in this question. The respondent could interpret it as meaning the toothpaste used this morning, this week, or over the past year.
Where	Not Specified
	At home, at the gym, on the road?

A more clearly defined question might read:

Which brand or brands of toothpaste have you personally used at home during the past month? In case of more than one brand, please list all the brands that apply.

(Correct)

Assessing the distribution of snack foods requires the use of words as ordinary and commonplace as snack foods themselves.

Use Simple Words

Simple, ordinary words that match the vocabulary level of the respondent should be used in a questionnaire. When choosing words, keep in mind that the average person in the United States has a high school, not a college, education. For certain respondent groups, the education level is even lower. Simplicity in wording and a conscious effort to avoid technical jargon should guide questionnaire development. As marketing professionals, it is also important to remember that most respondents do not understand marketing terminology. For example, instead of asking,

Is the distribution of snack foods adequate?

(Incorrect)

ask,

Are snack foods readily available when you want to buy them?

(Correct)

Use Unambiguous Words

When selecting words for a questionnaire, the questionnaire designer should choose words with only one meaning. This is not an easy task given that a number of words that appear unambiguous can have different meanings to different people. These include *usually, normally, frequently, often, regularly, occasionally,* and *sometimes.* Consider the following question:

In a typical month, how often do you go to a movie theater to see a movie?
1. Never   _____
2. Occasionally _____
3. Sometimes   _____
4. Often   _____
5. Regularly   _____

(Incorrect)

The categories of this multiple-choice question can have different meanings to different people, leading to response bias. Three respondents who go to movie theaters once a month may check three different categories: occasionally, sometimes, and often. The following is a much better worded question:

In a typical month, how often do you go to a movie theater to see a movie?
1. Less than once   _____
2. 1 or 2 times   _____
3. 3 or 4 times   _____
4. More than 4 times _____

(Correct)

This question is less ambiguous because each respondent is answering it from a consistent frame of reference. Response categories have been objectively defined, and respondents are no longer free to interpret them in their own way.

Avoid Producing Leading or Biasing Questions

leading question
A question that gives the respondent a clue as to what the answer should be.

A **leading question** is one that clues the respondent to what the answer should be, as in the following:

Do you think that America should provide financial aid to poor foreign countries when it is not our responsibility to do so?

1. Yes   _____
2. No   _____
3. Don't know _____

(Incorrect)

This question would lead respondents to a "No" answer. The answer would be unduly biased by the phrase "it is not our responsibility to do so." Therefore, this question would not help determine the preferences of Americans for providing aid to poor foreign countries. A better question would be:

Do you think that America should provide financial aid to poor foreign countries?

1. Yes   _____
2. No   _____
3. Don't know _____

(Correct)

Words can lead respondents in a particular direction. Identification of the research sponsor can have the same effect. When respondents are made aware of the sponsor, they tend to answer questions about that sponsor in a positive manner. The question,

Is Colgate your favorite toothpaste?

(Incorrect)

is likely to bias the responses in favor of Colgate. A more unbiased way of obtaining this information would be to ask,

What is your favorite brand of toothpaste?

(Correct)

Likewise, the mention of a prestigious or nonprestigious name can bias the response, as in, "Do you agree with the American Dental Association that Colgate is effective in preventing cavities?" Question wording should be objective, as in the World Vision vignette.

Balance Dual Statements

Many questions, particularly those measuring attitudes and lifestyles, are worded as statements to which respondents indicate their degree of agreement or disagreement using Likert scales. The statements in this type of questions can be worded either positively or negatively. Evidence shows that the responses obtained often depend on the direction of the wording of the questions—whether they are stated positively or negatively. Questions of this type should be balanced by using dual statements, some of which are positive and some negative. Two different questionnaires, which reverse the direction of the questions, could also be used to control for any bias introduced by the positive or negative nature of the statements. An example of dual statements was provided in the summated Likert scale in Chapter 10 that was designed to measure attitudes toward Macy's.

ARRANGE THE QUESTIONS IN PROPER ORDER

When arranging questions in a proper order, the researcher should consider the opening questions, the type of information sought, difficult questions, and the effect on subsequent questions. Questions should be arranged in a logical order, organized around topic areas.

Opening Questions

Opening questions set the stage for the remainder of the questionnaire. They serve a variety of purposes. They can introduce the topic, attempt to gain the confidence and cooperation of respondents, or establish the legitimacy of the study. The opening questions should be interesting, simple, and nonthreatening. Questions that ask respondents for their opinions are always good openers because most people like to express their opinions.

Sometimes opening questions may be asked to simply establish rapport. Some studies require a prescreening of the respondents to ensure that they are eligible to participate in the interview. In these cases, qualifying questions are used as opening questions.

E X A M P L E

QUALIFYING RESPONDENTS LEADS TO UNQUALIFIED SUCCESS FOR KELLOGG'S

Looking to expand its share of the ready-to-eat cereal category, Kellogg's conducted a telephone survey of users. The nonusers of ready-to-eat cereals were not relevant for this study and thus not part of the target population. The first question was: How often do you have ready-to-eat cereal for breakfast?

Less than twice a week   _____

Two or three times per week   _____

Four or five times per week   _____

More than five times per week _____

If the answer was "less than twice a week," that respondent was thanked and the interview terminated. Such respondents were operationally classified as nonusers and excluded from the study.

The results of the survey indicated that consumers were looking for a crunchy, tasty, yet low-fat and healthy cereal. Based on the findings of this survey, Kellogg's introduced Honey Crunch Corn Flakes. The oven-baked flake is 20 percent thicker than other flakes, offering a crunchier texture. It is low in fat, cholesterol-free, and a source of nine essential vitamins and minerals. The bright yellow package features Cornelius the Rooster, which has been on the Kellogg's Corn Flakes box since 1957. To support the product launch, Kellogg's ran a national TV spot emphasizing the cereal's "Taste of Honey, Heart of Gold." This new brand has been a great success in a very competitive cereal market.[5]

---

basic information
Information that relates directly to the marketing research problem.

classification information
Socioeconomic and demographic characteristics used to classify respondents.

identification information
A type of information obtained in a questionnaire that includes name, address, and phone number.

Type of Information

Three types of information are obtained from a questionnaire: (1) basic information, (2) classification information, and (3) identification information. **Basic information** relates directly to the research problem. **Classification information** consists of socioeconomic and demographic characteristics. It is used to classify the respondents in order to analyze results across different groups. **Identification information** includes name, address, and telephone number. Identification information may be obtained for a variety of purposes, including verifying that the respondents listed were actually interviewed, remitting promised incentives, and so on. Because basic information is the most important aspect of a study, it should be obtained first, followed by classification and then identification information. Classification and identification information is of a more personal nature. Respondents may resist answering a series of personal questions. Therefore, these types of questions should appear at the end of the questionnaire, as in the World Vision vignette.

Difficult Questions

Respondents can perceive questions as difficult for a variety of reasons. They may relate to sensitive issues or be embarrassing, complex, or dull. Questions that could be perceived as difficult should be placed late in the sequence after a relationship has been established and the respondent is involved in the process. The last question of the classification section is typically income information; the respondent's telephone number is the final item in the identification section for the same reasons.

Effect on Subsequent Questions

Initial questions can influence questions asked later in a questionnaire. As a rule, a series of questions should start with a general introduction to a topic, followed by specific questions related to the topic. This prevents specific questions from biasing responses to the general questions. Consider the following sequence of questions:

Q1: In selecting a department store, how important is convenience of location?
Q2: What considerations are important to you in selecting a department store?

(Incorrect)

The first question is specific in that it concerns a specific factor (convenience of location) while the second is general. Given the order of the questions, the respondents would be more likely to cite convenience of location as the response to the general question. This would bias the response to the general question. To prevent bias, the general question should be asked first followed by the specific question.

Q1: What considerations are important to you in selecting a department store?
Q2: In selecting a department store, how important is convenience of location?

(Correct)

Going from general to specific is called the **funnel approach**, because you begin with broader (more general) questions and then ask narrower (more specific) questions, reflecting the shape of a funnel (Figure 11.5).[6] The funnel approach was illustrated in the opening vignette when general information about motivations for giving was obtained before measuring awareness and perceptions of World Vision.

funnel approach
A strategy for ordering questions in a questionnaire in which the sequence starts with the general questions, which are followed by progressively specific questions, in order to prevent specific questions from biasing general questions.

Logical Order

Questions should be asked in a logical order, organized around topic areas. This was illustrated in the World Vision vignette. The order in which the questions were asked was as follows: (1) priorities and motivations for giving, (2) awareness of the organization (WV), (3) perceptions of the organization, (4) communication with donors, and (5) demographic information. When switching topics, brief transitional phrases or sentences should be used to help respondents switch their train of thought; for example, "In this section, we ask questions related to your purchase of a new car in the last six months."

Branching questions direct respondents to different places in the questionnaire based on their response to the question at hand. To avoid confusion, they should be designed carefully. Here is an example of a well-designed question: "If the answer to Question 4 (Have you purchased a new car in the last six months?) is No, go to Question 10; skip Questions 5 through 9 related to new car purchase." Branches enable respondents to skip irrelevant questions or elaborate in areas of specific interest. Skip patterns can become quite complex to the point that they are best administered in computer-assisted interviewing environments (CATI, CAPI, or Internet; see Chapter 7).

branching question
Question used to guide an interviewer through a survey by directing the interviewer to different spots on the questionnaire depending on the answers given.

FIGURE 11.5   The Funnel Approach to Ordering Questions

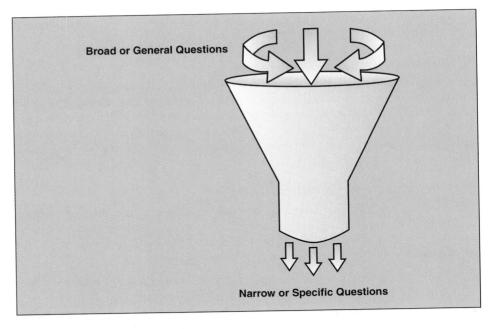

CHOOSE THE FORM AND LAYOUT

The physical characteristics of a questionnaire, such as the format, spacing, and positioning can have a significant effect on the results. This is particularly important for self-administered questionnaires. Experiments on mail questionnaires for the 1990 and 2000 censuses revealed that questions at the top of the page received more attention than those at the bottom. Instructions printed in red made little difference except that they made the questionnaire appear more complicated to the respondents.

Dividing a questionnaire into sections with separate topic areas for each section is a good practice, as illustrated in the World Vision project. Several parts may be needed for questions pertaining to the basic information. The questions in each part should be numbered, particularly when branching questions are used. Numbering also makes coding the responses easier. The questionnaires should preferably be precoded. In **precoding**, the codes to enter in the computer are printed on the questionnaire. Typically, the code identifies the line number and the column numbers in which a particular response will be entered. Note that when CATI or CAPI is used, the precoding is built into the software. Coding of questionnaires is explained in more detail in Chapter 15 on data preparation, but an example of the process in a questionnaire is shown below.

precoding
In questionnaire design, assigning a code to every conceivable response before data collection.

E X A M P L E

PRECODING A QUESTIONNAIRE

RESIDENTIAL CARPETING SURVEY

(1–3)

(Please ignore the numbers alongside the answers. They are only to help us in data processing)

Please answer the following questions pertaining to household carpeting by following the specified directions.

Part A

Q1. Does your household currently own carpeting?

1. Yes _____   (5)

2. No _____

(IF YES, GO TO QUESTION Q2; IF NO, GO TO QUESTION Q7)

Q2. Which of the following styles of carpeting do you have in your home? Please check as many as apply.

1. One Color; Traditional Style _____   (6)
2. Multicolor; Traditional Style _____   (7)
3. One Color; Fashion Style   _____   (8)
4. Multicolor; Fashion Style   _____   (9)
5. Other   _____   (10)

Please indicate your agreement with each of the following statements (Q3 to Q6).

Q3. Carpeting is an important part of my home.

Strongly Disagree			Neutral			Strongly Agree	
1	2	3	4	5	6	7	(11)

Q4. Carpeting is a fashion item for the home.

Strongly Disagree			Neutral			Strongly Agree	
1	2	3	4	5	6	7	(12)

In the preceding example, the first precoding value (1–3) indicates that the first three columns are used for the questionnaire ID. In general, the questionnaires themselves should be numbered serially as this enhances control of questionnaires in the field, as well as the coding and analysis. This numbering system alerts the researcher if questionnaires are misplaced or lost. A possible exception to this rule is mail questionnaires. Respondents are promised anonymity, and the presence of a questionnaire identifier may be interpreted as a breach of that promise. Some respondents may refuse to participate or answer differently if they believe the answers can be traced to them. However, recent research suggests that this loss of anonymity has little, if any, influence on the results.

REPRODUCE THE QUESTIONNAIRE

The quality of the paper and print process used for the questionnaire also influence response. For example, if the questionnaire is reproduced on poor-quality paper or is otherwise shabby in appearance, the respondents may conclude that the project is unimportant, and this perception will be reflected in the quality of the responses. Therefore, the questionnaire should be reproduced on good-quality paper and have a professional appearance, as illustrated in the World Vision study. Multipage questionnaires should be presented in booklet form rather than simply stapled or clipped. This format is easier for the interviewer to handle and it also enhances the overall appearance.

Questions should not be continued from one page to the next. In other words, researchers should avoid splitting a question, including its response categories. Respondents may be misled into thinking that a split question has ended at the bottom of a page and base their answers on the incomplete question.

The tendency to crowd questions together to make the questionnaire look shorter should be avoided. Overcrowding leaves little space for responses, which results in shorter answers. It also increases errors in data transcription. In addition, crowded questionnaires appear more complex, resulting in lower cooperation and completion rates. While shorter questionnaires are more desirable than longer ones, reduction in size should not be obtained at the expense of crowding.

PRETEST THE QUESTIONNAIRE

pretesting
The testing of the questionnaire on a small sample of respondents for the purpose of improving the questionnaire by identifying and eliminating potential problems before using it in the actual survey.

Pretesting refers to testing the questionnaire on a small sample of respondents, usually 15 to 30, to identify and eliminate potential problems. Even the best questionnaire can be improved by pretesting. As a general rule, a questionnaire should not be used in the field study without extensive pretesting, as in the World Vision vignette. All aspects of the questionnaire, including question content, wording, sequence, form and layout, question difficulty, and instructions should be tested. Additionally, pretesting should be conducted with a subset of the respondent group. The pretest groups should be similar to the respondents in terms of their background characteristics, familiarity with the topic, and attitudes and behaviors of interest.[7]

Pretests are best done by personal interviews, even if the actual survey is to be conducted by telephone, mail, or electronically, so that interviewers can observe respondent reactions and attitudes. After the necessary changes have been made, another pretest could be administered using the actual data collection approach if it is mail, telephone, or electronic. This stage of the pretest will reveal any potential problems in the interviewing method to be used in the actual survey. The pretest should be conducted in an environment and context similar to that of the actual survey.

Based on feedback from the pretest, the questionnaire should be edited, and the identified problems corrected. After each significant revision of the questionnaire, another pretest should be conducted, using a different sample of respondents. Pretesting should be continued until no further changes are needed. As a final step, the responses obtained during the pretest should be coded and analyzed. The analysis of pretest responses can serve as a check on the adequacy of the problem definition and provide insight into the nature of the data as well as analytic techniques that will be required. Table 11.1 outlines the questionnaire design process in the form of a checklist.

OBSERVATIONAL FORMS

Observational forms are designed to record respondent reaction to new products, advertising, packaging, or some other marketing stimuli. Since there is no questioning of the respondents, the researcher need not be concerned with the psychological impact of the questions and the way they are asked. Observational forms are designed primarily for the field work and the tabulation phase, providing a guide for recording information accurately and to simplify coding, entry, and analysis of data.

Observational forms should specify the who, what, when, where, why, and way of behavior to be observed. Suppose McDonald's wants to observe consumers' reactions to the

TABLE 11.1   Questionnaire Design Checklist

STEP 1   SPECIFY THE INFORMATION NEEDED

1. Ensure that the information obtained fully addresses all the components of the problem.
2. Have a clear idea of the target population.

STEP 2   TYPE OF INTERVIEWING METHOD

1. Review the type of interviewing method determined based on considerations discussed in Chapter 7.

STEP 3   INDIVIDUAL QUESTION CONTENT

1. Is the question necessary?
2. Are several questions needed instead of one to obtain the required information in an unambiguous manner?
3. Do not use double-barreled questions.

STEP 4   OVERCOMING INABILITY AND UNWILLINGNESS TO ANSWER

1. Is the respondent informed?
2. If respondents are not likely to be informed, filter questions that measure familiarity, product use, and past experience should be asked before questions about the topics themselves.
3. Can the respondent remember?
4. Questions that do not provide the respondent with cues can underestimate the actual occurrence of an event.
5. Can the respondent articulate?
6. Minimize the effort required of the respondents.
7. Make the request for information seem legitimate.
8. Is the information sensitive?

STEP 5   CHOOSING QUESTION STRUCTURE

1. Open-ended questions are useful in exploratory research and as opening questions.
2. Use structured questions whenever possible.
3. In multiple-choice questions, the response alternatives should include the set of all possible choices and should be mutually exclusive.
4. In a dichotomous question, if a substantial proportion of the respondents can be expected to be neutral, include a neutral alternative.
5. Consider the use of the split ballot technique to reduce order bias in dichotomous and multiple-choice questions.
6. If the response alternatives are numerous, consider using more than one question.

STEP 6   CHOOSING QUESTION WORDING

1. Define the issue in terms of who, what, when, where, why, and way (the six Ws).
2. Use ordinary words. Words should match the vocabulary level of the respondents.
3. Avoid ambiguous words: *usually, normally, frequently, often, regularly, occasionally, sometimes,* and so on.
4. Avoid leading questions that clue the respondent to what the answer should be.
5. Avoid implicit alternatives that are not explicitly expressed in the options.
6. Avoid implicit assumptions.
7. Respondent should not have to make generalizations or compute estimates.
8. Use positive and negative statements.

(continues)

T A B L E 1 1 . 1   (continued)

STEP 7   DETERMINE THE ORDER OF QUESTIONS

1. The opening questions should be interesting, simple, and nonthreatening.
2. Qualifying questions should serve as the opening questions.
3. Basic information should be obtained first, followed by classification, and, finally, identification information.
4. Difficult, sensitive, or complex questions should be placed late in the sequence.
5. General questions should precede specific questions.
6. Questions should be asked in a logical order.

STEP 8   FORM AND LAYOUT

1. Divide a questionnaire into several parts.
2. Number the questions in each part.
3. Precode the questionnaire.
4. Serially number the questionnaires themselves.

STEP 9   REPRODUCTION OF THE QUESTIONNAIRE

1. The questionnaire should have a professional appearance.
2. Use a booklet format for long questionnaires.
3. Reproduce each question on a single page (or double-page spread).
4. Avoid the tendency to crowd questions to make the questionnaire look shorter.
5. Place directions or instructions for individual questions as close to the questions as possible.

STEP 10   PRETESTING

1. Always pretest
2. Test all aspects of the questionnaire, including question content, wording, sequence, form and layout, question difficulty, and instructions.
3. Use respondents in the pretest that are similar to those who will be included in the actual survey.
4. Begin the pretest by using personal interviews.
5. Conduct the pretest by mail, telephone, or electronically if those methods are to be used in the actual survey.
6. Use a variety of interviewers for pretests.
7. The pretest sample size should be small, varying from 15 to 30 respondents for the initial testing.
8. After each significant revision of the questionnaire, conduct another pretest, using a different sample of respondents.
9. Code and analyze the responses obtained from the pretest.

deluxe sandwiches being considered for possible national introduction. An observational form to record customer reaction would include space for all of the following information.

ARE MCDONALD'S DELUXE SANDWICHES TRULY DELUXE?

Who: Purchasers, adults, parents with children, teenagers
What: Deluxe sandwiches, other sandwiches and menu items considered/ purchased, influence of children or other family members

When: Day, hour, and date of observation
Where: At checkout counter, inside the store in the eating area, outside the store
        upon exit
Why: Influence of promotion or family members on the purchase
Way: Personal observer disguised as sales clerk, undisguised personal observer,
        hidden camera, or obtrusive mechanical device

The same physical design considerations of layout and reproduction apply to both questionnaires and observational forms. A well-designed form guides the observer to appropriately record the details of the observation rather than merely summarize them. Finally, like questionnaires, observational forms also require adequate pretesting.

SUMMARY ILLUSTRATION USING THE OPENING VIGNETTE

We summarize and illustrate the questionnaire design process by returning to the opening vignette. Notice that the information obtained for World Vision and the order in which it was obtained were clearly specified. The questionnaire was kept simple, and detailed instructions were provided because it had to be administered by mail. Only necessary questions were asked, and combined questions were avoided. To increase the willingness of the donors and potential donors to participate and complete the questionnaire, the context of the survey was made clear, and the effort required of the respondents was minimized. Most of the questions were structured questions, requiring the respondents to simply circle a number on the scale. However, a few unstructured or open-ended questions were included where it was felt that the respondents needed the freedom to express underlying motivations for giving to charity.

Words with unequivocal meaning but familiar to the donors were used. Special effort was made to not bias the responses in any direction. The ordering of the questions was logical, and the funnel approach was used. General questions about priorities and motivations for giving were asked first; questions about awareness and perceptions of World Vision followed. The questionnaire was divided into parts, with a separate part devoted to each type of information sought. Information on name and address was optional and obtained at the end of the questionnaire. The questionnaire was professionally reproduced and thoroughly pretested.

MARKETING RESEARCH AND TQM

Research based on questionnaire administration can help companies measure quality ratings, as well as establish quality improvement areas and goals. Often, questions are formulated and specific scales are selected based on how management would like to hear respondents articulate attitudes, instead of the customers' own descriptions of those feelings. If the goal of a company is "100 percent satisfaction," there may be a tendency for this company to ask customers about their satisfaction using this exact wording as the top box (highest category) with the other categories being 75 percent, 50 percent, and 25 percent (or less) satisfaction. The problem is that customers may check the top box even when they are not 100 percent satisfied because it is the closest to the way they feel. Thus, a customer who is only 90 percent satisfied will check "100 percent satisfaction," rather than 75 percent, thereby biasing the results. This bias can be avoided by using various

FOCUS ON
ELRICK & LAVIDGE

The project manager is largely responsible for questionnaire design at Elrick & Lavidge (E&L) and follows the steps outlined in this chapter. The project managers are also very concerned with the cost and time involved in having the field workers ask the questions and record the answers, as well as the cost and time in processing the responses. If a longer question will obtain better information than a shorter question, the project manager must weigh the added value of that better information against the cost of the additional time involved in obtaining and processing this information. Quite often, the client's budget will not allow a "best" question, but only an "adequate" one.

E&L pretests every questionnaire before the survey is actually implemented. However, the extent of this pretest depends on the urgency with which the client requires the results of the survey. In a full-scale pretest involving a CATI survey implementation, the phone interviewers conduct several interviews using actual respondents who are taken from the survey sample. E&L's CATI system allows the project manager to monitor phone calls made on the system. Typically, the project manager, client, and interviewer all listen to calls made during this pretest in order to look for problems, such as unclear instructions or misunderstood questions. They also monitor the overall length of time required to finish the interview. The pretesting is thorough, checking on all aspects of the questionnaire.

types of questions, including open-ended questions that allow respondents to express themselves in their own words.

In addition, questionnaires should be well designed and cover all the salient aspects of quality and customer satisfaction, as demonstrated by Best Western.

EXAMPLE

BEST WESTERN REALIZES IT CANNOT BE BEST WITHOUT QUALITY

A global research project conducted by PricewaterhouseCoopers indicated that Best Western hotels and motels were not meeting the quality expectations of consumers and travel agents. As a result, Best Western realized the need for a chainwide dedication to TQM and improvement of quality. The company decided that a good way to begin was by listening directly to consumers and gathering their ideas as to how the company could improve overall quality and raise its image.

Accordingly, the company's marketing research department designed and administered a questionnaire in various hotels/motels across the country. The questionnaire was printed on small cards and placed inside the guestrooms so as to be very visible to consumers. The consumers had the choice of completing the survey and leaving it in the hotel room or of taking it with them and mailing it back to Best Western at their convenience. Part of the questionnaire dealing with the evaluation of the hotel is shown.

- The questionnaire is personalized for each respondent by inserting the name and answers to previous questions, as appropriate. This increases the respondent's involvement.

SPSS

SPSS Data Entry can help the researcher in designing the questionnaire, facilitated by the drag-and-drop feature of the program.

SUMMARY

To collect quantitative primary data, a researcher must design a questionnaire or an observation form. A questionnaire has three objectives. It must (1) translate the information needed into a set of specific questions, (2) motivate respondents to complete the interview, and (3) minimize response error.

Designing a questionnaire is as much an art as it is a science. We can provide guidelines for development, but no one optimal questionnaire design fits every research need. The process begins by specifying the information needed and the type of interviewing method. The next step is to decide on the content of individual questions.

Questions must be written to overcome the respondents' inability to answer. Respondents may be unable to answer if they are not informed, cannot remember, or cannot articulate the response. When too much effort is required, or the research context seems inappropriate, respondents will be unwilling to participate. Questions that attempt to collect sensitive information may also be met with resistance. Questions can be unstructured (open-ended) or structured to a varying degree. Structured questions include multiple-choice, dichotomous questions, and scales.

Determining the wording of each question involves defining the issue, using ordinary words, using unambiguous words, and using dual statements. The issue should be clearly defined in terms of at least who, what, when, and where. Ordinary and unambiguous words should be used. The researcher should avoid leading questions. Once the questions have been worded, the order in which they will appear in the questionnaire must be decided. Special consideration should be given to opening questions, type of information, difficult questions, and the effect on subsequent questions. The questions should be arranged in a logical order.

The stage is now set for determining the form and layout of the questions. The physical considerations in reproducing the questionnaire include: appearance, use of booklets, fitting entire question on a page, response category format, avoiding overcrowding, placement of directions, color coding, and cost. The effectiveness of all these design decisions must be assessed in a pretest.

The design of observational forms requires explicit decisions about what is to be observed and how that behavior is to be recorded. It is useful to specify the who, what, when, where, why, and way of the behavior to be observed.

Questionnaire design and administration is an important part of any quality improvement effort. The questionnaire or research instrument should be adapted to the specific cultural environment and should not be biased in terms of any one culture. Several software packages are available to facilitate questionnaire design. In consideration of the respondents, overly long questionnaires or questions that exceed the respondents' willingness or ability to respond should be avoided. The questionnaire should be designed to obtain information in an unbiased manner. Several firms supply software and services for designing Internet questionnaires.

KEY TERMS AND CONCEPTS

Questionnaire, 310
Double-barreled
  question, 314
Filter questions, 315
Unstructured
  questions, 318
Structured
  questions, 319

Order or position
  bias, 320
Dichotomous
  question, 320
Leading question, 322
Basic information, 324
Classification
  information, 324

Identification
  information, 324
Funnel approach, 325
Branching questions, 325
Precoding, 326
Pretesting, 328

ACRONYMS

The objectives and steps involved in developing a questionnaire may be defined by the acronym QUESTIONNAIRE:

Objectives	Q uestions that respondents can answer
	U plift the respondent
	E rror elimination
Steps	S pecify the information needed
	T ype of interviewing method
	I ndividual question content
	O vercoming inability and unwillingness to answer
	N onstructured versus structured questions
	N onbiased question wording
	A rrange the questions in proper order
	I dentify form and layout
	R eproduction of the questionnaire
	E liminate bugs by pretesting

The guidelines for question wording may be summarized by the acronym WORDS:

W ho, what, when, where, why, and way
O bjective questions: Avoid leading questions
R egularly, normally, usually, etc., should be avoided
D ual statements (positive and negative)
S imple, ordinary words

The guidelines for deciding on the order of questions may be summarized by the acronym ORDER:

O pening questions: simple
R udimentary or basic information should be obtained first
D ifficult questions toward the end
E xamine the influence on subsequent questions
R eview the sequence to ensure a logical order

EXERCISES

1. What is the purpose of questionnaires and observation forms?
2. Explain how the mode of administration affects questionnaire design.
3. How would you determine whether a specific question should be included in a questionnaire?

4. What is a double-barreled question?
5. What are the reasons that respondents are unable to answer the question asked?
6. Explain the concepts of aided and unaided recall.
7. What are the reasons that respondents are unwilling to answer specific questions?
8. What can a researcher do to make the request for information seem legitimate?
9. What are the advantages and disadvantages of unstructured questions?
10. What are the issues involved in designing multiple-choice questions?
11. What are the guidelines available for deciding on question wording?
12. What is a leading question? Give an example.
13. What is the proper order for questions intended to obtain basic, classification, and identification information?
14. What guidelines are available for deciding on the form and layout of a questionnaire?
15. Describe the issues involved in pretesting a questionnaire.
16. What are the major decisions involved in designing observational forms?

PROBLEMS

1. Develop three double-barreled questions related to flying and passengers' airline preferences. Also develop corrected versions of each question.
2. List at least 10 ambiguous words that should not be used in framing questions.
3. Do the following questions define the issue? Why or why not?
   a. What is your favorite brand of shampoo?
   b. How often do you go on a vacation?
   c. Do you consume orange juice?
      1. Yes   2. No
4. Design an open-ended question to determine whether households engage in gardening. Also develop a multiple-choice and a dichotomous question to obtain the same information. Which form is the most desirable?
5. Formulate five questions that ask respondents to provide generalizations or estimates.
6. A new graduate hired by the marketing research department of a major telephone company is asked to prepare a questionnaire to determine household preferences for telephone calling cards. The questionnaire is to be administered in mall intercept interviews. Using the principles of questionnaire design, critically evaluate this questionnaire.

HOUSEHOLD TELEPHONE CALLING CARD SURVEY

1. Your name _____
2. Age _____
3. Marital status _____
4. Income _____
5. Which, if any, of the following telephone calling cards do you have?

   1. AT&T _____   2. MCI/World Com _____   3. US Sprint _____   4. Others _____

6. How frequently do you use a telephone calling card?

   Infrequently   Very Frequently
        1   2   3   4   5   6   7

7. What do you think of the telephone calling card offered by AT&T?

_____

8. Suppose your household were to select a telephone calling card. Please rate the importance of the following factors in selecting a card.

	Not Important			Very Important	
a. Cost per call	1	2	3	4	5
b. Ease of use	1	2	3	4	5
c. Local and long distance charges included in the same bill	1	2	3	4	5
d. Rebates and discounts on calls	1	2	3	4	5
e. Quality of telephone service	1	2	3	4	5
f. Quality of customer service	1	2	3	4	5

9. How important is it for a telephone company to offer a calling card?

Not Important					Very Important	
1	2	3	4	5	6	7

10. Do you have children living at home? _____

Thank You for Your Help!

INTERNET AND COMPUTER EXERCISES

1. IBM would like to conduct an Internet survey to determine the image of IBM PCs and the image of its major competitiors (Compaq, Dell, and Hewlett Packard). Develop such a questionnaire. Relevant information may be obtained by visiting the Web sites of these companies *(www.ibm.com, www.compaq.com, www.dell.com, www.hp.com)*.

2. Using an electronic questionnaire design package, design a questionnaire to measure consumer preferences for sneakers. Then, develop the same questionnaire manually. Compare your experiences in designing this questionnaire electronically and manually.

3. Visit the Web site of one of the online marketing research firms (e.g., Greenfield Online Research Center, Inc. at *www.greenfieldonline.com*). Locate a survey being currently administered at this site. Critically analyze the questionnaire using the priniciples discussed in this chapter.

ACTIVITIES

ROLE PLAYING

1. You have just been hired as a management trainee by a firm that manufactures major appliances. Your boss has asked you to develop a questionnaire to determine how households plan, purchase, and use major appliances. This questionnaire is to be used in a nationwide study. However, you feel that you do not have the expertise or the experience to construct such a complex questionnaire. Explain this to your boss (role played by a fellow student).

2. You are working as an assistant marketing research manager with a national department store chain. Management, represented by a group of students, is concerned about the extent of shoplifting by employees. You are assigned the task of developing a questionnaire to determine the extent of employee shoplifting. This questionnaire would be mailed to employees nationwide. Explain your approach to designing the questionnaire to management.

FIELD WORK

1. Develop a questionnaire for determining how students select restaurants. Pretest the questionnaire by administering it to 10 students using personal interviews. How would you modify the questionnaire based on the pretest?

2. Develop a questionnaire for determining household preferences for popular brands of cold cereals. Administer the questionnaire to 10 female heads of household using personal interviews. How would you modify the questionnaire if it was to be administered by telephone? What changes would be necessary if it was to be administered by mail?

GROUP DISCUSSION

1. "Since questionnaire design is an art, it is useless to follow a rigid set of guidelines. Rather, the process should be left entirely to the creativity and ingenuity of the researcher." Discuss in a small group.

2. In a small group, discuss the role of questionnaire design in minimizing total research error.

3. Discuss the importance of form and layout in questionnaire construction.

NOTES

1. Based on *www.worldvision.org*, "Aussies Targeted for World Vision," October 20, 2000; Alicia Orr, "Raising Commitment," *Target Marketing*, 22(8) (August 1999): 58–59; and Greg Gattuso, Elaine Santoro, and George R. Reis, "Notebooks Open Hearts of Sponsors," *Fund Raising Management*, 27(10) (December 1966): 10–11.

2. Based on Ken Gronbach, "Generation Y—Not Just 'Kids'," *Direct Marketing*, 63(4) (August 2000): 36–38; Tom McGee, "Getting Inside Kids' Heads," *American Demographics*, 19(1) (January 1997): 52–55; and Joseph Rydholm, "Omnibus Study Talks to Kids," *Quirk's Marketing Research Review*, 5(6) (June/July 1991): 42, 41.

3. Based on Alan Rosenspan, "Making an Offer They Can't Refuse," *Direct Marketing*, 61(7) (November 1998): 46–50; Kenneth C. Schneider and James C. Johnson, "Link Between Response-Inducing Strategies and Uninformed Response," *Marketing Intelligence & Planning*, 12(1) (1994): 29–36; and Del I. Hawkins and Kenneth. A. Coney, "Uninformed Response Error in Survey Research," *Journal of Marketing Research* (August 1981): 373.

4. Based on Keith Naughton, "Bring on the Junk Food," *Newsweek*, 136(2) (July 10, 2000): 44; Stephanie Thompson, "Was It the Meals or Was It the Miles?" *Brandweek*, 40(10) (March 8, 1999): 44; and "Edison, American Marketing Association, Best New Product Awards," *Marketing News*, 31(6) (March 17, 1997): E5.

5. Based on Christine Bannister, "Taste Not Sacrificed in Low Fat," *Retail World*, 53(6) (April 3–14, 2000): 14; Judann Pollack and Beth Snyder, "Kellogg Shifts Two JWT Brands to Burnett in Rift," *Advertising Age*, 70(5) (February 1, 1999): 3, 44; and "Edison, American Marketing Association, Best New Product Awards."

6. Rating a brand on specific attributes early in a survey may affect responses to a later overall brand evaluation. For example, see Harry Seymour, "Conducting and Using Customer Surveys," *Marketing News*, 31(12) (June 9, 1997): H24, H39; and Barbara A. Bickart, "Carryover and Backfire Effects in Marketing Research," *Journal of Marketing Research*, 30 (February 1993): 52–62.

7. Elizabeth Martin and Anne E. Polivka, "Diagnostics for Redesigning Survey Questionnaires," *Public Opinion Quarterly*, 59(4) (Winter 1995): 547–567; and A. Diamantopoulos, Bodo B. Schlegelmilch, and Nina Reynolds, "Pretesting in Questionnaire Design: The Impact of Respondent Characteristics on Error Detection," *Journal of the Market Research Society*, 36 (October 1994): 295–314.

8. Jeff Higley, "Best Western Governors Support Changes," *Hotel and Motel Management*, 215(4) (March 6, 2000): 3–4; and Jeff Higley, "Quality Issue Concerns Best Western," *Hotel and Motel Management*, 213(21) (December 14,1998): 4, 42.

9. Based on Peter Coolsen, "Opinion Surveys Uncover Cultural Preferences," *Nonprofit World*, 17(2) (March–April 1999): 17–18; and Edgar P. Hibbert, *International Market Research—A Financial Perspective*, Blackwell Publishers Inc., 1996.

10. Thomas Donalson and Thomas Dunfee, "When Ethics Travel: The Promise and Peril of Global Business Ethics," *California Management Review*, 41(4) (Summer 1999): 45–63; and R. W. Armstrong, "An Empirical Investigation of International Marketing Ethics: Problems Encountered by Australian Firms," *Journal of Business Ethics*, 11 (1992): 161–171.

12

SAMPLING: DESIGN AND PROCEDURES

SAMPLING IS THE ONLY FEASIBLE WAY TO COLLECT MARKETING RESEARCH DATA IN MOST SITUATIONS. FORTUNATELY, SAMPLING ERRORS ARE ONLY A SMALL PART OF THE TOTAL RESEARCH ERROR.

Sue Johnson, Vice President/Sr. Research Director, Elrick & Lavidge.
Sue Johnson is responsible for designing and managing various research projects and programs for several clients, and supervises the Research Services group in Kansas City. Sue has experience in a variety of industries including the package goods industry.

Opening Questions

1. How do we differentiate a sample from a census, and what conditions favor the use of a sample versus a census?

2. What steps are involved in the sampling design process?

3. How can sampling techniques be classified, and what is the difference between nonprobability and probability sampling techniques?

4. What are the various nonprobability sampling techniques, and when are they used?

5. What are the various probability sampling techniques, and when are they used?

6. What conditions favor the use of nonprobability sampling versus probability sampling?

7. What is the role of sampling in total quality management?

8. How are sampling techniques used in international marketing research?

9. How does technology interface with sampling?

10. What ethical issues relate to the sampling design process and the use of appropriate sampling techniques?

11. What is the role of the Internet in the sampling design process?

GILLETTE CLEAR STICK CLEARS THE WAY FOR GROWTH IN THE DEODORANT MARKET

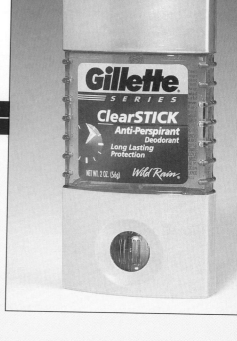

In August 2000, Gillette's struggling stationery unit, Paper Mate, was sold to Newell Rubbermaid, Inc. One reason Gillette sold the unit was to focus on three core product areas—razors and blades, grooming products, and Duracell batteries—so as to cut costs and increase profits. New product development and introduction have always been the backbone of Gillette's marketing strategy, as illustrated by the introduction of the Clear Stick deodorant.

After spending over $30 million to develop the Clear Stick technology, Gillette undertook consumer research to introduce a successful new antiperspirant/deodorant based on this technology. The sampling procedures played a critical role in revealing important findings that guided new product development and introduction. The company defined the population of interest, which is the target population, as male heads of households. Then it developed a questionnaire to measure preferences for stick deodorants versus other forms, such as sprays and roll-ons, and to compare the clear stick to conventional sticks.

Given the large size of the target population and limited time and money, it was clearly not feasible to interview the entire population, that is to take a census. So a sample was taken and a subgroup of the population was selected for participation in the research. The basic unit sampled was households and within the selected households the male heads of households were interviewed. Probability sampling, where each element of the population has a fixed chance of being selected, was chosen because the results had to be generalizable, that is, projectable to all male heads of households in the United States. Simple random sampling was used to select 1,000 households. This sample size was selected based on qualitative considerations, such as the importance of the decision, nature of the research, statistical analyses that would be required, resource constraint, and the sample sizes used in similar studies Gillette had conducted on new product development. The technique of simple random sampling was selected because efficient computer programs were available to randomly generate household telephone numbers, and minimize wastage due to nonexisting household telephone numbers. The respondents were recruited over the telephone by promising a monetary incentive and then mailed the survey questionnaire package, including a sample of the new clear stick deodorant.

The results indicated that 56 percent of men preferred stick deodorants. Moreover, clear sticks were preferred to conventional sticks on a variety of attributes: gliding on without dragging, ease of application, and no white residue on the skin or clothing. Based on these findings, Gillette introduced Clear Stick. The product packaging was designed to create a high-tech dispensing system. Inspired by the mouse control on most personal computers, Gillette designers created a powerball to replace the dial mechanism found on conventional sticks and solids. The launch was successful, and Clear Stick accelerated the retail value growth of the entire antiperspirant/deodorant market. Sound sampling procedures adopted in this research resulted in clear-cut findings that aided in the development and launch of a successful product.[1]

OVERVIEW

Sampling design issues are a part of the research design process. By this point in the research process, the researcher has identified the information needs of the study as well as the nature of the research design (exploratory, descriptive, or causal) (Chapters 3 through 8). Furthermore, the researcher has specified the scaling and measurement procedures (Chapters 9 and 10) and has designed the questionnaire (Chapter 11). The next step is to design suitable sampling procedures. Figure 12.1 briefly explains the focus of the chapter, the relationship of this chapter to the previous ones, and the step of the marketing research process on which this chapter concentrates.

Five basic questions are addressed in the sample design phase: (1) Should a sample be taken? (2) If so, what process should be followed? (3) What kind of sample should be taken? (4) How large should it be? (5) What can be done to adjust for incidence—the rate of occurrence of eligible respondents—and completion rates?

This chapter addresses the first three questions of the sample design. (Chapter 13 addresses the last two questions.) We will discuss sampling in terms of the qualitative considerations underlying the sampling design process. We first address the question of whether or not to sample and describe the steps involved in sampling. Next, we present nonprobability and probability sampling techniques. These issues were introduced in the opening vignette, in which Gillette used a probability sampling scheme to select the respondents. We then discuss the use of sampling techniques in total quality management and in international marketing research. We also discuss the interface of technology with sampling and identify the relevant ethical issues and Internet applications. Figure 12.2 gives an overview of the topics discussed in this chapter and how they flow from one to the next.

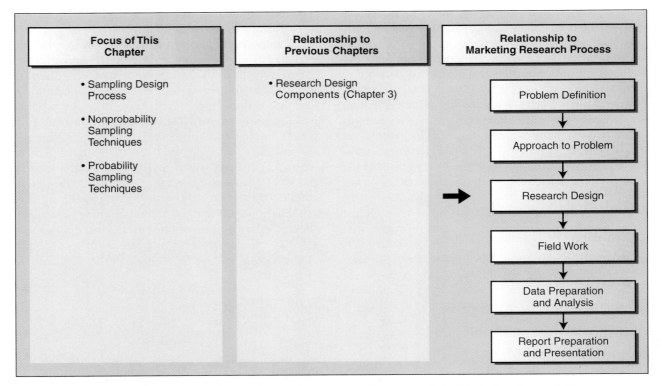

FIGURE 12.1　Relationship of Sampling Design to the Previous Chapters and the Marketing Research Process

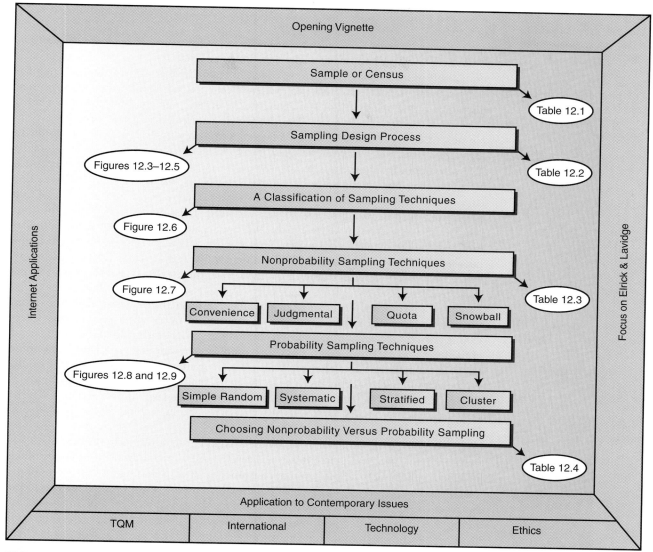

FIGURE 12.2   Sampling Design Procedures: An Overview

SAMPLE OR CENSUS

In sampling, an **element** is the object (or person) about which or from which the infor-mation is desired. In survey research, the element is usually the respondent. A **population** is the total of all the elements that share some common set of characteristics. Each mar-keting research project has a uniquely defined population that is described in terms of its parameters. The objective of most marketing research projects is to obtain information about the characteristics or parameters of a population. The proportion of consumers loyal to a particular brand of toothpaste is an example of a population parameter.

The researcher can obtain information about population parameters by taking either a census or a sample. A **census** involves a complete count of each element in a population. On the other hand, a **sample** is a subgroup of the population. In the open-ing vignette, the percentage of male heads of household that preferred a stick deodor-

element
Objects that possess the information the researcher seeks and about which the researcher will make inferences.

population
The aggregate of all the elements, sharing some common set of characteristics, which comprise the universe for the purpose of the marketing research problem.

census
A complete enumeration of the elements of a population or study objects.

sample
A subgroup of the elements of the population selected for participation in the study.

ant was a population parameter. This parameter was estimated via sampling to be 56 percent.

Table 12.1 summarizes the conditions favoring the use of a sample versus a census. The primary considerations favoring a sample are budget and time limits. A census is both costly and time consuming to conduct. In research studies involving large populations, such as users of consumer products, it is generally not feasible to take a census, as illustrated in the opening vignette. Therefore, a sample is the only viable option. On the other hand, business-to-business research involving industrial products typically involves a much smaller population. A census becomes not only possible but also desirable in many such situations. For example, while investigating the use of certain machine tools by U.S. automobile manufacturers, a census would be preferable to a sample since the population of automobile manufacturers is small. A census also becomes more attractive when large variations exist in the population. For example, large differences in machine tool usage from Ford to Honda would suggest the need for taking a census instead of sampling. In this case, if a sample were taken, it is unlikely to be representative of the population because the machine tool usage of automobile manufacturers not included in the sample is likely to be substantially different than those in the sample. Small populations, which vary widely in terms of the characteristics of interest to the researcher, lend themselves to a census.

The cost of sampling error (e.g., omitting a major manufacturer such as Ford from the machine tool study above) must be weighted against nonsampling error (e.g., interviewer errors). In many business-to-business studies, concerns involving sampling error argue for a census. However, in most other studies, nonsampling errors are found to be the major contributor to total error. While a census eliminates sampling errors, the resulting nonsampling errors may increase to the point that total error in the study becomes unacceptably high. In these instances, sampling would be favored over a census. This is one of the reasons the U.S. Census Bureau checks the accuracy of its census by conducting sample surveys.[2]

Sampling is also preferable if the measurement process results in the destruction or consumption of the product. In this case, a census would mean that a large quantity of the product would have to be destroyed or consumed, greatly increasing the cost. An example would be product usage tests that result in the consumption of the product, such as a new brand of cereal. Sampling may also be necessary to focus attention on individual cases, as in the case of depth interviews. Finally, other pragmatic considerations, such as the need to keep the study secret (an important consideration for firms such as Coca-Cola), may favor a sample over a census. In the opening vignette, Gillette chose sampling over a census as the size of the population of male heads of households in the United States is too

T A B L E 1 2 . 1   Sample Versus Census

	CONDITIONS FAVORING THE USE OF	
	Sample	**Census**
1. Budget	Small	Large
2. Time available	Short	Long
3. Population size	Large	Small
4. Variance in the characteristic	Small	Large
5. Cost of sampling error	Low	High
6. Cost of nonsampling errors	High	Low
7. Nature of measurement	Destructive	Nondestructive
8. Attention to individual cases	Yes	No

large to make a census feasible, particularly given limited time and money. Also, as is generally the case in consumer research, the cost of sampling errors was small as compared to the cost of nonsampling errors. As explained in Chapter 3, sampling error is the error due to the particular sample selected being an imperfect representation of the population of interest. On the other hand, nonsampling errors result from a variety of causes, including errors in problem definition, approach, scales, questionnaire design, survey methods, interviewing techniques, and data preparation and analysis. Evidence shows that in consumer research the cost of sampling error is small as compared to the cost of nonsampling errors.

THE SAMPLING DESIGN PROCESS

The sampling design process includes five steps, which are shown sequentially in Figure 12.3. Each step is closely related to all aspects of the marketing research project, from problem definition to presentation of the results. Therefore, sample design decisions should be integrated with all other decisions in a research project.

Define the Target Population

Sampling design begins by specifying the target population. The **target population** is the collection of elements or objects that possess the information the researcher is seeking. It is essential that the researcher precisely define the target population if the data generated are to address the marketing research problem. Defining the target population involves translating the research problem into a precise statement of who should and should not be included in the sample. In the opening vignette, the target population was defined as all male heads of households in the United States.

The target population should be defined in terms of elements, sampling units, extent, and time frame. As stated earlier, an element is the object (or person) about which or from which the information is desired, for example, the respondent. A **sampling unit** may be the element itself, or it may be a more readily available entity containing the element. Suppose that Revlon wanted to assess consumer response to a new line of lipsticks and wanted to sample women over 18 years of age. In this study, Revlon's sampling ele-

target population
The collection of elements or objects that possess the information the researcher seeks and about which the researcher will make inferences.

sampling unit
The basic unit containing the elements of the population to be sampled.

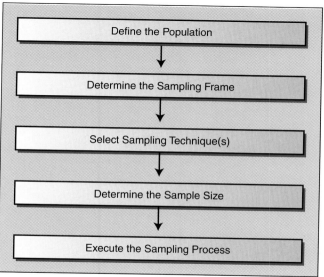

FIGURE 12.3
Sampling Design Process

The target population should be clearly defined if Revlon wants to assess consumer response to a new line of lipsticks.

ment would be women over 18 years of age. It may be possible to sample them directly, in which case the sampling unit will be the same as an element. More typically, Revlon would use a sampling unit such as households, interviewing one woman over 18 in each selected household. Here, the sampling unit and the population element are different. As another illustration, in the opening vignette, the sampling element was male head of household, and the sampling unit was a household.

Extent refers to geographical boundaries. In our example, Revlon is interested only in the domestic U.S. market. The time frame is the time period of interest. Revlon may be interested in studying lipstick demand for the upcoming summer market. This target population is defined in Figure 12.4.

Determine the Sampling Frame

A **sampling frame** is a representation of the elements of the target population. It consists of a list or set of directions for identifying the target population. A sampling frame can come from the telephone book, a computer program for generating telephone numbers, an association directory listing the firms in an industry, a mailing list purchased from a commercial organization, a city directory, or a map. If a listing is not readily available, it must be compiled. Specific instructions for identifying the target population should be developed, such as procedures for generating random telephone numbers of households mentioned in the opening vignette.

The process of compiling a list of population elements is often difficult and imperfect, leading to sampling frame error. Elements may be omitted, or the list may contain more than the desired population (Figure 12.5). For example, the telephone book is often used as a sampling frame for telephone surveys. However, at least three sources of sampling frame error are present in the telephone book: (1) It does not contain unlisted

FIGURE 12.4
Defining the Target Population

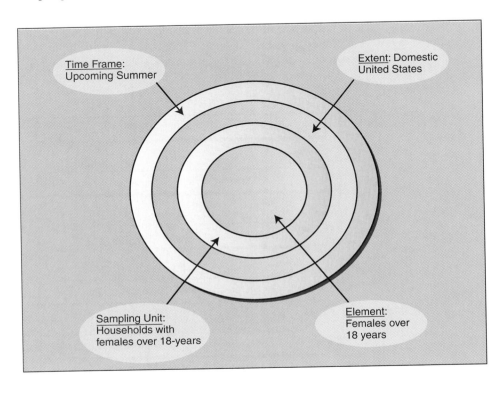

numbers, (2) it does not contain the telephone numbers of people who have moved into the area after the telephone book was published, and (3) it lists the inactive telephone numbers of people who have moved out of the area since the telephone book was published. Small differences between the sample frame and the population can be ignored. However, in most cases, the researcher should recognize and treat the sampling frame error. The researcher has three options:

1. The population can be redefined in terms of the sampling frame. When the telephone book is used as the sampling frame, the population may be defined as households with a correct listing in the telephone book in a given area. This approach is quite simple and eliminates any misinterpretation of the definition of the population under study.[3]

2. The representativeness of the research frame can be verified during the data collection process. Basic demographic, product familiarity, product usage, and other relevant information can be collected to ensure that the elements of the sampling frame satisfy the criteria for the target population. While inappropriate elements can be identified and eliminated from the sample in this way, this procedure does not correct for elements that have been omitted.

3. The data can be statistically adjusted by weighting under- or overrepresented segments to achieve a more representative sample. While sample frame error can be minimized through this type of adjustment, it assumes the researcher has accurate knowledge of the makeup of the target population.

The researcher can adopt any combination of these adjustments. The important point is to recognize and attempt to eliminate sampling frame error, so that inappropriate population inferences can be avoided.

Select a Sampling Technique

Selecting a sampling technique involves choosing nonprobability or probability sampling (Figure 12.6). **Nonprobability sampling** relies on the personal judgment of the researcher, rather than chance, in selecting sample elements. The researcher may select the sample arbitrarily, based on convenience, or make a conscious decision about which elements to include in the sample. Examples of nonprobability sampling include interview-

sampling frame
A representation of the elements of the target population. It consists of a list or set of directions for identifying the target population.

nonprobability sampling
Sampling techniques that do not use chance selection procedures. Rather, they rely on the personal judgment of the researcher.

FIGURE 12.5
Sampling Frame Error

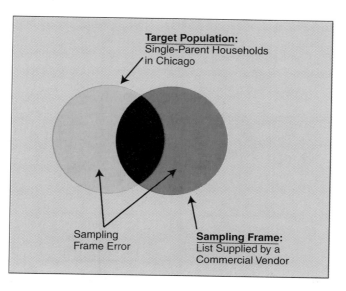

Target Population:
Single-Parent Households in Chicago

Sampling Frame Error

Sampling Frame:
List Supplied by a Commercial Vendor

precision
Precision refers to the level of uncertainty about the characteristic being measured, with greater precision implying smaller sampling error.

ing people at street corners, in retail stores, or in the malls. While nonprobability sampling produces good estimates of population characteristic, these techniques are limited. There is no way to objectively evaluate the **precision** of the sample results. Precision refers to the level of uncertainty about the characteristic being measured. Suppose the researcher wanted to determine how much an average household spends on Christmas shopping and surveyed people in the malls. Due to the convenience nature of the sample, there would be no way of knowing how precise the results of this survey are. The greater the precision, the smaller the sampling error. The probability of selecting one element over another is unknown. Therefore, the estimates obtained cannot be projected to the population with any specified level of confidence.

probability sampling
A sampling procedure in which each element of the population has a fixed probabilistic chance of being selected for the sample.

In **probability sampling,** sampling elements are selected by chance, that is, randomly. The probability of selecting each potential sample from a population can be prespecified. While every potential sample need not have the same probability of selection, it is possible to specify the probability of selecting a particular sample of a given size. Confidence intervals can be calculated around the sample estimates, and it is meaningful to statistically project the sample results to the population, that is, draw inferences about the target population. Since projectability of the sample results to the population of all male heads of households was important, Gillette used probability rather than nonprobability in the opening vignette. We will discuss the various nonprobability and probability sampling techniques later.

Determine the Sample Size

sample size
The number of units to be included in a study.

Sample size refers to the number of elements to be included in the study. Determining the sample size involves both qualitative and quantitative considerations. We discuss the qualitative factors in this section and discuss the quantitative factors in Chapter 13. Important qualitative factors that the researcher should consider in determining the sample size are (1) the importance of the decision, (2) the nature of the research, (3) the number of variables, (4) the nature of the analysis, (5) sample sizes used in similar studies, and (6) resource constraints.

As a general rule, the more important the decision, the more precise the information must be. This implies the need for larger samples. The need for greater precision must be weighed against the increase in cost that comes with the collection of information from each additional element.

The nature of the research also has an impact on the sample size. Exploratory research, such as a focus group, employs qualitative techniques that are typically based on small samples. Conclusive research, such as a descriptive survey, requires large samples. As the number of variables in a study increases, the sample size must grow accordingly. For example, problem identification surveys that measure a large number of variables typically require large samples of 1,000 to 2,500 (Table 12.2).

FIGURE 12.6
Classification of Sampling Techniques

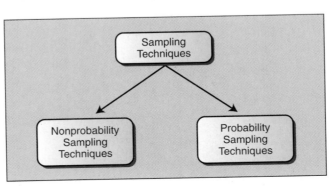

TABLE 12.2   Sample Sizes Used in Marketing Research Studies

TYPE OF STUDY	MINIMUM SIZE	TYPICAL RANGE
Problem identification research (e.g., market potential)	500	1,000–2,500
Problem solving research (e.g., pricing)	200	300–500
Product tests	200	300–500
Test marketing studies	200	300–500
TV/radio/print advertising (per commercial or ad tested)	150	200–300
Test-market audits	10 stores	10–20 stores
Focus groups	6 groups	10–15 groups

The type of analysis planned also influences the sample size requirements. Sophisticated analysis of the data using advanced techniques, or analysis at the subgroup rather than the total population level, requires larger samples, as in the case of Gillette in the opening vignette.

Prior studies can serve as a guide for estimating sample sizes. Table 12.2 gives an idea of sample sizes used in different marketing research studies. These sample sizes have been determined based on experience and can serve as rough guidelines, particularly when nonprobability sampling techniques are used, but they should be applied with caution. Finally, the sample size decisions are guided by money, personnel, and time limitations. In any marketing research project, resources are limited, in turn limiting the sample size. In the opening vignette, the sample size of 1,000 was based on the following considerations: Gillette would use the results to make an important decision involving the introduction of clear stick deodorants, quantitative analysis would be conducted, and this sample size had been adequate in similar studies conducted by Gillette in the past.

Execute the Sampling Process

Execution of the sampling process refers to implementing the various details of the sample design. The population is defined, the sampling frame is compiled, and the sampling units are drawn using the appropriate sampling technique so as to achieve the required sample size. If households are the sampling unit, an operational definition of a household is needed. Procedures should be specified for vacant housing units and for callbacks in case no one is home. Sometimes, it is necessary to qualify the potential respondents to make sure that they belong to the target population. In such a case, the criteria used to qualify the respondents should be specified and the qualifying questions should be asked at the beginning of the interview (see Chapter 11). For example, in a survey of heavy users of online services at home, a criterion for identifying heavy users is needed (for example, those using online services for more than 30 hours per week at home). Detailed information must be provided for all sampling design decisions. We will illustrate with a survey done for the Florida Department of Tourism.

EXAMPLE

TOURISM DEPARTMENT TELEPHONES BIRTHDAY BOYS AND GIRLS

A telephone survey was conducted for the Florida Department of Tourism related to the travel behavior of in-state residents. The sampling unit was the household. Probability sampling was used. Data were collected using a stratified random sample from three regions: north, central, and south Florida. To participate in the study, respondents had to meet the following qualifying criteria:

1. Age 25 or older.
2. Live in Florida at least seven months of the year.
3. Have lived in Florida for at least two years.
4. Have a Florida driver's license.

All household members meeting these four qualifications were eligible to participate in the study. The person with the next birthday in the household was selected. Repeated callbacks were made to reach that person. Each step in this sampling design process is spelled out below:

1. Target population: Adults meeting the four qualifications (element) in a household with a working telephone number (sampling unit) in the state of Florida (extent) during the survey period (time).
2. Sampling frame: Computer program for generating random telephone numbers.
3. Sampling technique: Probability sampling.
4. Sample size: 868
5. Execution: Allocate the sample among the north, central, and southern strata; use the probability sampling technique of computerized random-digit dialing; list all the members in the household who meet the four qualifications; select one member of the household using the next birthday method.[4]

A CLASSIFICATION OF SAMPLING TECHNIQUES

Sampling techniques may be broadly classified as nonprobability or probability (see Figure 12.6). Commonly used nonprobability sampling techniques include convenience sampling, judgmental sampling, quota sampling, and snowball sampling (Figure 12.7). The important probability sampling techniques are simple random sampling, systematic sampling, stratified sampling, and cluster sampling.

NONPROBABILITY SAMPLING TECHNIQUES

Convenience Sampling

convenience sampling
A nonprobability sampling technique that attempts to obtain a sample of convenient elements. The selection of sampling units is left primarily to the interviewer.

Convenience sampling, as the name implies, attempts to obtain a sample of elements based on the convenience of the researcher. The selection of sampling units is left primarily to the interviewer. Often, respondents are selected because they happen to be in the right place at the right time. Examples of convenience sampling are (1) use of students, church groups, and members of social organizations, (2) mall intercept interviews conducted without qualifying the respondents, (3) department stores using charge account lists, (4) tear-out questionnaires included in a magazine, (5) "people on the street" interviews, and (6) Internet browsers.

Convenience sampling has the advantages of being both inexpensive and fast. Additionally, the sampling units tend to be accessible, easy to measure, and cooperative. In spite of these advantages, this form of sampling has serious limitations. Primary

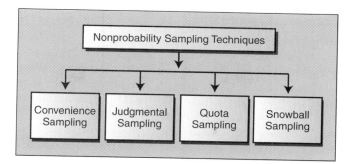

FIGURE 12.7
Nonprobability Sampling
Techniques

among them is the fact that the resulting sample is not representative of any definable target population. This sampling process suffers from selection bias, which means the individuals who participate in a convenience sample may have characteristics that are systematically different than the characteristics that define the target population. Because of these limitations, it is not theoretically meaningful to generalize to any population from a convenience sample.

Convenience samples are not appropriate for descriptive or causal research where the aim is to draw population inferences. However, in exploratory research where the objective is to generate ideas, gain insights, or develop hypotheses, convenience samples are useful. They can be used for focus groups, pretesting questionnaires, or pilot studies. Even in these cases, caution should be exercised in interpreting the results. Despite these limitations, this technique is sometimes used even in large surveys, as in the example that follows.

EXAMPLE

STARBUCKS BUCKS UP ON ICE CREAM

When Starbucks wanted to assess the brand equity behind its name in order to consider possible line extensions, researchers used convenience sampling to select a group of people patronizing its various coffee shops and retail outlets. Using convenience sampling in this manner was justified because the core market for the line extensions would consist of existing Starbucks customers.

A survey was administered that obtained information on the respondents' preference and loyalty for Starbucks coffee and other products they would like to see branded with the Starbucks name. Results of this survey revealed a tremendous potential to extend the Starbucks name to ice creams. Accordingly, Starbucks leveraged the strong equity of its coffee and loyal customer base to create a line of ice cream based on its coffee. The product is a rich, creamy ice cream that delivers on the intense flavor of Starbucks coffee. According to IRI (Information Resources, Inc.) data, it became the nation's number one brand of coffee ice cream three months after it was introduced.[5]

Judgmental Sampling

judgmental sampling
A form of convenience sampling in which the population elements are purposively selected based on the judgment of the researcher.

Judgmental sampling is a form of convenience sampling in which the population elements are selected based on the researcher's judgment. The researcher chooses the sampling elements because she or he believes they represent the population of interest. Common examples of judgmental sampling include (1) test markets selected to determine the potential of a new product, (2) purchase engineers selected in industrial marketing research because they are considered to be representative of the company, (3) bellwether precincts selected in voting behavior research, (4) expert witnesses used in court, and (5) department stores selected to test a new merchandising display system.

Judgmental sampling has appeal because it is inexpensive, convenient, and quick. However, it is subjective, depending largely on the expertise and creativity of the researcher. Therefore, generalizations to a specific population cannot be made, usually because the population is not defined explicitly. This sampling technique is most appropriate in research in which broad population generalizations are not required. For example, in 1997, Frito-Lay test marketed the WOW! line of Ruffles, Lays, and Doritos chips, all made with Olestra, in Indianapolis, Indiana. Indianapolis was selected because the researcher felt it would provide a good indicator of initial response to the new line. Note that Frito-Lay was looking only to evaluate the initial response to WOW!, not to make projections of how much WOW! would sell nationally.

An extension of judgmental sampling involves the use of quotas.

Quota Sampling

quota sampling
A nonprobability sampling technique that is a two-stage restricted judgmental sampling. The first stage consists of developing control categories or quotas of population elements. In the second stage, sample elements are selected based on convenience or judgment.

Quota sampling introduces two stages to the judgmental sampling process. The first stage consists of developing control categories, or quotas, of population elements. Using judgment to identify relevant categories such as age, sex, or race, the researcher estimates the distribution of these characteristics in the target population. For example, white women aged 18 to 35 may be considered the relevant control category for a study involving cosmetic purchases. The researcher would then estimate the proportion of the target population falling into this category based on past experience or secondary information sources. Sampling would then be done to ensure that the proportion of white women aged 18 to 35 in the target population would be reflected in the sample. Quotas are used to ensure that the composition of the sample is the same as the composition of the population with respect to the characteristics of interest.

Once the quotas have been assigned, the second stage of the sampling process takes place. Elements are selected using a convenience or judgment process. There is considerable freedom in selecting the elements to be included in the sample. The only requirement is that the elements that are selected fit the control characteristics. This technique is illustrated in the following example.

EXAMPLE

HOW METRO IS *METROPOLITAN* MAGAZINE READERSHIP?

A readership study was conducted for *Metropolitan* magazine using a quota sample. One thousand adults living in a metropolitan area of 500,000 people were selected. Age, sex, and race were used to define the makeup of the sample. Based on the composition of the adult population in that community, the quotas were assigned as follows:

CONTROL CHARACTERISTIC	POPULATION COMPOSITION PERCENTAGE	SAMPLE COMPOSITION PERCENTAGE	SAMPLE COMPOSITION NUMBER
Sex			
Male	48	48	480
Female	52	52	520
	100	100	1,000
Age			
18–30	27	27	270
31–45	39	39	390
46–60	16	16	160
Over 60	18	18	180
	100	100	1,000
Race			
White	59	59	590
Black	35	35	350
Other	6	6	60
	100	100	1,000

By imposing quotas proportionate to the population distribution, the researcher was able to select a sample that reflected the composition of the metropolitan area fairly well.

In the above example, proportionate quotas are assigned so that the composition of the population in the community is reflected in the sample. However, in certain situations, it is desirable either to under- or oversample elements with certain characteristics. For example, heavy users of a product may be oversampled in order to examine their behavior in greater detail. While this type of sample is not representative, it may nevertheless be quite relevant.

However, a number of potential problems are associated with this sampling technique. Relevant characteristics may be overlooked in the quota-setting process, resulting in a sample that does not mirror the population on relevant control characteristics. Since the elements within each quota are selected based on convenience or judgment, many sources of selection bias are potentially present. Interviewers may be tempted to select areas in which they believe they will have success in soliciting participants. They may avoid people who look unfriendly, who are not well dressed, or who live in undesirable locations. Quota sampling is also limited in that it does not permit assessment of sampling error.

Quota sampling attempts to obtain representative samples at a relatively low cost. Quota samples are also relatively convenient to draw. With adequate controls, quota sampling obtains results close to those for conventional probability sampling.

Snowball Sampling

In **snowball sampling,** an initial group of respondents is selected, usually at random. After being interviewed, these respondents are asked to identify others who belong to the target population of interest. This process is continued, resulting in a snowball effect as one referral is obtained from another. Thus, the referral process effectively produces the

snowball sampling
A nonprobability sampling technique in which an initial group of respondents is selected randomly. Subsequent respondents are selected based on the referrals or information provided by the initial respondents. This process may be carried out in waves by obtaining referrals from referrals.

sampling frame from which respondents are selected. Despite the fact that this sampling technique begins with a probability sample, it results in a nonprobability sample. This is because referred respondents will tend to have demographic and psychographic characteristics that are more similar to the person referring them than would occur by chance.

Snowball sampling is used when studying characteristics that are relatively rare or difficult to identify in the population. For example, the names of users of some government or social services, such as food stamps, are kept confidential. Groups with special characteristics such as widowed men under 35 or members of a scattered minority population may be impossible to locate without referrals. In industrial research, snowball sampling is used to identify buyer/seller pairs.

The major advantage of snowball sampling is that it substantially increases the likelihood of locating the desired characteristic in the population. It also results in relatively low sampling variance and costs. Snowball sampling is illustrated by the following example.

EXAMPLE

SURVEY SNOWBALL

To study the demographic profile of marketing research interviewers in Ohio, a sample of interviewers was generated using a variation of snowball sampling. Interviewers were initially contacted by placing classified advertisements in the newspapers of seven major metropolitan areas. These notices asked experienced marketing research interviewers willing to answer 25 questions about their job to write to the researcher. These responses were increased through a referral system: Each interviewer was asked for the names and addresses of other interviewers. Eventually, this process identified interviewers from many communities throughout the state who had not seen the original newspaper notices. Only 27 percent of returned questionnaires resulted from the classified notices; the remainder could be traced to referrals and referrals from referrals.[6]

In this example, the initial groups of respondents were contacted using a nonrandom selection technique, through classified advertisements. In this instance, this procedure was more efficient than random selection. In other cases, random selection of respondents through probability sampling techniques is more appropriate.

PROBABILITY SAMPLING TECHNIQUES

Probability sampling techniques vary in terms of sampling efficiency. Sampling efficiency is a concept that reflects a trade-off between sampling cost and precision. However, costs increase with improved precision. The trade-off comes into play as researchers balance the need for greater precision with higher sampling costs. The efficiency of a probability sampling technique may be assessed by comparing it to that of simple random sampling (Figure 12.8).

Simple Random Sampling

simple random sampling (SRS)
A probability sampling technique in which each element in the population has a known and equal probability of selection. Every element is selected independently of every other element, and the sample is drawn by a random procedure from a sampling frame.

In **simple random sampling (SRS)**, each element in the population has a known and equal probability of selection. Furthermore, each possible sample of a given size (n) has a known and equal probability of being the sample actually selected. The implication in a random sampling procedure is that each element is selected independently of every other element.

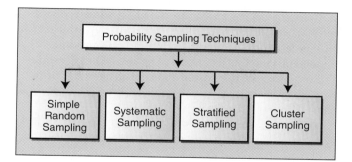

FIGURE 12.8
Probability Sampling Techniques

Placing the names in a container, shaking the container, and selecting the names in a lottery-style drawing is an example of a random sampling procedure. To draw a simple random sample, the research frame is compiled by assigning each element a unique identification number. Then, random numbers, generated using a computer routine or random number table (see Table 1 shown in the Appendix of Statistical Tables), are used to determine which element to select.

In telephone surveys, the **random-digit dialing (RDD)** technique is often used to generate a random sample of telephone numbers. RDD consists of randomly selecting all 10 digits of a telephone number (area code, prefix or exchange, suffix). While this approach gives all households with telephones an approximately equal chance of being included in the sample, not all the numbers generated in this way are working telephone numbers. Several modifications have been proposed to identify and eliminate the nonworking numbers. This makes the use of SRS in telephone surveys quite attractive, as illustrated in the case of Gillette in the opening vignette.

SRS has many benefits. It is easily understood and attempts to produce data that are representative of a target population. Most statistical inference approaches assume that random sampling was used. However, SRS suffers from at least four significant limitations: (1) Constructing a sampling frame for SRS is difficult; (2) SRS can be expensive and time consuming because the sampling frame may be widely spread over a large geographical area; (3) SRS often results in lower precision, producing samples with large standard error; and (4) samples generated by this technique may not be representative of the target population, particularly if the sample size is small. Although samples drawn will represent the population well on average, a given simple random sample may grossly misrepresent the target population. For these reasons, SRS is not widely used in marketing research. Procedures such as systematic sampling are more popular.

Systematic Sampling

In **systematic sampling,** the sample is chosen by selecting a random starting point and then picking every ith element in succession from the sampling frame. The frequency with which the elements are drawn, i, is called the sampling interval. It is determined by dividing the population size N by the sample size n and rounding to the nearest integer. For example, suppose there are 100,000 elements in the population and a sample of 1,000 is desired. In this case, the sampling interval, i, is 100. A random number between 1 and 100 is selected. If, for example, this number is 23, the sample consists of elements 23, 123, 223, 323, 423, 523, and so on.[7]

The population elements used in systematic sampling are typically organized in some fashion. If the telephone book is used as the sampling frame, the elements are alphabetically organized. In some cases, this order may be related to some characteristic of interest to the researcher. For example, credit card customers may be listed in order of

random-digit dialing (RDD)
A technique used to overcome the bias of unpublished and recent telephone numbers by selecting all telephone number digits at random.

systematic sampling
A probability sampling technique in which the sample is chosen by selecting a random starting point and then picking every ith element in succession from the sampling frame.

outstanding balance, or firms in a given industry may be ordered according to annual sales. When the population elements are organized in a manner related to the characteristics under study, systematic sampling may produce results quite different from SRS. Systematic sampling from a list of industrial firms, organized in increasing order by sales, will produce a sample that includes small and large firms. A simple random sample may be less representative. For example, only small firms or a disproportionate number of small firms may be drawn.

On the other hand, when sampling frames are organized in a cyclical pattern, systematic sampling tends to be less representative. To illustrate, consider the use of systematic sampling to generate a sample of monthly department store sales from a sampling frame containing monthly sales for the last 60 years. If a sampling interval of 12 is chosen, the resulting sample would not reflect the month-to-month variation in sales.

Systematic sampling is less costly and easier than SRS because random selection is done only once. Systematic sampling can also be applied without knowledge of the makeup of the sampling frame. For example, every *i*th person leaving a department store or mall can be intercepted. For these reasons, systematic sampling is often employed in consumer mail, telephone, and mall intercept interviews, as illustrated by the following example.

EXAMPLE

TENNIS'S SYSTEMATIC SAMPLING RETURNS A SMASH

Tennis magazine conducted a mail survey of its subscribers to gain a better understanding of its market. A systematic sample was drawn from the subscription list to produce a sample of 1,472 subscribers. The list was ordered according to the duration of subscription to ensure that recent as well as long-time subscribers would be included. If we assume that the subscriber list had 1,472,000 names, the sampling interval would be 1,000 (1,472,000/ 1,472). A starting point was selected between 1 and 1,000. Suppose this was 589. The sample would then be collected by selecting every 1,000th subscriber, that is, subscribers numbered 589, 1589, 2589, 3589, and so on.

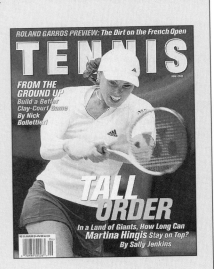

Systematic sampling was chosen because a sampling frame was conveniently available and this procedure is easier to implement than SRS.

An incentive in the form of a brand new dollar bill was included in the mail survey to boost participation in the study. The respondents were sent an alert postcard one week before the survey. A second, follow-up questionnaire was sent to the whole sample 10 days after the initial questionnaire. Of the 1,472 questionnaires mailed, 76 were returned with no forwarding address, so the net effective mailing was 1,396. Six weeks after the first mailing, 778 completed questionnaires were returned, yielding a response rate of 56 percent.[8]

Stratified Sampling

Stratified sampling involves a two-step sampling process, producing a probability rather than a convenience or judgment sample. First, the population is divided into subgroups called strata. Every population element should be assigned to one and only one stratum, and no population elements should be omitted. Second, elements of each stratum are then randomly selected. Ideally, SRS should be used to select elements from each stratum. However, in practice, systematic sampling and other probability sampling procedures may be used.

A major objective of stratified sampling is to increase precision without increasing cost. The population is partitioned using stratification variables. The strata are formed based on four criteria: (1) homogeneity, (2) heterogeneity, (3) relatedness, and (4) cost. The following guidelines should be observed:

- Elements within strata must be similar or homogeneous.
- Elements must differ or be heterogeneous between strata.
- The stratification variables must be related to the characteristic of interest.
- The number of strata usually varies between two and six. Beyond six strata, any gain in precision is more than offset by the increased costs.

Stratification offers two advantages. Sampling variation is reduced when the research follows the criteria listed above. Sampling costs can also be reduced when the stratification variables are selected in a way that is easy to measure and apply. Variables commonly used for stratification include demographic characteristics (as illustrated in the example for quota sampling), type of customer (credit card versus non–credit card), size of firm, or type of industry. Stratified sampling improves the precision of SRS. Therefore, it is a popular sampling technique, as illustrated in the BMW 5-Series survey.

stratified sampling
A probability sampling technique that uses a two-step process to partition the population into subpopulations, or strata. Elements are selected from each stratum by a random procedure.

EXAMPLE

STRATIFYING THE SUCCESS OF BMW 5-SERIES

Extensive marketing research went into the design of the recently introduced BMW 5-Series models. When a survey of luxury car buyers was conducted to project preferences for specific luxury car features, stratified random sampling was used. This procedure was selected because it includes all the important subpopulations, and results in good precision. The variables chosen for stratification were age and income, variables known to correlate with the purchase of luxury cars. The results indicated that the luxury car buyers put a premium on performance, handling, engineering, and, of course, luxury.

Based on this feedback, the new 5-Series advanced the concept of a four-door sedan that embodies performance, easy handling, active and passive safety engineering, and luxury. In both U.S. models, the six-cylinder 528I and the V-8 540I, the engine was larger, delivering greater torque for more effortless performance. For the first time, automatic climate control was standard in 5-Series models offered in the United States. There were extensive innovations and new features in virtually every area of the vehicle. The results? Both models were a roaring success.[9]

Cluster Sampling

In **cluster sampling,** the target population is first divided into mutually exclusive and collectively exhaustive subpopulations, or clusters. Then a random sample of clusters is selected, based on a probability sampling technique, such as SRS. For each selected cluster, either all the elements are included in the sample or a sample of elements is drawn probabilistically. If all the elements in each selected cluster are included in the sample, the procedure is called one-stage cluster sampling. If a sample of elements is drawn probabilistically from each selected cluster, the procedure is two-stage cluster sampling (Figure 12.9).

There are a number of key differences between cluster and stratified sampling. They are summarized in the following table.

CLUSTER SAMPLING	STRATIFIED SAMPLING
• Only a sample of the subpopulations (clusters) is selected for sampling.	• All of the subpopulations (strata) are selected for sampling.
• Within a cluster, elements should be different (heterogeneous), while homogeneity or similarity is maintained between different clusters.	• Within a strata, elements should be homogeneous, with clear differences (heterogeneity) between the strata.
• A sampling frame is needed only for the clusters selected for the sample.	• A complete sampling frame for the entire stratified subpopulations should be drawn.
• Increases sample efficiency by decreasing cost.	• Increases precision.

One common form of cluster sampling is area sampling. **Area sampling** relies on clustering based on geographic areas, such as counties, housing tracts, or blocks. Sampling can be achieved using either one or more stages. Single-stage area sampling

FIGURE 12.9
Types of Cluster
Sampling

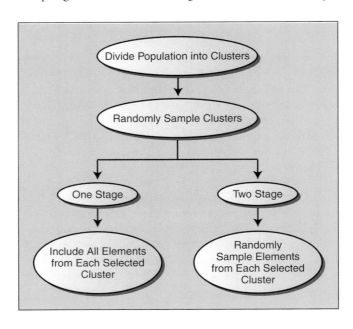

involves sampling all the elements within a particular cluster. For example, if city blocks were used as the clusters, then all the households within the selected blocks would be included within a single-stage sample. In the case of two-stage cluster sampling, only a portion of the households within each block would be sampled.

Cluster sampling has two major advantages: feasibility and low cost. Since sampling frames are often available in terms of clusters rather than population elements, cluster sampling may be the only feasible approach. Given the resources and constraints of the research project, it may be extremely expensive, perhaps not feasible, to compile a list of all consumers in a population. However, lists of geographical areas, telephone exchanges, and other clusters of consumers can be constructed relatively easily. Cluster sampling is the most cost-effective probability sampling technique. This advantage must be weighed against several limitations. Cluster sampling produces imprecise samples in which distinct, heterogeneous clusters are difficult to form. For example, households in a block tend to be similar rather than dissimilar. It can be difficult to compute and interpret statistics based on clusters. The strengths and weaknesses of cluster sampling and the other basic sampling techniques are summarized in Table 12.3.

CHOOSING NONPROBABILITY VERSUS PROBABILITY SAMPLING

Choosing between nonprobability and probability samples is based on considerations such as the nature of the research, the error contributed by the sampling process relative to nonsampling error, variability in the population, and statistical and operational considerations (see Table 12.4). For example, in exploratory research the findings are treated as preliminary and the use of probability sampling may not be warranted. On the other hand, in conclusive research in which the researcher wishes to generalize results to the target population, as in estimating market shares, probability sampling is favored. Probability samples allow statistical projection of the results to a target population. For these reasons, Gillette decided to use probability sampling in the opening vignette.

When high levels of sampling accuracy are required, as is the case when estimates of population characteristics are made, probability sampling is preferred. In these situations, the researcher needs to eliminate selection bias and calculate the effect of sampling error. In order to do this, probability sampling is required. Even with this added sampling precision, probability sampling will not always result in more accurate results. Nonsampling error, for example, cannot be controlled with probability sampling. If nonsampling error is likely to be a problem, then nonprobability sampling techniques such as judgment samples may be preferable, allowing greater control over the sampling process.

When choosing between sampling techniques, the researcher must also consider the similarity or homogeneity of the population with respect to the characteristics of interest. For example, probability sampling is more appropriate in highly heterogeneous populations, in which it becomes important to draw a representative sample. Probability sampling is also preferable from a statistical viewpoint, as it is the basis of the most common statistical techniques.

While probability sampling has many advantages, it is sophisticated and requires statistically trained researchers. It generally costs more and takes longer than nonprobability sampling. In many marketing research projects, it is difficult to justify the additional time and expense. Therefore, in practice, the objectives of the study dictate which sampling method will be used, as illustrated in the following example.

TABLE 12.3   Strengths and Weaknesses of Basic Sampling Techniques

TECHNIQUE	STRENGTHS	WEAKNESSES
Nonprobability Sampling		
Convenience sampling	Least expensive, least time consuming, most convenient	Selection bias, sample not representative, not recommended for descriptive or causal research
Judgmental sampling	Inexpensive, convenient, not time consuming	Does not allow generalization, subjective
Quota sampling	Sample can be controlled for certain characteristics	Selection bias, no assurance of representativeness
Snowball sampling	Can estimate rare characteristics	Time consuming
Probability Sampling		
Simple random sampling (SRS)	Easily understood, results projectable	Difficult to construct sampling frame, expensive, lower precision, no assurance of representativeness
Systematic sampling	Can increase representativeness, easier to implement than SRS, sampling frame not necessary	Can decrease representativeness
Stratified sampling	Includes all important subpopulations, precision	Difficult to select relevant stratification variables, not feasible to stratify on many variables, expensive
Cluster sampling	Easy to implement, cost effective	Imprecise, difficult to compute and interpret results

TABLE 12.4   Choosing Nonprobability Versus Probability Sampling

	CONDITIONS FAVORING THE USE OF	
FACTORS	NONPROBABILITY SAMPLING	PROBABILITY SAMPLING
Nature of research	Exploratory	Conclusive
Relative magnitude of sampling and nonsampling errors	Nonsampling errors are larger	Sampling errors are larger
Variability in the population	Homogeneous (low)	Heterogeneous (high)
Statistical considerations	Unfavorable	Favorable
Operational considerations	Favorable	Unfavorable

THE ALLURING CHARM OF ALLURE

Chanel, Inc., wanted to launch a major new fragrance in department and specialty stores that would reach and sustain at least the sales volume of Chanel No. 5. The target population was defined as women 18 and older who would appreciate a unique and broadly appealing fragrance. In conducting a survey to determine women's preferences for perfumes, a nonprobability sampling scheme making use of quota sampling was adopted in conjunction with mall intercept interviews. Quotas were assigned for age, income, and marital status. A nonprobability sampling scheme was chosen because the main objective of this exploratory research was qualitative: to understand what constituted a desirable, classic yet contemporary fragrance that women would choose to wear.

The results of the survey indicated a strong preference for a perfume that was fresh, clean, warm, and sexy. Moreover, women were looking for a perfume that would enable them to express themselves uniquely. Based on these findings, the company launched Allure, a unique and innovative fragrance created by Chanel perfumer Sacques Polge—packaged in a signature beige carton and a sleek bottle. Diversity and individuality were successfully communicated through multi-image ads in a breakthrough print and TV campaign. The advertising portrayed many different women because every woman expresses Allure in her own way. After being launched, Allure achieved top 10 ranking in major retail accounts and sales volume equivalent to Chanel No. 5. The success of Allure could be attributed in no small part to the carefully designed sampling procedures that resulted in important survey findings on which the new perfume was developed and marketed.[10]

SUMMARY ILLUSTRATION USING THE OPENING VIGNETTE

In the Gillette Clear Stick antiperspirant/deodorant survey, the target population was defined as male heads of households. Given the large size of the target population and the limited time and money, the company decided to take a sample rather than a census. The sampling unit was households and the sampling element, or the respondents, were male heads of households. The sampling frame consisted of telephone numbers of all U.S. households, randomly generated by efficient computer programs. The researchers chose probability sampling because the results had to be generalizable, that is, projectable to all male heads of households. The technique of simple random sampling was selected because efficient computer programs were available to randomly generate household telephone numbers and minimize wastage due to nonexisting household telephone numbers. The respondents were recruited over the telephone by promising a monetary incentive and then mailed the survey questionnaire package, including a sample of the new clear stick deodorant. Thus, simple random sampling was used to select 1,000 households. This sample size was selected based on qualitative considerations such as the importance of the decision, the nature of the research, resource constraints, and the sample sizes used in similar studies conducted by Gillette.

MARKETING RESEARCH AND TQM

Firms seeking to enhance customer value should implement sampling concepts, from definition of the target population to selection of a particular sampling technique, by taking into account the specific objectives of the research. If Levi Strauss wanted to assess customer satisfaction with its jeans, the target population should be defined as users of Levi jeans. Nonusers, including exclusive users of other brands, such as Lee, Wrangler, Guess?, and so on, should be excluded.

Likewise, the sampling method should fit the research goals. Nonprobability sampling allows for exploratory research of issues related to quality and value but does not allow for a reliable projection to the population. With probability sampling, the results can be projected to the population with known accuracy, and conclusions on questions of quality and value can be reached. Stratified random sampling may be attractive if, as in the case of jeans, usage varies with known demographic characteristics. On the other hand, if a suitable sampling frame is available internally, such as a complete list, simple random sampling has a great appeal.

EXAMPLE

SAMPLING DESIGN AIDS LEVI'S IN DESIGNING QUALITY JEANS

Levi's 501 faced a challenging task when this generation changed its style from the traditional close fitting 501 button-fly jeans to loose-fitting jeans. Obviously, the consumers' definition of quality jeans had changed, and in 2001 Levi's wanted to capture this shift by conducting a survey. The Levi's marketing research team adopted the following sampling design.

Target Population

The target population is consumers, male and female, between the ages of 13 and 25. The sampling unit is households, and the extent is the United States. The time frame is Fall 2001.

Sampling Frame

The sampling frame is a computer program for random-digit dialing.

Sampling Technique

Use GENESYS, a computer program that provides an accurate random-digit dialing (RDD) sample. This technique will avoid wasting time and money by eliminating nonproductive numbers during the Levi survey. GENESYS will provide RDD samples that will include both listed and unlisted telephone numbers. This method is easy and efficient, and the results can be applied to the target population.

Sample Size

The sample size, based on statistical and nonstatistical considerations, will be 3,000, with 500 interviews conducted in each of the six cities of Atlanta, Boston, Chicago, Los Angeles, Miami, and Seattle.

FOCUS ON ELRICK & LAVIDGE

Sampling is important to all research performed at Elrick & Lavidge (E&L). The type of sampling used depends to a great extent on the needs of the research involved. For example, qualitative research often uses convenience sampling, in which the sample is drawn from readily available lists or locations. Quantitative research, on the other hand, attempts to provide conclusions about the population being studied, so it is important to develop a sample that is representative of the population.

Much of E&L's business-to-business research is quantitative in nature. In these cases, the sampling process begins with a definition of the target population that is to be studied. Quite often, this population is small, consisting of existing or potential business customers of the client's product. The client may further define the target population by adding additional screening characteristics. For instance, a client may wish to target only those businesses that have purchased the client's or a competitor's product within the last six months and whose revenues are above a certain level.

The sampling frame is typically a list of current customers generated internally by the client, supplemented with lists of potential customers generated from a business database using the North American Industry Classification System (NAICS) codes or some other identifying information. Many of the existing and potential customers found in this sampling frame will not match the desired characteristics. They may not have bought the product within the last six months, or their revenues may be too low. This is an example of a sampling frame error. E&L attempts to correct for this error during the data collection phase of the research by asking screening questions. Data are discarded for those companies that do not pass the screening.

A sample is then generated using the sampling frame. E&L predominantly uses simple random sampling and versions of systematic sampling to select the elements to be included in the sample. When attributes are known and attached to the list that comprises the sampling frame, E&L can employ stratified sampling to select the elements to be included in the sample.

Execution of the Sampling Process

Use the random-digit dialing technique to select a random sample. Use the next birthday method to choose if more than one person in the selected household is between 13 and 25 years of age. In this case, the person with the next birthday in the household is selected. If no persons between these ages reside in the house, a new random number should be selected.

Continual improvement in quality leads to reduced costs, fewer mistakes, fewer delays, and better use of time and materials. By finding out exactly who the consumers are and what they want, Levi's can improve the quality of its jeans and enhance customer satisfaction and loyalty.[11]

INTERNATIONAL MARKETING RESEARCH

Implementing the sampling design process in international marketing research is seldom an easy task. Several factors should be considered in defining the target population. Identifica-

American Marketing Association directory. The respondents were selected based on a systematic sampling plan from the directory. Systematic random sampling was chosen over simple random sampling, as it is easier to implement. Respondents were asked to indicate the degree of ethicalness of various scenarios and promised a copy of the results in an attempt to boost response rates.

The study revealed that female marketing professionals, in general, demonstrated higher levels of research ethical judgments than their male counterparts. Similar findings have been obtained in other studies. Thus, the systematic random sampling plan was not only efficient but resulted in findings that were generalizable to the target population.[14]

When conducting research with small populations, such as in business-to-business marketing or employee research, researchers must be sensitive to preserving the respondents' anonymity. The results should be presented in such a way that respondents cannot be identified or linked to specific comments and findings.

INTERNET APPLICATIONS

Sampling potential respondents who are surfing the Internet is meaningful if the sample that is generated is representative of the target population. More and more industries are meeting this criterion. In software, computers, networking, technical publishing, semiconductors, and graduate education, it is rapidly becoming feasible to use the Internet for sampling respondents for quantitative research, such as surveys. For internal customer surveys, in which the client's employees share a corporate e-mail system, an intranet survey is practical even if workers have no access to the external Internet. However, sampling on the Internet is not yet practical for many noncomputer-oriented consumer products.

To avoid sampling errors, the researcher must be able to control the pool that the respondents are selected from. Also, it must be ensured that the respondents do not respond multiple times ("stuff the ballot box"). These requirements are met by e-mail surveys, where the researcher selects specific respondents. Furthermore, the surveys can be encoded to match the returned surveys with their corresponding outbound e-mailings. This can also be accomplished with Web surveys by e-mailing invitations to selected respondents and asking them to visit the Web site where the survey is posted. In this case, the survey is posted in a hidden location on the Web, which is protected by a password. Hence, noninvited Web surfers are unable to access it.

Nonprobability as well as probability sampling techniques can be implemented on the Internet. Moreover, the respondents can be prerecruited or recruited online while surfing the Internet. Recruiting visitors to a Web site is an example of convenience sampling. Based on the researcher's judgment, certain qualifying criteria can be introduced to prescreen the respondents. Even quotas can be imposed.

Likewise, simple random sampling is commonly used. Some companies, such as Millward Brown Intelliquest *(www.intelliquest.com)* use a "click-stream intercept," which randomly samples online users and gives them the opportunity to participate or decline. Various other forms of probability sampling can be implemented, some techniques, such as systematic random sampling, with relative ease.

Furthermore, the Internet can be used to order and access samples generated by marketing research suppliers, as illustrated by the following example.

SSI-SNAP™ ONLINE ORDERING SYSTEM IS A SNAP

Over the years, Survey Sampling, Inc. (SSI) *(www.surveysampling.com)* has become widely recognized by survey research professionals as a reliable and cost-effective source of samples for studies of all types. Customers can place sample orders online by using SSI-SNAP proprietary software. Samples generated by using different sampling techniques are available, for example:

Random-digit (RDD) samples

Listed household samples

Age samples

Income samples

Race and ethnic group samples

SSI's Sample Screening Service is available to reduce nonworking numbers in the sample. This lowers labor costs and related overhead and shortens time in the field without compromising the integrity of the probability sample. Once retrieved, the sample can be transferred to a computer-assisted telephone interviewing (CATI) system and reports can be printed.

SUMMARY

Researchers can obtain information about the characteristics of a population by conducting either a sample or a census. Samples tend to be preferred because of budget and time limits, large population sizes, and small variances in the characteristics of interest. Sampling is also preferred when the cost of sampling error is low, the cost of nonsampling error is high, the nature of measurement is destructive, and attention must be focused on individual cases. The opposite conditions favor the use of a census.

Sampling design begins by defining the target population in terms of elements, sampling units, extent, and time. Then the sampling frame should be determined. A sampling frame is a list of the elements of the target population. Directions for constructing the sampling frame should also be included. Sampling techniques are applied to the sample frame to develop the eventual sample. The sample size is determined based on both quantitative and qualitative considerations. Finally, execution of the sampling process requires detailed specifications for each step in the process.

Sampling techniques may be classified as nonprobability and probability techniques. Nonprobability sampling techniques rely on the researcher's judgment. Consequently, they do not permit an objective evaluation of the precision of the sample results, and the estimates obtained are not statistically projectable to the population. The commonly used nonprobability sampling techniques include convenience sampling, judgmental sampling, quota sampling, and snowball sampling.

In probability sampling techniques, sampling units are selected by chance. Each sampling unit has a nonzero chance of being selected, and the researcher can prespecify every potential sample of a given size that could be drawn from the population, as well as the probability of selecting each sample. It is also possible to determine the precision of the sample estimates and inferences and make projections to the target population. Probability sampling techniques include simple random sampling, systematic sampling, stratified sampling, and cluster sampling. The choice between probability and nonprobability sampling should be based on the nature of the research, degree of error tolerance, relative magnitude of sampling and nonsampling errors, variability in the population, and statistical and operational considerations.

Companies focusing on customer value adopt appropriate sampling procedures and techniques when collecting data for quality initiatives. When conducting international marketing research, it is desirable to achieve comparability in sample composition and representativeness even though this may require using different sampling techniques in different countries. Several computer programs are available for implementing nonprobability and probability sampling schemes. It is unethical and misleading to treat nonprobability samples as probability samples and project the results to a target population. Nonprobability as well as probability sampling techniques can be implemented on the Internet, with the respondents being prerecruited or tapped online.

KEY TERMS AND CONCEPTS

Element, 345
Population, 345
Census, 346
Sample, 346
Target population, 347
Sampling unit, 347
Sampling frame, 348
Nonprobability sampling, 349

Precision, 350
Probability sampling, 350
Sample size, 350
Convenience sampling, 352
Judgmental sampling, 354
Quota sampling, 354
Snowball sampling, 355

Simple random sampling (SRS), 356
Random-digit dialing (RDD), 357
Systematic sampling, 357
Stratified sampling, 359
Cluster sampling, 360
Area sampling, 360

ACRONYMS

The sampling design process and the steps involved may be represented by the acronym SAMPLE:

S ampling design process
A mount: sample size determination
M ethod: sampling technique selection
P opulation definition
L ist: sampling frame determination
E xecution of the sampling process

EXERCISES

1. What is the major difference between a sample and a census?
2. Under what conditions is a sample preferable to a census? A census preferable to a sample?
3. Describe the sampling design process.
4. How should the target population be defined?
5. What is a sampling unit? How is it different from the population element?
6. What qualitative factors should be considered in determining the sample size?
7. How do probability sampling techniques differ from nonprobability sampling techniques?

8. What is the least expensive and least time consuming of all sampling techniques? What are the major limitations of this technique?

9. What is the major difference between judgmental and convenience sampling?

10. What is the relationship between quota sampling and judgmental sampling?

11. What are the distinguishing features of simple random sampling?

12. Describe the procedure for selecting a systematic random sample.

13. Describe stratified sampling. What are the criteria for the selection of stratification variables?

14. Describe the cluster sampling procedure. What is the key distinction between cluster sampling and stratified sampling?

15. What factors should be considered in choosing between probability and nonprobability sampling?

PROBLEMS

1. Define the appropriate target population and the sampling frame in each of the following situations:

   a. The manufacturer of a new cereal brand wants to conduct in-home product usage tests in Chicago.

   b. A national chain store wants to determine the shopping behavior of customers who have its store charge card.

   c. A local TV station wants to determine households' viewing habits and programming preferences.

   d. The local chapter of the American Marketing Association wants to test the effectiveness of its new member drive in Atlanta.

2. A manufacturer would like to survey users to determine the demand potential for a new power press. The new press has a capacity of 500 tons and costs $225,000. It is used for forming products from lightweight and heavyweight steel and can be used by automobile, construction equipment, and major appliance manufacturers.

   a. Identify the population and sampling frame that could be used.

   b. Describe how a simple random sample can be drawn using the identified sampling frame.

   c. Could a stratified sample be used? If so, how?

   d. Could a cluster sample be used? If so, how?

   e. Which sampling technique would you recommend? Why?

INTERNET AND COMPUTER EXERCISES

1. Procter & Gamble would like to conduct a survey of consumer preferences for premium ice cream brands in Los Angeles. Stratified random sampling will be used. Visit *www.census.gov* to identify information that will be relevant in determining income and age strata.

2. Using a microcomputer or mainframe program, generate a set of 1,000 random numbers for selecting a simple random sample.

3. Visit the SurveySite Web site *(www.surveysite.com)*. Examine the Internet surveys being conducted. Write a report about the sampling plans being used.

ACTIVITIES

ROLE PLAYING

1. The alumni office of your university would like to conduct a survey to determine alumni's attitudes toward a new fund-raising program. As a consultant, you must develop a quota sample. What quota variables and levels of variables should be used? How many alumni should be included in each cell? Obtain the necessary information from the alumni office or the library on your campus and present your results to a group of students representing the alumni office.

2. You work as a marketing research manager for a major New York City bank. Management would like to know if the banking habits of different ethnic groups differ. They wonder whether, given the varied population of New York City, it is meaningful to segment the market according to ethnic background. A survey will be conducted. You have been asked to design an appropriate sampling process. Complete the assignment and make a presentation of your results to a group of students representing bank management.

FIELD WORK

1. A major software firm wants to determine the use of spreadsheets by (1) manufacturing firms, (2) service organizations, and (3) educational institutions located in the state of California. Using the resources available in your library, develop an appropriate sampling plan.

2. Visit a local marketing research firm. Determine what procedures the firm uses for online sample control in telephone interviews. Summarize your findings in a report.

GROUP DISCUSSION

1. "Given that the U.S. Census Bureau uses sampling to check on the accuracy of various censuses, a constitutional amendment should be passed replacing the decennial census with a sample." Discuss as a small group.

2. "Because nonsampling errors are greater in magnitude than sampling errors, it really does not matter which sampling technique is used." Discuss this statement.

NOTES

1. Based on Judy Newman, "Newell Rubbermaid Buys Pen Plant in Janesville; Gillette Decides to Sell Its Stationery Division to Focus on It's More Successful Line of Grooming Products," *Madison Newspaper* (August 23, 2000): 1E; Alice Naude, "Men's Toiletries in a New Age," *Chemical Market Reporter,* 257(19) (May 8, 2000): FR20–FR21; Martin Croft, "Men's Toiletries Come of Age," *Marketing Week,* 22(16) (May 20, 1999): 40–41; and "Edison, American Marketing Association, Best New Product Awards," *Marketing News,* 31(6) (March 17, 1997): E5.

2. Carol O. Rogers, "Census 2000 Update," *Indiana Business Review,* 75(1) (Spring 2000): 12; and "Just a Traditional Census," *U.S. News & World Report* (July 29, 1991): 10.

3. For the effect of sample frame error on research results see Seymour Sudman and Edward Blair, "Sampling in the Twenty-First Century," *Journal of the Academy of Marketing Science,* 27(2) (Spring 1999): 269–277; and Wayne Smith, Paul Mitchell, Karin Attebo, and Stephen Leeder, "Selection Bias From Sampling Frames: Telephone Directory and Electoral Roll Compared with Door-to-Door Population Census: Results from the Blue Mountains Eye Study," *Australian & New Zealand Journal of Public Health,* 21(2) (April 1997): 127–133.

4. Martin Oppermann, "Database Marketing by Travel Agencies," *Journal of Travel Research,* 37(3) (February 1999): 231–237; Donn Tilson and Don Stacks, "To Know Us Is to Love Us: The Public Relations

Campaign to Sell a 'Business-Tourist-Friendly' Miami," *Public Relations Review*, 23(2) (Summer 1997): 95–115; and "Florida Travel Habits Subject of Phone Survey," *Quirk's Marketing Research Review* (May 1987): 10, 11, 31, 56, 60.

5. Based on Richard L. Papiernik, "Starbucks Detours Away From Internet Crash Site, Turns Toward Core Operations," *Nation's Restaurant News*, 34(35) (August 28, 2000): 1–3; "Edison, American Marketing Association, Best New Product Awards," *Marketing News*, 31(6) (March 17, 1997): E11.

6. Gary T. Henry, *Practical Sampling* (Thousand Oaks, CA: Sage Publications, 1995); and Raymond F. Barker, "A Demographic Profile of Marketing Research Interviewers," *Journal of the Market Research Society* (July 1987): 279–292.

7. When the sampling interval, i, is not a whole number, the easiest solution is to use as the interval the nearest whole number below or above i. If rounding has too great an effect on the sample size, add or delete the extra cases.

8. Lisa Granatstein, "Tennis Moves to Net Readers," *Mediaweek*, 8(44) (November 23, 1998): 32; and "Readership Survey Serves Tennis Magazine's Marketing Needs," *Quirk's Marketing Research Review* (May 1988): 75–76.

9. Based on David Welch, "Luxury Cars Get Even More So; And Price Tags Go Up Accordingly. Here Are Autos That Will Draw All the Envious Glances You Could Want," *Business Week* (3678) (April 24, 2000): 180; and "Edison, American Marketing Association, Best New Product Awards," *Marketing News*, 31(6) (March 17, 1997): E4.

10. Based on "Teen Fragrances Flourish," *Global Cosmetic Industry*, 166(2) (February 2000): 44; and "Edison, American Marketing Association, Best New Product Awards," *Marketing News*, 31(6) (March 17, 1997): E4.

11. Louise Lee, "Can Levi's Be Cool Again? It's Trying to Woo Kids—Without Turning Off Grown-ups," *Business Week* (3672) (March 13, 2000): 144; "Levi's Repositions as 'Trendy' Label," *Marketing Week*, 22(33) (September 16, 1999): 6; and Alice Z. Cuneo, "Levi's 501 Stephen Wilkie," *Advertising Age*, 67 (June 1996): 36.

12. For the use of different nonprobability and probability sampling techniques in cross-cultural research, see Thomas Miller, "Cultural Affinity, Personal Values Factors in Marketing," *Marketing News*, 33(17) (August 16, 1999): H22–H23; Humphrey Taylor, "The Very Different Methods Used to Conduct Telephone Surveys of the Public," *Journal of the Market Research Society*, 39(3) (July 1997): 421–432; and Saeed Samiee and Insik Jeong, "Cross-Cultural Research in Advertising: An Assessment of Methodologies," *Journal of the Academy of Marketing Science*, 22 (Summer 1994): 205–215.

13. Andrew McIntosh, "The Sampling of Non-Domestic Populations," *Journal of the Market Research Society*, 38(4) (October 1996): 429–446; and B. J. Verhage, U. Yavas, R. T. Green, and E. Borak, "The Perceived Risk Brand Loyalty Relationship: An International Perspective," *Journal of Global Marketing*, 3(3) (1990): 7–22.

14. Daulatram B. Lund, "An Empirical Examination of Marketing Professional's Ethical Behavior in Differing Situations," *Journal of Business Ethics*, 24(4) (April 2000): 331–342; William A. Weeks, Carlos W. Moore, Joseph A. McKinney, and Justin G. Longenecker, "The Effects of Gender and Career Stage on Ethical Judgment," *Journal of Business Ethics*, 20(4) (Part 2) (July 1999): 301–313; Marshall Schminke and Maureen L. Ambrose, "Asymmetric Perceptions of Ethical Frameworks of Men and Women in Business and Nonbusiness Settings," *Journal of Business Ethics*, 16(7) (May 1997): 719–729; and I. P. Akaah, "Differences in Research Ethics Judgments Between Male and Female Marketing Professionals," *Journal of Business Ethics*, 8 (1989): 375–381.

13

SAMPLING: FINAL AND INITIAL SAMPLE SIZE DETERMINATION

THE SIZE OF THE SAMPLE IS DETERMINED NOT ONLY BY STATISTICAL CALCULATIONS, BUT ALSO MANAGERIAL CONSIDERATIONS INCLUDING TIME AND COST.

Opening Questions

1. What key concepts and symbols are pertinent to sampling?
2. How are the sampling distribution, statistical inference, and standard error relevant to sampling?
3. What is the statistical approach to determining sample size based on simple random sampling and the construction of confidence intervals?
4. How can we derive the formulas to statistically determine the sample size for estimating means and proportions?
5. How should the sample size be adjusted to account for incidence and completion rates?
6. Do statistical sampling concepts play a role in total quality management?
7. Why is it difficult to statistically determine the sample size in international marketing research?
8. What is the interface of technology with sample size determination?
9. What ethical issues are related to sample size determination, particularly the estimation of population variance?
10. What role does the Internet play in determining the sample size?

John Pelham, Sr. Research Director, Elrick & Lavidge.
John Pelham is responsible for the management of research programs. He has several years of experience in managing a variety of client research projects.

SIZING THE SAMPLE SIZE PROBLEM

An article in the *Chicago Tribune* suggested that as television has reduced the audiences for both theater and radio, so are online services reducing the audience for television. To support his claim, the author offered up survey data about America Online, which found that online subscribers watch less television than the average U.S. household. An executive at the research company that performed the survey said, "It doesn't matter why people watch less television. It only matters that they do."

The general reader and the general businessperson might read this piece and walk away with the notion that, indeed, increasing online use is directly related to decreasing television viewing. You can almost imagine the buzzing of such discussions at breakfast tables, water coolers, and in car pools: "Hey, I just read in the paper this morning that . . ."

A more skeptical reader would rightly question much of the study's findings and its application to everyday consumer media preferences. A closer look at the report reveals that the sample size comprised only 262 members of the online service's more than 30 million subscribers. Is this enough to mitigate random sampling error? Is this sample large enough to make such bold claims about TV viewing? To make decisions and set policy and strategy? The confidence level—the level of certainty—is not reported, only the margin of error as "probably" about five percentage points. Was it five or not? How confident are we that this conclusion is accurate? What is the confidence level and what is the confidence interval—the range likely to contain the true population parameter? Moreover, the completion rate was not reported. Without considering the appropriate sampling specifications, it is not appropriate to draw inferences from the sample about the population. Therefore, based on this study, it is not appropriate to conclude that users of online services, in general, watch less television.[1]

OVERVIEW

In Chapter 12, we considered the role of sampling in research design formulation, described the sampling process, and presented the various nonprobability and probability sampling techniques. This chapter focuses on the determination of sample size in simple random sampling. Figure 13.1 briefly explains the focus of the chapter, the relationship of this chapter to the previous ones, and the step of the marketing research process on which this chapter concentrates.

The opening vignette illustrates the importance of statistically determining the sample size and the random sampling error before generalizing the sample findings to the population. In order to understand and appreciate these issues, we will define various concepts and symbols and discuss the properties of the sampling distribution. Then we will describe statistical approaches to sample size determination based on confidence intervals. We will present the formulas for calculating the sample size with these approaches and illustrate their use.

The sample size determined statistically is the final or net sample size that represents the number of interviews or observations that need to be completed. For example, a sample size of 1,000 for a telephone survey means that the interviewers must complete 1,000 interviews. However, to obtain this final sample size, a much larger number of potential respondents have to be contacted initially. Thus, to complete 1,000 interviews it may be necessary to initially contact as many as, say, 3,000 respondents as only some of the potential respondents may qualify to participate; that is, the incidence rate is generally less than 100 percent. Furthermore, some of those who do qualify may refuse to participate or complete the survey; the completion rate is also less than 100 percent. This chapter will describe the adjustments that need to be made to the statistically determined sam-

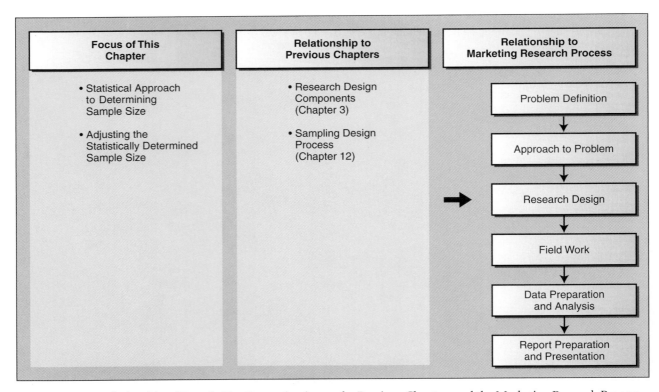

FIGURE 13.1 Relationship of Sample Size Determination to the Previous Chapters and the Marketing Research Process

ple size to account for incidence and completion rates and calculate the initial sample size. The chapter will also discuss the role of sample size in quality management, the difficulty of statistically determining the sample size in international marketing research, applications of technology, the relevant ethical issues, and Internet applications. Figure 13.2 gives an overview of the topics discussed in this chapter and how they flow from one to the next.

Statistical determination of sample size requires knowledge of the normal distribution and the use of normal probability tables. The **normal distribution** is bell-shaped and symmetrical. Its mean, median, and mode are identical (see Chapter 16). Information on the normal distribution and the use of normal probability tables is presented in Appendix 13A. You should also review the textbook from your statistics course. We begin with some basic definitions and symbols.

normal distribution
A basis for classical statistical inference that is bell-shaped and symmetrical in appearance. Its measures of central tendency are all identical.

DEFINITIONS AND SYMBOLS

The statistical concepts used in sample size determination are defined in the following list.

Parameter: A summary description of a fixed characteristic or measure of the target population. A parameter denotes the true value that would be obtained if a census (a survey of the complete population), rather than a sample, were undertaken.

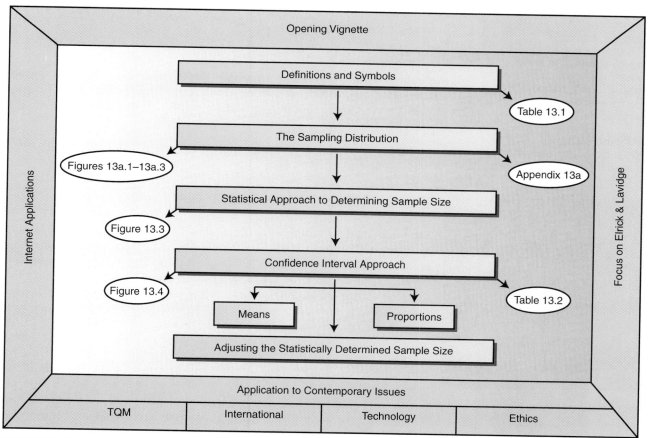

FIGURE 13.2   Final and Initial Sample Size Determination: An Overview

TABLE 13.1   **Symbols for Population and Sample Variables**

VARIABLE	POPULATION	SAMPLE
Mean	μ	$\overline{X}$
Proportion	π	p
Variance	σ^2	s^2
Standard deviation	σ	s
Size	N	n
Standard error of the mean	$\sigma_{\overline{x}}$	$S_{\overline{x}}$
Standard error of the proportion	σ_p	S_p
Standardized variate (z)	$\dfrac{X - \mu}{\sigma}$	$\dfrac{X - \overline{X}}{s}$

Statistic: A summary description of a characteristic or measure of the sample. The sample statistic is used as an estimate of the population parameter.

Precision level: When estimating a population parameter by using a sample statistic, the precision level is the desired size of the estimating interval. This is the maximum permissible difference between the sample statistic and the population parameter.

Confidence interval: The range into which the true population parameter will fall, assuming a given level of confidence.

Confidence level: The probability that a confidence interval will include the population parameter.

Random sampling error: The error that results when the particular sample selected is an imperfect representation of the population of interest (see Chapter 3). Note that this is different from the random error in measurement discussed in Chapter 10.

sampling distribution
The distribution of the values of a sample statistic computed for each possible sample that could be drawn from the target population under a specified sampling plan.

statistical inference
The process of generalizing the sample results to the population results.

The symbols used in statistical notation for describing population and sample characteristics are summarized in Table 13.1.

THE SAMPLING DISTRIBUTION

The **sampling distribution** is the distribution of the values of a sample statistic, for example, the sample mean. These values are computed for each possible sample of a given size. Under a specified sampling plan, it is possible to draw several different samples of a given size from the target population.[2] The sampling distribution should not be confused with the distribution of the values of the elements in a sample. Suppose a simple random sample of five steel mills is to be drawn from a population of 20 steel mills. There are $(20 \times 19 \times 18 \times 17 \times 16)/(1 \times 2 \times 3 \times 4 \times 5)$, or 15,504 different samples of five steel mills that can be drawn from this population. If the values of the means associated with these 15,504 samples were assembled, they would form the sampling distribution of the mean.

Several different samples of five steel mills can be drawn from a population of 20 steel mills.

An important task in marketing research is to calculate statistics, such as the sample mean and sample proportion, and to use them to estimate the corresponding true population values. This process of generalizing the sample results to the population results is referred to as **statistical inference.** In practice, a single sample of predetermined size is selected, and the sample statistics (such as means or proportions) are computed. The sample statistics become the basis for making inferences about the population values. This inferential process is possible because sampling distribution enables us to use probability theory to make inferences about the population values.

We will now describe the important properties of the sampling distribution of the mean and the corresponding properties for the proportion for large samples (30 or more). Please refer to Table 13.1 for a definition of the symbols used in these formulas.

1. The sampling distribution of the mean is a normal distribution (see Appendix 13A). Strictly speaking, the sampling distribution of a proportion is a binomial that approximates the normal distribution in large samples ($n = 30$ or more).

2. The mean (the average) of the sampling distribution of the mean $\left(\overline{X} = \left(\sum_{i=1}^{n} X_i\right) / n\right)$ or of the proportion (p) equals the corresponding population parameter value, μ or π, respectively.

3. The standard deviation of the sampling distribution is called the **standard error** of the mean or the proportion. This distinction is made to clarify the point that we are talking about a sampling distribution of the mean or the proportion, not about a distribution of elements in a sample or a population.

   The formula for the mean is:

   $$\sigma_{\overline{x}} = \frac{\sigma}{\sqrt{n}}$$

   The formula for the proportion is:

   $$\sigma_p = \sqrt{\frac{\pi (1 - \pi)}{n}}$$

standard error
The standard deviation of the sampling distribution of the mean or proportion.

4. Often the population standard deviation, σ, is not known. In these cases, it can be estimated from the sample by using the following formula:

   $$s = \sqrt{\frac{\sum_{i=1}^{n}(X_i - \overline{X})^2}{n - 1}}$$

   or

   $$s = \sqrt{\frac{\sum_{i=1}^{n} X_i^2 - \frac{\left(\sum_{i=1}^{n} X_i\right)^2}{n}}{n - 1}}$$

   In cases in which σ is estimated by s, the standard error of the mean becomes

   $$\text{est. } \sigma_{\overline{X}} = \frac{s}{\sqrt{n}}$$

   "est." denotes the fact that s has been used as an estimate of σ.

5. Likewise, the standard error of the proportion can be estimated by using the sample proportion p as an estimator of the population proportion, π, as:

   $$\text{est. } s_p = \sqrt{\frac{p (1 - p)}{n}}$$

z value
The number of standard errors that a point is away from the mean.

6. The area under the sampling distribution (normal distribution) curve between any two points can be calculated in terms of z values. The **z value** for a point is the number of standard errors that point is away from the mean. The z values may be computed as follows:

$$z = \frac{\bar{X} - \mu}{\sigma_{\bar{x}}}$$

For example, 34.13 percent of the area under one side of the curve lies between the mean and a z value of 1.0. The area from the mean to z value of 2.0 and 3.0 is equal to 0.4772 and 0.4986, respectively. (See Table 2 in the Appendix of Statistical Tables.) The same percentages of the area under the sampling distribution curve lie between the mean and z values of −1.0, −2.0, and −3.0. This is because the sampling distribution curve is symmetric around the mean. In the case of proportion, the computation of z values is similar.

STATISTICAL APPROACHES TO DETERMINING SAMPLE SIZE

In addition to statistical considerations, several qualitative factors should be considered when determining the sample size (see Chapter 12). These include the importance of the decision, the nature of the research, the number of variables, the nature of the analysis, sample sizes used in similar studies, incidence rates, completion rates, and resource constraints. The statistically determined sample size is the net or final sample size—the sample remaining after eliminating potential respondents who do not qualify or who do not complete the interview. Depending on incidence and completion rates, the initial sample may need to be much larger than the net or final sample requirements. In commercial marketing research, limits on time, money, and expert resources can exert an overriding influence on sample size determination.

The statistical approach to determining sample size is based on traditional statistical inference using the formulas (equations) presented in the previous section. In this approach, the precision level is specified in advance. This approach is based on the construction of confidence intervals around sample means or proportions (Figure 13.3).

THE CONFIDENCE INTERVAL APPROACH

Confidence intervals around sample means or proportions are estimated using the standard error formula. As an example, suppose that a researcher has taken a simple random sample of 300 households to estimate the monthly expenses on department store shopping, and has found that the mean household monthly expense for the

FIGURE 13.3
The Confidence Interval Approach and Determining Sample Size

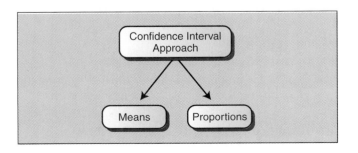

sample is $182. Past studies indicate that the population standard deviation σ can be assumed to be $55.

We want to find an interval within which a fixed proportion of the sample means would fall. Suppose we want to determine an interval around the population mean that will include 95 percent of the sample means, based on samples of 300 households. That is, we choose 95 percent as the confidence level. The 95 percent could be divided into two equal parts, half below and half above the mean, as shown in Figure 13.4. Calculation of the confidence interval involves determining a distance below ($\overline{X}_L$) and above ($\overline{X}_U$) the population mean ($\overline{X}$), which contains a specified area of the normal curve.

The z values corresponding to $\overline{X}_L$ and $\overline{X}_U$ may be calculated as

$$z_L = \frac{\overline{X}_L - \mu}{\sigma_{\overline{x}}}$$

$$z_U = \frac{\overline{X}_U - \mu}{\sigma_{\overline{x}}}$$

where $z_L = -z$ and $z_U = +z$. Therefore, the lower value of $\overline{X}$ is

$$\overline{X}_L = \mu - z\sigma_{\overline{x}}$$

and the upper value of $\overline{X}$ is

$$\overline{X}_U = \mu + z\sigma_{\overline{x}}$$

Note that μ is estimated by $\overline{X}$. The confidence interval is given by

$$\overline{X} \pm z\sigma_{\overline{x}}$$

We can now set a 95 percent confidence interval around the sample mean of $182. As a first step, we compute the standard error of the mean:

$$\sigma_{\overline{x}} = \frac{\sigma}{\sqrt{n}} = 55/\sqrt{300} = 3.18$$

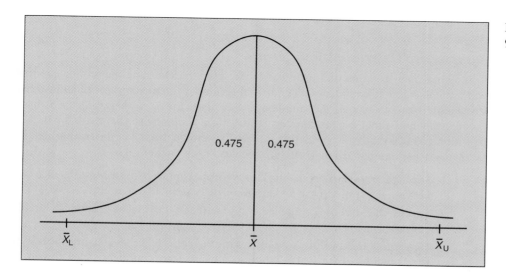

FIGURE 13.4
95% Confidence Interval

Monthly household expenses on department store shopping can be estimated with only a certain degree of confidence.

From Table 2 in the Appendix of Statistical Tables, we can see that the central 95 percent of the normal distribution lies within ±1.96 z values. The 95 percent confidence interval is given by

$$\overline{X} \pm 1.96\ \sigma_{\overline{x}}$$
$$= 182.00 \pm 1.96(3.18)$$
$$= 182.00 \pm 6.23$$

Thus, the 95 percent confidence interval ranges from \$175.77 to \$188.23. The probability of finding the true population mean to be within \$175.77 and \$188.23 is 95 percent. If the confidence interval is not reported, or cannot otherwise be calculated from the information given, we have no way of knowing how precise the sample estimates are. This was illustrated in the opening vignette, where it was difficult to evaluate the precision of the results of the America Online survey.

Confidence intervals are often associated with scales used to measure customer satisfaction, as illustrated by the American Customer Satisfaction Index.

EXAMPLE

THE AMERICAN CUSTOMER SATISFACTION INDEX

The American Customer Satisfaction Index (ACSI) is a national measure of satisfaction with quality that provides a resource for examining the differences in satisfaction among customers of different industries by their demographic and socioeconomic characteristics. The ACSI is based on about 42,000 customer interviews and is converted to a 0 to 100 scale.

The first national measure of ACSI gave an index reading of 74.5 with a 95 percent confidence interval of 74.3 to 74.7. This narrow confidence interval is due to a large sample size and indicates that customer satisfaction was measured with a high degree of precision. The ACSI is also broken down by economic sectors and industries. The ACSI is a useful new tool for companies to benchmark their customer satisfaction scores against those of other companies in their own and other industries.[3]

Sample Size Determination: Means

Confidence interval estimation formulas can be used to determine the sample size that will result in a desired confidence interval. In this case, we use the same formulas but have a different unknown, namely the sample size, n. Suppose the researcher wants to estimate the monthly household expense on department store shopping so that the estimate will be within ±\$5.00 of the true population value. What should the size of the sample be? The following steps, summarized in Table 13.2, will lead to an answer.

1. **Specify the level of precision.** This is the maximum permissible difference (D) between the sample mean and the population mean. In our example, $D = \pm\$5.00$.

2. **Specify the level of confidence.** Suppose that a 95 percent confidence level is desired.

3. **Determine the z value associated with the confidence level using Table 2 in the Appendix of Statistical Tables.** For a 95 percent confidence level, the prob-

TABLE 13.2   Sample Size Determination for Means and Proportions

STEPS	MEANS	PROPORTIONS
1. Specify the level of precision.	$D = \pm \$5.00$	$D = p - \pi = \pm 0.05$
2. Specify the confidence level (CL).	CL = 95%	CL = 95%
3. Determine the z value associated with the CL.	z value is 1.96	z value is 1.96
4. Determine the standard deviation of the population.	Estimate σ $\sigma = 55$	Estimate π $\pi = 0.64$
5. Determine the sample size using the formula for the standard error.	$n = \dfrac{\sigma^2 z^2}{D^2}$ $n = \dfrac{55^2(1.96)^2}{5^2}$ $= 465$	$n = \dfrac{\pi(1-\pi)z^2}{D^2}$ $n = \dfrac{0.64\,(1-0.64)\,(1.96)^2}{(0.05)^2}$ $= 355$
6. If necessary, reestimate the confidence interval by employing s to estimate σ.	$= \bar{X} \pm zs_{\bar{x}}$	$p \pm z\,s_p$

ability that the population mean will fall outside one end of the interval is 0.025 (0.05/2) with an associated z value of 1.96.

4. **Determine the standard deviation of the population.** The standard deviation of the population may be available from secondary sources, estimated from pilot study data, or based on the researcher's judgment. For example, the range of a normally distributed variable is approximately equal to plus or minus three standard deviations. The standard deviation of sample data can therefore be estimated by dividing the range of that data by six. The researcher can often estimate the range based on knowledge of the phenomenon or knowledge of the scale used. For example, the traditional Likert scale has a range of 4 (5–1).

5. **Determine the sample size using the formula for the standard error of the mean.** Let us use the formula for z and derive the formula for the sample size, n. Recall that

$$z = \frac{\bar{X} - \mu}{\sigma_{\bar{x}}}$$

because $D = \bar{X} - \mu$

$$z = \frac{D}{\sigma_{\bar{x}}}$$

Solving for $\sigma_{\bar{x}}$

$$\sigma_{\bar{x}} = \frac{D}{z}$$

But $\sigma_{\bar{x}} = \dfrac{\sigma}{\sqrt{n}}$

Therefore,

$$\frac{\sigma}{\sqrt{n}} = \frac{D}{z}$$

Solving for n

$$n = \frac{\sigma^2 z^2}{D^2}$$

In our example,

$$n = \frac{55^2 (1.96)^2}{5^2}$$

$$= 464.83$$

$$= 465 \text{ (rounded to the next higher integer)}$$

It can be seen from the above formulas that sample size is influenced by three factors. It increases as population variability increases, as greater confidence is required (that is, as confidence level increases), and as the precision level required of the estimate increases.

6. **If the population standard deviation, σ, is unknown and an estimate is used, it should be reestimated once the sample has been drawn.** The sample standard deviation, s, is used as an estimate of σ. A revised confidence interval should then be calculated to determine the precision level actually obtained.

Suppose that the value of 55.00 used for σ was an estimate because the true value was unknown. A sample of size ($n =$) 465 is drawn, and these observations generate a mean ($\bar{X}$) of 180.00 and a sample standard deviation s of 50.00. The revised confidence interval then is

$$= \bar{X} \pm z s_{\bar{x}}$$

$$= 180.00 \pm 1.96(50.0/\sqrt{465})$$

$$= 180.00 \pm 4.55$$

or

$$175.45 \leq \mu \leq 184.55$$

Note that the confidence interval obtained is narrower than planned because the population standard deviation was overestimated to be 55 compared to the sample standard deviation of only 50.

It is very important to note that the population size, N, does not directly affect the size of the sample. An example will make this point more obvious. Suppose all the population elements are identical on a characteristic of interest. A sample size of one would then be sufficient to estimate the mean perfectly. This would be true regardless of whether there were 50, 500, 5,000, or 50,000 elements in the population. The sample size is directly affected by the variability of the characteristic in the population. This variability enters into the sample size calculation by way of population variance σ^2 or sample variance s^2.

Sample Size Determination: Proportions

Proportions are estimated when the choice is dichotomous, meaning there are only two categories (for example, yes or no). The researcher is examining the percentage of elements that are in one of the two categories. If the statistic of interest is a proportion, rather than a mean, the approach to sample size determination is similar. Suppose that the researcher is interested in estimating the proportion of households possessing a department store credit card. The researcher should follow these six steps:

1. **Specify the level of precision.** Suppose the desired precision is such that the allowable interval is set as $D = p - \pi = \pm 0.05$ (that is, 5 percent expressed as a decimal equivalent).

2. **Specify the level of confidence.** Suppose that a 95 percent confidence level is desired.

3. **Determine the z value associated with the confidence level.** As explained in the case of estimating the mean, this will be $z = 1.96$.

4. **Estimate the population proportion, π.** As explained earlier, the population proportion may be estimated from secondary sources or from a pilot study, or based on the judgment of the researcher. Suppose that based on secondary data the researcher estimates that 64 percent of the households in the target population possess a department store credit card. In this case, $\pi = 0.64$.

5. **Determine the sample size using the formula for the standard error of the proportion.** The derivation of the formula for sample size is similar to that used for means. We know that

$$z = \frac{p - \pi}{\sigma_p}$$

Hence,

$$\sigma_p = \frac{p - \pi}{z}$$

Substituting D for $p - \pi$ we get

$$\sigma_p = \frac{D}{z}$$

We also know that

$$\sigma_p = \sqrt{\frac{\pi(1 - \pi)}{n}}$$

Therefore, setting

$$\frac{D}{z} = \sqrt{\frac{\pi(1 - \pi)}{n}}$$

and solving for n, we get

$$n = \frac{\pi(1 - \pi)z^2}{D^2}$$

In our example,

$$n = \frac{0.64(1 - 0.64)(1.96)^2}{(0.05)^2}$$

$$= 354.04$$

$$= 355 \text{ (rounded to the next higher integer)}$$

6. **If the estimate of π turns out to be poor, the confidence interval will be more or less precise than desired.** Suppose that after the sample has been taken, the proportion p is calculated to have a value of 0.55. The confidence interval is then reestimated by employing s_p to estimate the unknown σ_p as

$$p \pm z\, s_p$$

where

$$s_p = \sqrt{\frac{p\,(1-p)}{n}}$$

In our example,

$$s_p = \sqrt{\frac{0.55\,(1\text{-}0.55)}{355}}$$

$$= 0.0264$$

The confidence interval, then, is

$$= 0.55 \pm 1.96\,(0.0264)$$

$$= 0.55 \pm .052$$

which is wider than that specified. This could be attributed to the fact that the sample standard deviation determined from our actual sample was based on $p = 0.55$. This was larger than our original estimate of the population standard deviation determined from secondary data and based on $\pi = 0.64$.

If the resulting confidence interval is too wide, the sample size can be recalculated, using the maximum possible variation in the population. Maximum variation occurs when the product $\pi(1 - \pi)$ is at a maximum. This occurs when π is set at 0.5. This result can also be seen intuitively. If a population were evenly divided in terms of one value of a characteristic, more evidence would be required to obtain a valid inference than if the majority of the population possessed that characteristic. In our example, this leads to a sample size of

$$n = \frac{0.5\,(0.5)\,(1.96)^2}{(0.05)^2}$$

$$= 384.16$$

$$= 385 \text{ rounded to the next higher integer.}$$

Thus, in our opening vignette, if the proportion of online users is to be estimated with 95 percent confidence level and with a margin of error (allowable interval) not to exceed ±5 percent, the sample size should have been at least 385. However, the sample size was only 262, falling substantially short of the required size.

ADJUSTING THE STATISTICALLY DETERMINED SAMPLE SIZE

The sample size specified by these statistical methods is a final, or net, sample size. It represents the number of returned mail questionnaires or the number of completed interviews. Initial oversampling, in which a much larger number of respondents are originally contacted, is required to achieve the desired net sample. This is due to two factors, incidence rates and completion rates.

Incidence Rate

Incidence rate refers to the rate of occurrence. It is influenced by the proportion of people in the population with the characteristics under study. When studying a characteristic with a low incident rate, the researcher will have to initially contact many more people than if the characteristic has a high incidence rate, screening out those who do not meet the study requirements. Suppose a study of jewelry calls for a sample of female heads of households aged 25 to 55. Of the women between the ages of 20 and 60 who might reasonably be approached to see if they qualify, approximately 75 percent are heads of households between 25 and 55. That is, the incidence rate or the rate of occurrence is 0.75. This means that, on average, 1.33 (1/0.75) women need to be approached in order to obtain one qualified respondent.

> **incidence rate**
> The rate of occurrence of persons eligible to participate in the study expressed as a percentage.

Additional criteria for qualifying respondents (for example, they must be using a specific product or brand) will further decrease the incidence rate and therefore increase the number of contacts. Suppose it is decided that respondents must have worn jewelry in the past week in order to be eligible to participate in the study. It is estimated that 60 percent of the women contacted would meet this criterion of wearing jewelry. Then the incidence rate drops from 75 percent to 45 percent (= 0.75 × 0.60). To deliver one qualified respondent to the sample, 2.22 individuals (1/0.45) must be initially contacted.

Completion Rate

The number of initial contacts must also be increased in anticipation of refusals coming from people qualified to participate. The **completion rate** denotes the percentage of qualified respondents who complete the interview. For example, if the researcher expects an interview completion rate of 80 percent of eligible respondents, the number of contacts should be increased by a factor of 1.25 (= 1/0.8).

> **completion rate**
> The percentage of qualified respondents who complete the interview. It enables researchers to take into account anticipated refusals by people who qualify.

Combined Adjustment

Combining the expected incident and completion rates results in a contacted sample that is 2.22 × 1.25 or 2.77 times the final sample size requirement. In general,

$$\text{Initial sample size} = \frac{\text{Final sample size}}{\text{Incidence rate} \times \text{Completion rate}}$$

The number of units that will have to be sampled is equal to the initial sample size. The following example illustrates a variety of variables that can be used to qualify potential respondents. It also shows that as the number of qualifying variables increases, the incidence rate will fall.

EXAMPLE

TARGETING WOMEN'S LIPS

When Lancome Paris was conducting a survey to determine women's preferences for lip color, they defined the target population very precisely. The screening criteria for a respondent to be included in the survey were: (1) female, (2) age 25 to 55, and (3) annual household income of at least $30,000. Having three qualifying factors resulted in a highly targeted sample, although it boosted the initial sample size because of a much lower incidence rate. Survey results showed that these women were looking for a lipstick that provided more moisturizing comfort, a more even application and coverage, and less caking and feathering.

Based on these findings, Lancome developed and introduced Rouge Idole. It was the first transfer-resistant lipstick that won't smudge off when you eat, drink, or kiss, and it filled a large gap in consumer product needs. Rouge Idole was positioned for women who want an ultra-long-wearing lipstick with improved comfort. Six months after introduction, Rouge Idole accounted for 50 percent of Lancome's successful lipstick business.[4]

SUMMARY ILLUSTRATION USING THE OPENING VIGNETTE

The statistical approaches to determining sample size based on confidence intervals may involve the estimation of the mean (mean hours spent watching TV or using online services) or proportion (proportion of respondents using online services). Statistical calculation of sample size requires specification of precision level, confidence level, and population standard deviation. Only the precision level was disclosed in the opening vignette, about 5 percent. Therefore, we could not determine whether the sample size of 262 in the America Online survey was adequate and whether the conclusion reached was warranted. However, we know that the sample size required to estimate a proportion near 0.5 with 95 percent confidence level and 5 percent precision level is 385. The sample size in the opening vignette falls substantially short of this mark.

MARKETING RESEARCH AND TQM

Often, quality and value are assessed by measuring consumers' perceptions. These measures are subjective because they are influenced by the individuality of respondents. This translates into higher variances and standard deviations for samples. In light of these high standard deviations, large samples should be used. Compaq, for example, may be concerned about the ratings of its personal computers (PCs) on certain attributes that enhance the quality of the experience for the users. Confidence intervals could be established for the quality ratings based on the mean scores and the standard deviations. In order to control the width of the confidence intervals, the researcher can determine the appropriate sample sizes.

When measuring the quality of objective product characteristics (for example, in design and manufacturing), a much higher level of precision may be required as compared to measuring the consumer's quality perceptions. This may also call for a much higher confidence level. Both of these requirements will imply the need for a larger sam-

FOCUS ON
ELRICK & LAVIDGE

When conducting conclusive research, Elrick & Lavidge (E&L) will try to obtain 200 to 400 respondents per major groupings within the study. E&L's staff statistician noted that a sample of 400 responses to a particular question would be accurate within a 95 percent confidence interval (±5 percent precision) when there is no previous information available to guide the development or analysis of the question. In the case in which previous research has been performed and the researcher is confident that the population is fairly homogeneous, accurate information can be obtained from smaller samples.

When the research involves business-to-business research, the respondents are typically a fairly homogeneous group of customers or suppliers that the client wishes to survey. In such cases, the survey sample need not be as large because one is fairly sure that the smaller sample is representative of the total population.

Statistical issues are not the only issues that E&L considers when it consults with clients about sample size. The statistical determination of sample size may be overruled by cost and time considerations. To some extent, clients have to weigh the issues of quality of data against cost and time in collecting that data. This is especially true when the incidence rate in the available sampling frame is small, leading to a high cost per completed response.

As a rule, E&L tries to strongly discourage a client who is considering implementing research using small sample sizes that will give only 80 percent confidence intervals. As a long-term relationship issue, E&L tries to educate clients so they understand how to interpret and use results of the research at the different confidence levels.

ple size. However, variability may be small because of the tight production control, thereby reducing the sampling size. The use of sampling concepts in ensuring product quality is illustrated by the following example.

EXAMPLE

STATISTICAL QUALITY CONTROL FOR CONTROLLING PRODUCT QUALITY

Hartmarx is a 112-year-old clothing company that has teamed up with Tommy Hilfiger to distribute clothing to the apparel industry. Hartmarx is now licensed to handle all of Tommy Hilfiger's clothing and slacks.

Due to the agreement, the two companies' differences concerning total quality management had to be addressed. Hartmarx was already known for its excellence in product quality; however, Tommy Hilfiger had more than just product quality in mind. Mr. Hilfiger wanted to fully capitalize on the growing market, and to do this he demanded quality in every aspect of the operation, from production to the sales floor. One step the companies took to implement total quality management was very strict statistical quality control in the warehouse.

Statistical quality control uses principles similar to those in sample size determination. Using this, managers can determine whether the variations in the products are within or beyond expected limits. If the variation is within the limits, the process can be left alone. However, intervening action is necessary if the variation is beyond expected limits. Hartmarx has paid particular attention to their statistical quality control not only in the plant but also when goods arrive at the warehouse to ensure that they conform to quality standards. Thus, every Hilfiger garment is guaranteed to be of superior quality.[5]

INTERNATIONAL MARKETING RESEARCH

When conducting marketing research in foreign countries, statistical estimation of sample size may be difficult since estimates of the population variance may be unavailable. Hence, the sample size is often determined by qualitative considerations, as discussed in Chapter 12. When statistical estimation of sample size is attempted, the differences in estimates of population variance should be recognized and factored in if possible. For example, consumer preferences for certain products may be relatively heterogeneous in markets where those products have been newly introduced. Thus, it may be a mistake to assume that the population variance is the same, or to use the same sample size across countries, as the following example shows.

EXAMPLE

THE CHINESE TAKE TO THE SKY

The airline industry seems to have a strong and promising market in China. Spending billions of dollars, China is trying to satisfy a surging demand and catch up with the rest of the world. The domestic airline traffic is growing as much as 30 percent a year in some markets. Strong economic growth, surging foreign trade, and a revival in tourism have helped to fuel this boom. China is making rapid progress in increasing its fleet and training pilots. Whereas in 1984 the country had only 15 commercial aircraft—mostly outdated Soviet-made models—the fleet is now more than 50 times as large, with air-crafts from Boeing, McDonnell Douglas, and Airbus. The Civil Aviation Administration of China (once known as "Chinese Airlines Always Cancel") has granted much flexibility to the individual airlines.

Yet, for millions of Chinese, air travel is a relatively new experience, and many more millions have never flown. Hence, Chinese preferences for air travel are likely to exhibit much more variability as compared to Americans. In a survey by Delta Airlines to compare the attitude toward air travel in China and the United States, the sample size of the Chinese survey would have to be larger than the American survey in order for the two survey estimates to have comparable precision.[6]

TECHNOLOGY AND MARKETING RESEARCH

Computer-based systems are available to determine the sample size for various sampling techniques. For simple applications, appropriate sample size formulas can be programmed using spreadsheet programs. The researcher specifies the desired precision level, confidence level, and population variance. The program then determines the appropriate sample size for the study. By incorporating the cost of each sampling unit, the sample size can be adjusted based on budget considerations.

Several marketing research firms supply sample design software and services, including statistical determination of sample sizes and estimation of sample statistics. Survey Sampling, Inc. *(www.surveysampling.com),* has a line of sampling products. Its Contact and Cooperation Rate Adjustment software statistically adjusts sample sizes by taking into account the expected incidence and completion rates.

ETHICS IN MARKETING RESEARCH

The sample size is one of the major determinants of cost in a marketing research project. It may seem that if the sample size is statistically determined, this procedure is free from ethical conflicts. However, this may not be true. As we have seen in this chapter, the sample size is directly proportional to the variance of the variable. Estimates of the population variance are based on small pilot studies, related research, and the judgment of the researcher. Because judgment is involved, the researcher has the ethical responsibility to not use large estimates of the population variance simply to increase the cost of the project by inflating the sample size. Using the sample size formula, we can see that increasing the standard deviation by 20 percent, for example, will increase the sample size by 44 percent. This practice is clearly unethical.

Furthermore, the researcher may be faced with ethical dilemmas when the sample standard deviation varies widely from that assumed. In this case, the confidence interval will be larger than required if the actual sample standard deviation turns out to be much larger than that used to estimate the sample size. If this happens, the researcher should disclose the larger confidence interval to the client and jointly arrive at a corrective action. The ethical ramifications of miscommunicating the confidence intervals of survey estimates based on statistical samples are underscored in the case of political polling.

EXAMPLE

SURVEYS SERVE UP ELECTIONS

The release of political polling results during an election has been strongly criticized as manipulative and unethical. Critics have claimed that the general public is mislead by these results. Polling results released before an election are thought to discourage voters from casting votes for candidates that are clearly trailing. Prediction of election results on election night has come under even harsher criticism. For example, in the 1996 elections polls by NBC and Associated Press had projected Clinton as the winner when polling was still open in several West Coast states. Opponents of this practice feel that this predisposes voters to vote for the projected winner or it may even discourage voter turnout if a race appears to be decided. Not only are the effects of such projections criticized, but frequently the accuracy of the projections is questionable as well. In the closely contested Bush versus Gore 2000 presidential election, some of the projections had to be reversed. Although voters may be told a candidate has a certain percentage of the votes within ±1 percent, the confidence interval may be much larger, depending on the sample size.[7]

INTERNET APPLICATIONS

The Internet has information on calculating the sample size or determining the margin of error for a given sample size. For electronic mail surveys, prior e-mails sent by the sponsor to announce the survey are strongly suggested by many of the Internet marketing research firms. These firms also send reminder e-mails to nonrespondents a few days after the initial survey has been sent. Another way to motivate respondents to complete electronic surveys is to tell them that the results will be used to enhance service. Another motivator is to provide incentives for completion of surveys, such as entry into cash drawings or points redeemable for merchandise. One of the biggest challenges in online research is the ability to generate a truly random sample that is representative of the target population. This is more problematic when conducting a consumer survey. However, in the case of business surveys, these sampling limitations can be overcome, as illustrated by DataWorld Research.

EXAMPLE

THE (DATA)WORLD OF SAMPLING FOR ONLINE RESEARCH

DataWorld Research Inc. (*www.surveys-online.com*) is a marketing firm specializing in online marketing research and surveying. Other services include diskette by mail surveys, traditional telephone surveys, and face-to-face interviews.

    The sample size for online surveys generally exceeds that determined by statistical methods. The reason for this is that the marginal cost of collecting and analyzing larger samples is low. Moreover, larger samples permit a more detailed level of analysis at the subgroup or segment level.

    DataWorld has developed an innovative way for clients to control respondent selection when conducting an online business-to-business survey. Through the use of an "alert postcard," which includes a respondent password, DataWorld can limit the distribution of the survey to a select group of respondents within the clients' target group. In essence, the firm has complete control over who will participate, which is normally difficult to achieve when conducting online surveys. This allows traditional sampling techniques to be implemented in the Internet environment. In addition to sample control, DataWorld provides incentives to respondents, such as printout of gift certificates or product give-aways, to improve the response rate.

SPSS

SamplePower by SPSS can be used to calculate confidence intervals and statistically adjust the sample size. The sample size calculations are available for means as well as proportions.

SUMMARY

The statistical approaches to determining sample size are based on confidence intervals. These approaches may involve the estimation of the mean or proportion. When estimating the mean or the proportion, determination of sample size using the confidence interval approach requires the specification of precision level, confidence level, and population standard deviation. The sample size determined statistically represents the final or net sample size that must be achieved. The initial sample size has to be much larger to account for incidence rates and completion rates in order to deliver the final sample size.

When measuring the quality of objective product characteristics, a much higher level of precision may be required as compared to measuring the consumers' quality perceptions. The statistical estimation of sample size is even more complicated in international marketing research as the population variance may differ from one country to the next. Several computer programs are available for statistically estimating the sample size and making adjustments for incidence and completion rates. The preliminary estimation of population variance for the purpose of determining the sample size also has ethical ramifications. While conducting online surveys, we can use larger samples and exercise high sampling control in business-to-business research.

KEY TERMS AND CONCEPTS

Normal distribution, 377
Parameter, 377
Statistic, 378
Precision level, 378
Confidence interval, 378
Confidence level, 378

Random sampling
  error, 378
Sampling
  distribution, 378
Statistical inference, 378

Standard error, 379
z value, 380
Incidence rate, 387
Completion rate, 387

ACRONYMS

The statistical considerations involved in determining the sample size may be summarized by the acronym SIZE:

S ampling distribution
I nterval (confidence)
Z value
E stimation of population standard deviation

EXERCISES

1. Define the *sampling distribution.*
2. What is the standard error of the mean?
3. Define a *confidence interval.*
4. What is the procedure for constructing a confidence interval around a mean?
5. How do the degree of confidence and the degree of precision differ?
6. Describe the procedure for determining the sample size necessary to estimate a population mean, given the degree of precision and confidence and a known population variance. After the sample is selected, how is the confidence interval generated?

7. Describe the procedure for determining the sample size necessary to estimate a population mean, when the degree of precision and confidence level are known but the population variance is unknown. After the sample is selected, how is the confidence interval generated?

8. How is the sample size affected when the absolute precision with which a population mean is estimated is doubled?

9. How is the sample size affected when the degree of confidence with which a population mean is estimated is increased from 95 percent to 99 percent?

10. Describe the procedure for determining the sample size necessary to estimate a population proportion given the degree of precision and confidence. After the sample is selected, how is the confidence interval generated?

11. How can the researcher ensure that the generated confidence interval will be no larger than the desired interval when estimating a population proportion?

PROBLEMS

1. Using Table 2 of the Appendix of Statistical Tables, calculate the probability that:
   a. z is less than 1.48.
   b. z is greater than 1.90.
   c. z is between 1.48 and 1.90.
   d. z is between -1.48 and 1.90.

2. What is the value of z if:
   a. 60% of all values of z are larger?
   b. 10% of all values of z are larger?
   c. 68.26% of all possible z values (symmetrically distributed around the mean) are to be contained in this interval?

3. The management of a local restaurant wants to determine the average monthly amount spent by households in fancy restaurants. Management wants to be 95 percent confident of the findings and does not want the error to exceed plus or minus $5.
   a. After the survey was conducted, the average expenditure was found to be $90.30 and the standard deviation was $45. Construct a 95 percent confidence interval.
   b. What sample size would have resulted in a standard deviation of $45?

4. To determine the effectiveness of the advertising campaign for a new VCR, management would like to know what percentage of the households are aware of the new brand. The advertising agency thinks that this figure is as high as 70 percent. The management would like a 95 percent confidence interval and a margin of error no greater than ±2 percent.
   a. What sample size should be used for this study?
   b. Suppose that management wanted to be 99 percent confident but could tolerate an error of ±3 percent. How would the sample size change?

5. Assuming that $n = 100$ and $\sigma = 5$, compute the standard error of the mean.

INTERNET AND COMPUTER EXERCISES

1. Using a spreadsheet (e.g., EXCEL), program the formulas for determining the sample size under the various approaches.

2. Solve problems 3 through 5, using the programs that you have developed.

3. Visit the Gallup organization Web site *(www.gallup.com)*. Identify some of the surveys recently completed by the Gallup organization. What were the sample sizes and how were they determined in these surveys.

ACTIVITIES

ROLE PLAYING

1. You work in the marketing research department of a large fast-food chain. The chain has developed a new cooking process that makes the hamburgers taste better. However, before the new hamburger is introduced in the market, taste tests will be conducted. How should the sample size for these taste tests be determined? What approach would you recommend? Justify your recommendations to a group of students representing the chain's management.

2. A major electric utility would like to determine the average amount spent per household for cooling during the summer. The management believes that a survey should be conducted. You are appointed as a consultant. What procedure would you recommend for determining the sample size? Make a presentation about this project to three students who represent the chief operating officer, chief financial officer, and the chief marketing officer of this utility.

FIELD WORK

1. Visit a local marketing research firm. Find out how the sample sizes were determined in several recent surveys or experiments. Write a report about your findings.

GROUP DISCUSSION

1. "Quantitative considerations are more important than qualitative considerations in determining the sample size." Discuss as a small group. Alternatively, split a group into two smaller subgroups. One subgroup develops arguments for this statement, the other against.

2. Discuss the various options available for estimating incidence rates.

NOTES

1. Based on M. Shoukri and M. Demirkaya, "Sample Size Requirements to Test the Equality of Rater's Precision," *Journal of Applied Statistics,* 27(4) (May 2000): 483–494; Phillip E. Pfeifer, "The economic selection of sample sizes for list testing," *Journal of Interactive Marketing,* 12(3) (Summer 1998): 5–20; and "The 'Infocritical' Eye," *Marketing Research: A Magazine of Management & Applications,* 9(1) (Spring 1997): 37–39.

2. A discussion of the sampling distribution may be found in any basic statistics textbook. For example, see Mark L. Berenson and David M. Levine, *Basic Business Statistics: Concepts and Applications,* 7th ed. (Upper Saddle River, NJ: Prentice Hall, 1999).

3. "ACSI to Measure Customer Satisfaction for Government Agencies," *Quality Progress,* 32(8) (August 1999): 14; and Barbara Everitt Bryant and Jaesung Cha, "Crossing the Threshold: Some Customers Are Harder to Please Than Others, so Analyze Satisfaction Scores Carefully," *Marketing Research: A Magazine of Management & Applications,* 8(4) (Winter 1996): 21–28.

4. Based on Alexandra Jardine, "L'Oreal Puts Brands Under One Roof," *Marketing* (May 27, 1999): 4; "Edison, American Marketing Association, Best New Product Awards," *Marketing News,* 31(6) (March 17, 1997): E6.

5. Based on Kathleen Sampey, "Tommy Ads Tout Americana," *Adweek,* 41(28) (July 10, 2000): 4; Mercedes Cardona, "Hilfiger's New Apparel Lines Getting Individual Ad Efforts," *Advertising Age,* 70(6) (February 8, 1999): 24; and Gordon Cohen, "Hartmarx Embraces Change," *Industry Magazine,* 56(5) (May 1995): 98.

6. Terry Kosdrosky, "Carriers Scramble for China," *Crain's Detroit Business,* 16(10) (March 6, 2000): 1–2; Kristin S. Krause, "China Airlines' Big Buy," *Traffic World,* 259(7) (August 16, 1999): 37; and "Another Chinese Take-off," *The Economist* (December 19, 1992).

7. Nick Panagakis and Warren Mitofsky, "The Polls—Response: Response to 'Was 1996 a Worse Year for Polls than 1948?'" *Public Opinion Quarterly,* 63(2) (Summer 1999): 276–284; and Vicki G. Morwitz and Carol Pluzinski, "Do Polls Reflect Opinions or Do Opinions Reflect Polls? The Impact of Political Polling on Voters' Expectations, Preferences, and Behavior," *Journal of Consumer Research,* 23(1) (June 1996): 53–67.

APPENDIX 13A

THE NORMAL DISTRIBUTION

In this appendix, we provide a brief overview of the normal distribution and the use of the normal distribution table. The normal distribution is used in calculating the sample size, and it serves as the basis for classical statistical inference. Many continuous phenomena follow the normal distribution or can be approximated by it. The normal distribution can, likewise, be used to approximate many discrete probability distributions.[1]

The normal distribution has some important theoretical properties. It is bell-shaped and symmetrical in appearance. Its measures of central tendency (mean, median, and mode) are all identical. Its associated random variable has an infinite range ($-\infty < x < +\infty$).

The normal distribution is defined by the population mean μ and population standard deviation σ. Since an infinite number of combinations of μ and σ exist, an infinite number of normal distributions exist and an infinite number of tables would be required. However, by standardizing the data, we need only one table, such as Table 2 given in the Appendix of Statistical Tables. Standardization is the process of rescaling data to have a mean of 0 and a standard deviation of 1. Any normal random variable X can be converted to a standardized normal random variable z by the formula:

$$z = \frac{X - \mu}{\sigma}$$

Note that the random variable z is always normally distributed with a mean of 0 and a standard deviation of 1. The normal probability tables are generally used for two purposes: (1) finding probabilities corresponding to known values of X or z, and (2) finding values of X or z corresponding to known probabilities. We will discuss each of these uses.

FINDING PROBABILITIES CORRESPONDING TO KNOWN VALUES

Suppose Figure 13A.1 represents the distribution of the number of engineering contracts an engineering firm receives per year. Since the data span the entire history of the firm, Figure 13A.1 represents the population. Therefore, the probabilities or proportion of area under the curve must add up to 1.0. The vice president of marketing wishes to determine the probability that the number of contracts received next year will be between 50 and 55. The answer can be determined by using Table 2 in the Appendix of Statistical Tables.

Table 2 gives the probability or area under the standardized normal curve from the mean (zero) to the standardized value of interest, z. Only positive entries of z are listed in the table. For a symmetrical distribution with zero mean, the area from the mean to $+z$ (that is, z standard deviations above the mean) is identical to the area from the mean to $-z$ (z standard deviations below the mean).

Note that the difference between 50 and 55 ($= 5$) corresponds to a difference in z values of 1.00 ($= 1.00 - 0.00$). Note that to use Table 2, all z values must be recorded to two decimal places. To read the probability or area under the curve from the mean to $z = +1.00$, scan down the z column of Table 2 until the z value of interest (in tenths) is located. In this case, stop in the row $z = 1.00$. Then, read across this row until you intersect the column containing the hundredth place of the z value. Thus, in Table 2, the tabulated probability for $z = 1.00$ corresponds to the intersection of the row $z = 1.0$ with the column $z = .00$. This probability is 0.3413 (or 34.135). As shown in Figure 13A.1, the probability is 0.3413 that the number of contracts received by the firm next

FIGURE 13A.1
Finding Probabilities
Corresponding to Known
Values

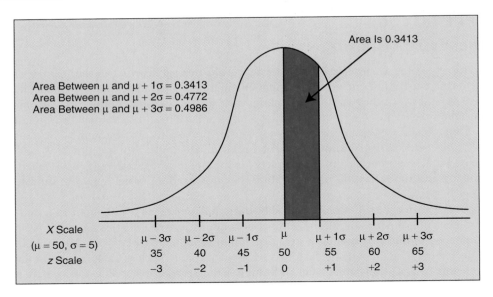

Area Between μ and μ + 1σ = 0.3413
Area Between μ and μ + 2σ = 0.4772
Area Between μ and μ + 3σ = 0.4986

Area Is 0.3413

X Scale ($\mu = 50$, $\sigma = 5$)	$\mu - 3\sigma$	$\mu - 2\sigma$	$\mu - 1\sigma$	μ	$\mu + 1\sigma$	$\mu + 2\sigma$	$\mu + 3\sigma$
	35	40	45	50	55	60	65
z Scale	−3	−2	−1	0	+1	+2	+3

year will be between 50 and 55. It can also be concluded that the probability is 0.6826 (2×0.3413) or 68.26 percent that the number of contracts received next year will be between 45 and 55.

This result could be generalized to show that for any normal distribution, the probability is 0.6826 that a randomly selected item will fall within ±1 standard deviations above or below the mean. Also, it can be verified from Table 2 that there is a 0.9544 probability that any randomly selected normally distributed observation will fall within ±2 standard deviations above or below the mean; and a 0.9973 probability that the observation will fall within ±3 standard deviations above or below the mean.

FINDING VALUES CORRESPONDING TO KNOWN PROBABILITIES

Suppose the vice president of marketing wishes to determine how many contracts must come in so that they represent 5 percent of the contracts expected for the year. If 5 percent of the contracts have come in, 95 percent of the contracts have yet to come. As shown in Figure 13A.2, this 95 percent can be broken down into two parts: contracts above the mean (that is, 50 percent) and contracts between the mean and the desired z value (that is, 45 percent). The desired z value can be determined from Table 2 since the area under the normal curve from the standardized mean, 0, to this z must be 0.4500. From Table 2, we search for the area or probability 0.4500. The closest value is 0.4495 or 0.4505. For 0.4495, we see that the z value corresponding to the particular z row (1.6) and z column (.04) is 1.64. However, the z value must be recorded as negative (that is, $z = -1.64$) since it is below the standardized mean of 0. Similarly, the z value corresponding to the area of .4505 is −1.65. Since .4500 is midway between .4495 and .4505, the appropriate z value could be midway between the two z values and estimated as −1.645. The corresponding X value can then be calculated from the standardization formula, as follows:

$$X = \mu + z\sigma$$

or

$$X = 50 + (-1.645)\,5 = 41.775$$

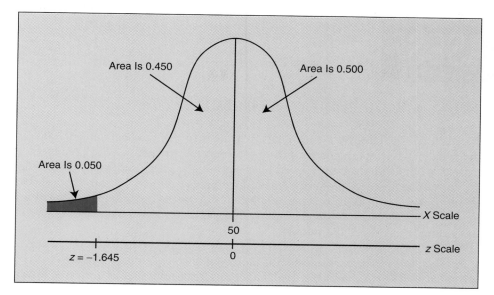

FIGURE 13A.2
Finding Values
Corresponding to Known
Probabilities

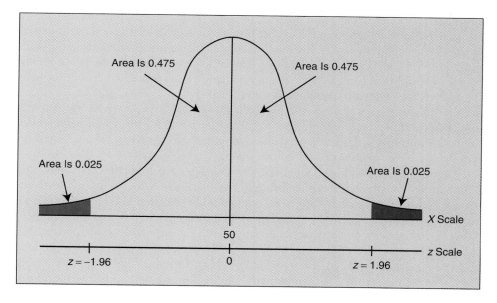

FIGURE 13A.3
Finding Values
Corresponding to Known
Probabilities: Confidence
Interval

Suppose the vice president wanted to determine the interval in which 95 percent of the contracts for next year are expected to lie. As can be seen from Figure 13A.3, the corresponding z values are ± 1.96. This corresponds to X values of $50 \pm (1.96)$ 5, or 40.2 and 59.8. This range represents the 95 percent confidence interval.

NOTE

1. This material is drawn from Mark L. Berenson and David M. Levine, *Basic Business Statistics: Concepts and Applications,* 7th ed. (Upper Saddle River, NJ: Prentice Hall, 1999).

CASES

CASE 2.1 ■ MAXFLI: GOING FOR THE LONG BALL

For decades, Maxfli has been one of the top names in quality golf equipment. A division of the international sports company Dunlop Slazenger Corporation, Maxfli produces golf balls, clubs, and other golf accessories. In its early stages, Maxfli's approach to the industry was similar to others: produce good products marketed through the traditional channels (pro shops, golf specialty stores, and using PGA professionals to market their products). This was a standard formula, but one that was challenged in the 1990s as more and more companies entered the industry.

By 1998, Maxfli Golf discovered that its growth in market share dropped below par. It lost sight of its target markets and the understanding of what people in those markets needed. Maxfli began conducting exploratory research because it was unclear as to what direction to steer the company.

Maxfli began exploratory research by conducting focus groups to uncover the motivations behind golf ball purchases. They wanted to understand how consumers identified golf balls (by brand name, manufacturer, or some unique identifier). The focus group research indicated that every golf ball needs an identifier. This identifier allows one golfer to tell another about the type of golf balls they use. The ability to do this is important to most golfers. "This signaled to us that we needed to not only get the Maxfli brand into people's minds but also to give them the nomenclature hook that allows them to be inside the games," Rooke, Maxfli's head of marketing, explains.

The focus groups also revealed that golf was as much a mental challenge as it was a physical one. Therefore, Maxfli's goal became to quiet that little voice inside golfer's heads. They wanted to figure out what types of products golfers were looking for and present them in a way that eased their state of mind.

Following the focus groups, in order to research deeper, Maxfli conducted a telephone survey. Maxfli used a market facts national panel as a cost-effective means to generate a representative sample of golfers who could be accessed via the telephone. The sample was then stratified by purchase points, where they played golf, and other variables. There are several different types of golfers, and each category had to be represented for the findings to be meaningful and conclusive. "The research showed that while many golfers were quality oriented, there was an even bigger segment that could be called the fashion crowd of golf." Maxfli then wanted to find out if its brand fit the needs of the so-called "fashion crowd."

Based on the research findings, Maxfli determined that it should offer all levels of golf balls and position its product with a youthful attitude. Each ball had its own identity so that it could be discussed among golfers. In golf, "the ball you choose says a lot about you." Maxfli used exploratory and descriptive research in the form of a telephone survey to make sure its line of golf balls met consumer needs.

For Maxfli, creating products that met consumer needs is the first step in maintaining itself as one of the leaders in the golf industry. To that end, Maxfli became an industry leader in forging relationships with companies outside the golf industry to create cross promotions and premium incentive activities. Maxfli is continually looking for the edge that will pull customers to their products.

A recent example of this is Dunlop/Maxfli's tie-in with the 1999 special edition release of the classic golf movie *Caddyshack*. A $500,000 print campaign in *Sports Illustrated, Golf,* and *People* magazines pushed the video and its tie to Dunlop's Precision and Titanium balls. They hoped to reap the same rewards received by Taylor Made when their equipment glistened on the silver screen in the recent movie *Tin Cup*. Obviously, not all co-promotions have been limited to film. Maxfli previously had successful cross-promotional relationships with both General Motors and Delta Airlines. More recently, Dunlop established frequent-purchase points redeemable for Greg Norman Collection merchandise for buyers of Shark Attack balls, and the Maxfli brand had several "gift with purchase" lures such as embroidered hats, golf tools, and the like.

Not every company in the industry joined in on the new approach. In fact, the list remains relatively short. Aside from the two previously mentioned companies, only Wilson, Callaway, and Nicklaus Golf have created cross relationships in recent years. Maxfli has been successful at solidifying their place in the market through good consumer research and creative marketing approaches.

Questions

1. What was the research design adopted by Maxfli in determining a direction for the company?

2. Discuss the role of qualitative research in uncovering the motivations behind golf ball purchases. Are focus groups the most appropriate technique for this purpose?

3. Is a telephone survey the most appropriate method for determining the preferences of golfers for golf balls? If not, what survey method would you recommend for this purpose?

4. Discuss the role of the Internet in locating information about golf.

References

1. Chuck Stogel, "Golf Biz Needs to Go Off-Course," *Brandweek*, 7(40) (February 15, 1999): 24.
2. Mike Beirne, "All Fired Up and Going for the Long Ball," *Brandweek*, 29(41) (July 17, 2000): 75.
3. Chuck Stogel, "Maxfli Takes Aim at Unmet Needs; Hot Gray Market Prompts Responses," *Brandweek*, 7(41) (February 14, 2000): 14.

CASE 2.2 ■ KELLOGG'S: DANCING WITH THE MOUSE

Kellogg's Company manufactures and markets ready-to-eat cereal and convenience food products worldwide. These products are manufactured in 20 countries and distributed in more than 160 countries around the world. The company's products are generally marketed under the Kellogg's and Morningstar Farms names, and are sold principally to the grocery trade through direct sales forces for resale to consumers. Kellogg's sales for ready-to-eat cereal dropped, while the sales of its closest competitor, General Mills, increased in the late 1990s. This forced Kellogg's to look for different avenues to market its products. In 2000, Kellogg's launched a $20 million promotional deal with Walt Disney. Kellogg's began marketing its cereals with free Disney "mini-bean" toys, as well as Walt Disney sweepstakes.

Kellogg's was very excited about this newly formed alliance with Walt Disney. It was the first company that Disney allowed to manufacture its characters in plush form. More than 80 million boxes of Kellogg's cereal contained one of these plush Disney characters.

Other Kellogg's products also offered Walt Disney vacation sweepstakes. Kellogg's expected this promotion to increase overall sales of its products. "Everyone knows and loves Disney characters," said Credit Suisse First Boston analyst, David Nelson.

Despite this enthusiastic approach, many analysts were worried about Kellogg's poor track record when it came to large promotions. This apprehensive attitude was especially illustrated by one midwestern grocery executive who stated, "Kellogg's is in such a state of screw-up that I don't know whether I'll be able to support the Disney program, because they'll likely botch it somehow. If they could execute the program, it could help them. But they don't have enough people, and they don't have the right people." In an effort to pump up grocery retailers, Kellogg's offered a $4,000 grand prize and a $2,000 first prize to those retailers who put out the most creative Disney displays in their place of business.

Kellogg's felt that the new Disney promotion would be a booming success and would help lift its decreased cereal sales. It was possible that Kellogg's could achieve success in this promotion, steal back market share from other competitors, and regain its number one reputation.

Questions

1. What kind of research design should Kellogg's adopt in order to determine consumer preferences for Kellogg's cereals versus General Mills brands?

2. What types of syndicated data would be useful in determining consumers' consumption of different cereal brands?

3. Kellogg's has developed three versions of a new commercial for its Product 19 cereal brand. It wants to determine which commercial will lead to the greatest sales of Product 19. What research should Kellogg's undertake?

4. Kellogg's has developed a new cereal brand and would like to determine consumers' preferences for it before deciding whether it should be marketed nationally. If a survey is to be conducted, which survey method would you recommend and why?

5. Develop a sampling plan for the survey of question 4.

Reference

1. Stephanie Thompson, "Kellogg's, Disney Link for Promo," *Advertising Age*, 71(43) (October 26, 2000): 4, 80.

CASE 2.3 ■ RESEARCH PROMPTS HCA-HEALTHCARE TO REEVALUATE ITS INTERNET FOCUS

HCA-Healthcare Corporation, formerly known as Columbia-HCA Healthcare Corp., is the largest U.S. hospital chain. HCA owns and operates approximately 200 hospitals and other health care facilities in 24 states, England, and Switzerland. HCA's Internet site was created in May 1995 as a channel to promote the company and its health care information. It averaged 400 hits per month the first few months it was online. However, a change in the company's Internet focus increased the figure to more than 500,000 hits per week by the summer of 1997.

The change in focus was spurred by secondary research initiatives conducted to determine the demand for information over the Internet. For example, a study by FIND/SVP using focus groups, Internet users, and a national telephone survey revealed that health care information was the seventh largest category of information requested by Internet users. FIND/SVP is a consulting and research company that produces more than 140 syndicated research reports annually. Organizations in the health care industry can access studies like these from FIND/SVP, order market and industry studies done by FIND/SVP, or order customized research.

Based on the information in an Internet survey that FIND/SVP did soon after HCA set up its home page, HCA saw the opportunity to be more than just an advertising or messaging site. The company reevaluated its Internet strategy and decided to create a health information resource with a focus on the Internet user's health information needs.

Users of the Web site include patients, consumers, physicians, vendors, employers, and clinicians. The site allows HCA to provide high-quality interactive content for the users. This interaction is in line with the organization's mission to provide a continuum of cost-effective, high-quality health care. The HCA homepage includes interactive opportunities, information about the organization, contests and games, announcements of special programs and events, gifts and products such as flowers that users can order, information on the latest medical research, health tips, e-mail links for comments and questions, and a survey that users can complete concerning their information needs.

E-mail and surveys are means of ongoing data collection. Tracking and measurement of the Web site provide additional data related to hits, time of day, day of week, domains seeking access, and so on. This information allows HCA to offer online products and services targeted and customized to users. By researching and responding to market needs, HCA has been able to expand its original Internet project into a national information resource.

In May 2000, Columbia Healthcare Corporation announced that the company was officially changing its name to HCA-The Healthcare Company. The new name reflects a return to the values that are the foundation of the current company. Putting patients first, focusing on local hospitals, and creating a mission and values statement based on input from across the company are all hallmarks of the culture the company has been recreating since 1997. "Returning the company's name to HCA is an affirmation of the culture and values of our more than 168,000 employees," said Thomas F. Frist, Jr., MD, chairman and chief executive officer of HCA. "We have restructured this company based on the principles on which the company was originally founded and our name reflects that change." However, the company's reliance on marketing research has not changed. Marketing research will continue to be HCA's guiding light in the years to come.

Questions

1. What data can HCA collect from visitors to its Web site?
2. Are surveys posted to an Internet Web site, such as HCA's related to consumers' health care needs? Why or why not?
3. Devise the following scales to measure users' overall satisfaction with the health care services provided by HCA:
   a. Likert scale
   b. Semantic Differential scale
   c. Stapel scale
   d. Binary or Dichotomous scale

4. Discuss the sampling problems associated with recruiting visitors to HCA's Web site as respondents to a health care survey.

References

1. Tod Fetherling, "Columbia: Sitting an Online Opportunity," *Marketing Health Services,* 17(2) (Summer 1997): 40–44.
2. *http://www.hcahealthcare.com.*
3. *http://www.findsvp.com.*
4. *http://etrg.findsvp.com.*

CASE 2.4 ■ TRUE COLORS BEHIND MANY COMPANY REPUTATIONS

During fall 2000, Harris Interactive, Inc., conducted an Internet-based marketing research survey, which rated the reputations of many corporate companies. Throughout the United States, random subjects were chosen from the company's 7 million-person database, to participate in the study. Harris conducted thousands of online and telephone interviews to find pertinent information on the reputations of many well-known companies.

In order to thoroughly study company reputations, the study consisted of two phases: nominations and ratings. During the nominations phase, 4,651 online interviews and 1,010 telephone interviews were conducted in the United States. Survey participants were asked to nominate two companies with the best overall reputations and two companies with the worst overall reputations. The objective of the Harris survey was to study companies that operate nationally and report financial results. Therefore, many telecommunications service providers, media companies, and wholly owned subsidiaries were excluded. From all the nominations reported, Harris generated a list of 45 companies that participants reported most frequently.

During the second phase of this study, 26,011 online participants were randomly selected to give a detailed rating on one or more companies. Respondents were asked to rate a company based on six categories that included 20 attributes. The major categories included financial performance, products and services, emotional appeal, vision and leadership, social responsibility, and workplace environment. Each company was rated on each attribute using a five-point scale, with 1 = poor, and 5 = excellent.

From all the major categories, the study revealed that many people based their ratings on emotional appeal, which included attributes such as respect, trust, admiration, and a general good feeling. Findings showed that stock price performance did not affect the ratings of a company. Furthermore, the reputation ratings of technology companies dropped, while many older and more traditional companies' reputations increased significantly. For example, Procter & Gamble Company, General Motors Corporation, and Sony Corporation all increased their rankings by nearly 50 percent.

To ultimately determine a company's rank, Harris computed a "reputation quotient." A company's reputation quotient was calculated based on the participant's ratings of 20 attributes found in the six major categories. A score of 100 was the highest score possible. When comparing two reputation quotients, a 1.96 difference was considered significantly different at the 90 percent confidence interval.

The following table illustrates the companies that received the highest ratings in each category:

Rank	Emotional Appeal	Products and Services	Workplace Environment	Social Responsibility	Vision and Leadership	Financial Performance
1	Johnson & Johnson	Johnson & Johnson	Anheuser-Busch	Home Depot	Microsoft	Microsoft
2	Sony	Sony	Johnson & Johnson	Johnson & Johnson	Anheuser-Busch	Maytag
3	Home Depot	Maytag	Maytag	Daimler-Chrysler	Disney	Anheuser-Busch
4	FedEx	Intel	Home Depot	Anheuser-Busch	Intel	Disney
5	Intel	Home Depot	IBM	McDonald's	Maytag	Sony

In general, the corporate company reputation study concluded that, "No news was good news" when dealing with company reputations. Of the companies that were ranked the lowest, participants remembered hearing about them through the news and media last year. In 1999, Phillip Morris held the title of the worst rated company. However, for year 2000, Bridgestone/Firestone held that title. Bridgestone/Firestone had a huge tire recall due to its tire failures, which resulted in many serious auto accidents. Many marketing experts said this company would never fully recover their reputation.

Questions

1. How do you think the six categories and 20 attributes used to measure company reputation were identified?
2. Is an Internet survey appropriate for measuring the reputation of companies? Why or why not?
3. The scale ranking the companies represents what type of measurement level?
4. Each company was rated on each attribute using what type of scale? What was the measurement level of the resulting data?

Reference

1. Ronald Alsop, "Survey Rates Companies' Reputations, and Many Are Found Wanting," *Wall Street Journal* (February 7, 2001): B1.

CASE 2.5 ■ UNITED STATES POSTAL SERVICE: DOES ITS SERVICE MEASURE UP?

The United States Postal Service (USPS) has been delivering mail for its customers for over 200 hundred years. Throughout our nation's history, the USPS has helped to bind our nation together, support the growth of commerce, and ensure the free flow of ideas and information. Today, the Postal Service delivers hundreds of millions of messages and billions of dollars in financial transactions each day to 10 million businesses and more than 250 million Americans.

Despite the Postal Service's excellent history, the marketplace's competitive forces have recently started to attack its once solid monopoly, specifically in the growing market for parcel delivery. The overnight delivery giants of Federal Express (FedEx) and United Parcel Service (UPS) have developed into market leaders in terms of customer service. In order to meet the challenge, the USPS has been forced to reexamine its approach to customer service.

During the summer of 1998, the USPS engaged in numerous marketing research efforts, one of which was a series of focus groups with the objective of better understanding parcel customers' requirements. The focus groups were composed of both USPS parcel customers and noncustomers.

Ten-member groups were formed for two-hour sessions. The respondents knew that the focus group was being conducted by the USPS and were therefore blunt in their criticisms. The focus groups brought forth many issues. Most participants rated the private carriers' parcel delivery service well above the USPS's, but conceded that their costs were much higher. The Postal Service's image was stated as being a primary problem. Respondents felt that service with UPS and FedEx was superior.

Respondents stated that a key factor leading to this perception was the Postal Service's inability to provide exact delivery times. The two- to three-day nonguaranteed delivery window that the USPS provided was not enough for most of the participants. Most customers wanted to know exactly when their packages were going to arrive and guaranteeing that time was critical. Another factor leading to the image problem was the USPS's inability to provide timely information about the status of a particular package. Both FedEx and UPS provide a track and trace system that allows a customer to know exactly where a package is from the time it is picked up to the point of delivery.

The USPS was particularly concerned with the latter of these two issues because it was preparing to launch its own information service. Their new system provides delivery confirmation for its Priority Mail service, but does not provide track and trace capability. Most respondents had not heard of the new system and when it was explained to them, the majority agreed that they still preferred the systems provided by FedEx and UPS.

The information provided by the focus group allowed the USPS to create some valuable benchmarks for their customer service. It was clear that the Postal Service had significant ground to cover in order to catch up with the corporate giants. The obvious issues unearthed were the USPS's inability to provide a guaranteed delivery schedule and timely information about the status of a particular package. Perhaps, more importantly, the Postal Service learned that there was little customer awareness about its attempts at improving its services. Furthermore, what little information customers have is overshadowed by the negative image of the USPS.

Thus, research made it clear that USPS's service did not measure up to consumer expectations. Significant improvements had to be made if the USPS expected to compete with FedEx and UPS for parcel delivery in the twenty-first century.

Questions

1. Conduct an Internet search to obtain data on the volume and breakdown of parcel delivery (e.g., ground parcel, expedited parcel).

2. Were the focus groups conducted by the USPS appropriate? Would you use any projective techniques? If so, which projective techniques would you use and why?

3. A survey of catalog marketers must be conducted to determine their usage of parcel delivery services. Please answer the following questions:

   a. Which type of survey method should be used and why?

b. What type of scales would be most appropriate to measure the image of the USPS, FedEx, UPS, and other major parcel delivery service providers?

c. Design a questionnaire to measure the image of the USPS, FedEx, and UPS.

d. What sampling technique should be used to select the respondents for the survey?

References

1. Paul Miller, "Focus Group Scolds USPS," *Catalog Age,* 15 (1998): 7.

2. Peter Bradley, Jim Thomas, Toby Gooley, and James Cooke, "Postal Service to Unveil Delivery Confirmation," *Logistics Management & Distribution Report,* 38(2) (February 1999): 23–24.

3. Paul Miller, "The Future of Parcel Shipping," *Catalog Age,* 15(7) (June 1998): 163–164.

4. *http://www.usps.gov/history/his1.htm,* "History of the United States Postal Service."

5. Robert J. Posch, Jr., "Strategic Opportunities for the 'Industry' and USPS," *Direct Marketing,* 63(3): 23.

6. Anonymous, "USPS Takes Two Awards," *Traffic World,* 262(12): 23.

CASE 2.6 ■ BLOOMINGDALE'S: INVITING THE BLOOM INTO THE STORE

Federated Department Stores operates full-line department stores under the names Macy's, Rich's, Lazarus, Goldsmith's, Bloomingdale's, Burdines, and The Bon Marché. The company operates more than 400 department stores in 33 states and sells a wide range of merchandise including men's, women's, and children's apparel and accessories, cosmetics, home furnishings, and other consumer goods. The company also operates direct-mail catalog businesses under the names Bloomingdale's By Mail and Macy's By Mail and an electronic commerce business that provides goods and services online under the name macys.com.

It is no secret that marketing emphasis should focus on satisfying customers' needs, but it is important to note that when it comes to customers, wants are considered needs. This is exactly why it is vital to the success of any business today to research and find out precisely what customers want. Bloomingdale's took these issues to heart when it developed its new customer-friendly design philosophy.

As part of the new philosophy, when planning the design of its new department store in Miami, Florida, Bloomingdale's looked to its focus groups for input on the needs of customers. The focus groups revealed that the most frequent complaint focuses on the lack of lighting in Bloomingdale's department stores. The groups also brought to the design committee's attention the potential benefit of having natural light and artificial light in the store. Their claim was that when buying clothing it is very beneficial to be able to see what the articles of clothing will look like in both types of lighting because different lighting can affect the way colors look.

The design committee took the suggestions of the focus groups into consideration and designed the new Miami location accordingly. This was accomplished through the use of a 220-foot façade made entirely out of glass. The glass is covered by a steel screen for protection, complying with the building codes of the area. Fortunately, the light gets through the metal because it is cloven and is therefore effective in letting light through the glass dome. As explained by architect Kevin Kennon, "The perforations are very small, like fine sieve, and create a sense of transparency so that light can penetrate into the building." Not only does the steel screen protect the glass, but it also combats the glare from the southern sun, which protects the clothes from sun damage and creates a more efficient cooling environment.

Because the steel screen was required, artificial light was also necessary. This was not a setback since focus groups suggested both types of light. The control of the steel screen allowed the two types of lighting to blend. The final product was excellent. The glass windows and façade more than doubled the lighting of the other Bloomingdale's department stores, and the design committee was thrilled with the results. In fact, Creative Director Michael Wilkins said, "It's the first new Bloomingdale's designed store so that the introduction of natural light represents a logical progression for the customer from the outside into the store environment."

It is vital for businesses today to keep their customers' interests close in mind in almost every aspect of the business. Bloomingdale's took a big step forward by establishing the new customer-friendly design philosophy. By using the input of focus groups, the department store was able to address a problem it has faced for years: bad lighting. With the new design, Bloomingdale's created a user-friendly environment, inviting the bloom into the store.

Questions

1. Was Bloomingdale's correct in making changes in the store architecture and design based solely on the findings of focus groups? If not, what type of research design should have been adopted?

2. Identify possible sources of secondary data for information on department store sales.

3. What type of information available from syndicated firms would be useful for understanding consumer preferences for department stores?

4. Discuss the role of projective techniques in understanding consumers' preference for department stores.

5. If a survey is to be conducted for determining consumer preferences for department stores, which survey method should be used and why?

6. Design a questionnaire to determine consumer preferences and evaluations of the various department store chains operated by Federal Department Stores as mentioned in this case.

7. Given the survey method you have selected in question 5, what sampling technique should be used and why? Would a sample size of 500 be appropriate? Why or why not?

References

1. Sharan Barnett and Frank Barnett, "Bloomingdale's Embraces One-to-One Marketing Opportunities," *Direct Marketing*, 61(9) (January 1999): 24–27.
2. Peter Girard, "Bloomie's Takes Trends to the Market," *Catalog Age*, 17(6) (May 2000): 16.

CASE 2.7 ■ CAN THE CADDIE MAKE A COMEBACK?

At one time, the Cadillac was the ultimate representation of American affluence and success. Unfortunately for General Motors, Cadillac's customer base is aging. With the aging of its customer base, Cadillac sales are slipping. Record sales of over 350,000 Cadillacs in 1978 slipped to just 155,000 cars in 1999. Even though total sales easily outnumbered that of Lexus, Mercedes, or BMW, the sales trends for these competing models are improving.

The average age of a Cadillac buyer is 64. The average age of the entry-level luxury car owner, someone who is first buying an upscale car with a starting price of approximately $30,000, is 46. Cadillac is traditionally not an entry-level automobile.

One reason Cadillac has faltered is because it can't make cars that appeal to anyone under 60. When drivers think Cadillac, they inevitably think "old," not "with it." In order to combat the loss of the Cadillac division, GM is trying to attract younger buyers, including women and minorities. One effort to do this is focused on producing smaller, sleeker cars, but this effort must be tailored so as not to alienate the established customers. The first efforts set forth to attract a younger clientele failed miserably with the introduction of the Cadillac Cimarron. In order to prevent a repeat of this, Cadillac hired 35-year-old Joe Kennedy as general director of marketing and product planning.

Kennedy's new plans formally began when Cadillac unveiled the Catera, a small (by Cadillac standards) luxury car. The Catera is a clone of the European Opel Omega MV6, which is produced by GM's Adam Opel AG unit. The Catera is priced as an entry-level luxury car, ranging between $30,000 and $40,000. With the Catera, Cadillac hoped to build a new identity. Even the name, Catera, which was coined by a GM employee, is new.

Cadillac attempted to emphasize the benefits of the vehicle itself, rather than focus on the name of Cadillac alone. Once the car is established, GM hopes to more closely associate it with Cadillac. The difference between the Cimarron and the Catera is that the Catera is based on a luxury model, whereas the Cimarron was basically an upscaled pedestrian car. Even so, the success of Cadillac may be a thing of the past. In its heyday, Cadillac stood for the American Dream.

Cadillac also attempted to enter the sports utility vehicle (SUV) market with the introduction of the Escalade, which costs $46,000. But many SUV drivers will not be in the market for an Escalade because they "can't justify spending that much" when "it's basically a (GMC Yukon) Denali," according to Todd Kaluzny, a 27-year-old assistant prosecutor in Oakland County, Michigan. "It's a lot cheaper to get a Denali."

The decline of the Cadillac can be directly linked to two incidents in the past. The first is the oil embargo of the early 1970s. As gas prices rose, the Cadillac became less and less popular with cost-conscious consumers. The small car became king, and the large car out of vogue. The real blow came, though, in 1981. U.S. automakers persuaded the U.S. government to limit the number of vehicles Japan could sell in the United States. The result was that Japan shifted exports to the United States from low-cost models to higher-profit, higher-cost luxury models. The invasion of the Japanese luxury car had begun. Additionally, BMW became the symbol for yuppie success during the 1980s, causing Cadillac's market share to dip from 32.3 percent in 1978 to 16.5 percent in 1999.

One reason for Cadillac's slide is that during the 1960s and 1970s there was little direct foreign competition. As small cars became popular, GM failed to respond to these changing values. Meanwhile, younger customers were enticed by the sleek engineering of the European luxury cars and the new Japanese models. Luxury brands such as Mercedes and BMW started at the high side and used their success to spin off smaller, less expensive models. They had a distinct advantage: just one brand to carry the flag. Cadillac's problem is that it has too many brothers and sisters. If Cadillac did that, it would rob from Buick and Pontiac. One point still in GM's favor is that customer satisfaction for new Cadillacs is very high. Cadillac consistently scores high marks for quality and power.

The goal of GM is to reincarnate the Cadillac division by tearing it down and rebuilding it. Additionally, Cadillac plans to make its cars even more luxurious, hoping to rival top-of-the-line Mercedes models. Cadillac also plans on exporting more cars to European and Japanese markets. There is also a push to gain more sales in the women's market. Currently, Cadillac sells 30 percent of its cars to women, but it hopes to get that figure up to at least 37 percent. To this end, Cadillac is more actively targeting the female consumer in its advertising and marketing. In addition, Cadillac is employing more top-level female executives in the development of new models. Women want smaller cars with more safety devices and more comfortable interiors.

While doubts remain about the Cadillac division, the future of GM looks bright. GM recorded net sales and revenues of $176.6 billion in calendar year 1999, an increase of 13.6 percent over 1998's $155.4 billion. Income totaled $5.6 billion in 1999 compared with $3.0 billion in 1998. GM Automotive's net margin was 3.2 percent in 1999 compared to 1.8 percent for 1998.

Questions

1. Identify the management decision problem facing Cadillac.
2. Define the marketing research problem.
3. Identify sources of secondary data for luxury cars.
4. For each year from 1996 to 2001, search the Internet to determine what is the total number of cars sold by Cadillac, Lincoln, Lexus, Mercedes, and BMW? Do you discover any trends?
5. What role can qualitative research play in helping Cadillac revive its sales and market share? Which qualitative research techniques would you recommend and why?
6. If a survey is to be conducted to determine consumer preferences for luxury cars, which survey method should be used and why?
7. What role can observation methods play in helping Cadillac redesign its models? Which observation method, if any, should be used?
8. Would you use the Likert, semantic differential, or Stapel scale to obtain consumers' evaluations of Cadillac and competing brands on important attributes?
9. Design a questionnaire to obtain consumers' evaluations of Cadillac and competing brands on important attributes.
10. What sampling technique should be used to select survey respondents?

References

1. www.generalmotors.com or www.gm.com.
2. Terril Yue Jones, "A Cadillac with a Foreign Accent," Forbes, 162(13) (December 14, 1998): 64–66.
3. Sue Zesiger, "Can Cadillac Come Back?" Fortune, 142(6) (September 18, 2000): 170.
4. David Welch, "Cadillac Hits the Gas; GM Is Spending Big to Revive the Brand, But Is It Too Late?" Business Week (3697) (September 4, 2000): 50.

CASE 2.8 ■ BURGER KING IS FRYING TO BECOME NUMBER ONE IN FRENCH FRIES

For many years in a row, the number two hamburger chain, Burger King, beat out McDonald's in taste tests of hamburgers, but has continuously finished second when it comes to french fries. McDonald's had a firm grasp on the best tasting fry, and with french fries returning 80 cents on the dollar, McDonald's was not going to give up the spot easily. However, Burger King wanted to become the french fry king, and was willing to do whatever it took to win over the fast-food customers.

Burger King began developing its new fry in 1996. Marketing research showed that people wanted a fry that was crispy and would remain hot. Burger King envisioned that a crunchy fry would differentiate its fry from McDonald's, and would help develop a loyal customer base, in a price sensitive market. The development team came up with 19 pages worth of fry specifications. These new fries were to each produce seven audible crunches and remain hot for more than 10 minutes (average previous time was seven minutes). At this time, a team of marketing executives was formed to investigate a starch-coated fry. While fries were cooked and tasted in test kitchen conditions, most testers agreed that the coated fries held up to the specifications. Before introducing this fry to the market, each fry supplier had to be equipped with new equipment, and at the same time 300,000 Burger King managers had to be comfortable with the new operations and frying techniques.

Burger King introduced this new version of its fry to the market in 1998. Burger King spent a lot of money on the development of this product and set forth $70 million for ad campaigns featuring the new fry. Mr. Potato Head became the new spokesman for the fry, and on Friday, January 2, 1998, Burger King introduced the new fry by handing out 15 million free orders of fries to the public. This day was declared "Free Fryday."

How did the new fry taste? "It tasted terrible," said the managers and customers across the country. Fast food thrives on consistency, and this fry was too complex to get right under anything less than perfect conditions. The fry also seemed to get a little too crunchy and lacked in potato taste. This led to a large decrease in fry sales at Burger King and convinced a large percent of customers to completely avoid Burger King because of their fries. Managers across the franchise were getting very frustrated with the loss of sales. This new product was considered a flop. Blame was placed on the potato suppliers, a lack of marketing research, an overengineered product, and poor fry cookers. Whatever the problem was, Burger King would have to put forth enormous effort in order to regain the sales that were lost.

Thirty months after the launch of this new fry, Burger King executives finally agreed that something needed to be done. A "new" fry was developed and introduced in 2001. This fry contained less coating and more potato taste. The supply chain and the 19 pages of specifications were simplified. Burger King said that they had it all under control. With fry taste scores higher than they were three years ago, Burger King believed that they were in a good position to challenge McDonald's again with this newer fry. It had learned from its mistakes and was not going to give up its fight to obtain the number-one tasting fry.

Questions

1. Define the management decision problem facing Burger King regarding its french fries.

2. Define the marketing research problem corresponding to the management decision problem you have identified in question 1.

3. What type of research design would be appropriate for investigating consumer preferences for french fries?

4. Use the Internet to determine the annual U.S. sales for McDonald's, Burger King, and Wendy's for 1996 to 2000. Interpret the data.

5. Do consumers have deeply felt emotions about french fries? If so, what are these emotions? How can Burger King find an answer to these questions?

6. If a survey is to be conducted to determine consumers' preference for french fries, which survey method should be used and why?

7. Which scaling technique would you use to measure preference for french fries made by McDonald's, Burger King, and Wendy's? Develop the appropriate scales.

8. Design a questionnaire that will obtain the information needed to address the marketing research problem defined in question 2.

9. Develop a sampling plan to conduct the survey specified in question 6.

10. If Burger King were to conduct the survey specified in question 6 in the United Kingdom, how would the research process be different?

11. Discuss the ethical issues involved in researching people's emotions, as in question 5.

Reference

1. Jennifer Ordonez, "How Burger King Got Burned in Quest to Make the Perfect Fry," *Wall Street Journal*, 237(11) (January 16, 2001): A1.

CASE 2.9 ■ IS AMTRAK ON TRACK?

Amtrak was created in 1970 when Congress passed the Rail Passenger Service Act. The Act created Amtrak as a private company intended to operate a nationwide rail system dedicated to passenger service. Amtrak began operation in early 1971, and started as a federally subsidized corporation with the intention of becoming self-sufficient within a few years.

Unfortunately, that has yet to happen. Amtrak fell under much criticism in the 1980s as the government continued to pump hundreds of millions of dollars into what seemed like a losing battle for profitability. The poor performance of Amtrak was even more scrutinized due to the fact that the board of directors were primarily active or former politicians with little or no business experience, much less experience in the transportation industry. Amtrak was finding it very difficult to compete with the airlines, and customer service was increasingly becoming a serious issue.

Amtrak continued to remain crippled by a collapsing infrastructure, disgruntled employees, and unhappy passengers. In the late 1990s, Amtrak began trying to revitalize its image. The firm undertook marketing research to determine how to win back some of the market share it lost to the airlines. By late 1997, Amtrak had gathered the opinions of more than 20,000 customers through focus groups and prequalified, self-administered phone surveys. Due to the high population density and the high frequency of business travel, the primary focus of the research was directed at the Northeast corridor.

Results from the research revealed key points on which Amtrak would direct its customer service strategy. Respondents were clear in stating that in order for the rail carrier to compete in the Northeast corridor, they had to stay within a three-hour transit time between the region's major markets (Boston to New York and New York to Washington). The transit time issue was viewed more as an order qualifier than an order winner. Meeting the time requirement only bought you the right to compete in the market.

It was clear that in order for Amtrak to steal customers back from the airlines, it would need to provide a superior level of service at a lower cost. Amtrak felt that there were several factors that would allow it to compete. First, due to an aging fleet and complex weather patterns, the airlines were struggling to maintain on-time performance. Second, the entire process around air travel, parking, check-in, and baggage claim was very cumbersome and increased the "actual" travel time to time frames with which rail service could easily compete. Finally, the customer environment while on board an airplane, with the exception of first class, could be related to a bus ride.

Amtrak executives set about planning their answer to these issues, and the result of their efforts was an entirely new high-speed rail service for the Northeast corridor, dubbed Acela (Ah-SELL-uh). The new brand is derived from the words *acceleration* and *excellence*. The purpose of renaming the line was to allow Amtrak to separate itself from its bad public image. Amtrak used research to design everything—redecorated cars, passenger-pleasing seats, lighting, restrooms, storage compartments—and even started to provide laptop connections at every seat. Additional information from the surveys led to redesigned beverage and food service, at both the first-class and coach levels. In addition to the cosmetic changes, the new service will provide more reliable transportation between the major markets because it will not be hindered by weather and the more frequent mechanical failures associated with air travel. It will also do this under the three-hour time window.

Acela began service on December 11, 2000, and it soon came under heavy fire. Critics pointed out that calling the new service "high speed" is simply Amtrak's new folly; citing the fact that the original trains on the corridor (28 years ago) made the run from New York to Boston in 2 hours and 41 minutes. This was exactly the estimated transit time for the new Acela rail service. To complicate the issue even further, many of the major airlines that serve a high volume of customers in the region have already prepared their own counterattack to Amtrak's new plan. The aging fleet of Boeing 737s was planned to be replaced by newer, more comfortable Airbus A-320 jets. The new jets will provide laptop connections at every seat and most likely improve on-time performance due to the increased reliability of the new aircraft.

There are many major problems that Amtrak needs to evaluate and act on in order to succeed. Outside of the major northeastern cities, Amtrak's trains are extremely slow and usually are limited to one trip a day; the tracks are muddy and in constant need of repair; and Amtrak trains miss some of the nations largest cities and most traveled routes. Amtrak is slowly running out of time. Resulting from a 1997 edict from Congress, Amtrak must operate without federal operating subsidies by 2003. If they are unable to do so, Amtrak may face major restructuring or liquidation. Only time will tell if Amtrak's new service will be sufficient to get it "back on track."

Questions

1. Define the management decision problem facing Amtrak.
2. Define the marketing research problem corresponding to the management decision problem identified in question 1.
3. What type of research design should be adopted to determine customer satisfaction with Acela?
4. What type of syndicated data would be useful to Amtrak and in what way?
5. As reported in the case, Amtrak conducted several focus groups. Do you think that depth interviews would be useful to Amtrak? If so, in what way?
6. If a survey is to be conducted to determine customer satisfaction toward Acela, which survey method should be used and why?
7. Should the Liker, semantic, differential, or Stapel scales be used to measure customer satisfaction toward Acela? Develop such a scale.
8. Design a questionnaire to measure customer satisfaction toward Acela.

9. Develop a sampling plan to conduct the customer satisfaction survey.

10. If marketing research to assess consumer preferences for traveling by train were to be conducted in Europe, how would the research process be different?

11. Discuss the ethical issues involved in researching consumer preferences for alternative modes of transportation.

References

1. Peter Howe, "Amtrak Chief Pumps up New Trains, Claims Superiority over Air Shuttles," *Boston Globe* (June 29, 1999): D6.

2. "A Loser? Amtrak's Numbers Say 'No,'" *Railway Age,* 201(8) (August 2000): 26.

3. William Vantuono, "Get Ready For a Great Ride," *Railway Age,* 201(5) (May 2000): 35.

4. Daniel Machalara, "Amtrak Boss Struggles to Get Train Service on Track in The U.S.," *Wall Street Journal* (January 16, 2001): A1.

5. "Acela Express: Off to a Good Start," *Railway Age,* 202(1) (January 2001): 26.

CASE 2.10 ■ HIGH PRICE OF CEREAL GETTING YOU DOWN? GENERAL MILLS THINKS SO

Marketing research is often used to explore strategic-level policies, such as pricing, packaging, promotional offers, and so on. In order to determine the impact of an important strategic move, such as lowering prices, it is essential to use marketing research.

In 1998, General Mills ran into problems when a pesticide scare hurt sales and private-label makers started to cut into their market share. In addition, four of General Mills' newest products produced only a four-tenth of a percentage point increase in market share. This was a disappointing sign since most products would not survive without having at least an eight-tenths of a percentage point of the market share.

Additional competition has emerged from private-label cereal makers, and store brands have become increasingly popular with consumers. Store owners took advantage of cereal prices of up to $5 per box, resulting in almost a five-tenth of a percentage point increase for the store brands. At least one cereal maker, Quaker Oats, started making a house brand version of its cereal. Quaker's lower priced bagged copies of leading brands have grown rapidly and advanced Quaker's market share to over 10 percent. Ralcorp Holdings Inc., the leading maker of private-label cereals, expects the trend of house brands gaining increased market share to continue, because only about half of the leading cereals have private-label competition. Ralcorp expects to gain a larger portion of the market as it continues to introduce more knockoffs. Some industry experts believe that unless the big brand name cereal prices are cut or the promotions increased, this trend will continue.

In order to address this problem, General Mills conducted problem-solving research to determine what, if any, changes it should make to its price and promotions strategy. In order to determine the effects of changes, consumer surveys were undertaken followed by test marketing. The results of General Mills' test markets suggested several pricing and promotional changes that would help increase its success.

General Mills cut prices on several of its cereal lines in the fall of 1998. Along with this price reduction, General Mills cut its coupon and promotion budget in an effort to halt spiraling costs and to reduce the price gap between General Mills' products and the competition, which had been as high as 25 percent in the past. The moves have increased General Mills' sales and profits. Overall for 2000, General Mills owned a 32.2 percent market share, compared to Kellogg's 30.7 percent.

The strategy of low prices was consistently followed through the year 2000, yielding gratifying results. In second quarter fiscal year 2000, General Mills reported diluted earnings of 62 cents per share, up 11 percent from 56 cents in fiscal 1999. Sales for the period ending November 28, 1999, totaled $1.82 billion. With an 8 percent increase in second-quarter shipments, General Mills' U.S. foods unit volume was up 7 percent through the first six months of fiscal 2000. Cereal unit volume grew 5 percent in the second quarter. This included gains by major brands including Cheerios, Lucky Charms, Golden Grahams, and Honey Nut Chex. Unit volume for the company's convenience foods businesses (snacks and yogurts) grew 18 percent in the second quarter. This included double-digit growth in both the fruit snacks and yogurt divisions.

Overall, General Mills was on track to deliver low double-digit growth in earnings per share (EPS) for fiscal year 2000, and the "prospects remain excellent for delivering double-digit EPS growth over the longer term," according to Steve Sanger, General Mills' chairman and CEO. The strategy of consistently low prices, supported by marketing research, is paying high dividends for General Mills.

Questions

1. General Mills would like to increase its share from 32.2 percent in 2000 to 37 percent. The management thinks that the way to achieve this growth is by introducing new brands. Define the management decision problem.

2. Define an appropriate marketing research problem corresponding to the management decision problem you have identified.

3. In what way can General Mills make use of the Census 2000 data?

4. What type of data available from syndicate firms will be helpful to General Mills?

5. Discuss the role of qualitative research in helping General Mills achieve the target market share. Which qualitative research technique(s) should be used and why?

6. If a survey is to be undertaken to determine consumer preferences for ready-to-eat cereals, which survey method should be used and why?

7. Can the observation method provide useful information to General Mills? If so, which observation method should be used and why?

8. Design an experiment to help General Mills determine whether the price of Cheerios should be decreased by 5 percent, 10 percent, 15 percent, or whether it should remain unchanged.

9. Develop Likert, semantic differential, and Stapel scales to measure consumers' preferences for Golden Grahams.

10. Design a sampling plan for administering the survey of question 6.

11. If General Mills were to conduct the survey specified in question 6 in India, how would the research process be different?

12. Discuss the ethical issues involved in researching consumer preferences for ready-to-eat cereals.

References

1. *www.generalmills.com.*

2. Ronald W. Cotterill and Andrew W. Franklin, "Forum—An Estimation of Consumer Benefits from the Public Campaign to Lower Cereal Prices," *Agribusiness,* 15(2) (Spring 1999): 273–287.

VIDEO CASE 2.1 ■ LANDS' END USES MARKETING RESEARCH TO LAND CUSTOMERS

Lands' End is a direct marketer of traditionally styled, casual clothing for men, women, and children; accessories; domestics; shoes; and soft luggage. The company offers its products through multiple distribution channels consisting of regular mailings of its catalogs, prospecting catalogs, and specialty catalogs as well as through the Internet, its international businesses, and its retail stores. Lands' End continually conducts marketing research to identify potential product improvements and ways to keep customers happy and satisfied.

Four ingredients make Lands' End a success in the business: people, products, services, and company policies.

- *People:* It's not just people that are important, but the type of people. Lands' End's 7,000 employees are chosen for their natural friendliness, good communication skills, willingness to work, and cooperativeness. From the telephone operators to management, everyone is motivated to do a good job, and employees are empowered to do what it takes to get the job done.

- *Products:* Quality products from the days of sailing gear through the introduction of clothing and luggage have dominated the offerings at Lands' End. Recently, they have introduced three new catalogs: "Coming Home" with soft household goods, "Lands' End Kids," and "Beyond Buttondowns," featuring menswear. The introduction of "Coming Home" illustrates Lands' End's commitment to customer needs. Their catalog featured a bedsheet with a 12-inch pocket that was an instant success because mattress makers were making mattresses thicker, but most sheet makers were unaware of this and people couldn't get their sheets to stay on the bed.

- *Services:* Whether its hemming; monogramming; friendly, fast, reliable service; or fast shipment, consumers have come to expect wonderful service from Lands' End, made possible because of the high caliber of people employed there.

- *Company policies:* Published and posted everywhere are the eight principles of business:

  1. Make quality products a priority.
  2. Price products honestly.
  3. Accept any return for any reason.
  4. Ship product faster than anyone else.
  5. What's best for the customer is best for the company.
  6. Eliminate the middleman and markup.
  7. Keep prices down by operating efficiently.
  8. Don't operate fancy and expensive stores.

Excellence in the above categories was only possible due to Lands' End's superb marketing research team. Although keeping up with customer needs was a tough task, Lands' End used a secret weapon; it just asked the consumers what they wanted. Through surveys and personal contacts, Lands' End asked its customers how it can go about improving certain products. Lands' End employees used their excellent listening skills and their brilliant product development team to produce more pleasing products. Every year Lands' End conducts a market survey of its customers. The survey asks basic information, such as age and education level, and follows up with questions about the products offered, the customer service received, the amount of time spent reading the catalogs, and whether or not they read the articles and customer testimonials inside the catalog. All of this new information generated each year helps Lands' End continue to build its customer base throughout the world.

Lands' End also specifically asks its customers how it can improve its products. Recently, Lands' End surveyed buyers of its mesh shirt. This was already a popular item but Lands' End wanted to see if improvements could be made. Buyers were asked questions like how the shirt could be improved, what they already like, and what would they not want to see changed. Four months after the survey, some improvements were made, and later that year the mesh shirt received top honors and was highlighted on a Lands' End catalog cover. This helps to illustrate that good products, happy customers, well-trained employees, and marketing research equals business success.

QUESTIONS

1. How does Lands' End involve customer research in its product development?

2. What type of research design do you think Lands' End adopted in conducting marketing research while developing the "Coming Home" catalog?

3. How would you use the Internet to determine men's preferences for clothes?

4. How do women perceive dresses? Do they attach deeply felt emotions to the clothes they wear? What qualitative research approach should be used to determine these answers?

5. What survey method would be appropriate for the annual survey of customers that Lands' End conducts?

6. Develop a questionnaire that Lands' End can use to survey its customers to find out whether or not it is successfully implementing the eight principles of business mentioned in the case.

7. Develop a complete sampling plan for administering the questionnaire developed in question 6 assuming the survey method you have recommended in question 5.

REFERENCES

1. *www.landsend.com/cd/frontdoor/.*

2. Janet Purdy, "Adapting Products and Services for Global E-Commerce," *World Trade,* 14(1) (January 2001): 52.

3. Mark Del Franco, "Lands' End: Turning the Tide?" *Catalog Age,* 18(3) (March 1, 2001): 1.

VIDEO CASE 2.2 ■ STARBUCKS: BUCKING THE TREND

Starbucks Corporation purchases and roasts quality whole-bean coffees and sells them, along with rich-brewed coffees, Italian-style espresso beverages, cold blended beverages, a variety of pastries and confections, coffee-related accessories and equipment, and a line of premium teas, primarily through its company-operated retail stores. In addition to sales through its company-operated retail stores, Starbucks sells primarily whole-bean coffees through a specialty sales group, a direct response business, supermarkets, and online at *starbucks.com*. Additionally, Starbucks produces and sells bottled Frappuccino® coffee drink and a line of premium ice creams through its joint venture partnerships and offers a line of innovative premium teas produced by its wholly owned subsidiary, Tazo Tea Company.

Coffee sales have gone down over the last few years, so how has Starbucks continued to grow? According to *Fortune* magazine, Starbucks affected a fundamental change in U.S. life. How? By focusing not on the product, but on the coffeehouse experience. By following its unique premise that "everything matters," it created an experience that elevates coffee drinking to an art form and coffeehouses to the place where Americans choose to relax and socialize. Through extensive marketing research, Starbucks created a place where you can meet and drink good coffee that did not resemble work or home, but fell somewhere in between. Today, consumers have little patience for brands that have worn out their welcome or have become disconnected. This makes it necessary for Starbucks to continuously research its customers and the market in order to continue its successful growth.

To keep its uniqueness, it shunned mass marketing and relied on conducting marketing research. It wanted to build the brand through resonance and relevance (the emotional side of coffee drinking), rather than through breadth and depth of taking the product to the market (breadth is more stores and depth is geographic expansion).

To create a unique environment, Starbucks hired an architect from Disney, who put together a creative team that designed standardized coffeehouse interiors that can be built affordably under a number of real estate limitations. The story of Starbucks is built around the siren in its logo. She's mischievous; she mesmerizes coffee drinkers and lures them to the cup. To tie everything together, the team created a logo for each coffee, which was seen beside the coffee's name on the menu board. This same logo or stamp appeared in color on the package of the coffee. The logo was designed to capture the spirit of the coffee.

Another unique emphasis of Starbucks is the emphasis on its people. By studying its competition, Starbucks was able to discover where certain companies were going wrong, and how it could improve the employee atmosphere in order to utilize its employees to the full extent. Employees received stock shares and were made to feel part of the company. Starbucks expanded this focus on people in each community in which it located by sharing their values and showing compassion for its citizens by making the community a better place to live, not just work. The company has traditionally been linked to assistance for causes such as AIDS, Hospice, and food banks. Starbucks recently initiated the Starbucks Foundation, which focuses on children in need.

The company's objective is to establish Starbucks as the most recognized and respected brand in the world. To achieve this goal, the company plans to invest heavily in marketing research. With the use of such research, Starbucks can determine target locations to rapidly expand its retail operations, grow its specialty sales and other operations, and selectively pursue opportunities to leverage the Starbucks brand through the introduction of new products and the development of new distribution channels. These tasks can be accomplished only with extensive marketing research, and Starbucks is taking steps to ensure these goals are achieved.

In expanding abroad, Starbucks has partners who share the same values. As the president said, they cannot share the same cultures, but they can share such values as treating employees with respect and dignity and caring for the product they sell. Starbucks first entered Japan because of the caliber of the partner it found there. Its slow global expansion process enables Starbucks to continue emphasizing all of its core policies.

Starbucks' current challenge is to retain its uniqueness and intimacy with the customer. Its founder and CEO said it must retain the ability to constantly entertain customers, provide them with special moments, and even surprise them, which is not easy when there are over a 1,000 stores, some of which are licenses and some of which are joint ventures. This makes continuous marketing research a very important tool for Starbucks. With the onslaught of so many different coffee shops opening up worldwide, it has become extremely important for Starbucks to stay on top of what its customers are looking for in a café and understand the steps its competitors are taking in order to gain a larger customer base. Starbucks must conduct marketing research in order to understand why it is that customers come to its shop and what it will take to keep them coming back. Starbucks can also use marketing research in order to get a grasp on what its competition is doing so that it can counter with a better option in order to retain and grow its customer base.

QUESTIONS

1. Using the Internet, identify secondary sources of information pertaining to coffee consumption in the United States.

2. What are consumers looking for in a coffeehouse experience? How do they view the Starbucks coffee shop experience? How can Starbucks determine answers to such questions?

3. A survey is to be conducted to determine the image coffee drinkers have of Starbucks and other coffee shop chains. Which survey method should be used and why?

4. Starbucks is thinking of introducing a new gourmet coffee with a strong aroma. Can the observation method be used to determine the consumer reaction to this coffee prior to national introduction? If so, which observation method should be used?

5. What type of scale would be appropriate for measuring the image of Starbucks? Design such a scale.

6. Design a sampling plan for administering the survey in question 3.

REFERENCES

1. *www.starbucks.com/*.

2. Sean Mehegan, "The Fourth Annual Restaurant Business High Performance Restaurant Leaderships Awards: The Stars Come Out," *Restaurant Business*, 100(5) (March 1, 2001): 22.

3. Richard Papiernik, "Starbucks Still Taking Bows in Long-Running Coffeehouse Show," *Nation's Restaurant News*, 35(7) (February 12, 2001): 11.

VIDEO CASE 2.3 ■ THE Y: WHY YOU SHOULD JOIN

Traditionally thought of as an all-American organization, the YMCA was actually formed in London, England, over 150 years ago. The YMCA was initially formed in response to unhealthy social conditions arising in big cities at the end of the Industrial Revolution. Currently, there are more than 2,000 YMCAs in the United States, and an additional 120 located in other countries around the world. YMCA's historical name stands for Young Men's Christian Association; however, that name has taken on a new meaning today. The YMCA caters to an extremely diverse group of people and communities, and therefore, the YMCA name has been shortened to the "Y." The Y is for people of all ages, incomes, races, religions, and abilities, and no one is turned away for the inability to pay. Through the use of marketing research, Ys around the world can determine the specific and beneficial needs of people in various communities and provide certain programs to help those people.

Throughout the history of the Y, the organization's mission has remained constant. That mission is illustrated in this case to show how the Y continues to meet the changing needs of society by providing exercise and recreation facilities; health, fitness, and educational programs; and other services needed by communities. In meeting society's changing needs, the Y reaches across many cultural and social barriers to help others. International efforts have long been important to the Y, and the Y will continue to maintain a global presence in other countries around the world.

The Y in the United States meets the changing needs of families by conducting marketing research to gather important information. Researchers have found that the Y's target market has changed over time and now they must focus on providing services to meet the needs of families with children, teens, and senior citizens. Today, the Y offers programs in such areas as aquatics; arts and humanities, which includes reading, writing, and performing; camping; child care services; community development, which includes job training, drug prevention, and economic development programs; family nights and support groups; health and fitness programs; international programs, which include educational exchange programs; older adult programs, which include social clubs and volunteering; sports programs such as basketball, soccer, and baseball; and finally, teen leadership programs.

Just as the Y in the United States seeks to help those in need, the Y in the United Kingdom, called YCare, helps young people who face severe social and economic problems. Through nearly 40 different programs, YCare provides third world assistance to those who live in poverty and struggle to survive. While the United States Y and YCare may differ, they both standardize their international marketing by focusing on helping disadvantaged segments of society through education and services. What changes are the needs, but even some of those remain constant. In the United States, the need for exercise and recreation is constant; however, each Y provides different programs for adults and children depending on choices of the community.

Raising funds for the Y varies from the United States to the United Kingdom. YCare in the United Kingdom raises funds through direct marketing by calling individuals and requesting donations. Personal donations contribute far more income than the business communities in the United Kingdom. YCare invests very little in media, television, and radio coverage to promote its services. However, YCare does invest a great deal in maintaining existing, qualified donors. Marketing research is helpful in determining which method of fund raising is the most effective for different YCare locations.

YMCA marketing worldwide must be customized to meet the needs of particular regions and communities. In order to customize, marketing researchers must determine such demographics as race, age, sex, marital status, morals, and income to better understand a particular region's needs that a Y can provide. By breaking down segments of a community, Ys can tailor specific programs that will truly benefit all that live in a particular community.

In order to begin a new Y facility in a community, other research must be conducted as well. Researchers must determine if there will be enough citizens who will contribute initially to the Y, if there will be enough people who are interested in volunteering to work at the Y, and if there will be enough people in the community to keep the Y going. After a Y has been developed, decisions such as programs offered, staffing, and style of operation are all made based on local choices of the community. All of the above criteria are very important in determining the success of a new Y, and marketing researchers must determine all factors that contribute to success to help a Y to make sure that it does in fact continue its mission.

QUESTIONS

1. What benefit can marketing research provide to Ys worldwide?
2. The management of the Y is seeking to reach more families in the United States. Define the management decision problem.
3. Give an appropriate definition of the corresponding marketing research problem.
4. Why do people patronize organizations such as the Y? Develop two hypotheses.
5. To develop a successful new YMCA in a community, what research design should be adopted to understand the needs of particular regions and communities?
6. What type of secondary data would be useful to the Y seeking to develop a new YMCA in a community in the United States? From where can such data be obtained?
7. Would focus groups or depth interviews be more useful in determining a community's preferences for programs that a local Y should offer? Defend your reasoning.
8. If a survey is to be conducted to determine a community's preferences for programs that a local Y should offer, which survey method should be used?
9. Develop a sampling plan for administering the survey in question 8.

REFERENCES

1. www.ymca.org.
2. Sandra Dolbow, "YMCA on the Mark with PepsiCo. Champion," *Brandweek,* 41(39) (October 9, 2000): 16.
3. Lauren Wiley, "Showing the Other YMCA of R.I.," *Adweek,* 37(5) (January 31, 2000): 8.

VIDEO CASE 2.4 ■ NIKE: ONE STEP AHEAD OF THE COMPETITION

Nike, Inc., designs, develops, and markets footwear, apparel, equipment, and accessory products. Nike is the largest seller of athletic footwear and athletic apparel in the world.

The company sells its products to approximately 19,000 retail accounts in the United States and approximately 140 countries around the world. Nike grew from $8,000 in sales in 1963 to a more than $6.5 billion company today. CEO Philip H. Knight's original goal is now Nike's mission: to serve the athlete. Marketing personnel at Nike believe that the mission means being inside the sport, understanding it from the participant's perspective, and creating a great product that enhances the athlete's performance. They believe the key to their success is motivating people to play a sport using a great product—a Nike product.

To communicate its message, Nike chose athletes to endorse products because they understand how the product works to enhance performance. To be chosen as an endorser, an athlete must excel at his or her sport and be willing to get involved with the company's marketing effort. Michael Jordan was involved in the design of the products he endorsed; he was not just a spokesperson. The communication goal is to touch people, to move them, to create an emotional bond with them through fresh, unexpected communications. Because the job of these spokespeople is so critical, it is very important that Nike selects the right people for the job. Therefore, Nike must use marketing research in order to continuously stay on top of the sports market. Nike researches its consumers in order to uncover the market's perspective on who the current leaders of the sports world are. This reinforces the centrality of the product in Nike's strategy.

Nike's initial attempts to enter international markets were not successful because it did not pay enough attention to the sports played in those markets. The necessary market research was not conducted or used properly. Although Nike has a great basketball shoe, basketball is not that popular outside the United States. So, Nike had to relearn its own creative process by getting close to the athletes in the popular sports, whether it was rugby in Australia or soccer in Europe. Nike researched the players to find out what they wanted out of athletic shoes, and also closely studied the consumers to not only find out who their sports heroes were and what they wanted out of a shoe, but also researched to learn why people wanted to play these sports. It is this information that is used to help develop successful marketing campaigns.

Nike had to learn the sport from the inside; it had to know what it takes to excel at the sport, and it had to create good products for the sport. Marketing Director Liz Dolan admits that they made mistakes—that the Nike soccer shoe was not that good. However, today, after conducting numerous studies on the market, Nike has continuously worked on improving its products and signing celebrity athletes to endorse its products. You need to be in the market in order to understand and sometimes it takes a couple of seasons to get it right. Nike is obviously using the same strategy overseas as it did in the United States: Improve your product (i.e., a better soccer shoe) and sign the major stars to endorse the product.

The most important marketing tool for Nike is the product itself, and that product needs to solve a problem. In order for Nike to accomplish this, it must continuously study the overall footwear market as well as its consumers in order to produce products that will solve consumer problems. Nike can use market research to not only stay on top of what its consumers want out of their footwear, but can also study what its competition is doing in order to stay one step ahead.

What has Nike learned from this experience? One thing is that the company should never be afraid to make mistakes. It has also learned to create marketing teams in its major markets that know the culture and sports and adapt the Nike strategy to the different markets. Liz Dolan comments that Nike has the same values as a big company that it had as a small company and that it is highly entrepreneurial. Tolerating mistakes is important in simulating the entrepreneurial spirit. Of course, systematic use of marketing research can help in reducing managerial mistakes.

QUESTIONS

1. Nike would like to increase its share of the athletic shoe market. Define the management decision problem.

2. Define an appropriate marketing research problem corresponding to the management decision problem you have identified.

3. Develop a graphical model explaining consumer selection of a specific brand of athletic shoes.

4. How can qualitative research be used to strengthen the image of Nike? Which qualitative research technique(s) should be used and why?

5. Should Nike invest by opening more upscale company retail stores such as Nike Town? Management is wondering if survey research can provide an answer. How should such a survey be administered?

6. Develop Likert, semantic differential, and Stapel scales for evaluating the durability of Nike running shoes.

7. Develop a sampling plan for administering the survey in question 5.

REFERENCES

1. *www.nike.com/.*
2. H. M. Fattah, "Just Doing It with Nike," *MC Technology Marketing Intelligence,* 21(2) (February 2001): 36.
3. "AdMarket 50—Profile of the Week: Nike," *Advertising Age,* 72(10) (March 5, 2001): 38.

VIDEO CASE 2.5 ■ WEST POINT: MAKING A POINT TO POTENTIAL CADETS

West Point's role in our nation's history dates back to the Revolutionary War, when both sides realized the strategic importance of the commanding plateau on the west bank of the Hudson River. Continental soldiers built forts, batteries, and redoubts and extended a l50-ton iron chain across the Hudson to control river traffic. The British, despite Benedict Arnold's treason, never captured fortress West Point. West Point is the oldest continuously occupied military post in America. While West Point offers a great Ivy League education, its mission is to train individuals to become army officers. Through the use of marketing research, West Point can determine effective ways to target potential cadets and more effective ways to promote the education and officer training it offers.

This case discussed the integrated promotions used by the United States Military Academy (USMA). The USMA uses promotions in the form of catalogs, brochures, and the like, which are combined with direct mailings, personal selling (recruiters and cadets), electronic media (Web site), and publicity. Marketing research determined which forms of promotion are the most effective, in terms of costs, candidate appeal, candidate scope, and most of all how to improve these promotions. The USMA's promotions all have a consistent theme or message of advertising—being willing to die for your country.

Once potential cadets are identified, they receive a series of increasingly tailored messages throughout their junior year in high school. Identification can start as early as the eighth grade, and personal recruiters may even help candidates select a high school curriculum. The final form of promotion is the campus tour or visit, which allows plenty of scope for more personal selling. Marketing researchers determine which method of campus visits is most effective in selling a candidate to West Point. Research showed that many potential candidates enjoy touring with a first-year cadet because they feel they can relate better to someone close to their own age. By recognizing this, West Point has a greater opportunity to attract new candidates.

Marketing researchers have discovered the need to use current technologies such as the Internet to facilitate the application process for potential candidates. Given the difficulty of applying to the USMA, they have set up a nine-step process to facilitate admission, which guides candidates throughout the process and allows them to check on their application at any time. West Point is implementing a video for its Web site. Research showed that not many students are familiar with everything that West Point offers, so an informative video seems to be a valuable tool to inform and attract an interested audience.

Marketing researchers have found that attracting new candidates involves a number of factors. First of all, the method of promotion directly affects how a new candidate will perceive West Point. Therefore, it is very important to research promotional methods in order to attract the best candidates to uphold the honor and integrity West Point is founded on. Competition is a very significant factor that cannot be overlooked. Marketing researchers must find out what the college market looks like in order to attract potential students to West Point. By focusing on West Point's strengths, they can sell their education and officer training to prospective students. Research shows that the historical background of West Point interests many students; therefore, they incorporate their unique history into many of their promotions. Marketing researchers gather feedback from the USMA's Web site *(www.usma.edu)* by measuring the number of hits and repeats, how often the candidate visits, what questions are asked, what parts of the Web site attract the most attention, how frequently candidates come to the Web site, and where they stay the longest. These data provide useful information to researchers to help USMA improve its Web site, attract potential cadets, and remain ahead of other college competitors. As the USMA considers America's military needs for the twenty-first century, the Academy realizes that it must increase both the quantity and quality of potential cadets that are recruited. Marketing research can play a crucial role in this process.

QUESTIONS

1. How can marketing research directly affect the success of West Point in attracting new cadets?

2. Define the management decision problem facing the USMA and the corresponding market research problem.

3. Besides studying feedback from West Point's Web site *(www.usma.edu),* what are some other ways marketing researchers can gain valuable information on improving promotions so they are successful?

4. Discuss the role of qualitative research in identifying the motivations that potential cadets have in applying to the USMA. Which qualitative research technique should be used for this purpose?

5. Would the use of surveys be very helpful in this type of marketing research? Which survey method should be used?

6. Develop Likert, semantic differential, and Stapel scales to measure the values of duty and honor that appear in the USMA mission statement *(www.usma.edu).*

7. Develop a sampling plan for surveying potential cadets by assuming the survey method you have recommended in question 5.

REFERENCES

1. *www.usma.edu/*.

2. Mark Rotella, "Duty First: West Point and the Making of American Leaders," *Publishers Weekly,* 248(1) (January 1, 2001): 79.

VIDEO CASE 2.6 ■ KODAK: TAKING PICTURES FURTHER

Eastman Kodak Company is engaged primarily in developing, manufacturing, and marketing consumer, professional, health, and other imaging products and services. Kodak began as a company that made it easy for everyone to take pictures. Its guiding principle has been, "No one but Kodak makes it easier to unleash the power of principles." Cameras going digital provided a challenge for Kodak. One of their original slogans was "You push the button, we do the rest." While introducing digital imaging, that slogan could change to "You click on the icon and we do the rest." Kodak's movement into the digital market was partially motivated by the need to avoid competition with Fuji. As illustrated in this video case, Kodak's use of marketing research enables it to provide customers with leading technology and convenience products.

Kodak is committed to the digital imaging business, believing that it is the next growth spurt of photography (the previous ones being black and white home photography and then color photography). Initially, Kodak tried to sell consumers on digital imaging from the ground up—meaning that consumers had to buy a digital camera and learn to use it and work with their pictures on a computer. This is quite a large behavioral and price modification for consumers.

However, the Picture CD was a vastly pared down means of getting consumers into digital imaging. The only change that a consumer had to make in picture taking is to ask for the CD when they got their pictures developed. This CD enabled the consumer to store their pictures on a disk or online, rotate the pictures, remove red eye, crop pictures, e-mail pictures, and so on. The goal was to get people to use their pictures rather than just taking them home and sticking them into an album. Putting pictures on CD or disk enabled consumers to better organize and more efficiently store their pictures. This advantage was one of the key benefits stressed in advertising for the CD.

Kodak is not a technology company, and to make the CD and all of the digital imaging and support for this new way of taking pictures, Kodak had to find partners. Therefore, Kodak teamed up with Intel, Microsoft, Adobe, and Hewlett Packard to have the software, processing, and printing capability needed to bring consumers fully into the digital picture age. In order to provide customers with the leading technology, Kodak conducted marketing research on several technology firms. Kodak chose the above firms on the innovativeness and quality they could provide to meet Kodak's needs.

Their hope, of course, was that the Picture CD would turn people on to digital photography so that consumers would eventually buy digital cameras. One element not mentioned in the video is the fact that Kodak has a service called PhotoNet Online. What Kodak ultimately hoped was that consumers would use this service to store, rotate, crop and e-mail pictures. To appeal to Generation d (Digital), Kodak realized it must keep up with current technological advances. Therefore, it felt this service would deliver new technology and keep Kodak on the cutting edge. The online service brought Kodak closer to consumers and broadened the ways in which Kodak could profit from the new technology.

Marketing research was an important aspect in the development and continued growth of this new product. Kodak test marketed the Picture CD in Salt Lake City and Indianapolis. These two cities were picked because they are very self-contained; promotions in one market do not spill over into others. Each city also has a different level of PC penetration, so Kodak could test how that would affect demand for the Picture CD. In each test site, Kodak ran different advertising and promotions to see which worked best.

Marketing research can be an especially powerful tool for companies in the technology field. Concepts and ideas are continuously changing along with consumer needs and demands. Kodak understands that the future is always a moving target. It is extremely important for Kodak to stay on top of where the market is moving so that they can make the most profitable and successful steps into the future.

Continuous marketing research will be necessary in order to keep the product updated with consumer needs. The results from research studies help Kodak come up with updated versions that meet new consumer demands. They also help Kodak discover what attributes of their products are not popular so that they can be replaced with more useful options. Thus, Kodak realizes that they must rely on marketing research in order to introduce innovative new products and services, as well as improve the existing ones so that they can remain competitive in the years to come.

QUESTIONS

1. How can marketing research help Kodak in developing innovative new products and services?

2. Kodak would like to increase the adoption of Picture CD. Define the management decision problem.

3. Kodak's marketing research department realizes that the key to increasing the adoption of the Picture CD is to understand the photography behavior, demographics, and lifestyles of the current adopters. Define an appropriate marketing research problem.

4. Identify possible sources of secondary data helpful in understanding the photographic behavior of camera users.

5. Discuss the role of qualitative research in understanding how Kodak can encourage the users of the Picture CD to start using digital cameras.

6. A lot of pictures are taken when a baby is born in the family. Kodak would like to survey mothers with newborns about their photography habits. Which survey method should be used to conduct such a survey?

7. Develop a questionnaire for the survey mentioned in question 6.

8. Develop a sampling plan for the survey mentioned in question 6.

REFERENCES

1. *www.kodak.com/.*

2. Laura Heller, "Shared Technologies Give Convention New Dimension," *DSN Retailing Today,* 40(3) (February 5, 2001): 69.

3. Todd Wasserman, "Kodak Rages in Favor of the Machines, *Brandweek,* 42(9) (February 26, 2001): 6.

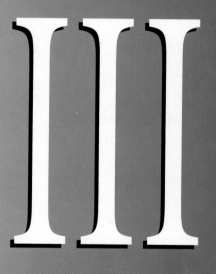

Data Collection, Analysis, and Reporting

III

14

FIELD WORK

THE SELECTION,
TRAINING,
SUPERVISION,
EVALUATION, AND
VALIDATION OF FIELD
WORKERS ARE
CRUCIAL FOR
COLLECTING HIGH
QUALITY DATA.

Opening Questions

1. What is meant by field work and what is the field work process?
2. In what aspects of interviewing should field workers be trained?
3. How should the field workers be supervised to enhance their effectiveness and efficiency?
4. How should field workers be evaluated?
5. What is the role of field work in total quality management?
6. How should field work be conducted in international marketing research?
7. How does technology facilitate field work?
8. What ethical issues are involved in field work?
9. What is the role of the Internet in field work?

Paul Sherrington, Vice President–Elrick &
Lavidge.
Paul is responsible for data processing and collec-
tion that includes E&L's telephone interviewing
centers and several field operations offices.

GALLUP'S GALLOPING FIELD WORK

Now more than ever, Americans are hanging up on interviewers. The primary difficulty of telephone interviewing is declining response rates and, more specifically, increasing refusal rates. Many techniques and procedures have been used to combat this problem, including incentives, aggressive call designs, shorter interviews, and special introductory statements. The most critical variable, however, may be the interviewers themselves.

Refusals are largely a function of interviewing skill. Top interviewers are rarely turned down. The Gallup organization, a prestigious marketing research and consulting firm that specializes in survey research, has identified the following characteristics of an outstanding interviewer:

- **Work orientation.** Works hard and sees work as more than a job, but an expression of oneself.
- **Teamwork.** Forms good team relationships with others.
- **Aptitude.** Has a natural affinity for telephone research—enjoys collecting opinions via the telephone.
- **Pride.** Is positive, quality conscious, and likes being recognized for a job well done.
- **Discipline.** Stays focused on a task and completes it.
- **Third ear.** Empathizes with a respondent and tailors presentation accordingly.
- **Command.** "Takes charge"—can turn refusals around by conveying the purpose of the survey and its importance.

- **Ability to woo.** Gets people to like him or her quickly; convinces people to cooperate who might not otherwise respond.
- **Ethics.** Is honest and behaves ethically at all times.

Using this theme, the hiring process for interviewers at the Gallup organization has become very selective, hiring only 1 out of every 16 candidates. The selected interviewers are carefully trained in all aspects of interviewing, from making the initial contact to terminating the interview. The Council of American Survey Research Organizations' guidelines for effective interviewing (discussed later in this chapter) are followed. The interviewers' work is closely supervised by experienced and qualified supervisors who make sure that appropriate procedures are being followed and the interviews are being properly conducted.

Validation of field work and the evaluation of interviewers are continuous activities. As a result, the Gallup organization has not only increased the retention rate of its field workers but has significantly increased the productivity and quality of its data collection. Gallup interviews more than three million people every year in the United States and has built a worldwide reputation for the high quality of its data collection process.[1]

OVERVIEW

Field work is the fourth step in the marketing research process. It follows problem definition and development of the approach (Chapter 2), and formulation of the research design (Chapters 3 through 13). Figure 14.1 briefly explains the focus of the chapter, the relationship of this chapter to the previous ones, and the step of the marketing research process on which this chapter concentrates.

During this phase, the field workers make contact with the respondents, administer the questionnaires or observation forms, record the data, and turn in the completed forms for processing. Field workers include a personal interviewer administering questionnaires door-to-door, an interviewer intercepting shoppers in a mall, a telephone interviewer calling from a central location, a worker mailing questionnaires from an office, an observer counting customers in a particular section of a store, and others involved in data collection and supervision of the process. The opening vignette gives the characteristics of outstanding interviewers, who form the backbone of field work.

This chapter describes the nature of field work and the field work/data collection process. This process involves the selection, training, and supervision of field workers, the validation of field work, and the evaluation of field workers. Care taken at each of these stages of the field work process can pay big dividends, as illustrated by the Gallup organization in the opening vignette. We also discuss field work in the context of total quality management, international marketing research, and technology and marketing research, and identify the relevant ethical issues and Internet applications. Figure 14.2 gives an overview of the topics discussed in this chapter and how they flow from one to the next.

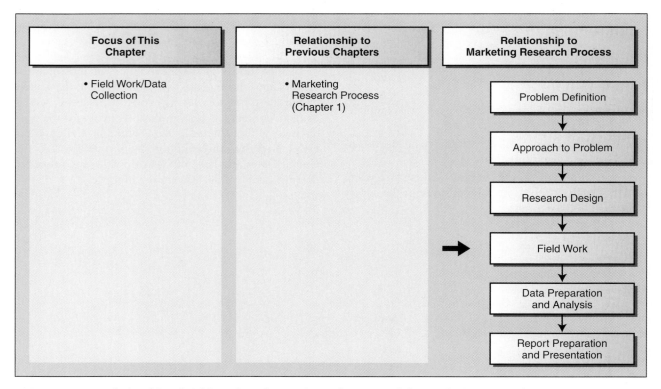

FIGURE 14.1   Relationship of Field Work to the Previous Chapters and the Marketing Research Process

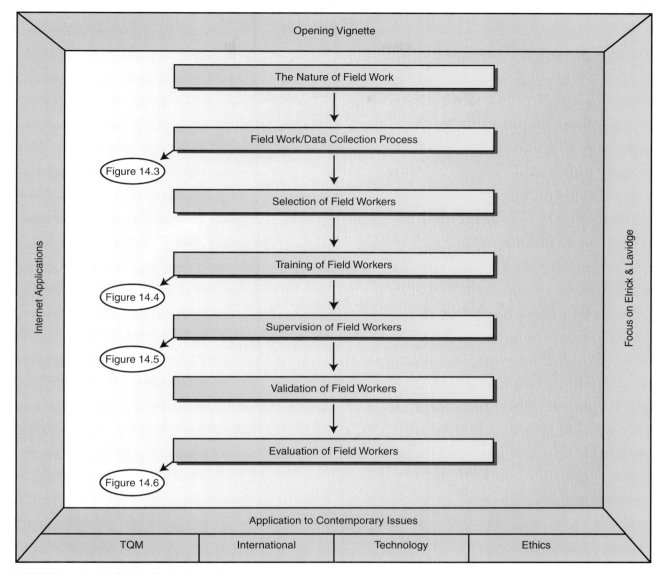

FIGURE 14.2 Field Work: An Overview

THE NATURE OF FIELD WORK

Those who design the research rarely collect marketing research data. Researchers have two major options for collecting their data: They can develop their own organizations, or they can contract with a field work agency. In either case, data collection involves using some kind of field force. This field force may operate either in the field (personal in-home, mall intercept, computer-assisted personal interviewing, and observation) or from an office (telephone/CATI, mail/mail panel, and electronic surveys). The field workers who collect the data typically have little research background or training. Therefore, to ensure high quality, the field work/data collection process should be streamlined and well controlled, as discussed in the following section.

FIELD WORK/DATA COLLECTION PROCESS

All field work involves the selection, training, and supervision of persons who collect data. The validation of field work and the evaluation of field workers are also parts of the process. All of these aspects were seen in the opening vignette, which described how Gallup selected, trained, supervised, monitored, and evaluated its field workers. Figure 14.3 represents a general framework for the field work/data collection process. While we describe a general process, it should be recognized that the nature of field work varies with the mode of data collection and that the relative emphasis on the different steps will vary for telephone, personal, mail, and electronic interviews.

SELECTION OF FIELD WORKERS

The first step in the field work process is the selection of field workers. The researcher should: (1) develop job specifications for the project, taking into account the mode of data collection; (2) decide what characteristics the field workers should have; and (3) recruit appropriate individuals. Interviewers' background characteristics, opinions, perceptions, expectations, and attitudes can affect the responses they elicit.

To the extent possible, interviewers should be selected to match respondents' demographic characteristics since this increases the probability of a successful interview. Thus, interviewers who are senior citizens would be best for interviewing respondents who are senior citizens. The job requirements will also vary with the nature of the problem and the type of data collection method. However, some general qualifications of field workers were outlined in the opening vignette: work orientation, teamwork, aptitude, pride, discipline, third ear, command, the ability to woo, and ethics. Interviewers with these qualifications will have a high likelihood of being successful in conducting the field work. Field workers are generally paid an hourly rate or on a per-interview basis. The typical interviewer is a married woman aged 35 to 54, with an above-average education and an above-average household income.[2]

FIGURE 14.3
The Field Work/Data Collection Process

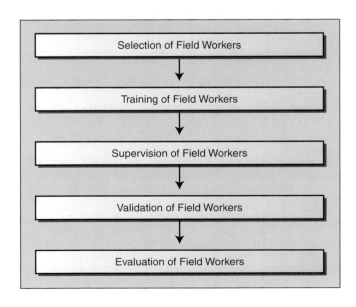

TRAINING OF FIELD WORKERS

Training field workers is critical to the quality of data collected. Training may be conducted in person at a central location, or, if the interviewers are geographically dispersed, by mail. Training ensures that all interviewers administer the questionnaire in the same manner so that the data can be collected uniformly. Training should cover all phases of the interviewing process (see opening vignette): making the initial contact, asking the questions, probing, recording the answers, and terminating the interview (Figure 14.4).

The initial contact can result in the cooperation or the loss of potential respondents. Interviewers should be trained to make opening remarks that will convince potential respondents that their participation is important. Questions that directly ask permission, such as "May I have some of your valuable time?" or "Would you like to answer a few questions?" should be avoided because people can answer "No." Interviewers should also be instructed on handling objections and refusals. For example, if the respondent says, "This is not a convenient time for me," the interviewer should respond, "What would be a more convenient time for you? I will call back then."

Asking questions is an art. Even a slight change in the wording, sequence, or manner in which a question is asked can distort its meaning and bias the response. Training in asking questions can yield high dividends by eliminating potential sources of bias. One method used to reduce response bias is to probe respondents. **Probing** is intended to motivate respondents to elaborate, clarify, or explain their answers. Probing also helps respondents focus on the specific content of the interview and provide only relevant information. Probing should not introduce any bias. Commonly used probes include questions such as: Any others? Anything else? Could you tell me more about your thinking on that?

Although recording respondent answers seems simple, several mistakes are common. All interviewers should use the same format and conventions to record the interviews and edit completed interviews. While the rules for recording answers to structured questions vary with each questionnaire, the general rule is to check the box that reflects the respondent's answer. The general rule for recording answers to unstructured questions is to record the responses verbatim.

probing
A motivational technique used when asking survey questions to induce the respondents to enlarge on, clarify, or explain their answers and to help the respondents focus on the specific content of the interview.

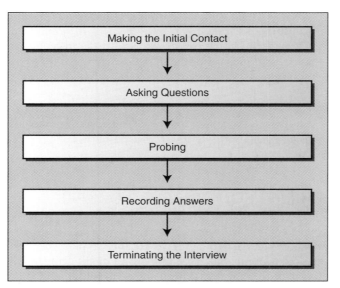

FIGURE 14.4
Training Field Workers

Before terminating, the interviewer should answer the respondent's questions about the project. The respondent should be left with a positive feeling about the interview. It is important to thank the respondent and express appreciation for their participation. The following example shows the importance of well-trained interviewers in the data collection process and the effect that has on new product development research.

EXAMPLE

BRUSHING INTERVIEWERS RESULTS IN A SUCCESSFUL NEW TOOTHBRUSH

When Chesebrough Pond's USA was conducting a survey to determine the market potential for a new toothbrush, the company realized that this research would be crucial to the development and introduction of a new product. To obtain high-quality data, the interviewers were carefully trained in all aspects of interviewing.

Training in making the initial contact resulted in a much lower refusal rate. The interviewers were instructed to ask the questions as written, to diligently probe the respondents for open-ended questions, and to record the answers fully and accurately. Many of the questions were unstructured or open-ended and required probing, for example, "Why are you (dis)satisfied with the brands of toothbrush currently available in the market?" Probing and recording answers to open-ended questions were particularly important since the company was seeking to identify some creative solutions to the oral care problems consumers faced.

One innovative idea that emerged from the survey findings was a toothbrush that not only cleaned teeth but also offered an additional benefit of gum care. Based on this finding, Chesebrough Pond's developed and launched the Mentadent Oral Care Toothbrush. This was the first toothbrush to offer an additional therapeutic benefit of gum care, thereby pioneering the advanced therapeutic segment of the category. The toothbrush was designed with multilevel interior bristles to clean teeth effectively and with flared side bristles to gently massage and stimulate gums. It is positioned as the state-of-the-art choice for people who are serious about oral care.

The launch was a strong success because the product addressed an unmet consumer need: care for both teeth and gums. A major factor contributing to this success was the careful training of the interviewers that was instrumental in discovering the need for this innovative toothbrush.[3]

SUPERVISION OF FIELD WORKERS

Supervision of field workers means making sure that they are following the procedures and techniques in which they were trained, as illustrated by the Gallup organization in the opening vignette. Supervision involves quality control and editing, sampling control, control of cheating, and central office control (Figure 14.5).

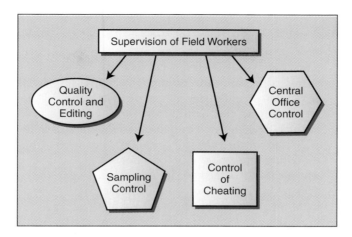

FIGURE 14.5
Supervising Field Workers

Quality control of field workers requires checking to see if the field procedures are being properly implemented. If any problems are detected, the supervisor should discuss them with the field workers and provide additional training if necessary. To understand the interviewers' problems, the supervisors should also do some interviewing. Supervisors should collect questionnaires and edit them daily. They should examine the questionnaires to make sure all appropriate questions have been completed, unsatisfactory or incomplete answers have not been accepted, and the writing is legible. Supervisors should also keep a record of hours worked and expenses. This will make it easy to determine the cost per completed interview, whether the job is moving on schedule, and whether any interviewers are having problems.

An important aspect of supervision is **sampling control,** which attempts to ensure that the interviewers are strictly following the sampling plan rather than selecting sampling units based on convenience or accessibility. To control these problems, supervisors should keep daily records of the number of calls made, the number of not-at-homes, the number of refusals, the number of completed interviews for each interviewer, and the total for all interviewers under their control.

sampling control
An aspect of supervision that ensures that the interviewers strictly follow the sampling plan rather than select sampling units based on convenience or accessibility.

Cheating involves falsifying part of a question or the entire questionnaire. An interviewer may falsify part of an answer to make it acceptable or may fake answers. The most blatant form of cheating occurs when the interviewer falsifies the entire questionnaire, filling in answers without contacting a respondent. Cheating can be minimized through proper training, supervision, and validation of field work.

Central office control involves tabulating the responses to important demographic characteristics and key questions. It also includes checking on the quotas to make sure they are being met. Supervisors provide quality and cost-control information to the central office so that a progress report can be maintained.

The following example illustrates the importance of close supervision in collecting high-quality data.

EXAMPLE

LITE BAR IS FROM MARS

M&M Mars, a Division of Mars, Inc., frequently conducts mall intercept interviews to identify and test new product concepts. Shoppers are intercepted at various locations in the mall and taken to a central facility where they can taste candy bars under development and then respond to surveys. The surveys contain a fair number of unstructured or open-ended questions, and interviewers are required to probe the respondents. Probing provides rich insights into the respondents' underlying values, attitudes, and beliefs. Since all such interviews are conducted at a central location, supervision of the interviewers is greatly facilitated. Completed questionnaires are available to the supervisors immediately after the interview for editing and quality control. Sampling control is easily exercised, and cheating is eliminated, which eliminates the need for validation. This procedure is also good for implementing quota sampling, which is often used, and also facilitates other aspects of central office control, such as tabulation of responses to key questions.

A recent mall intercept survey indicated that respondents had a strong preference for a low-fat candy bar, as such a product would allow people the opportunity to indulge without feeling guilty. Accordingly, M&M Mars introduced Milky Way Lite Bar, a reduced-fat candy bar. This was the first nationally advertised candy bar labeled to meet regulations of the U.S. Food and Drug Administration's Nutrition Labeling and Education Act of 1990 for "lite" products. It has five grams of fat, half the fat of the average leading chocolate brands per 44.5 gram-serving. Close supervision of field workers, made possible by mall intercept interviewing, facilitated the research responsible for introducing yet another winner for M&M Mars.[4]

VALIDATION OF FIELD WORK

Validation of field work means verifying that field workers are submitting authentic interviews. To validate the study, the supervisors call 10 to 25 percent of the respondents to inquire whether the field workers actually conducted the interviews. The supervisors ask about the length and quality of the interview, reaction to the interviewer, and basic demographic data. The demographic information is cross-checked against the information reported by the interviewers on the questionnaires.

EVALUATION OF FIELD WORKERS

It is important to evaluate field workers to provide them with feedback on their performance. Evaluation helps identify the more effective field workers in order to build a better, higher-quality field force. As in the case of the Gallup organization in the opening vignette, the evaluation of field workers should be an ongoing process. The evaluation criteria should be clearly communicated to the field workers during their training. The evaluation of field workers should be based on the criteria of quantity (cost and time, response rates) and quality (quality of interviewing, quality of data), as shown in Figure 14.6.

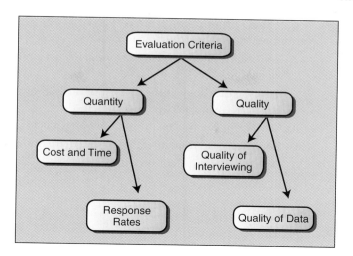

FIGURE 14.6
Evaluating Field Workers

Interviewers can be compared in terms of the total cost (salary and expenses) per completed interview. Field workers should also be evaluated on how they spend their time. Time should be broken down into categories such as actual interviewing, travel, and administration. It is important to monitor response rates on a timely basis so that corrective action can be taken if these rates are too low. Supervisors can help interviewers with an inordinate number of refusals by listening to the introductions they use and providing immediate feedback. When all the interviews are over, different field workers' percentage of refusals can be compared to identify the better workers.

To evaluate interviewers on the quality of interviewing, the supervisor must directly observe the interviewing process. The supervisor can do this in person, or the field worker can tape record the interview. The completed questionnaires of each interviewer should be evaluated for the quality of data. Some indicators of quality data are: (1) the recorded data are legible; (2) all instructions, including skip patterns (discussed in Chapter 11), are followed; (3) the answers to unstructured questions are recorded verbatim; (4) the answers to unstructured questions are meaningful and complete enough to be coded (discussed in Chapter 11); and (5) for structured questions, item nonresponse occurs infrequently.

SUMMARY ILLUSTRATION USING THE OPENING VIGNETTE

Notice the care the Gallup organization took in selecting its interviewers, choosing only 1 out of every 16 possible candidates. In selecting interviewers, Gallup looks for the following qualities: work orientation, teamwork, aptitude, pride, discipline, third ear, command, the ability to woo, and ethics. These interviewers are thoroughly trained by following the guidelines on interviewing by the Council of American Survey Research Organizations. Experienced and qualified supervisors closely supervise the interviewers. The interviewers' work is validated and evaluated, and they are continuously provided with feedback on performance. As a result, Gallup has been very successful in cultivating and retaining high-quality field workers who contribute significantly to the data collection process and the reputation of the organization.

The Council of American Survey Research Organizations has provided guidelines for effective interviewing:

1. Provide his or her full name, if asked by the respondent, as well as a phone number for the research firm.

2. Read each question exactly as written. Report any problems to the supervisor as soon as possible.

3. Read the questions in the order indicated on the questionnaire, following the proper skip sequences.

4. Clarify any question by the respondent in a neutral way.

5. Do not mislead respondents as to the length of the interview.

6. Do not reveal the identity of the ultimate client unless instructed to do so.

7. Keep a tally on each terminated interview and the reason for each termination.

8. Remain neutral in interviewing. Do not indicate agreement or disagreement with the respondent.

9. Speak slowly and distinctly so that words will be understood.

10. Record all replies verbatim, not paraphrased.

11. Avoid unnecessary conversations with the respondent.

12. Probe and clarify for additional comments on all open-ended questions, unless otherwise instructed. Probe and clarify in a neutral way.

13. Write neatly and legibly.

14. Check all work for thoroughness before turning it in to the supervisor.

15. When terminating a respondent, do so in a neutral way such as, "Thank you," or "Our quota has already been filled in this area, but thank you anyway."

16. Keep all studies, materials, and findings confidential.

17. Do not falsify any interviews or any answers to any questions.

18. Thank the respondent for participating in the study.

MARKETING RESEARCH AND TQM

Just as field work benefits from quality control procedures, it can also contribute to them. To monitor quality enhancement programs that have been implemented, a firm has to collect data and, hence, undertake field work. For example, quality and value-conscious firms periodically conduct customer satisfaction and employee satisfaction surveys. However, the quality programs can be monitored properly only if the field work or the data collection process conforms to high-quality standards.

Hiring external data collection firms can make quality control more difficult. This removes the company from having direct control over the selection, training, supervision, and evaluation of field workers. This problem can be addressed by working with field service agencies that have implemented quality management programs. Quality control is also enhanced when clear goals and guidelines are set for the data collection agency. The agency can then be evaluated on how well it has met the goals while following the guidelines. When the data are collected in-house, the company has more control and can focus on implementing proper field work procedures. Training and education of field workers are crucial. Recent Malcolm Baldrige award winners train each of their employees an average of 100 to 150 hours per year.

Regardless of whether field work is done using company field workers or an outside firm, validation of the quality of the work should be done inside the com-

FOCUS ON
ELRICK & LAVIDGE

At Elrick & Lavidge (E&L), field work is performed by full-time and part-time E&L employees and by employees of contract field work organizations. To illustrate the process of selecting the field force, we will describe the selection of telephone interviewers at E&L.

After a prospective telephone interviewer contacts E&L about employment, the candidate is told to leave a voice mail message listing his or her qualifications for the position. In reality, this is the first test of the candidate. The telephone center manager screens out many candidates at this time based on the vocal quality of their messages. Those who pass this first test are brought into E&L for an interview. The interview includes a typing test, a spelling test, a session in which the applicant reads passages out loud for the interviewer to hear, and a "detail test," which examines the applicant's ability to listen to and retain detailed information. The applicant's ability to successfully complete these tasks is highly correlated with his or her success in telephone interviewing.

After field workers are hired, they are entered into an "accelerated learning" program, a formalized, structured training program. The telephone interviewer training program consists of a two- to four-week training period. The new interviewer attends training sessions covering diverse topics, such as the use of the equipment, interviewing policies and techniques, and even probing techniques. These training sessions are augmented with formal, printed manuals that the interviewer keeps for review.

When the interviewer has completed training, she or he will enter the normal working environment. The phone center managers continue to monitor the administration of the interviews, randomly plugging into interviewer's conversations throughout the day. E&L's policy is to monitor each interviewer at least once per shift. The interviewer is reviewed using a standard form that rates her or his interviewing skills and lists areas for improvement.

E&L has implemented a number of controls that are used to validate the data and to identify error levels for each interviewer. By making follow-up phone calls to a random 10 percent sample of each interviewer's completed calls, E&L verifies that the respondents were actually contacted and actually gave the recorded responses. In a more positive light, this follow-up audit can also help E&L identify problems that individual interviewers may be having with the questionnaire. This can lead to additional training opportunities for the interviewer.

pany. As discussed earlier, well-designed validation procedures that are meticulously followed can go a long way toward enhancing the quality of data collection, and in turn, the quality of quality enhancement programs. The following example shows how AT&T uses a high-quality data collection process to gain a high level of customer satisfaction.

EXAMPLE
WINNING THE MALCOLM BALDRIGE NATIONAL QUALITY AWARD

AT&T's Customer Communications Services division (CCS) is one of its largest. It operates in the rapidly changing and highly competitive consumer long-distance service sector, vying with 500 other long-distance companies. CCS maintains a customer base of 100 million and interacts with 90 million customers on any given day. Needless to say, customer satisfaction is paramount for CCS. To ensure that CCS continues to offer the services its customers desire, the company constantly collects marketing research data.

A large majority of CCS's research is performed in-house. The data are collected by operators and other trained staff who are in direct contact with the customers. The selection, training, and supervision of these field workers are closely monitored, resulting in high-quality data. The data are used for a wide range of quality improvement efforts, including executive compensation. By focusing on the customers and building quality in all its operations, the CCS has won the Malcolm Baldrige National Quality Award and millions of satisfied customers.[5]

INTERNATIONAL MARKETING RESEARCH

The selection, training, supervision, and evaluation of field workers are critical in international marketing research. Because local field work agencies are unavailable in many countries, it may be necessary to recruit and train local field workers or import trained foreign workers. Using local field workers is preferable, however, since they are familiar with the local language and culture and can create an appropriate climate for the interview and be sensitive to the concerns of the respondents.

Extensive training of field workers may be required, and close supervision may be necessary. In many countries, interviewers tend to help respondents with the answers and select households or sampling units based on personal considerations rather than the sampling plan. Also, interviewer cheating may be more of a problem in many foreign countries than in the United States. For these reasons, validation of field work is critical. Proper application of field work procedures can greatly reduce these difficulties and result in consistent and useful findings, as the following example demonstrates.

EXAMPLE

AMERICANISM UNITES EUROPEANS

An image study conducted in 1999 by Research International, a U.K. market research company, showed that despite unification of the European market, European consumers still increasingly favor U.S. products. The survey was conducted in Germany, the United Kingdom, Italy, and the Netherlands. In each country, local interviewers and supervisors were used because it was believed that they would be better able to identify with the respondents. However, the field workers were trained extensively and supervised closely to ensure that appropriate procedures were followed. The validation efforts were doubled: 20 percent, rather than the minimum 10 percent, of the interviews were validated. These procedures ensured quality results and minimized the variability in country-to-country results due to differences in field work.

A total of 6,724 personal interviews were conducted. Europeans gave U.S. products high marks for being innovative; some countries also regarded them as fashionable and of high quality. Interestingly, France, often considered anti-American, also emerged as pro-American. Among the 1,034 French consumers surveyed, 40 percent considered U.S. products fashionable and 38 percent believed they were innovative, although only 15 percent said U.S. products were of high quality. In addition, when asked what nationality they preferred for a new company in their area, a U.S. company was the first choice. These findings were comparable and consistent across the four countries. A key to the discovery of these findings was the use of local field workers and extensive training and supervision that resulted in uniformly high-quality data across the different countries.

These findings are very useful for U.S. firms marketing in Europe. "Rather than trying to hide the fact that they are American, we think companies ought to stress or try to exploit their American heritage," says Eric Salaam, director of European operations for the Henley Center, the U.K. economic forecasting consultancy. U.S. firms have, in fact, capitalized on the "made in America" equity. As a result, exports to Europe have been soaring in recent years.[6]

TECHNOLOGY AND MARKETING RESEARCH

A new computer technology, predictive dialing, is allowing marketing research companies using telephone surveys to double their call attempts. A computer accesses a file of phone numbers and does the dialing. When a call is answered, it is instantly sent to an interviewer. The interviewer's computer terminal displays the caller's name and the appropriate survey to use for the caller. If the computer dials a number that is not answered, it will recycle that number. The computer selects the telephone numbers in such a way as to maximize the probability of contact by predicting that a respondent will be at home and will participate at that time. These systems also include provisions for long, complicated questionnaires with computer-assisted quota control, telephone number management, interviewer monitoring and supervision, and management reports. Computer technology has also made personal interviewing more efficient. Many field workers now use Palmtop personal computers to collect data that are then transmitted to a central computer using a wireless system.

New technology makes it possible for companies to conduct telephone interviews without the use of a live interviewer. As discussed earlier (Chapter 7), interviews can be conducted using Completely Automated Telephone Survey (CATS). These systems use "interactive voice response technology." Because no human interviewer is used, CATS greatly reduces interviewer biases by conducting standardized interviews.

ETHICS IN MARKETING RESEARCH

High ethical standards should be used when collecting data. Researchers and field workers should make the respondents feel comfortable by addressing their apprehensions and concerns. This can be done by providing respondents with adequate information about the project, addressing their questions, and clearly stating the responsibilities and expectations of both the field workers and the respondents at the beginning of the interview. Otherwise, respondents may be unsure about how their answers will be used and may not respond candidly. Researchers and field workers should respect respondents' time, feelings, privacy, and right to self-determination.

Researchers and the field work agencies are also responsible to the clients for following the accepted procedures for the selection, training, supervision, validation, and evaluation of field workers. Field work procedures should be carefully documented and made available to clients. As illustrated by the following example, ethical codes are available for guiding field work/data collection.

EXAMPLE

AN ETHICAL CODE FOR DATA COLLECTION AND CODING

The Marketing Research Association (MRA) recently designed a new Code of Data Collection Standards for marketing and opinion researchers that clarifies expectations by delineating specific acceptable practices. The new code addresses the following issues:

- The accuracy of statements given to respondents to secure cooperation
- The protection of respondent anonymity and the need to obtain consent when anonymity cannot be assured
- Respect for the respondent's right to refuse cooperation
- The need for parental consent before interviewing children
- Treating respondents with respect and not attempting to influence responses

The code covers rules (better stated as guidelines) regarding data collection companies' responsibilities to clients, clients' responsibilities to data collectors, and data collection companies' responsibilities to the general public and business community.

The guidelines regarding data collection companies' responsibilities to clients require that:

- Research be conducted per client specifications.
- The confidentiality of techniques, information, clients, and respondents will be protected.
- Multiple surveys are not administered sequentially during one interview without express permission to do so.
- Research results are reported accurately and promptly.
- No misrepresentations are made with regard to qualifications, experience, skills, or facilities.
- Membership in the MRA not be used as proof of competency.

The guidelines regarding clients' responsibilities to data collectors state that clients will:

- Provide safe products/services and disclose all product contents.
- Provide instructions.
- Not request activities that violate the code or are prohibited by law.

The guidelines regarding data collection companies' responsibilities to the general public and business community require that:

> • Public confidence in marketing research not be abused.
> • Interviewers be made aware of special conditions applicable to minors.
>
> Adherence to these guidelines will go a long way in resolving many of the ethical dilemmas encountered in field work.[7]

INTERNET APPLICATIONS

The Internet can play a valuable role in all the phases of field work: selection, training, supervision, validation, and evaluation of field workers. As far as selection is concerned, interviewers can be located, interviewed, and hired by using the Internet. This process can be initiated, for example, by posting job vacancies notices for interviewers at the company Web site, bulletin boards, and other suitable locations. While this would confine the search to only Internet-savvy interviewers, this may well be a qualification for the job.

Similarly, the Internet with its multimedia capabilities can be a good supplementary tool for training the field workers in all aspects of interviewing. Training in this manner can complement personal training programs and add value to the process. Supervision is enhanced by facilitating communication between the supervisors and the interviewers via e-mail and secured chatrooms. Central office control can be strengthened by posting progress reports, quality, and cost-control information on a secured location at a Web site, so that it is easily available to all the relevant parties.

Validation of field work, especially for personal and telephone interviews, can be easily accomplished for those respondents who have an e-mail address or access to the Internet. These respondents can be sent a short verification survey by e-mail or asked to visit a Web site where the survey is posted. Finally, the evaluation criteria can be communicated to field workers during the training stage by using the Internet, and performance feedback can also be provided to them using this medium.

SPSS

SPSS offers several programs to assist in the field work or data collection. Moreover, a number of different methods of administering the survey can be accommodated, including telephone, electronic, mail, and personal interviewing.

1. *SPSS Data Entry Station:* This deployment method will put a copy of the questionnaire on a computer so that a data entry operator or respondent can enter the answers on the screen using the keyboard and mouse (without giving them the ability to edit the form). In this way, to some extent, Data Entry can simulate a proper CATI system because you can prepopulate the data with the phone number and basic details of the respondent so the information appears as the operator moves through the list. However, this system completely lacks the ability to keep a call log and a callback list, which most good, true CATI systems should do.

2. *SPSS Data Entry Enterprise Server (DEES):* This deployment method will upload a copy of the questionnaire to a Web server so that data entry operators or respondents can log on using a password and enter their results without having to install anything to their local machine. DEES can be used on both

intranet and Internet settings. This software also includes technology that prevents Ballot Stuffing (a respondent answering the survey multiple times).

3. *Printing the Form:* This can be done by using SPSS DE Builder to simply print the form after it has been designed for a mail survey or personal interviewing. This is the least sophisticated because the researcher will not be able to take advantage of space-saving pull-down menus or any of the rules that were included. The rules can be used when the follow-up data entry is done into the computer, but in many situations if there is an error it may be too late to correct it. For a personal interview, it may be a better option for the interviewer to use a laptop with the form in DE Station as the rules would "fire" as the questions are answered, thus allowing for quick corrections if required.

SUMMARY

Researchers have two major options for collecting data: developing their own organizations or contracting with field work agencies. In either case, data collection involves the use of a field force. Field workers should be carefully selected and trained in important aspects of field work, including making the initial contact, asking the questions, probing, recording the answers, and terminating the interview. Supervision of field workers involves quality control and editing, sampling control, control of cheating, and central office control. Validation of field work can be accomplished by calling 10 to 25 percent of those who have been identified as respondents and inquiring whether the interviews actually took place. Field workers should be evaluated on the basis of cost and time, response rates, quality of interviewing, and quality of data collection.

Field work can both contribute to and benefit from quality control procedures. The selection, training, supervision, and evaluation of field workers is even more critical in international marketing research, as local field work agencies are not available in many countries. Computer technology is available to facilitate and even completely automate data collection. Ethical issues include making the respondents feel comfortable in the data collection process so that their experience is positive. Every effort must be undertaken to ensure that the data are of high quality. The Internet can greatly facilitate the field work/data collection process.

KEY TERMS AND CONCEPTS

Probing, 433

Sampling control, 435

ACRONYMS

In the field work/data collection process, the organization VESTS in the field workers:

V alidation of field work

E valuation of field workers

S election of field workers

T raining of field workers

S upervision of field workers

The areas in which field workers should be trained may be summarized by the acronym TRAIN:

> T erminating the interview
> R ecording the answers
> A sking the questions
> I nitial contact development
> N osy behavior: probing

EXERCISES

1. What options are available to researchers for collecting data?
2. Describe the field work/data collection process.
3. What qualifications should field workers possess?
4. What are the guidelines for asking questions?
5. What is probing?
6. How should the answers to unstructured questions be recorded?
7. How should the field worker terminate the interview?
8. What aspects are involved in the supervision of field workers?
9. How can respondent selection problems be controlled?
10. What is validation of field work? How is this done?
11. Describe the criteria that should be used for evaluating field workers.

PROBLEMS

1. Write interviewer instructions for in-home personal interviews to be conducted by students.
2. Comment on the following field situations, making recommendations for corrective action.
   a. One of the interviewers has an excessive rate of refusals in in-home personal interviewing.
   b. In a CATI situation, many phone numbers are giving a busy signal during the first dialing attempt.
   c. An interviewer reports that, at the end of the interviews, many respondents asked if they had answered the questions correctly.
   d. While validating the field work, a respondent reports that she cannot remember being interviewed over the telephone, but the interviewer insists that the interview was conducted.

INTERNET AND COMPUTER EXERCISES

1. Visit the Web sites of some marketing research suppliers. Make a report of all the material related to field work that is posted on these sites.
2. Visit the Marketing Research Association Web site *(www.mra-net.org)* and examine the ethical codes relating to data collection. Write a brief report.

3. Using PERT/CPM software such as MacProject, Timeline, Harvard Project Manager, Microsoft Project, or Category PERTmaster, develop a field work schedule for conducting a national survey of consumer preferences for fast foods involving 2,500 mall intercept interviews in Los Angeles, Salt Lake City, Dallas, St. Louis, Milwaukee, New Orleans, Cincinnati, Orlando, Atlanta, New York City, and Boston.

ACTIVITIES

ROLE PLAYING

1. You are a field supervisor. Ask a fellow student to assume the role of an interviewer and another student the role of a respondent. Train the interviewer to conduct in-home personal interviews by giving a live demonstration.
2. Exchange the roles of interviewer and supervisor in the role-playing situation described above.

FIELD WORK

1. Arrange a field trip to a marketing research firm or data collection agency. Ask the field work supervisor to describe the agency's field work process. How does it compare to the one described in this book?
2. Arrange a visit to a mall intercept interviewing facility when interviews are being conducted. Observe the interviewing process. Write a report about your visit.

GROUP DISCUSSION

1. Discuss the impact of women's changing lifestyles on field work during the last decade. Conduct an Internet search for the relevant materials.
2. Discuss the notion of interviewer cheating. Why do interviewers cheat? How can cheating be detected and prevented?

NOTES

1. Based on: "Gallup to Measure Postal Customer Satisfaction," *Fund Raising Management,* 28(11) (January 1998): 7; and Gale D. Muller and Jane Miller, "Interviewers Make the Difference," *Marketing Research: A Magazine of Management & Applications,* 8(1) (Spring 1996): 8–9.

2. Ted Samson, "Interviewing 101–For Managers," *InfoWorld,* 22(13) (March 27, 2000): 101; Peggy Lawless, "Empathic Interviewing Equals Insightful Results," *Marketing News,* 33(1) (January 4, 1999): 20; and Bud Phillips, "The Four Faces of Interviewers," *Journal of Data Collection,* 23 (Winter 1983): 35–40.

3. Based on Susan Kuchinskas, "iPlac," *Adweek,* 49(18) (May 3, 1999): 5; and "Edison, American Marketing Association, Best New Product Awards," *Marketing News,* 31(6) (March 17, 1997): E6.

4. Based on Kevin O'Rourke, "New Milky Way Seizes the Night," *Drug Store News,* 22(9) (June 26, 2000): 212; and "Edison, American Marketing Association, Best New Product Awards," *Marketing News,* 31(6) (March 17, 1997): E6.

5. Todd Wasserman, "AT&T Repeats 'All Day, Every Day' All Day," *Brandweek,* 41(13) (March 27, 2000): 5; Beth Snyder, "AT&T Jumps in with 7 Cents Call Plan vs. MCI, Sprint," *Advertising Age,* 70(37) (September 6, 1999): 14; and "AT&T Consumer Communication Services," *Industrial & Commercial Training,* 27(10) (1995): 35–36.

6. Dana Blankenhorn, "Export Sites Help Marketers Go Global," *Advertising Age's Business Marketing,* 84(4) (April 1999): 2, 38; and Laurel Wentz, "Poll: Europe Favors U.S. Products," *Advertising Age* (September 23, 1991).

7. "DMA Board Authorizes Revisions on Data Use," *Direct Marketing,* 60(12) (April 1998): 7; Betsy Peterson, "Data Collection: Ethics Revisited," *Marketing Research: A Magazine of Management & Applications,* 8(4) (Winter 1996): 47–48.

15

DATA PREPARATION AND ANALYSIS STRATEGY

THE RESEARCHER MUST RESIST THE URGE TO ANALYZE THE DATA BEFORE THEY HAVE BEEN PROPERLY EDITED, CODED, CLEANED, AND PREPARED FOR ANALYSIS.

Opening Questions

1. What is the nature and scope of data preparation, and how can the data preparation process be described?
2. What is involved in questionnaire checking and editing?
3. How should questionnaires be coded to prepare the data for analysis?
4. What methods are available for cleaning the data and treating missing responses?
5. How do we select a data analysis strategy?
6. What is the role of data analysis in implementing quality management programs?
7. How should data collected in international marketing research projects be prepared?
8. What is the role of technology in facilitating data preparation?
9. Which ethical issues are important in data preparation and analysis?
10. What is the role of the Internet in the data preparation process?

Howard L. Sanders, Director—Data Management, Elrick & Lavidge.
Howard "Bud" Sanders is responsible for the company's programming and processing of data. He supervises a staff located in the various Elrick & Lavidge offices.

DATABASE AWAKENS
A SLEEPING GIANT

Since its introduction, Sears, Roebuck and Company has been a leading department store retailer of apparel, home products, and automobile products and services. In the late 1990s, Sears tried to lose its reputation as a "hardware and tools" store in order to create a more trendy and modern store image for customers. Once held up as a textbook example of a mighty marketer failing to adapt to changing consumer demands, Sears, Roebuck and Company has since become an innovator in the retail world, pulling off a comeback that has even the retailer's harshest critics gushing.

One crucial element in its success was building a high-quality database about its customers and potential customers. By the beginning of 2001, Sears had built a massive database of more than two thirds of U.S. households. The data are collected from a variety of primary and secondary sources. One hallmark is the care taken to prepare the data before they become a part of the database. In the case of primary data, the completed questionnaires returned from the field are carefully checked and edited for incomplete responses (e.g., questions that are incorrectly skipped) or inconsistent responses (e.g., a respondent reports purchases made on Sears credit card but does not have one). Any questionnaires with unsatisfactory responses are simply discarded, as the proportion of such respondents is small, and the sample size is large. The data are coded by following appropriate procedures. To ensure uniformity in coding, Sears has prepared a codebook containing the coding instructions and the necessary information about the variables in the data set. The data are then transcribed from the questionnaires into the computer, using state-of-the art technology.

Further checks are performed on the data to ascertain their consistency and accuracy. An effort is made to identify data that are out of range (e.g., a response of 8 on a 1 to 7 scale) or logically inconsistent (e.g., sum of percentages totaling more than 100 percent), or have extreme values (e.g., household size of 11). Missing values are kept to a minimum by proper selection, training, and supervision of field workers and are treated by following a variety of methods to determine the impact on the results. A similar process is followed for data collected from secondary sources.

This superior database enables Sears to identify the needs of the marketplace and target its marketing efforts accordingly. Guided by these findings, Sears spent $4 billion renovating its stores. It markedly improved store layout, design, cleanliness, and merchandising mix. The move is clearly paying off, with Sears reporting higher sales and revenue per selling square foot than it did in the twentieth century.[1]

OVERVIEW

After the researcher has defined the research problem and developed a suitable approach (Chapter 2), formulated an appropriate research design (Chapters 3 through 13), and conducted field work (Chapter 14), she or he can move on to data preparation and analysis, the fifth step of the marketing research process. Figure 15.1 briefly explains the focus of the chapter, the relationship of this chapter to the previous ones, and the step of the marketing research process on which this chapter concentrates.

Before the raw data contained in the questionnaires can be subjected to statistical analysis, they must be converted into a suitable form. Care exercised in the data preparation phase can substantially improve the quality of the findings, resulting in better managerial decisions, as explained in the Sears opening vignette. On the other hand, inadequate attention to data preparation can seriously compromise statistical results, leading to biased findings and incorrect interpretation.

This chapter describes the data preparation process, which begins with checking the questionnaires for completeness. Then, we discuss the editing of data and provide guidelines for handling illegible, incomplete, inconsistent, ambiguous, or otherwise unsatisfactory responses. We also describe coding, transcribing, and data cleaning, emphasizing the treatment of missing responses. We then discuss selecting a data analysis strategy, data preparation issues in total quality management and international marketing research, the role of technology, and the ethical issues and Internet applications related to data processing. Figure 15.2 gives an overview of the topics discussed in this chapter and how they flow from one to the next.

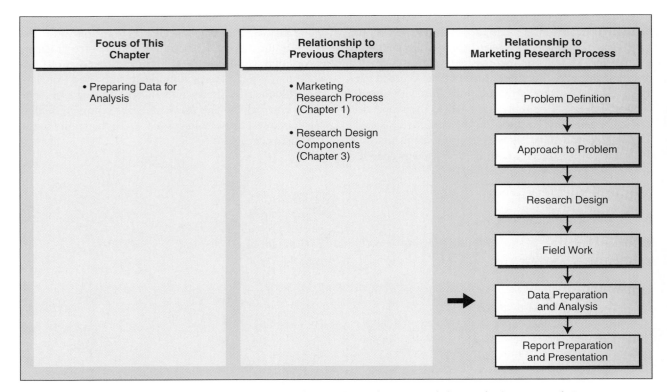

FIGURE 15.1 Relationship of Data Preparation to the Previous Chapters and the Marketing Research Process

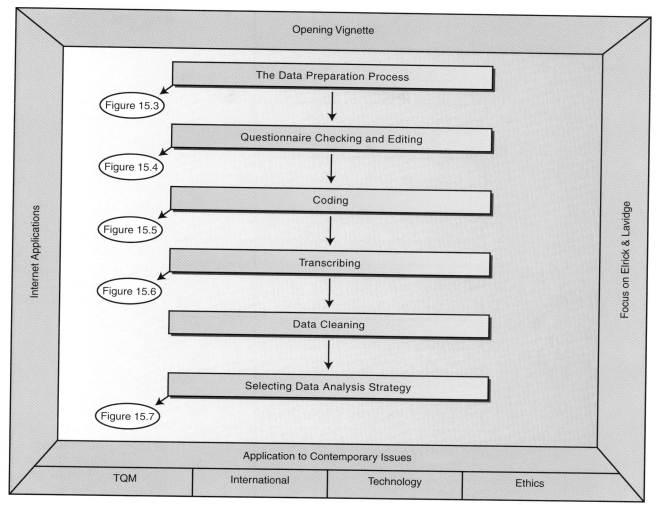

FIGURE 15.2 Data Preparation: An Overview

THE DATA PREPARATION PROCESS

The data preparation process is shown in Figure 15.3. Sears followed a similar process, as explained in the opening vignette. The entire process is guided by the preliminary plan of data analysis that was formulated in the research design phase (Chapter 3). As the first step, the field work supervisor checks for acceptable questionnaires. This is followed by editing, coding, and transcribing the data, all done by the data collection agency as part of field work (see Chapter 14). The researcher cleans the data then performs further checks for consistency and specifies how missing responses will be treated. The researcher then selects an appropriate data analysis strategy. The final data analysis strategy differs from the preliminary plan of data analysis due to the information and insights gained since the preliminary plan was formulated. Data preparation should begin as soon as the first batch of questionnaires is received from the field, while the field work is still going on. Thus, if any problems are detected, the field work can be modified to incorporate corrective action.

FIGURE 15.3
Data Preparation
Process

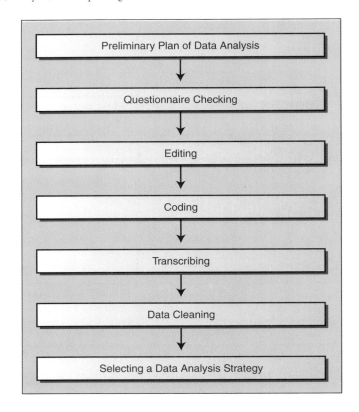

QUESTIONNAIRE CHECKING

The initial step in questionnaire checking involves checking for completeness and interviewing quality. This is a continuous process and begins as soon as the first set of questionnaires is returned, while field work is still underway. Thus, any problems can be detected early on and corrective action taken before too many surveys have been completed. A questionnaire returned from the field may be unacceptable for several reasons. For example, parts of the questionnaire may be incomplete, skip patterns may not have been followed (see Chapter 11), one or more pages may be missing, and so on.

If quotas or cell group sizes have been imposed (see Chapter 12), the acceptable questionnaires should be classified and counted accordingly. Any problems in meeting the sampling requirements should be identified and corrective action taken, such as conducting additional interviews in the underrepresented cells.

EDITING

editing
A review of the questionnaires with the objective of increasing accuracy and precision.

Editing involves reviewing questionnaires to increase accuracy and precision. It consists of screening questionnaires to identify illegible, incomplete, inconsistent, or ambiguous responses, as in the opening vignette.

Responses may be illegible if they have been poorly recorded, such as answers to unstructured or open-ended questions. Likewise, questionnaires may be incomplete to varying degrees. A few or many questions may be unanswered. At this stage, the researcher makes a preliminary check for consistency. Certain obvious inconsistencies can be easily detected. For example, a respondent reports an annual income of less than $20,000, yet indicates frequent shopping at prestigious department stores such as Saks

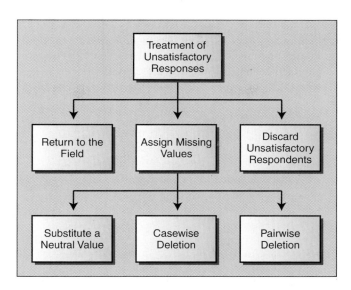

FIGURE 15.4
Treatment of
Unsatisfactory Responses

Fifth Avenue and Neiman-Marcus. A response is ambiguous if, for example, the respondent has circled both 4 and 5 on a seven-point scale.

Unsatisfactory responses are commonly handled by returning to the field to get better data, by assigning missing values, or by discarding unsatisfactory respondents (Figure 15.4). The questionnaires with unsatisfactory responses may be returned to the field, where the interviewers recontact the respondents. This approach is particularly attractive for business and industrial marketing surveys in which the sample sizes are small and the respondents are easily identifiable. If returning the questionnaires to the field is not feasible, the editor may assign missing values to unsatisfactory responses. This approach may be desirable if (1) the number of respondents with unsatisfactory responses is small, (2) the proportion of unsatisfactory responses for each of these respondents is small, or (3) the variables with unsatisfactory responses are not the key variables.

Alternatively, the respondents with unsatisfactory responses are simply discarded. This approach may have merit when (1) the proportion of unsatisfactory respondents is small (less than 10 percent), (2) the sample size is large, (3) the unsatisfactory respondents do not differ from satisfactory respondents in obvious ways (for example, demographics, product usage characteristics), (4) the proportion of unsatisfactory responses for each of these respondents is large, or (5) responses on key variables are missing (see the opening vignette). However, unsatisfactory respondents may differ from satisfactory respondents in systematic ways, and the decision to designate a respondent as unsatisfactory may be subjective. Both of these factors related to unsatisfactory respondents may bias the results. If the researcher decides to discard unsatisfactory respondents, the procedure adopted to identify these respondents and their number should be reported by the researcher in the project report, as in the following example.

EXAMPLE

A COMPLAINT AGAINST CONSUMER COMPLAINTS

In a study examining consumer complaints, 1,000 questionnaires were mailed to households in each of three service categories: automotive repair, medical care, and banking services. The numbers of responses received were: automotive repair, 155; medical care, 166; and banking services, 172. The returned questionnaires were carefully checked and edited. Respondents who did not meet the qualifying criteria (being able to recall a recent dissatisfying experience) and those with a large number of missing values or missing values on key variables were discarded. The usable samples that remained were: automotive repair, 116; medical care, 125; and banking services, 104.

The researchers complained that a large number of respondents had to be discarded because of failure to meet the qualifying criteria or a high incidence of missing values. These complaints are justified because discarding such a high proportion of returned questionnaires (25.2 percent for automotive repair, 24.7 percent for medical care, and 39.5 percent for banking services) is not a good research practice. According to the general guidelines, no more than 10 percent of the returned questionnaires should be discarded.[2]

CODING

coding
The assignment of a code to represent a specific response to a specific question along with the data record and column position that code will occupy.

codebook
A book containing coding instructions and the necessary information about variables in the data set.

Coding means assigning a code, usually a number, to each possible response to each question. The code includes an indication of the column position (field) and data record it will occupy. For example, sex of respondents may be coded as 1 for females and 2 for males. A field represents a single item of data, such as sex of the respondent. A record consists of related fields, such as sex, marital status, age, household size, occupation, and so on. Thus, each record can have several columns. Generally, all the data for a respondent will be stored on a single record, although a number of records may be used for each respondent. It is often helpful to prepare a **codebook** containing the coding instructions and the necessary information about the variables in the data set (see opening vignette).

The data (all the records) for all the respondents are stored in a computer file, as illustrated in Table 15.1. In this table, the columns represent the fields, and the rows represent the records or respondents, as there is one record per respondent. Table 15.1 presents coded data for part of the record. These data have been coded according to the coding scheme specified in Figure 15.5. Columns 1–3 represent a single field and contain the

TABLE 15.1   Illustrative Computer File: Department Store Patronage Project

| | Fields Column Numbers | | | | | |
RESPONDENT	1–3	4	5–6	7–8..........	26........35	77
1	001	1	31	01	6544234553	5
2	002	1	31	01	5564435433	4
3	003	1	31	01	4655243324	4
4	004	1	31	01	5463244645	6
Record #271	271	1	31	55	6652354435	5

Column Number	Variable Number	Variable Name	Question Number	Coding Instructions	
1–3	1	Respondent ID		001 to 890 add leading zeros as necessary	
4	2	Record Number		1 (same for all respondents)	
5–6	3	Project Code		31 (same for all respondents)	
7–8	4	Interview Code		As coded on the questionnaire	
9–14	5	Date Code		As coded on the questionnaire	
15–20	6	Time Code		As coded on the questionnaire	
21–22	7	Validation Code		As coded on the questionnaire	
23–24		Blank		Leave these columns blank	
25	8	Who shops	I	Male head	=1
				Female head	=2
				Other	=3
				Punch the number circled	
				Missing values	=9
26	9	Familiarity with store 1	IIa	For question II parts a through j	
				Punch the number circled	
27	10	Familiarity with store 2	IIb	Not so familiar	=1
				Very familiar	=6
				Missing Values	=9
28	11	Familiarity with store 3	IIc		
35	18	Familiarity with store 10	IIj		

FIGURE 15.5 A Codebook Excerpt

respondent numbers coded 001 to 271. Column 4 contains the record number. This column has a value of 1 for all the rows since only one record is used for each respondent. Columns 5–6 contain the project code, which is 31. The next two columns, 7–8, display the interviewer code, which varies from 01 to 55 for respondent number 271. Columns 26–35, each representing one field, contain familiarity ratings for the 10 stores, with values ranging from 1 to 6. Finally, column 77 represents the rating of store 10 on prices. There are 271 rows, indicating that data for 271 respondents are stored in this file. One can also use a spreadsheet program to enter the data, as most analysis programs can import data from a spreadsheet. In this case, the data for each respondent for each field is a cell.

If the questionnaire contains only structured questions or very few unstructured questions, it is precoded. This means that codes are assigned before field work is conducted. If the questionnaire contains unstructured questions, codes are assigned after the questionnaires have been returned from the field (postcoding). While precoding was briefly discussed in Chapter 11 on questionnaire design, we provide further guidelines in the next section.

Coding Questions

The respondent code and the record number should appear on each record in the data. The following additional codes should be included for each respondent: project code, interviewer code, date and time codes, and validation code. **Fixed field codes** are highly desirable. This means that the number of records for each respondent is the same and the same data appear in the same column(s) for all respondents. If possible, standard codes should be used for missing data. For example, a code of 9 could be used for a single-column variable (responses coded on a 1 to 7 scale), 99 for a double-column variable

fixed field code
A code in which the number of records for each respondent are the same, and the same data appear in the same columns for all respondents.

(responses coded on a 1 to 11 scale), and so on. The missing value codes should be distinct from the codes assigned to the legitimate responses.

Coding structured questions is relatively simple since the response options are predetermined. The researcher assigns a code for each response to each question and specifies the appropriate record and columns in which the response codes are to appear. For example,

In the last month, have you bought a product or service over the Internet?

1. Yes   2. No   (94)

For this question, a "Yes" response is coded 1 and a "No" response receives a 2. The numbers in parentheses indicate that the code assigned will appear in column 94 for this respondent. Because only one response is allowed and there are only two possible responses (1 or 2), a single column is sufficient. In general, a single column is sufficient to code a structured question with a single response if there are less than nine possible responses.

In questions that permit multiple responses, each possible response option should be assigned a separate column. Such questions include those about brand ownership or usage, television viewing, and magazine readership, as in the following example.

EXAMPLE

READING MAGAZINE READERSHIP

Which magazines have you read during the last two months? ("X" as many as apply)

Time	❑	(102)
Newsweek	❑	(103)
Business Week	❑	(104)
Forbes	❑	(105)
Fortune	❑	(106)
Economist	❑	(107)
Other magazines	❑	(108)

Suppose a respondent checked *Time, Newsweek,* and other magazines. On the record for this respondent, a 1 will be entered in the column numbers 102, 103, and 108. All the other columns (104, 105, 106, and 107) will receive a 0.

Coding unstructured or open-ended questions is more complex. Respondents' verbatim responses are recorded on the questionnaire. Codes are then developed and assigned to these responses. The following guidelines are suggested for coding unstructured questions and questionnaires in general.

Category codes should be mutually exclusive and collectively exhaustive. Categories are mutually exclusive if each response fits into one and only one category code. Categories should not overlap. Categories are collectively exhaustive if every response fits into one of the assigned category codes. This can be achieved by adding a category code of "other" or "none of the above." However, only a few (10 percent or less) of the responses should fall into this category. The vast majority of the responses should be classified into meaningful categories.

Data should be coded to retain as much detail as possible. For example, if data on the exact number of trips made on commercial airlines by business travelers have been obtained, they should be coded as such, rather than grouped into two category codes of "infrequent fliers" and "frequent fliers." Obtaining information on the exact number of trips allows the researcher to later define categories of business travelers in several different ways (for example, less than 3 trips per month, 4 to 6 trips per month, 7 to 10 trips per month, 11 to 15 trips per month, and more than 15 trips per month). If the categories were predefined (for example, infrequent fliers and frequent fliers), the subsequent analysis of data would be limited by those categories.

TRANSCRIBING

Transcribing data involves transferring the coded data from the questionnaires or coding sheets onto disks or directly into computers by key punching or other means, as in the opening vignette. If the data have been collected via computer-assisted telephone interviewing (CATI) or personal interviewing (CAPI), this step is unnecessary since the data are entered directly into the computer as they are collected. Besides keypunching, the data can be transferred by using mark sense forms, optical scanning, or computerized sensory analysis (Figure 15.6).

Mark sense forms require responses to be recorded with a special pencil in a predesignated area coded for that response. A machine can then read the data. Optical scanning involves direct machine reading of the codes and simultaneous transcription. A familiar example of optical scanning is the transcription of UPC (universal product code) data at supermarket checkout counters. Technological advances have resulted in computerized sensory analysis systems, which automate the data collection process. The questions appear on a computerized gridpad, and responses are recorded directly into the computer using a sensing device.

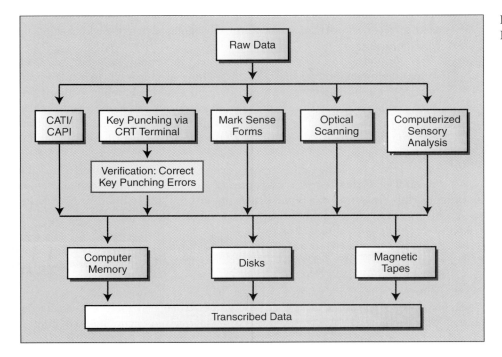

FIGURE 15.6
Data Transcription

When CATI, CAPI, or electronic methods are used, data are verified as they are collected. In the case of inadmissible responses, the computer will prompt the interviewer or respondent. In case of admissible responses, the interviewer or the respondent can see the recorded response on the screen and verify it before proceeding.

The selection of a data transcription method is guided by the type of interviewing method used and the availability of equipment. If CATI, CAPI, or electronic methods are used, the data are entered directly into the computer. Keypunching into a computer is most frequently used for ordinary telephone, in-home, mall intercept, and mail interviews. However, the use of computerized sensory analysis systems in personal interviews is growing with the increasing use of gridpads and handheld computers. Optical scanning can be used in structured and repetitive surveys, and mark sense forms are used in special cases.

DATA CLEANING

data cleaning
Thorough and extensive checks for consistency and treatment of missing responses.

Data cleaning includes consistency checks and treatment of missing responses. While preliminary consistency checks have been made during editing, the checks at this stage are more thorough and extensive since they are made by computer.

Consistency Checks

consistency checks
A part of the data cleaning process that identifies data that are out of range, or logically inconsistent, or that have extreme values. Data with values not defined by the coding scheme are inadmissible.

Consistency checks identify data that are out of range, logically inconsistent, or have extreme values (see opening vignette). Out-of-range data values are inadmissible and must be corrected. For example, respondents have been asked to express their degree of agreement with a series of lifestyle statements on a 1 to 5 scale. Assuming that 9 has been designated for missing values, data values of 0, 6, 7, and 8 are out of range. These out-of-range responses can arise due to respondent errors or interviewer errors. Computer packages such as SPSS, SAS, MINITAB, and EXCEL can be programmed to identify out-of-range values for each variable and print out the respondent code, variable code, variable name, record number, column number, and out-of-range value.[3] This makes it easy to check each variable systematically for out-of-range values. The correct responses can be determined by going back to the edited and coded questionnaire.

Responses can be logically inconsistent in various ways. For example, a respondent may indicate that she charges long-distance calls to a calling card, even though she does not have one. Or a respondent might report both unfamiliarity with and frequent use of the same product. The necessary information (respondent code, variable code, variable name, record number, column number, and inconsistent values) can be printed to locate these responses and take corrective action.

Finally, extreme values should be closely examined. Not all extreme values result from errors, but they may point to problems with the data. For example, an extremely low evaluation of a brand may be the result of the respondent's indiscriminately circling 1s (on a 1 to 7 rating scale) on all attributes of this brand.

Consistency checks are valuable in identifying problems with the data.

EXAMPLE

CUSTOM CLEANING

According to Joann Harristhal of Custom Research, completed questionnaires from the field often have many small errors because of the inconsistent quality of interviewing. For example, qualifying responses are not circled or skip patterns are not followed accurately.

These small errors can be costly. When responses from such questionnaires are put into a computer, Custom Research runs a cleaning program that checks for completeness and logic. Discrepancies are identified on a computer printout, which the tabulation supervisors check. Once the errors are identified, appropriate corrective action is taken before data analysis is carried out. Custom Research has found that this procedure substantially increases the quality of statistical results.

Treatment of Missing Responses

Missing responses represent values of a variable that are unknown, either because respondents provided ambiguous answers or their answers were not properly recorded. The incidence of missing responses should be minimized by proper selection, training, and supervision of field workers (see Chapter 14), as illustrated by Sears in the opening vignette. Treatment of missing responses poses problems, particularly if the proportion of missing responses is more than 10 percent. The following options are available for the treatment of missing responses (Figure 15.4):

1. **Substitute a neutral value.** A neutral value, typically the mean response to the variable, is substituted for missing responses. Thus, the mean of the variable remains unchanged and other statistics, such as correlations, may not be affected much if the proportion of missing values is small. While this approach has some merit, the logic of substituting a mean value (say 4) for respondents who, if they had answered, might have used either high ratings (6 or 7) or low ratings (1 or 2) is questionable.

2. **Casewise deletion.** In **casewise deletion,** cases or respondents with any missing responses are discarded from the analysis. Suppose 20 percent of the respondents do not respond to the income questions. All of these respondents will be excluded from analysis that involves the income variable, thus reducing the sample size by 20 percent. If several variables are involved in the analysis (for example, income, education, occupation), respondents with missing values on any of those variables will be excluded. Because many respondents may have missing responses on several variables, this approach could result in a small sample. Throwing away large amounts of data is undesirable because it is costly and time consuming to collect data. Furthermore, respondents with missing responses could differ from respondents with complete responses in systematic ways. If so, casewise deletion could seriously bias the results.

3. **Pairwise deletion.** In **pairwise deletion,** instead of discarding all cases with any missing values, the researcher uses only the cases or respondents with complete responses for each calculation. Suppose the researcher is interested in calculating pairwise correlations (see Chapter 18) between a set of variables—say awareness, attitude, preference, and purchase intention—all measured on a 1 to 7 scale. Then, in calculating the correlation between attitude and preference, all respondents with legitimate responses on the two variables will be included in the analysis, even though these respondents may have missing values on the other two variables, namely, awareness and purchase intentions. In contrast, in casewise deletion, respondents with missing values on any of the four variables would be excluded from the analysis.

missing responses
Values of a variable that are unknown as these respondents did not provide unambiguous answers to the question.

casewise deletion
A method for handling missing responses in which cases or respondents with any missing responses are discarded from the analysis.

pairwise deletion
A method of handling missing values in which for each calculation or analysis, only the cases or respondents with complete responses are considered.

Pairwise deletion may be appropriate when: (1) the sample size is large, (2) there are few missing responses, and (3) the variables are not highly related. Yet, this procedure can produce results that are unappealing or even infeasible as different calculations in an analysis may be based on different sample sizes. For example, statistics, such as pairwise correlations, may be based on different sample sizes, making comparisons more difficult.

The different procedures for the treatment of missing responses may yield different results, particularly when the responses are not missing at random and the variables are related. The researcher should carefully consider the implications of the various procedures before selecting a particular method for the treatment of nonresponse. It is also recommended that the data be analyzed using different options for handling missing responses to determine the impact on the results, as illustrated by Sears in the opening vignette.

SELECTING A DATA ANALYSIS STRATEGY

Selecting a data analysis strategy should be based on the earlier steps of the marketing research process, known characteristics of the data, properties of statistical techniques, and the background and philosophy of the researcher (Figure 15.7).

When selecting a data analysis strategy, the researcher must begin by considering the earlier steps in the process: problem definition (step 1), development of an approach (step 2), and research design (step 3). The researcher should use as a springboard the preliminary plan of data analysis that was prepared as part of the research design. It may be necessary to make changes to the preliminary plan in light of additional information generated in subsequent stages of the research process.

The next step is to consider the known characteristics of the data. The measurement scales used exert a strong influence on the choice of statistical techniques (see Chapter 9). In addition, the research design may favor certain techniques. The insights into the data obtained during data preparation can be valuable in selecting a strategy for analysis.

FIGURE 15.7
Selecting a Data
Analysis Strategy

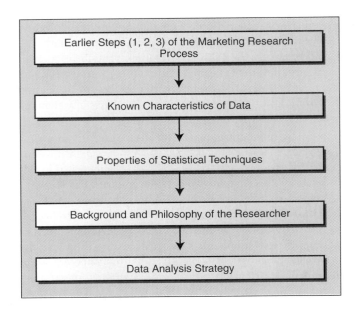

It is also important to take into account the properties of the statistical techniques, particularly their purpose and underlying assumptions. Some statistical techniques are appropriate for examining differences in variables, others for assessing the magnitudes of the relationships between variables, and others are appropriate for making predictions (see Chapters 16, 17, and 18). The techniques also involve different assumptions, and some techniques can withstand violations of the underlying assumptions better than others. The statistical techniques may be broadly classified as univariate or multivariate. **Univariate techniques** are used for analyzing data when there is a single measurement of each element or unit in the sample or, if there are several measurements of each element, each variable is analyzed in isolation. On the other hand, **multivariate techniques** are used for analyzing data when there are two or more measurements on each element and the variables are analyzed simultaneously.

Finally, the researcher's background and philosophy affect the choice of a data analysis strategy. The experienced, statistically trained researcher will employ a range of techniques.

univariate techniques
Statistical techniques appropriate for analyzing data when there is a single measurement of each element in the sample; or, if there are several measurements of each element, each variable is analyzed in isolation.

multivariate techniques
Statistical techniques suitable for analyzing data when there are two or more measurements on each element and the variables are analyzed simultaneously. Multivariate techniques are concerned with the simultaneous relationships among two or more phenomena.

SUMMARY ILLUSTRATION USING THE OPENING VIGNETTE

While collecting primary data, the completed questionnaires returned from the field are carefully checked and edited for incomplete (for example, questions that are incorrectly skipped) or inconsistent responses (for example, a respondent reports purchases made on Sears credit card but does not have one). Any respondents with unsatisfactory responses are simply discarded as the proportion of such respondents is small, the sample size is large, and Sears' research has shown that the unsatisfactory respondents do not differ from satisfactory respondents on the key variables. The data are coded by following the standard procedures given in Sears' codebook. Then the data are transcribed from the questionnaires into the computer using state-of-the art technology. As part of data cleaning, further checks are performed on the data to ascertain their consistency and accuracy. An effort is made to identify data that are out of range (for example, a response of 8 on a 1 to 7 scale) or logically inconsistent (for example, sum of percentages adding to more than 100 percent), or have extreme values (for example, household size of 11). Missing values are kept to a minimum by proper selection, training, and supervision of field workers. In addition, the data are analyzed by different procedures for treating missing values, including casewise and pairwise deletion, to determine the impact on the results. A similar process is followed for data collected from secondary sources. This care taken in preparing the data has resulted in a high-quality database that enables Sears to identify the needs of the marketplace and target its marketing efforts accordingly.

MARKETING RESEARCH AND TQM

Data must be analyzed to design, implement, and control quality management programs. It is extremely important that the data preparation procedures described in this chapter be followed to ensure the quality of these data. The quality of the data should be checked at each stage of the data preparation process: questionnaire checking, editing, coding, transcribing, and data cleaning. Business and nonbusiness firms that meticulously follow the data preparation procedures are reaping the benefits of superior quality in their quality management programs.

FOCUS ON

ELRICK & LAVIDGE

The data processing (DP) group is responsible for most of the steps involved in data preparation at Elrick & Lavidge (E&L). The data preparation process begins with the research director and/or project manager. This person develops a preliminary plan of data analysis as part of the research proposal well before the field organization actually collects the data.

For a typical telephone survey, E&L uses Hewlett Packard (HP) mainframe computers and market research software from CfMC (Computers for Marketing Corporation). CfMC has developed a number of software packages to perform functions that include questionnaire implementation (including phone center management), editing and checking of data, and tabulation of questionnaire results.

Because most questionnaires are implemented using CATI, the CfMC software performs most of the questionnaire checking and editing steps. One of the primary advantages to using CATI is that many of these checks and edits can be performed while the interviewer is talking with the respondent, offering an opportunity for correcting mistakes while the respondent is still on the phone. Since the interviewer types the respondents' answers to open-ended questions, CATI eliminates issues of illegibility. Training of the interviewers helps reduce ambiguous and incomplete responses, as discussed in Chapter 14.

The CATI software eliminates the need for transcribing the data and substantially reduces the cleaning effort. Rules within the software prevent data from being entered that are out of range or otherwise incorrect. In addition, the software can be configured to replace missing responses with a neutral value, such as a 4 on a scale from 1 to 7.

All structured questions are precoded. However, many of the structured questions have an "other" option to capture those responses that do not fit in the precoded categories. In addition, some questions are unstructured or open-ended. For both of these question types, the interviewer types the response into "Survent" software exactly as the respondent has said it (verbatim).

The CfMC software produces daily status reports of the study and phone system performance. Included in these daily reports are reports of verbatim answers to questions. The data are now ready for analysis. The data processing group does not perform data analysis but prepares the data for others to analyze.

EXAMPLE

CUSTOMER SATISFACTION RESEARCH LINKS AMERICAN CANCER SOCIETY TO THE SOCIETY

The American Cancer Society (ACS) has instituted ongoing customer satisfaction research as part of its total quality management program. These surveys ask the donors and the general public what is most important to them in the fight against cancer and what role they expect the ACS to play.

Before any analysis is done, the data are thoroughly checked for quality. Any unsatisfactory questionnaires discovered during checking or editing are sent back to the field, as the response of every single respondent is considered important. A standard coding scheme is used and as most of the data are collected using CATI, subsequent transcription is unnecessary. Several procedural and logical checks are built into the CATI system so that inconsistencies can be identified and rectified while the data are being collected during the course of the interview. These high-quality data provide ACS with an accurate measurement of what is important to donors and the public, enabling it to effectively address those issues in its marketing campaigns and charitable programs. As a result, contributions are at an all-time high, and the ACS is well connected to the society at large.[4]

INTERNATIONAL MARKETING RESEARCH

The researcher should ensure that the data have been prepared in a comparable manner across countries or cultural units. This means that comparable procedures must be followed for checking questionnaires, editing, and coding. Note that the procedures must be comparable, although the questionnaire itself, and therefore the coding scheme, could vary. Certain adjustments may be necessary to make the data comparable across countries. For example, the data may have to be adjusted to establish currency equivalents or metric equivalents. Furthermore, transformation of the data may be necessary to make meaningful comparisons and achieve consistent results, as in the example that follows.

EXAMPLE

ACER PULLS OUT AN ACE

In just a few years, Taiwan-based Acer has transformed itself from a no-name cloner into the seventh-largest personal computer (PC) manufacturer in the world. Acer, which forged brand-name recognition for itself by developing sleekly styled computers aimed at the home market, set its goals high. It wanted to become one of the top five PC suppliers in the world by exceeding $10 billion in revenue by 2001. A crucial factor in Acer's success was the knowledge of consumer preferences for PCs obtained by conducting surveys in different countries. Great pains are taken at the data preparation stage to ensure that the data are comparable. For example, the price of PCs in each country is transformed to a common unit. This transformation is necessary as the prices are specified in different local currencies, and a common basis is needed for comparison across countries. Also, in each country, the premium price is defined in relation to the prices of competing brands.

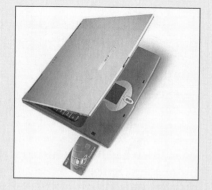

The care taken at the data preparation stage has resulted in rich findings. For example, Acer found that, though the relative importance varies from country to country, eight product attributes contribute to brand preference for desktop PCs on a worldwide basis: price, ease of installation and use, service and support, features, performance, reliability, scope of usage, and compatibility on a network. Such findings enabled Acer to launch global marketing strategies that are responsive to variations in local preferences.[5]

TECHNOLOGY AND MARKETING RESEARCH

Advances in technology have greatly facilitated the data preparation process. When the data are collected by computer-assisted interviewing (CATI or CAPI) or electronic surveys (Internet, e-mail), several error checks can be programmed into the questionnaire administration process, and the data are transcribed directly into the computer.

Other advances have also been made. For example, National Computer Systems (NCS), Minneapolis, has released a new data capture system designed to automatically read handwritten information from documents or faxes and process it for a variety of applications. Called NCS Accra, the system verifies and corrects inaccurate information and stores it on optical media. The NCS Accra system features high-production scanners, proven recognition engines for accurate data capture, advanced contextual editing, including address validation and correction, remote fax input capabilities, and robust image archive storage and retrieval options. The system can read hand-printed, machine-printed, and bar-coded data as well as optical marks, including check marks, Xs, and tick marks, from documents and images. Once the data have been validated and verified, the ASCII record is transferred to a database or user application file.[6]

ETHICS IN MARKETING RESEARCH

Ethical issues can arise during the data preparation and analysis step, particularly in areas where the researcher has to exercise judgment. While checking, editing, coding, transcribing, and cleaning, the researcher can get some idea about the quality of the data. Sometimes it is easy to identify respondents who did not take the questionnaire seriously or who otherwise provided data of questionable quality. Consider, for example, a respondent who checks the "neither agree nor disagree" response to all the 30 items measuring attitude toward spectator sports. Decisions about whether such respondents should be discarded, that is, not included in the analysis, can raise ethical concerns. A good rule of thumb is to make such decisions during the data preparation phase before conducting any analysis. Discarding respondents after analyzing the data raises ethical concerns, particularly if this information is not fully disclosed in the written report. Moreover, the procedure used to identify unsatisfactory respondents and the number of respondents discarded should be clearly disclosed, as in the following example.

EXAMPLE

ETHICAL EDITING OF DATA

In a study of MBAs' responses to marketing ethics dilemmas, respondents were required to respond to 14 questions regarding ethically ambiguous scenarios by writing a simple sentence regarding what action they would take if they were the manager in those situations. The responses were then analyzed to determine if they were indicative of ethical behavior. However, in the data preparation phase, six respondents out of the 561 total respondents were eliminated from further analysis because their responses indicated that they did not follow the directions that told them to clearly state their choice of action. This is an example of ethical editing of the data. The criterion for unsatisfactory responses is clearly stated, the unsatisfactory respondents are identified before the analysis, and the number of respondents eliminated is disclosed.[7]

Another ethical concern relates to interpretation of the results, drawing conclusions, and making recommendations. While interpretations, conclusions, and recommendations necessarily involve the subjective judgment of the researcher, this judgment must be exercised honestly, free from any personal biases or agendas of the researcher or the client. Suppose, a survey reveals that 31 percent of the respondents preferred the client's brand while 30.8 percent preferred the closest competing brand, with all the other brands being preferred to a much less extent. For the researcher to state that the client's brand is the most preferred brand in the marketplace, without disclosing that a competing brand is a very close second, may be misleading if it conveys the false impression that the client's brand is the dominant brand.

INTERNET APPLICATIONS

Major statistical packages such as SPSS *(www.spss.com)*, SAS *(www.sas.com)*, MINITAB *(www.minitab.com)*, and EXCEL *(www.microsoft.com/office/excel/)* have Internet sites that can be accessed for a variety of information. The use of SPSS is discussed in the following section while Figure 15.8 details how to use the other packages to make consistency checks. These packages also contain options for handling missing responses and for statistically adjusting the data. In addition, a number of statistical packages can now be found on the Internet. While some of these programs may not offer integrated data analysis and management, they can nevertheless be very useful for conducting specific statistical analyses.

Information useful for formulating a data analysis strategy is readily available on the Internet. A great deal of information can be obtained about the appropriateness of using certain statistical techniques in specific settings. It is possible to surf the net for new statistical techniques that are not yet available in commonly used statistical packages. News groups and special interest groups are useful sources for a variety of statistical information.

SPSS

SPSS

Using the SPSS Base module, out-of-range values can be selected using the SELECT IF command. These cases, with the identifying information (subject ID, record number, variable name, and variable value) can then be printed using the LIST or PRINT com-

---

Similar programs are available in the mainframe and the microcomputer versions of all the packages. Hence, we won't distinguish between mainframes and microcomputers.

SAS

The IF, IF-THEN, and IF-THEN/ELSE statements can be used to select cases with missing or out-of-range values. The select statement executes one of several statements or groups of statements. The LIST statement is useful for printing suspicious input lines. The LOSTCARD statement can be used to identify missing records in the data. The PRINT and PRINTTO procedures can be used to identify cases and print variable names and variable values. In addition, the OUTPUT and PUT statements can be used to write the values of variables.

MINITAB

There are control statements that permit the control of the order of commands in a macro. The IF command allows implementation of different blocks of commands. This includes IF, ELSEIF, ELSE, and ENDIF.

EXCEL

The IF statement can be used to make logical checks and check out-of-range values. The IF statement can be assessed under the INSERT>FUNCTION>ALL>IF.

FIGURE 15.8   Other Computer Programs for Data Preparation

mands. The Print command will save active cases to an external file. If a formatted list is required, the SUMMARIZE command can be used.

SPSS Data Entry can facilitate data preparation. You can verify respondents have answered completely by setting rules. These rules can be used on existing datasets to validate and check the data, whether or not the questionnaire used to collect the data was constructed in Data Entry. Data Entry allows you to control and check the entry of data through three type of rules: validation, checking, and skip and fill rules.

While the missing values can be treated within the context of the Base module, SPSS Missing Values Analysis can assist in diagnosing missing values and replacing missing values with estimates.

TextSmart by SPSS can help in the coding and analysis of open-ended responses.

SUMMARY

Data preparation begins with a preliminary check of all questionnaires for completeness and interviewing quality. Then more thorough editing takes place. Editing consists of screening questionnaires to identify illegible, incomplete, inconsistent, or ambiguous responses. Such responses may be handled by returning questionnaires to the field, assigning missing values, or discarding the unsatisfactory respondents.

The next step is coding. A numerical or alphanumeric code is assigned to represent a specific response to a specific question, along with the column position that code will occupy. It is often helpful to prepare a codebook containing the coding instructions and the necessary information about the variables in the data set. The coded data are transcribed onto disks or entered into computers via keypunching. Mark sense forms, optical scanning, or computerized sensory analysis may also be used.

Cleaning the data requires consistency checks and treatment of missing responses. Options available for treating missing responses include substitution of a neutral value, such as the mean, casewise deletion, and pairwise deletion. The selection of a data analysis strategy should be based on the earlier steps of the marketing research process, known characteristics of the data, properties of statistical techniques, and the background and philosophy of the researcher.

Proper data preparation is essential before analyzing data for quality management programs such as customer satisfaction. While analyzing the data in international marketing research, the researcher should ensure that the units of measurement are comparable across countries or cultural units. Technological advances are resulting in new ways to capture, edit, code, and prepare data. Several ethical issues are related to data processing, particularly the discarding of unsatisfactory respondents, and evaluation and interpretation of results. Major statistical packages such as SPSS, SAS, MINITAB, and EXCEL have Internet sites that can be accessed for useful information

KEY TERMS AND CONCEPTS

Editing, 452	Data cleaning, 458	Pairwise deletion, 459
Coding, 454	Consistency checks, 458	Univariate techniques, 461
Codebook, 454	Missing responses, 459	Multivariate
Fixed field codes, 455	Casewise deletion, 459	techniques, 461

ACRONYMS

The data preparation process may be summarized by the acronym DATA PREP:

D ata consistency checks
A djusting the data for missing values
T ranscribing
A nalysis strategy

P ost field work questionnaire checking
R ecording numerical or alphanumerical values: Coding
E diting
P reliminary plan of data analysis

EXERCISES

1. Describe the data preparation process.
2. What activities are involved in the preliminary checking of questionnaires that have been returned from the field?
3. What does editing a questionnaire mean?
4. How are unsatisfactory responses that are discovered in editing treated?
5. What is the difference between precoding and postcoding?
6. Describe the guidelines for the coding of unstructured questions.
7. What does transcribing the data involve?
8. What kinds of consistency checks are made in cleaning the data?
9. What options are available for the treatment of missing data?
10. What considerations are involved in selecting a data analysis strategy?

PROBLEMS

1. Shown below is part of a questionnaire used to determine consumer preferences for cameras. Set up a coding scheme for these three questions.

---

9. Please rate the importance of the following features you would consider when shopping for a new camera.

	Not so important				Very important
a. DX film speed setting	1	2	3	4	5
b. Auto-film advance	1	2	3	4	5
c. Autofocus	1	2	3	4	5
d. Autoloading	1	2	3	4	5

10. If you were to buy a new camera, which of the following outlets would you visit? Please check as many as apply.

a. _____ Drugstore
b. _____ Camera store
c. _____ Discount/mass merchandiser
d. _____ Supermarket
e. _____ Other

---

11. Where do you get most of your photo processing done? Please check only one option.

    a. _____ Drugstore
    b. _____ Mini labs
    c. _____ Camera stores
    d. _____ Discount/mass merchandiser
    e. _____ Supermarkets
    f. _____ Mail order
    g. _____ Kiosk/other

INTERNET AND COMPUTER EXERCISES

1. Explain how you would make consistency checks for the questionnaire given in problem 1 above using SPSS, SAS, MINITAB, or EXCEL.
2. Use an electronic questionnaire design and administration package such as Ci3 (*www.sawtooth.com*) to program the camera preference questionnaire given in problem 1. Add one or two questions of your own. Administer the questionnaire to five students and prepare the data for analysis. Does computer administration of the questionnaire facilitate data preparation?

ACTIVITIES

ROLE PLAYING

1. You are a project supervisor with SDR, Inc., a data analysis firm based in Atlanta. You are supervising the data preparation process for a large survey conducted for a leading manufacturer of paper towels. The data are being collected via in-home personal interviews, and 1,823 questionnaires have been returned from the field. In cleaning the data, you find that 289 questionnaires have missing responses. The data analyst preparing the data (a student in your class), not knowing how to deal with these missing responses, approaches you for help and instructions. Please explain to the data analyst how the missing responses should be handled.
2. You are the marketing research manger for General Electric. GE has developed a luxury refrigerator model that has several innovative features and will be sold for a premium price of $1,995. A national survey was conducted to determine consumer response to the proposed model. The data were obtained by conducting mall intercept interviews in 10 major U.S. cities. The resulting sample of 2,639 contains 13 respondents who have low incomes but yet report the purchase of luxury goods. The marketing research analyst, who reports to you, would like to know how to handle the data for these 13 respondents. Discuss this question with the analyst (a student in your class).

FIELD WORK

1. Visit a marketing research firm or a business firm with an in-house marketing research department. Investigate the data preparation process this firm followed in a

recently completed project. How does this process compare with the one described in this book?

2. Obtain a codebook or coding instructions used by a marketing research firm for a completed project. Examine the codebook or coding instructions carefully. Can you improve on the coding scheme the firm used?

GROUP DISCUSSION

As a small group, discuss the following statements:

1. Data preparation is a time-consuming process. In projects with severe time constraints, data preparation should be circumvented.

2. The researcher should always use computer-assisted interviewing (CATI or CAPI) to collect the data, as these methods greatly facilitate data preparation.

NOTES

1. Based on "Sears Joins Forces with Check Free," *Home Textiles Today,* 22(4) (September 22, 2000): 4; Aaron Baar, "Sears Opts for Unified Tagline," *Adweek* (Midwest Ed.) 40(25) (June 21, 1999): 6; Cyndee Miller, "Redux Deluxe: Sears Comeback an Event Most Marketers Would Kill For," *Marketing News,* 30(15) (July 15, 1996): 1, 14.

2. David Lipton, "Now Hear This . . . Customer Complaints Are Not Bad if Viewed as Business-Building Occasions," *Nation's Restaurant News,* 34(35) (August 28, 2000): 30–31; Gordon A. Wyner, "Anticipating Customer Priorities," *Marketing Research: A Magazine of Management & Applications,* 11(1) (Spring 1999): 36–38; and Jagdip Singh and Robert E. Wilkes, "When Consumers Complain: A Path Analysis of the Key Antecedents of Consumer Complaint Response Estimates," *Journal of the Academy of Marketing Science,* 24 (Fall 1996): 350–365.

3. See the SPSS, SAS, MINITAB, and EXCEL manuals available for microcomputers and mainframes.

4. Vincent Coppola, "Cancer Society Pays Its Way," *Adweek,* 21(14) (April 3, 2000): 3; Don Heinz and Richard K. Robinson, "Nonprofits Need Surveys in Order to Serve Better," *Marketing News,* 33(12) (June 7, 1999): H36; and "American Cancer Society Initiative," *Fund Raising Management,* 29(2) (April 1998): 7.

5. Based on Faith Hung, "Compaq Signs Major Laptop Deal With Taiwan's Quanta," *Electronic Buyer's News* (July 10, 2000): 4; Jonathan Moore, "In Asia, Thin Margins Could Mean Fat City," *Business Week* (3626) (April 26, 1999): 38; and Geoffrey James "U.S. Computer Market: Where East Meets West," *Upside,* 8(12) (December 1996): 78–81.

6. New data capture system from NCS, *Quirk's Marketing Research* (April 1996).

7. Barbara Libby, "Ethical Decision Making and the Law," *Journal of Business Ethics,* 26(3) (August 2000): 223–232; Frederick Greenman and John Sherman, "Business School Ethics: An Overlooked Topic," *Business & Society Review,* 104(2) (Summer 1999): 171–177; Cheryl MacLellan and John Dobson, "Women, Ethics, and MBAs," *Journal of Business Ethics,* 16(11) (August 1997): 1201–1209; and G. M. Zinkhan, M. Bisesi, and M. J. Saxton, "MBAs' Changing Attitudes Toward Marketing Dilemmas: 1981–1987," *Journal of Business Ethics,* 8 (1989): 963–974.

16

FREQUENCY DISTRIBUTION, HYPOTHESIS TESTING, AND CROSS-TABULATION

FREQUENCY DISTRIBUTIONS AND CROSS-TABULATIONS ARE BASIC TECHNIQUES THAT PROVIDE RICH INSIGHTS INTO THE DATA AND LAY THE FOUNDATION FOR MORE ADVANCED ANALYSIS.

Opening Questions

1. Why is preliminary data analysis desirable, and what insights can be obtained from such an analysis?

2. What is meant by frequency counts, and what measures are associated with such an analysis?

3. What is the general procedure for hypothesis testing, and what steps are involved?

4. How should cross-tabulation analysis be conducted, and what are the associated statistics?

5. How is the chi-square statistic calculated, and for what purpose is it used? What other statistics are used to test association between two variables, and when are they used?

6. What computer programs are available for conducting frequency and cross-tabulation analyses?

Eli Miller, Vice President–Marketing Sciences, Elrick & Lavidge.
Eli Miller is responsible for the Marketing Science group. He is involved with all aspects of research design and analysis. He has over 20 years of marketing research experience.

CONSUMERS CONSUME COUPONS

A recent Promotional Attitudes and Practices Study surveyed 682 female primary grocery shoppers who were members of the Market Facts Consumer Mail Panel. The survey data were analyzed by calculating frequency counts, percentages, and means. This survey found that 93 percent liked coupons, 99 percent had used coupons in the last year, and 95 percent had used a coupon within the last 30 days. The survey also reported that 642 (94 percent) said coupons were helpful in order to reduce the cost of groceries, 593 (87 percent) used coupons for brands they normally bought, and 212 (31 percent) used coupons to try new products. Despite the growing influence of frequent customer clubs, frequency counts indicated that most of the respondents did not limit their shopping to a single store. Of the 44 percent who are club members, 19 percent said that their membership makes them more likely to shop at that store, while 51 percent shop at other stores for specials. The average number of stores shopped was 2.9 per household.

As illustrated here, survey data are often analyzed to obtain frequency counts (593 respondents used coupons for brands they normally bought), percentages (95 percent had used a coupon within the last 30 days), and means (the average number of stores shopped was 2.9 per household). A cross-tabulation of coupon usage with income indicated that households at all income levels were cashing coupons. Furthermore, lower-income households had higher coupon usage as compared to middle- and higher-income households, and this association was statistically significant. Supermarkets can use such findings to target their coupon and promotional strategies. It is clear that supermarkets cannot rely exclusively on frequent customer clubs; coupons and price specials also play a major role in attracting shoppers.[1]

OVERVIEW

Once the data have been prepared for analysis (Chapter 15), the researcher should conduct some basic analyses. Often, this involves computing frequency counts, percentages, and averages, as in the opening vignette. This chapter describes basic data analysis, including frequency distribution, hypothesis testing, and cross-tabulation. Figure 16.1 briefly explains the focus of the chapter, the relationship of this chapter to the previous ones, and the step of the marketing research process on which this chapter concentrates.

First, we describe the frequency distribution of a single variable and explain how it provides both an indication of the number of out-of-range, missing, or extreme values, as well as insight into the central tendency and variability of the underlying distribution. Next, we discuss hypothesis testing and present a general procedure. Then, we consider the use of cross-tabulation for understanding the associations between variables taken two at a time. While the nature of the association can be observed from tables, statistics are available for testing the significance and strength of the association. Figure 16.2 gives an overview of the topics discussed in this chapter and how they flow from one to the next.

Many commercial marketing research projects do not go beyond basic data analysis. These findings are often displayed using tables and graphs, as discussed further in Chapter 19. While the findings of basic analysis are valuable in their own right, the insights gained from the basic analysis are also invaluable in interpreting the results obtained from more sophisticated statistical techniques. Therefore, before conducting more advanced statistical analysis, it is useful to examine the frequency distributions of the relevant variables.

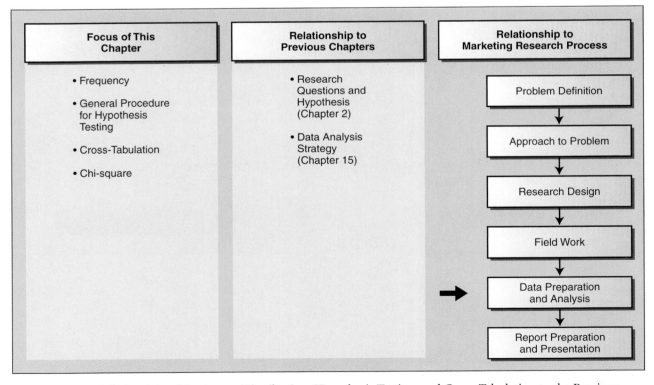

FIGURE 16.1   Relationship of Frequency Distribution, Hypothesis Testing, and Cross-Tabulation to the Previous Chapters and the Marketing Research Process

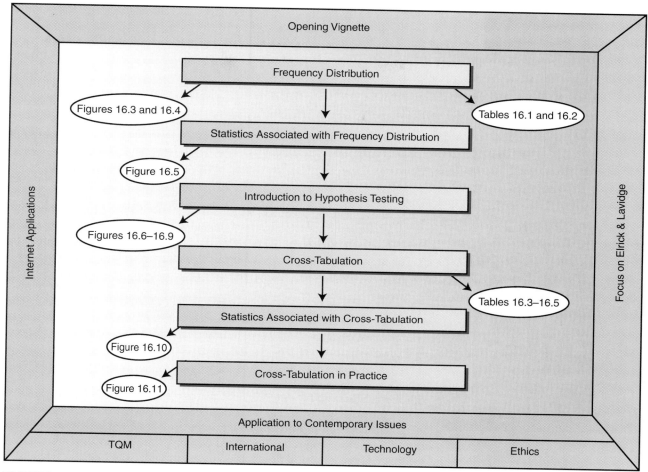

FIGURE 16.2 Frequency Distribution, Hypothesis Testing, and Cross-Tabulation: An Overview

FREQUENCY DISTRIBUTION

Marketing researchers often need to answer questions about a single variable. For example:

- What is the percentage of shoppers using coupons (see opening vignette)?
- What percentage of the market consists of heavy users, medium users, light users, or nonusers?
- How many customers are very familiar with a new product offering? How many are familiar, somewhat familiar, or unfamiliar with the brand? What is the mean rating on familiarity with the brand? Is there much variance in the extent to which customers are familiar with the new product?
- What is the income distribution of brand users? Is this distribution skewed toward low-income brackets?

The answers to these kinds of questions can be determined by examining frequency distributions. In a **frequency distribution,** one variable is considered at a time. The objective is to obtain a count of the number of responses associated with different values of the variable. The relative occurrence, or frequency, of different values of the variable is expressed in percentages, as in the opening vignette. A frequency distribution for a vari-

frequency distribution
A mathematical distribution whose objective is to obtain a count of the number of responses associated with different values of one variable and to express these counts in percentage terms.

able produces a table of frequency counts, percentages, and cumulative percentages for all the values associated with that variable.

The steps involved in conducting frequency analysis are given in Figure 16.3. We illustrate the frequency procedure with the data of Table 16.1, which gives the attitude toward Nike, usage, and sex of a sample of Nike users. Attitude is measured on a seven-point Likert-type scale (1 = very unfavorable, 7 = very favorable). The users have been coded as 1, 2, or 3, representing light, medium, or heavy users. The sex has been coded as 1 for females and 2 for males.

Table 16.2 gives the frequency distribution of attitude. In the table, the first column contains the labels assigned to the different categories of the variable. The second column indicates the code or value assigned to each label or category. The third column gives the number of respondents for each value, including the missing value. For example, of the 45 respondents who participated in the survey, six respondents have a value of 2 denoting an unfavorable attitude. One respondent did not answer and has a missing value denoted by 9. The fourth column displays the percentage of respondents checking each value. These percentages are obtained by dividing the frequencies in column 3 by 45. The next column shows percentages calculated by excluding the cases with missing values, that is, by dividing the frequencies in column 3 by 44 (= 45 − 1). As can be seen, 8 or 18.2 percent have an attitude value of 5. If there are no missing values, columns 4 and 5 are identical. The last column represents cumulative percentages after adjusting for missing cases. The cumulative percentage corresponding to the value of 5 is 70.5. In other words, 70.5 percent of the respondents have a value of 5 or less.

A frequency distribution of responses can help in understanding attitude toward Nike.

A frequency distribution helps determine the extent of illegitimate responses. Values of 0 and 8 would be illegitimate responses, or errors. The cases with these values can be identified and corrective action taken. The presence of outliers, or cases with extreme values, can also be detected. In the case of a frequency distribution of household size, a few isolated families with household sizes of 9 or more might be considered outliers. A frequency distribution also indicates the shape of the empirical distribution of the variable. The frequency data may be used to construct a histogram or a vertical bar chart in which the values of the variable are portrayed along the X-axis and the absolute or relative frequencies of the values are placed along the Y-axis.

FIGURE 16.3
Conducting Frequency Analysis

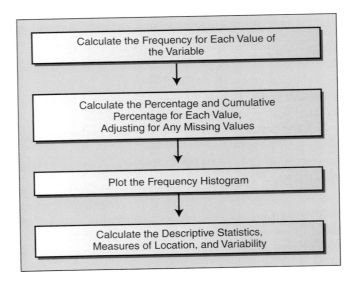

TABLE 16.1 Usage and Attitude Toward Nike Shoes

SPSS
Data File

NO.	USER GROUP	SEX	ATTITUDE
1	3.00	2.00	7.00
2	1.00	1.00	2.00
3	1.00	1.00	3.00
4	3.00	2.00	6.00
5	3.00	2.00	5.00
6	2.00	2.00	4.00
7	2.00	1.00	5.00
8	1.00	1.00	2.00
9	2.00	2.00	4.00
10	1.00	1.00	3.00
11	3.00	2.00	6.00
12	3.00	2.00	6.00
13	1.00	1.00	2.00
14	3.00	2.00	6.00
15	1.00	2.00	4.00
16	1.00	2.00	3.00
17	3.00	1.00	7.00
18	2.00	1.00	6.00
19	1.00	1.00	1.00
20	3.00	1.00	5.00
21	3.00	2.00	6.00
22	2.00	2.00	2.00
23	1.00	1.00	1.00
24	3.00	1.00	6.00
25	1.00	2.00	3.00
26	2.00	2.00	5.00
27	3.00	2.00	7.00
28	2.00	1.00	5.00
29	1.00	1.00	9.00
30	2.00	2.00	5.00
31	1.00	2.00	1.00
32	1.00	2.00	4.00
33	2.00	1.00	3.00
34	2.00	1.00	4.00
35	3.00	1.00	5.00
36	3.00	1.00	6.00
37	3.00	2.00	6.00
38	3.00	2.00	5.00
39	3.00	2.00	7.00
40	1.00	1.00	4.00
41	1.00	1.00	2.00
42	1.00	1.00	1.00
43	1.00	1.00	2.00
44	1.00	1.00	3.00
45	1.00	1.00	1.00

T A B L E   1 6 . 2   **Frequency Distribution of Attitude Toward Nike**

VALUE LABEL	VALUE	FREQUENCY	PERCENTAGE	VALID PERCENTAGE	CUMULATIVE PERCENTAGE
Very unfavorable	1	5	11.1	11.4	11.4
	2	6	13.3	13.6	25.0
	3	6	13.3	13.6	38.6
	4	6	13.3	13.6	52.3
	5	8	17.8	18.2	70.5
	6	9	20.0	20.5	90.9
Very favorable	7	4	8.9	9.1	100.0
	9	1	2.2	Missing	___
	Total	45	100.0	100.0	

Output File

Figure 16.4 is a histogram of the attitude data in Table 16.2. From the histogram, one could examine whether the observed distribution is consistent with an expected or assumed distribution. In this case, the observed distribution does not look like the standard normal distribution. This may be important in determining what type of statistical test is appropriate. For further illustration, consider the following example.

E X A M P L E

THE SIGNAL IS GREEN FOR YELLOW PAGES ADVERTISING BY PHYSICIANS

A census was conducted of every physician's yellow pages listing in Atlanta, Chicago, and Charlotte, and the contents of these listings were analyzed to determine the types of ads. The various types of yellow pages ads were as follows:

TYPE OF YELLOW PAGE AD	FREQUENCY	PERCENTAGE
Nondisplay listings: lightface	5,454	46.0
Nondisplay listings: face	1,656	14.0
Display ads	4,694	40.0
Total advertisements	11,804	100.0

Based on the frequency counts, the study concluded that yellow page listings are a widely used form of physician advertising: 11,804 ads were located in the three areas. However, the majority of the physicians (46 + 14 = 60 percent) were using nondisplay (lightface/face) listings, which are more appropriate for physicians with established practices who have all the patients they want. Only 40 percent were using the larger display ads that have a much higher likelihood of being seen by potential patients who consult yellow pages when looking for a physician. Since a majority of the physicians were looking for new patients, the study concluded that more physicians should use the display, rather than nondisplay, ads in the Yellow Pages.[2]

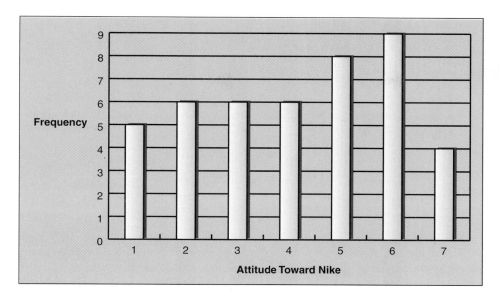

FIGURE 16.4
Frequency Histogram

Output File

Note that the numbers and percentages in the preceding example indicate the extent of advertising. Since numbers are involved, a frequency distribution can be used to calculate descriptive or summary statistics. We discuss some of the statistics associated with frequency distribution in the next section.

STATISTICS ASSOCIATED WITH FREQUENCY DISTRIBUTION

As illustrated in the previous section, a frequency distribution is a convenient way of looking at the values of a variable. A frequency table is easy to read and provides basic information, but sometimes this information may be too detailed and the researcher must summarize it by the use of descriptive statistics. The most commonly used statistics associated with frequencies are measures of location (mean, mode, and median) and measures of variability (range and standard deviation).

Measures of Location

The **measures of location** that we discuss are measures of central tendency because they tend to describe the center of the distribution (see Chapter 13). If the entire sample is changed by adding a fixed constant to each observation, then the mean, mode, and median change by the same fixed amount. Suppose we added the number 10 to the attitude ratings of all the 44 (45 − 1) respondents who expressed attitude toward Nike in Table 16.1. Then the mean, mode, and median will all increase by 10.

MEAN The **mean,** or average value, is the most commonly used measure of central tendency, or center of a distribution (see opening vignette). It is used to estimate the average when the data have been collected using an interval or ratio scale (see Chapter 9). The data should display some central tendency, with most of the responses distributed around the mean.

The mean, $\overline{X}$ is given by

$$\overline{X} = \sum_{i=1}^{n} X_i/n$$

measures of location
A statistic that describes a location within a data set. Measures of central tendency describe the center of the distribution.

mean
The average; that value obtained by summing all elements in a set and dividing by the number of elements.

where,

X_i = Observed values of the variable X

n = Number of observations (sample size)

Generally, the mean is a robust measure and does not change markedly as data values are added or deleted. For the frequency counts given in Table 16.2, the mean value is calculated as follows:

$$\overline{X} = (5 \times 1 + 6 \times 2 + 6 \times 3 + 6 \times 4 + 8 \times 5 + 9 \times 6 + 4 \times 7)/44$$
$$= (5 + 12 + 18 + 24 + 40 + 54 + 28)/44$$
$$= 181/44$$
$$= 4.11$$

mode
A measure of central tendency given as the value that occurs the most in a sample distribution.

MODE The **mode** is the value that occurs most frequently. It represents the highest peak of the distribution. The mode is a good measure of location when the variable is inherently categorical or has otherwise been grouped into categories. The mode in Table 16.2 is 6 as this value occurs with the highest frequency, that is, 9 times (see also the histogram in Figure 16.4).

median
A measure of central tendency, given as the value above which half of the values fall and below which half of the values fall.

MEDIAN The **median** of a sample is the middle value when the data are arranged in ascending or descending rank order (see Chapter 9). If the number of data points is even, the median is usually estimated as the midpoint between the two middle values—by adding the two middle values and dividing their sum by 2. The middle value is the value at which 50 percent of the values are greater than that value, and 50 percent are less. Thus, the median is the 50th percentile. The median is an appropriate measure of central tendency for ordinal data. In Table 16.2, the middle value is the average of the 22nd and 23rd observations when the data are arranged in ascending or descending order. This average is 4, and so the median is 4. The median can be easily determined by using cumulative percentages in the frequency table. Note that at a value of 4, the cumulative percentage is only 52.3 percent, but for 5 it is 70.5 percent, and for 3 it is 38.6 percent. Therefore, the 50 percent point occurs at the value of 4.

As can be seen, for Table 16.2 the three measures of central tendency for this distribution are different (mean = 4.11, mode = 6, median = 4). This is not surprising since each measure defines central tendency in a different way. The three values are equal only when the distribution is symmetric. In a symmetric distribution, the values on either side of the center of the distribution are the same, and the mean, mode, and median are equal (Figure 16.5). The normal distribution discussed earlier in Chapter 13 is a symmetric distribution, and the three measures of central tendency are equal. An advantage of calculating all three measures of central tendency is that we can determine whether the distribution is symmetric or asymmetric. The asymmetry of the distribution of Table 16.2 can also be seen from the histogram of Figure 16.4.

If the distribution is asymmetric, which measure should be used? If the variable is measured on a nominal scale, the mode should be used. If the variable is measured on an ordinal scale, the median is appropriate. If the variable is measured on an interval or ratio scale, the mode is a poor measure of central tendency. This can be seen from Table 16.2. While the modal value of 6 has the highest frequency of 9, it represents only 20.5 percent of the sample. In general, for interval or ratio data, the median is a better measure of central tendency, although it too ignores available information about the variable. The actual values of the variable above and below the median are ignored. The

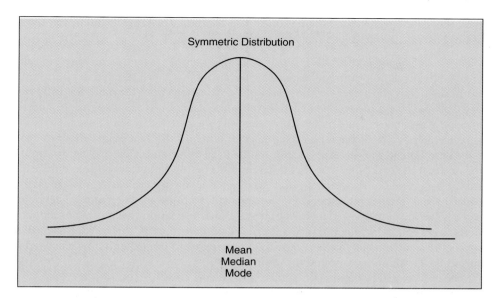

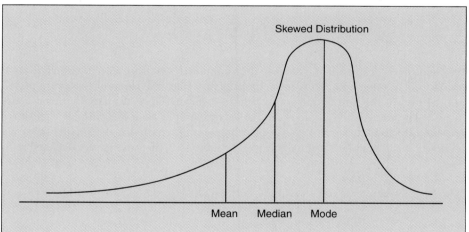

FIGURE 16.5
Skewness of a Distribution

mean is the most appropriate measure of central tendency for interval or ratio data. The mean makes use of all the information available since all of the values are used in computing it. However, the mean is sensitive to isolated cases with extremely small or extremely large values, called outliers. When outliers are in the data, the mean is not a good measure of central tendency and it is useful to consider both the mean and the median.

Measures of Variability

The most common **measures of variability,** which are calculated on interval or ratio data, are the range and variance or standard deviation.

RANGE The **range** measures the spread of the data. It is simply the difference between the largest and smallest values in the sample. As such, the range is directly affected by outliers.

$$\text{Range} = X_{\text{largest}} - X_{\text{smallest}}$$

measures of variability
A statistic that indicates the distribution's dispersion.

range
The difference between the smallest and largest values of a distribution.

variance
The mean squared deviation of all the values from the mean.

If all the values in the data are multiplied by a constant, the range is multiplied by the same constant. The range in Table 2 is $7 - 1 = 6$.

VARIANCE AND STANDARD DEVIATION The difference between the mean and an observed value is called the deviation from the mean. The **variance** is the mean squared deviation from the mean, that is, the average of the square of the deviations from the mean for all the values. The variance can never be negative. When the data points are clustered around the mean, the variance is small. When the data points are scattered, the variance is large. The variance helps us to understand how similar or different the data points are. If the data points are similar, the variance is small and their distribution is clustered tightly around the mean. If the data points are very different in value, the variance is large and their distribution is spread more widely around the mean. If all the data values are multiplied by a constant, the variance is multiplied by the square of the constant. The **standard deviation** is the square root of the variance. Thus, the standard deviation is expressed in the same units as the data, while the variance is expressed in squared units. The standard deviation serves the same purpose as the variance in helping us to understand how clustered or spread the distribution is around the mean value.

standard deviation
The square root of the variance.

The standard deviation of a sample, s_x, is calculated as:

$$s_x = \sqrt{\sum_{i=1}^{n} \frac{(X_i - \bar{X})^2}{n-1}}$$

We divide by $n - 1$ instead of n because the sample is drawn from a population and we are trying to determine how much the responses vary from the mean of the entire population. However, the population mean is unknown; therefore, the sample mean is used instead. The use of the sample mean makes the sample seem less variable than it is in actuality. By dividing by $n - 1$, instead of n, we compensate for the smaller variability observed in the sample. For the data given in Table 16.2, the variance is calculated as follows:

$$
\begin{aligned}
\text{Variance} = s_x^2 &= \{5 \times (1 - 4.11)^2 + 6 \times (2 - 4.11)^2 + 6 \times (3 - 4.11)^2 \\
&\quad + 6 \times (4 - 4.11)^2 + 8 \times (5 - 4.11)^2 + 9 \times (6 - 4.11)^2 \\
&\quad + 4 \times (7 - 4.11)^2\}/43 \\
&= \{48.36 + 26.71 + 7.39 + 0.07 + 6.34 + 32.15 + 33.41\}/43 \\
&= 154.43/43 \\
&= 3.59
\end{aligned}
$$

The standard deviation, therefore, is calculated as:

$$
\begin{aligned}
\text{Standard deviation} = S_x &= \sqrt{3.59} \\
&= 1.90
\end{aligned}
$$

INTRODUCTION TO HYPOTHESIS TESTING

Hypotheses were defined and illustrated in Chapter 2. It may be recalled that hypotheses are unproven statements or propositions that are of interest to the researcher. Hypotheses are declarative and can be tested statistically. Often, hypotheses are possible answers to research questions. Basic analysis invariably involves some hypothesis testing. Examples of hypotheses generated in marketing research follow:

- The average number of stores shopped for groceries is 3.0 per household (see opening vignette).
- The department store is being patronized by more than 10 percent of the households.
- The heavy and light users of a brand differ in terms of psychographic characteristics.
- One hotel has a more upscale image than its close competitor.
- Familiarity with a restaurant results in greater preference for that restaurant.

Chapter 13 covered the concepts of the sampling distribution, standard error of the mean or the proportion, and the confidence interval.[3] Because all of these concepts are relevant to hypothesis testing, it would be wise to review them. Below, we describe a general procedure for hypothesis testing that can be applied to test a wide range of hypotheses.

A GENERAL PROCEDURE FOR HYPOTHESIS TESTING

The following steps are involved in hypothesis testing (Figure 16.6).

1. Formulate the null hypothesis H_0 and the alternative hypothesis H_1.
2. Select an appropriate statistical technique and the corresponding test statistic.

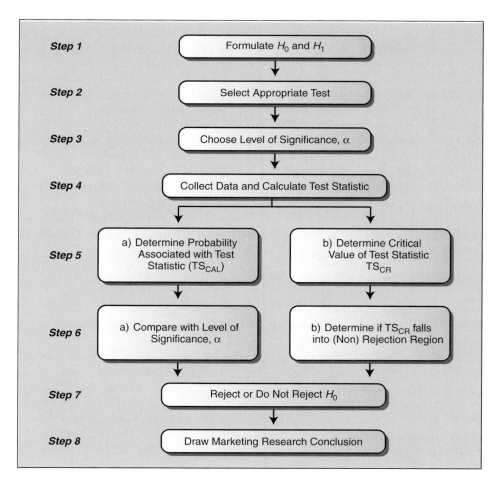

FIGURE 16.6
A General Procedure for Hypothesis Testing

3. Choose the level of significance, α.

4. Determine the sample size and collect the data. Calculate the value of the test statistic.

5. (a) Determine the probability associated with the test statistic calculated from the sample data under the null hypothesis, using the sampling distribution of the test statistic. (b) Alternatively, determine the critical value associated with the test statistic that divides the rejection and nonrejection regions, given the level of significance, α.

6. (a) Compare the probability associated with the test statistic with the level of significance specified. (b) Alternatively, determine whether the test statistic calculated from the sample data falls into the rejection or the nonrejection region.

7. Make the statistical decision to reject or not reject the null hypothesis.

8. Arrive at a conclusion. Express the statistical decision in terms of the marketing research problem.

Step 1: Formulating the Hypothesis

null hypothesis
A statement in which no difference or effect is expected. If the null hypothesis is not rejected, no changes will be made.

The first step is to formulate the null and alternative hypothesis. A **null hypothesis** is a statement of the status quo, one of no difference or no effect. If the null hypothesis is not rejected, no changes will be made. An **alternative hypothesis** is one in which some difference or effect is expected. Accepting the alternative hypothesis will lead to changes in opinions or actions. Thus, the alternative hypothesis is the opposite of the null hypothesis.

alternative hypothesis
A statement that some difference or effect is expected. Accepting the alternative hypothesis will lead to changes in opinions or actions.

The null hypothesis is always the hypothesis that is tested. The null hypothesis refers to a specified value of the population parameter (e.g., μ, σ, π), not a sample statistic (e.g., $\overline{X}$). A null hypothesis may be rejected, but it can never be accepted based on a single test. A statistical test can have one of two outcomes. One is that the null hypothesis is rejected and the alternative hypothesis accepted. The other outcome is that the null hypothesis is not rejected based on the evidence. However, it would be incorrect to conclude that since the null hypothesis is not rejected, it can be accepted as valid. In classical hypothesis testing, there is no way to determine whether the null hypothesis is true.[4]

In marketing research, the null hypothesis is formulated in such a way that its rejection leads to the acceptance of the desired conclusion. The alternative hypothesis represents the conclusion for which evidence is sought. For example, America Online (AOL) is considering the introduction of a new servicing plan. The plan will be introduced if it is preferred by more than 40 percent of customers. The appropriate way to formulate the hypotheses is as follows:

$$H_0: \pi \leq 0.40$$
$$H_1: \pi > 0.40$$

If the null hypothesis H_0 is rejected, then the alternative hypothesis H_1 will be accepted and the new service plan introduced. On the other hand, if H_0 is not rejected, the new service plan should not be introduced unless additional evidence is obtained.

one-tailed test
A test of the null hypothesis where the alternative hypothesis is expressed directionally.

The test of the null hypothesis is a **one-tailed test** because the alternative hypothesis is expressed directionally: The proportion of customers who express a preference is greater than 0.40. On the other hand, suppose the researcher wanted to determine whether the new service plan is different (superior or inferior) from the current plan, which is preferred by 40 percent of customers. Then a **two-tailed test** would be required, and the hypotheses would be expressed as:

two-tailed test
A test of the null hypothesis where the alternative hypothesis is not expressed directionally.

$$H_0: \pi = 0.40$$
$$H_1: \pi \neq 0.40$$

In commercial marketing research, the one-tailed test is used more often than a two-tailed test. Typically, there is some preferred direction for the conclusion for which evidence is sought. For example, the higher the profits, sales, and product quality, the better. The one-tailed test is more powerful than the two-tailed test. The power of a statistical test is discussed further in step 3.

Step 2: Selecting an Appropriate Test

To test the null hypothesis, it is necessary to select an appropriate statistical technique. The researcher should take into consideration how the test statistic is computed and the sampling distribution that the sample statistic (e.g., the mean) follows. The **test statistic** measures how close the sample has come to the null hypothesis. The test statistic often follows a well-known distribution, such as the normal, t, or chi-square distributions. Guidelines for selecting an appropriate test or statistical technique are discussed later in this chapter, as well as in Chapter 17.

In our AOL example, the **z test,** which is based on the standard normal distribution, would be appropriate. The z statistic would be computed as follows for proportions (see Chapter 13):

$$z = \frac{p - \pi}{\sigma_p}$$

where

$$\sigma_p = \sqrt{\frac{\pi(1 - \pi)}{n}}$$

test statistic
A measure of how close the sample has come to the null hypothesis. It often follows a well-known distribution, such as the normal, t, or chi-square distribution.

z test
A univariate hypothesis test using the standard normal distribution.

Step 3: Choosing a Level of Significance

Whenever we draw inferences about a population, there is a risk that an incorrect conclusion will be reached. Two types of error can occur:

TYPE I ERROR **Type I error** occurs when the sample results lead to the rejection of the null hypothesis when it is in fact true. In our example, a type I error would occur if we concluded, based on the sample data, that the proportion of customers preferring the new service plan was greater than 0.40, when in fact it was less than or equal to 0.40. The probability of type I error (α) is also called the **level of significance.** The type I error is controlled by establishing the tolerable level of risk of rejecting a true null hypothesis. The selection of a particular risk level should depend on the cost of making a type I error. The level of significance, α, when expressed as a percent is equal to 100 percent minus the confidence level (see Chapter 13).

type I error
Also known as alpha error, occurs when the sample results lead to the rejection of a null hypothesis that is in fact true.

level of significance
The probability of making a Type I error.

TYPE II ERROR **Type II error** occurs when, based on the sample results, the null hypothesis is not rejected when it is in fact false. In our example, the type II error would occur if we concluded, based on sample data, that the proportion of customers preferring the new service plan was less than or equal to 0.40 when, in fact, it was greater than 0.40. The probability of type II error is denoted by β. Unlike α, which is specified by the researcher, the magnitude of β depends on the actual value of the population parameter (that is, mean or proportion). The probability of type I error (α) and the probability of type II error (β) are shown in Figure 16.7. The complement $(1 - \beta)$ of the probability of a type II error is called the power of a statistical test.

type II error
Also known as beta error, occurs when the sample results lead to nonrejection of a null hypothesis that is in fact false.

FIGURE 16.7
Type I Error (α) and Type
II Error (β)

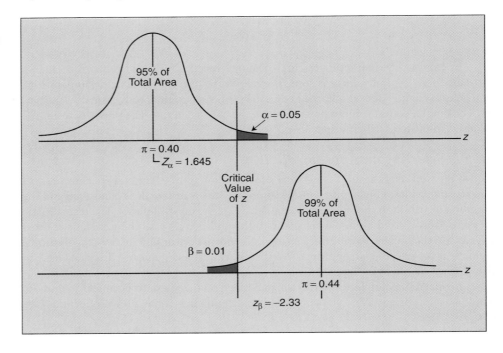

power of a test
The probability of rejecting the
null hypothesis when it is in fact
false and should by rejected.

POWER OF A TEST The **power of a test** is the probability $(1 - \beta)$ of rejecting the null hypothesis when it is false and should be rejected. Although β is unknown, it is related to α. An extremely low value of α (for example, 0.001) will result in intolerably high β errors. So, it is necessary to balance the two types of errors. As a compromise, α is often set at 0.05; sometimes it is 0.01; other values of α are rare. The level of α, along with the sample size, will determine the level of β for a particular research design. The risk of both α and β can be controlled by increasing the sample size. For a given level of α, increasing the sample size will decrease β, thereby increasing the power of the test.

Step 4: Data Collection

Sample size is determined after taking into account the desired α and β errors, incidence and completion rates, and other qualitative considerations, such as budget constraints (see Chapter 13). Then the required data are collected and the value of the test statistic is computed. In our example, suppose 500 customers were surveyed and 220 expressed a preference for the new service plan. Thus, the value of the sample proportion is $\hat{p} = 220/500 = 0.44$.

The value of σ_p can be determined as follows:

$$\sigma_p = \sqrt{\frac{\pi (1 - \pi)}{n}}$$

$$= \sqrt{\frac{(0.40)(0.6)}{500}}$$

$$= 0.0219$$

The test statistic z can be calculated as follows:

$$z = \frac{\hat{p} - \pi}{\sigma_{\hat{p}}}$$

$$= \frac{0.44 - 0.40}{0.0219}$$

$$= 1.83$$

Step 5: Determining the Probability (Critical Value)

(a) Using standard normal tables (Table 2 of the Statistical Appendix), the probability of obtaining a z value of 1.83 can be calculated (see Figure 16.8). The shaded area between $-\infty$ and 1.83 is 0.9664. Therefore, the area to the right of z = 1.83 is $1.0000 - 0.9664 = 0.0336$. Most computer programs automatically calculate this value.

(b) Alternatively, the critical value of z, which will give an area to the right side of the critical value of 0.05, is between 1.64 and 1.65 and equals 1.645. Note, that in determining the critical value of the test statistic, the area to the right of the critical value is either α or $\alpha/2$. It is α for a one-tail test and $\alpha/2$ for a two-tail test.

Steps 6 and 7: Comparing the Probability (Critical Value) and Making the Decision

(a) The probability associated with the calculated or observed value of the test statistic calculated from the sample data is 0.0336. This is the probability of getting a p value of 0.44 when $\pi = 0.40$. This is less than the level of significance of 0.05. Hence, the null hypothesis is rejected.

(b) Alternatively, the calculated value of the test statistic $z = 1.83$ lies in the rejection region, beyond the value of 1.645. Again, the same conclusion to reject the null hypothesis is reached. Note that the two ways of testing the null hypothesis are equivalent but mathematically opposite in the direction of comparison. If the probability associated with the calculated or observed value of the test statistic (TS_{CAL}) is *less than* the level of significance (α), the null hypothesis is rejected. However, if the calculated value of the test statistic (TS_{CAL}) is *greater*

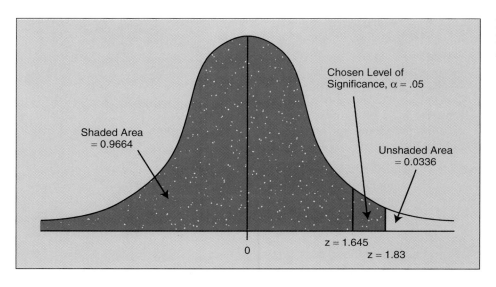

FIGURE 16.8
Probability of z with a One-Tailed Test

critical value
The value of the test statistic that divides the rejection and nonrejection regions. If the calculated value of the test statistic is greater than the critical value of the test statistic, the null hypothesis is rejected.

than the **critical value** of the test statistic (TS_{CR}), the null hypothesis is also rejected. The critical value is the value of the test statistic that divides the rejection and nonrejection regions. The reason for this sign shift is that the larger the value of TS_{CAL}, the smaller the probability of obtaining a more extreme value of the test statistic under the null hypothesis. This sign shift can be easily seen as follows.

Under (a), step 7 is:

if probability of TS_{CAL} < significance level (α), then reject H_0,

but, under (b) step 7 is:

if TS_{CAL} > TS_{CR}, then reject H_0.

Step 8: Marketing Research Conclusion

The conclusion reached by hypothesis testing must be expressed in terms of the marketing research problem and managerial action that should be taken. In our example, we conclude that there is evidence that the proportion of customers preferring the new service plan is significantly greater than 0.40. Hence, the recommendation would be to introduce the new service plan. Another illustration of hypothesis testing is provided by the following example.

EXAMPLE

INTERNATIONAL BRAND EQUITY— THE NAME OF THE GAME

In the twenty-first century, the trend is toward global marketing. How can marketers market a brand abroad where there are diverse historical and cultural differences? According to Bob Kroll, the former president of Del Monte International, uniform packaging may be an asset, yet catering to individual countries' culinary taste preferences is more important. Marketing executives now believe it's best to think globally, but act locally.

A suitable research question might be: Do consumers in different countries prefer to buy global name brands with different packaging customized to suit their local needs? Based on this research question, one can frame the hypothesis that, other factors being constant, standardized branding with customized packaging for a well-established name brand will result in greater market share. The hypotheses may be formulated as follows:

H_0:   Standardized branding with customized packaging for a well-established name brand will not lead to greater market share in the international market.

H_1:   Other factors remaining equal, standardized branding with customized packaging for a well-established name brand will lead to greater market share in the international market.

> To test the null hypothesis, a well-established brand such as Colgate toothpaste, which has followed a mixed strategy, can be selected. The market share in countries with standardized branding and standardized packaging can be compared with market share in countries with standardized branding and customized packaging, after controlling for the effect of other factors. Note that this is a one-tail test.

Hypotheses testing can be related to either an examination of associations or an examination of differences (Figure 16.9). In tests of associations, the null hypothesis is that there is no association between the variables (H_0: . . . is NOT related to . . .). In tests of differences, the null hypothesis is that there is no difference (H_0: . . . is NOT different than . . .). Tests of differences could relate to means or proportions. First, we discuss hypotheses related to associations in the context of cross-tabulations.

CROSS-TABULATIONS

While answers to questions related to a single variable are interesting, they often raise additional questions about how to link that variable to other variables. To introduce the frequency distribution, we posed several representative marketing research questions. For each of these, a researcher might pose additional questions to relate these variables to other variables. For example:

- What percentage of coupon users have annual household incomes of more than $35,000? (See opening vignette.)
- Is product use (measured in terms of heavy users, medium users, light users, and nonusers) related to interest in outdoor activities (high, medium, and low)?
- Is familiarity with a new product (unfamiliar, familiar) related to education levels (high school or less, some college, college degree)?
- Is the income (high, medium, and low) of brand users related to the geographic region in which they live (north, south, east, and west)?

The answers to such questions can be determined by examining cross-tabulations. While a frequency distribution describes one variable at a time, a **cross-tabulation** describes two or more variables simultaneously. Cross-tabulation results in tables that

cross-tabulation
A statistical technique that describes two or more variables simultaneously and results in tables that reflect the joint distribution of two or more variables that have a limited number of categories or distinct values.

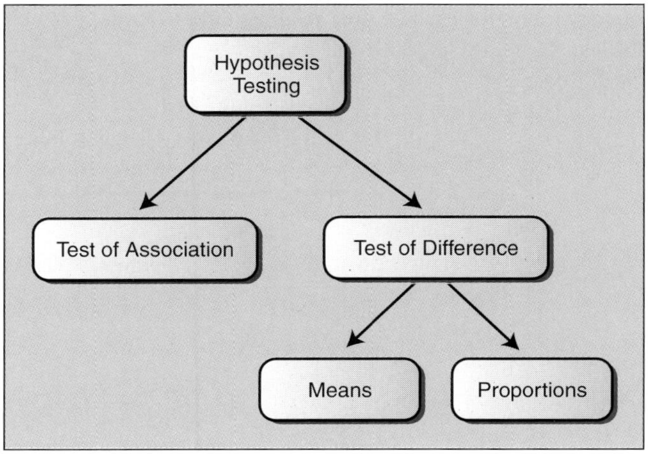

FIGURE 16.9
A Broad Classification of Hypothesis Testing Procedures

Output File

T A B L E 1 6 . 3   A Cross-Tabulation of Sex and Usage of Nike Shoes

USAGE	SEX		ROW TOTAL
	Female	Male	
Light Users	14	5	19
Medium Users	5	5	10
Heavy Users	5	11	16
Column Total	24	21	45

reflect the joint distribution of two or more variables with a limited number of categories or distinct values. The categories of one variable are cross-classified with the categories of one or more other variables. Thus, the frequency distribution of one variable is subdivided according to the values or categories of the other variables. This was illustrated in the opening vignette where coupon usage was cross-classified with income. The analysis revealed that lower income households had higher coupon usage as compared to middle and higher income households.

Suppose Nike was interested in determining whether sex was associated with the degree of usage of Nike shoes. In Table 16.1, the respondents were divided into three categories of light (denoted by 1), medium (2), or heavy users (3) based on reported wear time per week. There were 19 light users, 10 medium users, and 16 heavy users. While data on attitude were missing for one respondent, information on usage and sex was available for all. Sex was coded as 1 for females and 2 for males. There were 24 females and 21 males.

The cross-tabulation is shown in Table 16.3. A cross-tabulation includes a cell for every combination of the categories of the two variables. The number in each cell shows how many respondents gave that combination of responses. In Table 16.3, 14 respondents were females and light users. The marginal totals (column totals and row totals) in this table indicate that, of the 45 respondents with valid responses on both the variables, 19 were light users, 10 were medium users, and 16 were heavy users, confirming the classification procedure adopted.

Furthermore, 21 respondents were males, and 24 were females. Note that this information could have been obtained from a separate frequency distribution for each variable. In general, the margins of a cross-tabulation show the same information as the frequency tables for each of the variables. Cross-tabulation tables are also called **contingency tables.**

contingency table
A cross-tabulation table. It contains a cell for every combination of categories of the two variables.

Output File

T A B L E 1 6 . 4   Usage of Nike Shoes by Sex

USAGE	SEX	
	Female	Male
Light Users	58.4%	23.8%
Medium Users	20.8%	23.8%
Heavy Users	20.8%	52.4%
Column Total	100.0%	100.0%

TABLE 16.5   Sex by Usage of Nike Shoes

USAGE	SEX		ROW TOTAL
	Female	Male	
Light Users	73.7%	26.3%	100.0%
Medium Users	50.0%	50.0%	100.0%
Heavy Users	31.2%	68.8%	100.0%

Cross-tabulation is widely used in commercial marketing research because (1) cross-tabulation analysis and results can be easily interpreted and understood by managers who are not statistically oriented; (2) the clarity of interpretation provides a stronger link between research results and managerial action; and (3) cross-tabulation analysis is simple to conduct and more appealing to less sophisticated researchers. We will discuss cross-tabulation for two variables, the most common form in which this procedure is used.

Cross-tabulation with two variables is also known as bivariate cross-tabulation. Consider again the cross-classification of sex and usage of Nike shoes given in Table 16.3. Is usage of Nike shoes related to sex? It might be. We see from Table 16.3 that disproportionately more of the males are heavy users and disproportionately more of the females are light users. Computation of percentages can provide more insights.

Since two variables have been cross-classified, percentages could be computed either columnwise, based on column totals (Table 16.4), or rowwise, based on row totals (Table 16.5). Which of these tables is more useful? The answer depends on which variable will be considered as the independent variable and which as the dependent variable. The general rule is to compute the percentages in the direction of the independent variable, across the dependent variable. In our analysis, sex would be considered as the independent variable, and usage as the dependent variable. Therefore, the correct way of calculating percentages is as shown in Table 16.4. Note that while 52.4 percent of the males are heavy users, only 20.8 percent of females are heavy users. This seems to indicate that as compared to females, males are more likely to be heavy users of Nike shoes. The recommendation to management may be to promote more heavily to women to increase their usage rate or to promote more heavily to men to prevent brand loyalty erosion. Obviously, additional variables would need to be analyzed before management would act upon such variables. Nevertheless, this illustrates how hypotheses tests should be linked to recommended managerial actions.

Note that computing percentages in the direction of the dependent variable across the independent variable, as shown in Table 16.5, is not meaningful in this case. Table 16.5 implies that heavy usage of Nike shoes causes people to be males. This latter finding is not meaningful. As another example, consider the following study.

EXAMPLE

OLD IS GOLD BUT SOME MARKETERS TREAT IT AS DUST

A study examined whether older models are depicted in an undesirable light in TV commercials. The researchers analyzed television commercials emanating from the three major networks, one local station, and five cable companies. The results were as follows in terms of the number and percentage of models of different age groups that were depicted in a desirable or undesirable light:

AGE OF THE MODEL	DESIRABLE		UNDESIRABLE		TOTAL	
	NO.	%	NO.	%	NO.	%
Under 45	415	83.1	85	16.9	500	100
45–64	64	66.0	33	34.0	97	100
65 and over	28	54.0	24	46.0	52	100

Note that as age of the model increases, the percentages in the undesirable column increase. Therefore, the study concluded that older models do tend to be depicted in an undesirable manner. Thus, some marketers may be pursuing self-defeating strategies by depicting older consumers unfavorably. Marketers should note that the older consumers represent a large and growing segment that controls substantial income and wealth.[5]

General Comments on Cross-Tabulation

While three or more variables can be cross-tabulated, the interpretation can be quite complex. Also, because the number of cells increases multiplicatively, maintaining an adequate number of respondents or cases in each cell can be problematic. As a general rule, there should be at least five expected observations in each cell for the chi-square statistic used for testing cross-tab hypothesis to be reliable. Thus, cross-tabulation is an inefficient way of examining relationships when there are several variables. Note that cross-tabulation examines association between variables, not causation. To examine causation, the causal research design framework should be adopted (see Chapter 8).

STATISTICS ASSOCIATED WITH CROSS-TABULATION

In this section, we will discuss the statistics commonly used for assessing the statistical significance and strength of association of cross-tabulated variables. The statistical significance of the observed association is commonly measured by the chi-square statistic. The strength of association, or degree of association, is important from a practical or managerial perspective. Generally, the strength of an association is of interest only if the association is statistically significant. The strength of the association can be measured by the phi correlation coefficient, the contingency coefficient, Cramer's *V*, and the lambda coefficient.

Chi-Square

chi-square statistic
The statistic used to test the statistical significance of the observed association in a cross-tabulation. It assists us in determining whether a systematic association exists between the two variables.

The **chi-square statistic** (χ^2) is used to test the statistical significance of the observed association in a cross-tabulation. It assists us in determining whether a systematic association exists between two variables. This is illustrated in the opening vignette where a systematic association exists between coupon usage and income, with lower-income households consuming more coupons than middle- or higher-income households. The null hypothesis, H_0, is that there is no association between the variables. The test is conducted by computing the cell frequencies that would be expected if no association were present between the variables, given the existing row and column totals. These expected cell frequencies, denoted f_e, are then compared to the actual observed frequencies, f_o, found in the cross-tabulation to calculate the chi-square statistic. The greater the discrepancies between the expected and actual frequencies, the larger the value of the statistic. Assume that a cross-tabulation has r rows and c columns and a random sample of n observations. Then the expected frequency for each cell can be calculated by using a simple formula:

$$f_e = \frac{n_r n_c}{n}$$

where

n_r = total number in the row
n_c = total number in the column
n = total sample size

For the data in Table 16.3, the total number in the row, n_r, is 19 for light users, 10 for medium users, and 16 for heavy users. The total number in each column, n_c, is 24 for females and 21 for males. Therefore, the expected cell frequencies for the six cells from left to right and top to bottom are:

$f_e = (24 \times 19)/45 = 10.1$ $f_e = (21 \times 19)/45 = 8.9$
$f_e = (24 \times 10)/45 = 5.3$ $f_e = (21 \times 10)/45 = 4.7$
$f_e = (24 \times 16)/45 = 8.5$ $f_e = (21 \times 16)/45 = 7.5$

Generally, the expected cell frequency will be different for each cell, as is the case here. Only when all the row totals are the same and all the column totals are the same will the expected cell frequency be the same for each cell.

Once the expected cell frequencies are calculated, the value of χ^2 is calculated as follows:

$$\chi^2 = \sum_{\substack{\text{all} \\ \text{cells}}} \frac{(f_o - f_e)^2}{f_e}$$

For the data in Table 16.3, in which there are six cells, the value of χ^2 is calculated as:

$$\chi^2 = \frac{(14 - 10.1)^2}{10.1} + \frac{(5 - 8.9)^2}{8.9}$$

$$+ \frac{(5 - 5.3)^2}{5.3} + \frac{(5 - 4.7)^2}{4.7}$$

$$+ \frac{(5 - 8.5)^2}{8.5} + \frac{(11 - 7.5)^2}{7.5}$$

$$= 1.51 + 1.71 + 0.02 + 0.02 + 1.44 + 1.63$$

$$= 6.33$$

To determine whether a systematic association exists, the probability of obtaining a value of chi-square as large or larger than the one calculated from the cross-tabulation is estimated (see step 5 in the general procedure for hypothesis testing, Figure 16.6). An important characteristic of the chi-square statistic is the number of degrees of freedom (df) associated with it. In general, the number of degrees of freedom is equal to the number of observations less the number of constraints needed to calculate a statistical term. In the case of a chi-square statistic associated with a cross-tabulation, the number of degrees of freedom is equal to the product of number of rows (r) less one and the number of columns (c) less one. That is, $df = (r - 1) \times (c - 1)$. The null hypothesis (H_0) of no association between the two variables will be rejected only when the calculated value of the test statistic is greater than the critical value of the chi-square distribution with the appropriate degrees of freedom, as shown in Figure 16.10. (See step 6 in the general procedure for hypothesis testing, Figure 16.6.)

chi-square distribution
A skewed distribution whose shape depends solely on the number of degrees of freedom. As the number of degrees of freedom increases, the chi-square distribution becomes more symmetrical.

Unlike the normal distribution, the **chi-square distribution** is a skewed distribution whose shape depends solely on the number of degrees of freedom. As the number of degrees of freedom increases, the chi-square distribution becomes more symmetrical. Table 3 in the Statistical Appendix contains upper-tail areas of the chi-square distribution for different degrees of freedom. In this table, the value at the top of each column indicates the area in the upper portion (the right side, as shown in Figure 16.10) of the chi-square distribution. To illustrate, for 2 degrees of freedom, the critical value of chi-square (χ^2_{CR}) for an upper-tail area of .05 is 5.991. This indicates that for 2 degrees of freedom the probability of exceeding a chi-square value of 5.991 is 0.05. In other words, at the 0.05 level of significance with 2 degrees of freedom, the critical value of the chi-square statistic is 5.991.

For the cross-tabulation given in Table 16.3, there are $(3 - 1) \times (2 - 1) = 2$ degrees of freedom. The calculated chi-square statistic had a value of 6.33. Since this is greater than the critical value of 5.991, the null hypothesis of no association is rejected, indicating that the association is statistically significant at the 0.05 level.

The chi-square statistic can also be used in goodness-of-fit tests to determine whether certain models fit the observed data. These tests are conducted by calculating the significance of sample deviations from assumed theoretical (expected) distributions and can be performed on cross-tabulations as well as on frequencies (one-way tabulations). The calculation of the chi-square statistic and the determination of its significance is the same as illustrated above.

The chi-square statistic should be estimated only on counts of data. When the data are in percentage form, they should first be converted to absolute counts or numbers. In addition, an underlying assumption of the chi-square test is that the observations are drawn independently. This means that respondents do not influence each other's responses in any way. As a general rule, chi-square analysis should not be conducted when the expected or theoretical frequencies in any of the cells is less than five. Low expected frequencies would cause the calculated value of chi-square to be higher than it should be

FIGURE 16.10
Chi-Square Test of Association

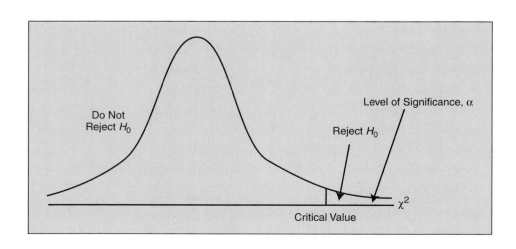

(bias it upward) and make it more likely to commit a type I error. The issue of cell sizes is directly related to statistical determination of sample size discussed in Chapter 13. In the case of a 2×2 table, the chi-square is related to the phi coefficient.

Phi Coefficient

The **phi coefficient** (ϕ) is used as a measure of the strength of association in the special case of a table with two rows and two columns (a 2×2 table). The phi coefficient is proportional to the square root of the chi-square statistic. For a sample of size n, this statistic is calculated as:

phi coefficient
A measure of the strength of association in the special case of a table with two rows and two columns (a 2×2 table).

$$\phi = \sqrt{\frac{\chi^2}{n}}$$

It takes the value of 0 when there is no association, which would be indicated by a chi-square value of 0 as well. When the variables are perfectly associated, phi assumes the value of 1 and all the observations fall just on the main or minor diagonal. (In some computer programs, phi assumes a value of -1 rather than 1 when there is perfect negative association.) In the more general case involving a table of any size, the strength of association can be assessed by using the contingency coefficient.

Contingency Coefficient

While the phi coefficient is specific to a 2×2 table, the **contingency coefficient** (C) can be used to assess the strength of association in a table of any size. This index is also related to chi-square, as follows:

contingency coefficient
A measure of the strength of association in a table of any size.

$$C = \sqrt{\frac{\chi^2}{\chi^2 + n}}$$

The contingency coefficient varies between 0 and 1. The 0 value occurs in the case of no association (that is, the variables are statistically independent) but the maximum value of 1 is never achieved. Rather, the maximum value of the contingency coefficient depends on the size of the table (number of rows and number of columns). For this reason, it should be used only to compare tables of the same size.

Output File

Normally, the strength of association is not meaningful and hence not calculated when the null hypothesis of no association is not rejected. If there is no relationship between the two variables, there can be no strength. In our case, the null hypothesis was rejected and so it is meaningful to calculate the contingency coefficient. The value of the contingency coefficient for Table 16.3 is:

$$C = \sqrt{\frac{6.33}{6.33 + 45}}$$
$$= \sqrt{.1235}$$
$$= 0.351$$

This value of C indicates that the association is low to moderate.

Cramer's V

Cramer's V is a modified version of the phi correlation coefficient, ϕ, and is used in tables larger than 2×2. When phi is calculated for a table larger than 2×2, it has no upper limit.

Cramer's V
A measure of the strength of association used in tables larger than 2×2.

Cramer's V is obtained by adjusting phi for either the number of rows or the number of columns in the table, based on which of the two is smaller. The adjustment is such that V will range from 0 to 1. A large value of V merely indicates a high degree of association. It does not indicate how the variables are associated. As a rule of thumb, values of V below 0.3 indicate low association, values between 0.3 and 0.6 indicate low to moderate association, and values above 0.6 indicate strong association. For a table with r rows and c columns, the relationship between Cramer's V and the phi correlation coefficient is expressed as:

$$V = \sqrt{\frac{\phi^2}{\min{(r-1),(c-1)}}}$$

or

$$V = \sqrt{\frac{\chi^2/n}{\min{(r-1),(c-1)}}}$$

The value of Cramer's V for Table 16.3 is:

$$V = \sqrt{\frac{6.33/45}{1}}$$

or

$$V = \sqrt{.01409}$$
$$= 0.375$$

Thus, the association is low to moderate.

Given that the null hypothesis was rejected and we have determined the strength of association as low to moderate, we can interpret the pattern of relation by looking at the percentages in Table 16.4. There is a low to moderate association between sex and usage of Nike shoes. Males tend to be heavy users, while females tend to be light users.

CROSS-TABULATION IN PRACTICE

While conducting cross-tabulation analysis in practice, it is useful to proceed along the following steps (Figure 16.11):

1. Construct the cross-tabulation table.
2. Test the null hypothesis that there is no association between the variables using the chi-square statistic (see the procedure described in Figure 16.6).
3. If you fail to reject the null hypothesis, there is no relationship.
4. If H_0 is rejected, determine the strength of the association using an appropriate statistic (phi coefficient, contingency coefficient, or Cramer's V), as discussed earlier.
5. If H_0 is rejected, interpret the pattern of the relationship by computing the percentages in the direction of the independent variable, across the dependent variable. Draw marketing conclusions.

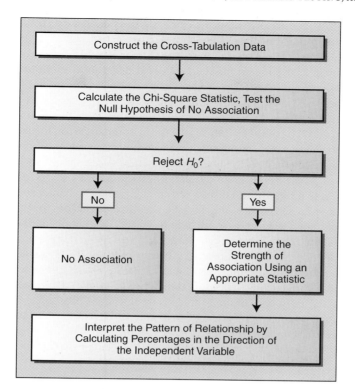

FIGURE 16.11
Conducting Cross-Tabulation Analysis

SUMMARY ILLUSTRATION USING THE OPENING VIGNETTE

Basic data analysis provides valuable insights, as in the case of the coupon usage study. A frequency distribution produces a table of frequency counts, percentages, and cumulative percentages for all the values associated with that variable. The mean, mode, and median of a frequency distribution are measures of central tendency. Some of the important statistics and the insights they provided in the opening vignette were: frequency counts (593 respondents used coupons for brands they normally bought), percentages (95 percent had used a coupon within the last 30 days), and means (the average number of stores shopped was 2.9 per household).

Hypotheses are declarative statements. Basic analysis invariably involves some hypothesis testing. Based on the data collected in the opening vignette, one could test the hypothesis that the average number of stores shopped for groceries is 3.0 per household. Cross-tabulations are tables that reflect the joint distribution of two or more variables. The chi-square statistic provides a test of the statistical significance of the observed association in a cross-tabulation. In the opening vignette, a cross-tabulation of coupon usage with income indicated that households at all income levels were cashing coupons. Yet, lower-income households had higher coupon usage as compared to middle- and higher-income households, and this association was statistically significant. Such findings can be used by supermarkets to target their coupon and promotional strategies.

INTERNET AND COMPUTER APPLICATIONS

SPSS and SAS have similar programs in their microcomputer and mainframe versions for computing frequency distributions, cross-tabulations, and testing hypotheses. The major programs for frequency distribution are FREQUENCIES (SPSS) and UNIVARIATE

(SAS). Other programs provide only the frequency distribution (FREQ in SAS) or only some of the associated statistics (Figure 16.12).

In MINITAB, the main function is Stats>Descriptive Statistics. The output values include the mean, median, standard deviation, minimum, maximum, and quartiles. Histogram in the form of a bar chart or graph can be produced from the Graph>Histogram selection. Several of the spreadsheets can also be used to obtain frequencies and descriptive statistics. In EXCEL, the Tools>Data Analysis function computes the descriptive statistics. The output produces the mean, standard error, median, mode, standard deviation, variance, range, minimum, maximum, sum, count, and confidence level. Frequencies can be selected under the histogram function. A histogram can be produced in bar format.

The major cross-tabulation programs are CROSSTABS (SPSS) and FREQ (SAS). These programs will display the cross-classification tables and provide cell counts, row and column percentages, the chi-square test for significance, and all the measures of the strength of the association that have been discussed. In addition, the TABULATE (SAS) program can be used for obtaining cell counts and row and column percentages, although it does not provide any of the associated statistics. In MINITAB, cross-tabulations (cross tabs) and chi square are under the Stats>Tables function. Each of these features must be selected separately under the Tables function. The Data>Pivot Table function performs cross-tabs in EXCEL. To do additional analysis or customize data, select a different summary function such as max, min, average, or standard deviation. ChiTest can be assessed under the Insert>Function>Statistical>ChiTest function. The following section describes the SPSS programs while Figures 16.12 and 16.13 give more details about the other programs.

SPSS

The main program in SPSS is FREQUENCIES. It produces a table of frequency counts, percentages, and cumulative percentages for the values of each variable. It gives all of the associated statistics. If the data are interval scaled and only the summary statistics are

---

SAS

The main program in SAS is UNIVARIATE. In addition to providing a frequency table, this program provides all of the associated statistics. Another procedure available is FREQ. For one-way frequency distribution, FREQ does not provide any associated statistics. If only summary statistics are desired, procedures such as MEANS, SUMMARY, and TABULATE can be used. It should be noted that FREQ is not available as an independent program in the microcomputer version.

MINITAB

The main function is Stats>Descriptive Statistics. The output values include the mean, median, mode, standard deviation, minimum, maximum, and quartiles. Histogram in a bar chart or graph can be produced from the Graph>Histogram selection.

EXCEL

The Tools>Data Analysis function computes the descriptive statistics. The output produces the mean, standard error, median, mode, standard deviation, variance, range, minimum, maximum, sum, count, and confidence level. Frequencies can be selected under the histogram function. A histogram can be produced in bar format.

FIGURE 16.12   Other Computer Programs for Frequencies

SAS

Cross-tabulation can be done by using FREQ. This program will display the cross-classification tables and provide cell counts, row and column percentages. In addition, the TABULATE (SAS) program can be used for obtaining cell counts and row and column percentages, although it does not provide any of the associated statistics.

MINITAB

In MINITAB, cross-tabulations (cross-tabs) and chi-square are under the Stats>Tables function. Each of these features must be selected separately under the Tables function.

EXCEL

The Data>Pivot Table function performs crosstabs in EXCEL. To do additional analysis or customize data, select a different summary function such as max, min, average, or standard deviation. In addition, a custom calculation can be selected to analyze values based on other cells in the data plane. ChiTest can be assessed under the Insert>Function>Statistical>ChiTest function.

FIGURE 16.13   Other Computer Programs for Cross-Tabulation

desired, the DESCRIPTIVES procedure can be used. All of the statistics computed by DESCRIPTIVES are available in FREQUENCIES. However, DESCRIPTIVES is more efficient because it does not sort values into a frequency table. Moreover, the DESCRIPTIVES procedure displays summary statistics for several variables in a single table and can also calculate standardized values (z scores). The EXPLORE procedure produces summary statistics and graphical displays, either for all of cases or separately for groups of cases. Mean, median, variance, standard deviation, minimum, maximum, and range are some of the statistics that can be calculated.

To select these procedures click:

Analyze > Descriptive Statistics > Frequencies

or   Analyze > Descriptive Statistics > Descriptives

or   Analyze > Descriptive Statistics > Explore

The major cross-tabulation program is CROSSSTABS. This program will display the cross-classification tables and provide cell counts, row and column percentages, the chi-square test for significance, and all the measures of the strength of the association that have been discussed.

To select this procedure click:

Analyze > Descriptive Statistics > Crosstabs

SUMMARY

Basic data analysis provides valuable insights and guides the rest of the data analysis as well as the interpretation of the results. A frequency distribution should be obtained for each variable in the data. This analysis produces a table of frequency counts, percentages, and cumulative percentages for all the values associated with that variable. It indicates the extent of out-of-range, missing, or extreme values. The mean, mode, and median of a frequency distribution are measures of central tendency. The variability of the distribution is described by the range and the variance or standard deviation.

Cross-tabulations are tables that reflect the joint frequency distribution of two or more variables. In cross-tabulation, the cell percentages can be computed either column-wise, based on column totals, or rowwise, based on row totals. The general rule is to compute the percentages in the direction of the independent variable, across the dependent variable. The chi-square statistic provides a test of the statistical significance of the observed association in a cross-tabulation. The phi coefficient, contingency coefficient, and Cramer's *V* provide measures of the strength of association between the variables.

KEY TERMS AND CONCEPTS

Frequency
    distribution, 473
Measures of location, 477
Mean, 477
Mode, 478
Median, 478
Measures of
    variability, 479
Range, 479
Variance, 480
Standard deviation, 480

Null hypothesis, 482
Alternative
    hypothesis, 482
One-tailed test, 482
Two-tailed test, 482
Test statistic, 483
z test, 483
Type I error, 483
Level of significance, 483
Type II error, 483
Power of a test, 484

Critical value, 486
Cross-tabulation, 487
Contingency tables, 488
Chi-square statistic, 490
Chi-square
    distribution, 492
Phi coefficient, 493
Contingency
    coefficient, 493
Cramer's *V*, 493

ACRONYMS

The statistics associated with frequencies may be summarized by the acronym FREQUENCIES:

F requency histogram

R ange

E stimate of location: mean

Q uotients: percentages

U ndulation: variance

E stimate of location: mode

N umbers or counts

C umulative percentage

I ncorrect and missing values

E stimate of location: median

S hape of the distribution

The salient characteristics of cross-tabulations may be summarized by the acronym TABULATE:

T wo variables at a time

A ssociation and not causation is measured

B ased on cell count of at least five

U derstood easily by managers

L imited number of categories

A ssociated statistics

T wo ways to calculate percentages

E xpected cell frequencies

EXERCISES

1. Describe the procedure for computing frequencies.
2. What measures of location are commonly computed for frequencies?
3. What measures of variability are commonly computed for frequencies?
4. What is the major difference between cross-tabulation and frequency distribution?
5. What is the general rule for computing percentages in cross-tabulation?
6. Describe the chi-square distribution.
7. What is meant by the expected cell frequency?
8. How is the chi-square statistic calculated?
9. When is it meaningful to determine the strength of association in a cross-tabulation?
10. What statistics are available for determining the strength of association in cross-tabulation?
11. Discuss the reasons for the frequent use of cross-tabulations. What are some of its limitations?

PROBLEMS

1. In each of the following situations, indicate the statistical analysis you would conduct and the appropriate test or test statistic that should be used.
   a. Respondents in a survey of 1,000 households were classified as heavy, medium, light, or nonusers of ice cream. They were also classified as being in high-, medium-, or low-income categories. Is the consumption of ice cream related to income level?
   b. In a survey using a representative sample of 2,000 households from the Market Facts consumer mail panel, the respondents were asked whether or not they preferred to shop at Sears. The sample was divided into small and large households based on a median split of the household size. Does preference for shopping in Sears vary by household size?
2. The current advertising campaign for a major soft drink brand would be changed if less than 30 percent of the consumers like it.
   a. Formulate the null and alternative hypotheses.
   b. Discuss the Type I and Type II errors that could occur in hypothesis testing.
3. A major department store chain is having an end-of-season sale on refrigerators. The number of refrigerators sold during this sale at a sample of ten stores was:

80	110	0	40	70	80	100	50	80	30

   a. Compute the mean, mode, and median. Which measure of central tendency is most appropriate in this case and why?
   b. Compute the variance and the standard deviation.
   c. Construct a histogram and discuss whether this variable is normally distributed.

INTERNET AND COMPUTER EXERCISES

1. A pilot survey was conducted with 30 respondents to examine Internet usage for personal (nonprofessional) reasons. The following table contains the resulting data giving each respondent's sex (1 = male, 2 = female), familiarity with the Internet (1 = very unfamiliar, 7 = very familiar), Internet usage in hours per week, attitude toward Internet and toward technology, both measured on a seven-point scale (1 = very unfavorable, 7 = very favorable), whether the respondents has done shopping or banking on the Internet (1 = yes, 2 = no).

INTERNET USAGE DATA

Respondent Number	Sex	Familiarity	Internet Usage	Attitude Toward Internet	Technology	Shopping	Usage of Internet for Banking
1	1.00	7.00	14.00	7.00	6.00	1.00	1.00
2	2.00	2.00	2.00	3.00	3.00	2.00	2.00
3	2.00	3.00	3.00	4.00	3.00	1.00	2.00
4	2.00	3.00	3.00	7.00	5.00	1.00	2.00
5	1.00	7.00	13.00	7.00	7.00	1.00	1.00
6	2.00	4.00	6.00	5.00	4.00	1.00	2.00
7	2.00	2.00	2.00	4.00	5.00	2.00	2.00
8	2.00	3.00	6.00	5.00	4.00	2.00	2.00
9	2.00	3.00	6.00	6.00	4.00	1.00	2.00
10	1.00	9.00	15.00	7.00	6.00	1.00	2.00
11	2.00	4.00	3.00	4.00	3.00	2.00	2.00
12	2.00	5.00	4.00	6.00	4.00	2.00	2.00
13	1.00	6.00	9.00	6.00	5.00	2.00	1.00
14	1.00	6.00	8.00	3.00	2.00	2.00	2.00
15	1.00	6.00	5.00	5.00	4.00	1.00	2.00
16	2.00	4.00	3.00	4.00	3.00	2.00	2.00
17	1.00	6.00	9.00	5.00	3.00	1.00	1.00
18	1.00	4.00	4.00	5.00	4.00	1.00	2.00
19	1.00	7.00	14.00	6.00	6.00	1.00	1.00
20	2.00	6.00	6.00	6.00	4.00	2.00	2.00
21	1.00	6.00	9.00	4.00	2.00	2.00	2.00
22	1.00	5.00	5.00	5.00	4.00	2.00	1.00
23	2.00	3.00	2.00	4.00	2.00	2.00	2.00
24	1.00	7.00	15.00	6.00	6.00	1.00	1.00
25	2.00	6.00	6.00	5.00	3.00	1.00	2.00
26	1.00	6.00	13.00	6.00	6.00	1.00	1.00
27	2.00	5.00	4.00	5.00	5.00	1.00	1.00
28	2.00	4.00	2.00	3.00	2.00	2.00	2.00
29	1.00	4.00	4.00	5.00	3.00	1.00	2.00
30	1.00	3.00	3.00	7.00	5.00	1.00	2.00

Data File

a. Obtain the frequency distribution of familiarity with the Internet. Calculate the relevant statistics.

b. For the purpose of cross-tabulation, classify respondents as light or heavy users. Those reporting 5 hours or less usage should be classified as light users and the remaining are heavy users. Run a cross-tabulation of sex and Internet usage. Interpret the results. Is Internet usage related to sex?

2. Use one of the mainframe statistical packages (SPSS, SAS, or MINITAB, or EXCEL) to conduct the following analysis for the data that you have collected as part of your field work (described later).

a. Obtain a frequency distribution of the weekly soft drink consumption.

b. Obtain the summary statistics related to the weekly amount spent on soft drinks.

c. Conduct a cross-tabulation of the weekly consumption of soft drinks with sex of the respondent? Does your data show any association?

ACTIVITIES

ROLE PLAYING

You have been hired as a marketing research analyst by a major industrial marketing company in the country. Your boss, the market research manager, is a high-powered statistician who does not believe in using rudimentary techniques such as frequency distributions and cross-tabulations. Convince your boss (a student in your class) of the merits of conducting these analyses.

FIELD WORK

1. Develop a questionnaire to obtain the following information from students on your campus.
   a. Average amount per week spent on the consumption of soft drinks.
   b. Average amount per week spent on the consumption of other nonalcoholic beverages (milk, coffee, tea, fruit juices).
   c. Frequency of weekly soft drink consumption. Measure this as categorical variable with the following question: "How often do you consume soft drinks? (1) once a week or less often, (2) two or three times a week, (3) four to six times a week, and (4) more than six times a week."
   d. Sex of the respondent.

   Administer this questionnaire to 40 students. Code the data and transcribe them to a data file for computer analysis.

GROUP DISCUSSION

1. "Because cross-tabulation has certain basic limitations, this technique should not be used extensively in commercial marketing research." Discuss as a small group.
2. "Why waste time doing basic data analysis? Why not just conduct sophisticated multivariate data analysis (see Chapter 15)?" Discuss.

NOTES

1. Based on David Wellman, "Click 'n' Save," *Supermarket Business,* 54(4) (April 1999): 19–22; "Cox Direct Releases Survey of Promotional Practices," *Direct Marketing,* 61(7) (November 1998): 15–16; and "Coupons, In-store Promotions Motivate Consumer Purchasing," *Marketing News* (October 9, 1995).

2. Terese Hudson, "Selling Brand MD," *Hospitals & Health Networks,* 73(8) (August 1999): A14–A16; and Daniel D. Butler and Avery M. Abernethy, "Yellow Pages Advertising by Physicians," *Journal of Health Care Marketing,* 16 (Spring 1996): 45–50.

3. For our purposes, no distinction will be made between formal hypothesis testing and statistical inference by means of confidence intervals.

4. Technically, a null hypothesis cannot be accepted. It can be either rejected or not rejected. This distinction, however, is inconsequential in applied research.

5. Paula Hendrickson, "Clutter: More Commercial time, More Buyer Complaints," *Advertising Age,* 70(20) (May 10, 1999): S4; and Robin T. Peterson and Douglas T. Ross, "A Content Analysis of the Portrayal of Mature Individuals in television Commercials," *Journal of Business Ethics,* 16 (1997): 425–433.

17

HYPOTHESIS TESTING RELATED TO DIFFERENCES

HYPOTHESIS TESTING RELATED TO DIFFERENCES PROVIDES RICH INSIGHTS INTO DIFFERENCES BETWEEN GROUPS MEASURED ON INTERVAL OR RATIO SCALES.

Opening Questions

1. What is the role of the *t* distribution in testing hypotheses related to differences?

2. How would you test the hypothesis related to one sample?

3. How does hypothesis testing change when there are two independent samples rather than one? Does the hypothesis testing procedure change when we are testing for difference in proportions rather than means?

4. What about hypothesis testing for paired samples? How is it done?

5. How can the analysis of variance procedure be used for testing hypotheses related to more than two samples?

6. What computer programs are available for testing hypotheses related to differences?

Kenneth Athaide, Managing Director/Vice President, Elrick & Lavidge.
Ken is responsible for the Research Services in Elrick & Lavidge's Atlanta office. He works closely with key clients to develop new and ongoing research programs. He works with clients in a variety of industries including telecommunications, cable, and consumer products/services.

LOYALTY VERSUS PROMISCUITY AND CONVENIENCE VERSUS PRICE

As of the year 2001, grocery store shoppers have actually been able to save money by spending more. How is this possible? Through the Internet, consumers now have access to a rewards and rebate program offered by grocery stores and other merchants. The program, Microrebate Investing, moves a percentage of loyal consumers' purchases directly into an investment account. The program is designed for customers at all income levels, with no prequalifications to membership. This is only one of many ways in which supermarkets and grocery stores are attempting to build customer loyalty.

A recent study examined the differences between 138 loyal shoppers (LS) and 110 promiscuous (disloyal) shoppers (PS) of a major supermarket. Both groups of shoppers were asked to indicate the importance of 15 shopping attributes on a seven-point scale (1 = not important, 7 = very important). Based on the two independent sample t-tests, which are used to test the hypothesis of differences between means of two samples, significant differences were identified on five of the 15 attributes, as indicated in the following table.

While the promiscuous shoppers were motivated by the low prices, the loyal shoppers gave significantly greater importance to convenience (access, parking, and opening hours), and displays and internal decor. Thus, even discount supermarkets such as Cub Foods, who have positioned themselves as low price leaders, cannot compete on the basis of price alone. To attract loyal shoppers, they must offer convenience and good aisle displays and internal decor.[1]

Attribute	Mean Importance Rating		Significance Level
	PS	LS	
Low prices	6.30	6.14	0.044
Convenient access	6.24	6.49	0.045
Convenient parking	6.17	6.63	0.030
Convenient opening hours	5.99	6.46	0.001
Attractive displays and decor	4.67	5.14	0.026

OVERVIEW

Chapter 16 described basic data analysis, including frequency distribution, cross-tabulation, and the general procedure for hypothesis testing. As we explained, hypothesis testing procedures are classified as tests of associations or tests of differences. We also discussed statistics for examining the significance and strength of association. In this chapter, we present tests for examining hypotheses related to differences, as in the opening vignette. Figure 17.1 briefly explains the focus of the chapter, the relationship of this chapter to the previous ones, and the step of the marketing research process on which this chapter concentrates.

The parametric tests that we discuss assume that the data are at least interval scaled. We first discuss the case for difference in means for one sample followed by hypothesis testing for two samples. We then make the extension to more than two samples and also examine hypothesis testing associated with differences in proportions. Figure 17.2 gives an overview of the topics discussed in this chapter and how they flow from one to the next.

HYPOTHESIS TESTING RELATED TO DIFFERENCES

In Chapter 16, we considered hypothesis testing related to associations. These hypothesis are of the form that two variables are associated with or related to each other. For example, the values of homes purchased are related to the buyers' incomes. We now focus on hypothesis testing related to differences. These hypotheses are of the form that two variables are different from each other. For example, people living in the suburbs have higher

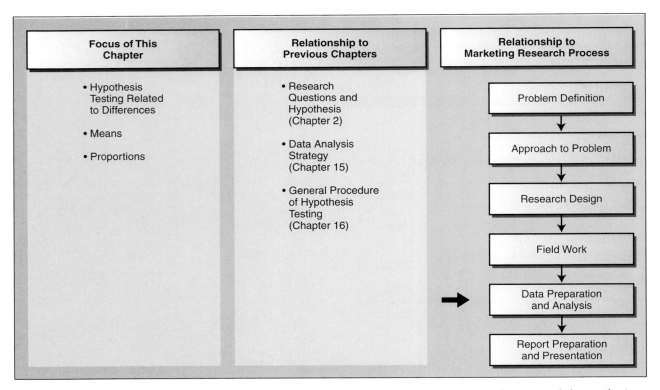

FIGURE 17.1   Relationship of Hypothesis Testing Related to Differences to the Previous Chapters and the Marketing Research Process

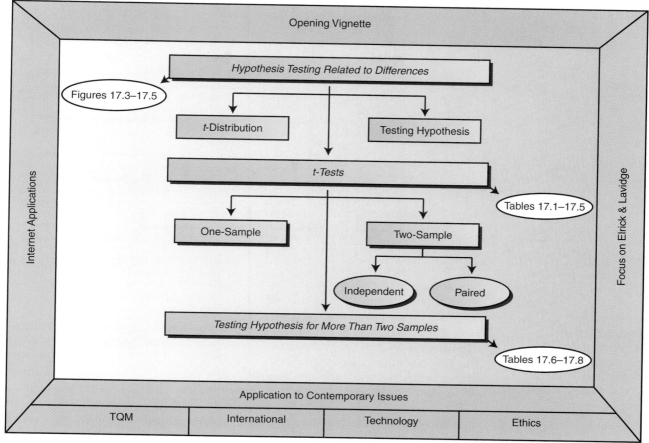

FIGURE 17.2   Hypothesis Testing Related to Differences: An Overview

incomes than people living in the downtown areas. A classification of hypothesis testing procedures for examining differences is presented in Figure 17.3. These procedures are related to examining differences in means or proportions. First, we focus on hypothesis testing procedures examining differences in means. These procedures are also called **para-metric tests** because they assume that the variables of interest are measured on at least an interval scale. For example, the average household spends less than $30 per month on long distance telephone calls. Here, the monthly expenditure on long distance telephone calls is measured on a ratio scale. The most popular parametric test is the *t*-test conducted for examining hypotheses about means. The *t*-test can be conducted on the means of one sample or two samples of observations. In the case of two samples, the samples can be independent or paired. The opening vignette provided an application of a *t*-test for the difference in means of two independent samples—loyal shoppers and promiscuous shoppers. All *t*-tests are based on the *t* distribution.

The t Distribution

Parametric tests provide inferences for making statements about the means of parent populations. A **t-test** is commonly used for this purpose. This test is based on Student's *t* statistic. The **t statistic** is calculated by assuming that the variable is normally distributed, the mean is known, and the population variance is estimated from the sample. Assume that the random variable *X* is normally distributed, with mean μ and unknown popula-

parametric tests
Hypothesis testing procedures that assume the variables of interest are measured on at least an interval scale.

t-test
A univariate hypothesis test using the *t* distribution, which is used when the standard deviation is unknown and the sample size is small.

t statistic
A statistic that assumes that the variable has a symmetric bell-shaped distribution and the mean is known (or assumed to be known), and the population variance is estimated from the sample.

FIGURE 17.3
Hypothesis Tests Related to Differences

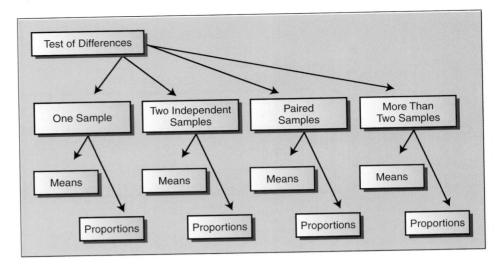

tion variance σ^2, which is estimated by the sample variance s^2. Recall that the standard deviation of the sample mean, $\bar{X}$, is estimated as $s_{\bar{x}} = s/\sqrt{n}$. Then, $t = (\bar{X} - \mu)/s_{\bar{x}}$ is t distributed with $n - 1$ degrees of freedom.

_t_ distribution
A symmetric bell-shaped distribution that is useful for small sample ($n < 30$) testing.

The **_t_ distribution** is similar to the normal distribution in appearance. Both distributions are bell-shaped and symmetric. However, the t distribution has more area in the tails and less in the center than the normal distribution. This is because population variance σ^2 is unknown and is estimated by the sample variance s^2. Given the uncertainty in the value of s^2, the observed values of t are more variable than those of z. Thus, we must go to a larger number of standard deviations from 0 to encompass a certain percentage of values from the t distribution than is the case with the normal distribution. However, as the number of degrees of freedom increases, the t distribution approaches the normal distribution. In fact, for large samples of 120 or more, the t distribution and the normal distribution are virtually indistinguishable. Table 4 in the Statistical Appendix shows selected percentiles of the t distribution. Although normality is assumed, the t-test is quite robust to departures from normality.

Testing Hypothesis Based on the t Statistic

For the special case when the t statistic is used, the general procedure for hypothesis testing discussed in the previous chapter is applied as follows (Figure 17.4):

1. Formulate the null (H_0) and the alternative (H_1) hypotheses.
2. Select the appropriate formula for the t statistic.
3. Select a significance level, α, for testing H_0. Typically, the 0.05 level is selected.
4. Take one or two samples and compute the mean and standard deviation for each sample. Calculate the t statistic assuming H_0 is true. Calculate the degrees of freedom.
5. (a) Estimate the probability of getting a more extreme value of the statistic from Table 4. (b) Alternatively, calculate the critical value of the t statistic. Note that in determining the critical value of the test statistic, the area to the right of the critical value is either α or $\alpha/2$. It is α for a one-tailed test and $\alpha/2$ for a two-tailed test.
6. (a) Compare the probability computed in step 5 with the significance level selected in step 3. (b) Alternatively, compare the calculated t statistic in step 4 with the critical value determined in step 5.

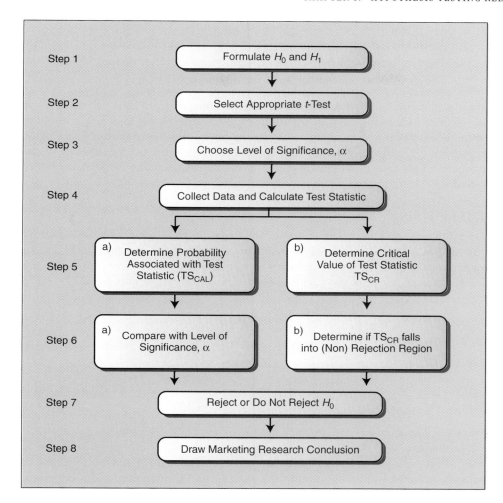

FIGURE 17.4
Conducting *t*-Tests

7. Make the statistical decision to reject or not reject the null hypotheses. If the probability computed in step 5 is smaller than the significance level selected in step 3, reject H_0. If the probability is larger, do not reject H_0. Alternatively, if the value of the calculated *t* statistic in step 4 is larger than the critical value determined in step 5, reject H_0. If the calculated value is smaller than the critical value, do not reject H_0. Failure to reject H_0 does not necessarily imply that H_0 is true. It means only that the true state is not significantly different than that assumed by H_0.[2]

8. Express the conclusion reached by the *t*-test in terms of the marketing research problem.

We illustrate the general procedure for conducting *t*-tests in the following sections, beginning with the one-sample case.

ONE-SAMPLE *t*-TESTS

In marketing research, the researcher is often interested in making statements about a single variable against a known or given standard. The following are examples of such statements:

- The market share for the new product will exceed 15 percent.
- At least 65 percent of customers will like the new package design.
- The average monthly household expenditure on groceries exceeds $500.00.
- The new service plan will be preferred by at least 70 percent of the customers.

These statements can be translated to null hypotheses that can be tested using a one-sample test, such as the z-test or the t-test. In the case of a t-test for a single mean, the researcher is interested in testing whether the population mean conforms to a given hypothesis (H_0). In the opening vignette, the hypotheses that the mean rating of each attribute for the overall sample (loyal shoppers and promiscuous shoppers combined) exceeded 5.0 would be tested using the one-sample t-test.

Test for a Single Mean

Suppose a new machine attachment would be introduced if it receives a mean of at least 7 on a 10-point scale. A sample of 20 purchase engineers are shown the attachment and asked to evaluate it. The results indicate a mean rating of 7.9 with a standard deviation of 1.6. A significance level of $\alpha = 0.05$ is selected. Should the part be introduced?

$$H_0: \mu \leq 7.0$$
$$H_1: \mu > 7.0$$
$$t = (\overline{X} - \mu)/s_{\overline{X}}$$
$$s_{\overline{X}} = s/\sqrt{n}$$
$$s_{\overline{X}} = 1.6/\sqrt{20} = 1.6/4.472 = 0.358$$
$$t = (7.9 - 7.0)/0.358 = 0.9/0.358 = 2.514$$

The degrees of freedom for the t statistic to test a hypothesis about one mean are $n - 1$. In this case, $n - 1 = 20 - 1$ or 19. From Table 4 in the Statistical Appendix, the probability of getting a more extreme value than 2.514 is between 0.025 and 0.01, which is less than 0.05. Alternatively, the critical t value for 19 degrees of freedom and a significance level of 0.05 is 1.7291, which is less than the calculated value of 2.514. Therefore, the null hypothesis is rejected, favoring the introduction of the part.

Note that if the population standard deviation was assumed to be known as 1.5, rather than estimated from the sample, a **z-test** would be appropriate. In this case, the value of the z statistic would be:

z-test
A univariate hypothesis test using the standard normal distribution.

$$z = (\overline{X} - \mu)/\sigma_{\overline{X}}$$

where

$$\sigma_{\overline{X}} = 1.5/\sqrt{20} = 1.5/4.472 = 0.335$$

and

$$z = (7.9 - 7.0)/0.335 = 0.9/0.335 = 2.687$$

From Table 2 in the Statistical Appendix, the probability of getting a more extreme value of z than 2.687 is 0.0036, which is less than 0.05. Alternatively, the critical z value for a one-tailed test and a significance level of 0.05 is 1.645, which is less than the calculated value of 2.687. Therefore, the null hypothesis is rejected, and we can reach the same conclusion arrived at earlier by the t-test.

We further illustrate the one-sample t-test using the data of Table 17.1. This table contains data from two samples, each consisting of 10 respondents. The sample sizes have been kept small so that we can show the detailed calculations (by hand). Sample one consists of teenagers (ages 13 to 19), whereas sample two consists of adults 20 years old or older. The respondents were asked to indicate their preferences for Disney theme parks, immediately before and immediately after their visit, using a 10-point scale. The null hypothesis, based on a previous survey, is that the preference for sample one before entering the theme park will be 5.0. It is possible that the preference for Disney parks could have increased or decreased since the last survey. Hence, the hypotheses are:

$$H_0: \mu = 5.0$$
$$H_1: \mu \neq 5.0$$

A one-sample t-test was conducted using a statistical program. The results are described in Table 17.2.

It can be seen from this table that the mean preference of sample one before entering the park is 5.5 with a standard deviation (SD) of 1.08. These calculations are as follows:

$$\overline{X}_1 = (7 + 6 + 5 + 6 + 4 + 6 + 5 + 4 + 7 + 5)/10$$
$$= 55/10$$
$$= 5.5$$

TABLE 17.1   Preference for Disney Before and After Visiting the Resort

RESPONDENT NUMBER	SAMPLE	PREFERENCE FOR DISNEY	
		Before	After
1	1.00	7.00	9.00
2	1.00	6.00	8.00
3	1.00	5.00	8.00
4	1.00	6.00	9.00
5	1.00	4.00	7.00
6	1.00	6.00	8.00
7	1.00	5.00	7.00
8	1.00	4.00	7.00
9	1.00	7.00	9.00
10	1.00	5.00	7.00
1	2.00	3.00	7.00
2	2.00	4.00	8.00
3	2.00	4.00	7.00
4	2.00	3.00	6.00
5	2.00	6.00	8.00
6	2.00	5.00	8.00
7	2.00	4.00	9.00
8	2.00	3.00	6.00
9	2.00	3.00	7.00
10	2.00	5.00	9.00

Data File

Output File

TABLE 17.2   One-Sample *t*-Test: Teenager's Preference Before Visiting

VARIABLE	NUMBER OF CASES	MEAN	STANDARD DEVIATION	STANDARD ERROR OF MEAN
Preference Before Visiting	10	5.5000	1.080	.342

Test Value = 5

MEAN DIFFERENCE	95% CONFIDENCE INTERVAL		*t* VALUE	DEGREES OF FREEDOM	TWO-TAILED SIGNIFICANCE
	Lower	Upper			
.50	−.273	1.273	1.46	9	.177

$$\sum (X_i - \bar{X}_1)^2 = (7 - 5.5)^2 + (6 - 5.5)^2 + (5 - 5.5)^2 + (6 - 5.5)^2 + (4 - 5.5)^2$$
$$+ (6 - 5.5)^2 + (5 - 5.5)^2 + (4 - 5.5)^2 + (7 - 5.5)^2 + (5 - 5.5)^2$$
$$= 2.25 + 0.25 + 0.25 + 0.25 + 2.25$$
$$+ 0.25 + 0.25 + 2.25 + 2.25 + 0.25$$
$$= 10.50$$

$$S_{x1}^2 = 10.50/(10 - 1)$$
$$S_{x1} = \sqrt{(10.5)/(10 - 1)}$$
$$= 1.08$$

Therefore,

$$t = (\bar{X} - \mu)/s_{\bar{X}}$$
$$s_{\bar{X}} = s/\sqrt{n}$$
$$s_{\bar{X}} = 1.08/\sqrt{10} = 1.08/3.16 = 0.342$$
$$t = (5.5 - 5.0)/0.342 = 0.5/0.342 = 1.46$$

With nine degrees of freedom, the probability of getting a more extreme value of *t* is 0.18. Hence, the null hypothesis cannot be rejected. In other words, the mean preference of sample one before entering the theme park is no different than 5.0. Thus, based on the results, there has been no change in the preference of teenagers since the last survey.

Test for a Single Proportion

Such hypotheses relate to the proportion or percentage pertaining to a single population. For example, the proportion of brand-loyal users of Coca-Cola exceeds 0.2, or 70 percent of the households eat out at least once a week. The procedure for testing a hypothesis associated with a proportion for one sample was illustrated in Chapter 16 in the section "A General Procedure for Hypothesis Testing."

TWO-SAMPLE *t*-TESTS

As can be seen from Figure 17.3, the two samples can be either independent or paired. Furthermore, the hypotheses and the related tests could pertain to examining differences in means or proportions.

Two Independent Samples

Samples drawn randomly from different populations are termed **independent samples.** Several hypotheses in marketing relate to parameters from two different populations:

- The populations of users and nonusers of a brand differ in terms of their perceptions of the brand.
- The high-income consumers spend more on entertainment than low-income consumers.
- The proportion of brand-loyal users in Segment I is more than the proportion in Segment II.
- The proportion of households with an Internet connection in the United States exceeds those in Germany.

In each of the foregoing hypotheses, we have two different populations: users and nonusers, high-income and low-income consumers, Segment I and Segment II, and the United States and Germany. Samples drawn randomly from these populations will be independent samples. In the opening vignette, the loyal shoppers (LS) and the promiscuous shoppers (PS) constituted two independent samples. As in the case for one sample, the hypotheses can relate to means or proportions. The first two hypotheses in the introduction to this section relate to means while the latter two relate to proportions.

MEANS   In the case of means for two independent samples, the hypotheses take the following form:

$$H_0: \mu_1 = \mu_2$$
$$H_1: \mu_1 \neq \mu_2$$

In the opening vignette, the hypotheses tested for the importance of each attribute by the LS and the PS were:

$$H_0: \mu_{LS} = \mu_{PS}$$
$$H_1: \mu_{LS} \neq \mu_{PS}$$

The two populations are sampled and the means and variances computed based on samples of sizes n_1 and n_2. If both populations are found to have the same variance, a pooled variance estimate is computed from the two sample variances as follows:

$$s^2 = \frac{\sum_{i=1}^{n_1} (X_{i_1} - \overline{X}_1)^2 + \sum_{i=1}^{n_2} (X_{i_2} - \overline{X}_2)^2}{n_1 + n_2 - 2}$$

or

$$s^2 = \frac{(n_1 - 1)\, s_1^{\,2} + (n_2 - 1)\, s_2^{\,2}}{n_1 + n_2 - 2}$$

The standard deviation of the test statistic can be estimated as:

$$s_{\overline{x}_1 - \overline{x}_2} = \sqrt{s^2 \left(\frac{1}{n_1} + \frac{1}{n_2} \right)}$$

independent samples
Two samples that are not experimentally related. The measurement of one sample has no effect on the values of the other sample.

The appropriate value of t can be calculated as:

$$t = \frac{(\bar{X}_1 - \bar{X}_2) - (\mu_1 - \mu_2)}{s_{\bar{x}_1 - \bar{x}_2}}$$

The degrees of freedom in this case are $(n_1 + n_2 - 2)$.

If the two populations have unequal variances, an exact t cannot be computed for the difference in sample means. For example, consumers in the United States have well-developed preferences for brands, whereas such preference formation seems to be weak for consumers in developing countries. Thus, preferences for shampoo brands in the United States are expected to exhibit lower variance as compared to preferences in the developing country of Sierra Leone in West Africa. In these cases, an approximation to t is computed. The number of degrees of freedom in this case is usually not an integer, but a reasonably accurate probability can be obtained by rounding to the nearest integer.[3] In this case, the standard deviation of the test statistic can be estimated as:

$$s_{\bar{x}_1 - \bar{x}_2} = \sqrt{\left(\frac{s_1^2}{n_1} + \frac{s_2^2}{n_2}\right)}$$

F-test
A statistical test of the equality of the variances of two populations.

An **F-test** of sample variance may be performed if it is not known whether the two populations have equal variance. In this case, the hypotheses are:

$$H_0: \sigma_1^2 = \sigma_2^2$$
$$H_1: \sigma_1^2 \neq \sigma_2^2$$

F statistic
The F statistic is computed as the ratio of two sample variances.

The **F statistic** is computed from the sample variances as follows:

$$F_{(n_1 - 1),(n_2 - 1)} = \frac{s_1^2}{s_2^2}$$

where

n_1 = size of sample 1
n_2 = size of sample 2
$n_1 - 1$ = degrees of freedom for sample 1
$n_2 - 1$ = degrees of freedom for sample 2
s_1^2 = sample variance for sample 1
s_2^2 = sample variance for sample 2

F distribution
A frequency distribution that depends on two sets of degrees of freedom: the degrees of freedom in the numerator and the degrees of freedom in the denominator.

As can be seen, the critical value of the **F distribution** depends on two sets of degrees of freedom—those in the numerator and those in the denominator. The critical values of F for various degrees of freedom for the numerator and denominator are given in Table 5 of the Statistical Appendix. If the probability of F is greater than the significance level α, H_0 is not rejected, and t based on the pooled variance estimate can be used. On the other hand, if the probability of F is less than or equal to α, H_0 is rejected, and t based on a separate variance estimate is used.

Using the data of Table 17.1, we can examine whether the teenagers have a different preference than adults before entering the park. A two-independent-samples t-test is conducted. Since the difference could be in either direction, a two-tailed test is used. The results are presented in Table 17.3. It can be seen that sample one has a mean of 5.5 with a standard deviation of 1.080 or a variance of $(1.080)^2 = 1.166$.

TABLE 17.3 *t*-Tests for Independent Samples: Preference Before Visiting

Output File

Variable Sample	Number of Cases	Mean	Standard Deviation	Standard Error of Mean
Teenagers	10	5.5000	1.080	.342
Adults	10	4.0000	1.054	.333

Mean Difference = 1.5000
Test for Equality of Variances: $F = 1.05$; $P = .472$

_t_-Test for Equality of Means

Variances	*t*-Value	Degrees of Freedom	Two-Tailed Significance	Standard Error of Difference	95% CI for Difference
Equal	3.14	18	.006	.477	(.497, 2.503)
Unequal	3.14	17.99	.006	.477	(.497, 2.503)

These calculations were illustrated earlier for the one-sample test. Similar calculations will show that sample two has a mean of 4.0 and a standard deviation of 1.054 or a variance of 1.111. The value of the *F* statistic for testing the equality of variances is

$$F_{9,9} = (1.166/1.111) = 1.05$$

Note that the *F*-test of sample variances has a probability that exceeds 0.05.

Alternatively, the critical value of $F_{9,9}$ is 3.18. Accordingly, the null hypothesis of equal variances cannot be rejected, and the *t*-test based on the pooled variance estimate should be used.

The pooled variance estimate may be calculated as

$$s^2 = \frac{(10 - 1)\ 1.166 + (10 - 1)\ 1.111}{10 + 10 - 2}$$
$$= 1.139$$

Thus,

$$s_{\bar{x}_1 - \bar{x}_2} = \sqrt{1.139 \left(\frac{1}{10} + \frac{1}{10}\right)}$$

$$= 0.477$$

Under the null hypothesis, the value of the *t* statistic is

$$t = (5.5 - 4.0)/0.477$$
$$= 3.14$$

The *t* value is 3.14, and with $20 - 2 = 18$ degrees of freedom, this gives us a probability of 0.006, which is less than the significance level of $0.05/2 = 0.025$. Alternatively, the critical value of *t* is 2.1009. Note that in determining the critical value of the test statistic (TS_{CR}), the area to the right of the critical value is $\alpha/2$ for the two-tailed test being conducted. Since the calculated value of *t* exceeds the critical value, the null hypothesis of equal means is rejected. Thus, the conclusion is that the teenagers and adults differ in their preferences for Disney theme parks before entering the park. Table 17.3 also shows the *t*-test using separate variance estimate since most computer programs automatically conduct the *t*-test both ways.

Suppose we wanted to determine whether teenagers have a higher preference for Disney parks as compared to adults. In this case, a one-tailed rather than a two-tailed test should be used. The hypotheses are:

$$H_0: \mu_1 \leq \mu_2$$
$$H_1: \mu_1 > \mu_2$$

The *t* statistic is calculated in exactly the same way as in the two-tailed test. However, in determining the critical value of the test statistic (TS_{CR}), the area to the right of the critical value is α for a one-tailed test (see Figure 17.5). In this case, the critical value of *t* is 1.7341, leading to the same conclusion as arrived at earlier.

As an application of *t*-test, consider the following example.

EXAMPLE

ETHICS IN MARKETING EDUCATION: PRIVATE VERSUS PUBLIC SCHOOLS

A survey of undergraduate marketing students at private and public business schools was undertaken to determine their perceptions of the coverage of ethical topics in marketing courses. There were 101 respondents from private schools and 171 from public schools. Respondents were asked to indicate their degree of (dis)agreement with three statements, using a five-point scale (1 = strongly disagree, 5 = strongly agree). Based on two-independent-samples *t*-tests, students from private schools indicated a greater emphasis on ethics than students from public schools.

STATEMENT	MEAN RATINGS Private	Public	LEVEL OF SIGNIFICANCE
In the marketing program at my school, there is a substantial emphasis on teaching ethics.	2.88	2.62	0.02
In my marketing courses, I have the opportunity to initiate discussion of ethical issues.	3.50	3.09	0.00
My professor seems to be concerned about ethical issues.	3.50	3.30	0.06

The mean responses also indicate that schools are merely doing an adequate job of covering ethical issues in marketing courses. Given the importance of the topic, both private and public business schools need to improve the emphasis on ethical issues in marketing courses.[4]

In this example, we tested the difference between means. A similar test is available for testing the difference between proportions for two independent samples.

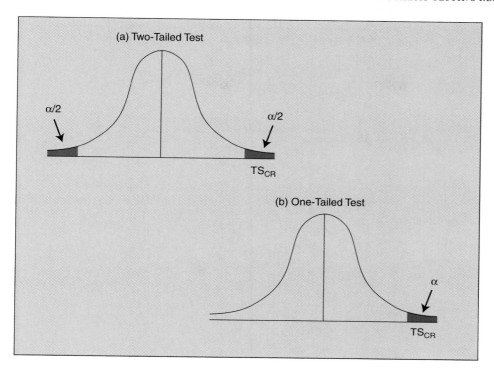

FIGURE 17.5
Calculating the Critical Value of the Test Statistic: TS_{CR} for Two-Tailed and One-Tailed Tests

PROPORTIONS   A case involving proportions for two independent samples is illustrated in Table 17.4, which gives the number (and percentage) of users and nonusers of jeans in the United States and Hong Kong. Is the proportion of users the same in the United States and Hong Kong samples?

The null and alternative hypotheses are:

$$H_0: \pi_1 = \pi_2$$
$$H_1: \pi_1 \neq \pi_2$$

A z-test is used as in testing the proportion for one sample. This is a large sample problem. The samples from each population must be large so that the binomial distribution of sample proportions can be approximated by the normal distribution. As a rule of thumb, both np and $n(1 - p)$ must be greater than 10 for each sample. In this case, the test statistic is given by:

$$z = \frac{P_1 - P_2}{S_{P_1 - P_2}}$$

TABLE 17.4   **Comparing the Proportions of Jeans Users for the United States and Hong Kong**

SAMPLE	USAGE OF JEANS		ROW TOTALS
	Users	Nonusers	
United States	160	40	200
Hong Kong	120	80	200
Column Totals	280	120	

In the test statistic, the numerator is the difference between the proportions in the two samples, P_1 and P_2. The denominator is the standard error of the difference in the two proportions and is given by

$$s_{P_1 - P_2} = \sqrt{P(1-P)\left[\frac{1}{n_1} + \frac{1}{n_2}\right]}$$

where

$$P = \frac{n_1 P_1 + n_2 P_2}{n_1 + n_2}$$

A significance level of $\alpha = 0.05$ is selected. Given the data of Table 17.4, the test statistic can be calculated as:

$$P_1 - P_2 = 0.8 - 0.6 = 0.20$$

$$P = (200 \times 0.8 + 200 \times 0.6)/(200 + 200) = 0.7$$

$$s_{P_1 - P_2} = \sqrt{0.7 \times 0.3\left[\frac{1}{200} + \frac{1}{200}\right]} = 0.04583$$

$$z = 0.2/0.04583 = 4.36$$

Given a two-tailed test, the area to the right of the critical value is $\alpha/2$ or 0.025. Hence, the critical value of the test statistic is 1.96. Since the calculated value exceeds the critical value, the null hypothesis is rejected. Thus, the proportion of users (0.80 for the United States and 0.60 for Hong Kong) is significantly different for the two samples.

As an alternative to the parametric z-test considered earlier, one could also use the cross-tabulation procedure to conduct a chi-square test. In this case, we will have a 2×2 table. One variable will be used to denote the sample, and will assume the value 1 for sample 1 and the value of 2 for sample 2. The other variable will be the dichotomous variable of interest. The t-test in this case is equivalent to a chi-square test for independence in a 2×2 contingency table. The relationship is

$$\chi^2_{(1)} = t^2_{(n_1 + n_2 - 2)}$$

For large samples, the t distribution approaches the normal distribution and so the t-test and the z-test are equivalent.

Paired Samples

paired samples
In hypothesis testing, the observations are paired so that the two sets of observations relate to the same respondents.

In many marketing research applications, the observations for the two groups are not selected from independent samples. Rather, the observations relate to **paired samples** in that the two sets of observations relate to the same respondents. Examples of hypotheses related to paired samples include:

- Shoppers consider brand name to be more important than price while purchasing fashion clothing.
- Households spend more money on pizza than they do on hamburgers.
- The proportion of households who subscribe to a daily newspaper exceeds the proportion subscribing to magazines.
- The proportion of a bank's customers who have a checking account exceeds the proportion who have a savings account.

Each of the foregoing hypotheses relates to the same set of people. Furthermore, the first two hypotheses relate to means while the latter two relate to proportions.

MEANS A sample of respondents may rate two competing brands, indicate the relative importance of two attributes of a product, or evaluate a brand at two different times. The difference in these cases is examined by a **paired samples *t*-test.** In the opening vignette, the hypotheses that the loyal shoppers (LS) consider convenient parking as more important than low prices would be tested by using a paired samples *t*-test. To compute *t* for paired samples, the paired difference variable, denoted by *D*, is formed and its mean and variance calculated. Then the *t* statistic is computed. The degrees of freedom are $n - 1$, where n is the number of pairs. The relevant formulas are:

paired samples *t*-test
A test for differences in the means of paired samples.

$$H_0: \mu_D = 0$$
$$H_1: \mu_D \neq 0$$

$$t_{n-1} = \frac{\bar{D} - \mu_D}{s_{\bar{D}}}$$

or

$$t_{n-1} = \frac{\bar{D} - \mu_D}{\frac{s_D}{\sqrt{n}}}$$

where,

$$\bar{D} = \frac{\sum_{i=1}^{n} D_i}{n}$$

$$s_D = \sqrt{\frac{\sum_{i=1}^{n} (D_i - \bar{D})^2}{n-1}}$$

$$s_{\bar{D}} = \frac{s_D}{\sqrt{n}}$$

SPSS
Output File

For the data given in Table 17.1, a paired *t*-test could be used to determine if there is a difference in the preference before and after visiting the Disney theme park for respon-

T A B L E 1 7 . 5   *t*-Tests for Paired Samples: Teenagers

Variable	Number of Pairs	Correlation	Two-Tailed Significance	Mean	Standard Deviation	Standard Error of Mean
Preference Before Visiting				5.5000	1.080	.342
	10	.881	.001			
Preference After Visiting				7.9000	.876	.277

PAIRED DIFFERENCES

Mean	Standard Deviation	Standard Error of Mean	*t* Value	Degrees of Freedom	Two-Tailed Significance	95% Confidence Interval
−2.4000	.516	.163	−14.70	9	.000	(−2.769, −2.031)

dents in sample one (teenagers). The resulting output is shown in Table 17.5. The mean difference between the variables is 2.4, with a standard deviation of 0.516 and a standard error of 0.163. These calculations are as follows:

$$
\begin{aligned}
\bar{D} &= ((9-7)+(8-6)+(8-5)+(9-6)+(7-4)+ \\
&\quad (8-6)+(7-5)+(7-4)+(9-7)+(7-5))/10 \\
&= (2+2+3+3+3+2+2+3+2+2)/10 \\
&= 2.4
\end{aligned}
$$

$$
\begin{aligned}
S_D^2 &= ((2-2.4)^2+(2-2.4)^2+(3-2.4)^2+(3-2.4)^2+(3-2.4)^2+ \\
&\quad (2-2.4)^2+(2-2.4)^2+(3-2.4)^2+(2-2.4)^2+(2-2.4)^2)/(10-1) \\
&= (0.16+0.16+0.36+0.36+0.36+ \\
&\quad 0.16+0.16+0.36+0.16+0.16)/9 \\
&= 0.2667
\end{aligned}
$$

Thus,

$$
\begin{aligned}
S_D &= \sqrt{0.2667} \\
&= 0.516
\end{aligned}
$$

and

$$
\begin{aligned}
S_{\bar{D}} &= \frac{0.516}{\sqrt{10}} \\
&= 0.516/3.162 \\
&= 0.163
\end{aligned}
$$

This results in a t value of

$$
\begin{aligned}
&2.4/0.163 \\
&= 14.7
\end{aligned}
$$

With $10 - 1 = 9$ degrees of freedom, this has a probability of less than 0.001. Therefore, the preferences of teenagers before and after visiting the Disney theme parks are significantly different. A one-tailed test would have the same value for the t statistic except that the area to the right of the critical value is α (Figure 17.5). Thus, if we wanted to test whether the preferences after visiting the theme park were significantly greater than before the visit, a one-tailed test would also lead to the rejection of the null hypothesis

$$
\begin{aligned}
H_0 &: \mu_D \leq 0 \\
H_1 &: \mu_D > 0
\end{aligned}
$$

where D = preference after the visit − preference before the visit.

Another application is provided in the context of determining the effectiveness of advertising.

EXAMPLE

ROCKPORT ROCKS THE SHOE MARKET WITH COMFORT APPEAL

Focus groups followed by a mall intercept survey indicated that men prefer individuality and comfort in footwear as both a physical goal and a life philosophy.

Rockport Company designed a new advertising campaign based on these findings. The advertising used real people from various walks of life, including Web site expert Clint Rosemund of Razorfish and Robert F. Kennedy Jr., environmental lawyer for Riverkeeper. In the Kennedy ad, Kennedy was seen holding a Harris hawk with copy that reads, "I'm comfortable suing polluters." The TV campaign also featured noncelebrities, including a telephone repairman and a pastor. All advertising ended with a new tagline: "Be comfortable. Uncompromise. Start with your feet."

The TV commercials, as well as the print ads, were carefully tested before they were released to the media. A group of 200 men were asked to respond to a series of 10 scales designed to measure attitude toward Rockport shoes. They were then exposed to the TV commercial as part of an entertaining program. After the program, attitude toward Rockport shoes was again measured using the same 10 scales (see the one-group pretest–posttest design in Chapter 8). A paired t-test indicated a significant increase in attitude after exposure to the commercial.

The TV commercials and the print ads not only fared well in the test but also were successful in achieving sales growth. Rockport saw unit sales rise 21.6 percent in the first year of the campaign, even as the total footwear category declined 6 percent to one billion pairs.[5]

PROPORTIONS The difference in proportions for paired samples can be tested by the chi-square test explained in Chapter 16.

TESTING HYPOTHESES FOR MORE THAN TWO SAMPLES

Procedures for examining differences between more than two means are called **analysis of variance (ANOVA)**. The null hypothesis, typically, is that all means are equal. Marketing researchers are often interested in examining the differences in the mean values of more than two groups. For example:

analysis of variance (ANOVA)
A statistical technique for examining the differences among means for two or more populations.

- Do the various segments differ in terms of their volume of product consumption?
- Do the brand evaluations of groups exposed to different commercials vary?
- Do retailers, wholesalers, and agents differ in their attitudes toward the firm's distribution policies?
- Do the users, nonusers, and former users of a brand differ in their attitude toward the brand?

The answer to these and similar questions can be determined by conducting ANOVA. To further explain this procedure, suppose the researcher was interested in examining whether heavy, medium, light, and nonusers of shampoo differed in their preference for Pert shampoo, measured on a nine-point Likert scale. The null hypothesis that the four groups were not different in their preference for Pert could be tested using analysis of variance. When conducting analysis of variance, it is necessary to distinguish between dependent and independent variables.

Dependent and Independent Variables

In its simplest form, ANOVA must have a dependent variable (preference for Pert shampoo) that is metric (measured using an interval or ratio scale). There must also be one or more independent variables, also called **factors** (product use: heavy, medium, light, and nonusers). The independent variables must be all categorical (nonmetric). The differ-

factors
Categorical independent variables. The independent variables must be all categorical (nonmetric) to use ANOVA.

one-way analysis of variance
An ANOVA technique in which there is only one factor.

treatment
In ANOVA, a particular combination of factor levels or categories.

ences in preference of heavy, medium, light, and nonusers would be examined by one-way analysis of variance. **One-way analysis of variance** involves only one categorical variable, or a single factor that defines the different samples or groups. These groups are also called **treatment** conditions. Thus, the different independent samples are treated as categories of a single independent variable. In this case, heavy, medium, light, and nonusers of shampoo would constitute different samples or groups and would be treated as categories of a single independent variable called shampoo usage.

In the opening vignette, suppose the respondents were classified into three groups: loyal shoppers (LS2—loyal to only one supermarket), multiloyal shoppers (MS2—loyal to two or three supermarkets), and promiscuous shoppers (PS2—nonloyal shoppers). The differences in the mean importance ratings attached to each attribute by the LS2, MS2, and PS2 groups would be tested using one-way ANOVA.

The dependent variable is denoted by Y and the independent variable by X. X is a categorical variable having c categories. There are n observations on Y for each category of X. Thus, the sample size in each category of X is n, and the total sample size $N = n \times c$. While the sample sizes in the categories of X (the group sizes) are assumed to be equal for the sake of simplicity, this is not a requirement.

Decomposition of the Total Variation

decomposition of the total variation
In one-way ANOVA, separation of the variation observed in the dependent variable into the variation due to the independent variables plus the variation due to error.

In examining the differences among means, one-way analysis of variance involves the **decomposition of the total variation** observed in the dependent variable. This variation is measured by the sums of squares corrected for the mean (SS). Analysis of variance is so named because it examines the variability or variation in the sample (dependent variable) and, based on the variability, determines whether there is reason to believe that the population means differ.

The total variation in Y, denoted by SS_y, can be decomposed into two components:

$$SS_y = SS_{between} + SS_{within}$$

SS_y
The total variation in Y.

$SS_{between}$
Also denoted as SS_x, the variation in Y related to the variation in the means of the categories of X. This represents variation between the categories of X, or the portion of the sum of squares in Y related to X.

SS_{within}
Also referred to as SS_{error}, the variation in Y due to the variation within each of the categories of X. This variation is not accounted for by X.

where the subscripts *between* and *within* refer to the categories of X. **$SS_{between}$** is the variation in Y related to the variation in the means of the categories of X. It represents variation between the categories of X. In other words, $SS_{between}$ is the portion of the sum of squares in Y related to the independent variable or factor X. For this reason, $SS_{between}$ is also denoted as SS_x. **SS_{within}** is the variation in Y related to the variation within each category of X. SS_{within} is not accounted for by X. Therefore, it is referred to as SS_{error}. The total variation in Y may be decomposed as:

$$SS_y = SS_x + SS_{error}$$

where

$$SS_y = \sum_{i=1}^{N} (Y_i - \overline{Y})^2$$

$$SS_x = \sum_{j=1}^{c} n(\overline{Y}_j - \overline{Y})^2$$

$$SS_{error} = \sum_{j}^{c} \sum_{i}^{n} (Y_{ij} - \overline{Y}_j)^2$$

Y_i = individual observation
$\overline{Y}_j$ = mean for category j
$\overline{Y}$ = mean over the whole sample, or grand mean
Y_{ij} = ith observation in the jth category

Measurement of Effects

The effects of X on Y are measured by SS_x. Since SS_x is related to the variation in the means of the categories of X, the relative magnitude of SS_x increases as the differences among the means of Y in the categories of X increase. The relative magnitude of SS_x also increases as the variations in Y within the categories of X decrease. The strength of the effects of X on Y are measured as follows:

$$\eta^2 = SS_x/SS_y = (SS_y - SS_{error})/SS_y$$

The value of eta^2 (η^2) varies between 0 and 1. It assumes a value of 0 when all the category means are equal, indicating that X has no effect on Y. The value of η^2 will be 1 when there is no variability within each category of X but there is some variability between categories. Thus, **eta^2 (η^2)** is a measure of the variation in Y that is explained by the independent variable X. Not only can we measure the effects of X on Y, but we can also test for their significance.

eta^2 (η^2)
The strength of the effects of X (independent variable or factor) on Y (dependent variable) is measured by eta^2 (η^2). The value of η^2 varies between 0 and 1.

Significance Testing

In one-way ANOVA, the interest lies in testing the null hypothesis that the category means are equal in the population. In other words,

$$H_0: \mu_1 = \mu_2 = \mu_3 = \ldots = \mu_c$$

Under the null hypothesis, SS_x and SS_{error} come from the same source of variation. In such a case, the estimate of the population variance of Y can be based on either between category variation or within category variation. In other words, the estimate of the population variance of Y

$S_y^2 = SS_x/(c-1)$
    = Mean square due to X
    = MS_x

or

$S_y^2 = SS_{error}/(N-c)$
    = **Mean square** due to error
    = MS_{error}

The **significance of the overall effect** in terms of the null hypothesis may be tested by the F statistic based on the ratio between these two estimates:

mean square
The sum of squares divided by the appropriate degrees of freedom.

significance of the overall effect
A test that some differences exist between some of the treatment groups.

$$F = \frac{SS_x/(c-1)}{SS_{error}/(N-c)} = \frac{MS_x}{MS_{error}}$$

This statistic follows the F distribution, with $(c-1)$ and $(N-c)$ degrees of freedom (df). A table of the F distribution is given as Table 5 in the Statistical Appendix at the end of the book. As mentioned earlier, the F distribution is a probability distribution of the ratios of sample variances. It is characterized by degrees of freedom for the numerator and degrees of freedom for the denominator.[6]

Illustrative Applications of One-Way Analysis of Variance

We illustrate these concepts first with an example showing calculations done by hand, followed by computer analysis. Suppose that a major supermarket is attempting to determine the effect of in-store advertising (X) on sales (Y). In-store advertising is varied at three levels: high, medium, and low. Fifteen stores are randomly selected, and five stores are randomly assigned to each treatment condition. The experiment lasts for four weeks. Sales are monitored, normalized to account for extraneous factors (store size, traffic, etc.) and converted to a 0-to-10 scale. The data obtained (Y_{ij}) are reported in Table 17.6. The one-way ANOVA output is shown in Table 17.7.

The null hypothesis is that the category means are equal:

$$H_0: \mu_1 = \mu_2 = \mu_3$$

To test the null hypothesis, the various means and sums of squares are computed as follows:

Category means: $\bar{Y} = 45/5 \quad 25/5 \quad 20/5$
$$= 9 \quad = 5 \quad = 4$$

Grand mean: $\bar{Y} = (45 + 25 + 20)/15 = 6$

$$
\begin{aligned}
SS_y &= (10-6)^2 + (9-6)^2 + (10-6)^2 + (8-6)^2 + (8-6)^2 \\
&\quad + (6-6)^2 + (4-6)^2 + (7-6)^2 + (3-6)^2 + (5-6)^2 \\
&\quad + (5-6)^2 + (6-6)^2 + (5-6)^2 + (2-6)^2 + (2-6)^2 \\
&= 16 + 9 + 16 + 4 + 4 \\
&\quad + 0 + 4 + 1 + 9 + 1 \\
&\quad + 1 + 0 + 1 + 16 + 16 \\
&= 98
\end{aligned}
$$

$$
\begin{aligned}
SS_x &= 5(9-6)^2 + 5(5-6)^2 + 5(4-6)^2 \\
&= 45 + 5 + 20 \\
&= 70
\end{aligned}
$$

$$
\begin{aligned}
SS_{error} &= (10-9)^2 + (9-9)^2 + (10-9)^2 + (8-9)^2 + (8-9)^2 \\
&\quad + (6-5)^2 + (4-5)^2 + (7-5)^2 + (3-5)^2 + (5-5)^2 \\
&\quad + (5-4)^2 + (6-4)^2 + (5-4)^2 + (2-4)^2 + (2-4)^2 \\
&= 1 + 0 + 1 + 1 + 1 \\
&\quad + 1 + 1 + 4 + 4 + 0 \\
&\quad + 1 + 4 + 1 + 4 + 4 \\
&= 28
\end{aligned}
$$

Data File

T A B L E   1 7 . 6   **Effect of In-Store Promotion on Sales**

STORE NO.	LEVEL OF IN-STORE PROMOTION		
	High	Medium	Low
		Normalized Sales	
1	10	6	5
2	9	4	6
3	10	7	5
4	8	3	2
5	8	5	2

TABLE 17.7   One-Way Analysis of Variance

Source of Variation	Sum of Squares	Degrees of Freedom	Mean Square	F	Significance of F
Main effects	70.00	2	35.00	15.00	.001
In-store promotion	70.00	2	35.00	15.00	.001
Explained (Between Groups)	70.00	2	35.00	15.00	.001
Residual (Within Groups)	28.00	12	2.33		
Total	98.00	14	7.00		

It can be verified that

SPSS

Output File

$$SS_y = SS_x + SS_{error}$$

as follows:

$$98 = 70 + 28$$

The strength of the effects of X on Y are measured as follows:

$$\eta^2 = SS_x/SS_y$$

$$= 70/98$$

$$= 0.714$$

In other words, 71.4 percent of the variation in sales (Y) is accounted for by in-store advertising (X), indicating a strong effect. The null hypothesis may now be tested.

$$F = \frac{SS_x/(c-1)}{SS_{error}/(N-c)} = \frac{MS_X}{MS_{error}}$$

$$F = \frac{70/(3-1)}{28/(15-3)}$$

$$= 15.0$$

From Table 5 in the Statistical Appendix, we see that for 2 and 12 degrees of freedom and $\alpha = 0.05$, the critical value of F is 3.89. Since the calculated value of F is greater than the critical value, we reject the null hypothesis. Therefore, we can conclude that the population means for the three levels of in-store advertising are indeed different. The relative magnitudes of the means for the three categories indicate that a high level of in-store advertising leads to significantly higher sales.

Proportions

To test differences in proportions for more than two samples, one could also use the cross-tabulation procedure to conduct a chi-square test (see Chapter 16). In this case, we will have a $2 \times c$ table. One variable will be used to denote the sample, and will assume the value of 1 for sample 1, the value of 2 for sample 2, and the value of c for sample c. The other variable will be the dichotomous variable of interest. The various hypothesis testing procedures for examining differences in means and proportions are summarized in Table 17.8.

TABLE 17.8   A Summary of Hypothesis Testing

Sample	Test/Comments
One sample	
Means	t-test, if variance is unknown
	z-test, if variance is known
Proportions	z-test
Two independent samples	
Means	Two-group t-test
	F-test for equality of variances
Proportions	z-test
	Chi-square test
Paired samples	
Means	Paired t-test
Proportions	Chi-square test
More than two samples	
Means	One-way analysis of variance
Proportions	Chi-square test

EXAMPLE

ONE-WAY ANALYSIS OF VARIANCE FAVORS "LEVI'S. THEY GO ON."

Levi Strauss & Company was battling competition from designer labels and private-label brands. Designers such as Ralph Lauren Polo, Calvin Klein, Guess?, and Tommy Hilfiger, as well as traditional competitors such as Gap, had launched substantial marketing and advertising campaigns. At the same time, JCPenney Company and Sears, Roebuck & Company had in place strong national branding efforts for their own private-label jeans.

In response to such stiff competition, Levi Strauss developed three alternative image themes: "Levi's. They go on," "They're not Levi's jeans until we say they are," and "A story in every pair." The three themes were tested. Three groups of 150 respondents each were recruited. Each group was asked to evaluate one theme by rating both the theme and Levi's jeans. The theme ratings by the three groups were compared using a one-way analysis of variance to examine the differences in the jeans ratings provided by the three groups. "Levi's. They go on" received significantly higher ratings than the other two alternatives in both of the analyses. Thus, this campaign was chosen for rollout on the national media. Levi Strauss & Company spent more than $90 million on this campaign in an attempt to ward off competition and capture a larger share of the $9 billion jeans market.[7]

SUMMARY ILLUSTRATION USING THE OPENING VIGNETTE

Hypotheses about means of one or two populations are commonly examined by using a t-test. Different forms of the t-test are suitable for testing hypotheses based on one sample, two independent samples, or paired samples. In the opening vignette, the hypothesis that the mean rating of each attribute for the overall sample (LS and PS combined) exceeded 5.0 would be tested using the one sample t-test. The hypotheses related to differences in the mean importance ratings attached to each attribute by the loyal shoppers (LS) and the promiscuous shoppers (PS) would be tested using the two-independent-samples t-test. The hypotheses that the LS consider convenient parking as more important than low prices would be tested by using a paired-samples t-test. Similar tests could be used for testing differences in proportions.

One way ANOVA involves tests of differences in the means of more than two independent samples. The samples are treated as categories of a single independent variable. The null hypothesis of equal means is tested by an F statistic, which is the ratio of the mean square related to the independent variable to the mean square related to error. In the opening vignette, suppose the respondents were classified into three groups: loyal shoppers (LS2—loyal to only one supermarket), multiloyal shoppers (MS2—loyal to two or three supermarkets), and promiscuous shoppers (PS2—nonloyal shoppers). The differences in the mean importance ratings attached to each attribute by the LS2, MS2, and PS2 groups would be tested using one-way ANOVA. The differences in the proportion of females among the LS2, MS2, and PS2 could be tested using the cross-tabulation procedure to conduct a chi-square test (see Chapter 16).

INTERNET AND COMPUTER APPLICATIONS

The major program for conducting t tests in SPSS is T-TEST. This program can be used to conduct t-tests on independent as well as paired samples. In SAS, the program TTEST can be used. Parametric tests available in MINITAB in descriptive stat function are z-test mean, t-test of the mean, and two-sample t-test. The available parametric tests in EXCEL and other spreadsheets include the t-test: paired two sample for means; t-test: two independent samples assuming equal variances; t-test: two independent samples assuming unequal variances; z-test: two samples for means; and F-test: two samples for variances (see Figure 17.6). SPSS and SAS also have programs for conducting analysis of variance available for the microcomputer and mainframe versions. In addition to the basic analysis that we have considered, these programs can also perform more complex analysis. MINITAB and EXCEL also offer programs. Figure 17.7 contains a description of the relevant programs for conducting analysis of variance. Refer to the user manuals for these packages for more details.

SAS
In SAS, the program TTEST can be used to conduct t-tests on independent as well as paired samples.

MINIMTAB
Parametric tests available in MINITAB in descriptive stat function are z-test mean, t-test of the mean, and two-sample t-test.

EXCEL
The available parametric tests in EXCEL and other spreadsheets include the t-test; paired sample for means; t-test: two independent samples assuming equal variances; t-test: two independent samples assuming unequal variances, z-test: two samples for means, and F-test: two samples for variances.

FIGURE 17.6   Other Computer Programs for t-Tests

SAS
The main program for performing analysis of variance is ANOVA. This program can handle data from a wide variety of experimental designs. For more complex designs, the more general GLM procedure can be used. While GLM can also be used for analyzing simple designs, it is not as efficient as ANOVA for such models.

MINIMTAB
Analysis of Variance can be accessed from the Stats>ANOVA function. This function performs one-way ANOVA and can also handle more complex designs. In order to compute the mean and standard deviation, the cross-tab function must be used. To obtain F and p values, use the balanced ANOVA.

EXCEL
Both a one-way ANOVA and more complex designs can be analyzed under the Tools>Data Analysis function.

FIGURE 17.7   Other Computer Programs for ANOVA

SPSS

The major program for conducting *t*-tests in SPSS is T-TEST. This program can be used to conduct *t*-tests on one sample or independent or paired samples. One-way ANOVA can be efficiently performed using the program ONEWAY. To select these procedures using SPSS for Windows click:

> Analyze > Compare Means > Means . . .
> Analyze > Compare Means > One-Sample T Test . . .
> Analyze > Compare Means > Independent-Samples T Test . . .
> Analyze > Compare Means > Paired-Samples T Test . . .
> Analyze > Compare Means > One-Way ANOVA . . .

SUMMARY

Hypotheses related to differences in the population means and proportions can be tested using the *t* distribution. Different forms of the *t*-test are suitable for testing hypotheses based on one sample, two independent samples, or paired samples.

One-way ANOVA involves a single metric dependent variable and a single independent categorical variable. Interest lies in testing the null hypothesis that the category means are equal in the population. The total variation in the dependent variable is decomposed into two components: variation related to the independent variable and variation related to error. The variation is measured in terms of the sums of squares corrected for the mean (*SS*). The mean square is obtained by dividing the *SS* by the corresponding degrees of freedom (df). The null hypothesis of equal means is tested by an *F* statistic, which is the ratio of the mean square related to the independent variable to the mean square related to error.

KEY TERMS AND CONCEPTS

Parametric tests, 505	*z*-test, 508	*F* statistic, 512
t-test, 505	Independent	*F* distribution, 512
t statistic, 505	samples, 511	Paired samples, 516
t distribution, 506	*F*-test, 512	Paired samples *t*-test, 517

ACRONYMS

The major characteristics of *t*-tests can be summarized by the acronym TTEST:

      T distribution is similar to the normal distribution

      T est of difference: Means or proportions

      E stimate of variance from the sample

      S ingle sample

      T wo samples: independent or paired

EXERCISES

1. Present a classification of hypothesis testing procedures.
2. Describe the general procedure for conducting a *t*-test.
3. Give the formula for the *t* statistic when examining hypothesis related to a single mean.
4. Give the formula for the *t* statistic when examining hypothesis related to a single proportion.
5. Give the formula for the *t* statistic when examining hypothesis related to means of two independent samples.
6. Give the formula for the *t* statistic when examining hypothesis related to means of paired samples.
7. What is the relationship between analysis of variance and the *t*-test?
8. What is total variation? How is it decomposed in a one-way analysis of variance?
9. What is the null hypothesis in one-way ANOVA? What basic statistic is used to test the null hypothesis in one-way ANOVA? How is this statistic computed?

PROBLEMS

1. In each of the following situations, indicate the statistical analysis you would conduct and the appropriate test or test statistic that should be used.

   a. Consumer preferences for Camay soap were obtained on an 11-point Likert scale. The same consumers were then shown a commercial about Camay. After the commercial, preferences for Camay were again measured. Has the commercial been successful in inducing a change in preferences?

   b. Respondents in a survey of 1,000 households were asked to indicate the frequency of domestic air travel on an interval scale. They were also classified as being in high-, medium-, or low-income categories. Is the frequency of domestic air travel related to income level?

   c. In a telephone survey using a representative sample of 3,000 households, the respondents were asked to indicate preference for fast-food restaurants using a seven-point Likert-type scale. The sample was divided into small and large households based on a median split of the household size. Does preference for fast-food restaurants vary by household size?

2. The current advertising campaign for a major automobile brand would be changed if fewer than 70 percent of the consumers like it.

    a. Formulate the null and alternative hypotheses.

    b. Which statistical test would you use? Why?

    c. A random sample of 300 consumers was surveyed, and 204 respondents indicated that they liked the campaign. Should the campaign be changed? Why?

3. A major computer manufacturer is having an end-of-season sale on computers. The number of computers sold during this sale at a sample of 10 stores was:

    800 1,100 0 400 700 800 1,000 500 800 300

    a. Is there evidence that an average of more than 500 computers per store were sold during this sale? Use $\alpha = 0.05$.

    b. What assumption is necessary to perform this test?

4. After receiving complaints from readers, your campus newspaper decides to redesign its front page. Two new formats, B and C, are developed and tested against the current format, A. A total of 75 students are randomly selected, and 25 students are randomly assigned to each of three format conditions. The students are asked to evaluate the effectiveness of the format on a 11-point scale (1 = poor, 11 = excellent).

    a. State the null hypothesis.

    b. What statistical test should you use?

    c. What are the degrees of freedom are associated with the test statistic?

5. A marketing researcher wants to test the hypothesis that, in the population, there is no difference in the importance attached to shopping by consumers living in the northern, southern, eastern, and western United States. A study is conducted and ANOVA is used to analyze the data. The results obtained are presented in the following table.

Source	df	Sum of Squares	Mean Squares	F Ratio	F Prob.
Between groups	3	70.212	23.404	1.12	0.3
Within groups	996	20812.416	20.896		

    a. Is there sufficient evidence to reject the null hypothesis?

    b. What conclusion can be drawn from the table?

    c. If the average importance was computed for each group, would you expect the sample means to be similar or different?

    d. What was the total sample size in this study?

6. In a pilot study examining the effectiveness of three commercials (A, B, and C), 10 consumers were assigned to view each commercial and rate it on a nine-point Likert scale. The data obtained are shown in the table below.

COMMERCIAL		
A	B	C
4	7	8
5	4	7
3	6	7
4	5	6
3	4	8
4	6	7

4	5	8
3	5	8
5	4	5
5	4	6

a. Calculate the category means and the grand mean.

b. Calculate SS_y, SS_x, and SS_{error}.

c. Calculate η^2.

d. Calculate the value of F.

e. Are the three commercials equally effective?

INTERNET AND COMPUTER EXERCISES

1. Conduct the following analyses for the Internet usage data given in Internet and Computer Exercises 1 in Chapter 16.

   a. Test the hypothesis that the mean familiarity with the Internet exceeds 4.0.

   b. Is the Internet usage different for males as compared to females? Formulate the null and alternative hypotheses and conduct the test.

   c. Is the proportion of respondents using the Internet for shopping the same for males and females? Formulate the null and alternative hypotheses and conduct the test.

   d. Do the respondents differ in their attitude toward the Internet and attitude toward technology? Formulate the null and alternative hypotheses and conduct the test.

2. In a pretest, respondents were asked to express their preference for an outdoor lifestyle using a 7-point scale, 1 = not at all preferred, 7 = greatly preferred (V1). They were also asked to indicate the importance of the following variables on a 7-point scale, 1 = not at all important, 7 = very important.

   V2 = enjoying nature
   V3 = relating to the weather
   V4 = living in harmony with the environment
   V5 = exercising regularly
   V6 = meeting other people

   The sex of the respondent was coded as one for females and two for males. The location of residence was coded as: 1 = midtown/downtown, 2 = suburbs, and 3 = countryside. The data obtained are given in the following:

Data File

V1	V2	V3	V4	V5	V6	V7	V8
7.00	3.00	6.00	4.00	5.00	2.00	1.00	1.00
1.00	1.00	1.00	2.00	1.00	2.00	1.00	1.00
6.00	2.00	5.00	4.00	4.00	5.00	1.00	1.00
4.00	3.00	4.00	6.00	3.00	2.00	1.00	1.00
1.00	2.00	2.00	3.00	1.00	2.00	1.00	1.00
6.00	3.00	5.00	4.00	6.00	2.00	1.00	1.00
5.00	3.00	4.00	3.00	4.00	5.00	1.00	1.00

6.00	4.00	5.00	4.00	5.00	1.00	1.00	1.00
3.00	3.00	2.00	2.00	2.00	2.00	1,00	1,00
2.00	4.00	2.00	6.00	2.00	2.00	1.00	1.00
6.00	4.00	5.00	3.00	5.00	5.00	1.00	2.00
2.00	3.00	1.00	4.00	2.00	1.00	1.00	2.00
7.00	2.00	6.00	4.00	5.00	6.00	1.00	2.00
4.00	6.00	4.00	5.00	3.00	3.00	1.00	2.00
1.00	3.00	1.00	2.00	1.00	4.00	1.00	2.00
6.00	6.00	6.00	3.00	4.00	5.00	2.00	2.00
5.00	5.00	6.00	4.00	4.00	6.00	2.00	2.00
7.00	7.00	4.00	4.00	7.00	7.00	2.00	2.00
2.00	6.00	3.00	7.00	4.00	3.00	2.00	2.00
3.00	7.00	3.00	6.00	4.00	4.00	2.00	2.00
1.00	5.00	2.00	6.00	3.00	3.00	2.00	3.00
5.00	6.00	4.00	7.00	5.00	6.00	2.00	3.00
2.00	4.00	1.00	5.00	4.00	4.00	2.00	3.00
4.00	7.00	4.00	7.00	4.00	6.00	2.00	3.00
6.00	7.00	4.00	2.00	1.00	7.00	2.00	3.00
3.00	6.00	4.00	6.00	4.00	4.00	2.00	3.00
4.00	7.00	7.00	4.00	2.00	5.00	2.00	3.00
3.00	7.00	2.00	6.00	4.00	3.00	2.00	3.00
4.00	6.00	3.00	7.00	2.00	7.00	2.00	3.00
5.00	6.00	2.00	6.00	7.00	2.00	2.00	3.00

Using a statistical package of your choice, please answer the following questions. In each case, formulate the null and the alternative hypotheses and conduct the appropriate statistical test(s).

a. Does the mean preference for an outdoor lifestyle exceed 3.0?

b. Does the mean importance of enjoying nature exceed 3.5?

c. Does the mean preference for an outdoor lifestyle differ for males and females?

d. Does the importance attached to V2 to V6 differ for males and females?

e. Do the respondents attach more importance to enjoying nature than they do to relating to the weather?

f. Do the respondents attach more importance to relating to the weather than they do to meeting other people?

g. Do the respondents attach more importance to living in harmony with the environment than they do to exercising regularly?

3. Using the appropriate microcomputer and mainframe programs in the package of your choice (SPSS, SAS, MINITAB, or EXCEL), analyze the data collected in field work assignment 2. Should the campus newspaper change the format of the cover page? What is your conclusion?

ACTIVITIES

ROLE PLAYING

1. You have been hired as the marketing research manager by a major consumer marketing company in the country. Your boss, the vice president of marketing, has a ten-

dency to shun statistical techniques such as *t*-tests and analysis of variance. Convince your boss (a student in your class) of the merits of conducting these analyses.

FIELD WORK

1. Develop a questionnaire to obtain the following information from students on your campus.

   a. Average amount per week spent at fast-food restaurants.

   b. Average amount per week spent at other (full-service, dine-in) restaurants.

   c. Frequency of weekly consumption of fast foods. Measure this as categorical variable with the following question: "How often do you eat fast foods? (1) once a week or less often, (2) two or three times a week, (3) four to six times a week, and (4) more than six times a week."

   d. Sex of the respondent

   Administer this questionnaire to 50 students. Code the data and transcribe them for computer analysis.

2. Contact your campus newspaper. Collect data for the experiment described in problem 4. Since this may be too much work for one student, this project may be handled in teams of three.

GROUP DISCUSSION

1. "*t*-Tests are so simple to conduct that they should be used more often in analyzing marketing research data." Discuss as a small group.

2. Which procedure is more useful in marketing research—*t*-test or analysis of variance? Discuss as a small group.

NOTES

1. "A Trip to the Grocery Store Could Help Fund Your Child's College Education," *www.idcresearch.com* (November 13, 2000); Elizabeth Ban, "Grocery Shopping Survey," *Retail World,* 51(20) (October 12–25, 1998): 6–7; and Peter J. McGoldrick and Elisabeth Andre, "Consumer Misbehavior: Promiscuity or Loyalty in Grocery Shopping," *Journal of Retailing and Consumer Services,* 4(2) (1997): 73–81.

2. Technically, a null hypothesis cannot be accepted. It can be either rejected or not rejected. This distinction, however, is inconsequential in applied research.

3. The condition when the variances cannot be assumed to be equal is known as the Behrens–Fisher problem. There is some controversy over the best procedure in this case.

4. Roger N. Conaway, "Ethical Preferences Among Business Leaders: Implications for Business Schools," *Business Communication Quarterly,* 63(1) (March 2000): 23–38; Lori T. Martens and Kristen Day, "Five Common Mistakes in Designing and Implementing a Business Ethics Program," *Business & Society Review,* 104(2) (Summer 1999): 163–170; and Richard J. Shannon and Robert L. Berl, "Are We Teaching Ethics in Marketing?: A Survey of Students' Attitudes and Perceptions," *Journal of Business Ethics,* 16 (1997): 1059–1075.

5. Based on "Comfort Zone," *Adweek* (Eastern Ed.) 39(28) (July 13, 1998): 31; and Carol Krol, "Rockport Updates Image with Comfort Philosophy," *Advertising Age* (August 11, 1997): 6.

6. The *F*-test is a generalized form of the *t*-test. If a random variable is *t* distributed with *n* degrees of freedom, then t^2 is *F* distributed with 1 and *n* degrees of freedom. Where there are two factor levels or treatments, ANOVA is equivalent to the two-sided *t*-test.

7. Based on Alice Z. Cuneo, "Levi's Makes Move to Drop All the Hype and Push Products," *Advertising Age,* 71(17) (April 17, 2000): 4–5; Wayne Friedman, "Levi's Uses Music to Heat Up 'Coolness' Factor," *Advertising Age,* 70(10) (March 8, 1999): 3, 56; and Alice Z. Cuneo, "Levi's Unleashing New Image Ads," *Advertising Age* (July 28, 1997): 1, 31.

18

CORRELATION AND REGRESSION

Opening Questions

1. What is product moment correlation, and how does it provide a foundation for regression analysis?

2. What are the nature and methods of bivariate regression analysis, and how can you describe the general model?

3. How can you explain the estimation of parameters, standardized regression coefficient, significance testing, and prediction accuracy in bivariate regression?

4. How does multiple regression differ from bivariate regression?

5. What is the meaning of partial regression coefficients?

6. What computer programs are available for conducting correlation and regression analysis?

CORRELATION IS A SIMPLE BUT POWERFUL WAY TO LOOK AT THE LINEAR RELATIONSHIP BETWEEN TWO METRIC VARIABLES. THE EXTENSION TO MULTIPLE REGRESSION ENABLES THE RESEARCHER TO EXAMINE THE RELATIONSHIP BETWEEN ONE VARIABLE AND SEVERAL OTHERS.

Matt Garrett, Vice President Marketing and Database Analytics, Elrick & Lavidge. Matt has 12 years experience in marketing and database analytics, and is responsible for the design and analysis using various multivariate techniques.

REGRESSION MODELS MODEL THE MARKETING STRATEGY OF ADIDAS

In November 2000, Adidas began pushing through the market to introduce a very expensive and well-engineered basketball shoe called Kobe, named after the Los Angeles Lakers basketball star, Kobe Bryant. After millions of dollars were spent in research and design, endorsements, and marketing agreements, Adidas finally produced a shoe that is extremely competitive with Nike's newest shoe, NikeShox. Many officials believe that the new Kobe shoe will bring Adidas' dwindling sales to an end and create a successful turnaround for the company.

Adidas realized that preference for athletic shoes has strong positive correlations with sports-related variables such as interest in sports, attitude toward sports personalities, attendance at sports events, and time spent watching sports on television. Research by the company revealed that consumers with a greater interest in sports, a more favorable attitude toward sports personalities, higher attendance at sports events, or those who spent more time watching sports on television exhibited a stronger preference for brand name athletic shoes. A multiple regression model with preference for athletic shoes as the dependent variable, and interest in sports, attitude toward sports personalities, attendance at sports events, and time spent watching sports on television as the independent variables had a very good fit. The model fit was determined by strength of association (a measure of how strongly the dependent variable and the independent variables are related) and the accuracy of predicted values of the dependent variable. The coefficient (partial regres-

sion coefficient) associated with each independent variable was positive and significant, indicating that higher values on each independent variable were associated with stronger preference for athletic shoes. Thus, the model had the following form:

Estimated Preference for athletic shoes = $a + b_1$ (interest in sports) + b_2 (attitude toward sports personalities) + b_3 (attendance at sports events) + b_4 (time spent watching sports on television)

where a = constant, and b_1, b_2, b_3, and b_4 are positive partial regression coefficients.

Armed with such information, Adidas, the nation's fourth ranked athletic footwear company, attempted to boost the visibility of its brand with a $5 million TV campaign centered on National Football League star Troy Aikman. Another TV campaign in New York supported its 10-year, $91 million sponsorship of the Yankees. The spots focused on Yankee fans, not players, and featured the tagline "Only in New York." Adidas also launched a national push featuring National Basketball Association star, Kobe Bryant. The latter effort was linked to the company's new marketing alliance with the NBA. Thus, regression models have played a key role in modeling the marketing strategy of Adidas.[1]

OVERVIEW

This chapter describes regression analysis, which is widely used for explaining variation in a dependent variable in terms of a set of independent variables. In marketing, the dependent variable could be market share, sales, or brand preference while the independent variables are marketing management variables such as advertising, price, distribution, product quality, and demographic and lifestyle variables. This was illustrated in the opening vignette, in which the regression model had preference for athletic shoes as the dependent variable and sports-related lifestyle variables as the independent variables.

However, before discussing regression, we will describe the concept of the product moment correlation or the correlation coefficient, which lays the conceptual foundation for regression analysis. Figure 18.1 briefly explains the focus of the chapter, the relationship of this chapter to the previous ones, and the step of the marketing research process on which this chapter concentrates.

In introducing regression analysis, we discuss the simple bivariate case first. We describe estimation, standardization of the regression coefficients, and testing and examination of the strength and significance of association between variables, prediction accuracy, and the assumptions underlying the regression model. Next, we discuss the multiple regression model, emphasizing the interpretation of parameters, strength of association, significance tests, and examination of residuals. Figure 18.2 gives an overview of the different topics discussed in this chapter and how they flow from one to the next.

Fundamental to regression analysis is an understanding of the product moment correlation.

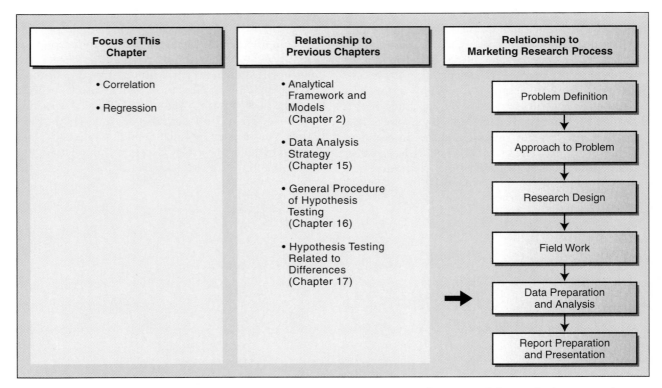

FIGURE 18.1   Relationship of Correlation and Regression to the Previous Chapters and the Marketing Research Process

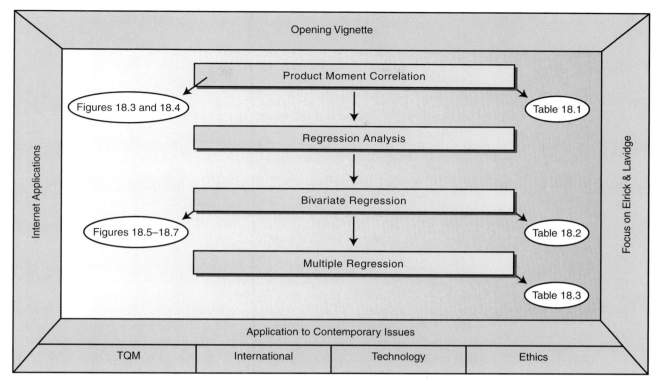

FIGURE 18.2   Correlation and Regression: An Overview

PRODUCT MOMENT CORRELATION

In marketing research, we are often interested in summarizing the strength of association between two metric variables, as in the following situations:

- How strongly are sales related to advertising expenditures?
- Is there an association between market share and size of the sales force?
- Are consumers' perceptions of quality related to their perceptions of prices?

In situations like these, the **product moment correlation** is used. It is denoted by *r*. It is the most widely used statistic that summarizes the strength and direction of association between two metric (interval or ratio scaled) variables, say *X* and *Y*. It is an index used to determine whether a linear or straight line relationship exists between *X* and *Y*. It indicates the degree to which the variation in one variable, *X*, is related to the variation in another variable, *Y*. Karl Pearson originally proposed it, so it is also known as the *Pearson correlation coefficient*. It is also referred to as *simple correlation, bivariate correlation,* or merely the *correlation coefficient*.

In the opening vignette, preference for athletic shoes showed strong positive correlations with sports-related variables such as interest in sports, attitude toward sports personalities, attendance at sports events, and time spent watching sports on television. From a sample of *n* observations, *X* and *Y,* the product moment correlation, *r,* can be calculated as:

product moment correlation
A statistic summarizing the strength of association between two metric variables.

$$r = \frac{\sum_{i=1}^{n} (X_i - \overline{X})(Y_i - \overline{Y})}{\sqrt{\sum_{i=1}^{n} (X_i - \overline{X})^2 \sum_{i=1}^{n} (Y_i - \overline{Y})^2}}$$

Division of the numerator and denominator by $(n-1)$ gives

$$r = \frac{\sum_{i=1}^{n} \dfrac{(X_i - \overline{X})(Y_i - \overline{Y})}{n-1}}{\sqrt{\sum_{i=1}^{n} \dfrac{(X_i - \overline{X})^2}{n-1} \sum_{i=1}^{n} \dfrac{(Y_i - \overline{Y})^2}{n-1}}}$$

$$= \frac{\text{COV}_{xy}}{S_x S_y}$$

covariance
A systematic relationship between two variables in which a change in one implies a corresponding change in the other (COV_{xy}).

In these equations, $\overline{X}$ and $\overline{Y}$ denote the sample means and S_x and S_y the standard deviations. COV_{xy}, the **covariance** between X and Y, measures the extent to which X and Y are related. The covariance may be either positive or negative. Division by $S_x S_y$ achieves standardization, so that r varies between -1.0 and $+1.0$. Note that the correlation coefficient is an absolute number and is not expressed in any unit of measurement. The correlation coefficient between two variables will be the same regardless of their underlying units of measurement.

As an example, suppose a researcher wants to explain attitudes toward sports cars in terms of the number of years the respondent has owned a sports car. The attitude is measured on an 11-point scale (1 = do not like sports cars, 11 = very much like sports cars), and the duration of car ownership is measured in terms of the number of years the respondent has owned one or more sports cars. In a pretest of 12 respondents, the data shown in Table 18.1 were obtained.

Data File

TABLE 18.1   Explaining Attitude Toward Sports Cars

Respondent No.	Attitude Toward Sports Cars	Duration of Sports Car Ownership	Importance Attached to Performance
1	6	10	3
2	9	12	11
3	8	12	4
4	3	4	1
5	10	12	11
6	4	6	1
7	5	8	7
8	2	2	4
9	11	18	8
10	9	9	10
11	10	17	8
12	2	2	5

The correlation coefficient may be calculated as follows:

Output File

$$\overline{X} = (10 + 12 + 12 + 4 + 12 + 6 + 8 + 2 + 18 + 9 + 17 + 2)/12$$
$$= 9.333$$
$$\overline{Y} = (6 + 9 + 8 + 3 + 10 + 4 + 5 + 2 + 11 + 9 + 10 + 2)/12$$
$$= 6.583$$

$$\sum_{i=1}^{n} (X_i - \overline{X})(Y_i - \overline{Y}) = (10 - 9.33)(6 - 6.58) + (12 - 9.33)(9 - 6.58)$$

$$+ (12 - 9.33)(8 - 6.58) + (4 - 9.33)(3 - 6.58)$$
$$+ (12 - 9.33)(10 - 6.58) + (6 - 9.33)(4 - 6.58)$$
$$+ (8 - 9.33)(5 - 6.58) + (2 - 9.33)(2 - 6.58)$$
$$+ (18 - 9.33)(11 - 6.58) + (9 - 9.33)(9 - 6.58)$$
$$+ (17 - 9.33)(10 - 6.58) + (2 - 9.33)(2 - 6.58)$$

$$= -0.3886 + 6.4614 + 3.7914 + 19.0814$$
$$+ 9.1314 + 8.5914 + 2.1014 + 33.5714$$
$$+ 38.3214 - 0.7986 + 26.2314 + 33.5714$$

$$= 179.6668$$

$$\sum_{i=1}^{n} (X_i - \overline{X})^2 = (10 - 9.33)^2 + (12 - 9.33)^2 + (12 - 9.33)^2 + (4 - 9.33)^2$$

$$+ (12 - 9.33)^2 + (6 - 9.33)^2 + (8 - 9.33)^2 + (2 - 9.33)^2$$
$$+ (18 - 9.33)^2 + (9 - 9.33)^2 + (17 - 9.33)^2 + (2 - 9.33)^2$$
$$= 0.4489 + 7.1289 + 7.1289 + 28.4089$$
$$+ 7.1289 + 11.0889 + 1.7689 + 53.7289$$
$$+ 75.1689 + 0.1089 + 58.8289 + 53.7289$$

$$= 304.6668$$

$$\sum_{i=1}^{n} (Y_i - \overline{Y})^2 = (6 - 6.58)^2 + (9 - 6.58)^2 + (8 - 6.58)^2 + (3 - 6.58)^2$$

$$+ (10 - 6.58)^2 + (4 - 6.58)^2 + (5 - 6.58)^2 + (2 - 6.58)^2$$
$$+ (11 - 6.58)^2 + (9 - 6.58)^2 + (10 - 6.58)^2 + (2 - 6.58)^2$$
$$= 0.3364 + 5.8564 + 2.0164 + 12.8164$$
$$+ 11.6964 + 6.6564 + 2.4964 + 20.9764$$
$$+ 19.5364 + 5.8564 + 11.6964 + 20.9764$$

$$= 120.9168$$

Thus,

$$r = \frac{179.6668}{\sqrt{(304.6668)(120.9168)}}$$

or

$$r = \frac{179.6668}{(17.4547)(10.9962)}$$
$$= 0.9361$$

In this example, $r = 0.9361$, a value close to 1.0. This means that the number of years a respondent has owned a sports car is strongly associated with attitude toward sports cars. Thus, the length of time a person has owned a sports car is positively related to degree of favorableness of the attitude toward sports cars. Furthermore, the positive sign of r implies a positive relationship; the longer the duration of car ownership, the more favorable the attitude and vice versa. If John has owned a sports car much longer than Paul, John is likely to have a much more favorable attitude toward sports cars than Paul. Over many years of ownership, John sees his sports car as a treasured possession. On the other hand, Paul has only recently purchased a sports car and has yet to develop such strong feelings toward it. This can be seen from a plot of Y (attitude toward sports cars) against X (duration of sports car ownership) given in Figure 18.3. The points seem to be arranged in a band running from the bottom left to the top right.

Since r indicates the degree to which variation in one variable is related to variation in another, it can also be expressed in terms of the decomposition of the total variation (see Chapter 17). In other words,

$$r^2 = \frac{\text{Explained variation}}{\text{Total variation}}$$

$$= \frac{SS_x}{SS_y}$$

$$= \frac{\text{Total variation} - \text{Error variation}}{\text{Total variation}}$$

$$= \frac{SS_y - SS_{error}}{SS_y}$$

FIGURE 18.3
Plot of Attitude with Duration of Sports Car Ownership

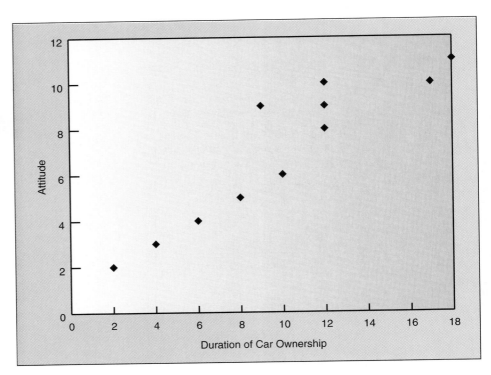

Therefore, r^2 measures the proportion of variation in one variable that is explained by the other. Both r and r^2 are symmetric measures of association. In other words, the correlation of X with Y is the same as the correlation of Y with X. It does not matter which variable is considered the dependent variable and which the independent. The product moment coefficient measures the strength of the linear relationship and is not designed to measure nonlinear relationships. Thus, $r = 0$ merely indicates that there is no linear relationship between X and Y. It does not mean that X and Y are unrelated. There could well be a nonlinear relationship between them, which would not be captured by r (see Figure 18.4).

When it is computed for a population rather than a sample, the product moment correlation is denoted by ρ, the Greek letter rho. The coefficient r is an estimator of ρ. Note that the calculation of r assumes that X and Y are metric variables whose distributions have the same shape. If these assumptions are not met, r is deflated and underestimates ρ. In marketing research, data obtained by using rating scales with a small number of categories may not be strictly interval. This tends to deflate r, resulting in an underestimation of ρ.

The statistical significance of the relationship between two variables measured by using r can be conveniently tested. The hypotheses are:

$$H_0: \rho = 0$$
$$H_1: \rho \neq 0$$

The test statistic is:

$$t = r \left[\frac{n-2}{1-r^2} \right]^{1/2}$$

which has a t distribution with $n - 2$ degrees of freedom. For the correlation coefficient calculated based on the data given in Table 18.1,

$$t = 0.9361 \left[\frac{12-2}{1-(0.9361)^2} \right]^{1/2}$$

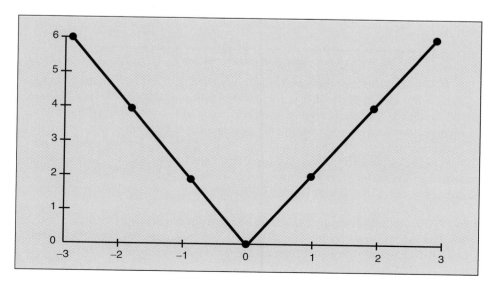

FIGURE 18.4
A Nonlinear Relationship for Which $r = 0$

or

$$t = 0.9361 \left[\frac{10}{0.1237}\right]^{1/2}$$

or

$$t = 0.9381[80.8407]^{1/2}$$
$$= 0.9361 \times 8.991$$
$$= 8.414$$

and the degrees of freedom $= 12 - 2 = 10$. From the t distribution table (Table 4 in the Statistical Appendix), the critical value of t for a two-tailed test and $\alpha = 0.05$ is 2.228. Since the calculated value of t is greater than the critical value, the null hypothesis of no relationship between X and Y is rejected. This, along with the positive sign of r, indicates that attitude toward sports cars is positively related to the duration of car ownership. Moreover, the high value of r indicates that this relationship is strong. The usefulness of the product moment correlation, r, in assessing relationships is illustrated by the following example.

EXAMPLE

IT'S A SMALL WORLD

A recent study analyzed the ratings of 186 countries on seven dimensions of quality of life (QOL): favorable cost of living (COL), culture (CUL), economy (ECON), freedom (FREE), infrastructure (INFRA), health (HEA), and environment (ENV). The simple correlations between these dimensions are as follows:

	COL	CUL	ECON	FREE	INFRA	HEA	ENV
COL	1.0						
CUL	−.03	1.0					
ECON	.27*	.66*	1.0				
FREE	−.05	.57*	0.46*	1.0			
INFRA	−.26*	.76*	.85*	.55*	1.0		
HEA	−.03	.78*	.59*	.47*	.70*	1.0	
ENV	−.05	.04	−.02	.10	−.01	−.07	1.0

* Indicates correlation is statistically significant at $\alpha = .05$.

The magnitude of the correlation indicates the extent to which the two QOL dimensions are interrelated. The highest correlation of 0.85 is observed between INFRA and ECON, indicating that infrastructure and economic development are highly interrelated. In contrast, there is no relationship between infrastructure and environment ($r = -.01$). Based on ratings on the QOL dimensions, the 186 countries were classified into 12 clusters or groups. The highest quality of life was represented by the 10th cluster that consisted of 19 developed countries, including the United States, Canada, the United Kingdom, Japan, France, Germany, and the Scandinavian countries.

This information can be used by country policy makers to identify possible rival countries for direct investment and to form alliances with countries having complementary resources, cultures, and economic development.[2]

The product moment provides a conceptual foundation for bivariate as well as multiple regression analysis.

REGRESSION ANALYSIS

Regression analysis is a powerful and flexible procedure for analyzing associative relationships between a metric-dependent variable and one or more independent variables. It can be used in the following ways:

1. Determine whether the independent variables explain a significant variation in the dependent variable: whether a relationship exists.
2. Determine how much of the variation in the dependent variable can be explained by the independent variables: strength of the relationship.
3. Determine the structure or form of the relationship: the mathematical equation relating the independent and dependent variables.
4. Predict the values of the dependent variable.
5. Control for other independent variables when evaluating the contributions of a specific variable or set of variables.

Although the independent variables may explain the variation in the dependent variable, this does not necessarily imply causation. The use of the terms *dependent* or *criterion* variables, and *independent* or *predictor* variables in regression analysis arises from the mathematical relationship between the variables. These terms do not imply that the criterion variable is dependent on the independent variables in a causal sense, as at least two of the three criteria for causation discussed in Chapter 8 (time order of occurrence of variables and absence of other causal factors) may not be satisfied. Regression analysis is concerned with the nature and degree of association between variables and does not imply or assume any causality. We will discuss bivariate regression first, followed by multiple regression.

regression analysis
A statistical procedure for analyzing associative relationships between a metric dependent variable and one or more independent variables.

BIVARIATE REGRESSION

Bivariate regression is a procedure for deriving a mathematical relationship, in the form of an equation, between a single metric dependent or criterion variable and a single metric independent or predictor variable. The analysis is similar in many ways to determining the simple correlation between two variables. However, since an equation has to be derived, one variable must be identified as the dependent and the other as the independent variable. For example, the growth rate of the U.S. economy has a positive correlation with the level of consumer spending. Thus, a **bivariate regression model** could be constructed with growth rate of the U.S. economy as the dependent variable and the level of consumer spending as the independent variable. The examples of simple correlation given earlier can be translated into the regression context:

bivariate regression
A procedure for deriving a mathematical relationship, in the form of an equation, between a single metric dependent variable and a single metric independent variable.

bivariate regression model
The basic regression line $Y_i = \beta_0 + \beta_1 X_i + e_i$

- Can variation in sales be explained in terms of variation in advertising expenditures? What is the structure and form of this relationship, and can it be modeled mathematically by an equation describing a straight line?
- Can the variation in market share be accounted for by the size of the sales force?
- Are consumers' perceptions of quality determined by their perceptions of price?

CONDUCTING BIVARIATE REGRESSION ANALYSIS

The steps involved in conducting bivariate regression analysis are described in Figure 18.5. Suppose the researcher wants to explain attitudes toward sports cars in terms of the duration of car ownership (see Table 18.1). In deriving such relationships, it is often useful to first examine a scatter diagram.

Scatter Diagram

scatter diagram
A plot of the values of two variables for all the cases or observations; also known as a scattergram.

A **scatter diagram,** or scattergram, is a plot of the values of two variables for all the cases or observations. It is customary to plot the dependent variable on the vertical axis and the independent variable on the horizontal axis. A scatter diagram is useful for determining the form of the relationship between the variables. A scatter plot can alert the researcher to any patterns or problems in the data. Any unusual combinations of the two variables can be easily identified. A plot of Y (attitude toward sports cars) against X (duration of sports car ownership) is given in Figure 18.3. The points seem to be arranged in a band running from the bottom left to the top right.

FIGURE 18.5
Conducting Bivariate Regression Analysis

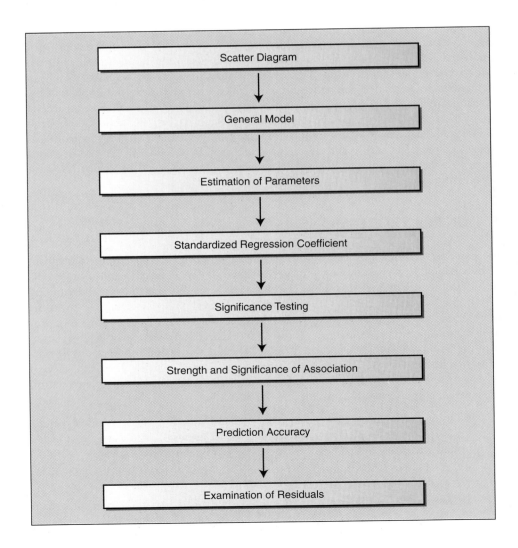

One can see the pattern: As one variable increases, so does the other. It appears from this scattergram that the relationship between X and Y is linear and that it could be well described by a straight line. By fitting the best straight line to the data, the equation of the line gives the estimate of the underlying relationship in the data. How should the straight line be fitted to best describe the data?

The most commonly used technique for fitting a straight line to a scattergram is the **least-squares procedure.** This technique determines the best-fitting line by minimizing the vertical distances of all the points from the line. The best fitting line is called the *regression line.* Any point that does not fall on the regression line is not fully accounted for. The vertical distance from the point to the line is the error, e_j (see Figure 18.6). The distances of all the points from the line are squared and added together to arrive at the **sum of the squared errors,** which is a measure of total error, Σe_j^2. In fitting the line, the least-squares procedure minimizes the sum of squared errors. If Y is plotted on the vertical axis and X on the horizontal axis, as in Figure 18.6, the best-fitting line is called the regression of Y on X since the vertical distances are minimized. The scatter diagram indicates whether the relationship between Y and X can be modeled as a straight line, and, consequently, whether the bivariate regression model is appropriate.

least-squares procedure
A technique for fitting a straight line to a scattergram by minimizing the vertical distances of all the points from the line.

sum of the squared errors
The distances of all the points from the regression line are squared and added together, Σe_j^2.

Bivariate Regression Model

In the bivariate regression model, the general form of a straight line is:

$$Y = \beta_0 + \beta_1 X$$

where

Y = dependent or criterion variable
X = independent or predictor variable
β_0 = intercept of the line
β_1 = slope of the line

This equation is very similar to the equation of a straight line that you are familiar with: $y = mx + b$), with $b = \beta_0$, and $m = \beta_1$. This model implies a deterministic relationship,

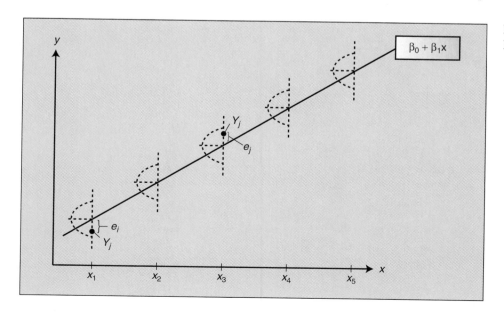

FIGURE 18.6
Bivariate Regression

in that Y is completely determined by X. The value of Y can be perfectly predicted if β_0 and β_1 are known. In marketing research, however, very few relationships are deterministic. So the regression procedure adds an error term to account for the probabilistic or stochastic nature of the relationship. It is assumed that the error terms are independent and normally distributed with a mean of zero and a constant variance. The basic regression equation becomes:

$$Y_i = \beta_0 + \beta_1 X + e_i$$

where e_i is the error term associated with the ith observation.[3] Estimation of the regression parameters, β_0 and β_1, is relatively simple.

Estimation of Parameters

In most cases, β_0 and β_1 are unknown and are estimated from the sample observations using the equation

$$\hat{Y}_i = a + b x_i$$

Where $\hat{Y}_i$ is the **estimated or predicted value** of Y_i, and a and b are estimators of β_0 and β_1, respectively. The constant b is usually referred to as the nonstandardized **regression coefficient.** It is the slope of the regression line, and it indicates the expected change in Y when X is changed by one unit. The formulas for calculating a and b are simple. The slope, b, may be computed in terms of the covariance between X and Y (COV_{xy}) and the variance of X as:

estimated or predicted value
The value $\hat{Y}_i = a + b x_i$ where $\hat{Y}_i$ is the estimated or predicted value of Y_i, and a and b are estimators of β_0 and β_1, respectively.

regression coefficient
The estimated parameter b is usually referred to as the nonstandardized regression coefficient.

$$b = \frac{COV_{xy}}{S_x^2}$$

$$= \frac{\sum_{i=1}^{n}(X_i - \bar{X})(Y_i - \bar{Y})}{\sum_{i=1}^{n}(X_i - \bar{X})^2}$$

$$= \frac{\sum_{i=1}^{n}X_i Y_i - n\bar{X}\bar{Y}}{\sum_{i=1}^{n}X_i^2 - n\bar{X}^2}$$

The intercept, a, may then be calculated using:

$$a = \bar{Y} - b\bar{X}$$

For the data in Table 18.1, the estimation of parameters may be illustrated as follows:

$$\sum_{i=1}^{12} X_i Y_i = (10)(6) + (12)(9) + (12)(8) + (4)(3) + (12)(10) + (6)(4)$$
$$+ (8)(5) + (2)(2) + (18)(11) + (9)(9) + (17)(10) + (2)(2)$$
$$= 917$$

$$\sum_{i=1}^{12} X_i^2 = 10^2 + 12^2 + 12^2 + 4^2 + 12^2 + 6^2$$
$$+ 8^2 + 2^2 + 18^2 + 9^2 + 17^2 + 2^2$$
$$= 1350$$

It may be recalled from earlier calculations of the simple correlation that

$$\overline{X} = 9.333$$
$$\overline{Y} = 6.583$$

Given that $n = 12$, b can be calculated as:

$$b = \frac{917 - (12)(9.333)(6.583)}{1350 - (12)(9.333)^2}$$

or

$$b = \frac{917 - 737.370}{1350 - 1045.259}$$

$$= \frac{179.73}{304.741}$$

$$= 0.5897$$

$$a = \overline{Y} - b\overline{X}$$
$$= 6.583 - (0.5897)(9.333)$$
$$= 6.583 - 5.504$$
$$= 1.079$$

Note that these coefficients have been estimated on the raw (untransformed) data. Should standardization of the data be considered desirable, the calculation of the standardized coefficients is also straightforward.

Using a computer program, the regression of attitude on duration of sports car ownership, using the data shown in Table 18.1, yielded the results shown in Table 18.2. The intercept, a, equals 1.0793, and the slope, b, equals 0.5897, as shown earlier by hand calculations. Therefore, the estimated equation is:

$$\text{Attitude }(\overline{Y}) = 1.0793 + 0.5897 \text{ (Duration of sports car ownership)}$$

Standardized Regression Coefficients

Standardization is the process by which the raw data are transformed into new variables that have a mean of 0 and a variance of 1. This process is similar to the calculation of Z values discussed earlier (Chapters 13, 16, and 17). To standardize a variable, simply subtract the mean and divide the difference by the standard deviation. When the data are standardized, the intercept assumes a value of 0. The term **beta coefficient,** or *beta weight,* is used to denote the **standardized regression coefficient.** Standardization may be desirable because it is easier to compare the beta coefficients than it is to compare the raw coefficients. In this case, the slope obtained by the regression of Y on X, B_{yx}, is the same as the slope obtained by the regression of X on Y, B_{xy}. Moreover, each of these regression coefficients is equal to the simple correlation between X and Y.

Attitude toward sports cars can be explained by the duration of sports car ownership using bivariate regression.

standardization
The process by which the raw data are transformed into new variables that have a mean of 0 and a variance of 1.

beta coefficient
The term used to denote the standardized regression coefficient (also called *beta weight*).

Output File

TABLE 18.2   Bivariate Regression

Multiple R	.9361
R^2	.8762
Adjusted R^2	.8639
Standard Error of the Estimate	1.2233

ANALYSIS OF VARIANCE

	Degrees of Freedom	Sum of Squares	Mean Square
Regression	1	105.9522	105.9522
Residual	10	14.9644	1.4964

$F = 70.8027$ Significance of $F = .0000$

COEFFICIENTS

Variable	b	Standard Error b	Beta (β)	T	Significance
(Constant)	1.0793	.7434		1.452	.1772
Duration	.5897	.0700	.9361	8.414	.0000

Dependent Variable: Attitude Toward Sports Cars

$$B_{yx} = B_{xy} = r_{xy}$$

standardized regression coefficient
Also termed the beta coefficient, this is the slope obtained by the regression of y on x when the data are standardized.

Thus, instead of running Pearson correlations in the opening vignette, we could have alternatively run four bivariate regressions with preference for athletic shoes as the dependent variable. Each of the independent variables in turn would serve as the independent or predictor variable: interest in sports, attitude toward sports personalities, attendance at sports events, and time spent watching sports on television.

There is also a simple relationship between the standardized and nonstandardized regression coefficients:

$$B_{yx} = b_{yx} (S_x/S_y)$$

For the regression results given in Table 18.2, the value of the beta coefficient is estimated as 0.9361. Note that this is also the value of r calculated earlier in this chapter.

Once the parameters have been estimated, they can be tested for significance.

Significance Testing

The statistical significance of the linear relationship between X and Y may be tested by examining the hypotheses:

$$H_0: \beta_1 = 0$$
$$H_1: \beta_1 \neq 0$$

The null hypothesis implies that there is no linear relationship between X and Y. The alternative hypothesis is that there is a relationship, positive or negative, between X and Y. For example, the relationship between income and the number of times people dine out in a month can be statistically tested via bivariate regression. The null hypothesis would be that income has no relationship with the number of times people dine out in a month. The alternative hypothesis would be that income has a positive relationship with the number of times people dine out in a month. If the null hypothesis is not rejected, then we conclude that there is no relationship between X and Y even though the regression coefficient may not be exactly zero. Typically, a two-tailed test is done. A t statistic with $n - 2$ degrees of freedom can be used, where

$$t = \frac{b}{SE_b}$$

SE_b denotes the standard deviation of b and is called the **standard error.**[4] The t distribution was discussed in Chapter 17.

    The standard error or standard deviation of b is estimated as 0.07008 and the value of the t statistic is $t = 0.5897/0.0700 = 8.414$, with $n - 2 = 10$ degrees of freedom (Table 18.2). From Table 4 in the Statistical Appendix, we see that the critical value of t with 10 degrees of freedom and $\alpha = 0.05$ is 2.228 for a two-tailed test. Since the calculated value of t is larger than the critical value, the null hypothesis is rejected. Hence, there is a significant linear relationship between attitude toward sports cars and duration of car ownership. The positive sign of the slope coefficient indicates that this relationship is positive. In other words, those who have owned cars for a longer time have more favorable attitudes toward sports cars, indicating a stronger liking for these cars.

Strength and Significance of Association

A related inference involves determining the strength and significance of the association between Y and X. The strength of association is measured by the **coefficient of determination,** r^2. In bivariate regression, r^2 is the square of the simple correlation coefficient obtained by correlating the two variables. The coefficient r^2 varies between 0 and 1. It signifies the proportion of the total variation in Y that is accounted for by the variation in X. The decomposition of the total variation in Y is similar to that for analysis of variance (Chapter 17).

    As shown in Figure 18.7, the total variation, SS_y, may be decomposed into the variation accounted for by the regression line, SS_{reg}, and the error or **residual** variation, SS_{error} or SS_{res}, as follows:

$$SS_y = SS_{reg} + SS_{res}$$

where

$$SS_y = \sum_{i=1}^{n} (Y_i - \bar{Y})^2$$

$$SS_{reg} = \sum_{i=1}^{n} (\hat{Y}_i - \bar{Y})^2$$

$$SS_{res} = \sum_{i=1}^{n} (Y_i - \hat{Y}_i)^2$$

The strength of association may then be calculated as follows:

$$r^2 = \frac{SS_{reg}}{SS_y}$$

$$= \frac{SS_y - SS_{res}}{SS_y}$$

standard error
SE_b denotes the standard deviation of b and is called the standard error.

coefficient of determination
The strength of association is measured by the coefficient of determination, r^2.

residual
The difference between the observed value of Y and the value predicted by the regression equation $\hat{Y}_i$.

FIGURE 18.7
Decomposition of the
Total Variation in Bivariate
Regression

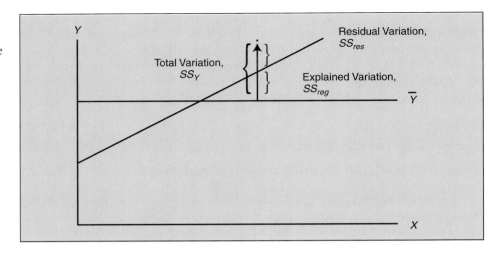

To illustrate the calculations of r^2, let us consider again the effect of the duration of sports car ownership on attitude toward sports cars. It may be recalled from earlier calculations of the simple correlation coefficient that:

$$SS_y = \sum_{i-1}^{n} (Y_i - \bar{Y})^2$$

$$= 120.9166$$

The predicted values $(\hat{Y})$ can be calculated using the regression equation:

$$\text{Attitude } (\hat{Y}) = 1.0793 + 0.5897 \text{ (Duration of sports car ownership)}$$

For the first observation in Table 18.1, this value is:

$$(\hat{Y}) = 1.0793 + 0.5897 \times 10 = 6.9763$$

For each successive observation, the predicted values are, in order, 8.1557, 8.1557, 3.4381, 8.1557, 4.6175, 5.7969, 2.2587, 11.6939, 6.3866, 11.1042, and 2.2587. Therefore,

$$SS_{reg} = \sum_{i=1}^{n} (\hat{Y}_i - \bar{Y})^2 = (6.9763 - 6.5833)^2 + (8.1557 - 6.5833)^2$$

$$+ (8.1557 - 6.5833)^2 + (3.4381 - 6.5833)^2$$
$$+ (8.1557 - 6.5833)^2 + (4.6175 - 6.5833)^2$$
$$+ (5.7969 - 6.5833)^2 + (2.2587 - 6.5833)^2$$
$$+ (11.6939 - 6.5833)^2 + (6.3866 - 6.5833)^2$$
$$+ (11.1042 - 6.5833)^2 + (2.2587 - 6.5833)^2$$
$$= 0.1544 + 2.4724 + 2.4724 + 9.8922 + 2.4724$$
$$+ 3.8643 + 0.6184 + 18.7021 + 26.1182$$
$$+ 0.0387 + 20.4385 + 18.7021$$

$$= 105.9522$$

$$SS_{res} = \sum_{i=1}^{n} (Y_i - \hat{Y}_i)^2 = (6 - 6.9763)^2 + (9 - 8.1557)^2 + (8 - 8.1557)^2$$

$$
\begin{aligned}
&+ (3 - 3.4381)^2 + (10 - 8.1557)^2 + (4 - 4.6175)^2 \\
&+ (5 - 5.7969)^2 + (2 - 2.2587)^2 + (11 - 11.6939)^2 \\
&+ (9 - 6.3866)^2 + (10 - 11.1042)^2 + (2 - 2.2587)^2 \\
&= 14.9644
\end{aligned}
$$

It can be seen that $SS_y = SS_{reg} + SS_{res}$. Furthermore,

$$
\begin{aligned}
r^2 &= SS_{reg}/SS_y \\
&= 105.9524/120.9168 \\
&= 0.8762
\end{aligned}
$$

Another equivalent test for examining the significance of the linear relationship between X and Y (significance of b) is the test for the significance of the coefficient of determination. The hypotheses in this case are:

$$H_0: R^2_{pop} = 0$$
$$H_1: R^2_{pop} > 0$$

The appropriate test statistic is the F statistic:

$$F = \frac{SS_{reg}}{SS_{res}/(n-2)}$$

which has an F distribution with 1 and $n - 2$ degrees of freedom. The F test is a generalized form of the t test (see Chapter 15). If a random variable is t distributed with n degrees of freedom, then t^2 is F distributed with 1 and n degrees of freedom. Hence, the F test for testing the significance of the coefficient of determination is equivalent to testing the following hypotheses:

$$H_0: \beta_1 = 0$$
$$H_0: \beta_1 \neq 0$$

or

$$H_0: \rho = 0$$
$$H_0: \rho \neq 0$$

From Table 18.2, it can be seen that:

$$
\begin{aligned}
r^2 &= 105.9522/(105.9522 + 14.9644) \\
&= 0.8762
\end{aligned}
$$

Which is the same as the value calculated earlier. The value of the F statistic is:

$$
\begin{aligned}
F &= 105.9522/(14.9644/10) \\
&= 70.8027
\end{aligned}
$$

with 1 and 10 degrees of freedom. The calculated F statistic exceeds the critical value of 4.96 determined from Table 5 in the Statistical Appendix. Therefore, the relationship is significant at $\alpha = 0.05$, corroborating the results of the *t*-test. If the relationship between X and Y is significant, it is meaningful to predict the values of Y based on the values of X and to estimate prediction accuracy.

Prediction Accuracy

standard error of estimate
The standard deviation of the actual *Y* values from the predicted $\hat{Y}$ values.

To estimate the accuracy of predicted values, $\hat{Y}$, it is useful to calculate the **standard error of estimate** (SEE). This statistic is the standard deviation of the actual Y values from the predicted $\hat{Y}$ values. The larger the SEE, the poorer the fit of the regression. From Table 18.2, it can be seen that the SEE is 1.2233. The SEE can be used for constructing confidence intervals around predicted values of Y (see Chapter 13).

EXAMINATION OF RESIDUALS

A residual is the difference between the observed value of Y_i and the value predicted by the regression equation $\hat{Y}_i$. Residuals are used in the calculation of several statistics associated with regression. Scattergrams of the residuals, in which the residuals are plotted against the predicted values, $\hat{Y}_i$, time, or predictor variables, provide useful insights in examining the appropriateness of the underlying assumptions and regression model fitted. For example, the assumption of a normally distributed error term can be examined by constructing a histogram of the residuals. A visual check reveals whether the distribution is normal. Additionally, if the pattern of residuals is not random, then some of the underlying assumptions are being violated.

The following example illustrates how regression analysis can result in findings with great managerial relevance.

EXAMPLE

AVOIDING DISSATISFACTION TO ENHANCE OVERALL SATISFACTION

A large health maintenance organization (HMO) collects data regularly as part of its ongoing patient satisfaction measurement program. In a recent study, data on patient satisfaction, quality of interaction, and related variables were obtained from 4,517 patients who subscribed to 501 primary care physicians (PCPs) affiliated with the HMO. The survey was conducted by telephone. To estimate the impact of the quality of interaction with the primary care physician (PCP) on patient satisfaction, the researchers conducted regression analysis.

The dependent variable was patient satisfaction, and the independent variable was the quality of PCP interaction. Three regressions were run: for satisfied patients, for dissatisfied patients, and for all patients. The estimates of the regression coefficient for these three regressions were 1.04,

3.73, and 2.02, respectively. As can be seen, the value of the coefficient was the highest for dissatisfied patients, indicating that dissatisfied patients are differentially more sensitive to the quality of PCP interaction. The implication is that, in order to enhance overall patient satisfaction, health care providers should accord greater attention to those aspects of PCP interaction that lead to dissatisfaction than to those that lead to satisfaction.[5]

MULTIPLE REGRESSION

Multiple regression involves a single dependent variable and two or more independent variables. Just as bivariate regression attempts to fit a best line to the data, regression with two independent variables tries to fit a best plane to the data. To extend the bivariate regression example considered earlier, the growth rate of the U.S. economy has a positive correlation with the level of consumer spending and the level of interest rates. Thus, a **multiple regression model** could be constructed with growth rate of the U.S. economy as the dependent variable and the level of consumer spending and the level of interest rates as the independent variables. The concept is similar in regression with more than two independent variables. The questions raised in the context of bivariate regression can also be answered via multiple regression by considering additional independent variables:

multiple regression
A statistical technique that simultaneously develops a mathematical relationship between two or more independent variables and an interval-scaled dependent variable.

multiple regression model
An equation used to explain the results of multiple regression analysis.

- Can variation in sales be explained in terms of variation in advertising expenditures, prices, and level of distribution?
- Can variation in market shares be accounted for by the size of the sales force, advertising expenditures, and sales promotion budgets?
- Are consumers' perceptions of quality determined by their perceptions of prices, brand image, and brand attributes?

Additional questions can also be answered by multiple regression:

- How much of the variation in sales can be explained by advertising expenditures, prices, and level of distribution?
- What is the contribution of advertising expenditures in explaining the variation in sales when the levels of prices and distribution are controlled?
- What levels of sales may be expected given the levels of advertising expenditures, prices, and level of distribution?

The general form of the multiple regression model is as follows:

$$Y = \beta_0 + \beta_1 X_1 + \beta_2 X_2 + \beta_3 X_3 + \ldots + \beta_k X_k + e$$

which is estimated by the following equation:

$$\hat{Y} = a + b_1 X_1 + b_2 X_2 + b_3 X_3 + \ldots + b_k X_k$$

As before, the coefficient a represents the intercept, but the b's are now the partial regression coefficients. The least-squares criterion estimates the parameters in such a way as to minimize the total error, SS_{res}. This process also maximizes the correlation between the actual values of Y and the predicted values of $\hat{Y}$. All the assumptions made in bivariate regression also apply in multiple regression.

CONDUCTING MULTIPLE REGRESSION ANALYSIS

The steps involved in conducting multiple regression analysis are similar to those for bivariate regression analysis. The discussion focuses on partial regression coefficients, strength of association, and significance testing.

Partial Regression Coefficients

To understand the meaning of a partial regression coefficient, let us consider again the multiple regression model with growth rate of the U.S. economy as the dependent variable and the level of consumer spending and the level of interest rates as the independent variables. In this case, there are two independent variables, so that:

$$\hat{Y} = a + b_1X_1 + b_2X_2$$

First, note that the relative magnitude of the partial regression coefficient of an independent variable is, in general, different from that of its bivariate regression coefficient. In other words, the partial regression coefficient, b_1, will be different from the regression coefficient, b, obtained by regressing Y on only X_1. This happens because X_1 and X_2 are usually correlated. In bivariate regression, X_2 was not considered, and any variation in Y that was shared by X_1 and X_2 was attributed to X_1. However, in the case of multiple independent variables, this is no longer true. Thus, in modeling the growth rate of the U.S. economy, the (partial) regression coefficient for the level of consumer spending in the multiple regression model will be different than that for bivariate regression.

partial regression coefficient
The partial regression coefficient, b_1, denotes the change in the predicted value of Y when X_1 is changed by one unit but the other independent variables, X_2 to X_k, are held constant.

The interpretation of the **partial regression coefficient,** b_1, is that it represents the expected change in Y when X_1 is changed by one unit but X_2 is held constant or otherwise controlled. Thus, the partial regression coefficient for the level of consumer spending will be different in multiple regression than the coefficient in bivariate regression. Likewise, b_2 represents the expected change in Y for a unit change in X_2, when X_1 is held constant. Thus, calling b_1 and b_2 partial regression coefficients is appropriate. It can also be seen that the combined effects of X_1 and X_2 on Y are additive. In other words, if X_1 and X_2 are each changed by one unit, the expected change in Y would be $(b_1 + b_2)$.

Extension to the case of k variables is straightforward. The partial regression coefficient, b_1, represents the expected change in Y when X_1 is changed by one unit and X_2 through X_k are held constant. It can also be interpreted as the bivariate regression coefficient, b, for the regression of Y on the residuals of X_1, when the effect of X_2 through X_k has been removed from X_1.

In the opening vignette, a multiple regression model was estimated with preference for athletic shoes as the dependent variable, and interest in sports, attitude toward sports personalities, attendance at sports events, and time spent watching sports on television as the independent variables. The partial regression coefficient associated with each independent variable was positive and significant, indicating that higher values on each independent variable were associated with stronger preference for athletic shoes. The partial regression coefficient for interest in sports would represent the expected change in preference for athletic shoes when interest in sports is changed by one unit and attitude toward sports personalities, attendance at sports events, and time spent watching sports on television are held constant.

The beta coefficients are the partial regression coefficients obtained when all the variables ($Y, X_1, X_2, \ldots X_k$) have been standardized to a mean of 0 and a variance of 1 before estimating the regression equation. The relationship of the standardized to the nonstandardized coefficients remains the same as before:

$$B_1 = b_1 \, (S_{x1}/S_y)$$
.
.
.
$$B_k = b_k \, (S_{xk}/S_y)$$

The intercept and the partial regression coefficients are estimated by solving a system of simultaneous equations derived by differentiating and equating the partial derivatives to 0. Since the various computer programs automatically estimate these coefficients, we will not present the details. However, it is worth noting that the equations cannot be solved if: (1) the sample size, n, is smaller than or equal to the number of independent variables, k; or (2) one independent variable is perfectly correlated with another.

Suppose that in explaining the attitude toward sports cars, we now introduce a second variable—the importance of performance. The data for the 12 pretest respondents on attitude toward sports cars, duration of sports car ownership, and importance attached to performance are given in Table 18.1. The results of multiple regression analysis are depicted in Table 18.3. The partial regression coefficient for duration (X_1) is now 0.4811, different from what it was in the bivariate case. The corresponding beta coefficient is 0.7636. The partial regression coefficient for importance attached to per-

TABLE 18.3   Multiple Regression

Output File

Multiple R	.9721
R^2	.9450
Adjusted R^2	.9330
Standard Error of the Estimate	.8597

ANALYSIS OF VARIANCE

	Degrees of Freedom	Sum of Squares	Mean Square
Regression	2	114.2643	57.1321
Residual	9	6.6524	.7392

$F = 77.2936$ Significance of $F = .0000$

COEFFICIENTS

Variable	b	Standard Error b	Beta (β)	T	Significance
(Constant)	.3373	.56736		.595	.5668
Duration	.4811	.05895	.7636	8.160	.0000
Importance	.2887	.08608	.3138	3.353	.0085

Dependent Variable: Attitude Toward Sports Cars

formance (X_2) is 0.2887, with a beta coefficient of 0.3138. The estimated regression equation is:

$$(\hat{Y}) = 0.3373 + 0.4811\, X_1 + 0.2887\, X_2$$

or

$$\text{Attitude} = 0.3373 + 0.4811\,(\text{Duration}) + 0.2887\,(\text{Importance})$$

This equation can be used for a variety of purposes, including predicting attitudes toward sports cars, given a knowledge of the respondents' duration of car ownership and the importance they attach to performance.

Strength of Association

The strength of the relationship stipulated by the regression equation can be determined by using the appropriate measures of association. The total variation is decomposed as in the bivariate case:

$$SS_y = SS_{reg} + SS_{res}$$

where

$$SS_y = \sum_{i=1}^{n} (Y_i - \bar{Y})^2$$

$$SS_{reg} = \sum_{i=1}^{n} (\hat{Y}_i - \bar{Y})^2$$

$$SS_{res} = \sum_{i=1}^{n} (Y_i - \hat{Y}_i)^2$$

The strength of association is measured by the square of the multiple correlation coefficient, R^2, which is also called the **coefficient of multiple determination.**

coefficient of multiple determination
In multiple regression, the strength of association is measured by the square of the multiple correlation coefficient, R^2, which is called the coefficient of multiple determination.

$$R^2 = \frac{SS_{reg}}{SS_y}$$

The multiple correlation coefficient, R, can also be viewed as the simple correlation coefficient, r, between Y and $\hat{Y}$. Several points about the characteristics of R^2 are worth noting. The coefficient of multiple determination, R^2, cannot be less than the highest bivariate, r^2, of any individual independent variable with the dependent variable. R^2 will be larger when the correlations between the independent variables are low. If the independent variables are statistically independent (uncorrelated), then R^2 will be the sum of bivariate r^2 of each independent variable with the dependent variable. R^2 cannot decrease as more independent variables are added to the regression equation. However, diminishing returns do set in, so that after the first few variables, the additional independent variables do not make much of a contribution. For this reason, R^2 is adjusted for the number of independent variables and the sample size by using the following formula:

adjusted R^2
The value of R^2 adjusted for the number of independent variables and the sample size.

$$\textbf{Adjusted } R^2 = R^2 - \frac{k(1 - R^2)}{n - k - 1}$$

For the regression results given in Table 18.3, the value of R^2 is:

$$R^2 = 114.2643/(114.2643 + 6.6524)$$
$$= 114.2643/120.9167$$
$$= .9450$$

This is higher than the r^2 value of 0.8762 obtained in the bivariate case. The r^2 in the bivariate case is the square of the simple (product moment) correlation between attitude toward sports cars and duration of sports car ownership. The R^2 obtained in multiple regression is also higher than the square of the simple correlation between attitude and importance attached to performance (which can be estimated as 0.5379). The adjusted R^2 is estimated as:

$$\text{Adjusted } R^2 = 0.9450 - 2 \, (1.0 - 0.9450)/(12 - 2 - 1)$$
$$= 0.9450 - 0.0122$$
$$= 0.9328$$

Note that the value of adjusted R^2 is close to R^2 and both are higher than r^2 for the bivariate case. This suggests that the addition of the second independent variable, importance attached to performance, makes a contribution in explaining the variation in attitude toward sports cars. Of course, R^2 should be significant and higher values of R^2 are more desirable than lower values. However, in commercial marketing research values of R^2 as high as 0.9 or higher are uncommon. Values of R^2 in the 0.5 to 0.8 range may be reasonable in many commercial marketing research projects.

Significance Testing

Significance testing involves testing the significance of the overall regression equation as well as specific partial regression coefficients. The null hypothesis for the overall test is that the coefficient of multiple determination in the population, R^2_{pop}, is zero.

$$H_0: R^2_{pop} = 0$$

This is equivalent to the following null hypothesis:

$$H_0: \beta_1 = \beta_2 = \beta_3 = \ldots = \beta_k = 0$$

The overall test can be conducted by using an F statistic:

$$F = \frac{SS_{reg}/k}{SS_{res}/(n-k-1)}$$

$$= \frac{R^2/k}{(1-R^2)/(n-k-1)}$$

which has an F distribution with k and $(n - k - 1)$ degrees of freedom. For the multiple regression results given in Table 18.3,

$$F = \frac{114.2643/2}{6.6524/9} = 77.2936$$

which is significant at $\alpha = 0.05$.

If the overall null hypothesis is rejected, one or more population partial regression coefficients have a value different from 0. To determine which specific coefficients (b_i's) are nonzero, additional tests are necessary. Testing for the significance of the b_i's can be done in a manner similar to that in the bivariate case by using *t*-tests. The significance of the partial coefficient for importance attached to performance may be tested by the following equation:

$$t = \frac{b}{SE_b}$$
$$= 0.2887/0.08608$$
$$= 3.353$$

which has a *t* distribution with $n - k - 1$ degrees of freedom. This coefficient is significant at $\alpha = 0.05$. The significance of the coefficient for duration of car ownership is tested in a similar way and found to be significant. Therefore, both the duration of car ownership and the importance attached to performance are important in explaining attitude toward sports cars. However, if any of the regression coefficients are not significant, they should be treated as zero.

Some computer programs provide an equivalent *F*-test, often called the partial *F*-test. This involves a decomposition of the total regression sum of squares, SS_{reg}, into components related to each independent variable. We further illustrate the application of multiple regression with an example.

EXAMPLE

THE NEW YORK TIMES CAMPAIGN REFLECTS CHANGING TIMES

The *New York Times* surveyed a representative sample of 2,500 households by telephone to determine their interest in reading daily newspapers. The survey found that the United States had become much more global or "world minded." One of the most important factors influencing interest in reading a newspaper was that it provides "sensitive insight into the world," regardless of whether it was a local or national newspaper. Other important factors that emerged were that a newspaper should reflect intelligence, quality, and trustworthiness.

A multiple regression model was estimated with interest in reading a daily newspaper as the dependent variable and insight into the world, intelligence, quality, and trustworthiness as the independent variables. This model had an excellent fit as determined by a high R^2, and the partial regression coefficient for each of the independent variables was positive and significant.

The *New York Times* built a campaign around these findings. The $20 million national image campaign had the tagline "Expect the World," and it reflected all four of the important factors that influence interest in a daily newspaper: insight into the world, intelligence, quality, and trustworthiness. TV spots appeared during the news magazine and analysis shows *48 Hours, Dateline, Primetime Live, 20/20,* and *Nightline,* as well as during *News at Sunrise, The Today Show, Good Morning America,* CNN's *Headline News,* and the *Jim Lehrer News Hour.* In addition, the commercials ran on the CNN airport network in 30 major metropolitan airports and on network and local radio. The campaign was successful, substantially increasing circulation in its very first year.[6]

SUMMARY ILLUSTRATION USING THE OPENING VIGNETTE

The Pearson product moment correlation coefficient measures the linear association between two metric variables. In the opening vignette, preference for athletic shoes showed strong positive correlations with sports-related variables such as interest in sports, attitude toward sports personalities, attendance at sports events, and time spent watching sports on television.

Bivariate regression derives a mathematical equation, in the form of a straight line between a single metric criterion variable and a single metric predictor variable. Instead of running Pearson correlations, we could have alternatively run four bivariate regressions with preference for athletic shoes as the dependent variable. Each of the independent variables in turn would serve as the predictor variable: interest in sports, attitude toward sports personalities, attendance at sports events, and time spent watching sports on television.

Multiple regression involves a single dependent variable and two or more independent variables. The partial regression coefficient represents the expected change in the dependent variable when one of the independent variables is changed by one unit and the other independent variables are held constant. A multiple regression model with preference for athletic shoes as the dependent variable, and interest in sports, attitude toward sports personalities, attendance at sports events, and time spent watching sports on television as the independent variables had very good strength of association. The partial regression coefficient associated with each independent variable was positive and significant, indicating that higher values on each independent variable were associated with stronger preference for athletic shoes. The partial regression coefficient for interest in sports would represent the expected change in preference for athletic shoes when interest in sports is changed by one unit and attitude toward sports personalities, attendance at sports events, and time spent watching sports on television are held constant.

INTERNET AND COMPUTER APPLICATIONS

The computer programs available for conducting correlation analysis are described in Figure 18.8. In SPSS, CORRELATIONS can be used for computing Pearson product moment correlations, while in SAS the corresponding program is CORR. In MINITAB, correlation can be computed using STAT>BASIC STATISTICS>CORRELATION function. It calculates Pearson's product moment. Correlations can be determined in EXCEL by using the TOOLS>DATA ANALYSIS>CORRELATION function. Use the Correlation Worksheet Function when a correlation coefficient for two cell ranges is needed.

SAS

CORR produces metric and nonmetric correlations between variables, including Pearson's product moment correlation.

MINITAB

Correlation can be computed using STAT>BASIC STATISTICS>CORRELATION function. It calculates Pearson's product moment using all the columns.

EXCEL

Correlations can be determined in EXCEL by using the TOOLS>DATA ANALYSIS>CORRE-LATION function. Use the Correlation Worksheet Function when a correlation coefficient for two cell ranges is needed.

FIGURE 18.8   Other Computer Programs for Correlations

As described in Figure 18.9, the microcomputer and mainframe packages contain several programs for performing regression analysis, calculating the associated statistics, performing tests for significance, and plotting the residuals. In SPSS, the main program is REGRESSION. In SAS, the most general program is REG. Other specialized programs such as RSREG, ORTHOREG, GLM, and NLIN are also available, but readers not familiar with the intricate aspects of regression analysis are advised to stick to REG when using SAS. In MINITAB, regression analysis, under the STATS>REGRESSION function can perform simple and multiple analysis. In EXCEL, regression can be accessed from the

---

The mainframe and microcomputer packages contain the same programs.

SAS

REG is a general purpose regression procedure that fits bivariate and multiple regression models using the least-squares procedure. All the associated statistics are computed, and residuals can be plotted.

MINITAB

Regression analysis output under the STATS>REGRESSION function can perform simple and multiple analysis. The output includes a linear regression equation, table of coefficients, R square, R squared adjusted, analysis of variance table, a table of fits and residuals that provide unusual observations. Other available features include fitted line plot, and residual plots.

EXCEL

Regression can be assessed from the TOOLS>DATA ANALYSIS menu. Depending on the features selected, the output can consist of a summary output table, including an ANOVA table, a standard error of y estimate, coefficients, standard error of coefficients, R^2 values, and the number of observations. In addition, the function computes a residual output table, a residual plot, a line fit plot, normal probability plot, and a two-column probability data output table.

FIGURE 18.9   Other Computer Programs for Regression

TOOLS>DATA ANALYSIS menu. These programs are available in mainframe and micro-computer versions.

SPSS

The CORRELATIONS program computes Pearson product moment correlations with significance levels. Univariate statistics, covariance, and cross-product deviations may also be requested. Significance levels are included in the output. To select this procedure using SPSS for Windows click:

Analyze > Correlate > Bivariate . . .

Scatterplots can be obtained by clicking:

Graphs > Scatter . . .> Simple > Define

REGRESSION calculates bivariate and multiple regression equations, associated statistics, and plots. It allows for an easy examination of residuals. This procedure can be run by clicking:

Analyze > Regression > Linear . . .

SUMMARY

The product moment correlation coefficient, r, measures the linear association between two metric (interval or ratio scaled) variables. Its square, r^2, measures the proportion of variation in one variable explained by the other.

Bivariate regression derives a mathematical equation between a single metric crite-rion variable and a single metric predictor variable. The equation is derived in the form of a straight line by using the least-squares procedure. When the regression is run on stan-dardized data, the intercept assumes a value of 0, and the regression coefficients are called beta weights. The strength of association is measured by the coefficient of determination, r^2, which is obtained by computing a ratio of SS_{reg} to SS_y. Scattergrams of the residuals are useful for examining the appropriateness of the underlying assumptions and the regres-sion model fitted.

Multiple regression involves a single dependent variable and two or more indepen-dent variables. The partial regression coefficient, b_1, represents the expected change in Y when X_1 is changed by one unit and X_2 through X_k are held constant. The strength of association is measured by the coefficient of multiple determination, R^2. The significance of the overall regression equation may be tested by the overall F-test. Individual partial regression coefficients may be tested for significance using the t-test.

KEY TERMS AND CONCEPTS

Product moment correlation, 535
Covariance, 536
Regression analysis, 541
Bivariate regression, 541
Bivariate regression model, 541
Scatter diagram, 542

Least-squares procedure, 543
Sum of the squared errors, 543
Estimated or predicted value, 544
Regression coefficient, 544

Standardization, 545
Beta coefficient, 545
Standardized regression coefficient, 545
Standard error, 547
Coefficient of determination, 547
Residual, 547

ACRONYMS

The main features of regression analysis may be summarized by the acronym REGRES-SION:

R esidual analysis is useful

E stimation of parameters: solution of simultaneous equations

G eneral model is linear

R^2 strength of association

E rror terms are independent and $N(0, \sigma^2)$

S tandardized regression coefficients

S tandard error of estimate: prediction accuracy

I ndividual coefficients and overall F-tests

O ptimal: minimizes total error

N onstandardized regression coefficients

EXERCISES

1. What is the product moment correlation coefficient? Does a product moment correlation of 0 between two variables imply that the variables are not related to each other?
2. Give an example of a bivariate regression model and identify the dependent and the independent variables.
3. What are the main uses of regression analysis?
4. What is the least-squares procedure?
5. Explain the meaning of standardized regression coefficients.
6. How is the strength of association measured in bivariate regression? In multiple regression?
7. What is meant by prediction accuracy?
8. What is the standard error of estimate?
9. What assumptions underlie the error term?
10. What is multiple regression? How is it different from bivariate regression?
11. Explain the meaning of a partial regression coefficient. Why is it so called?
12. State the null hypothesis in testing the significance of the overall multiple regression equation. How is this null hypothesis tested?

PROBLEMS

1. A major supermarket chain wants to determine the effect of promotion on relative competitiveness. Data were obtained from 15 states on the promotional expenses relative to a major competitor (competitor expenses = 100) and on sales relative to this competitor (competitor sales = 100).

STATE NO.	RELATIVE PROMOTIONAL EXPENSE	RELATIVE SALES
1	95	98
2	92	94
3	103	110
4	115	125
5	77	82
6	79	84
7	105	112
8	94	99
9	85	93
10	101	107
11	106	114
12	120	132
13	118	129
14	75	79
15	99	105

You are assigned the task of telling the manager whether there is any relationship between relative promotional expense and relative sales.

a. Plot the relative sales (Y axis) against the relative promotional expense (X axis), and interpret this diagram.

b. Which measure would you use to determine whether there is a relationship between the two variables? Why?

c. Run a bivariate regression analysis of relative sales on relative promotional expense.

d. Interpret the regression coefficients.

e. Is the regression relationship significant?

f. If the company matched the competitor in terms of promotional expense (if the relative promotional expense was 100), what would the company's relative sales be?

g. Interpret the resulting r^2.

2. To understand the role of quality and price in influencing the patronage of drugstores, 14 major stores in a large metropolitan area were rated in terms of preference to shop, quality of merchandise, and fair pricing. All the ratings were obtained on an 11-point scale, with higher numbers indicating more positive ratings.

STORE NO.	PREFERENCE	QUALITY	PRICE
1	6	5	3
2	9	6	11
3	8	6	4
4	3	2	1
5	10	6	11
6	4	3	1
7	5	4	7
8	2	1	4
9	11	9	8
10	9	5	10
11	10	8	8
12	2	1	5
13	9	8	5
14	5	3	2

a. Run a multiple regression analysis explaining store preference in terms of quality of merchandise and pricing.

b. Interpret the partial regression coefficients.

c. Determine the significance of the overall regression.

d. Determine the significance of the partial regression coefficients.

3. You come across a magazine article reporting the following relationship between annual expenditure on prepared dinners (*PD*) and annual income (*INC*):

$$PD = 23.4 + 0.003\ INC$$

The coefficient of the *INC* variable is reported as significant.

a. Does this relationship seem plausible? Is it possible to have a coefficient that is small in magnitude and yet significant?

b. From the information given, can you tell how good the estimated model is?

c. What are the expected expenditures on prepared dinners of a family earning $30,000?

d. If a family earning $40,000 spent $130 annually on prepared dinners, what is the residual?

e. What is the meaning of a negative residual?

INTERNET AND COMPUTER EXERCISES

1. Conduct the following analyses for the Internet usage data given in Internet and Computer Exercises 1 in Chapter 16.

a. Find the simple correlations between the following sets of variables: Internet usage and attitude toward Internet, Internet usage and attitude toward technology, and attitude toward Internet and attitude toward technology. Interpret the results.

    b. Run a bivariate regression with Internet usage as the dependent variable and attitude toward Internet as the independent variable. Interpret the results.

    c. Run a bivariate regression with Internet usage as the dependent variable and attitude toward technology as the independent variable. Interpret the results.

    d. Run a multiple regression with Internet usage as the dependent variable, and attitude toward Internet and attitude toward technology as the independent variables. Interpret the results.

2. Conduct the following analyses for the preference for an outdoor lifestyle data given in Internet and Computer Exercises 2 of Chapter 17.

    a. Calculate the simple correlations between V1 to V6 and interpret the results.

    b. Run a bivariate regression with preference for an outdoor lifestyle (V1) as the dependent variable and the importance of enjoying nature (V2) as the independent variable. Interpret the results.

    c. Run a multiple regression with preference for an outdoor lifestyle as the dependent variable and V2 to V6 as the independent variables. Interpret the results. Compare the coefficients for V2 obtained in the bivariate and the multiple regressions.

3. In a pretest, data were obtained from 20 respondents on preferences for sneakers on a 7-point scale, 1 = not at all preferred, 7 = greatly preferred (V1). The respondents also provided their evaluations of the sneakers on comfort (V2), style (V3), and durability (V4), also on 7-point scales, 1 = poor, and 7 = excellent. The resulting data are given in the following:

SPSS
Data File

V1	V2	V3	V4
6.00	6.00	3.00	5.00
2.00	3.00	2.00	4.00
7.00	5.00	6.00	7.00
4.00	6.00	4.00	5.00
1.00	3.00	2.00	2.00
6.00	5.00	6.00	7.00
5.00	6.00	7.00	5.00
7.00	3.00	5.00	4.00
2.00	4.00	6.00	3.00
3.00	5.00	3.00	6.00
1.00	3.00	2.00	3.00
5.00	4.00	5.00	4.00
2.00	2.00	1.00	5.00
4.00	5.00	4.00	6.00
6.00	5.00	4.00	7.00
3.00	3.00	4.00	2.00
4.00	4.00	3.00	2.00
3.00	4.00	3.00	2.00
4.00	4.00	3.00	2.00
2.00	3.00	2.00	4.00

  a. Calculate the simple correlations between V1 and V4 and interpret the results.

  b. Run a bivariate regression with preference for sneakers (V1) as the dependent variable and evaluation on comfort (V2) as the independent variable. Interpret the results.

  c. Run a bivariate regression with preference for sneakers (V1) as the dependent variable and evaluation on style (V3) as the independent variable. Interpret the results.

  d. Run a bivariate regression with preference for sneakers (V1) as the dependent variable and evaluation on durability (V4) as the independent variable. Interpret the results.

  e. Run a multiple regression with preference for sneakers (V1) as the dependent variable and V2 to V4 as the independent variables. Interpret the results. Compare the coefficients for V2, V3, and V4 obtained in the bivariate and the multiple regressions.

4. Use an appropriate microcomputer or mainframe program (SPSS, SAS, MINITAB, or EXCEL) to analyze the data for:

  a. Problem 1
  b. Problem 2
  c. Field work exercise

ACTIVITIES

FIELD WORK

1. Visit 10 drug stores in your area. Evaluate each store in terms of its overall image and quality of in-store service using an 11-point rating scale (1 = poor, 11 = excellent). Then analyze the data you have collected as follows:

  a. Plot the overall image (Y axis) against relative in-store service (X axis) and interpret this diagram.

  b. Which measure would you use to determine whether there is a relationship between the two variables? Why?

  c. Run a bivariate regression analysis of overall image on in-store service.

  d. Interpret the regression coefficients.

  e. Is the regression relationship significant?

  f. Interpret the resulting r^2.

GROUP DISCUSSION

1. As a small group, discuss the following statement: "Regression is such a basic technique that it should always be used in analyzing data."

2. As a small group, discuss the relationship between bivariate correlation, bivariate regression, and multiple regression.

NOTES

1. Based on Andy Dworkin, "Nike, Adidas Square Off With Competing Shoes Backed by Basketball Stars," *The Oregonian* (October 22, 2000); Terry Lefton, "Adidas Looks for More Retail Oomph Out of Team Sponsorship," *Brandweek,* 40(9) (March 1, 1999): 10; and Jeff Jensen and Alice Z. Cuneo, "Adidas Raises Profile in U.S. With a Three-Sport TV Push," *Advertising Age* (July 28, 1997): 6.

2. Mark Peterson and Naresh K. Malhotra, "Comparative Marketing Measures of Societal Quality of Life: Substantive Dimensions in 186 Countries," *Journal of Macromarketing,* 17(1) (Spring 1997): 25–38.

3. In a strict sense, the regression model requires that errors of measurement be associated only with the criterion variable and that the predictor variables be measured without error.

4. Technically, the numerator is $b - \beta$. However, since it has been hypothesized that $\beta = 0.0$, it can be omitted from the formula.

5. Based on Diane H. Friedman, "Quality Customer Service: It's Everyone's Job," *Healthcare Executive,* 15(3) (May/June 2000): 64–65; Julie Howard," Hospital Customer Service in a Changing Healthcare World: Does It Matter?" *Journal of Healthcare Management,* 44(4) (July/August 1999): 312–325; Vikas Mittal, William T. Ross, Jr., and Patrick M. Baldasare, "The Asymmetric Impact of Negative and Positive Attribute-Level Performance on Overall Satisfaction and Repurchase Intentions," *Journal of Marketing,* 62(1) (January): 33–47; and Vikas Mittal and Patrick M. Baldasare, "Eliminate the Negative: Managers Should Optimize Rather Than Maximize Performance to Enhance Patient Satisfaction," *Journal of Health Care Marketing,* 16(3) (Fall 1996): 24–31.

6. Based on Bob Garfield, "'Times' Ads May Be Moving but Won't Deliver Subscriptions," *Advertising Age,* 71(19) (May 1, 2000): 77; and Kelly Shermach, "Times Campaigns to Strengthen Brand Image," *Marketing News,* 31(6) (March 17, 1997): 2.

19

REPORT PREPARATION AND PRESENTATION

OFTEN THE QUALITY AND USEFULNESS OF THE ENTIRE MARKETING RESEARCH PROJECT IS EVALUATED BY THE CLIENT BASED ON THE FINAL REPORT AND ITS PRESENTATION.

Opening Questions

1. What process should be followed in preparing and presenting the final report?

2. Are any guidelines available for writing a report that includes graphs and tables?

3. How should an oral presentation be made, and what are some of the principles involved?

4. Why is the follow-up with the client important, and what assistance should be given to the client in implementing and evaluating the research project?

5. What is the role of report preparation in the total quality management process?

6. How is the report preparation and presentation process different in international marketing research?

7. How does technology facilitate report preparation and presentation?

8. What ethical issues are related to the interpretation and reporting of the research process and findings?

9. What is the role of the Internet in report preparation and presentation?

Reece Ritter, Vice President and Sr. Research Director, Elrick & Lavidge.
Reece Ritter works closely with various clients on the design and implementation of research programs. She is based in the company's Atlanta office.

RESEARCH REPORTS MAKE UNITED'S FRIENDLY SKIES EVEN MORE FRIENDLY

In 2000, United Airlines announced the testing of airport self-check-in kiosks as a way to improve customer service for passengers traveling throughout the United States. Aspen, San Diego, and Chicago were among the first cities chosen for this state-of-the art computer test. With the new kiosk computers, passengers are able to check in, check baggage, get seat assignments, and upgrade to business class. United Airlines feels that future customers will respond to the new check-in method with very positive feedback and high levels of customer satisfaction. The vice president of United Airline's customer satisfaction stated, "Our investment in this leading-edge technology further demonstrates United Airlines' commitment to providing our customers with an airport experience that involves less hassle and a faster check-in experience."

United Airlines does, indeed, put a premium on customer satisfaction. For its in-flight customer satisfaction tracking program, United surveys passengers on some 900 flights per month using a four-page scannable questionnaire. It administers 192,000 questionnaires, in nine languages, to people traveling to 40 different countries. The survey covers passenger satisfaction with the entire air travel process: reservations, airport service, flight attendants, meal service, and the aircraft itself.

The marketing research department at United prepares a monthly report summarizing the customer satisfaction data for about a hundred people worldwide, including airport, country, and regional managers; executive management; and others at United's headquarters. The report is very thorough and includes a title page, table of contents, executive summary, problem definition, approach, research design, data analysis, results, and conclusions and recommendations. Several tables and graphs are prepared to enhance the clarity of the findings. The report findings are also available online.

After issuing the monthly report, the marketing research department handles several requests from internal customers (various departments within United Airlines) for additional analysis. For example, the marketing department may request a breakdown of customer satisfaction rating by demographic characteristics for a specific route (city pair), such as Atlanta–Los Angeles. Since the data can be linked to operational data, such as arrival and departure times and number of passengers, United's researchers can dig deep to answer questions from internal customers. Alex Maggi, United's senior staff analyst, market research, says, "We have often used the data to identify the reasons why some ratings might differ from one airport to another or one segment to another, by looking at customer mix, by linking survey data to operational data. For example, we can take ratings for a given flight and link them to the on-time performance of the flight in that market and we can show that when on-time performance went down so did the ratings in specific categories."

This monthly report on customer satisfaction and the follow-up activities that it generates has helped United Airlines to become much more customer focused, thereby improving its competitive positioning and making its friendly skies even more friendly. The in-flight customer satisfaction tracking program also enabled United to identify and address new customer needs following the September 11, 2001 hijacking incidents.[1]

OVERVIEW

Report preparation and presentation constitutes the sixth and final step of the marketing research project. It follows problem definition, developing an approach, research design formulation, field work, and data preparation and analysis. This chapter describes the importance of this final step, as well as a process for report preparation and presentation. Figure 19.1 briefly explains the focus of the chapter, the relationship of this chapter to the previous ones, and the step of the marketing research process on which this chapter concentrates. As illustrated in the opening vignette, well-prepared marketing research reports and associated follow-up activities add substantial value to the marketing research process.

In this chapter, we provide guidelines for report preparation, including report writing and preparing tables and graphs. We discuss oral presentation of the report. We describe research follow-up, including assisting the client and evaluating the research process. We discuss special considerations for report preparation and presentation in total quality management (TQM) and international marketing research. In addition, we identify applications of technology, ethics, and the Internet. Figure 19.2 gives an overview of the topics discussed in this chapter and how they flow from one to the next.

IMPORTANCE OF THE REPORT AND PRESENTATION

The report and its presentation are the tangible products of the research effort, and the report serves as a historical record of the project. If inadequate attention is paid to this step, the value of the project to management will be greatly diminished. The involvement

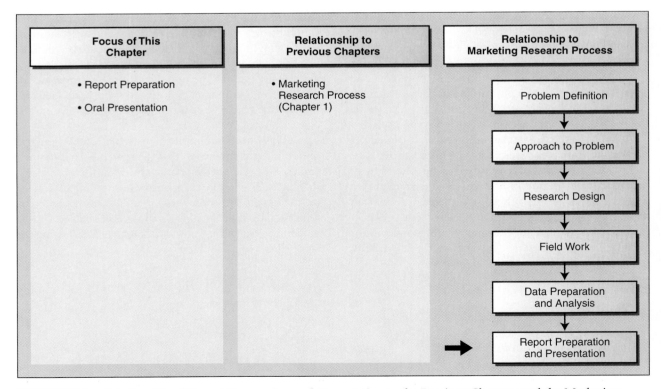

FIGURE 19.1 Relationship of Report Preparation and Presentation to the Previous Chapters and the Marketing Research Process

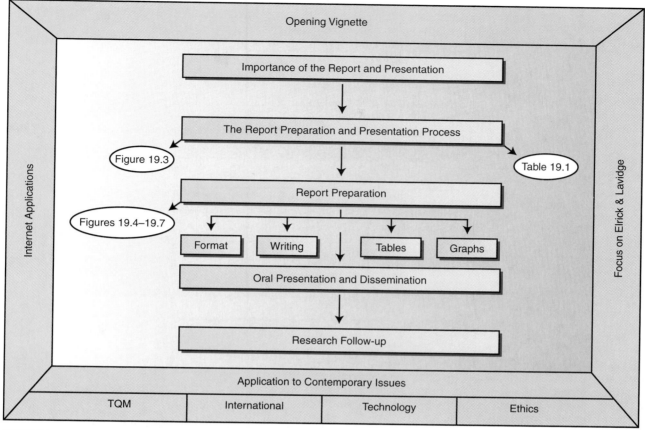

FIGURE 19.2   Report Preparation and Presentation: An Overview

of many marketing managers in the project is limited to the written report and the oral presentation. These managers evaluate the quality of the entire project based on the quality of the report and presentation. Management's decision to undertake marketing research in the future or to use the particular research supplier again will be influenced by the perceived usefulness of the report and the presentation. For these reasons, report preparation and presentation assume great importance.

THE REPORT PREPARATION AND PRESENTATION PROCESS

Figure 19.3 illustrates the report preparation and presentation process. The process begins by interpreting the results of data analysis in light of the marketing research problem, approach, research design, and field work. Instead of merely summarizing the statistical results, the researcher should present the findings in such a way that they can be used directly as input into decision making. Wherever appropriate, conclusions should be drawn and recommendations that management can act upon should be made. Before writing the report, the researcher should discuss the major findings, conclusions, and recommendations with the client's key decision makers. These discussions play a major role in ensuring that the report meets the client's needs and is ultimately accepted. These discussions should confirm specific dates for the delivery of the written report and other data.

FIGURE 19.3
The Report Preparation
and Presentation Process

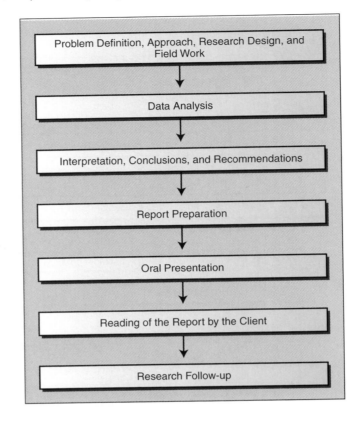

The entire marketing research project should be summarized in a single written report or in several reports addressed to different readers. For example, a report prepared for top management should emphasize the strategic aspects of the research project rather than the operating details. However, the reverse is true for a report prepared for operating managers. Generally, an oral presentation supplements these written documents. After the presentation, the client should be given an opportunity to read the report. After the client has read the report, the researcher should take the necessary follow-up actions. Such actions are found in the opening vignette, where United's marketing research department handles several requests for additional data analysis. The researcher should assist the client in understanding the report, implementing the findings, undertaking further research, and evaluating the research process in retrospect. The importance of the researcher being intimately involved in the report preparation and presentation process is highlighted by the following example.

EXAMPLE

FOCUS GROUP MODERATORS' GHOSTWRITERS CAN SHORTCHANGE CLIENTS

Thomas Greenbaum, president of a market research company focusing on qualitative research, notes a disturbing trend in recent years in the focus group service sector. Greenbaum of Groups Plus Inc. of Wilton, Connecticut, asserts that some moderators of focus groups misrepresent their work to clients because their reports are actually written by ghostwriters who did not participate in the focus group sessions.

According to Greenbaum, perhaps more than half of moderators use ghostwriters to develop their reports for clients. Often, junior researchers learning the business or part-time employees write these ghostwritten reports. Greenbaum criticizes such ghostwriting because those who merely listen to audiotapes or view videotapes of focus group sessions cannot always accurately report the nonverbal reactions of focus group participants. Greenbaum calls upon moderators to be forthright with clients about the authorship of focus group reports. He also calls upon clients to be more demanding of their contracted research teams.

"Although some people in the industry defend ghostwriting by saying they always review the reports before they are sent to the client, or perhaps even write certain key sections, this practice must be looked at carefully by clients who use focus group research," Greenbaum said. "If the clients know in advance that their reports will be written by someone else, it is clearly less of a problem, but they still do not get the best effort from their research consultants."[2]

REPORT PREPARATION

Researchers differ in the way they prepare a research report. The personality, background, expertise, and responsibility of the researcher, along with the decision maker (DM) to whom the report is addressed, interact to give each report a unique character. However, there are guidelines for formatting and writing reports and designing tables and graphs.

Report Format

Report formats are likely to vary with the researcher or the marketing research firm conducting the project, the client for whom the project is being conducted, and the nature of the project itself. Hence, the following is intended as a guideline from which the researcher can develop a format for the research project at hand. Most research reports, as in the opening vignette, include most of the following elements:

I. Title page
II. Letter of transmittal
III. Letter of authorization
IV. Table of contents
    a. List of tables
    b. List of graphs
    c. List of appendices
    d. List of exhibits
V. Executive summary
    a. Major findings
    b. Conclusions
    c. Recommendations
VI. Problem definition
    a. Background to the problem
    b. Statement of the problem

VII. Approach to the problem

VIII. Research design

    a. Type of research design

    b. Information needs

    c. Data collection from secondary sources

    d. Data collection from primary sources

    e. Scaling techniques

    f. Questionnaire development and pretesting

    g. Sampling techniques

    h. Field work

IX. Data analysis

    a. Methodology

    b. Plan of data analysis

X. Results

XI. Limitations and caveats

XII. Conclusions and recommendations

XIII. Exhibits

    a. Questionnaires and forms

    b. Statistical output

    c. Lists

This format closely follows the earlier steps of the marketing research process. However, the format should be flexible so that it can accommodate the unique features of a specific project. For example, the results may be presented in several chapters of the report. For example, in a national survey, data analysis may be conducted for the overall sample, and then the data for each geographic region may be analyzed separately. In this case, the results can be presented in five chapters instead of one.

TITLE PAGE The title page should include the title of the report, information (name, address, and telephone number) about the researcher or organization conducting the research, the name of the client for whom the report was prepared, and the date of release. The title should also indicate the nature of the project.

letter of transmittal
A letter that delivers the report to the client and summarizes the researcher's overall experience with the project without mentioning the findings.

LETTER OF TRANSMITTAL A formal report generally contains a **letter of transmittal** that delivers the report to the client and summarizes the researcher's overall experience with the project. The letter should also identify the need for further action on the part of the client, such as implementation of the findings or further research that should be undertaken.

LETTER OF AUTHORIZATION The client writes a letter of authorization to the researcher before work on the project begins. It authorizes the researcher to proceed with the project and specifies its scope and the terms of the contract. Often, it is sufficient to refer to the letter of authorization in the letter of transmittal. However, sometimes it is necessary to include a copy of the letter of authorization in the report. The letter of transmittal and the letter of authorization may be dispensed with in the case of recurring projects conducted internally by the marketing research department of the firm, as in the case of United Airlines in the opening vignette.

TABLE OF CONTENTS The table of contents should list the topics covered and the appropriate page numbers. In most reports, only the major headings and subheadings are included. A list of tables, list of graphs, list of appendices, and list of exhibits follow the table of contents.

EXECUTIVE SUMMARY The executive summary is an extremely important part of the report, as this is often the only portion of the report that executives read. The summary should concisely describe the problem, the approach, the research design, major results, conclusions, and recommendations. The executive summary should be written after the rest of the report because it is much easier for the writer to read through the body of the report and then summarize the most important points.

PROBLEM DEFINITION This section of the report gives the background to the problem, highlights discussions with the decision makers and industry experts, discusses the secondary data analysis, the qualitative research that was conducted, and the factors that were considered. It should contain a clear statement of the management decision problem and the marketing research problem (see Chapter 2).

APPROACH TO THE PROBLEM This section should discuss the broad approach that was adopted in addressing the problem. This section should also contain a description of the theoretical foundations that guided the research, any analytical models formulated, research questions, and hypotheses.

RESEARCH DESIGN The section on research design should specify the details of how the research was conducted (see Chapters 3 through 13). This should include the nature of the research design adopted, information needed, data collection from secondary and primary sources, scaling techniques, questionnaire development and pretesting, sampling techniques, and field work. These topics should be presented in a nontechnical, easy-to-understand manner. The technical details should be included in an appendix. This section of the report should justify the specific methods selected.

DATA ANALYSIS This section should describe the plan of data analysis and justify the data analysis strategy and techniques used. The techniques used for analysis should be described in simple, nontechnical terms.

RESULTS This section is normally the longest part of the report and may comprise several chapters. Often, the results are presented not only at the aggregate level but also at the subgroup (market segment, geographical area, etc.) level. The results should be organized in a coherent and logical way. The presentation of the results should be geared directly to the components of the marketing research problem and the information needs that were identified. The details should be presented in tables and graphs, with the main findings discussed in the text.

LIMITATIONS AND CAVEATS All marketing research projects have limitations caused by time, budget, and other organizational constraints. Furthermore, the research design adopted may be limited in terms of the various types of errors (see Chapter 3) that may be serious enough to warrant discussion. This section should be written with great care and a balanced perspective. On one hand, the researcher must make sure that management does not overly rely on the results or use them for unintended purposes, such as projecting them to unintended populations. On the other hand, this section should not erode their confidence in the research or unduly minimize its importance.

CONCLUSIONS AND RECOMMENDATIONS Presenting a mere summary of the statistical results is not sufficient. The researcher should interpret the results in light of the problem being addressed to arrive at major conclusions. Based on the results and conclusions, the researcher may make recommendations to the decision makers. Sometimes marketing researchers are not asked to make recommendations because they research only one area but do not understand the bigger picture at the client firm. If recommendations are made, they should be feasible, practical, actionable, and directly usable as inputs into managerial decision making. It is very important that the report of a conclusive research project (see Chapter 3) be written in such a way that the findings can be used as input into managerial decision making. Otherwise, the report is unlikely to get due attention from management, as illustrated by the following example.

EXAMPLE

DOES THE MANAGEMENT READ MARKETING RESEARCH REPORTS?

Every profession has its nagging doubts. Teachers sometimes wonder if their students are really learning anything; police officers occasionally question whether they're actually reducing crime. Once in a while, marketing researchers have a sneaking suspicion that no one is reading their reports.

Determined to resolve this doubt, one marketing researcher inserted a very undignified photo of himself from a recent office party in the middle of his report. Weeks went by as the report was passed through brand and category management with no response. Finally, the senior vice president of advertising called to ask if he needed a vacation. Evidently, this senior VP was the only one who had read the report in detail.

Who is responsible when research reports are ignored—the research department or management? According to a study recently released by the Advertising Research Foundation and the American Marketing Association, most marketing managers truly believe that marketing research can be valuable. They also claim that most of what they see isn't delivering the kind of information they need to make business decisions. Thus, the responsibility of writing readable reports lies with marketing researchers.[3]

Report Writing

A report should be written for a specific reader or readers: the marketing managers who will use the results. The report should take into account the readers' technical sophistication and interest in the project, as well as the circumstances under which they will read the report and how they will use it.

Technical jargon should be avoided. The researcher is often required to cater to the needs of several audiences with different levels of technical sophistication and interest in the project. Such conflicting needs may be met by including different sections in the report for different readers or separate reports entirely.

The report should be easy to follow. It should be structured logically and written clearly. An excellent check on the clarity of a report is to have two or three people who are unfamiliar with the project read it and offer critical comments. Several revisions of the report may be needed before the final document emerges.

Objectivity is a virtue that should guide report writing. The report should accurately present the methodology, results, and conclusions of the project, without slanting the findings to conform to the expectations of management.

It is important to reinforce key information in the text with tables, graphs, pictures, maps, and other visual devices. Visual aids can greatly facilitate communication and add to the clarity and impact of the report. The appearance of a report is also important. The report should be professionally reproduced with quality paper, typing, and binding. Guidelines for tabular and graphical presentation are discussed next.

Guidelines for Tables

Statistical tables are a vital part of the report and deserve special attention (see opening vignette). We illustrate the guidelines for tables using the data for Hewlett-Packard sales reported in Table 19.1. The numbers in parentheses in the following paragraphs refer to the numbered sections of the table.

TITLE AND NUMBER Every table should have a number (1a) and title (1b). The title should be brief, yet clearly describe the information provided. Arabic numbers are used to identify tables so that they can be referred to easily in the text.

ARRANGEMENT OF DATA ITEMS Data should be arranged in a table to emphasize the most significant aspect of the data. For example, when the data pertain to time, the items should be arranged by appropriate time period. When order of magnitude is most important, the data items should be arranged in that order (2a). If ease of locating items is critical, an alphabetical arrangement is most appropriate.

BASIS OF MEASUREMENT The basis or unit of measurement should be clearly stated (3a).

LEADERS, RULINGS, SPACES **Leaders**—dots or hyphens used to lead the eye horizontally—impart uniformity and improve readability (4a). Instead of ruling the table horizontally or vertically, use white spaces (4b) to set off data items. Skipping lines after different sections of the data can also assist the eye. Horizontal rules (4c) are often used after the headings.

EXPLANATIONS AND COMMENTS: HEADINGS, STUBS, AND FOOTNOTES Explanations and comments clarifying the table can be provided in the form of captions, stubs, and footnotes. Designations placed over the vertical columns are called headings (5a). Designations placed in the left-hand column are called **stubs** (5b). Information that cannot be incorporated into the table should be explained by footnotes (5c). Letters or symbols should be used for footnotes rather than numbers. The footnotes should come after the main table, but before the source note.

SOURCES OF THE DATA If the data contained in the table are secondary, the source of data should be cited (6a).

leaders
Dots or hyphens that are used to lead the eye horizontally, impart uniformity, and improve readability of a table.

stubs
Designations placed in the left-hand column of a table.

Guidelines for Graphs

As a general rule, graphic aids should be used whenever practical, as in the opening vignette. Graphical display of information can effectively complement the text and tables

TABLE 19.1 Hewlett-Packard Sales by Product Category: 2000

PRODUCT	PERCENTAGE SALES (%) 2000
Computing Systems	42
Imaging and Printing Systems	41
IT Services	14
Other*	3
Total	100

* Includes all other products.

Source: The 2000 Annual Report, Hewlett-Packard Company.

Graphs can be used to highlight the sales of Hewlett-Packard.

pie chart
A round chart divided into sections.

line chart
A chart that connects a series of data points using continuous lines.

pictograph
A graphical depiction that makes use of small pictures or symbols to display the data.

bar chart
A chart that displays data in bars positioned horizontally or vertically.

histogram
A vertical bar chart in which the height of the bars represents the relative or cumulative frequency of occurrence.

to enhance clarity of communication and impact. As the saying goes, a picture is worth a thousand words. The guidelines for preparing graphs are similar to those for tables. Therefore, this section focuses on the different types of graphical aids. We illustrate several of these using the data from Table 19.1 and other data for Hewlett-Packard (HP) reported in the same source (Table 19.2).[4]

GEOGRAPHIC AND OTHER MAPS Geographic and other maps, such as product positioning maps, can communicate relative location and other comparative information. Geographic maps can pertain to countries, states, counties, sales territories, and other divisions. For example, suppose the researcher wanted to display the percentage of HP sales by product category for each state in the United States. This information could be effectively communicated in a map in which each state was divided into three areas, proportionate to the percentage sales for each of the major product lines of HP: computing systems, imaging and printing, and IT services. Each area should be displayed in a different color or pattern.

ROUND OR PIE CHARTS In a **pie chart,** the area of each section, as a percentage of the total area of the circle, reflects the percentage associated with the value of a specific variable. A pie chart is not useful for displaying relationships over time or relationships among several variables. As a general guideline, a pie chart should not require more than seven sections. Figure 19.4 shows a pie chart for HP sales by product category for 2000, as given in Table 19.1.

LINE CHARTS A **line chart** connects a series of data points using continuous lines. This is an attractive way of illustrating trends and changes over time (see Figure 19.5). Several series can be compared on the same chart, and forecasts, interpolations, and extrapolations can be shown. If several series are displayed simultaneously, each line should have a distinctive color or form.

PICTOGRAPHS A **pictograph** uses small pictures or symbols to display the data. As Figure 19.6 shows, pictographs do not depict results precisely. Therefore, caution should be exercised when using them.

HISTOGRAMS AND BAR CHARTS A **bar chart** displays data in various bars that may be positioned horizontally or vertically. Bar charts can be used to present absolute and relative magnitudes, differences, and changes. The **histogram** is a vertical bar chart where the height of the bars represents the relative or cumulative frequency of occurrence of a specific variable (see Figure 19.7).

SCHEMATIC FIGURES AND FLOWCHARTS Schematic figures and flowcharts take on a number of different forms. They can be used to display the steps or components of a process, as in

TABLE 19.2   Hewlett-Packard Sales: 1996–2000

YEAR	NET REVENUE (BILLIONS OF DOLLARS)
1996........................	31.6
1997........................	35.5
1998........................	39.4
1999........................	42.4
2000........................	48.8

Source: The 2000 Annual Report, Hewlett-Packard Company.

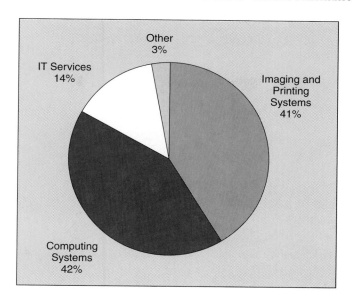

FIGURE 19.4
Pie Chart of 2000 Hewlett-Packard Sales by Product Category

Figure 19.3, or they can be used as classification diagrams. Examples of classification charts for classifying secondary data were provided in Chapter 4 (Figures 4.3 to 4.6).

ORAL PRESENTATION AND DISSEMINATION

The researcher should present the entire marketing research project to the management of the client firm. This presentation will help management understand and accept the written report. Any preliminary questions that the management may have can be addressed in the presentation. Since many executives form their first and lasting impressions about the project based on the presentation, its importance cannot be overemphasized.

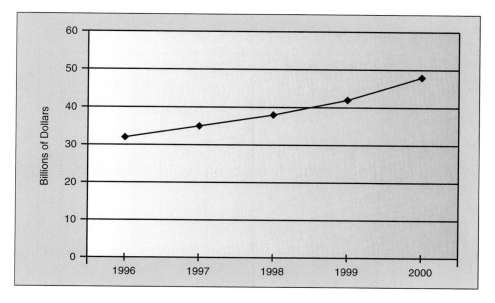

FIGURE 19.5
Line Chart of Total Hewlett-Packard Net Revenues

FIGURE 19.6
A Pictograph of Hewlett-Packard Net Revenues in Billions of Dollars

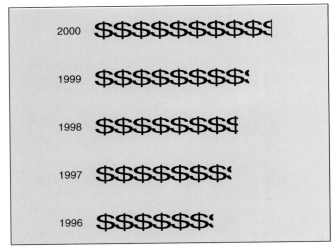

Each Symbol Equals Five Billion Dollars

The key to an effective presentation is preparation. A written script or detailed outline should be prepared following the format of the written report. The presentation must be geared to the audience. For this purpose, the researcher should determine their backgrounds, interests, and involvement in the project, as well as the extent to which they are likely to be affected by it. For example, a presentation prepared for the advertising department should put more emphasis on advertising decisions, including budget, media, copy, and execution details. The presentation should be rehearsed several times before it is made to management.

Visual aids, such as tables and graphs, should be displayed with a variety of media. It is important to maintain eye contact and interact with the audience during the presentation. Sufficient opportunity should be provided for questions, both during and after the presentation. The presentation should be made interesting and convincing with the use of appropriate stories, examples, experiences, and quotations. Filler words like "uh," "y'know," and "all right," should not be used.

The **"tell 'em" principle** is effective for structuring a presentation. This principle states: (1) tell 'em what you're going to tell 'em, (2) tell 'em, and (3) tell 'em what you've

"tell 'em" principle
An effective guideline for structuring a presentation. This principle states: (1) tell 'em what you're going to tell 'em, (2) tell 'em, and (3) tell 'em what you've told 'em.

FIGURE 19.7
Histogram of Hewlett-Packard's Net Revenues

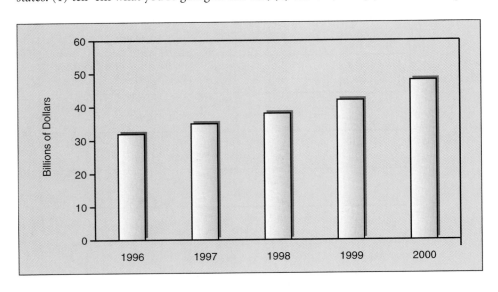

told 'em. Another useful guideline is the **"KISS 'em" principle,** which states: Keep It Simple and Straightforward (hence the acronym KISS).

Body language is also important. It helps the speaker to convey his or her ideas more emphatically. The body language can reinforce the issue or the point the speaker is trying to communicate to the audience. The speaker should vary the volume, pitch, voice quality, articulation, and rate while speaking. The presentation should terminate with a strong closing. To stress its importance, a top-level manager in the client's organization should sponsor the presentation.

Elrick & Lavidge (E&L) conducted a research project to measure the relative effectiveness of television, print, and radio as advertising media for a client firm. They also assessed the effectiveness of 10 TV commercials, radio commercials, and print ads. Given the nature of the project, the oral presentation of the report was particularly important in communicating the findings. In addition to an overhead projector and slide projector, E&L used a VCR (for playing TV commercials), a tape recorder (for playing radio commercials), and a storyboard (for showing print ads). The presentation was made to the client's top corporate officers, consisting of the president, all vice presidents, and all assistant vice presidents at one of their monthly meetings.[5]

The dissemination of the research results should go beyond the oral presentation. The marketing research report, or at least sections of it, should be widely distributed to key executives within the client firm and made available on demand, as by online distribution. This was illustrated in the opening vignette where United Airlines makes the monthly customer satisfaction report available online. After dissemination, key executives in the client firm should be given time to read the report in detail before follow-up activities are initiated.

RESEARCH FOLLOW-UP

The researcher's task does not end with the oral presentation. Two other tasks remain. First, the researcher should help the client understand and implement the findings and take any follow-up actions. Second, while it is still fresh in her or his mind, the researcher should evaluate the entire marketing research project.

Assisting the Client

After the client has read the report in detail, several questions may arise. The client may not understand parts of the report, particularly those dealing with technical matters. The researcher should provide any help that is needed, as routinely done by the marketing research department of United Airlines in the opening vignette. Sometimes the researcher helps implement the findings. Often, the client retains the researcher to help select a new product or advertising agency, or to develop a pricing policy, a market segmentation, or other marketing actions. An important reason for client follow-up is to discuss further research projects. For example, the researcher and management may agree to repeat the study after two years. Finally, the researcher should help the client firm make the information generated in the marketing research project a part of the firm's marketing (management) information system (MIS) or decision support system (DSS), as discussed in Chapter 1.

Evaluating the Research Project

While marketing research is scientific, it also involves creativity, intuition, and expertise. Hence, every marketing research project provides an opportunity for learning, and the researcher should critically evaluate the entire project to obtain new insights and knowl-

"KISS 'em" principle
A principle of report presentation that states: Keep It Simple and Straightforward.

edge. The key question to ask is, "Could this project have been conducted more effectively or efficiently?" This question, of course, raises several more specific questions. Could the problem have been defined differently so as to enhance the value of the project to the client or reduce the costs? Could a different approach have yielded better results? Was the research design the best? How about the mode of data collection? Should mall intercepts have been used instead of telephone interviews? Was the sampling plan the most appropriate? Were the sources of possible design error correctly anticipated and kept under control, at least in a qualitative sense? If not, what changes could have been made? How could the selection, training, and supervision of field workers be altered to improve data collection? Was the data analysis strategy effective in yielding information useful for decision making? Were the conclusions and recommendations appropriate and useful to the client? Was the report adequately written and presented? Was the project completed within the time and budget allocated? If not, what went wrong? The insights gained from such an evaluation will benefit the researcher and subsequent projects.

SUMMARY ILLUSTRATION USING THE OPENING VIGNETTE

Report preparation and presentation is the last, but not the least, step in the marketing research project. A formal report should be prepared and an oral presentation made. As in the case of United Airlines customer satisfaction survey, the report should be very thorough and include a table of contents, executive summary, problem definition, approach, research design, data analysis, results, and conclusions and recommendations. Several tables and graphs should be prepared to enhance the clarity of the findings. The report, or at least some portion of it, may need to be widely disseminated, for example, by making the findings available online, as United Airlines did. After management has read the report, the researcher should conduct a follow-up. The researcher should provide assistance to management and conduct a thorough evaluation of the marketing research project, as illustrated by the numerous requests that the marketing research department of United Airlines handled following each report.

MARKETING RESEARCH AND TQM

Firms seeking the highly coveted Malcolm Baldrige Award (see Chapter 1) have to prepare a detailed report duly documenting their quality enhancement programs. This process illustrates the importance of report preparation to quality management programs. The preparation of these reports follows the principles discussed here and covers all aspects of the quality programs. However, the motivation to document the quality programs in formal reports should go beyond attainment of the Malcolm Baldrige Award. Unless the quality programs are documented, it would be difficult to sustain, much less improve, them. It is difficult to communicate such programs to the employees, suppliers, customers, and other constituencies. Hence, the value of undocumented or poorly documented programs is greatly reduced. On the other hand, the value of quality programs documented in a formal report is substantially enhanced, as illustrated by the Bureau of Census.

EXAMPLE

QUALITY (CON)CENSUS

There seems to be a consensus that quality management programs can be implemented in all types of organizations. The Census Bureau, the largest single source

FOCUS ON ELRICK & LAVIDGE

Report preparation is a group effort at Elrick & Lavidge (E&L). Many of the people who were involved in the implementation of the research project also contribute to the final report. In general, the project manager is responsible for coordinating with the various contributors and collecting their contributions into a standard format. In most instances, the project manager will also write a considerable portion of the report. Throughout the life of the project, the project manager collects technical details and statistics generated at important milestones. For example, when the data processing group creates a sample for a survey, they send information to the project manager about the details of the sampling process. The field operations group continuously updates statistics about the data collection efforts, including incidence rates within the sample, invalid test units (perhaps unknown names and addresses), and uncooperative respondents (those who refuse to start the interview and those who refuse to complete the interview). These and other field statistics are important to the interpretation of the results of the research project. Therefore, the project manager includes in the report a summary of relevant information about the field work. The general format of E&L reports is consistent with the material presented in this chapter.

It is important to note that E&L's report to the client is not always the last step in the process. Some clients will take E&L's report and use it to create internal documents that are presented to important decision makers within their respective firms. Other clients will simply make copies of E&L's report and distribute the copies to all-important internal stakeholders. In the first case, E&L rarely takes part in any live presentations to decision makers. In the second case, the E&L research director is often the one leading the presentation.

of data in the world, has developed and practices Census Quality Management (CQM), patterned after the concept of total quality management. CQM is designed to help the Bureau become more customer oriented rather than more process or data oriented. The development of CQM was motivated by a desire to greatly increase the use of Census Bureau data by making them more user friendly.

The Census Bureau has prepared a formal report documenting the CQM procedures. Among other things, the report describes the quality procedures the Bureau follows to generate its various data. The quality procedures help users determine appropriate uses of the data. Formal documentation of the CQM procedures in an easily accessible report enhances the value and usability of census data.[6]

INTERNATIONAL MARKETING RESEARCH

The guidelines presented earlier in this chapter apply to international marketing research as well, although report preparation may be complicated by the need to prepare reports for management in different countries and in different languages. In such a case, the researcher should prepare different versions of the report, each geared to specific readers.

The reports should be comparable, although the formats may differ. The guidelines for oral presentation are also similar to those given earlier, with the added proviso that the presenter should be sensitive to cultural norms. For example, telling jokes, which is frequently done in the United States, is not appropriate in all cultures.

Most marketing decisions are made from facts and figures arising out of marketing research. But these figures have to pass the test and limits of logic, subjective experience, and gut feelings of decision makers. The subjective experience and gut feelings of managers could vary widely across countries, necessitating that different recommendations be made for implementing the research findings in different countries. This is particularly important when making innovative or creative recommendations such as advertising campaigns, as illustrated by the following example.

EXAMPLE

CAMRY CHICKEN FRIES FORD

"Why did the chicken cross the road?" Toyota asked in a continuing series of TV commercials aired recently in Australia. The answer: "To sell more Toyota Camrys, of course." The spots showing an animated chicken trying to cross the road and getting its feathers blown off by a passing Camry were created by Saatchi & Saatchi Advertising. When Bob Miller, Toyota's general manager for marketing, tried to explain the ad to their counterpart in Japan, they thought he was insane.

Maybe so, but the commercials did unbelievably well. Hoary old joke that it was, the gag helped Toyota topple Ford's dominance in Australia. As a continuing series, the next ad showed the featherless chicken sitting on a pile of eggs in the middle of the road and hatching chicks as the Camry sped past. While such use of humor would not have made sense to the Japanese, it solicited a favorable response from the Australians.[7]

TECHNOLOGY AND MARKETING RESEARCH

Video revolutionized business presentations in the late 1970s and 1980s and largely sounded the death knell for film- and slide-based corporate programs. Now video itself is under threat from the PC-based communications media of the twenty-first century. Computer-based systems are available for preparing reports and making presentations. These packages also have free-form capability for laying out records and fields anywhere on the screen. They have a what-you-see-is-what-you-get feature that permits the writer to view the finished report before it is stored on disk or sent to a printer.

Finally, a vast number of software programs are available for developing remarkable presentations with great ease. For example, Microsoft PowerPoint allows the user to develop a slide show as a presentation. The development process is simple, but the final product can be intricate. Some of the tools available with this presentation software include a variety of transitions between slides, including fade, dissolve, fly-in from various directions, and many other visual effects. Some presentation programs also allow for the addition of sound and video clips for a more complete representation of data. This means that news reports or audio commentaries can be easily added to a presentation. With a little more effort, presentation software such as Director or Authorware can be used to fully animate a presentation.

ETHICS IN MARKETING RESEARCH

Several ethical issues also arise during report preparation and presentation. These issues include ignoring pertinent data when drawing conclusions or making recommendations, not reporting relevant information (such as low response rates), deliberately misusing statistics, falsifying figures, altering research results, and misinterpreting the results with the objective of supporting a personal or corporate viewpoint. These issues should be addressed in a satisfactory manner, and the researchers should prepare reports that accurately and fully document the details of all the procedures and findings.

Like researchers, clients also have the responsibility for full and accurate disclosure of the research findings and are obligated to employ these findings honorably. For example, a client who distorts the research findings to make a more favorable claim in advertising can negatively affect the public. Ethical issues also arise when client firms, such as tobacco companies, use marketing research findings to formulate questionable marketing programs.

EXAMPLE

TOBACCO INDUSTRY IS A "SMOKING GUN"

It is well known that tobacco smoking is responsible for 30 percent of all cancer deaths in the United States, is a leading cause of heart disease, and is associated with colds, gastric ulcers, chronic bronchitis, emphysema, and other diseases. Should tobacco companies be ethically responsible for this situation? Is it ethical for these companies to employ marketing research to create glamorous images for cigarettes that have a strong appeal to the target market?

Based on the findings of extensive research, it is estimated that advertising by the tobacco industry plays a part in creating more than 3,000 teenage smokers each day in the United States. It has been estimated that advertising for Camel cigarettes through the Old Joe cartoon advertisements increased Camel's share of the illegal children's cigarette market segment from 0.5 percent to 32.8 percent—representing sales projected at $500 million per year.

These detrimental effects were not limited to the United States. Not only was the tobacco industry enticing children to smoke, it also targeted other, less informed populations, such as those living in Third World countries. This raises the question of whether this was a way for tobacco companies to replace those U.S. smokers who quit or die.[8]

INTERNET APPLICATIONS

Marketing research reports can be published or posted directly to the Web. Normally, these reports are not located in publicly accessible areas but in locations that are protected by passwords or on corporate intranets. The various word-processing, spreadsheet, and presentation packages have the capability to produce material in a format that can be posted directly to the Web, thus facilitating the process.

There are a number of advantages to publishing marketing research reports on the Web. These reports can incorporate all kinds of multimedia presentations, including graphs, pictures, animation, audio, and full-motion video. The dissemination is immediate, and an authorized person anywhere in the world can access the reports online. These reports can be searched electronically to identify materials of specific interest. For example, a Coca-Cola manager in Brazil can electronically locate the portions of the report that pertain to South America. Storage and future retrieval is efficient and effortless. It is easy to integrate these reports to become a part of the decision support system. The advantages of publishing marketing research reports on the Web are illustrated by the Gallup organization.

EXAMPLE

GALLUP IS ON A GALLOP

The Gallup Organization is a world leader in the measurement and analysis of people's attitudes, opinions, and behavior. Although Gallup is best known for the Gallup Poll, which dates from 1935, Gallup also provides marketing and management research, consulting, and training. Its Web site *(www.gallup.com)* contains several reports presenting the detailed methodology and findings of surveys they have conducted. For example, in November 2000, a survey was conducted to show how much the average American would spend on gifts during the 2000 holiday season. The results reported that the average American would spend approximately $797. This amount had decreased from the average of $857 in 1999. Six out of 10 American shoppers planned to spend at least $500 on gifts alone. The Gallup poll also found that only 21 percent of these shoppers planned to shop online. This percentage had only slightly increased from 1999's expected 19 percent of online shoppers. The usefulness of such reports to marketers and the general public has made the Gallup site very popular.[9]

SPSS

While the normal graphs can be produced using the Base module of SPSS, for more extensive graphing, the DeltaGraph package can be used. This package has extensive graphing capabilities with 80+ chart types and 200+ chart styles.

Likewise, SPSS Tables software enables the researcher to create even complicated tables. For example, the results of multiple response tables can be condensed into a single table. The researcher can create a polished look by changing column width, adding boldface, drawing lines, or aligning.

SPSS OLAP cubes are interactive tables that enable you to slice your data in different ways for data exploration and presentation.

SmartViewer enables the researcher to distribute reports, graphs, tables, even pivotal report cubes, over the web. Company managers can be empowered to interact with the results by putting a report cube on the Web, intranet, or extranet. Thus, they can answer their own questions by drilling down for more detail and creating new views of the data.

SUMMARY

Report preparation and presentation is the final step in the marketing research project. This process begins with interpretation of data analysis results and leads to conclusions and recommendations. Next, the formal report is written and an oral presentation made. After management has read the report, the researcher should conduct a follow-up, assisting management and undertaking a thorough evaluation of the marketing research project.

TQM procedures and programs should be formally documented so that they can be easily communicated to the various constituencies. In international marketing research, report preparation may be complicated by the need to prepare reports for management in different countries and in different languages. Available software can greatly facilitate report preparation and presentation. Several ethical issues are pertinent, particularly those related to the interpretation and reporting of the research process and findings to the client, and the subsequent ways the client uses these results.

KEY TERMS AND CONCEPTS

Letter of transmittal, 572
Leaders, 575
Stubs, 575
Pie chart, 576

Line chart, 576
Pictograph, 576
Bar chart, 576

Histogram, 576
"Tell 'em" principle, 578
"KISS 'em" principle, 579

ACRONYMS

The guidelines for constructing tables may be described by the acronym TABLES:

    T itle and number

    A rrangement of data items

    B asis of measurement

    L eaders, rulings, spaces

    E xplanations and comments: headings, stubs, and footnotes

    S ources of data

GRAPHS can be used as an acronym for guidelines for constructing graphs:

    G eographic and other maps

    R ound or pie chart

    A ssembly or line charts

    P ictographs

    H istograms and bar charts

    S chematic figures and flow charts

The guidelines for making a presentation can be summarized by the acronym PRESEN-TATION:

    P reparation

    R ehearse your presentation

    E ye contact

    S tories, experiences, examples, and quotations

    E quipment: multimedia

    N o filler words

    T ell 'em principle

    A udience analysis

    T erminate with a strong closing

    I nteract with the audience

    O utline or script should be prepared

    N umber one level manager should sponsor it

EXERCISES

1. Describe the process of report preparation.
2. Describe a commonly used format for writing marketing research reports.
3. Describe the following parts of a report: title page, table of contents, executive summary, problem definition, research design, data analysis, conclusions, and recommendations.
4. Why is the "Limitations and Caveats" section included in the report?
5. Discuss the importance of objectivity in writing a marketing research report.
6. Describe the guidelines for report writing.
7. How should the data items be arranged in a table?
8. What is a pie chart? For what type of information is it suitable? For what type of information is it not suitable?
9. Describe a line chart. What kind of information is commonly displayed using such charts?
10. Describe the role of pictographs. What is the relationship between bar charts and histograms?
11. What is the purpose of an oral presentation? What guidelines should be followed in an oral presentation?
12. Describe the "tell 'em" and "KISS 'em" principles.
13. Describe the evaluation of a marketing research project in retrospect.

PROBLEMS

1. The following passage is taken from a marketing research report prepared for a group of printers and lithographers without much formal business education who run a small family-owned business.

   > To measure the image of the printing industry, two different scaling techniques were employed. The first was a series of semantic differential scales. The second consisted of a set of Likert scales. The use of two different techniques for measurement could be justified based on the need to assess the convergent validity of the findings. Data obtained using both these techniques were treated as interval scaled. Pearson product moment correlations were computed between the sets of ratings. The resulting correlations were high, indicating a high level of convergent validity.

   Rewrite this paragraph so that it is suitable for inclusion in the report.

2. Graphically illustrate the consumer decision-making process described in the following paragraph:

   > The consumer first becomes aware of the need. Then the consumer simultaneously searches for information from several sources: retailers, advertising, word of mouth, independent publications, and the Internet. Next, the consumer develops a criterion for evaluating the available brands in the marketplace. Based on this evaluation, the consumer selects the most preferred brand.

INTERNET AND COMPUTER EXERCISES

1. For the data given in Table 19.1, use a graphics package or a spreadsheet, such as Excel, to construct the following graphs:
   a. Pie chart
   b. Line chart
   c. Bar chart
2. Visit *www.gallup.com* to identify a recent report prepared by this company. How does the format of this report compare to the one in the book?

ACTIVITIES

ROLE PLAYING

1. You are a researcher preparing a report for a high-tech firm: "The Demand Potential for Microcomputers in Europe." Develop a format for your report. How is it different from the one given in the book? Discuss your format with your boss (role-played by a student in your class).
2. Obtain a copy of a marketing research report from a local marketing research firm. (Many marketing research firms will provide copies of old reports for educational purposes). Suppose you were the researcher who wrote the report. Prepare an oral presentation of this report for senior marketing managers. Deliver your presentation to a group of students and ask them to critique it.

FIELD WORK

1. From the Internet, pull down the latest annual reports of two companies known for effective marketing (for example, Coca-Cola, Procter & Gamble, GE). Identify the strong and weak points of these reports based on the guidelines presented in this chapter.
2. Obtain a copy of a marketing research report from your library or a local marketing research firm. (Many marketing research firms will provide copies of old reports for educational purposes). Critically evaluate this report using the guidelines presented in this chapter.

GROUP DISCUSSION

1. As a small group, discuss the following statement: "All the graphical aids are really very similar; it doesn't matter which ones you use."
2. "Writing a report that is concise and yet complete is virtually impossible, as these two objectives are conflicting." Discuss.
3. "Writing, presenting, and reading reports is an acquired talent." Discuss as a small group.

NOTES

1. Based on Shannon Stevens, "United Testing Self Check-In Kiosks in San Diego," *www.united airlines.com* (October 23, 2000); "United Uses 'Old' Look to Flag Gains," *Brandweek,* 39(10) (March 9, 1998): 44; and Joseph Rydholm, "Surveying the Friendly Skies," *Quirk's Marketing Research Review* (May 1996): 11, 33–35.

2. Jonathan Hall, "Moderators Must Motivate Focus Group," *Marketing News,* 34(19) (September 11, 2000): 26–27; Thomas L. Greenbaum, "Note to Clients: Hands Off Moderator Report," *Marketing News,* 31(13) (June 23, 1997): 22; and Thomas L. Greenbaum, "Using 'Ghosts' to write Reports Hurts Viability of Focus Group," *Marketing News,* 27(19) (September 13, 1993): 25.

3. Joop van der Vegt, "We are Drowning in Data but We Want Information," *Marketing & Research Today,* 26(2) (May 1998): 73-79; and Jeannine Bergers Everett, "Value-Added Research Begins Where the Marketplace Meets Management," *Marketing Research: A Magazine of Management and Applications,* 9(1) (Spring 1997): 33–36.

4. Paul McDougall, "HP Expands Initiatives for Open Storage," *Information Week* (795) (July 17, 2000): 36; and Lee Gomes, "Hewlett-Packard Sets Its PC Bar Higher and Higher," *Wall Street Journal* (September 8, 1997): B4.

5. Information provided by Roger L. Bacik, senior vice president, Elrick & Lavidge, Atlanta.

6. Robert M. Lloyd, "Census 2000," *Business and Economic Review,* 46(4) (July–September 2000): 11–15; Howard Gleckman, "Census 2000: Math, Not Politics, Please," *Business Week* (3545) (September 22, 1997): 42; and Barbara Everitt Bryant, "Reflections of the Census Director," *American Demographics* (March 1993): 13–15.

7. "Drivers' Interest Group Slams Ad For Toyota Model," *Marketing* (August 24, 2000): 3; "Business Briefing," *Far Eastern Economic Review,* 160(35) (August 28, 1997): 65; and Lee Geoffrey, "Aussies Chicken Fries Ford," *Advertising Age* (January 18, 1993).

8. Marianne DelPo, "Tobacco Abroad: Legal and Ethical Implications of Marketing Dangerous United States Products Overseas," *Business & Society Review,* 104(2) (Summer 1999): 147–162; Elise Truly Sautter and Nancy A. Oretskin, "Tobacco Targeting: The Ethical Complexity of Marketing to Minorities," *Journal of Business Ethics,* 16(10) (July 1997): 1011–1017; Kenman L. Wong, "Tobacco Advertising and Children: The Limits of First Amendment Protection," *Journal of Business Ethics,* 15(10) (October 1996): 1051–1064; and S. Rapp, "Cigarettes: A Question of Ethics," *Marketing* (November 5, 1992): 17.

9. Mark Gillespie, "Average American Will Spend $797 on Gifts This Holiday Season," Gallup News Service (November 27, 2000), *www.gallup.com.*

CASES

PART 3A: CASES WITH EXTERNAL DATA

CASE 3.1 ■ FORD SEEKS A NEW IMAGE

Ford spent billions of dollars remaking the Taurus. The new body design for the 2000 Taurus was bold, with upgrades galore. As a result, the cost increased. Why did Ford add so much, pushing the price of the Taurus up? Ford believed it must win over baby boomers as a matter of survival. With sales of over 400,000 Taurus vehicles per year at roughly $7.5 billion, the Taurus accounts for over 10 percent of Ford's U.S. auto revenues. The Taurus and its Mercury version, the Sable, account for 6 percent of the entire U.S. car market. Despite Ford's hard work on the new Taurus, a failure to conduct appropriate market research resulted in a car too expensive for many consumers—and therefore decreased market share for Ford.

Historically, the Taurus did much better with sales among the older segment of the U.S. population than with the younger baby boomers. As this latter group makes up more of the auto buyer market, sales of the domestic Taurus could fall. Additionally, almost half of all Taurus sales are low-margin fleet buyers, such as automobile rental agencies and corporate-owned fleets. Ford wanted to reduce Taurus fleet sales to 40 percent of total sales, thereby increasing its overall profit margin.

Ford also felt compelled to upgrade the Taurus due to one of its major competitors, the Toyota Camry. The Camry was upgraded with many of the features of its luxury Lexus line, and Toyota's sales were increasing. Ford felt it had to beat the Camry in order to accomplish its goals. The Taurus is key to Ford's plans to displace General Motors as the number one auto manufacturer in the world, and to wrest the world-quality title away from Toyota.

One of the most difficult tasks was to change the look of the Taurus without changing its identity. Inspired by the familiar Taurus oval grille, designer Doug Gaffka and his team decided on an elliptical shape. The 2000 Taurus had an elongated oval shape; as did its headlights, rear window, door handles, control panel, airbag pad, and more. It did not have chrome trim or visible seams, but it did have a curving, dropped rear deck and a very steep, sloping windshield. "We tried to make it sleek, sleek, and sleeker," says Gaffka. "We wanted to suck the body molding right down over the mechanics as if it were carved out of a single piece of metal."

Despite the praise from designers and automotive critics, right from the beginning many felt that the Taurus was just too expensive. Ford listened to the protests of its dealers and stepped back a proposed 7 percent price increase for the new model, which had been intended to cover the high cost of bringing the car to the market. That would have pushed the basic model above the $20,000 mark, which research shows is the cutoff level for many middle-income buyers. Instead, the company opted for a 5.6 percent rise and priced the basic Taurus at $19,390.

Even this smaller increase had many analysts worried. "They're abandoning a lot of their former customers," says Susan Jacobs, a New Jersey marketing analyst. "I don't think this market can absorb price increases at all. So I think it'll be a challenge." Joseph Phillippi, an analyst with Lehman Brothers, called the Taurus "a wonderful automobile," but asked, "Is the market going to pay them for the amount of content they've engineered into the car? A lot of cost has crept in. It's a real issue."

589

However, the higher cost resulted in lowered sales, with Ford Taurus lagging behind the Toyota Camry, which was the best-selling car in 2000. Ford knew it needed to improve the Taurus, but it failed to determine the effect of the increased price on sales. Consumers constantly make trade-offs between benefits and costs. Consumers buy the level of benefits that they believe is worth the cost and that is within their means. Despite the increased benefits provided by the new Taurus, many consumers were not willing to pay the higher price Ford charged.

For future success and increased profits the Taurus must attract the yuppie crowd—the highly educated, affluent baby boomers—who tend to prefer imported vehicles. Since this group is one of the prime target groups for this car, Ford needed to ensure that it could compete in a market where the Toyota Camry and the Honda Accord offer stiff competition. Primary concerns for Ford were overcoming its conservative image with this group, determining if they should offer incentives on the Taurus, and the importance of styling and prestige when promoting to this market.

To address these concerns, 30 statements were constructed to measure attitudes toward these factors and to classify the respondents. The respondents used a nine-point Likert scale (1 = definitely disagree, 9 = definitely agree). The respondents were obtained from the mailing lists of *Car and Driver, Business Week,* and *Inc.* magazines, and they were telephoned at their homes by an independent surveying company. The statements used in the survey of 400 respondents are listed below:

1. I am in very good physical condition.
2. When I must choose between the two, I usually dress for fashion, not comfort.
3. I have more stylish clothes than most of my friends.
4. I want to look a little different from others.
5. Life is too short not to take some gambles.
6. I am not concerned about the ozone layer.
7. I think the government is doing too much to control pollution.
8. Basically, society today is fine.
9. I don't have time to volunteer for charities.
10. Our family is not too heavily in debt today.
11. I like to pay cash for everything I buy.
12. I pretty much spend for today and let tomorrow bring what it will.
13. I use credit cards because I can pay the bill off slowly.
14. I seldom use coupons when I shop.
15. Interest rates are low enough to allow me to buy what I want.
16. I have more self-confidence than most of my friends.
17. I like to be considered a leader.
18. Others often ask me to help them out of a jam.
19. Children are the most important aspect of a marriage.
20. I would rather spend a quiet evening at home than go out to a party.
21. American-made cars can't compare with foreign-made cars.
22. The government should restrict imports of products from Japan.
23. Americans should always try to buy American products.
24. I would like to take a trip around the world.
25. I wish I could leave my present life and do something entirely different.
26. I am usually among the first to try new products.
27. I like to work hard and play hard.

28. Skeptical predictions are usually wrong.
29. I can do anything I set my mind to.
30. Five years from now, my income will be a lot higher than it is now.

In addition, the criterion variable, attitude toward Taurus, was measured by asking each person to respond to the statement, "I would consider buying the Taurus made by Ford." This statement was measured on the same nine-point scale as the 30 predictor statements.

The data for the case are provided. In the enclosed ASCII text data file, the first variable represents attitude toward a Taurus automobile. The next 30 variables, in the order listed in the case, represent the ratings of the lifestyle statements. Each field occupies three columns. In addition, the SPSS data file is also provided.

Questions

The director of marketing for Ford is interested in knowing the psychological characteristics of the yuppies to configure the Taurus program. You have been presented with the responses from the survey outlined above. Analyze the data according to the following guidelines:

1. Frequency distribution: Ensure that each variable is appropriate for analysis by running a frequency distribution for each variable.
2. Categorize the attitude toward Taurus and the 30 lifestyle statements as follows: 1 to 5 = 1, 6 to 9 = 2. Run cross-tabs with attitude toward Taurus as the dependent variable and each categorized lifestyle variable as the independent variable. Thus, you will run 30 cross-tabs in all.
3. Now recategorize the 30 lifestyle statements as follows: 1 to 3 = 1, 4 to 6 = 2, and 7 to 9 = 3. Run one-way analyses of variance with attitude as the dependent variable and each of the following lifestyle variables as the independent variable. Thus, you will run 3 analyses of variance in all.
   a. I am in very good physical condition (#1).
   b. I have more stylish clothes than most of my friends (#3).
   c. I wish I could leave my present life and do something entirely different (#25).
4. Run product moment correlations between all possible pairs of lifestyle statements. Interpret the results.
5. Run a multiple regression with attitude toward the Taurus as the dependent variable. The independent variables are the following lifestyle statements. Interpret the results.
   a. When I must choose between the two, I usually dress for fashion, not comfort (#2).
   b. Americans should always try to buy American products (#23).
   c. I would like to take a trip around the world (#24).
   d. I am usually among the first to try new products (#26).
   e. Five years from now, my income will be a lot higher than it is now (#30).

Based on the analysis, prepare a report to management explaining the yuppie consumer and offering recommendations on the design of the Ford Taurus. Your recommendations should aid Ford in achieving what they seek: an image for the Taurus that is attractive to the yuppie market and that helps them outperform the competition.

References

1. www.ford.com.
2. "Have You Driven a Ford Taurus Lately?" *New Hampshire Business Review*, 22(20) (September 8, 2000): 5.

3. Tom Jensen and Cathy Luebke, "Taurus Redesign Makes It an All-American Choice," *Orlando Business Journal,* 17(1) (June 2, 2000): 18.

4. Koland Cordell, "Competition Getting Hotter For Ford Taurus," *Business Journal Serving San Jose & Silicon Valley,* 18(1) (April 28, 2000): 44.

Note: This case was prepared for class discussion purposes only and does not represent the views of Ford or its affiliates. The problem scenario is hypothetical and the data provided are simulated.

Data File

CASE 3.2 ■ MARRIOTT: A BOLD ENTRANCE INTO THE ASSISTED LIVING MARKET

Marriott Corporation opened its first hotel in 1957 after years of operation in the food services industry. Since then, Marriott has consistently been designated the leader in the hotel industry. As of the year 2000, Marriott opened a total of 2,000 operating units. The company's full-service hotels had an average occupancy of 78.8 percent versus the industry full-service average of 71.1 percent. Over the course of the company's history, Marriott has been quick to meet the needs of the changing hotel market. Marriott introduced its Courtyard chain of hotels to support the growing market for premium, extended-stay business travelers in 1983. Four years later, it acquired The Residence Inn Company to further supplement this market. Shortly thereafter, Marriott introduced its chain of Fairfield Inns to penetrate the short-stay, economy market.

Thus, past operations demonstrated Marriott's willingness to enter new markets in an effort to maintain their desired level of growth. Given this, it is not too surprising that Marriott entered the assisted living market for senior citizens in the late 1980s. However, Marriott did not enter this new segment without performing significant market research, especially since this market was not traditionally one of their core businesses.

As part of their research, Marriott made use of various secondary data, primarily U.S. Census information. Census information revealed some very enlightening facts. The senior segment of the population is growing at a faster rate than it ever has in the past. By the year 2030, the Census Bureau predicts that seniors will account for nearly 20 percent of the U.S. population. Other demographers also predict that the "graying of America" will last well into the new millennium. In fact, many predict that there is virtually no risk of overbuilding assisted living facilities due to the aging population.

Marriott's investigation confirmed that it should enter the market as soon as possible. Marriott created a new division, Senior Living Services, which promptly opened its first lifecare retirement community in 1989. Marriott continued with full force into the market by acquiring the Forum Group and its chain of 29 assisted living facilities a few years later. Since then, Marriott has continued to expand its number of facilities.

The Senior Living Services division has experienced much success, but not without a few bumps in the road along the way. The assessment that there was no risk in overbuilding was not entirely accurate. What was ignored was how seniors differed in their service needs and/or wants. Scores of independent and congregate care communities were built and marketed to the active elderly group (ages 65 to 74), including those built by Marriott. It turned out that very few in this group were willing to trade life in their own home for a few social activities and a prepared meal or two. Marriott was forced to reassess the market for the elderly.

Their response was to create different chains to address the needs of the different groups within the market segment as well as to offer tiered service within the chains. The tiered service approach allows residents to receive only the level of service they require. As more service is required, residents can move to the next service level. This helps prevent residents needing less care from subsidizing the care of more needy residents. The tiered service approach also helps reduce turnover, since most residents leave as a result of needing a higher level of service than can be provided in a single-tier environment. Marriott operates over 150 communities and plans on opening more throughout the next five years. These locations are operated through chains such as National Guest Homes, Hearthside Communities, Brighton Gardens, and the newly formed Village Oaks, which targets residents most interested in affordability.

Marriott's more segmented approach has vaulted it into the leadership position in the industry. The Senior Living Division has achieved solid profit growth and an astounding 94 percent occupancy rate for comparable communities. The division also relishes in an average gross operating margin of 27 percent for its senior communities. Marriott's aggressive growth strategy resulted in 117 percent sales growth in 1996, due in large part to acquisitions. The Senior Living Division is now the largest component in Marriott's Contract Services segment, which accounts for over 23 percent of Marriott's total revenue.

Marriott's success in this market might have been reached more quickly had they taken a deeper look into the intricacies of the senior demographic, as opposed to just looking at the big picture painted by the Census Bureau.

To remain on the cutting edge of customer needs, Marriott needs to continue to seek out and address exactly what consumers are searching for in the assisted living market. This kind of marketing research may be the key to enabling Marriott to have continued success in the assisted living market.

In this increasingly competitive assisted living market, Marriott's marketing department desired to formulate new approaches to the construction and marketing of its assisted living services to position it effectively against its competition. To do so, 300 elderly men and women, who fell into Marriott's target market age, were surveyed. Each was given a randomly selected assisted living brochure (either Marriott's or one of two competitors) and asked to rate that assisted living community on nine attributes and to give his or her overall preference for the community. These ratings were obtained on seven-point Likert scales. The study was designed so that each of the three competitors appeared 100 times. The goal of the study was to learn which attributes of assisted living communities were most important in influencing preference (Y). The nine attributes used in the study were:

VARIABLE	ATTRIBUTE	MARKETING OPTIONS
X_1	Value	Promote high value
X_2	Price	Charge a fair price
X_3	Medical Assistance	Qualified assistance
X_4	Dining	High quality and healthy dining options
X_5	Local Attractions	Large variety of local attractions
X_6	Entertainment	Daily
X_7	Comfort	Friendly employees
X_8	Wellness Programs	Exercise facilities and activities
X_9	Location	Convenience

Data were collected using in-home personal interviewing and are provided in an ASCII text file. The first variable represents brand preference (Y). The next nine variables represent the ratings of the brands on the nine attributes in the order listed in the case (X_1 to X_9). Each field occupies three columns. In addition, the SPSS data file is also provided.

Questions

You must analyze the data and prepare a report for the marketing department. The one-page memo you received suggested that you use the following procedures:

1. Frequency distribution: Run a frequency distribution for each variable and show bar graphs of the first three variables.

2. Cross-tabulations: Group brand preference as low, medium, and high under the formula low = 1 or 2, medium = 3 to 5, and high = 6 or 7. Group all independent variables as either: low = 1 to 3, medium = 4, and high = 5 to 7. Run cross-tabs of brand preference with each independent variable. Interpret these results for management.

3. Do a paired t-test with price and comfort as the two variables. Interpret the results.

4. Do a paired t-test with local attractions and entertainment as the two variables. Interpret the results.

5. One-way analysis of variance: Group all independent variables into low, medium, and high groups as you did for cross-tabulations. Run a one-way analysis of variance on each of the first three independent variables with brand preference. Explain the results to management.

6. Regression: Run a regression equation for preference that includes all independent variables for the model, and describe how meaningful the model is. Interpret the results for management.

Interpret the results of the survey and make recommendations based on your findings to the marketing department. They want your opinion about which of the nine attributes the elderly value most highly, as well as your ideas for specific actions that can increase market share for Marriott in today's market. The marketing department is counting on your recommendations to provide them with ways to continue to improve Marriott's image.

References

1. "Top Seniors Housing Firm: Marriott Senior Living Services," *National Real Estate Investor,* 41(7) (June 1999): L13.

2. Mike Giacopelli, "Marriott Ventures into Affordability," *Nursing Homes,* 48(3) (March 1999): 32.

3. Jim Mctague, "Hotelier's Detour," *Barron's,* 80(7) (February 14, 2000): 14.

4. Bruce Adams, "Marriott Targets International, Brand Growth," *Hotel and Motel Management,* 215(6) (April 3, 2000): 3.

Note: This case was prepared for class discussion purposes only and does not represent the views of the Marriott Corporation or its affiliates. The problem scenario is hypothetical and the data provided are simulated.

CASE 3.3 ■ SHOULD MICROSOFT "SOFTEN" UP TO RESCUE ITS IMAGE?

For over a decade, Microsoft has enjoyed near monopoly power in the market for computer operating systems. The Windows operating system has dominant control in both consumer and commercial computer systems. Microsoft was extremely successful in using its operating systems as a way to control and dominate other software markets. When it began its campaign in the Internet browser market (against Netscape), it started to draw attention from the Justice Department. Microsoft soon faced an antitrust lawsuit that greatly changed its environment.

Recently, Microsoft has learned that keeping up with the legal world is of great importance to business. The legal environment includes regulations, laws, governmental agencies, and pressure groups that influence and regulate society. The Justice Department is an example of such an entity.

In May 1998, the Justice Department filed a lawsuit against Microsoft because it felt that the company was using its monopoly power to act as a corporate predator by hindering competition and ultimately hurting the consumer. Microsoft was concerned about what effect this legal action had on the company's image. Microsoft decided to conduct a survey to analyze the image and perception of Microsoft. The polls were Microsoft's efforts to try and fight back against the Justice Department and its allegations. Microsoft wanted to keep in touch with customer perceptions and make sure that the pending lawsuit did not irreparably damage their image.

The polls were used for internal use only. Before the antitrust suit was filed, Microsoft had a very wholesome image, one of which it was extremely proud. Later, the Justice Department provided details that made customers' current perceptions change. A company's image is one of its most valuable assets and Microsoft scrambled to protect its own.

Any time a company is in trouble, or what they think might be trouble, they'll track groups to figure out how the public perceives them. That is exactly what Microsoft did. It tried to avoid a potential marketing research problem by conducting surveys to tap into the environmental changes occurring. The legal environment was ready to destroy Microsoft, but where did the customers stand?

Microsoft needed to keep focusing a good portion of its marketing effort toward maintaining its image, especially when consumers were more and more interested in not only purchasing a good product, but also feeling good about it.

Accordingly, the marketing research department of Microsoft designed a survey for its new Office software. The company wished to determine executives' willingness to buy Microsoft Office. Management particularly wanted information in three areas: the reactions of businesses of various sizes; the impact of familiarity with Microsoft Office on willingness to buy; and how American businesses were using PCs in the workplace. This led to the related question of whether sales of peripherals to technically competent PC users could be increased.

To address these issues, 1,080 companies throughout the United States were sent a questionnaire designed to uncover executives' willingness to purchase Microsoft Office assuming they were in the market for office productivity software. The companies were classified for research purposes along three variables—company size, familiarity with Microsoft Office, and business application of PCs. Each of these variables could assume one of three values as listed on the following page.

VARIABLE	VALUE
Company Size	
Small/entrepreneurial	1
Medium/private	2
Division of major corporation	3
Familiarity with Microsoft Office	
No experience	1
Has used Microsoft Office for less than three years	2
Has used Microsoft Office for more than three years	3
Business Applications	
Individual use (word processing and data analysis)	1
Departmental use (functional computing, networking)	2
Corporate use (enterprise integration)	3

Forty respondents were randomly assigned to each of the 27 possible combinations of variables (i.e., 40 respondents with Low-Low-Low ratings, 40 with Low-Low-Medium ratings, etc.). The respondents' stated willingness to purchase Microsoft Office was measured on an 11-point scale.

Questions

Using SPSS, SAS, MINITAB, or EXCEL (or a similar statistical software package), you have been assigned to analyze the data using the following procedures:

1. Frequency distribution: Ensure that the frequency distributions of all variables are appropriate for further analysis.

2. Cross-tabulations: Recode the dependent variable, Willingness to Buy, into three relatively equal groups (low, medium, and high). Run cross-tabulations on the dependent variable with each of the independent variables (Company Size, Familiarity, and Business Application). Interpret the results for management.

3. Do a two-group *t*-test with groups based on company size: Small (coded as 1) versus Division of Major Corporation (coded as 2). The dependent variable is willingness to purchase Microsoft Office.

4. One-way analysis of variance: Explain the variation in the dependent variable by running three ANOVAs of the dependent variable with each of the predictor variables (Company Size, Familiarity with Microsoft Office, and Business Application).

The data for this case are provided in an ASCII text file. In the enclosed data, the first variable represents the stated willingness to purchase Microsoft Office. The next three variables, in the order listed in the case, represent the variables used to classify the companies. Each field occupies six columns. In addition, the SPSS data file is also provided.

The principal consultant of your firm has asked you to analyze the data using a significance level of .05. You should prepare a thorough report detailing the results of the analysis and offering recommendations for Microsoft management on its promotional program for its Office software. Remember that your target is American business executives. Your mission, while not impossible, is a difficult one—help Microsoft retarget its market and regain its image.

References

1. David Segal, "Microsoft on Lookout for Cracks in Its Image," *Washington Post* (November 21, 1998): G01.

2. Harriet Marsh, "Microsoft's Real Trial Is Trust," *Marketing* (December 3, 1998): 16–17.

3. Stacy Collett, "Wintel Monopoly Thrives: Customer Confidence Won't," *Computerworld,* 33(25) (June 21, 1999): 6.

4. Bill Laberis, "Image Is Everything," *MC Technology Marketing Intelligence,* 19(2) (February 1999): 20.

5. Ian McCawley, "Microsoft Restructure to Focus on Customer Care," *Marketing Week,* 23(13) (April 27, 2000): 8.

Note: This case was prepared for class discussion purposes only and does not represent the views of Microsoft or its affiliates. The problem scenario is hypothetical and the data provided are simulated.

PART 3B: CASES WITHOUT EXTERNAL DATA

CASE 3.4 ■ ARE CATALOGS RISKY BUSINESS?

The catalog shopping habits of Americans show that parents and couples are the two main groups that use catalogs as a means of shopping. The most popular merchandise category of catalog purchases is women's apparel. So, why do people shop from catalogs as opposed to store shopping? The top reasons for catalog shopping are convenience, perceived value, unique merchandise, price, direct home delivery, and lack of time to store shop. However, people do not shop from catalogs for reasons such as not trusting ordering procedures, wanting to see a product before buying it, not wanting to wait for delivery and not seeing anything of interest to order. Many people feel that ordering from a catalog is very risky due to hidden taxes or service fees and possible problems with returning goods. In addition, many people would rather not deal with the hassle of paying for delivery costs when they can purchase the same item at a store without any extra charge.

Twelve product categories were examined to compare catalog to store shopping. For each product, each respondent evaluated the degree of risk perceived in buying that product from a retail store and from a catalog. The null hypothesis—that there is no significant difference in the overall amount of risk perceived when buying products by catalog compared to buying the same products in a retail store—was tested by computing 12 (one for each product) paired *t*-tests. Mean scores for overall perceived risk for some of the products in both buying situations are presented in the following table, with higher scores indicating greater risk.

MEAN SCORES OF OVERALL PERCEIVED RISK FOR PRODUCTS BY PURCHASE MODE

	OVERALL PERCEIVED RISK	
Product	Catalog	Retail Store
Stereo hi-fi	48.89	41.98[*]
Record albums	32.65	28.74[*]
Dress shoes	58.60	50.80[*]
13-inch color TV	48.53	40.91[*]
Athletic socks	35.22	30.22[*]
Pocket calculator	49.62	42.00[*]
35mm camera	48.13	39.52[*]
Perfume	34.85	29.79[*]

[*] Significant at 0.01 level

Questions

1. Interpret the statistical results. Are catalogs risky business? What is your conclusion?

2. Are paired t-tests appropriate in this case? Why or why not?

3. Suppose we wanted to test the hypothesis that the perceived risk of buying dress shoes from a catalog exceeded 50. Formulate the null and alternative hypothesis. Assume that the population variance is known to be 25 and the sample size is 400, test the null hypothesis.

4. Suppose the sample was split into two equal groups. One group evaluated the perceived risk of buying each product from a retail store whereas the other group evaluated the perceived risk of buying each product from a catalog. What would be the appropriate way of testing the null hypothesis.

5. Suppose the sample was split into three equal groups. One group evaluated the perceived risk of buying each product from a retail store, the second group evaluated the perceived risk of buying each product from a catalog, and the third group evaluated the perceived risk of buying each product on the Internet. What would be the appropriate way of testing the null hypothesis that there is no significant difference in the overall amount of risk perceived when buying products from a catalog, retail store, or the Internet?

References

1. Melissa Dowling, "To Go Direct—or Not," *Catalog Age,* 14(9) (September 1, 1997): 5.

2. Troy A. Festervand, Don R. Snyder, and John D. Tsalikis, "Influence of Catalog vs. Store Shopping and Prior Satisfaction on Perceived Risk," *Journal of the Academy of Marketing Science* (Winter 1986): 28–36.

3. Mary Ann Eastlick and Richard A. Feinberg, "Shopping Motives for Mail Catalog Shopping," *Journal of Business Research,* 45(3) (July 1999): 281–290.

CASE 3.5 ■ DOES ADVERTISING SUBSIDIZE THE PRICE OF CONSUMER MAGAZINES?

For many magazine publishers, advertising growth is likely to slow in the beginning of 2001 compared to the previous year's booming market, thanks in large part to cutbacks by dot-coms, telecommunications, computer and automotive marketers, as well as a general cooling off in the economy. However, according to Universal McCann's forecasters, total U.S. ad spending is expected to grow by 5.8 percent in 2001, to $250 billion. Although interest rate increases and the stock market's poor performance in 2000 was expected to keep the brakes on growth into the first half of 2001, Universal McCann's forecasters said the general economic expansion was expected to continue and strengthen spending numbers for the second half of 2001.

Many magazine companies rely heavily on advertising for revenue. The more magazines consumers buy, the more magazine companies can charge advertisers. It is widely believed that consumer magazines' prices are subsidized by the advertising carried within the magazines. A study examined the contribution of advertising to the price per copy of magazines.

Multiple regression analysis was used to examine the relationships among price per copy, circulation, percentage of newsstand circulation, promotional expenditures, percentage of color pages, and per copy advertising revenues. The form of the analysis was:

$$PPC = b_0 + b_1 \text{ (Ed Pages)} + b_2 \text{ (Circ)} + b_3 \text{ (\% News Circ)} + b_4$$
$$\text{(PE)} + b_5 \text{ (\% Color)} + b_6 \text{ (Ad Revs)}$$

where

PPC	= price per copy (in $)
Ed Pages	= editorial pages per average issue
Circ	= the log of average paid circulation (in 000s)
% News Circ	= percentage newsstand circulation
PE	= promotional expenditures (in $)
% Color	= percentage of pages printed in color
Ad Revs	= per copy advertising revenues (in $)

Table 1 shows the zero-order Pearson product moment correlations among the variables.

T A B L E 1   Zero-Order Correlation Matrix of Variables in Analyses

	Price per Copy	Circulation	Editorial Pages	Promotion Expenditures	% Color Pages	% Newsstand Circ.
Circulation	−.21*					
Editorial Pages	.52*	.29*				
Promotion Expenditures	−.22*	.42*	−.19			
% Color Pages	.01	.33*	.19	−.15		
% Newsstand Circ.	.46*	.09	.31*	.26*	.02	
Ad Revenues per Copy	.29*	−.25*	.30*	−.14	.15	.08

*p < .05

599

The results of the regression analysis using price per copy as the dependent variable are given in Table 2. Of the six independent variables, three were significant ($p < .05$): the number of editorial pages, average circulation, and percentage newsstand circulation. The three variables accounted for virtually all of the explained variance ($R^2 = .51$; adjusted $R^2 = .48$). The direction of the coefficients was consistent with prior expectations: The number of editorial pages was positive, circulation was negative, and percentage newsstand circulation was positive. This was expected, given the structure of the magazine publishing industry, and confirmed the hypothesized relationship.

Promotional expenditures, use of color, and per copy advertising revenues were found to have no relationship with price per copy, after the effects of circulation, percentage newsstand circulation, and editorial pages were controlled in the regression analysis.

TABLE 2   Regression Analysis Using Price per Copy as Dependent Variable

Dependent Variable: Price per Copy

Independent Variables	b	SE	F
Editorial Pages	.0084	.0017	23.04[*]
Circulation	−.4180	.1372	9.29[*]
Percentage Newsstand Circulation	.0067	.0016	18.46[*]
Promotional Expenditures	.13–04[**]	.0000	.59
Percentage Color Pages	.0227	.0092	.01
Per Copy Ad Revenues	.1070	.0412	.07
Overall R^2 = .51	df = 6,93	Overall F = 16.19[*]	

[*] $p < .05$
[**] Decimal moved in by four zeros

Questions

1. Interpret the correlations.
2. Interpret the results of the regression. Does advertising subsidize the price of consumer magazines? What is your conclusion?
3. What should be the nature of regression results for you to conclude that consumers who purchase magazines are, in fact, paying for the advertising in those magazines?

References

1. Helen Berman, "Selling the Advertising/Trade Show Partnership," *Folio: The Magazine for Magazine Management* (Special Sourcebook Issue for 1997 Supplement) 25(18) (1997): 214–215.

2. Lawrence Soley and R. Krishnan, "Does Advertising Subsidize Consumer Magazine Prices?", *Journal of Advertising*, 16 (Spring 1987): 4–9.

CASE 3.6 ■ CITIBANK BANKS ON DATABASE MARKETING

Since its inception in the early 1800s, Citibank has been considered one of the premier financial institutions in the United States. After the Federal Reserve Act was passed in

1913, which permitted national banks to open offices abroad, Citibank was one of the first banks to take advantage of the new opportunities by opening a branch in Buenos Aires. After surviving the depression, due in large part to the strength in foreign markets, Citibank became the largest commercial bank in the world. Furthermore, Citibank again led the financial industry by being one of the first banks to enter the credit card industry in 1965.

The credit card industry has become more competitive over time, with virtually every financial institution getting into the act. Credit cards soon became the standard way to conduct transactions, and customers could choose from hundreds of providers. In the late 1980s, Citibank realized that to be the preferred credit card provider, it would need to differentiate its service over and above its competitors. To accomplish this, Citibank began a strategic information initiative to gather and mine customer-specific data.

Citibank's new project was entitled Cards Analytical Model (CAM) and was composed of data warehouses and intricate data mining techniques. Citibank's plan was to develop mathematical models to track the activity of its customers. However, the end goal is not just to track customer activity, it is to predict future purchases and provide better warnings of potential fraud cases. The CAM project was a significant technical undertaking. Customer data would approach two terabytes of information. The sheer volume of information combined with the complexity of the analytical models would require a mainframe class processing system. However, Citibank knew it could not rely on the existing set of mainframes used for online transaction processing because of the drag on response times. Therefore, an entirely separate system was developed using the powerful network of IBM RS/6000 MPP (massively parallel processing) servers.

Citibank believed the rewards derived from the information would well outweigh the complexity and cost of implementing such a system. The most important benefit from having such a system was the ability to improve service to their customers and to develop new products and service offerings that would meet customer's changing needs. In addition to this key point, the analytical models would operate off of a continuous stream of information. Traditional marketing research often requires examining and updating models each time new data are collected. The CAM system helped to automate this task due to the continuous stream of data and the fact that the models were built into the system's data mining routines.

The CAM project was completed in 1997 and has been fully integrated into the credit card services divisions of Citibank. The results were used to create products and services that gave Citibank an edge over the competitors. In addition to traditional credit card offerings, Citibank found other uses for the powerful data in the worlds of online banking and e-commerce. The firm became so committed to this segment that it published the goal of expanding its customer base from 100 million to 1 billion worldwide by 2012. Citibank created a new division to spearhead its e-commerce effort and quickly began working overtime to deploy new products and services. The new division used information from the CAM system in exploring radical ways to make it easier for customers to interact with the company. The aggressiveness in the e-commerce segment is a requirement because of the much smaller, faster moving Internet only banks.

Citibank's competitors realized the threat posed by such information and many responded in kind by creating their own systems. First Union Corporation developed its own customer specific data warehouse and recently expanded its capacity to 27 terabytes, making it one of the largest data warehouse systems on record. In addition to consumers, the expansion will contain information about First Union's small business customers and commercial customers. The end objective is the same as Citibank's: improve service levels, customer retention, and customer profitability.

Database marketing and the use of mathematical models have become very popular in the credit card industry. However, it should be noted that getting value out of a data warehouse is not as simple as gathering data and loading it into a relational database. Several myths about this relatively new technology exist such as, "If we invest in the right database technology, everything will be fine." The right technology is not enough to get results. Organizations must change their entire operating models to function in a more customer-centric manner in order to take advantage of the information. Another popular myth is: "Once the data are collected, the hard part is over." Information has a relatively short life cycle and must be used quickly. Data must be cleansed and prepared before they can be analyzed. This step typically makes up 80 percent of the time spent data mining. Companies must realize that data quality is as important as quantity. Even though the amount of time and investment required to implement these large marketing data warehouses is extensive, the returns can be far greater, as in the case of Citibank.

Questions

1. Citibank would like to increase its share of the credit card market. Identify the appropriate management decision problem.
2. Define the marketing research problem corresponding to the management decisions problem you have identified in question 1.
3. Use the Internet to determine the current market share of Citibank and other major issuers of credit cards.
4. What do you think are some of the variables on which information is being stored in the CAM database. Discuss the relevance of the variables you have identified.
5. What role can qualitative research play in helping Citibank further its share of the credit card market? Which qualitative research technique should be used and why?
6. If a survey is to be conducted to determine consumers' evaluations of major banks issuing credit cards, which survey method should be used and why?
7. Design a questionnaire to measure Citibank's image of the credit card market.
8. What type of statistical analysis should be conducted to determine which consumer demographic variables explain credit card usage?
9. In the credit card usage survey, respondents were asked to express their degree of (dis)agreement with a number of lifestyle statements on a seven-point scale. What statistical analysis should be done to determine if the users and nonusers of Citibank credit cards differ in terms of lifestyles?

References

1. Bob Violino and Clinton Wilder, "Banking on E-business," *Informationweek* (732) (May 3, 1999): 44–52.
2. Carolyn Brzezinski, "Database Marketing: Separating Fact From Fiction," *Credit Union Executive,* 4(39) (July/August 1999): 20–24.
3. Tom Groenfeldt, "Customer Data, Right Here, Right Now," *USBanker,* 110(5) (May 2000): 73.
4. "Citibank Restored to the Throne," *Asiamoney,* 11(3) (April 2000): 4, 70.

CASE 3.7 ■ THE BIRTH OF GATORADE: FROM JORDAN TO THE UNKNOWN

The product Gatorade, as we know it, came to fruition in 1965. It was originally developed as a drink to help prevent dehydration and replace body salts lost during extreme physical activity in high temperatures for the University of Florida football team. This initial product was named Gatorade, after the mascot for the University of Florida. Thanks in part to their new sports drink, The Florida Gators enjoyed a winning season that year and attributed much of their success to the players' ability to play hard for the entire game.

Stokely-Van Camp purchased the brand in 1967. Sixteen years later, in 1983, Quaker Oats subsequently acquired Stokely-Van Camp. Since its impressive beginning, the Gatorade brand has enjoyed tremendous success in the beverage industry. Despite competition from beverage heavyweights, Coca-Cola (Poweraid) and PepsiCo (All Sport), Gatorade remained atop the sports drink industry. On May 1, 2001, PepsiCo Inc.'s shareholders approved a plan to merge with the Quaker Oats Company.

Gatorade attributes much of its long-term success to its marketing and marketing research abilities. Over time, Gatorade has used many different approaches to maintain their brand image. The most memorable is the use of NBA superstar Michael Jordan. Along with athletic shoe manufacturer Nike, Gatorade developed a long-term relationship with Jordan spanning most of his career, throughout the 1980s and 1990s.

In the early 1990s, the use of Michael Jordan in marketing campaigns came into question when his potential gambling problems came into public view. Many industry experts predicted that Jordan's public image would be forever tainted and his multimillion dollar endorsement contracts would quickly disappear. Gatorade soon began a marketing research project to determine whether or not the Jordan name would still provide the necessary return on their marketing dollars.

Gatorade conducted a series of phone surveys to better understand customers' opinion of Michael Jordan, in light of his recently disclosed predisposition to gambling. The results of the research showed that the vast majority of consumers associated Jordan with a certain style of play on the basketball court and leadership position with the NBA. The negative press and gambling charges affected Jordan the person, not Jordan the athlete, which was the image associated with Gatorade. Gatorade chose to stand firm with Michael Jordan as its primary spokesperson and it certainly was no worse for wear. Throughout Jordan's post-gambling tenure in the 1990s, Gatorade's sales continued to climb faster than the industry average.

The future of Jordan's marketing strength reappeared on the radar screen again in the late 1990s due to his announced retirement and the perception that Jordan had been overexposed. In fact, in late 1998, Jordan's agent finally put a hold on any new endorsement deals due to fear that the value of his name was decreasing. In addition to these issues, the whole idea of using a celebrity to market products was coming under criticism. The increase in the availability of information about athletes and products over the Web and the Internet was thought to hamper the effectiveness of "star power." It has also been argued that marketing by endorsement is simply old school. The fear is that the next generation of star athletes will just look like copycats of the Jordan era.

Gatorade's contract with Jordan kept him on the payroll through the year 2001. However, without explicitly stating, corporate executives at Gatorade seem to realize that the Jordan era is coming to a close. Over the coming years, Jordan spots will become less and less prevalent, as Gatorade attempts to expand their presence into new market areas. Gatorade feels that the next huge growth opportunity will be expanding their "active thirst" market share, which implies expanding beyond just sports activities. With that strategy in mind, waiting for the next Jordan to appear may not be the answer.

Questions

1. Describe the management decision problem as Gatorade attempts to expand its presence into new market areas.

2. Define an appropriate marketing research problem corresponding to the management decision problem you have identified.

3. To expand into new market areas, Gatorade would like to research consumer preferences for beverages via a mall intercept survey. Describe the field work process that should take place.

4. Discuss the role of supervision of field workers in the survey of question 3. How should the field workers be evaluated?

5. Using the Internet, compile additional background information on Gatorade since its inception. Write a detailed report summarizing your findings. Modify the format suggested in Chapter 19 as necessary. Your recommendation should focus on future research that Gatorade might undertake.

References

1. Sarah Theodore, "Gatorade Growth Taps 'Active Thirst,'" *Beverage Industry,* 89(4) (April 1998): 16–17.

2. Matthew Grimm, "Over Jordan," *Brandweek,* 40(6) (February 8, 1999): 24.

3. Terry Lefton, "The Post-Mike Millennium," *Brandweek,* 41(1) (January 3, 2000): 22–23.

4. Sarah Theodore, "Sports Drinks Leave Room for Many Players," *Beverage Industry,* 91(6) (June 2000): 18–20.

VIDEO CASE 3.1 ■ DUPONT: THE RIGHT INGREDIENTS FOR SUCCESS

DuPont is engaged in science and technology in a range of disciplines including high-performance materials, specialty chemicals, pharmaceuticals, and biotechnology. The company operates through 20 strategic business units, and within the strategic business units, approximately 80 businesses manufacture and sell a wide range of products to many different markets, including the transportation, textile, construction, automotive, agricultural, health, pharmaceuticals, packaging, and electronics markets. DuPont relies heavily on the use of marketing research in order to remain successful and efficient in all aspects of their business.

E. I. DuPont and company was making blasting powder before anyone thought of brands and even had Thomas Jefferson as a celebrity spokesperson in 1811. Today, DuPont sells over 30,000 products across 1,500 product lines. DuPont has made continual efforts at innovation, both in products and advertising. Because DuPont makes ingredients used in the production of other products, branding is a major challenge for this company—especially when one considers that the company has two markets.

Although DuPont sells directly to other manufacturers, to be successful, it must understand and respond to the needs of final consumers and communicate with them. DuPont uses marketing research when picking its direct customers. Useful information is gathered and direct customers are chosen carefully because the company wants not only to sell to them, but also to partner with them. The customer should become a partner in designing the final products to be made from the DuPont ingredient brands. For final consumers, DuPont engages in marketing research in order to understand the needs of the consumers, how they are living, and what they are thinking, in order to turn that knowledge into products meeting the needs that consumers sometimes don't even know they have.

To accomplish its goals, DuPont uses an umbrella strategy where the DuPont name is the umbrella under which the ingredient brands such as Corian, Kevlar, Nomex, Teflon, and Stainmaster are sheltered and marketed in a proactive manner. Thus, advertising and communication for the individual brands is also associated with the DuPont logo and slogan "Better things for better living." As the umbrella or parent brand, DuPont is presented as standing for respect for the individual, safety, health and the environment, honesty, and ethics. The ingredient brands are then promoted on the basis of the benefits that each provides.

DuPont adheres to five principles of Brand Management:

1. Personality—the company's culture, its goal of bringing solutions to consumer needs.
2. Visibility—projecting the company to its markets through a variety of advertising and promotional means that create awareness of the company's brands and make them visible in the marketplace as well as connecting with consumers.

3. Target Management—selecting partners and customers: With whom do we connect?

4. Marketing Management—managing the brand by understanding the dynamics of the marketplace: by seeing, feeling, and touching them.

5. Reputation Management—present DuPont globally in a way that builds on the core values of respect, health, environment, honesty, and ethics.

DuPont continues to follow the core values it built 200 years ago: Respect the individual, respect safety, and respect the environment. DuPont is always searching for new ideas and has a reputation as being an innovator. It has built this reputation by continuously studying its consumers and the market. DuPont uses a healthy dose of marketing research in the decision-making process. Marketing research has been and will continue to be an important part of DuPont's success. DuPont expends a lot of resources on listening to its customers and has been very successful in meeting their needs, some of which it didn't even know they had. DuPont understands that an external view of its products is a very important aspect that will help it make quality improvements. It has also been necessary for DuPont to conduct marketing research on its supply chain. It is important for DuPont to understand its suppliers because it wants them to continue to provide new products/designs and work together to better satisfy the consumers.

DuPont managers are tuned into the needs of customers via marketing research. They then translate those needs into product offerings that meet the need in a timely fashion and a quality way, at a price that the customers are willing and can afford to pay.

QUESTIONS

1. In a survey, consumers are asked to express their degree of agreement with the DuPont slogan "Better things for better living" using a standard Likert scale. They also expressed their degree of agreement using the same scale with the following six statements selected as independent variables: DuPont is presented as standing for (1) respect for the individual, (2) safety, (3) health, (4) the environment, (5) honesty, and (6) ethics. Which statistical technique(s) will you use to answer the following questions?

    a. Is the DuPont slogan associated individually with each of the six independent variables?

    b. Considered collectively, which independent variables best explain the ratings of the DuPont slogan?

    c. For the sample as a whole, do the ratings on safety differ significantly from the ratings on honesty?

    d. The sample is divided into two groups: those with a favorable (ratings of 4 or 5) and those with an unfavorable or neutral (ratings of 1, 2, or 3) response to the DuPont slogan. Do the two groups differ in their ratings of each of the six independent variables?

2. Consider again the survey mentioned in question 1. However, suppose that the agreement with the DuPont slogan and the six independent variables was measured using a categorical scale consisting of three categories: disagree, neutral, and agree. Which statistical technique(s) will you use to determine whether the DuPont slogan is associated individually with each of the six independent variables?

3. Consider again the survey mentioned in question 1. However, suppose that the agreement with the DuPont slogan was measured using the standard Likert scale but the six independent variables were measured using a categorical scale consisting of three categories: disagree, neutral, and agree. Which statistical technique(s) will you use to determine whether the DuPont slogan is associated individually with each of the six independent variables?

REFERENCES

1. *www.dupont.com/.*
2. Andrew Goldstein, "Making Another Big Score," *Time,* 157(10) (March 12, 2001): 66.
3. Bill Schmitt, "Expanding Six Sigma: Have You Signed Up Yet?" *Chemical Week,* 163(8) (February 21, 2001): 21.

VIDEO CASE 3.2 ■ DHL: DELIVERING DURING CRUNCH TIME

While most people think of FedEx and UPS when they think of air express, the business consumer knows that DHL has the largest market share in the international air express market. Beginning as an air shuttle service between San Francisco and Honolulu, DHL Worldwide Express has grown into the world's largest and most experienced international air express network, with service to 635,000 destinations in more than 228 countries and territories. Since DHL provides service to so many destinations, the use of marketing research is crucial for the company to prosper in the air express delivery industry.

Business-to-business customers tend to be demanding and vocal, competition is very intense, and new products and services are critical to a firm's success. The expanding global market has been an incredible opportunity for DHL, leading to both growth and challenges.

DHL plans to maintain its leadership through expansion of its services and products and its caring customer service. Marketing research has shown the demand for DHL's services in new countries, and relying on such useful information will help DHL to expand successfully. The use of surveys showed that customers were more than pleased with the service. This traces back to DHL employees and their training. The firm employees strive to be flexible and helpful. A story is told about a courier picking up a package from a customer in the midst of a traffic jam. Employees are noted for their "can do" attitude. Employees have been able to build this reputation by having access to the most updated technology, market research clarifying what customers want, and the ability to constantly improve customer service. Paying attention to details, such as clearing customs with packages, caused DHL to develop the technology and procedures to make the normal hassle a smooth experience.

The company uses its own people in most areas of the world, ensuring consistent service. Customer service is very important, and this is demonstrated by DHL using their own employees. The company also creates services, such as logistics services—the process of moving a good component from origin to destination without going through intermediary points. This is very valuable for the fashion and technology industries.

DHL was named "2000 Global Parcel Express Carrier of the Year" by Royal Philips Electronics, one of the world's leading electronics companies and Europe's largest. Logistics professionals at Philips business units worldwide selected DHL for its superior express delivery of parcels and documents internationally and its innovative global logistics services. In order for DHL to remain the number one international carrier and continue with its successful growth and expansion, it must continue to study the market and its competitors by using marketing research.

QUESTIONS

1. Qualitative research has shown that businesses evaluate air express carriers, such as DHL, FedEx, and UPS, on six factors: (1) customer service, (2) logistic service, (3) on-time delivery, (4) accurate delivery (delivery to the correct address), (5) cost, and (6) responsiveness to customer needs. In a global survey of businesses, the respondents rated their willingness to do business with DHL, FedEx, and UPS and also evaluated each of these carriers on each of the six factors using five-point scales, with higher ratings representing more favorable evaluations. What statistical analyses will you do to answer the following questions?

   a. Is the willingness to do business with an air express carrier related to evaluations on each of the six factors when the factors are considered individually?

   b. Is the willingness to do business with an air express carrier related to evaluations on all the six factors when the factors are considered simultaneously?

   c. Do the respondents evaluate DHL higher on customer service than on logistic service?

   d. Are businesses more willing to do business with DHL than they are with FedEx?

   e. Do the evaluations of DHL on the six factors differ for those who have used DHL and those who have not used DHL during the past one year?

   f. Are U.S.-based businesses more willing to use DHL than non–U.S.-based businesses?

   g. Respondent firms were classified into four size groups based on the number of employees as large, medium, small, or very small. Do the four groups differ in their willingness to do business with DHL?

   h. Willingness to do business with UPS was classified into three categories: unwilling (ratings of 1 and 2), neutral (rating of 3), and willing (ratings of 4 and 5). Do the four size groups of question g differ in their willingness to do business with UPS?

   i. Do the businesses based on North America, Europe, or Asia differ in their willingness to do business with DHL?

   j. Do the businesses based on North America, Europe, or Asia differ in their willingness to do business with UPS as classified in question h?

REFERENCES

1. *www.dhl.com/*.
2. Kristen Krause, "DHL Strikes Back," *Traffic World,* 265(7) (February 12, 2001): 21.
3. Gina DeLapa, "Helping Customers Help Themselves," *Sales and Marketing Management,* 152(11): (November 2000): 34.

Part IV

Comprehensive Cases

SPSS
Data File

Student Version
Data File

COMPREHENSIVE CASES WITH EXTERNAL DATA

CASE 4.1 ■ DUPONT HAS DESIGNS ON FASHION

DuPont is a company that delivers science-based solutions in food and nutrition; health care; apparel; home and construction; electronics; and transportation. The company was founded in 1802 and operates in 70 countries. DuPont's core values for nearly 200 years have remained constant: commitment to safety, health, and the environment; integrity and high ethical standards; and treating people with fairness and respect.

DuPont Fibers Division was wondering whether carpets could move "uptown" into the fashion-oriented world typically associated with clothing and furniture. Dupont, the longtime market share leader in the carpet industry, was searching for new ways to expand in a slow growth market. In addition, in the residential segment of the market, DuPont needed a way to differentiate its nylon fiber carpets from increased competition including the strong challenge of Amoco's new polypropylene fiber carpets.

The carpet industry can be divided into three end-use segments: commercial carpets for offices, hospitals, hotels, schools, government facilities, and industrial sites; contract residential carpets for large residential purposes like apartment complexes or subdivisions; and residential carpets for homes. DuPont estimated that 30 percent of carpet sales were from new residential construction, and the other 70 percent were from replacement purchases. In addition to different end-use segments, each segment's consumers were quite different from the other segment's consumers and each segment was serviced through different channels. Commercial carpets were typically bought by interior designers, architects, or specifiers for their clients. They had to be durable and, especially for some end uses like hotels, fashionable. Contract residential carpets were bought by designers or by the contractor who typically focused on price and durability. The residential segment differed from the other two because the purchaser was also the end user. Typically, the lady of the house purchased carpeting from a retail outlet in order to create the atmosphere she wanted in her home. In a recent trade journal article, carpet industry experts stated that retail stores are an important and effective component of the retail environment.

Ninety-seven percent of all carpeting is produced from man-made fibers derived from petroleum. The leading fiber in the industry has been nylon, which was invented by DuPont in the 1930s. Though the leader in the industry, DuPont was challenged by other high-quality nylon producers, like Monsanto, Allied, and BASF, and a host of generic low-end fiber producers. DuPont has 27 percent of the global nylon market and 58 percent of the nylon-6/6 market (the most advanced nylon fiber). Fiber producers sell their output to carpet mills, who then produce the carpeting. Until the 1980s, competition in the residential segment was based on the technical qualities of the fibers, mill price of fiber, and reliability in shipping—none of which directly affected the consumer. As such, the industry tended to be very production oriented.

In the early 1980s, a giant breakthrough benefiting the consumer emerged—stain-resistant carpets. By applying a chemical coating to the carpet fiber during production, the carpet was protected from permanent staining arising from most household soiling agents. Stains could be wiped off the carpet, thus alleviating the concern many people had

609

about entertaining or "living" on their carpet. The four major fiber producers quickly announced their versions of the stain-resistant carpets in an effort to remain competitive. Amoco also got into the game when it announced a "new revolution in carpeting," carpets made from polypropylene (PP) fibers rather than nylon. As a fiber, PP is inherently stain resistant. Thus, it offered the best overall protection from stains and it cost less to produce than nylon. However, it did not accept dyes as readily as nylon, nor was it as soft to the touch, thus making it less fashionable. As such, PP initially had difficulty entering the residential segment, but was well received by the commercial segment. Approximately 24 percent of the total U.S. carpet fiber market is PP.

In the mid-1980s, technical advancements in dyeing allowed Amoco to seriously compete in the residential segment. Amoco's objective was to lead the introduction of PP fibers to the residential market. DuPont, desiring to be the unquestionable leading fiber producer to the residential segment, relied more on marketing than other companies. It seemed to sense the threat of PP toward nylon fibers when it purchased Hercules fibers, a large PP extruder. However, DuPont believed that nylon was still the fiber for residential carpets and was bent on letting the consumer cast the deciding vote.

DuPont believed it could use its well-respected company name to attract consumers. As such, DuPont created the first fiber producer–backed carpets, DuPont Stainmaster carpets, which carried a guarantee backed by DuPont on stain resistance, wear, and antistatic, and was branded as a DuPont carpet. The results of the program were highly successful, with DuPont creating high brand recognition among consumers, the first time this had ever been achieved by a fiber company, thus differentiating it from the other fiber producers. DuPont took its Stainmaster carpet business and converted it to a premium carpet brand by increasing prices and reducing its distribution channels. DuPont spent over $10 million on television advertising beginning in 1995. A survey conducted by Video Storyboard Tests, Inc., rated the DuPont Stainmaster television commercial the fourth "most popular television commercial." Based on its success with DuPont Stainmaster, the industry leader decided to forge new ground.

For most of its history, the residential segment had typically been the most blasé segment of the carpet market. Styles tended to be simple, colors passive, and features uniform across all competitors in the industry. Technically, industry players maintained that differences did indeed exist, but in the words of one industry analyst, "The differences were there in style and fiber quality, but the housewife out shopping for carpet didn't really know or care—she only liked what she could see and feel." As such, DuPont wondered if the styles and designs so popular in the commercial segment could be transferred to the residential segment. Was the average household willing to make carpeting more than just a backdrop for other furnishings? If the program were to be successful, it would mean further differentiation from other nylon fiber producers by creating a new segment based on fashion and status for residential carpets; increasing brand awareness among consumers for DuPont (resulting in increased demand for DuPont fibers); and bringing in a new dimension to residential sales, which would be difficult for PP carpets to duplicate and would solidify DuPont as the leader in the residential segment. However, it would be an expensive undertaking, involving a significant amount of publicity and risking its reputation with its major fiber clients.

In addition, if DuPont were to proceed with the Designer Collection, it would have to move fast. The largest trade show in the industry—in which the companies announced their major designs and programs for the coming year—was coming up in three months. If DuPont wanted the Designer Collection to have maximal impact, it would have to have carpet samples and promotional materials ready for distribution at the show and its marketing program in line to begin shortly thereafter. As such, the go–no go decision would have to be made within six weeks.

In 2000, DuPont began an integrated marketing campaign to promote its Tactesse nylon carpet fiber. The fiber features two new deniers, 995 and 2,250, which DuPont engineers developed for added flexibility in loop constructions. The promotion included placing ads in several trade publications and a direct-mail piece to more than 5,000 carpet retailers. The mailer contained samples of carpet with Tactesse in loop and cutpile configurations. They provided carpet retailers an opportunity to test the fiber's "You have to feel it to believe it" theme. Overall, for the full year of 2000, consolidated sales totaled $28.3 billion compared to $26.9 billion in 1999.

References

1. Gregory Morris, "DuPont Canada Brings on Nylon-6/6 Expansion," *Chemical Week* (April 29, 1998): 19.

2. Marc Reisch, "New Texture in Carpet Fibers," *Chemical & Engineering News,* 76(4) (January 26, 1998): 20–21.

3. Andrew Wood, "DuPont Wants to Hitch Up Nylon's Performance," *Chemical Week* (October 29, 1997): 42.

4. Elaine Gross, "Dupont Shows New Tactesse Nylon Fiber for Carpets," *Textile World,* 150(6) (June 2000): 6.

5. *www.dupont.com.*

QUESTIONS

CHAPTER 1

1. Marketing research involves the identification, collection, analysis, and dissemination of information. Explain how each of these phases of marketing research applies to DuPont's problem.
2. Is the problem facing DuPont a case of problem identification research or problem solution research? Explain.
3. How can DuPont use limited service, external marketing research suppliers to assist them in their study?

CHAPTER 2

1. Identify two items that relate to each of the following factors to be considered in the environmental context of the problem.
2. What is the management decision problem facing DuPont? Should the Designer Collection line of carpets be introduced into the residential market?
3. What is the marketing research problem facing DuPont?
4. Break down the general marketing research problem statement into component parts.
5. What theoretical findings can assist in developing an approach to the problem?
6. Develop a graphical model of residential carpet purchasing.
7. Develop three suitable research questions and hypotheses from the marketing research problem.

CHAPTER 3

1. Can exploratory research be used in this case, and if so, how?
2. Can descriptive research be used in this case, and if so, how?
3. Can causal research be used in this case, and if so, how?

CHAPTERS 4 AND 5

1. What internal sources of secondary data can you identify that would be helpful?
2. What published sources of secondary data can you identify that would be helpful?
3. Which computerized databases can be used? What is their biggest disadvantage?
4. Assess the possible bias in the following sources of secondary data:
   a. An article interviewing designers on the new fashion trends in *Floorcovering News*.
   b. A DuPont sales history for 1997–2001 broken out by market regions.
   c. A chart of sales of residential carpet by region from the *Census of Retail Trade*.
   d. A list of bibliographic titles related to carpet fashion.

CHAPTER 6

1. Which exploratory research techniques would you recommend and why?
2. Develop a moderator's outline for a focus group to assess consumer desires in residential carpets with respect to the Designer Collection.
3. Devise word association techniques to measure consumer associations that may affect attitudes toward designer carpets.
4. Design sentence completion techniques to uncover underlying motives.

CHAPTER 7

1. Match the criteria for selecting survey methods with the survey method(s) offering the best results in this case.
2. Which survey method would you recommend to DuPont for conducting descriptive research, and why? What are the limitations of this mode?
3. Can observational methods be used to collect data and if so how? What are the limitations of your method?

CHAPTER 8

1. Based on the DuPont project, give an example of each of the conditions of causality for the relationship between purchase of designer carpets and income level.

2. Is causal research appropriate in this case? If so, which experimental designs would you recommend and why? If not, devise a scenario in which causal research would be appropriate.

3. Can a field experiment be used to conduct the test? Explain.

CHAPTERS 9 AND 10

1. What types of comparative scales can be used to gather the information needed on motivation, intentions, and preferences for carpets? Design these scales.

2. What types of noncomparative scales can be used to gather the information needed on psychographics, motivations, attitudes, and intentions?

3. In designing scales for the survey, which scales do you recommend?

4. How would you determine the reliability of the scales?

5. How would you assess the validity of the scales?

CHAPTER 11

1. Are each of the following questions well formulated? If not, what is the error?
   a. What is your favorite construction of carpet fibers?
      Nylon BCF _____
      Nylon Staple _____
      Polypropylene BCF _____
      Polypropylene Staple _____
      Polyester _____
   b. What style of carpeting do you have in your office?
      Uniform color; conservative style _____
      Uniform color; fashionable style _____
      Multicolor; conservative style _____
      Multicolor; fashionable style _____
   c. Do you intend to buy a new carpet soon?
      Yes _____
      No _____
   d. Do you believe, as most Americans do, that U.S. citizens should buy American-made carpets?
      Yes _____
      No _____
   e. Will you buy designer carpets given that they cost slightly more than traditional carpets?
      Yes _____
      No _____

2. Design a questionnaire to be used in a survey.

CHAPTER 12

Answer questions 1 through 4 assuming that a mall intercept interview is being conducted.

1. What is the target population for this study?
2. What sampling frame can you use?
3. What sampling technique do you recommend for this study, and why?
4. What nonresponse issues must be considered and how can they be overcome?
5. If a CATI were being conducted, which method of sampling would you recommend?

CHAPTER 13

1. Suppose DuPont conducts a preliminary market study of 30 respondents to determine the price per square yard they are willing to pay for carpets in the Designer Collection. The mean response is calculated to be $30.00. If DuPont wants to be 99 percent sure that the true value lies within $1 of this figure, how large a sample does it need to survey given that the population standard deviation is $5.00?
2. Suppose DuPont wants to know how many households are interested in the Designer Collection. To do so, it conducts a pilot study and learns that 21 of 30 respondents expressed an interest in designer carpets. (a) How large a sample does DuPont need to draw in order to be 99 percent sure that this result is within 5 percent of the true value? (b) What if they wanted it to be only within 20 percent of the true value at a 99 percent level of confidence? (c) What if DuPont required only an 80 percent level of confidence at a 20 percent level of precision?

CHAPTER 14

Answer the following questions assuming a mall intercept interview is being conducted.

1. What characteristics would you look for when hiring field workers for this survey?
2. What issues are most important in training your field workers for this survey?
3. What issues must you as the supervisor be most concerned with during the interviewing?
4. How would you validate the field work?
5. How would you evaluate the success of your field workers?

CHAPTER 15

1. Develop a codebook for the first eight questions in the questionnaire constructed for question 2 of Chapter 11.
2. Based on the codebook above, code the questionnaire for items 1 through 8.

CHAPTERS 16 AND 17

SPSS
Data File

Student Version
Data File

Suppose you administered the survey designed in Chapter 11 (see Dupont questionnaire), and you collected data from 240 respondents (provided for this case). Run the following analyses on the data and draw conclusions from the results obtained.

1. Run descriptive statistics and obtain frequency distributions for all variables.

2. Cross-tab Q3 (Is carpeting important?), Q4 (Is carpeting fashionable?), Q5 (Is carpeting central?), and Q6 (Is carpeting durable?) with the demographic variables in Q17 to Q21. If results are poor, you may have to regroup variables in order to obtain valid results. Interpret the results.

3. Conduct a *t*-test for each of the seven attributes listed in Q7 (importance ratings of attributes) by each of the four responses to Q2 (What carpet do you own?). There will be 28 *t*-tests run. *Note:* Respondents have been coded as either owning or not owning the style of carpet mentioned in question 2. Thus, the *t*-tests examine the differences between the owners and nonowners of carpets of a particular style. Interpret the results.

4. Conduct a *t*-test for each of the seven ratings listed in Q10 (Ratings of the Designer Collection) by the response to Q12 (Would you purchase Designer Collection?). There will be seven *t*-tests run. Interpret the results.

5. Do the respondents in the survey attach more importance to stain resistance (Q7a) than they do to long life (Q7b). Formulate the null and alternative hypotheses and prescribe an appropriate statistical test.

6. Do the respondents in the survey attach more importance to price (Q7e) than they do to warranty (Q7g). Formulate the null and alternative hypotheses and prescribe an appropriate statistical test.

7. Do those who prefer different styles of carpet (A, B, C, or D in Q9e) differ in terms of their agreement with the four statements of Q13? Conduct the appropriate analyses. Interpret the results.

8. Do the different age groups (Q19) differ in terms of their opinions about carpeting as expressed in Q13? Conduct the appropriate analyses. Interpret the results.

CHAPTER 18

1. Regress each of the four styles of designer carpets in Q9a, b, c, and d (rating for styles) on the seven attributes of Q7. Thus, there will be four regressions. Interpret the results.

2. Regress each of the styles in Q9a, b, c, and d on all attributes in Q10 (Designer Collection ratings), that is, there will be four regressions. Interpret the results.

CHAPTER 19

1. Prepare a report for management that explains your research results and provides an answer for their management decision problem.

CASE 1 - DUPONT QUESTIONNAIRE

Please answer ALL the questions whether or not your household currently has carpeting.

Part A

Q1. Does your household currently own carpeting?
    1. Yes_____
    2. No_____
(IF YES GO TO QUESTION Q2; IF NO, GO TO QUESTION Q7)

Q2. Which of the following styles of carpeting do you have in your home? Please check as many as apply. _____
    a. One color; traditional style _____
    b. Multicolor; traditional style_____
    c. One color; fashion style _____
    d. Multicolor; fashion style _____

Please indicate your agreement with each of the following statements (Q3 to Q6).

Q3. Carpeting is an important part of my home.

Strongly Disagree			Neutral			Strongly Agree
1	2	3	4	5	6	7

Q4. Carpeting is a fashion item for the home.

Strongly Disagree			Neutral			Strongly Agree
1	2	3	4	5	6	7

Q5. Carpeting is a central item in my interior design for my home.

Strongly Disagree			Neutral			Strongly Agree
1	2	3	4	5	6	7

Q6. It is more important for a carpet to last long than look pretty.

Strongly Disagree			Neutral			Strongly Agree
1	2	3	4	5	6	7

Q7. Suppose your household were to purchase new carpeting. Please rate the relative importance of the factors you would consider in selecting carpeting on a 1 to 7 scale in which 1 means "Not So Important" and 7 means "Very Important."

	Not So Important						Very Important
a. Stain resistance	1	2	3	4	5	6	7
b. Long life	1	2	3	4	5	6	7
c. Fashionable	1	2	3	4	5	6	7
d. Matches my furniture	1	2	3	4	5	6	7
e. Price	1	2	3	4	5	6	7
f. Made by a well-known company	1	2	3	4	5	6	7
g. Warranty	1	2	3	4	5	6	7

Q8. How likely is your household to buy carpeting in the next three months?

Not So Likely			Maybe/Maybe Not			Very Likely
1	2	3	4	5	6	7

Part B

(Show the respondent the samples of designer carpets.)

Q9. Please rate the attractiveness of the designer styles you have seen on a 1 to 7 scale in which 1 means "Definitely Not My Style" and 7 means "Definitely My Style."

	Definitely Not My Style						Definitely My Style
a. Style A	1	2	3	4	5	6	7
b. Style B	1	2	3	4	5	6	7
c. Style C	1	2	3	4	5	6	7
d. Style D	1	2	3	4	5	6	7

Q9e. Of the Designer Collection carpets you have just seen, which one would you most prefer to have in your home? (Check only one)

  i. Style A   _____
 ii. Style B   _____
iii. Style C   _____
 iv. Style D   _____

Q10. Please rate the Designer Collection carpets you have just seen on the following attributes. Use a 1 to 7 scale where 1 means Very Poor and 7 means Excellent.

	Very Poor						Excellent
a. Stain resistance	1	2	3	4	5	6	7
b. Long life	1	2	3	4	5	6	7
c. Fashionable	1	2	3	4	5	6	7
d. Matches my furniture	1	2	3	4	5	6	7
e. Price	1	2	3	4	5	6	7
f. Made by a well-known company	1	2	3	4	5	6	7
g. Warranty	1	2	3	4	5	6	7

Q11. Do you think it is desirable to have a designer carpet?

Yes_____
No_____

Please explain.

_____
_____

Q12. After viewing Designer Carpets, do you think you would purchase them for your home?

Yes _____
No _____

Why or why not?

_____

Q13. Listed below are statements that describe different opinions about carpeting. Please indicate how strongly you agree or disagree with each statement by using the following scale:

1 = Strongly Disagree
2 = Generally Disagree
3 = Somewhat Disagree
4 = Neither Agree nor Disagree
5 = Somewhat Agree
6 = Generally Agree
7 = Strongly Agree

	Strongly Disagree			Neither Agree nor Disagree			Strongly Agree
a. Carpeting is primarily a functional item.	1	2	3	4	5	6	7
b. I like to be associated with the latest styles.	1	2	3	4	5	6	7
c. It is important to buy the best quality.	1	2	3	4	5	6	7
d. I am fashionable.	1	2	3	4	5	6	7

Q14. Please rank the following colors of carpets in your order of preference when buying a residential carpet. Assign a rank of 1 to the most preferred color, 2 to the second most preferred color, and so on, with a rank of 6 to the least preferred color.

Color	Rank Order
a. Beige	_____
b. Gold	_____
c. Blue	_____
d. Crimson	_____
e. Green	_____
f. Brown	_____

Q15. In this section, there are several statements about interests and opinions. For each statement, indicate if you agree or disagree with the statement based on a 7-point scale in which 1 means Definitely Disagree and 7 means Definitely Agree.

	Definitely Disagree						Definitely Agree
a. Magazines are more interesting than television.	1	2	3	4	5	6	7
b. All men should be clean shaven every day.	1	2	3	4	5	6	7
c. When I must choose between the two, I usually dress for fashion, not comfort.	1	2	3	4	5	6	7
d. I am a homebody.	1	2	3	4	5	6	7
e. A subcompact car can meet my needs.	1	2	3	4	5	6	7
f. My friends come to me more than I go to them for advice on clothes.	1	2	3	4	5	6	7

		Definitely Disagree					Definitely Agree	

g. I like to buy new and
   different things.   1   2   3   4   5   6   7

h. I often wish for the good
   old days.   1   2   3   4   5   6   7

i. It is important to me to
   feel attractive to others.   1   2   3   4   5   6   7

j. I don't like to take chances.   1   2   3   4   5   6   7

k. I get personal satisfaction
   from using cosmetics.   1   2   3   4   5   6   7

Q16. Please answer the following questions as they relate to the way in which you have answered this questionnaire.

a. How interested were   Not So   Very
   you?   Interested   Interested
                             1   2   3   4   5   6   7

b. How committed were   Not So   Very
   you?   Committed   Committed
                             1   2   3   4   5   6   7

c. How much effort did   Not Much   Much
   you use?   Effort   Effort
                             1   2   3   4   5   6   7

d. How motivated were   Not So   Very
   you?   Motivated   Motivated
                             1   2   3   4   5   6   7

e. Did this questionnaire lead you to change your views about carpeting?
   No Change   A Lot of Change
        1   2   3   4   5   6   7

Part D

Q17. Your gender:
1. Male   _____
2. Female   _____

Q18. Marital status:
1. Married   _____
2. Never Married   _____
3. Divorced/Separated/Widowed _____

Q19. Your age:
1. 18–24   _____
2. 25–40   _____
3. 41–60   _____
4. 60+   _____

Q20. Your formal education:
1. Less than High School   _____
2. High School Graduate   _____
3. Some College   _____
4. College Graduate   _____

Q21. Which one of the following is your principal dwelling?
1. House _____
2. Condominium _____
3. Apartment _____
4. Trailer _____

Q22. What is your zip code?

_____

Q23. What is the approximate combined annual income of your household before taxes?
1. $10,000 or less _____
2. $10,001 to 30,000 _____
3. $30,001 to 50,000 _____
4. $50,001 to 90,000 _____
5. $90,001 to 150,000 _____
6. $150,001 and over _____

Thank you for your participation.

DUPONT CODING SHEET

(File - DPNEW.DAT)

Note: Fill variable column(s) with "9" if no response marked on questionnaire.

Column	Question/ Number Code Name	Variable Name	Coding Instructions
1–3	RESP	respondent id	001–099—add leading zeros
4		blank	
5	Q1	carpet in house	No = 0; Yes = 1
6	Q2a	single color—traditional	" "
7	Q2b	multi-color—traditional	" "
8	Q2c	single-color—designer	" "
9	Q2d	multi-color—designer	" "
10	Q3	carpet importance	code circled number
11	Q4	carpet as fashion item	"
12	Q5	carpet central to interior design	"
13	Q6	prefer durability to looks	"
14	Q7a	importance of stain resistance	"
15	Q7b	importance of long life	"
16	Q7c	importance of fashion-ableness	"
17	Q7d	importance of matches furniture	"
18	Q7e	importance of price	"
19	Q7f	importance of well-known maker	"
20	Q7g	importance of warranty	"

Column	Question/ Number Code Name	Variable Name	Coding Instructions
21	Q8	likelihood of carpet buy in 3 months	"
22	Q9a	attractiveness of style A	"
23	Q9b	attractiveness of style B	"
24	Q9c	attractiveness of style C	"
25	Q9d	attractiveness of style D	"
26	Q9e	preference for carpet style	"
27	Q10a	rating of stain resistance	"
28	Q10b	rating of long life	"
29	Q10c	rating of fashionableness	"
30	Q10d	rating of matches furniture	"
31	Q10e	rating of prices	"
32	Q10f	rating of well-known maker	"
33	Q10g	rating of warranty	"
34	Q11	desirability of designer carpet	No = 0, Yes = 1
35	Q12	would purchase designer carpet	" "
36	Q13a	carpeting is functional	code circled number
37	Q13b	like for fashion	"
38	Q13c	importance of best quality	"
39	Q13d	I am fashionable	"
40	Q14a	ranked preferences for beige	"
41	Q14b	ranked preferences for gold	"
42	Q14c	ranked preference for blue	"
43	Q14d	ranked preference for crimson	"
44	Q14e	ranked preference for green	"
45	Q14f	ranked preference for brown	"
46	Q15a	magazines preferred over TV	code circled number
47	Q15b	men should be clean shaven	"
48	Q15c	prefer fashion to comfort	"
49	Q15d	I am a homebody	"
50	Q15e	subcompact car meets my needs	"
51	Q15f	give advice more than seek it	"
52	Q15g	like to buy new things	"
53	Q15h	wish for good old days	"
54	Q15i	importance to feel attractive	"
55	Q15j	don't like to take chances	"
56	Q15k	satisfaction from using cosmetics	"
57	Q16a	interest in survey	code circled number
58	Q16b	commitment during survey	"
59	Q16c	effort during survey	"
60	Q16d	motivation during survey	"
61	Q16e	carpet ideas changed during survey	"
62	Q17	gender	0 = female; 1 = male

Column	Question/ Number Code Name	Variable Name	Coding Instructions
63–64	Q18	marital status	00 = married; 01 = never married; 10 = other
65–67	Q19	age	000 = 18–24; 100 = 25–40; 010 = 41–60; 001 = 60+
68–70	Q20	formal education	000 = less than HS; 100 = HS grad; 010 = some college; 001 = college grad
71–73	Q21	primary dwelling	000 = house; 100 = condo; 010 = apt.; 001 = trailer
74–77	Q22	zip code	limit to five digits
78–82	Q23	pre-tax household income	00000 = $10,000 or less 10000 = $10,001–30,000 01000 = $30,001–50,000 00100 = $50,001–90,000 00010 = $90,001–150,000 00001 = $150,001 or more

SPSS
Data File

Student Version
Data File

PREFACE TO DATA FILE EXTRACTS

One page of each data file is included in order to show how the data would look to the data entry person. Checking variables' column locations on these extracts must be done to ensure that data is not being misinterpreted during the analysis of computer runs. The data file must correspond with the coding sheet.

CASE 1 - DUPONT

Filename - DPNEW.DAT

1
1101174537612717567122525315111425325413622433114242555430000100010000010
000010
2
1010175716513726176131717516110717111624531171111617113522100001001010100
000010
3
1010164535424635164242525315111415336254122423113342665520001000010000001
000001
4
0999999991157362421574252252500253516342555255542525213440001000100010001100
000100
5
0999999993256353123564161161500171736254177177777171734144110000010001100
000010
6
1101011253256373622564262152400243516253445256442524222720001000010000000
000010

7
101102117325637312256426116160017171623547717776171713114000000001000001
000010
8
099999999115736251156427116160016262635146616666162623113100010010100001
000100
9
101114343115735272157427216160026174625316626655161647752000000010100100
001000
10
110101117434545444345343433411142434615323343311334232232000000001000100
000010
11
110101234434545413345426215240016262635146626755162614211100010010100001
000100
12
101017562761272746612261651611161612635141161111616134224000010001000100
000001
13
101016571542464555424343432311033342543163333421343312223100010010010001
000010

Note: There are two SPSS data files for Case 4.1. One is a full file that contains all the variables. This file cannot be run on the student version because the number of variables exceeds 50. The other file is a data file for the student version of SPSS. In the student version, questions 14, 15 and 16 in the DuPont questionnaire have not been coded to keep the number of variables below 50.

CASE 4.2 ■ DO GUCCI CATALOGS STACK UP IN DIRECT MARKETING?

SPSS
Data File

Student Version
Data File

Catalogs, one type of direct-mail merchandising, have been increasing in popularity as consumers look toward convenience in their shopping. Catalog business has even been expanding on the international horizon. Harris Catalog Library has offered 1,250 domestic and international catalogs for patrons to order from. Catalog libraries can be found close to home in U.S. libraries and as far away as Japanese department stores. The Japanese have been especially fond of shopping by catalog, since ordering American products directly from catalogs can save them up to 30 or 40 percent over local retailers.

Approximately 12 billion catalogs are produced each year in the United States. All catalog and mail-order sales combined accounted for about 4 percent of all U.S. retail sales. The largest catalogers were expected to generate 90 percent of the entire industry's revenues, which were projected to approach $102.4 billion in 2000 and reach an estimated $125.1 billion in 2004. This projection came from the "Future of Catalogs" report, which was prepared in October 2000 by W. A. Dean & Associates. According to the study, larger players would sell a wider array of products in the future. This growth won't be realized through a return to the "big book" catalog, it predicted, but through the distribution of specialized titles with a narrower product focus.

Closer to home, American catalog marketers have been striving to increase sales and promote catalog growth on the domestic horizon. The big dilemma facing these marketers is how to accomplish this goal—a difficult task, since look-alike catalogs and merchandising are standard in the industry. The problem is only compounded by the fact that attempts to break out of this trend are unusual for catalog marketers—especially due to the fact that the industry occupies one of the most conservative locations on the American marketing landscape.

A few catalog marketers have made attempts to break away from the traditional modes of catalog marketing. Gucci is one such company that employs innovative marketing techniques. Gucci's unorthodox style emerged in 1985 when the Gucci autumn/winter catalog took a new distribution route in the United States—for the first time Gucci catalogs were made available in bookstores.

Gucci fell on bad times in the early 1980s, but revitalized itself by the 1990s primarily by the leadership of Maurizio Gucci, the owner and original designer for the company. Despite the killing of Maurizio Gucci by his wife in March 1995, Gucci continued to expand its presence both globally and in the United States. It also more than tripled its revenues from 1993 to 2001. A great deal of its strategy involved creating a unified image for Gucci worldwide and discontinuing products that did not fit that image. Gucci's CEO, Domenico De Sole, personally traveled the globe to visit Gucci's stores and closed several that did not present Gucci's products effectively. Part of revitalizing Gucci's image has been with a catalog of very high standard. According to a company spokesperson, "The amount that Gucci spends on catalogs is unheard of in the industry."

Described as a product in itself, the Gucci catalog was predicted to generate interest that went beyond the typical catalog. It was said to even have an editorial appeal. Released in early September, the Gucci catalog came with a cover price of $5. Five thousand copies of the catalog were given to Crown Publishers for distribution, and Gucci began courting other booksellers such as Rizzoli, Endicott, Waldenbooks, and B. Dalton. Containing 96 color pages, the book was produced in-house at a very high budget.

Apart from bookstores, the Gucci catalog was also available in Gucci stores and was mailed out free of charge to 50,000 of Gucci's best customers. The merchandise shown in the catalog was available in the stores, by mail, or by telephone. Furthermore, this strategy allowed Gucci to determine where the customer got his or her catalog. The order forms in each catalog were coded to indicate whether the catalog was distributed through bookstores, the Gucci stores, or through the mail.

Although this campaign was not as successful as Gucci would have liked, the company did not give up on the idea of developing a new approach to generate growth and sales. In particular, Gucci hoped to gain a competitive advantage by capitalizing on the latest high-technology development for direct marketers—automated voice response.

Automated voice response (AVR), also known as audiotex, combines computer intelligence with telephone accessibility—a phenomenon with tremendous marketing applications. Recently, this technique has leapt to even greater heights with the introduction of interactive 900 numbers. Unlike an 800 number, wherein the marketer pays the cost, the cost of the 900 number call is passed on to the consumer. This is done by billing callers on their monthly phone bill, and the marketer receives any money that is left after the telephone company deducts its charge.

The marketing department at Gucci thought that it might use AVR technology to build catalog readership. They felt confident that they could do this by working under the assumption that ". . . the more time people spend poring over the pages of a catalog, the more likely they are to find something in there that they can't live without." In order to gain readership, a catalog readership game that required a touch-tone phone would be employed. On the cover of the catalog, the reader would be informed that there were lucky numbers scattered throughout the catalog. When lucky numbers were found, the person should dial the game phone number (which could be an 800 or 900 number) and punch in the lucky numbers, along with his or her personal identification code (PIN). The person should try to find as many lucky numbers as possible, since the more lucky numbers a person has, the greater the discount on purchases he or she makes from the catalog. This game, therefore, not only benefited Gucci by stimulating readership (due to the consumer's increased scrutiny of the catalog for lucky numbers), but also served as an inducement for the customer to make a catalog purchase.

Unfortunately, while Gucci's marketing department felt that they had a winning strategy, top management was not so sure. Before authorizing the implementation of this plan, top management wanted a marketing researcher to assess if the plan was a viable one. Based on the researcher's report, management would decide whether or not to give marketing the green light.

Despite how other retailers have begun to use the Internet to increase sales, Gucci has fought to keep its brand name under house control and is not keen on franchising through the Internet. As of 2001, it had no plans to sell products online and continued to sell products through its stores and catalogs.

REFERENCES

1. Gucci corporate spokesperson, catalog marketing department, personal interview, May 1998.
2. Gene G. Marcial, "Scuffed-up Gucci May Get a Shine," *Business Week* (August 4, 1997): 65.
3. Ida Picker, "Brand Rescue," *Institutional Investor* (April 1997): 25–26.
4. Faye Rice, "The Turnaround Champ of Haute Couture," *Fortune* (November 24, 1997): 305–306.
5. "Gucci Resurfaces as Fast-Growing Firm," *Wall Street Journal* (October 8, 1995): Col. 1, PA14(W), PA16(E).
6. Stephen Jewkes, "Italian Fashion Goes High-Click," *Europe* (401) (November 2000): 34.

QUESTIONS

CHAPTER 1

1. Marketing research involves the identification, collection, analysis, and dissemination of information. Explain how each of these phases of marketing research applies to Gucci's problem.

2. Is the problem facing Gucci a case of problem identification research or problem solution research? Explain.

3. How can Gucci use MIS or DSS to assist it in its study?

CHAPTER 2

1. Before marketing research can effectively be carried out, a marketing research problem must be defined. However, to arrive at a problem definition, the first thing that must occur is the analysis of the environmental factors of the problem. In the Gucci catalog scenario, what information, relevant to the construction of a problem definition, can be obtained from the environmental factors and how might it be obtained?

2. What is the management decision problem?

3. What is the marketing research problem?

4. The tasks undertaken to help define the problem (i.e., discussions with management, interviews with experts, secondary data analysis, and qualitative research) are also helpful in developing an approach to the marketing research problem. How can these tasks help in developing an approach?

5. Regardless of which techniques are used to develop the problem, the approach development process should produce several outputs. What output might result from the approach process applied to the Gucci scenario, in terms of:

   a. Objective/Theoretical Foundations
   b. Research Questions
   c. Hypotheses

CHAPTER 3

1. Can exploratory research be used in this case, and if so, how?
2. Can descriptive research be used in this case, and if so, how?
3. Can causal research be used in this case, and if so, how?

CHAPTERS 4 AND 5

1. What internal sources of secondary data can you identify that would be helpful to Gucci?
2. What published sources of secondary data can you identify that would be helpful?
3. Would you recommend using syndicate sources of secondary data? If so, which ones would you recommend?

CHAPTER 6

1. Which exploratory research techniques would you recommend and why?
2. Develop a moderator's outline for a focus group to assess consumer desires in catalog purchases with respect to Gucci.
3. Devise word association techniques to measure consumer associations that may affect attitudes toward catalogs.
4. Design sentence completion techniques to uncover underlying motives.

CHAPTER 7

1. Which of the criteria for selecting survey methods are most important in this case? Please explain your reasoning.
2. Which survey method would you recommend to Gucci to conduct descriptive research? Why? What are the limitations of this mode?
3. Can observational methods be used to collect data? How? What are the limitations of your method?

CHAPTER 8

1. Is causal research necessary in this case? If so, which experimental designs would you recommend and why? If not, devise a scenario in which it would be.

2. If a mall intercept interview is used and Gucci conducts causal research without randomizing respondents, which preexperimental design would you recommend?

3. Can you think of any way in which the static group design above can be randomized to increase its validity?

CHAPTERS 9 AND 10

1. In constructing an item for a questionnaire, Gucci decides to use a noncomparative itemized rating scale to measure attitudes (i.e., like or dislike) toward Gucci catalogs. They ask you to construct a Likert scale for this item. Construct the scale.

2. What types of comparative scales can be used to gather the information needed on motivation, attitudes, and intentions? Design these scales.

3. What types of noncomparative scales can be used to gather the information needed on psychographics, motivation, attitudes, and intentions?

4. How would you determine the reliability of the scales?

5. How would you assess the validity of the scales?

CHAPTER 11

1. What challenges exist in this case in meeting the three objectives of a questionnaire?

2. Design a questionnaire to be used in a survey.

CHAPTER 12

Answer questions 1 through 3 assuming that an in-home personal interview is being conducted.

1. What is the target population for this study?

2. What sampling frame can you use?

3. What sampling technique do you recommend for this study, and why?

CHAPTER 13

1. Suppose Gucci conducts a preliminary market study of 12 respondents to determine the average amount of a discount respondents would like from a promotional game. The mean response is calculated to be $5.00. If Gucci wants to be 90 percent sure that the true value lies within $0.50 of this figure, how large a sample does it need to survey given that the population standard deviation is $2.00? What is the confidence interval for the mean based on the preliminary market study?

2. Suppose after conducting the study in exercise 1, Gucci learns that these observations generated a mean of $6.00 and sample standard deviation of $3.00. What is a better estimate of the 90 percent confidence interval than previously calculated?

CHAPTER 14

Answer the following questions assuming an in-home personal interview is being conducted.

1. What characteristics would you look for when hiring field workers for this survey?
2. What issues are most important in training your field workers for this survey?
3. What issues must you as the supervisor be most concerned with during the interviewing?
4. How would you validate the field work?
5. How would you evaluate the success of your field workers?

CHAPTER 15

1. Suppose the following responses appeared on completed questionnaires that you as the supervisor of the project are editing. What is the problem with the responses and how would you treat them?

   a. How likely are you to participate in this promotional game?

Not So Likely			Maybe/Maybe Not			Very Likely
1	2	3	4	5	6	7

   Please explain why or why not.

   Games sometimes are fun.
   _____

   For the next two questions, assume that we cannot recontact the respondent. Only three unsatisfactory responses exist and the sample size is 250.

   b. How likely are you to participate in this promotional game?

Not So Likely			Maybe/Maybe Not			Very Likely
1	2	3	4	5	6X	7

   Please explain why or why not.

   I don't like games. They bore me and really don't save any money when you buy something.

   c. How likely are you to participate in this promotional game?

Not So Likely			Maybe/Maybe Not			Very Likely
1	2	3	4	5	6	7

   Please explain why or why not.

   I probably wouldn't play the game since it takes too much time to look through the whole catalog. I usually know what I want and go right to it.

2. Develop a codebook for the first seven questions in the questionnaire constructed in question 2 of Chapter 11.

CHAPTER 16

Suppose you administered the survey designed in Chapter 11, and you collected data from 250 respondents. Run the following analyses on the data (provided for this case) and draw conclusions from the results obtained.

1. Run descriptive statistics and obtain frequency distributions for all variables. Interpret the results.
2. Determine if receiving catalogs (Q1), playing promotional games (Q4), awareness of Gucci (Q8), receiving Gucci catalogs (Q9), looking through Gucci catalogs (Q10), and purchasing from a Gucci catalog (Q11) are related to any of the demographic variables (Q20–Q24, Q26).

CHAPTER 17

1. Conduct two-group *t*-tests to see if there is any difference in responses to the demonstration catalog shown (Q13) between those who are aware of Gucci and those who are not (Q8), those who have received a Gucci catalog and those who have not (Q9), those who have looked through a Gucci catalog and those who have not (Q10), and those who have purchased from a Gucci catalog and those who have not (Q11).
2. Determine whether the respondents have greater agreement with "Games save me money" (Q6c) than with "I play games for enjoyment" (Q6d) in answering the Gucci questionnaire. Formulate the null and alternative hypotheses and prescribe an appropriate statistical test.
3. Determine whether the respondents find promotional games in catalogs as being more fun (Q5a) than sophisticated (Q5b). Formulate the null and alternative hypotheses and prescribe an appropriate statistical test.
4. Conduct a one-way analysis of variance to see if there is any difference in responses to the demonstration catalog shown (Q13) among those who receive Gucci catalogs, those who receive other catalogs, and those who receive no catalogs (Q2).
5. Conduct one-way analysis of variance with each of the six statements of Q6 describing opinions about playing games in catalogs as the dependent variable. The independent variables will be the demographic variables (Q20–Q24, Q26). Thus, you will run $6 \times 6 = 36$ different analyses. Interpret the results.

CHAPTER 18

1. Regress the four dimensions of promotional games (Q5) on the respondents' attitudes towards playing promotional games (Q6). Thus, you will be running four separate regressions. Interpret the results.
2. Regress each of the six statements of Q13 describing Gucci catalog ratings against the four statements of Q12. Thus, you will be running six separate regressions. Interpret the results.

CHAPTER 19

1. Prepare an executive summary of the results from the study. Specifically, answer the research questions that were posed at the beginning of the study.

GUCCI QUESTIONNAIRE

Please answer ALL the questions whether or not your household currently receives a Gucci catalog.

Q1. Do you currently receive catalogs in the mail?
Yes _____
No _____

Q2. What catalogs are you currently receiving?
_____
_____

Q3. In the catalogs you have received in the past year, did any of them have a promotional game?
Yes _____
No _____
If YES, which catalogs had promotional games?
_____
_____

Q4. Did you play any of the promotional games in the catalogs?
Yes _____
No _____
(If NO, go to question Q8)

Q5. Please mark the scale below in terms of what the statement means to you.
Promotional games in catalogs are . . .
a. Fun |___|___|___|___|___|___|___| Dull
b. Sophisticated |___|___|___|___|___|___|___| Simplistic
c. Valuable |___|___|___|___|___|___|___| Not valuable
d. Worth my time |___|___|___|___|___|___|___| Not worth my time

Q6. Below are statements which describe different opinions about playing the games in catalogs which have been sent to you. Please indicate how strongly you agree or disagree with each statement by using the following scale:
1 = Strongly Disagree
2 = Disagree
3 = Somewhat Disagree
4 = Neither Agree nor Disagree
5 = Somewhat Agree
6 = Agree
7 = Strongly Agree

		Strongly Disagree		Neither Agree nor Disagree			Strongly Agree
a.	Promotional games in magazines add to the image of the magazine.	1	2	3	4	5	6	7
b.	I'm likely to buy something from a catalog that has a game in it.	1	2	3	4	5	6	7

	Strongly Disagree		Neither Agree nor Disagree			Strongly Agree	

c. Games save me money on my shopping. 1 2 3 4 5 6 7

d. I play games for the enjoyment. 1 2 3 4 5 6 7

e. I play games because I like to win. 1 2 3 4 5 6 7

f. It is important for a game to offer real savings on items in the catalog. 1 2 3 4 5 6 7

Q7. Please mark the scales below in terms of what the statement means to you. Company catalogs I receive in the mail are . . .

a. Helpful |___|___|___|___|___|___|___| A Bother

b. Informative |___|___|___|___|___|___|___| Not Informative

Shopping from a catalog is . . .

c. Convenient |___|___|___|___|___|___|___| Not Convenient

d. Inexpensive |___|___|___|___|___|___|___| Expensive

e. Easy |___|___|___|___|___|___|___| Difficult

f. Advisable |___|___|___|___|___|___|___| Not Advisable

Q8. Have you ever heard of Gucci?

Yes _____

No _____

Q9. Have you ever received a Gucci catalog in the mail?

Yes _____

No _____

Q10. Have you ever looked through a Gucci catalog?

Yes _____

No _____

Q11. Have you ever purchased anything from a Gucci catalog?

Yes _____

No _____

Q12. Please mark the scales below in terms of what the statement means to you. Gucci is . . .

a. Expensive |___|___|___|___|___|___|___| Inexpensive

b. Sophisticated |___|___|___|___|___|___|___| Common

c. High Status |___|___|___|___|___|___|___| Low Status

d. Poor Quality |___|___|___|___|___|___|___| Top Quality

I am going to show you a Gucci catalog. I would like you to look through the catalog for a few minutes before answering the next question. (Give the respondent a catalog.)

Q13. Please rate the catalog you have just seen on the following attributes. Use a 1 to 7 scale wherein 1 means Very Poor and 7 means Excellent.

	Very Poor						Excellent
a. Attention grabbing	1	2	3	4	5	6	7
b. Fun to look at	1	2	3	4	5	6	7
c. Matches the Gucci image	1	2	3	4	5	6	7
d. Shows quality products	1	2	3	4	5	6	7
e. Fashionable	1	2	3	4	5	6	7
f. Easy to place an order	1	2	3	4	5	6	7

Q14. Think about the promotional game you saw in the catalog. Please indicate how strongly you agree or disagree with each statement by using the following scale:

1 = Strongly Disagree
2 = Disagree
3 = Somewhat Disagree
4 = Neither Agree nor Disagree
5 = Somewhat Agree
6 = Agree
7 = Strongly Agree

	Strongly Disagree			Neither Agree nor Disagree			Strongly Agree
a. The game was fun to play.	1	2	3	4	5	6	7
b. The game caught my eye.	1	2	3	4	5	6	7
c. The game adds to the appeal of the catalog.	1	2	3	4	5	6	7
d. I am less likely to buy something from the catalog because of the game.	1	2	3	4	5	6	7
e. The game is right for Gucci.	1	2	3	4	5	6	7
f. Calling a 900 number to get my discounts when ordering is okay.	1	2	3	4	5	6	7

Q15. How likely are you to participate in this promotional game?

Not So Likely		Maybe/Maybe Not				Very Likely
1	2	3	4	5	6	7

Please explain why or why not.

_____

_____

Q16. Below are statements that describe different intentions toward shopping from catalogs. Please indicate how strongly you agree or disagree with each statement by using the following scale:

1 = Strongly Disagree
2 = Disagree
3 = Somewhat Disagree
4 = Neither Agree nor Disagree
5 = Somewhat Agree
6 = Agree
7 = Strongly Agree

		Strongly Disagree			Neither Agree nor Disagree			Strongly Agree
a.	I intend to play any game I find in a catalog.	1	2	3	4	5	6	7
b.	I intend to look through the catalogs sent to me.	1	2	3	4	5	6	7
c.	I intend to order goods from a catalog.	1	2	3	4	5	6	7
d.	Ordering on the phone with a computer voice response is okay.	1	2	3	4	5	6	7

Q17. Assume you are going to buy Gucci products. Please rank the following ways to purchase Gucci products based on your intended way to purchase goods. Assign a rank of 1 to the most preferred way, 2 to the second most preferred way, and a rank of 3 to the least preferred way.

	Way to Purchase	Rank Order
a.	Catalog mail order	_____
b.	Retail store	_____
c.	Catalog phone order	_____

Q18. In this section, there are several statements about interests and opinions. For each statement, indicate if you agree or disagree with the statement based on a seven-point scale where 1 means Definitely Disagree and 7 means Definitely Agree.

a.	Magazines are more interesting than television.	1	2	3	4	5	6	7
b.	I never know how much to tip.	1	2	3	4	5	6	7
c.	Most of my friends have graduated from college.	1	2	3	4	5	6	7
d.	I spend for today and don't worry about tomorrow.	1	2	3	4	5	6	7
e.	Advertising insults my intelligence.	1	2	3	4	5	6	7
f.	I am a bit of a swinger.	1	2	3	4	5	6	7
g.	I like to buy new and different things.	1	2	3	4	5	6	7
h.	Warranties aren't worth the paper they are printed on.	1	2	3	4	5	6	7
i.	It is important to me to feel attractive to others.	1	2	3	4	5	6	7
j.	I wish I knew how to relax.	1	2	3	4	5	6	7
k.	I shop often for specials.	1	2	3	4	5	6	7

Q19. Please answer the following questions as they relate to the way in which you have answered this questionnaire.

		Not So Interested						Very Interested
a.	How interested were you?	1	2	3	4	5	6	7

		Not So Committed						Very Committed
b.	How committed were you?	1	2	3	4	5	6	7

c. How much effort did you use?	Not Much Effort						Much Effort
	1	2	3	4	5	6	7

d. How motivated were you?	Not So Motivated						Very Motivated
	1	2	3	4	5	6	7

e. Did this questionnaire lead you to change your views about catalogs?	A Lot of Change						No change
	1	2	3	4	5	6	7

Q20. Your gender:
   1. Male   _____
   2. Female   _____

Q21. Marital status:
   1. Married   _____
   2. Never Married   _____
   3. Divorced/Separated/Widowed _____

Q22. Family size:
   1. 1   _____
   2. 2   _____
   3. 3   _____
   4. 4   _____
   5. 5+   _____

Q23. Your age:
   1. 18–24   _____
   2. 25–40   _____
   3. 41–60   _____
   4. 60+   _____

Q24. Your formal education:
   1. Less than High School   _____
   2. High School Graduate   _____
   3. Some College   _____
   4. College Graduate   _____

Q25. What is your address?

_____

Q26. What is the approximate combined annual income of your household before taxes?
   1. $10,000 or less   _____
   2. $10,001 to 30,000   _____
   3. $30,001 to 50,000   _____
   4. $50,001 to 90,000   _____
   5. $90,001 to 150,000   _____
   6. $150,001 and over   _____

Thank you for your participation.

_____

GUCCI CODING SHEET

(File - GCNEW.DAT)

Note: Fill variable column(s) with "9" and leading zeroes, if no response on questionnaire.

Column	Question/ Number Code Name	Variable Name	Coding Instructions
1–3	Respondent		
4		blank	
5	Q1	receive catalogs	No = 0; Yes = 1
6–7	Q2	current catalogs	00 = none; 10 = Gucci; 01 = other
8	Q3	catalogs had game	No = 0; Yes = 1
9	Q4	played catalog game	" "
10	Q5a	catalog games are fun	far left = 1; far right = 7
11	Q5b	catalog games are sophisticated	" "
12	Q5c	catalog games are valuable	" "
13	Q5d	catalog games are worth time	" "
14	Q6a	games improve magazine image	code circled number
15	Q6b	likely to buy from catalog with game	" "
16	Q6c	games save money	" "
17	Q6d	games played for enjoyment	" "
18	Q6e	games played to win	" "
19	Q6f	important for games to save money	" "
20	Q7a	mail catalogs helpful	" "
21	Q7b	mail catalogs informative	" "
22	Q7c	mail shopping convenient	" "
23	Q7d	mail shopping inexpensive	" "
24	Q7e	mail shopping easy	" "
25	Q7f	mail shopping advisable	" "
26	Q8	heard of Gucci	No = 0; Yes = 1
27	Q9	received Gucci catalog	" "
28	Q10	looked thru Gucci catalog	No = 0; Yes = 1
29	Q11	purchased from Gucci catalog	" "
30	Q12a	Gucci is expensive	far left = 1; far right = 7
31	Q12b	Gucci is sophisticated	" "
32	Q12c	Gucci is high status	" "
33	Q12d	Gucci is poor quality	" "
34	Q13a	Gucci catalog grabs attention	code circled number
35	Q13b	Gucci catalog fun to look at	" "
36	Q13c	Gucci catalog matches Gucci image	" "
37	Q13d	Gucci catalog shows quality products	" "
38	Q13e	Gucci catalog is fashionable	" "
39	Q13f	Gucci catalog easy to order from	" "
40	Q14a	Gucci catalog game fun to play	" "

Column	Question/ Number Code Name	Variable Name	Coding Instructions
41	Q14b	Gucci catalog game caught my eye	" "
42	Q14c	Gucci catalog game adds to catalog	" "
43	Q14d	Gucci catalog game reduces purchase likelihood	" "
44	Q14e	Gucci catalog game right for Gucci	" "
45	Q14f	900 number for discounts OK	" "
46	Q15	likely to participate in this game	" "
47	Q16a	intend to play any game	" "
48	Q16b	intend to look thru any catalog mailed	" "
49	Q16c	intend to order from a catalog	" "
50	Q16d	computer voice for phone order OK	" "
51	Q17a	ranked performance for mail order	code number entered
52	Q17b	ranked performance retail store	" "
53	Q17c	ranked performance phone order	" "
54	Q18a	prefer magazines to TV	code circled number
55	Q18b	confused on tipping	" "
56	Q18c	most friends college grads	" "
57	Q18d	spend for today	" "
58	Q18e	ads insult me	" "
59	Q18f	bit of a swinger	" "
60	Q18g	like to buy new things	" "
61	Q18h	warranties have little value	" "
62	Q18i	important to be attractive	" "
63	Q18j	wish I knew how to relax	" "
64	Q18k	shop often for specials	" "
65	Q19a	interest in survey	" "
66	Q19b	commitment during survey	" "
67	Q19c	effort during survey	" "
68	Q19d	motivation during survey	" "
69	Q19e	survey changed catalog opinions	" "
70	Q20	gender	0 = female; 1 = male
71–72	Q21	marital status	00 = married; 10 = never married 01 = other
73–76	Q22	family size	0000 = 1; 1000 = 2; 0100 = 3; 0010 = 4; 0001 = 5+
77–79	Q-23	age	000 = 18–24; 100 = 25–40; 010 = 41–60 001 = 60+

Column	Question/ Number Code Name	Variable Name	Coding Instructions
80-82	Q24	formal education	000 = some HS; 100 = HS grad; 010 = some coll.; 001 = coll. grad.
83-86	Q23	address	0000 = NE US 1000 = SE US 0100 = Midwest US 0010 = Western US 0001 = Non-US
87-91	Q26	income	00000 = $10,000 or less 10000 = $10,001–30,000 01000 = $30,001–50,000 00100 = $50,001–90,000 00010 = $90,001–150,000 00001 = $150,001–or more

PREFACE TO DATA FILE EXTRACTS

One page of each data file is included in order to show how the data would look to the data entry person. Checking variables' column locations on these extracts must be done to ensure that data is not being misinterpreted during the analysis of computer runs. The data file must correspond with the coding sheet.

GUCCI

Filename - GCNEW.DAT

```
1
0999999999999999999999910003322333212332232423112132222625333245411400000001
100100010001000
2
1000099999999999999999991000111143453445414674545132465353336774325310100000
000001100010000
3
1101156357435432542321111543465677565357545551322322116533465324010000
001010010000100
4
1000172512767755225561000332332353434323654535132213727343154426300000010
100100010001000
5
1101175767777666456461111554464755546637654665132323332213236644500000001
001010010000100
6
0999999999999999999999910003333313323234244524532133346463334444262630000100
100100010001000
```

7
110114555776545555535111155446567765365367646451322122213231365435000010 0
001010010000100
8
110117252275764411474100033337576676772775677631232354533334331420000001
100100010001000
9
110117666777766556261111543465564456534544644213212323323146644500000001
001010010000100
10
101117656765764354434111055455656777654574765631263627244344664451000100
010001001000010
11
110117655776775555525111143236677736763735575221332233233323653350000001
001010010000100
12
110117372377766621666100044446476554772776577631222252533334321320000001
100100010001000
13
110115253476655523555100011116647756732375672513211141343314552241000001
100100010001000

Note: There are two SPSS data files for Case 4.2. One is a full file that contains all the variables. This file cannot be run on the student version because the number of variables exceeds 50. The other file is a data file for the student version of SPSS. In the student version, questions 14, 15, 16, 17, 18, and 19 in the Gucci questionnaire have not been coded to keep the number of variables below 50.

COMPREHENSIVE VIDEO CASES

VIDEO CASE 4.1 ■ "THE PRICE IS RIGHT" FOR BOJANGLES'

Bojangles' is a regional southeastern restaurant chain, headquartered in Charlotte, North Carolina. Bojangles' has a distinctive menu built by two restaurant veterans. The restaurants are known for their breakfast biscuits and core Cajun and Southern-style chicken. The firm currently has 156 company-owned stores and 114 franchised units. There are some distinctive characteristics of Bojangles': Cajun-style products, high quality, made-from-scratch products, and a fun atmosphere. Bojangles' relies on marketing research to determine many key functions of its business strategy, operation, and profitability.

Pricing is one of the most unappreciated but key elements to profitability. Pricing decisions often directly influence the demand curve. The demand influence is dependent on the type of goods. Price is influenced by demand, product quality, promotion, price elasticity, and consumer perception. Bojangles' product attributes differentiate its products from competitors through distinct taste, high quality, and unique environment.

While important, product does not protect the restaurant chain from dealing with price elasticity of demand. Bojangles' uses marketing research to determine where to set the price of their products. By researching the competition, the company can make appropriate price changes. Bojangles' competition is all the other fast-food restaurants in the industry.

Promotions are also important as consumer perception affects the prices consumers are willing to pay. The more service and distinctiveness, the higher the price can be. Extensive marketing research must be conducted in order to determine which promotions will appeal to Bojangles' customers. Through marketing research, management has been able to provide effective promotions and the high-quality products consumers want. By studying past promotions that resulted either in success or failure, Bojangles' has a good idea of which promotional methods are best suited for their company. Various elements of business such as service, facilities, staffing, product quality, and uniqueness all affect the price of a product. By using marketing research, Bojangles' can improve these elements of their business and create a successful business strategy.

A significant pricing issue for Bojangles' was whether to pursue combo pricing. Combo pricing deals with the price point, which is usually 10 to 15 percent below what the individual elements would cost if purchased separately. The company heavily invested in marketing research to decide whether combo pricing would be a success or a flop. Bojangles' had to study its customer buying habits to see if customers wanted side items and a drink included with their meal or if they just wanted certain items a la carte. With the help of marketing research, management chose combo pricing, which has led to significant sales growth and profitability for the company.

In 2000, Bojangles' focused on introducing more portable foods, especially sandwiches and a reformulated nuggets recipe. Bojangles' decided on these new introductions by using marketing research to attract more customers, stay at par with other competitors, and ultimately increase profitability. In addition, the chain has had success with both fried chicken and Carolina-style barbecued pork sandwiches, which are a departure from its core menu. "We're repositioning to be more relevant to lunch, as well as dinner, with our sandwiches," said Tom Hesskamp, Bojangles' vice president for strategic planning, who expected to add 30 new franchised restaurants by the end of 2000 in the chain's fast-growing southeastern markets.

New advertising in 2000 increased the focus on meals with "good food photography both for point-of-purchase and TV," said senior vice president of marketing Randy Poindexter. "The food-quality image has always been very important. It's been Bojangles' strength." The chain spends about $6.5 million on advertising. Although it tends to use more broadcast media than print, Poindexter said Bojangles' would become more aggressive with print campaigns in the year 2001 and beyond.

QUESTIONS

1. Discuss the role that marketing research can play in helping a fast-food restaurant such as Bojangles' formulate sound marketing strategies.
2. Bojangles' is considering further expansion in the Southeast. Define the management decision problem.
3. Define an appropriate marketing research problem based on the management decision problem you have identified.
4. Use the Internet to determine the market shares of the major fast-food national chains for the last calendar year.
5. What type of syndicate data will be useful to Bojangles'?
6. Discuss the role of qualitative research in helping Bojangles' expand further in the Southeast.
7. Bojangles' has developed a new fish sandwich with a distinctive Cajun taste. It would like to determine consumers' response to this new sandwich before introducing it in the marketplace. If a survey is to be conducted to determine consumer preferences, which survey method should be used and why?
8. Develop a questionnaire for assessing consumer preferences for fast-food restaurants.
9. What sampling plan should be adopted for the survey of question 7?
10. According to Bojangles' vice president of marketing, Randy Poindexter, product quality, price, service, facilities, staffing, and uniqueness are all independent variables that affect the preference for a fast-food restaurant. Assume that in a survey of fast-food restaurants, each of the independent variables is measured on a seven-point scale with 1 = poor, and 7 = excellent. Preference for fast-food restaurants is also measured on a seven-point scale with 1 = not at all preferred, and 7 = greatly preferred. Each respondent rates Bojangles' and three competing restaurants on all the independent variables as well as preference to eat there. What statistical technique(s) would you use to answer the following questions:
    a. Is preference related to each of the independent variables considered individually? What is the nature of the relationship you expect?
    b. Is preference related to all the independent variables considered simultaneously?
    c. Do the respondents evaluate the fast-food restaurants more favorably on product quality than they do on price?

d. The sample is divided into two groups: regular patrons of Bojangles' and patrons of other restaurants. Do these two groups differ in terms of their ratings of Bojangles' on product quality?

e. The sample is divided in three groups: heavy, medium, and light users of fast-food restaurants. Do the three groups differ in terms of preference for Bojangles'?

11. If marketing research to determine consumer preferences for fast foods was to be conducted in Latin America, how would the research process be different?

12. Discuss the ethical issues involved in researching consumer preferences for fast foods.

REFERENCES

1. www.bojangles.com/.

2. Gregg Cebrzynski, "Bojangles' 'Basic' Strategy Fuels Same-Store Sales Growth," *Nation's Restaurant News,* 33(48) (November 29, 1999): 8.

3. Carolyn Walkup, "2nd 100's Chicken Flock Seeks to Feather Nest with Convenience," *Nation's Restaurant News,* 34(30) (July 24, 2000): 98.

VIDEO CASE 4.2 ■ MTV: AN AMERICAN INSTITUTION?

MTV was born on August 1, 1981, and immediately got the reputation as being "unpredictable and irreverent." It imitated the cutting edge of rock and roll with its graphic look, young scantly dressed video jockeys or VJs, continuous music news, rockumentaries (short movies on rock stars), original programming, and seemingly endless lines of less than censored music videos. Its programming consisted of what young people were interested in—sports, movies, music news, news from a different perspective, and specials. It became an American Institution—a cultural monolith.

MTV knew that the United States was the leading world exporter of entertainment, and when cable growth began to slow in the United States, MTV moved into the international market, debuting in Australia in 1987. Surprisingly, MTV has more viewers in Europe than in the United States. It has been hailed as the ultimate new-generation multinational and is seen in more than 256 million homes in 64 countries. Through marketing research, MTV produces a single global brand with customized local programming, although this strategy costs more, takes longer, and is harder to produce. Marketing research shows that programming must be localized to bond with viewers and for MTV to remain successful and popular among viewers.

MTV has six affiliates: MTV Europe (Pan-European and in English, with 40 percent of videos not in English); MTV Latino (from Miami and aimed at the U.S. Hispanic population and Latin and South American countries); MTV Brazil (in Portuguese); MTV Asia (which reaches 30 countries in English and Mandarin); and MTV Japan (which is customized for Japanese youth). Each MTV network is tailored to its audience.

While there are standardized shows, they are frequently dubbed with the local language and presented from the local point of view, although the footage may have been sent from the United States. To localize, MTV stations use local artists and videos, yet the mix and the programming is constantly changing. MTV uses marketing research to create new shows to appeal specifically to an international audience.

At the end, the video asks if this is the homogenization of youth internationally—whether they are losing their cultural identity. Comments from the VP of International Operations indicate that each MTV affiliate has its own style. MTV Brazil is very rock oriented, whereas MTV Europe is more pop, and MTV Asia is very glossy and stylish. Marketing research is conducted to determine which style is best suited for the youth segment in different countries. Failure to conduct such marketing research would result in a huge flop for that particular affiliate and could potentially discredit MTV. So, maybe the youth are not being exposed to such a standardized product, after all. But what will it be like in 10 years?

MTV faces increasing competition from local music channels. MTV's attitude is that competition is good and so much is changing so quickly that competition has a hard time keeping up, let alone surpassing them. With continuous changes in the market, it is very critical that MTV continuously conducts marketing research. Marketing research can help MTV discover what it is that attracts people to view its channel and what can be done to draw more viewers. The public opinion can also lead to the birth of new programming or possibly a completely new channel. MTV must also conduct marketing research in order to stay aware of what music is popular in its different markets so it can provide the music that people want to hear. The majority of MTV's new ideas come from its viewers, and it will be these viewers that will continuously shape MTV for the next generation.

QUESTIONS

1. Discuss the role of marketing research in determining the preferences of youth for television channels.

2. While expanding abroad, MTV wants to remain strong in the U.S. domestic market and would like to further increase its presence in this market. Define the management decision problem.

3. Define an appropriate marketing research problem based on the management decision problem you have identified.

4. What type of secondary data would be useful to MTV? What are the possible sources of such data?

5. Discuss the role of qualitative research in determining the preferences of youth for television channels? Which qualitative research technique(s) should be used and why?

6. If a survey is to be conducted to determine the preferences of youth for television channels, which survey method should be used and why?

7. Develop Likert, semantic differential, and Stapel scales for measuring preferences of youth for MTV.

8. Develop a sampling plan for the survey in question 6.

9. As mentioned in the case, youth's overall evaluation of a TV channel are determined by type of music (rock and roll, pop, etc.), appearance of VJs and stars, programming, movies, news (music, sports, etc.), and specials. Identify the dependent and the independent variables. In a global survey of youth, the respondents were asked to rate their overall evaluation of MTV as well as to rate the channel on the identified determining variables using seven-point scales, with 1 = poor, and 7 = excellent. What statistical techniques would you use to answer the following questions?

    a. Is the overall evaluation of MTV related to its evaluations on each of the independent variables?

    b. Is the overall evaluation of MTV related to its evaluations on all the independent variables considered simultaneously?

    c. Is the evaluation of MTV on type of music more favorable than its evaluation on programming? Formulate the null and alternative hypotheses and prescribe an appropriate statistical test.

    d. Do the youth in the United States and Europe differ in their overall evaluation of MTV? Formulate the null and alternative hypotheses and prescribe an appropriate statistical test.

    e. Do the youth in South America, North America, Europe, and Asia differ in their overall evaluation of MTV? Formulate the null and alternative hypotheses and prescribe an appropriate statistical test.

10. How should marketing research conducted for MTV in Asia be different from the research conducted in the United States?

11. Discuss the ethical issues involved in conducting research on youth.

REFERENCES

1. *www.mtv.com/*.

2. Karen Anderson Prikios, "MTV Networks Listens Up," *Broadcasting & Cable,* 131(12) (March 19, 2001): 68.

3. Anonymous, "MTV's Buzzworthy," *Adweek,* 42(11) (March 12, 2001): CT1.

VIDEO CASE 4.3 ■ NASCAR: DRIVING TO CONNECT WITH FANS

The National Association of Stock Car Auto Racing (NASCAR) is the second most popular sport in America, behind football, and has grown 65 percent over the last few years. The recent growth has been attributed to the ability of people to identify with the cars and drivers, the large corporate sponsorships and their involvement, consistent weekly races, tremendous regional and national exposure, and fan loyalty. Starting in the South from the dubious past, NASCAR now has a race every weekend of the year in some part of the United States. The France family, which largely controls the sport, has managed it into a product and a specific brand. NASCAR sees its role as helping its sponsors build their brand images and corporate sponsorships. NASCAR uses marketing research in many aspects of its business, and especially when determining which sponsors to chose.

Marketing objectives are key to making a sponsor and branding effort work. Sponsors need to understand their customers in using NASCAR as a branding vehicle. Licensing and promotions like the $30 million effort Coke made are two of the marketing programs NASCAR helps its sponsors develop and implement.

NASCAR views itself as a resource of information for sponsors that helps them better market their products and as a doorway to various venues, magazines, shows, television, online sites, and so on, to communicate with the public. A second way NASCAR helps its sponsors is by constantly updating their image, which automatically provides sponsors with new product images, enhancing repeat sales. Sponsors also benefit NASCAR by extending its reach through cooperative advertising.

A key element to NASCAR's marketing success has been its drivers. Marketing research shows that fans really connect with drivers, and this keeps the sport thriving. The drivers give back to both fans and sponsors through promotions, personal appearances, and marketing efforts. NASCAR gets 2,000 applications for a license each year and only about 50 are granted. One downside to NASCAR's success is the need to police the use of its trademarked name. It has to watch for misuse because of dilution of the brand name.

Despite all of this success, NASCAR will not expand into producing its own products. It will stay with endorsing other brands. Originally, licensing and branding tended to be of automotive products, but now it has spread to many nonautomotive product lines—games, Barbie dolls, and the like.

The NASCAR fan is one of the most devoted in all of sports. An important question is whether the devotion is to one man, one car, one team, or a single memory. The mourning of Dale Earnhardt's death in 2001 has been a tough time for NASCAR fans. The transition period for NASCAR will be very important. There will never be another Dale Earnhardt, but you can cling to the recollections only so long. There are many more races to be run. NASCAR needs to spend a little extra time researching the market so that it can understand what effects, if any, Earnhardt's death will have on its planned growth and how NASCAR can help strive to produce more drivers of his status.

QUESTIONS

1. Discuss the role that marketing research can play in helping NASCAR understand the devotion of fans to a particular sport.

2. In order to continue to grow, NASCAR must foster and build the loyalty of its fans. Define the management decision problem.

3. Define an appropriate marketing research problem based on the management decision problem you have identified.

4. In what way can NASCAR make use of Census 2000 data?

5. What type of data available from syndicate marketing research firms will be useful to NASCAR?

6. Discuss the role of qualitative research in understanding the devotion of fans to a particular sport. Which qualitative research technique(s) should be used and why?

7. If a survey is to be conducted to understand consumer preferences for various sports, which survey method should be used and why?

8. Design a questionnaire to measure consumers' evaluation of NASCAR.

9. Develop a sampling plan for the survey of question 7.

10. Qualitative research has indicated that the following factors influence the willingness of spectators to attend a sporting event (dependent variable): the extent to which an event is perceived as (1) entertaining, (2) exciting, (3) costly, (4) symbol of the American pastime, and (5) accessible and convenient to attend (independent variables). In a survey, consumers were asked to state their willingness to attend events sponsored by NASCAR, NBA, NFL, and NHL, using five-point scales with 1 = not at all willing, and 5 = very willing. The respondents were also asked to evaluate each of these sporting events on the

five independent variables, again using five-point scales with 1 = not at all, and 5 = very much. What statistical analyses will you perform to answer the following questions?

a. Is the willingness to attend a sporting event related to each of the five independent variables when the variables are considered individually?

b. Is the willingness to attend a sporting event related to all the five independent variables when the variables are considered simultaneously?

c. Do the respondents find NASCAR events more exciting than entertaining?

d. Are NFL events perceived as more of an American pastime than NASCAR events?

e. Do the evaluations of NASCAR on the five independent variables differ for those who have attended and those who have not attended a NASCAR event during the past year?

f. Are men more willing to attend NASCAR events than women?

g. Respondents were classified into four age groups: less than 25, 26 to 45, 46 to 65, and 66 or older. Do the four groups differ in their willingness to attend NASCAR events?

h. Willingness to attend NHL events was classified into three categories: unwilling (ratings of 1 and 2), neutral (rating of 3), and willing (ratings of 4 and 5). Do the four age groups of question g differ in their willingness to attend NHL events?

i. Do the never married, currently married, and divorced/separated/widowed groups differ in their willingness to attend NASCAR events?

j. Do the never married, currently married, and divorced/separated/widowed groups differ in their willingness to attend NHL events as classified in question h?

11. If NASCAR were to conduct marketing research to determine consumer preferences for auto racing events in Germany, how would the research process be different?

12. Discuss the ethical issues involved in researching consumer preferences for auto racing events.

REFERENCES

1. *www.nascar.com/.*
2. Stephanie Thompson, "Crash Affects Campaigns," *Advertising Age,* 72(9) (February 26, 2001): 4.
3. Laura Petrecca, "Nascar Sponsors Still On Track," *Advertising Age,* 72(9) (February 26, 2001): 4.

VIDEO CASE 4.4 ■ YAHOO!—THE NAME SAYS IT ALL

Yahoo! is a customized database designed to serve the needs of thousands of Internet users. Originating in 1994, Yahoo! is one of the first Internet entities to make a profit. Started by two techno-geeks as a hobby, Yahoo! averages an astounding 165 million hits a month. The name Yahoo! stands for "Yet Another Hierarchical Officious Oracle," but Yahoo!'s developers, Filo and Yang, insist they selected the name because they considered themselves yahoos. Yahoo! itself first resided on Yang's student workstation, "akebono" while the search engine was lodged on Filo's computer, "konishiki." (These machines were named after legendary Hawaiian sumo wrestlers.)

This case illustrates brand management and the strategy of dealing with competition. Yahoo!'s entire brand strategy is aimed at differentiating itself from its competitors and managing competition. Yahoo! used extensive marketing research to develop a successful brand strategy and to remain ahead of its competitors. The company developed new ways to grow, innovate, and create strategic brand marketing. Yahoo! used marketing research to determine consumers' preferences for Internet portals and search engines.

Marketing research showed that users want fun, easy-to-use, convenient, and accessible information and downloads from the Internet that are readily available. Therefore, Yahoo! positioned its strategy around these characteristics to provide consumers with exactly what they want. Basically, marketing research helped Yahoo! to better understand its customers and deliver quality services that would keep customers happy. By conducting marketing research and leveraging these consumer wants, Yahoo! felt it could become the first place a consumer goes to connect, buy, or communicate on the Internet. Marketing research helped Yahoo! to develop an easy, fun, convenient, and human brand, rather than a serious techy sort of brand. Management's thinking was that if consumers perceive Yahoo! to be fun, that will translate into easy, which translates into convenient. From their perspective, Yahoo! is a consumer brand that helps people do exactly what they want to do.

In order to remain ahead of competitors, Yahoo! differentiated its services. Yahoo!'s main competitors include AOL, Excite, Msn, GoTo, and NBCi. Yahoo! aimed at being a consumer brand. In order to please a wide range of users, Yahoo! offered consumers many different features. There are many factors that influence a consumer's selection of Internet portals. Consumers specifically choose Yahoo! as their Internet portal because its contents are presented in a fun and entertaining way and are different from competing, traditional technology portals whose information is presented in a rather bland fashion. Yahoo! uses bright colors to display its logo, and it also uses creative animations for different holidays. In addition, consumers choose Yahoo! because it is easy to use when looking for specified information. Yahoo! designed its search engines to display relevant information to users and allow those who have never used the Internet to search for information easily. Yahoo!'s name is another attraction for users, since it's a fun and easy-to-remember name. All these factors provided Yahoo! with a competitive edge.

Management wanted to give Yahoo! a sense of personality by creating an image as a consumer brand, a personality that's irreverent and a little offbeat, through their advertising. Breaking away from traditional technology companies, their ad campaigns are supported through kazoos, yoyos, T-shirts, surfer shirts, and the Yahoo! colors of yellow and purple. The friendly, fun commercials show that anyone can access the Internet through Yahoo!. Based on marketing research, Yahoo! discovered that ease of use and accessibility are very important to users. Yahoo! looks at its brand strategy as being the Safeway of the Internet, providing a wide variety of products and services. A fun commercial of a punk rocker knitting is shown to make this point.

Since users like a wide range of services, Yahoo! uses co-branding with companies like Amazon.com in order to offer more to consumers. To determine which companies Yahoo! should co-brand with, Yahoo! uses marketing research. This type of research provides Yahoo! with useful information about industries that consumers have an interest in, and which companies would be the best candidates to team up with. It is very important that Yahoo! chooses very well researched companies because it doesn't want to put its company brand name in danger by teaming up with a disreputable company. Yahoo! has brand partners, content partners, and distribution partners. In addition, marketing research must be carefully conducted on each type of Yahoo!'s partners. Yahoo! gives partners the opportunity to target very specific markets, from businesses to consumers. Yahoo! delved deeper into marketing research and discovered the need to target the youth segment, as well as adults. Therefore, Yahoo! developed Yahooligans (*www.yahooligans.com*), which is a Web site specifically aimed at attracting youth.

To expand markets, Yahoo! decided to go global and is now available in 15 countries. While many of the services and features of Yahoo! are the same around the globe, it also adapts its offerings to the local market. For example, local news, people, and events might be featured.

In an effort to attract new users, Yahoo! used marketing research to find a different avenue to target customers. Yahoo! turned to television advertising as part of this strategy. In addition, Yahoo! made some use of radio for targeted advertising, but television proved to be most beneficial. Yahoo!'s strategy is to reach the maximum audience by creating a consumer brand. The use of humor and silliness keeps Yahoo! from becoming too impressed with itself. Once users are comfortable with Yahoo!, the goal is to keep users at the site. Public relations is also an important element of Yahoo!'s communication strategy, but continues to carry the humor theme.

Yahoo! expects competition to remain tough and in fact become more difficult as it competes with new Internet portals. It can't outspend its larger competitors, so it has to keep its humor and zaniness working in the quality of the Yahoo! product. By continuing to use marketing research, Yahoo! can modify its strategies for branding, expanding its markets, attracting new users, keeping existing customers happy, and staying ahead of competitors.

QUESTIONS

1. Discuss the role that marketing research can play in helping Yahoo! formulate sound marketing strategies.

2. After the technology bear market of 2000 and 2001, the management would like to rebuild Yahoo!. They feel this can be best accomplished by increasing the market share of Yahoo!. Define the management decision problem.

3. Define an appropriate marketing research problem based on the management decision problem you have identified.

4. Use the Internet to determine the market shares of the major portals (AOL, Excite, Msn, GoTo, NBCi, and Yahoo!) for the last calendar year.

5. What type of syndicate data will be useful to Yahoo!?

6. Discuss the role of qualitative research in helping Yahoo! expand its market share.

7. If a survey is to be conducted to determine consumer preferences for Internet portals, which survey method should be used and why?

8. Develop a questionnaire for assessing consumer preferences for Internet portals.

9. What sampling plan should be adopted for the survey of question 7?

10. Exploratory research indicates that, fun, easy-to-use, convenient, accessible, human, and rich in content are all independent variables that affect the preference for Internet portals. Assume that in a survey of Internet portals, each of

the independent variables is measured on a seven-point scale with 1 = poor, and 7 = excellent. Preference for Internet portals is also measured on a seven-point scale with 1 = not at all preferred, and 7 = greatly preferred. Each respondent rates Yahoo! and three competing portals on all the independent variables as well as preference to use the portal. What statistical technique(s) would you use to answer the following questions?

   a. Is preference related to each of the independent variables considered individually? What is the nature of the relationship you expect?

   b. Is preference related to all the independent variables considered simultaneously?

   c. Do the respondents evaluate Yahoo! more favorably on ease of use than they do on fun?

   d. The sample is divided into two groups: regular users of Yahoo! and users of other portals. Do these two groups differ in terms of their ratings of Yahoo! on rich in content?

   e. The sample is divided in three groups: heavy, medium, and light users of the Internet. Do the three groups differ in terms of preference for Yahoo!?

11. Consider again the survey mentioned in question 10. However, suppose that the preference for Internet portals was measured using a categorical scale consisting of three categories: disliked, neutral, and liked. The independent variables were also measured using a categorical scale consisting of three categories: poor, neutral, and good. Which statistical technique(s) will you use to determine whether preference for Internet portals is associated individually with each of the six independent variables.

12. Consider again the survey mentioned in question 10. Suppose that preference for Internet portals was measured using the seven-point scale of question 10 but the six independent variables were measured using a categorical scale consisting of three categories: poor, neutral, and good. Which statistical technique(s) will you use to determine whether preference for portals is associated individually with each of the six independent variables.

13. If Yahoo! were to conduct marketing research to determine consumer preferences for Internet portals in Europe, how would the research process be different?

14. Discuss the ethical issues involved in researching consumer preferences for Internet portals.

REFERENCES

1. *www.yahoo.com/*.
2. Louise Banbury, "Yahoo! Brand Hits Its Toughest Week," *Marketing* (March 15, 2001): 7.
3. Normandy Madden, "Economy Hampering Yahoo!'s Global Goals," *Advertising Age,* 72(11) (March 12, 2001).

APPENDIX

Statistical Tables

T A B L E 1   Simple Random Numbers

Line/Col.	(1)	(2)	(3)	(4)	(5)	(6)	(7)	(8)	(9)	(10)	(11)	(12)	(13)	(14)
1	10480	15011	01536	02011	81647	91646	69179	14194	62590	36207	20969	99570	91291	90700
2	22368	46573	25595	85393	30995	89198	27982	53402	93965	34095	52666	19174	39615	99505
3	24130	48390	22527	97265	76393	64809	15179	24830	49340	32081	30680	19655	63348	58629
4	42167	93093	06243	61680	07856	16376	39440	53537	71341	57004	00849	74917	97758	16379
5	37570	39975	81837	16656	06121	91782	60468	81305	49684	60072	14110	06927	01263	54613
6	77921	06907	11008	42751	27756	53498	18602	70659	90655	15053	21916	81825	44394	42880
7	99562	72905	56420	69994	98872	31016	71194	18738	44013	48840	63213	21069	10634	12952
8	96301	91977	05463	07972	18876	20922	94595	56869	69014	60045	18425	84903	42508	32307
9	89579	14342	63661	10281	17453	18103	57740	84378	25331	12568	58678	44947	05585	56941
10	85475	36857	53342	53988	53060	59533	38867	62300	08158	17983	16439	11458	18593	64952
11	28918	69578	88231	33276	70997	79936	56865	05859	90106	31595	01547	85590	91610	78188
12	63553	40961	48235	03427	49626	69445	18663	72695	52180	20847	12234	90511	33703	90322
13	09429	93969	52636	92737	88974	33488	36320	17617	30015	08272	84115	27156	30613	74952
14	10365	61129	87529	85689	48237	52267	67689	93394	01511	26358	85104	20285	29975	89868
15	07119	97336	71048	08178	77233	13916	47564	81056	97735	85977	29372	74461	28551	90707
16	51085	12765	51821	51259	77452	16308	60756	92144	49442	53900	70960	63990	75601	40719
17	02368	21382	52404	60268	89368	19885	55322	44819	01188	65255	64835	44919	05944	55157
18	01011	54092	33362	94904	31273	04146	18594	29852	71685	85030	51132	01915	92747	64951
19	52162	53916	46369	58586	23216	14513	83149	98736	23495	64350	94738	17752	35156	35749
20	07056	97628	33787	09998	42698	06691	76988	13602	51851	46104	88916	19509	25625	58104
21	48663	91245	85828	14346	09172	30163	90229	04734	59193	22178	30421	61666	99904	32812
22	54164	58492	22421	74103	47070	25306	76468	26384	58151	06646	21524	15227	96909	44592
23	32639	32363	05597	24200	13363	38005	94342	28728	35806	06912	17012	64161	18296	22851
24	29334	27001	87637	87308	58731	00256	45834	15398	46557	41135	10307	07684	36188	18510
25	02488	33062	28834	07351	19731	92420	60952	61280	50001	67658	32586	86679	50720	94953
26	81525	72295	04839	96423	24878	82651	66566	14778	76797	14780	13300	87074	79666	95725
27	29676	20591	68086	26432	46901	20849	89768	81536	86645	12659	92259	57102	80428	25280
28	00742	57392	39064	66432	84673	40027	32832	61362	98947	96067	64760	64584	96096	98253
29	05366	04213	25669	26422	44407	44048	37937	63904	45766	66134	75470	66520	34693	90449
30	91921	26418	64117	94305	26766	25940	39972	22209	71500	64568	91402	42416	07844	69618
31	00582	04711	87917	77341	42206	35126	74087	99547	81817	42607	43808	76655	62028	76630
32	00725	69884	62797	56170	86324	88072	76222	36086	84637	93161	76038	65855	77919	88006
33	69011	65795	95876	55293	18988	27354	26575	08625	40801	59920	29841	80150	12777	48501

(continues)

T A B L E 1 (continued)

Line/Col.	(1)	(2)	(3)	(4)	(5)	(6)	(7)	(8)	(9)	(10)	(11)	(12)	(13)	(14)
34	25976	57948	29888	88604	67917	48708	18912	82271	65424	69774	33611	54262	85963	03547
35	09763	83473	73577	12908	30883	18317	28290	35797	05998	41688	34952	37888	38917	88050
36	91567	42595	27958	30134	04024	86385	29880	99730	55536	84855	29088	09250	79656	73211
37	17955	56349	90999	49127	20044	59931	06115	20542	18059	02008	73708	83517	36103	42791
38	46503	18584	18845	49618	02304	51038	20655	58727	28168	15475	56942	53389	20562	87338
39	92157	89634	94824	78171	84610	82834	09922	25417	44137	48413	25555	21246	35509	20468
40	14577	62765	35605	81263	39667	47358	56873	56307	61607	49518	89656	20103	77490	18062
41	98427	07523	33362	64270	01638	92477	66969	98420	04880	45585	46565	04102	46880	45709
42	34914	63976	88720	82765	34476	17032	87589	40836	32427	70002	70663	88863	77775	69348
43	70060	28277	39475	46473	23219	53416	94970	25832	69975	94884	19661	72828	00102	66794
44	53976	54914	06990	67245	68350	82948	11398	42878	80287	88267	47363	46634	06541	97809
45	76072	29515	40980	07391	58745	25774	22987	80059	39911	96189	41151	14222	60697	59583
46	90725	52210	83974	29992	65831	38857	50490	83765	55657	14361	31720	57375	56228	41546
47	64364	67412	33339	31926	14883	24413	59744	92351	97473	89286	35931	04110	23726	51900
48	08962	00358	31662	25388	61642	34072	81249	35648	56891	69352	48373	45578	78547	81788
49	95012	68379	93526	70765	10592	04542	76463	54328	02349	17247	28865	14777	62730	92277
50	15664	10493	20492	38301	91132	21999	59516	81652	27195	48223	46751	22923	32261	85653
51	16408	81899	04153	53381	79401	21438	83035	92350	36693	31238	59649	91754	72772	02338
52	18629	81953	05520	91962	04739	13092	97662	24822	94730	06496	35090	04822	86774	98289
53	73115	35101	47498	87637	99016	71060	88824	71013	18735	20286	23153	72924	35165	43040
54	57491	16703	23167	49323	45021	33132	12544	41035	80780	45393	44812	12515	98931	91202
55	30405	83946	23792	14422	15059	45799	22716	19792	09983	74353	68668	30429	70735	25499
56	16631	35006	85900	98275	32388	52390	16815	69293	82732	38480	73817	32523	41961	44437
57	96773	20206	42559	78985	05300	22164	24369	54224	35083	19687	11052	91491	60383	19746
58	38935	64202	14349	82674	66523	44133	00697	35552	35970	19124	63318	29686	03387	59846
59	31624	76384	17403	53363	44167	64486	64758	75366	76554	31601	12614	33072	60332	92325
60	78919	19474	23632	27889	47914	02584	37680	20801	72152	39339	34806	08930	85001	87820
61	03931	33309	57047	74211	63445	17361	62825	39908	05607	91284	68833	25570	38818	46920
62	74426	33278	43972	10119	89917	15665	52872	73823	73144	88662	88970	74492	51805	99378
63	09066	00903	20795	95452	92648	45454	69552	88815	16553	51125	79375	97596	16296	66092
64	42238	12426	87025	14267	20979	04508	64535	31355	86064	29472	47689	05974	52468	16834
65	16153	08002	26504	41744	81959	65642	74240	56302	00033	67107	77510	70625	28725	34191
66	21457	40742	29820	96783	29400	21840	15035	34537	33310	06116	95240	15957	16572	06004
67	21581	57802	02050	89728	17937	37621	47075	42080	97403	48626	68995	43805	33386	21597
68	55612	78095	83197	33732	05810	24813	86902	60397	16489	03264	88525	42786	05269	92532
69	44657	66999	99324	51281	84463	60563	79312	93454	68876	25471	93911	25650	12682	73572
70	91340	84979	46949	81973	37949	61023	43997	15263	80644	43942	89203	71795	99533	50501
71	91227	21199	31935	27022	84067	05462	35216	14486	29891	68607	41867	14951	91696	85065
72	50001	38140	66321	19924	72163	09538	12151	06878	91903	18749	34405	56087	82790	70925
73	65390	05224	72958	28609	81406	39147	25549	48542	42627	45233	57202	94617	23772	07896
74	27504	96131	83944	41575	10573	03619	64482	73923	36152	05184	94142	25299	94387	34925
75	37169	94851	39117	89632	00959	16487	65536	49071	39782	17095	02330	74301	00275	48280
76	11508	70225	51111	38351	19444	66499	71945	05422	13442	78675	84031	66938	93654	59894
77	37449	30362	06694	54690	04052	53115	62757	95348	78662	11163	81651	50245	34971	52974
78	46515	70331	85922	38329	57015	15765	97161	17869	45349	61796	66345	81073	49106	79860
79	30986	81223	42416	58353	21532	30502	32305	86482	05174	07901	54339	58861	74818	46942
80	63798	64995	46583	09785	44160	78128	83991	42865	92520	83531	80377	35909	81250	54238
81	82486	84846	99254	67632	43218	50076	21361	64816	51202	88124	41870	52689	51275	83556
82	21885	32906	92431	09060	64297	51674	64126	62570	26123	05155	59194	52799	28225	85762

(continues)

T A B L E   1   (**continued**)

Line/Col.	(1)	(2)	(3)	(4)	(5)	(6)	(7)	(8)	(9)	(10)	(11)	(12)	(13)	(14)
83	60336	98782	07408	53458	13564	59089	26445	29789	85205	41001	12535	12133	14645	23541
84	43937	46891	24010	25560	86355	33941	25786	54990	71899	15475	95434	98227	21824	19535
85	97656	63175	89303	16275	07100	92063	21942	18611	47348	20203	18534	03862	78095	50136
86	03299	01221	05418	38982	55758	92237	26759	86367	21216	98442	08303	56613	91511	75928
87	79626	06486	03574	17668	07785	76020	79924	25651	83325	88428	85076	72811	22717	50585
88	85636	68335	47539	03129	65651	11977	02510	26113	99447	68645	34327	15152	55230	93448
89	18039	14367	61337	06177	12143	46609	32989	74014	64708	00533	35398	58408	13261	47908
90	08362	15656	60627	36478	65648	16764	53412	09013	07832	41574	17639	82163	60859	75567
91	79556	29068	04142	16268	15387	12856	66227	38358	22478	73373	88732	09443	82558	05250
92	92608	82674	27072	32534	17075	27698	98204	63863	11951	34648	88022	56148	34925	57031
93	23982	25835	40055	67006	12293	02753	14827	23235	35071	99704	37543	11601	35503	85171
94	09915	96306	05908	97901	28395	14186	00821	80703	70426	75647	76310	88717	37890	40129
95	59037	33300	26695	62247	69927	76123	50842	43834	86654	70959	79725	93872	28117	19233
96	42488	78077	69882	61657	34136	79180	97526	43092	04098	73571	80799	76536	71255	64239
97	46764	86273	63003	93017	31204	36692	40202	35275	57306	55543	53203	18098	47625	88684
98	03237	45430	55417	63282	90816	17349	88298	90183	36600	78406	06216	95787	42579	90730
99	86591	81482	52667	61582	14972	90053	89534	76036	49199	43716	97548	04379	46370	28672
100	38534	01715	94964	87288	65680	43772	39560	12918	80537	62738	19636	51132	25739	56947

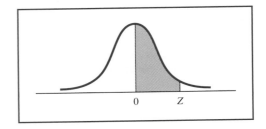

TABLE 2   Area Under the Normal Curve

Z	.00	.01	.02	.03	.04	.05	.06	.07	.08	.09
0.0	.0000	.0040	.0080	.0120	.0160	.0199	.0239	.0279	.0319	.0359
0.1	.0398	.0438	.0478	.0517	.0557	.0596	.0636	.0675	.0714	.0753
0.2	.0793	.0832	.0871	.0910	.0948	.0987	.1026	.1064	.1103	.1141
0.3	.1179	.1217	.1255	.1293	.1331	.1368	.1406	.1443	.1480	.1517
0.4	.1554	.1591	.1628	.1664	.1700	.1736	.1772	.1808	.1844	.1879
0.5	.1915	.1950	.1985	.2019	.2054	.2088	.2123	.2157	.2190	.2224
0.6	.2257	.2291	.2324	.2357	.2389	.2422	.2454	.2486	.2518	.2549
0.7	.2580	.2612	.2642	.2673	.2704	.2734	.2764	.2794	.2823	.2852
0.8	.2881	.2910	.2939	.2967	.2995	.3023	.3051	.3078	.3106	.3133
0.9	.3159	.3186	.3212	.3238	.3264	.3289	.3315	.3340	.3365	.3389
1.0	.3413	.3438	.3461	.3485	.3508	.3531	.3554	.3577	.3599	.3621
1.1	.3643	.3665	.3686	.3708	.3729	.3749	.3770	.3790	.3810	.3830
1.2	.3849	.3869	.3888	.3907	.3925	.3944	.3962	.3980	.3997	.4015
1.3	.4032	.4049	.4066	.4082	.4099	.4115	.4131	.4147	.4162	.4177
1.4	.4192	.4207	.4222	.4236	.4251	.4265	.4279	.4292	.4306	.4319
1.5	.4332	.4345	.4357	.4370	.4382	.4394	.4406	.4418	.4429	.4441
1.6	.4452	.4463	.4474	.4484	.4495	.4505	.4515	.4525	.4535	.4545
1.7	.4554	.4564	.4573	.4582	.4591	.4599	.4608	.4616	.4625	.4633
1.8	.4641	.4649	.4656	.4664	.4671	.4678	.4686	.4693	.4699	.4706
1.9	.4713	.4719	.4726	.4732	.4738	.4744	.4750	.4756	.4761	.4767
2.0	.4772	.4778	.4783	.4788	.4793	.4798	.4803	.4808	.4812	.4817
2.1	.4821	.4826	.4830	.4834	.4838	.4842	.4846	.4850	.4854	.4857
2.2	.4861	.4864	.4868	.4871	.4875	.4878	.4881	.4884	.4887	.4890
2.3	.4893	.4896	.4898	.4901	.4904	.4906	.4909	.4911	.4913	.4916
2.4	.4918	.4920	.4922	.4925	.4927	.4929	.4931	.4932	.4934	.4936
2.5	.4938	.4940	.4941	.4943	.4945	.4946	.4948	.4949	.4951	.4952
2.6	.4953	.4955	.4956	.4957	.4959	.4960	.4961	.4962	.4963	.4964
2.7	.4965	.4966	.4967	.4968	.4969	.4970	.4971	.4972	.4973	.4974
2.8	.4974	.4975	.4976	.4977	.4977	.4978	.4979	.4979	.4980	.4981
2.9	.4981	.4982	.4982	.4983	.4984	.4984	.4985	.4985	.4986	.4986
3.0	.49865	.49869	.49874	.49878	.49882	.49886	.49889	.49893	.49897	.49900
3.1	.49903	.49906	.49910	.49913	.49916	.49918	.49921	.49924	.49926	.49929
3.2	.49931	.49934	.49936	.49938	.49940	.49942	.49944	.49946	.49948	.49950
3.3	.49952	.49953	.49955	.49957	.49958	.49960	.49961	.49962	.49964	.49965
3.4	.49966	.49968	.49969	.49970	.49971	.49972	.49973	.49974	.49975	.49976
3.5	.49977	.49978	.49978	.49979	.49980	.49981	.49981	.49982	.49983	.49983
3.6	.49984	.49985	.49985	.49986	.49986	.49987	.49987	.49988	.49988	.49989
3.7	.49989	.49990	.49990	.49990	.49991	.49991	.49992	.49992	.49992	.49992
3.8	.49993	.49993	.49993	.49994	.49994	.49994	.49994	.49995	.49995	.49995
3.9	.49995	.49995	.49996	.49996	.49996	.49996	.49996	.49996	.49997	.49997

Entry represents area under the standard normal distribution from the mean to Z.

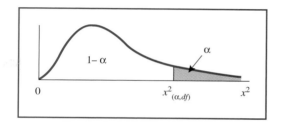

TABLE 3   Chi-Square Distribution

Degrees of Freedom	Upper Tail Areas (α)											
	.995	.99	.975	.95	.90	.75	.25	.10	.05	.025	.01	.005
1			0.001	0.004	0.016	0.102	1.323	2.706	3.841	5.024	6.635	7.879
2	0.010	0.020	0.051	0.103	0.211	0.575	2.773	4.605	5.991	7.378	9.210	10.597
3	0.072	0.115	0.216	0.352	0.584	1.213	4.108	6.251	7.815	9.348	11.345	12.838
4	0.207	0.297	0.484	0.711	1.064	1.923	5.385	7.779	9.488	11.143	13.277	14.860
5	0.412	0.554	0.831	1.145	1.610	2.675	6.626	9.236	11.071	12.833	15.086	16.750
6	0.676	0.872	1.237	1.635	2.204	3.455	7.841	10.645	12.592	14.449	16.812	18.548
7	0.989	1.239	1.690	2.167	2.833	4.255	9.037	12.017	14.067	16.013	18.475	20.278
8	1.344	1.646	2.180	2.733	3.490	5.071	10.219	13.362	15.507	17.535	20.090	21.955
9	1.735	2.088	2.700	3.325	4.168	5.899	11.389	14.684	16.919	19.023	21.666	23.589
10	2.156	2.558	3.247	3.940	4.865	6.737	12.549	15.987	18.307	20.483	23.209	25.188
11	2.603	3.053	3.816	4.575	5.578	7.584	13.701	17.275	19.675	21.920	24.725	26.757
12	3.074	3.571	4.404	5.226	6.304	8.438	14.845	18.549	21.026	23.337	26.217	28.299
13	3.565	4.107	5.009	5.892	7.042	9.299	15.984	19.812	22.362	24.736	27.688	29.819
14	4.075	4.660	5.629	6.571	7.790	10.165	17.117	21.064	23.685	26.119	29.141	31.319
15	4.601	5.229	6.262	7.261	8.547	11.037	18.245	22.307	24.996	27.488	30.578	32.801
16	5.142	5.812	6.908	7.962	9.312	11.912	19.369	23.542	26.296	28.845	32.000	34.267
17	5.697	6.408	7.564	8.672	10.085	12.792	20.489	24.769	27.587	30.191	33.409	35.718
18	6.265	7.015	8.231	9.390	10.865	13.675	21.605	25.989	28.869	31.526	34.805	37.156
19	6.844	7.633	8.907	10.117	11.651	14.562	22.718	27.204	30.144	32.852	36.191	38.582
20	7.434	8.260	9.591	10.851	12.443	15.452	23.828	28.412	31.410	34.170	37.566	39.997
21	8.034	8.897	10.283	11.591	13.240	16.344	24.935	29.615	32.671	35.479	38.932	41.401
22	8.643	9.542	10.982	12.338	14.042	17.240	26.039	30.813	33.924	36.781	40.289	42.796
23	9.260	10.196	11.689	13.091	14.848	18.137	27.141	32.007	35.172	38.076	41.638	44.181
24	9.886	10.856	12.401	13.848	15.659	19.037	28.241	33.196	36.415	39.364	42.980	45.559
25	10.520	11.524	13.120	14.611	16.473	19.939	29.339	34.382	37.652	40.646	44.314	46.928
26	11.160	12.198	13.844	15.379	17.292	20.843	30.435	35.563	38.885	41.923	45.642	48.290
27	11.808	12.879	14.573	16.151	18.114	21.749	31.528	36.741	40.113	43.194	46.963	49.645
28	12.461	13.565	15.308	16.928	18.939	22.657	32.620	37.916	41.337	44.461	48.278	50.993
29	13.121	14.257	16.047	17.708	19.768	23.567	33.711	39.087	42.557	45.722	49.588	52.336
30	13.787	14.954	16.791	18.493	20.599	24.478	34.800	40.256	43.773	46.979	50.892	53.672
31	14.458	15.655	17.539	19.281	21.434	25.390	35.887	41.422	44.985	48.232	52.191	55.003
32	15.134	16.362	18.291	20.072	22.271	26.304	36.973	42.585	46.194	49.480	53.486	56.328
33	15.815	17.074	19.047	20.867	23.110	27.219	38.058	43.745	47.400	50.725	54.776	57.648
34	16.501	17.789	19.806	21.664	23.952	28.136	39.141	44.903	48.602	51.966	56.061	58.964
35	17.192	18.509	20.569	22.465	24.797	29.054	40.223	46.059	49.802	53.203	57.342	60.275
36	17.887	19.233	21.336	23.269	25.643	29.973	41.304	47.212	50.998	54.437	58.619	61.581
37	18.586	19.960	22.106	24.075	26.492	30.893	42.383	48.363	52.192	55.668	59.892	62.883
38	19.289	20.691	22.878	24.884	27.343	31.815	43.462	49.513	53.384	56.896	61.162	64.181

(continues)

TABLE 3 (continued)

Degrees of Freedom	Upper Tail Areas (α)											
	.995	.99	.975	.95	.90	.75	.25	.10	.05	.025	.01	.005
39	19.996	21.426	23.654	25.695	28.196	32.737	44.539	50.660	54.572	58.120	62.428	65.476
40	20.707	22.164	24.433	26.509	29.051	33.660	45.616	51.805	55.758	59.342	63.691	66.766
41	21.421	22.906	25.215	27.326	29.907	34.585	46.692	52.949	56.942	60.561	64.950	68.053
42	22.138	23.650	25.999	28.144	30.765	35.510	47.766	54.090	58.124	61.777	66.206	69.336
43	22.859	24.398	26.785	28.965	31.625	36.436	48.840	55.230	59.304	62.990	67.459	70.616
44	23.584	25.148	27.575	29.787	32.487	37.363	49.913	56.369	60.481	64.201	68.710	71.893
45	24.311	25.901	28.366	30.612	33.350	38.291	50.985	57.505	61.656	65.410	69.957	73.166
46	25.041	26.657	29.160	31.439	34.215	39.220	52.056	58.641	62.830	66.617	71.201	74.437
47	25.775	27.416	29.956	32.268	35.081	40.149	53.127	59.774	64.001	67.821	72.443	75.704
48	26.511	28.177	30.755	33.098	35.949	41.079	54.196	60.907	65.171	69.023	73.683	76.969
49	27.249	28.941	31.555	33.930	36.818	42.010	55.265	62.038	66.339	70.222	74.919	78.231
50	27.991	29.707	32.357	34.764	37.689	42.942	56.334	63.167	67.505	71.420	76.154	79.490
51	28.735	30.475	33.162	35.600	38.560	43.874	57.401	64.295	68.669	72.616	77.386	80.747
52	29.481	31.246	33.968	36.437	39.433	44.808	58.468	65.422	69.832	73.810	78.616	82.001
53	30.230	32.018	34.776	37.276	40.308	45.741	59.534	66.548	70.993	75.002	79.843	83.253
54	30.981	32.793	35.586	38.116	41.183	46.676	60.600	67.673	72.153	76.192	81.069	84.502
55	31.735	33.570	36.398	38.958	42.060	47.610	61.665	68.796	73.311	77.380	82.292	85.749
56	32.490	34.350	37.212	39.801	42.937	48.546	62.729	69.919	74.468	78.567	83.513	86.994
57	33.248	35.131	38.027	40.646	43.816	49.482	63.793	71.040	75.624	79.752	84.733	88.236
58	34.008	35.913	38.844	41.492	44.696	50.419	64.857	72.160	76.778	80.936	85.950	89.477
59	34.770	36.698	39.662	42.339	45.577	51.356	65.919	73.279	77.931	82.117	87.166	90.715
60	35.534	37.485	40.482	43.188	46.459	52.294	66.981	74.397	79.082	83.298	88.379	91.952

For a particular number of degrees of freedom, entry represents the critical value of χ^2 corresponding to a specified upper tail area, α.

For larger values of degrees of freedom (DF) the expression $z = \sqrt{2\chi^2} - \sqrt{2(DF) - 1}$ may be used and the resulting upper tail area can be obtained from the table of the standardized normal distribution.

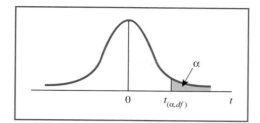

TABLE 4   *t* Distribution

Degrees of Freedom	Upper Tail Areas					
	.25	.10	.05	.025	.01	.005
1	1.0000	3.0777	6.3138	12.7062	31.8207	63.6574
2	0.8165	1.8856	2.9200	4.3027	6.9646	9.9248
3	0.7649	1.6377	2.3534	3.1824	4.5407	5.8409
4	0.7407	1.5332	2.1318	2.7764	3.7469	4.6041
5	0.7267	1.4759	2.0150	2.5706	3.3649	4.0322
6	0.7176	1.4398	1.9432	2.4469	3.1427	3.7074
7	0.7111	1.4149	1.8946	2.3646	2.9980	3.4995
8	0.7064	1.3968	1.8595	2.3060	2.8965	3.3554
9	0.7027	1.3830	1.8331	2.2622	2.8214	3.2498
10	0.6998	1.3722	1.8125	2.2281	2.7638	3.1693
11	0.6974	1.3634	1.7959	2.2010	2.7181	3.1058
12	0.6955	1.3562	1.7823	2.1788	2.6810	3.0545
13	0.6938	1.3502	1.7709	2.1604	2.6503	3.0123
14	0.6924	1.3450	1.7613	2.1448	2.6245	2.9768
15	0.6912	1.3406	1.7531	2.1315	2.6025	2.9467
16	0.6901	1.3368	1.7459	2.1199	2.5835	2.9208
17	0.6892	1.3334	1.7396	2.1098	2.5669	2.8982
18	0.6884	1.3304	1.7341	2.1009	2.5524	2.8784
19	0.6876	1.3277	1.7291	2.0930	2.5395	2.8609
20	0.6870	1.3253	1.7247	2.0860	2.5280	2.8453
21	0.6864	1.3232	1.7207	2.0796	2.5177	2.8314
22	0.6858	1.3212	1.7171	2.0739	2.5083	2.8188
23	0.6853	1.3195	1.7139	2.0687	2.4999	2.8073
24	0.6848	1.3178	1.7109	2.0639	2.4922	2.7969
25	0.6844	1.3163	1.7081	2.0595	2.4851	2.7874
26	0.6840	1.3150	1.7056	2.0555	2.4786	2.7787
27	0.6837	1.3137	1.7033	2.0518	2.4727	2.7707
28	0.6834	1.3125	1.7011	2.0484	2.4671	2.7633
29	0.6830	1.3114	1.6991	2.0452	2.4620	2.7564
30	0.6828	1.3104	1.6973	2.0423	2.4573	2.7500
31	0.6825	1.3095	1.6955	2.0395	2.4528	2.7440
32	0.6822	1.3086	1.6939	2.0369	2.4487	2.7385
33	0.6820	1.3077	1.6924	2.0345	2.4448	2.7333
34	0.6818	1.3070	1.6909	2.0322	2.4411	2.7284
35	0.6816	1.3062	1.6896	2.0301	2.4377	2.7238
36	0.6814	1.3055	1.6883	2.0281	2.4345	2.7195
37	0.6812	1.3049	1.6871	2.0262	2.4314	2.7154
38	0.6810	1.3042	1.6860	2.0244	2.4286	2.7116

(continues)

TABLE 4 (continued)

Degrees of Freedom	Upper Tail Areas					
	.25	.10	.05	.025	.01	.005
39	0.6808	1.3036	1.6849	2.0227	2.4258	2.7079
40	0.6807	1.3031	1.6839	2.0211	2.4233	2.7045
41	0.6805	1.3025	1.6829	2.0195	2.4208	2.7012
42	0.6804	1.3020	1.6820	2.0181	2.4185	2.6981
43	0.6802	1.3016	1.6811	2.0167	2.4163	2.6951
44	0.6801	1.3011	1.6802	2.0154	2.4141	2.6923
45	0.6800	1.3006	1.6794	2.0141	2.4121	2.6896
46	0.6799	1.3002	1.6787	2.0129	2.4102	2.6870
47	0.6797	1.2998	1.6779	2.0117	2.4083	2.6846
48	0.6796	1.2994	1.6772	2.0106	2.4066	2.6822
49	0.6795	1.2991	1.6766	2.0096	2.4049	2.6800
50	0.6794	1.2987	1.6759	2.0086	2.4033	2.6778
51	0.6793	1.2984	1.6753	2.0076	2.4017	2.6757
52	0.6792	1.2980	1.6747	2.0066	2.4002	2.6737
53	0.6791	1.2977	1.6741	2.0057	2.3988	2.6718
54	0.6791	1.2974	1.6736	2.0049	2.3974	2.6700
55	0.6790	1.2971	1.6730	2.0040	2.3961	2.6682
56	0.6789	1.2969	1.6725	2.0032	2.3948	2.6665
57	0.6788	1.2966	1.6720	2.0025	2.3936	2.6649
58	0.6787	1.2963	1.6716	2.0017	2.3924	2.6633
59	0.6787	1.2961	1.6711	2.0010	2.3912	2.6618
60	0.6786	1.2958	1.6706	2.0003	2.3901	2.6603
61	0.6785	1.2956	1.6702	1.9996	2.3890	2.6589
62	0.6785	1.2954	1.6698	1.9990	2.3880	2.6575
63	0.6784	1.2951	1.6694	1.9983	2.3870	2.6561
64	0.6783	1.2949	1.6690	1.9977	2.3860	2.6549
65	0.6783	1.2947	1.6686	1.9971	2.3851	2.6536
66	0.6782	1.2945	1.6683	1.9966	2.3842	2.6524
67	0.6782	1.2943	1.6679	1.9960	2.3833	2.6512
68	0.6781	1.2941	1.6676	1.9955	2.3824	2.6501
69	0.6781	1.2939	1.6672	1.9949	2.3816	2.6490
70	0.6780	1.2938	1.6669	1.9944	2.3808	2.6479
71	0.6780	1.2936	1.6666	1.9939	2.3800	2.6469
72	0.6779	1.2934	1.6663	1.9935	2.3793	2.6459
73	0.6779	1.2933	1.6660	1.9930	2.3785	2.6449
74	0.6778	1.2931	1.6657	1.9925	2.3778	2.6439
75	0.6778	1.2929	1.6654	1.9921	2.3771	2.6430
76	0.6777	1.2928	1.6652	1.9917	2.3764	2.6421
77	0.6777	1.2926	1.6649	1.9913	2.3758	2.6412
78	0.6776	1.2925	1.6646	1.9908	2.3751	2.6403
79	0.6776	1.2924	1.6644	1.9905	2.3745	2.6395
80	0.6776	1.2922	1.6641	1.9901	2.3739	2.6387
81	0.6775	1.2921	1.6639	1.9897	2.3733	2.6379
82	0.6775	1.2920	1.6636	1.9893	2.3727	2.6371
83	0.6775	1.2918	1.6634	1.9890	2.3721	2.6364
84	0.6774	1.2917	1.6632	1.9886	2.3716	2.6356
85	0.6774	1.2916	1.6630	1.9883	2.3710	2.6349

(continues)

T A B L E   4   (continued)

Degrees of Freedom	Upper Tail Areas					
	.25	.10	.05	.025	.01	.005
86	0.6774	1.2915	1.6628	1.9879	2.3705	2.6342
87	0.6773	1.2914	1.6626	1.9876	2.3700	2.6335
88	0.6773	1.2912	1.6624	1.9873	2.3695	2.6329
89	0.6773	1.2911	1.6622	1.9870	2.3690	2.6322
90	0.6772	1.2910	1.6620	1.9867	2.3685	2.6316
91	0.6772	1.2909	1.6618	1.9864	2.3680	2.6309
92	0.6772	1.2908	1.6616	1.9861	2.3676	2.6303
93	0.6771	1.2907	1.6614	1.9858	2.3671	2.6297
94	0.6771	1.2906	1.6612	1.9855	2.3667	2.6291
95	0.6771	1.2905	1.6611	1.9853	2.3662	2.6286
96	0.6771	1.2904	1.6609	1.9850	2.3658	2.6280
97	0.6770	1.2903	1.6607	1.9847	2.3654	2.6275
98	0.6770	1.2902	1.6606	1.9845	2.3650	2.6269
99	0.6770	1.2902	1.6604	1.9842	2.3646	2.6264
100	0.6770	1.2901	1.6602	1.9840	2.3642	2.6259
110	0.6767	1.2893	1.6588	1.9818	2.3607	2.6213
120	0.6765	1.2886	1.6577	1.9799	2.3578	2.6174
130	0.6764	1.2881	1.6567	1.9784	2.3554	2.6142
140	0.6762	1.2876	1.6558	1.9771	2.3533	2.6114
150	0.6761	1.2872	1.6551	1.9759	2.3515	2.6090
∞	0.6745	1.2816	1.6449	1.9600	2.3263	2.5758

For a particular number of degrees of freedom, entry represents the critical value of t corresponding to a specified upper tail area α.

TABLE 5 F Distribution

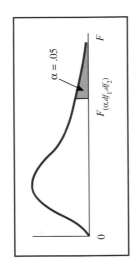

$\alpha = .05$

$F_{(\alpha, df_1, df_2)}$

	Numerator df_1																		
Denominator df_2	1	2	3	4	5	6	7	8	9	10	12	15	20	24	30	40	60	120	∞
1	161.4	199.5	215.7	224.6	230.2	234.0	236.8	238.9	240.5	241.9	243.9	245.9	248.0	249.1	250.1	251.1	252.2	253.3	254.3
2	18.51	19.00	19.16	19.25	19.30	19.33	19.35	19.37	19.38	19.40	19.41	19.43	19.45	19.45	19.46	19.47	19.48	19.49	19.50
3	10.13	9.55	9.28	9.12	9.01	8.94	8.89	8.85	8.81	8.79	8.74	8.70	8.66	8.64	8.62	8.59	8.57	8.55	8.53
4	7.71	6.94	6.59	6.39	6.26	6.16	6.09	6.04	6.00	5.96	5.91	5.86	5.80	5.77	5.75	5.72	5.69	5.66	5.63
5	6.61	5.79	5.41	5.19	5.05	4.95	4.88	4.82	4.77	4.74	4.68	4.62	4.56	4.53	4.50	4.46	4.43	4.40	4.36
6	5.99	5.14	4.76	4.53	4.39	4.28	4.21	4.15	4.10	4.06	4.00	3.94	3.87	3.84	3.81	3.77	3.74	3.70	3.67
7	5.59	4.74	4.35	4.12	3.97	3.87	3.79	3.73	3.68	3.64	3.57	3.51	3.44	3.41	3.38	3.34	3.30	3.27	3.23
8	5.32	4.46	4.07	3.84	3.69	3.58	3.50	3.44	3.39	3.35	3.28	3.22	3.15	3.12	3.08	3.04	3.01	2.97	2.93
9	5.12	4.26	3.86	3.63	3.48	3.37	3.29	3.23	3.18	3.14	3.07	3.01	2.94	2.90	2.86	2.83	2.79	2.75	2.71
10	4.96	4.10	3.71	3.48	3.33	3.22	3.14	3.07	3.02	2.98	2.91	2.85	2.77	2.74	2.70	2.66	2.62	2.58	2.54
11	4.84	3.98	3.59	3.36	3.20	3.09	3.01	2.95	2.90	2.85	2.79	2.72	2.65	2.61	2.57	2.53	2.49	2.45	2.40
12	4.75	3.89	3.49	3.26	3.11	3.00	2.91	2.85	2.80	2.75	2.69	2.62	2.54	2.51	2.47	2.43	2.38	2.34	2.30
13	4.67	3.81	3.41	3.18	3.03	2.92	2.83	2.77	2.71	2.67	2.60	2.53	2.46	2.42	2.38	2.34	2.30	2.25	2.21
14	4.60	3.74	3.34	3.11	2.96	2.85	2.76	2.70	2.65	2.60	2.53	2.46	2.39	2.35	2.31	2.27	2.22	2.18	2.13
15	4.54	3.68	3.29	3.06	2.90	2.79	2.71	2.64	2.59	2.54	2.48	2.40	2.33	2.29	2.25	2.20	2.16	2.11	2.07
16	4.49	3.63	3.24	3.01	2.85	2.74	2.66	2.59	2.54	2.49	2.42	2.35	2.28	2.24	2.19	2.15	2.11	2.06	2.01
17	4.45	3.59	3.20	2.96	2.81	2.70	2.61	2.55	2.49	2.45	2.38	2.31	2.23	2.19	2.15	2.10	2.06	2.01	1.96
18	4.41	3.55	3.16	2.93	2.77	2.66	2.58	2.51	2.46	2.41	2.34	2.27	2.19	2.15	2.11	2.06	2.02	1.97	1.92
19	4.38	3.52	3.13	2.90	2.74	2.63	2.54	2.48	2.42	2.38	2.31	2.23	2.16	2.11	2.07	2.03	1.98	1.93	1.88
20	4.35	3.49	3.10	2.87	2.71	2.60	2.51	2.45	2.39	2.35	2.28	2.20	2.12	2.08	2.04	1.99	1.95	1.90	1.84
21	4.32	3.47	3.07	2.84	2.68	2.57	2.49	2.42	2.37	2.32	2.25	2.18	2.10	2.05	2.01	1.96	1.92	1.87	1.81
22	4.30	3.44	3.05	2.82	2.66	2.55	2.46	2.40	2.34	2.30	2.23	2.15	2.07	2.03	1.98	1.94	1.89	1.84	1.78
23	4.28	3.42	3.03	2.80	2.64	2.53	2.44	2.37	2.32	2.27	2.20	2.13	2.05	2.01	1.96	1.91	1.86	1.81	1.76
24	4.26	3.40	3.01	2.78	2.62	2.51	2.42	2.36	2.30	2.25	2.18	2.11	2.03	1.98	1.94	1.89	1.84	1.79	1.73
25	4.24	3.39	2.99	2.76	2.60	2.49	2.40	2.34	2.28	2.24	2.16	2.09	2.01	1.96	1.92	1.87	1.82	1.77	1.71
26	4.23	3.37	2.98	2.74	2.59	2.47	2.39	2.32	2.27	2.22	2.15	2.07	1.99	1.95	1.90	1.85	1.80	1.75	1.69
27	4.21	3.35	2.96	2.73	2.57	2.46	2.37	2.31	2.25	2.20	2.13	2.06	1.97	1.93	1.88	1.84	1.79	1.73	1.67
28	4.20	3.34	2.95	2.71	2.56	2.45	2.36	2.29	2.24	2.19	2.12	2.04	1.96	1.91	1.87	1.82	1.77	1.71	1.65
29	4.18	3.33	2.93	2.70	2.55	2.43	2.35	2.28	2.22	2.18	2.10	2.03	1.94	1.90	1.85	1.81	1.75	1.70	1.64
30	4.17	3.32	2.92	2.69	2.53	2.42	2.33	2.27	2.21	2.16	2.09	2.01	1.93	1.89	1.84	1.79	1.74	1.68	1.62
40	4.08	3.23	2.84	2.61	2.45	2.34	2.25	2.18	2.12	2.08	2.00	1.92	1.84	1.79	1.74	1.69	1.64	1.58	1.51
60	4.00	3.15	2.76	2.53	2.37	2.25	2.17	2.10	2.04	1.99	1.92	1.84	1.75	1.70	1.65	1.59	1.53	1.47	1.39
120	3.92	3.07	2.68	2.45	2.29	2.17	2.09	2.02	1.96	1.91	1.83	1.75	1.66	1.61	1.55	1.50	1.43	1.35	1.25
∞	3.84	3.00	2.60	2.37	2.21	2.10	2.01	1.94	1.88	1.83	1.75	1.67	1.57	1.52	1.46	1.39	1.32	1.22	1.00

(continues)

TABLE 5 (continued)

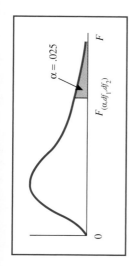

$\alpha = .025$

$F_{(\alpha, df_1, df_2)}$

Numerator df_1

Denominator df_2	1	2	3	4	5	6	7	8	9	10	12	15	20	24	30	40	60	120	∞
1	647.8	799.5	864.2	899.6	921.8	937.1	948.2	956.7	963.3	968.6	976.7	984.9	993.1	997.2	1001	1006	1010	1014	1018
2	38.51	39.00	39.17	39.25	39.30	39.33	39.36	39.37	39.39	39.40	39.41	39.43	39.45	39.46	39.46	39.47	39.48	39.49	39.50
3	17.44	16.04	15.44	15.10	14.88	14.73	14.62	14.54	14.47	14.42	14.34	14.25	14.17	14.12	14.08	14.04	13.99	13.95	13.90
4	12.22	10.65	9.98	9.60	9.36	9.20	9.07	8.98	8.90	8.84	8.75	8.66	8.56	8.51	8.46	8.41	8.36	8.31	8.26
5	10.01	8.43	7.76	7.39	7.15	6.98	6.85	6.76	6.68	6.62	6.52	6.43	6.33	6.28	6.23	6.18	6.12	6.07	6.02
6	8.81	7.26	6.60	6.23	5.99	5.82	5.70	5.60	5.52	5.46	5.37	5.27	5.17	5.12	5.07	5.01	4.96	4.90	4.85
7	8.07	6.54	5.89	5.52	5.29	5.12	4.99	4.90	4.82	4.76	4.67	4.57	4.47	4.42	4.36	4.31	4.25	4.20	4.14
8	7.57	6.06	5.42	5.05	4.82	4.65	4.53	4.43	4.36	4.30	4.20	4.10	4.00	3.95	3.89	3.84	3.78	3.73	3.67
9	7.21	5.71	5.08	4.72	4.48	4.32	4.20	4.10	4.03	3.96	3.87	3.77	3.67	3.61	3.56	3.51	3.45	3.39	3.33
10	6.94	5.46	4.83	4.47	4.24	4.07	3.95	3.85	3.78	3.72	3.62	3.52	3.42	3.37	3.31	3.26	3.20	3.14	3.08
11	6.72	5.26	4.63	4.28	4.04	3.88	3.76	3.66	3.59	3.53	3.43	3.33	3.23	3.17	3.12	3.06	3.00	2.94	2.88
12	6.55	5.10	4.47	4.12	3.89	3.73	3.61	3.51	3.44	3.37	3.28	3.18	3.07	3.02	2.96	2.91	2.85	2.79	2.72
13	6.41	4.97	4.35	4.00	3.77	3.60	3.48	3.39	3.31	3.25	3.15	3.05	2.95	2.89	2.84	2.78	2.72	2.66	2.60
14	6.30	4.86	4.24	3.89	3.66	3.50	3.38	3.29	3.21	3.15	3.05	2.95	2.84	2.79	2.73	2.67	2.61	2.55	2.49
15	6.20	4.77	4.15	3.80	3.58	3.41	3.29	3.20	3.12	3.06	2.96	2.86	2.76	2.70	2.64	2.59	2.52	2.46	2.40
16	6.12	4.69	4.08	3.73	3.50	3.34	3.22	3.12	3.05	2.99	2.89	2.79	2.68	2.63	2.57	2.51	2.45	2.38	2.32
17	6.04	4.62	4.01	3.66	3.44	3.28	3.16	3.06	2.98	2.92	2.82	2.72	2.62	2.56	2.50	2.44	2.38	2.32	2.25
18	5.98	4.56	3.95	3.61	3.38	3.22	3.10	3.01	2.93	2.87	2.77	2.67	2.56	2.50	2.44	2.38	2.32	2.26	2.19
19	5.92	4.51	3.90	3.56	3.33	3.17	3.05	2.96	2.88	2.82	2.72	2.62	2.51	2.45	2.39	2.33	2.27	2.20	2.13
20	5.87	4.46	3.86	3.51	3.29	3.13	3.01	2.91	2.84	2.77	2.68	2.57	2.46	2.41	2.35	2.29	2.22	2.16	2.09
21	5.83	4.42	3.82	3.48	3.25	3.09	2.97	2.87	2.80	2.73	2.64	2.53	2.42	2.37	2.31	2.25	2.18	2.11	2.04
22	5.79	4.38	3.78	3.44	3.22	3.05	2.93	2.84	2.76	2.70	2.60	2.50	2.39	2.33	2.27	2.21	2.14	2.08	2.00
23	5.75	4.35	3.75	3.41	3.18	3.02	2.90	2.81	2.73	2.67	2.57	2.47	2.36	2.30	2.24	2.18	2.11	2.04	1.97
24	5.72	4.32	3.72	3.38	3.15	2.99	2.87	2.78	2.70	2.64	2.54	2.44	2.33	2.27	2.21	2.15	2.08	2.01	1.94
25	5.69	4.29	3.69	3.35	3.13	2.97	2.85	2.75	2.68	2.61	2.51	2.41	2.30	2.24	2.18	2.12	2.05	1.98	1.91
26	5.66	4.27	3.67	3.33	3.10	2.94	2.82	2.73	2.65	2.59	2.49	2.39	2.28	2.22	2.16	2.09	2.03	1.95	1.88
27	5.63	4.24	3.65	3.31	3.08	2.92	2.80	2.71	2.63	2.57	2.47	2.36	2.25	2.19	2.13	2.07	2.00	1.93	1.85
28	5.61	4.22	3.63	3.29	3.06	2.90	2.78	2.69	2.61	2.55	2.45	2.34	2.23	2.17	2.11	2.05	1.98	1.91	1.83
29	5.59	4.20	3.61	3.27	3.04	2.88	2.76	2.67	2.59	2.53	2.43	2.32	2.21	2.15	2.09	2.03	1.96	1.89	1.81
30	5.57	4.18	3.59	3.25	3.03	2.87	2.75	2.65	2.57	2.51	2.41	2.31	2.20	2.14	2.07	2.01	1.94	1.87	1.79
40	5.42	4.05	3.46	3.13	2.90	2.74	2.62	2.53	2.45	2.39	2.29	2.18	2.07	2.01	1.94	1.88	1.80	1.72	1.64
60	5.29	3.93	3.34	3.01	2.79	2.63	2.51	2.41	2.33	2.27	2.17	2.06	1.94	1.88	1.82	1.74	1.67	1.58	1.48
120	5.15	3.80	3.23	2.89	2.67	2.52	2.39	2.30	2.22	2.16	2.05	1.94	1.82	1.76	1.69	1.61	1.53	1.43	1.31
∞	5.02	3.69	3.12	2.79	2.57	2.41	2.29	2.19	2.11	2.05	1.94	1.83	1.71	1.64	1.57	1.48	1.39	1.27	1.00

(continues)

659

TABLE 5 (continued)

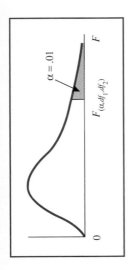

$\alpha = .01$

$F_{(\alpha, df_1, df_2)}$

Numerator df_1

Denominator df_2	1	2	3	4	5	6	7	8	9	10	12	15	20	24	30	40	60	120	∞
1	4052	4999.5	5403	5625	5764	5859	5928	5982	6022	6056	6106	6157	6209	6235	6261	6287	6313	6339	6366
2	98.50	99.00	99.17	99.25	99.30	99.33	99.36	99.37	99.39	99.40	99.42	99.43	99.45	99.46	99.47	99.47	99.48	99.49	99.50
3	34.12	30.82	29.46	28.71	28.24	27.91	27.67	27.49	27.35	27.23	27.05	26.87	26.69	26.60	26.50	26.41	26.32	26.22	26.13
4	21.20	18.00	16.69	15.98	15.52	15.21	14.98	14.80	14.66	14.55	14.37	14.20	14.02	13.93	13.84	13.75	13.65	13.56	13.46
5	16.26	13.27	12.06	11.39	10.97	10.67	10.46	10.29	10.16	10.05	9.89	9.72	9.55	9.47	9.38	9.29	9.20	9.11	9.02
6	13.75	10.92	9.78	9.15	8.75	8.47	8.26	8.10	7.98	7.87	7.72	7.56	7.40	7.31	7.23	7.14	7.06	6.97	6.88
7	12.25	9.55	8.45	7.85	7.46	7.19	6.99	6.84	6.72	6.62	6.47	6.31	6.16	6.07	5.99	5.91	5.82	5.74	5.65
8	11.26	8.65	7.59	7.01	6.63	6.37	6.18	6.03	5.91	5.81	5.67	5.52	5.36	5.28	5.20	5.12	5.03	4.95	4.86
9	10.56	8.02	6.99	6.42	6.06	5.80	5.61	5.47	5.35	5.26	5.11	4.96	4.81	4.73	4.65	4.57	4.48	4.40	4.31
10	10.04	7.56	6.55	5.99	5.64	5.39	5.20	5.06	4.94	4.85	4.71	4.56	4.41	4.33	4.25	4.17	4.08	4.00	3.91
11	9.65	7.21	6.22	5.67	5.32	5.07	4.89	4.74	4.63	4.54	4.40	4.25	4.10	4.02	3.94	3.86	3.78	3.69	3.60
12	9.33	6.93	5.95	5.41	5.06	4.82	4.64	4.50	4.39	4.30	4.16	4.01	3.86	3.78	3.70	3.62	3.54	3.45	3.36
13	9.07	6.70	5.74	5.21	4.86	4.62	4.44	4.30	4.19	4.10	3.96	3.82	3.66	3.59	3.51	3.43	3.34	3.25	3.17
14	8.86	6.51	5.56	5.04	4.69	4.46	4.28	4.14	4.03	3.94	3.80	3.66	3.51	3.43	3.35	3.27	3.18	3.09	3.00
15	8.68	6.36	5.42	4.89	4.56	4.32	4.14	4.00	3.89	3.80	3.67	3.52	3.37	3.29	3.21	3.13	3.05	2.96	2.87
16	8.53	6.23	5.29	4.77	4.44	4.20	4.03	3.89	3.78	3.69	3.55	3.41	3.26	3.18	3.10	3.02	2.93	2.84	2.75
17	8.40	6.11	5.18	4.67	4.34	4.10	3.93	3.79	3.68	3.59	3.46	3.31	3.16	3.08	3.00	2.92	2.83	2.75	2.65
18	8.29	6.01	5.09	4.58	4.25	4.01	3.84	3.71	3.60	3.51	3.37	3.23	3.08	3.00	2.92	2.84	2.75	2.66	2.57
19	8.18	5.93	5.01	4.50	4.17	3.94	3.77	3.63	3.52	3.43	3.30	3.15	3.00	2.92	2.84	2.76	2.67	2.58	2.49
20	8.10	5.85	4.94	4.43	4.10	3.87	3.70	3.56	3.46	3.37	3.23	3.09	2.94	2.86	2.78	2.69	2.61	2.52	2.42
21	8.02	5.78	4.87	4.37	4.04	3.81	3.64	3.51	3.40	3.31	3.17	3.03	2.88	2.80	2.72	2.64	2.55	2.46	2.36
22	7.95	5.72	4.82	4.31	3.99	3.76	3.59	3.45	3.35	3.26	3.12	2.98	2.83	2.75	2.67	2.58	2.50	2.40	2.31
23	7.88	5.66	4.76	4.26	3.94	3.71	3.54	3.41	3.30	3.21	3.07	2.93	2.78	2.70	2.62	2.54	2.45	2.35	2.26
24	7.82	5.61	4.72	4.22	3.90	3.67	3.50	3.36	3.26	3.17	3.03	2.89	2.74	2.66	2.58	2.49	2.40	2.31	2.21
25	7.77	5.57	4.68	4.18	3.85	3.63	3.46	3.32	3.22	3.13	2.99	2.85	2.70	2.62	2.54	2.45	2.36	2.27	2.17
26	7.72	5.53	4.64	4.14	3.82	3.59	3.42	3.29	3.18	3.09	2.96	2.81	2.66	2.58	2.50	2.42	2.33	2.23	2.13
27	7.68	5.49	4.60	4.11	3.78	3.56	3.39	3.26	3.15	3.06	2.93	2.78	2.63	2.55	2.47	2.38	2.29	2.20	2.10
28	7.64	5.45	4.57	4.07	3.75	3.53	3.36	3.23	3.12	3.03	2.90	2.75	2.60	2.52	2.44	2.35	2.26	2.17	2.06
29	7.60	5.42	4.54	4.04	3.73	3.50	3.33	3.20	3.09	3.00	2.87	2.73	2.57	2.49	2.41	2.33	2.23	2.14	2.03
30	7.56	5.39	4.51	4.02	3.70	3.47	3.30	3.17	3.07	2.98	2.84	2.70	2.55	2.47	2.39	2.30	2.21	2.11	2.01
40	7.31	5.18	4.31	3.83	3.51	3.29	3.12	2.99	2.89	2.80	2.66	2.52	2.37	2.29	2.20	2.11	2.02	1.92	1.80
60	7.08	4.98	4.13	3.65	3.34	3.12	2.95	2.82	2.72	2.63	2.50	2.35	2.20	2.12	2.03	1.94	1.84	1.73	1.60
120	6.85	4.79	3.95	3.48	3.17	2.96	2.79	2.66	2.56	2.47	2.34	2.19	2.03	1.95	1.86	1.76	1.66	1.53	1.38
∞	6.63	4.61	3.78	3.32	3.02	2.80	2.64	2.51	2.41	2.32	2.18	2.04	1.88	1.79	1.70	1.59	1.47	1.32	1.00

For a particular combination of numerator and denominator degrees of freedom, entry represents the critical values of F corresponding to a specified upper tail area α.

PHOTO CREDITS

CHAPTER 1

Page 3: Tom McCarthy/PhotEdit. Page 8: Chuck Nacke/Woodfin Camp & Associates. Page 12: © Shia Photos. Page 13: Copyright 2002 General Motors Corp. Used with permission of GM Media Archives. Page 27: Henry Westheim Photography.

CHAPTER 2

Page 35: Subaru of America, Inc. Page 42: Amy E. Conn/AP/Wide World Photos. Page 48: The Terry Wild Studio, Inc. Page 51: The Terry Wild Studio, Inc. Page 53: David Yound-Wolfe/PhotoEdit. Page 56 (Ad): Courtesy of Bozell Worldwide. Page 60: Michael Newman/PhotoEdit.

CHAPTER 3

Page 81: James Leynse/Corbis/SABA Press Photos, Inc. Page 88: © Shia Photos. Page 92: Frito-Lay, Inc. Page 94: Courtesy of BMW of North America. Page 94: Jeff Christensen/AP/Wide World Photos.

CHAPTER 4

Page 109: Frank LaBua, Inc. Page 116: Corbis/Stock Market. Page 118: General Electric Appliances. Page 122: VCG/FPG. Page 129: Jeff Greenberg/PhotoEdit. Page 130: The Terry Wild Studio, Inc.

CHAPTER 5

Page 137: Haggar Clothing Company. Page 144: The Terry Wild Studio, Inc. Page 146: Ford Motor Company. Page 150: © Shia Photos. Page 153: Chuck Nacke/Woodfin Camp & Associates. Page 155: Campbell Soup Company.

CHAPTER 6

Page 165: The Terry Wild Studio, Inc. Page 177: Richard B. Levine/Frances M. Roberts. Page 179: The Terry Wild Studio, Inc. Page 180: Ron Kimball Photography. Page 185: © Reuters NewMedia Inc./Corbis. Page 187: Bob Daemmrich Photography, Inc.

CHAPTER 7

Page 193: © Shia Photos. Page 199: Claus Guglberger/Black Star. Page 201: Amy C. Etra/PhotoEdit. Page 207: Bicycling Magazine. Page 208: Greg Mancuso/Stock Boston. Page 210: Steelcase Inc. Page 211: The Terry Wild Studio, Inc. Page 215: Yannis Vlamos/A Perfect Exposure.

CHAPTER 8

Page 223: Churchill & Klehr Photography. Page 226: David Hunter/AP/Wide World Photos. Page 230: Patti McConville/The Image Bank. Page 233: Pepsi Cola Company/AP/Wide World Photos. Page 242: Daimler/Chrysler Corporation. Page 245: Jean Clause/Moscetti/REA/Corbis/SABA Press Photos, Inc.

CHAPTER 9

Page 253: Dean Abramson/Stock Boston. Page 256: Dean Abramson/Stock Boston. Page 260: The Terry Wild Studio, Inc. Page 263: The Terry Wild Studio, Inc. Page 265: Tony Freeman/PhotoEdit. Page 266: David Lassman/© Syracuse Newspapers/The Image Works. Page 268: Steak and Ale Restaurants. Page 269: Elrick & Lavidge Inc..

CHAPTER 10

Page 279: Chuck Savage/Corbis/Stock Market. Page 283: Chuck Nacke/Woodfin Camp & Associates. Page 283: MSInteractive Multimedia Services. Page 285: Courtesy of BMW of North America. Page 286: Infante/eStock Photography LLC. Page 298: Xerox Corporation. Page 300: Chuck Nacke/Woodfin Camp & Associates.

CHAPTER 11

Page 307: Ellen Ericson Kupp/World Vision USA, Inc. Page 310: Churchill & Klehr Photography. Page 314: Dallal/SIPA Press. Page 321: Hulton/Archive. Page 322: Churchill & Klehr Photography.

CHAPTER 12

Page 343: The Terry Wild Studio, Inc. Page 348: Jaskson Smith/Pictor, New York. Page 353: Tony Freeman Photographs. Page 358: Tennis Magazine. Page 363: John Loggins/Shia Photos.

CHAPTER 13

Page 375: Peter Griffith/Masterfile Corporation. Page 378: Michael A. Dwyer/Stock Boston. Page 382: Chuck Nacke/Woodfin Camp & Associates. Page 388: Tony Freeman Photographs. Page 390: Patrick Zachmann/Magnum Photos, Inc.

CHAPTER 14

Page 429: Pearson Education/PH College. Page 434: Churchill & Klehr Photography. Page 436: Felicia Martinez/PhotoEdit.

CHAPTER 15

Page 449: © Dennis Nett/Syracuse Newspapers/The Image Works. Page 454: Frank Siteman/Stock Boston. Page 456: Steve Raymer/Corbis. Page 458: Al Campanie/© Syracuse Newspapers/The Image Works. Page 463: Acer America.

CHAPTER 16

Page 471: Jordan Harris/PhotoEdit. Page 474: Dallal/SIPA Press. Page 486: Christopher Liu/ChinaStock Photo Library.

CHAPTER 17

Page 503: Cub Foods, a SUPERVALU INC. Company.

CHAPTER 18

Page 533: The Terry Wild Studio, Inc. Page 545: Ron Kimball Photography. Page 550: Brian Pieters/Masterfile Corporation. Page 556: Teri Leigh Stratford/Pearson Education/PH College.

CHAPTER 19

Page 567: United Air Lines/AP/Wide World Photos. Page 576: Porter Novelli Convergence Group.

SUBJECT INDEX

COMPANY AND PRODUCT INDEX

NAME INDEX